W9-DFP-409

Contents at a Glance

MrExcel
LIBRARY

Excel® 2013 VBA and Macros

Bill Jelen

Tracy Syrstad

que®

800 East 96th Street,
Indianapolis, Indiana 46240 USA

Excel® 2013 VBA and Macros

ISBN-13: 978-0-7897-4861-4
ISBN-10: 0-7897-4861-4

Library of Congress Cataloging-in-Publication Data is on file.

Printed in the United States of America
Third Printing: December 2014

Trademarks

All terms mentioned in this book that are known to be trademarks or service marks have been appropriately capitalized. Que Publishing cannot attest to the accuracy of this information. Use of a term in this book should not be regarded as affecting the validity of any trademark or service mark.

Warning and Disclaimer

Every effort has been made to make this book as complete and as accurate as possible, but no warranty or fitness is implied. The information provided is on an "as is" basis. The authors and the publisher shall have neither liability nor responsibility to any person or entity with respect to any loss or damages arising from the information contained in this book.

Bulk Sales

Que Publishing offers excellent discounts on this book when ordered in quantity for bulk purchases or special sales. For more information, please contact

U.S. Corporate and Government Sales
1-800-382-3419
corpsales@pearsontechgroup.com

For sales outside of the U.S., please contact

International Sales
international@pearsoned.com

Editor-in-Chief
Greg Wiegand

Executive Editor
Loretta Yates

Development Editor
Charlotte Kughen

Managing Editor
Sandra Schroeder

Project Editor
Mandie Frank

Copy Editor
Cheri Clark

Indexer
Tim Wright

Proofreader
Paula Lowell

Technical Editor
Bob Umlas

Editorial Assistant
Cindy Teeters

Designer
Anne Jones

Compositor
Jake McFarland

Table of Contents

About the Author

Bill Jelen, Excel MVP and the host of MrExcel.com, has been using spreadsheets since 1985, and he launched the MrExcel.com website in 1998. Bill was a regular guest on *Call for Help* with Leo Laporte and has produced more than 1,500 episodes of his daily video podcast, *Learn Excel from MrExcel*. He is the author of 39 books about Microsoft Excel and writes the monthly Excel column for *Strategic Finance* magazine. His Excel tips appear regularly in CFO Excel Pro Newsletter and *CFO Magazine*. Before founding MrExcel.com, Bill Jelen spent 12 years in the trenches—working as a financial analyst for finance, marketing, accounting, and operations departments of a $500 million public company. He lives near Akron, Ohio, with his wife, Mary Ellen.

Tracy Syrstad is the project manager for the MrExcel consulting team. She was introduced to Excel VBA by a co-worker who encouraged her to learn VBA by recording steps, and then modifying the code as needed. Her first macro was a simple lookup and highlight for a part index, although it hardly seemed simple when she did it. She was encouraged by her success with that macro and others that followed. She'll never forget the day when it all clicked. She hopes this book will bring that click to its readers sooner and with less frustration. She lives near Sioux Falls, South Dakota, with her husband, John.

Dedication

Bill Jelen

For Mary Ellen Jelen

Tracy Syrstad

To Nate P. Oliver, who shared his love of Excel with the world.

Acknowledgments

Thanks to Tracy Syrstad for being a great coauthor and for doing a great job of managing all the consulting projects at MrExcel.com.

Bob Umlas is the smartest Excel guy I know and is an awesome technical editor. At Pearson, Loretta Yates is an excellent acquisitions editor.

Along the way, I've learned a lot about VBA programming from the awesome community at the MrExcel.com message board. VoG, Richard Schollar, and Jon von der Heyden all stand out as having contributed posts that led to ideas in this book. Thanks to Pam Gensel for Excel macro lesson #1. Mala Singh taught me about creating charts in VBA, and Oliver Holloway brought me up to speed with accessing SQL Server. Scott Ruble and Robin Wakefield at Microsoft helped with the charting chapter. And I give a tip of the cap to JWalk for that HWND trick.

At MrExcel.com, thanks to Barb Jelen, Wei Jiang, Tracy Syrstad, Tyler Nash, and Scott Pierson.

My family was incredibly supportive during this time. Thanks to Zeke Jelen, Dom Grossi, and Mary Ellen Jelen.

—Bill

Juan Pablo Gonzalez Ruiz is a great programmer, and I really appreciate his time and patience showing me new ways to write better programs.

Thank you to all the moderators at the MrExcel forum who keep the board organized, despite the best efforts of the spammers.

Programming is a constant learning experience, and I really appreciate the clients who have encouraged me to program outside my comfort zone so that my skills and knowledge have expanded.

And last, but not least, thanks to Bill Jelen. His site, MrExcel.com, is a place where thousands come for help. It's also a place where I, and others like me, have an opportunity to learn from and assist others.

—Tracy

We Want to Hear from You!

As the reader of this book, *you* are our most important critic and commentator. We value your opinion and want to know what we're doing right, what we could do better, what areas you'd like to see us publish in, and any other words of wisdom you're willing to pass our way.

We welcome your comments. You can email or write to let us know what you did or didn't like about this book—as well as what we can do to make our books better.

Please note that we cannot help you with technical problems related to the topic of this book.

When you write, please be sure to include this book's title and author as well as your name and email address. We will carefully review your comments and share them with the author and editors who worked on the book.

Email: feedback@quepublishing.com

Mail: Que Publishing
            ATTN: Reader Feedback
            800 East 96th Street
            Indianapolis, IN 46240 USA

Reader Services

Visit our website and register this book at quepublishing.com/register for convenient access to any updates, downloads, or errata that might be available for this book.

Introduction

Getting Results with VBA

As corporate IT departments have found themselves with long backlogs of requests, Excel users have discovered that they can produce the reports needed to run their business themselves using the macro language *Visual Basic for Applications* (VBA). VBA enables you to achieve tremendous efficiencies in your day-to-day use of Excel. Without your waiting for resources from IT, VBA helps you figure out how to import data and produce reports in Excel.

What Is in This Book?

You have taken the right step by purchasing this book. I can help you reduce the learning curve so that you can write your own VBA macros and put an end to the burden of generating reports manually.

Reduce the Learning Curve

This Introduction provides a case study of the power of macros. Chapter 1 introduces the tools and confirms what you probably already know: The macro recorder does not work reliably. Chapter 2 helps you understand the crazy syntax of VBA. Chapter 3 breaks the code on how to work efficiently with ranges and cells.

Chapter 4 covers the power of looping using VBA. The case study in this chapter creates a program to produce a department report, and then wraps that report routine in a loop to produce 46 reports.

Chapter 5 covers R1C1-style formulas. Chapter 6 covers names. Chapter 7 includes some great tricks that use event programming. Chapters 8 and 9 cover arrays, classes, records, and collections. Chapter 10 introduces custom dialog boxes that you can use to collect information from the human using Excel.

Excel VBA Power

Chapters 11 and 12 provide an in-depth look at Filter, Advanced Filter, and pivot tables. Any report automation tool will rely heavily on these concepts. Chapters 13 and 14 include 25 code samples designed to exhibit the power of Excel VBA and custom functions.

Chapters 15 through 20 handle charting, data visualizations, web queries, sparklines, and automating another Office program such as Word.

Techie Stuff Needed to Produce Applications

Chapter 21 handles reading and writing to Access databases and SQL Server. The techniques for using Access databases enable you to build an application with the multiuser features of Access while keeping the friendly front end of Excel.

Chapter 22 discusses advanced userform topics. Chapter 23 teaches some tricky ways to achieve tasks using the Windows application programming interface. Chapters 24 through 26 deal with error handling, custom menus, and add-ins. Chapter 27 is a brief introduction to building your own Java application within Excel. Chapter 28 summarizes the changes in Excel 2013.

Does This Book Teach Excel?

Microsoft believes that the ordinary Office user touches only 10 percent of the features in Office. I realize everyone reading this book is above average, and I have a pretty smart audience at MrExcel.com. Even so, a poll of 8,000 MrExcel.com readers shows that only 42 percent of smarter-than-average users are using any one of the top 10 power features in Excel.

I regularly present a Power Excel seminar for accountants. These are hard-core Excelers who use Excel 30 to 40 hours every week. Even so, two things come out in every seminar. First, half of the audience gasps when they see how quickly you can do tasks with a particular feature such as automatic subtotals or pivot tables. Second, someone in the audience routinely trumps me. For example, someone asks a question, I answer, and someone in the second row raises a hand to give a better answer.

The point? You and I both know a lot about Excel. However, I assume that in any given chapter, maybe 58 percent of the people have not used pivot tables before and maybe even fewer have used the "Top 10 Filter" feature of pivot tables. With this in mind, before I show how to automate something in VBA, I briefly cover how to do the same task in the Excel interface. This book does not teach you how to do pivot tables, but it does alert you when you might need to explore a topic and learn more about it elsewhere.

CASE STUDY: MONTHLY ACCOUNTING REPORTS

This is a true story. Valerie is a business analyst in the accounting department of a medium-size corporation. Her company recently installed an overbudget $16 million ERP system. As the project ground to a close, there were no resources left in the IT budget to produce the monthly report that this corporation used to summarize each department.

However, Valerie had been close enough to the implementation process to think of a way to produce the report herself. She understood that she could export General Ledger data from the ERP system to a text file with comma-separated values. Using Excel, Valerie was able to import the G/L data from the ERP system into Excel.

Creating the report was not easy. As with many companies, there were exceptions in the data. Valerie knew that certain accounts in one particular cost center needed to be reclassed as an expense. She knew that other accounts needed to be excluded from the report entirely. Working carefully in Excel, Valerie made these adjustments. She created one pivot table to produce the first summary section of the report. She cut the pivot table results and pasted them into a blank worksheet. Then she created a new pivot table report for the second section of the summary. After about three hours, she had imported the data, produced five pivot tables, arranged them in a summary, and neatly formatted the report in color.

Becoming the Hero

Valerie handed the report to her manager. The manager had just heard from the IT department that it would be months before they could get around to producing "that convoluted report." When Valerie created the Excel report, she became the instant hero of the day. In three hours, Valerie had managed to do the impossible. Valerie was on cloud nine after a well-deserved "atta-girl."

More Cheers

The next day, Valerie's manager attended the monthly department meeting. When the department managers started complaining that they could not get the report from the ERP system, this manager pulled out his department report and placed it on the table. The other managers were amazed. How was he able to produce this report? Everyone was relieved to hear that someone had cracked the code. The company president asked Valerie's manager if he could have the report produced for each department.

Cheers Turn to Dread

You can probably see this coming. This particular company had 46 departments. That means 46 one-page summaries had to be produced once a month. Each report required importing data from the ERP system, backing out certain accounts, producing five pivot tables, and then formatting the reports in color. Even though it had taken Valerie three hours to produce the first report, after she got into the swing of things, she could produce the 46 reports in 40 hours. This is horrible. Valerie had a job to do before she became responsible for spending 40 hours a month producing these reports in Excel.

VBA to the Rescue

Valerie found my company, MrExcel Consulting, and explained her situation. In the course of about a week, I was able to produce a series of macros in Visual Basic that did all the mundane tasks. For example, the macros imported the data, backed out certain accounts, did five pivot tables, and applied the color formatting. From start to finish, the entire 40-hour manual process was reduced to two button clicks and about four minutes.

Right now, either you or someone in your company is probably stuck doing manual tasks in Excel that can be automated with VBA. I am confident that I can walk into any company with 20 or more Excel users and find a case just as amazing as Valerie's.

The Future of VBA and Windows Versions of Excel

Several years ago, there were many rumblings that Microsoft might stop supporting VBA. There is now plenty of evidence to indicate that VBA will be around in Windows versions of Excel through 2030. When VBA was removed from the Mac version of Excel 2008, a huge outcry from customers led to its being included in the next Mac version of Excel.

Microsoft has hinted that in Excel 16, which is the next version of Excel, it will stop providing support for XLM macros. These macros were replaced by VBA in 1993, and 20 years later, they are still supported. Some would say that Microsoft introduced a new programming language for Excel with the JavaScript applications that are discussed in Chapter 28. Assuming that Microsoft continues to support VBA for 22 years after Excel 2013, you should be good through the mid-2030s.

Versions of Excel

This fourth edition of *VBA and Macros* is designed to work with Excel 2013. The previous editions of this book covered code for Excel 97 through Excel 2010. In 80 percent of the chapters, the code for Excel 2013 is identical to the code in previous versions. However, there are exceptions. For example, Microsoft offers new pivot table models and timelines that will add some new methods to the pivot table chapter.

Differences for Mac Users

Although Excel for Windows and Excel for the Mac are similar in their user interface, there are a number of differences when you compare the VBA environment. Certainly, nothing in Chapter 23 that uses the Windows API will work on the Mac. The overall concepts discussed in the book apply to the Mac, but differences exist. You can find a general list of differences as they apply to the Mac at `http://www.mrexcel.com/macvba.html`.

Special Elements and Typographical Conventions

The following typographical conventions are used in this book:

- *Italic*—Indicates new terms when they are defined, special emphasis, non-English words or phrases, and letters or words used as words
- `Monospace`—Indicates parts of VBA code such as object or method names, and filenames
- `Italic monospace`—Indicates placeholder text in code syntax
- `Bold monospace`—Indicates user input

In addition to these typographical conventions, there are several special elements. Each chapter has at least one case study that presents a real-world solution to common problems. The case study also demonstrates practical applications of topics discussed in the chapter.

In addition to the case studies, you will see New icons, Notes, Tips, and Cautions.

NOTE

Notes provide additional information outside the main thread of the chapter discussion that might be useful for you to know.

TIP

Tips provide quick workarounds and time-saving techniques to help you work more efficiently.

CAUTION

Cautions warn about potential pitfalls you might encounter. Pay attention to the Cautions; they alert you to problems that might otherwise cause you hours of frustration.

Code Files

As a thank-you for buying this book, the authors have put together a set of 50 Excel workbooks that demonstrate the concepts included in this book. This set of files includes all the code from the book, sample data, additional notes from the authors, and 25 bonus macros. To download the code files, visit this book's web page at http://www.quepublishing.com or http://www.mrexcel.com/getcode2013.html.

Next Steps

Chapter 1, "Unleash the Power of Excel with VBA," introduces the editing tools of the Visual Basic environment and shows why using the macro recorder is not an effective way to write VBA macro code.

Unleash the Power of Excel with VBA

1

The Power of Excel

Visual Basic for Applications (VBA) combined with Microsoft Excel is probably the most powerful tool available to you. VBA is sitting on the desktops of 500 million users of Microsoft Office, and most have never figured out how to harness the power of VBA in Excel. Using VBA, you can speed the production of any task in Excel. If you regularly use Excel to produce a series of monthly charts, you can have VBA do the same task for you in a matter of seconds.

Barriers to Entry

There are two barriers to learning successful VBA programming. First, Excel's macro recorder is flawed and does not produce workable code for you to use as a model. Second, for many who learned a programming language such as BASIC, the syntax of VBA is horribly frustrating.

The Macro Recorder Doesn't Work!

Microsoft began to dominate the spreadsheet market in the mid-1990s. Although it was wildly successful in building a powerful spreadsheet program to which any Lotus 1-2-3 user could easily transition, the macro language was just too different. Anyone proficient in recording Lotus 1-2-3 macros who tried recording a few macros in Excel most likely failed. Although the Microsoft VBA programming language is much more powerful than the Lotus 1-2-3 macro language, the fundamental flaw is that the macro recorder does not work when you use the default settings.

With Lotus 1-2-3, you could record a macro today and play it back tomorrow, and it would faithfully work. When you attempt the same feat in Microsoft

Excel, the macro might work today but not tomorrow. In 1995, when I tried to record my first Excel macro, I was horribly frustrated by this. In this book, I teach you the three rules for getting the most out of the macro recorder.

Visual Basic Is Not Like BASIC

The code generated by the macro recorder was unlike anything I had ever seen. It said this was "Visual Basic" (VB). I had the pleasure of learning half a dozen programming languages at various times; this bizarre-looking language was horribly unintuitive and did not resemble the BASIC language I had learned in high school.

To make matters worse, even in 1995 I was the spreadsheet wizard in my office. My company had forced everyone to convert from Lotus 1-2-3 to Excel, which meant I was faced with a macro recorder that didn't work and a language that I couldn't understand. This was not a good combination of events.

My assumption in writing this book is that you are pretty talented with a spreadsheet. You probably know more than 90 percent of the people in your office. I also assume that even though you are not a programmer, you might have taken a class in BASIC at some point. However, knowing BASIC is not a requirement—it actually is a barrier to entry into the ranks of being a successful VBA programmer. There is a good chance that you have recorded a macro in Excel and a similar chance that you were not happy with the results.

Good News: Climbing the Learning Curve Is Easy

Even if you've been frustrated with the macro recorder, it is really just a small speed bump on your road to writing powerful programs in Excel. This book teaches you not only why the macro recorder fails, but also how to change the recorded code into something useful. For all the former BASIC programmers in the audience, I decode VBA so that you can easily pick through recorded macro code and understand what is happening.

Great News: Excel with VBA Is Worth the Effort

Although you probably have been frustrated with Microsoft over the inability to record macros in Excel, the great news is that Excel VBA is powerful. Absolutely anything you can do in the Excel interface can be duplicated with stunning speed in Excel VBA. If you find yourself routinely creating the same reports manually day after day or week after week, Excel VBA will greatly streamline those tasks.

The authors of this book work for MrExcel Consulting. In this role, we have automated reports for hundreds of clients. The stories are often similar: The IT department has a several-month backlog of requests. Someone in accounting or engineering discovers that he or she can import some data into Excel and get the reports necessary to run the business. This is a liberating event—you no longer need to wait months for the IT department to write a program. However, the problem is that after you import the data into Excel and win accolades from your manager for producing the report, you will likely be asked to produce the same report every month or every week. This becomes very tedious.

Again, the great news is that with a few hours of VBA programming, you can automate the reporting process and turn it into a few button clicks. The reward is great. So hang with me as we cover a few of the basics.

This chapter exposes why the macro recorder does not work. It also walks through an example of recorded code and demonstrates why it works today but will fail tomorrow. I realize that the code you see in this chapter might not be familiar to you, but that's okay. The point of this chapter is to demonstrate the fundamental problem with the macro recorder. You also learn the fundamentals of the Visual Basic environment.

Knowing Your Tools: The Developer Tab

Let's start with a basic overview of the tools needed to use VBA. By default, Microsoft hides the VBA tools. You need to complete the following steps to change a setting in Excel options to access the Developer tab.

1. Open the File menu to get to the new Backstage view.
2. Along the left navigation bar, select Options near the bottom of the list.
3. In the Excel Options dialog, select Customize Ribbon from the left navigation.
4. In the right list box, the Developer tab is third from the bottom. Select the check box next to this item.
5. Click OK to return to Excel.

Excel displays the Developer tab shown in Figure 1.1.

Figure 1.1
The Developer tab provides an interface for running and recording macros.

The Code group on the Developer tab contains the icons used for recording and playing back VBA macros, as listed here:

- **Visual Basic icon**—Opens the Visual Basic Editor.
- **Macros icon**—Displays the Macro dialog, where you can choose to run or edit a macro from the list of macros.
- **Record Macro icon**—Begins the process of recording a macro.
- **Use Relative References icon**—Toggles between using relative or absolute recording. With relative recording, Excel records that you move down three cells. With absolute recording, Excel records that you selected cell A4.
- **Macro Security icon**—Accesses the Trust Center, where you can choose to allow or disallow macros to run on this computer.

The Add-Ins group provides icons for managing regular add-ins and COM add-ins.

The Controls group of the Developer tab contains an Insert menu where you can access a variety of programming controls that can be placed on the worksheet. See "Assigning a Macro to a Form Control, Text Box, or Shape," later in this chapter. Other icons in this group enable you to work with the on-sheet controls. The Run Dialog button enables you to display a custom dialog box or userform that you designed in VBA. For more on user-forms, see Chapter 10, "Userforms—An Introduction."

The XML group of the Developer tab contains tools for importing and exporting XML documents.

The Modify group enables you to specify whether the Document Panel is always dis-played for new documents. Users can enter keywords and a document description in the Document Panel. If you have SharePoint and InfoPath, you can define custom fields to appear in the Document Panel.

Understanding Which File Types Allow Macros

Excel 2013 offers support for four file types. Macros are not allowed to be stored in the XLSX file type, and this file type is the default file type! You have to use the Save As set-ting for all of your macro workbooks, or you can change the default file type used by Excel 2013.

The available files types are as listed here:

- **Excel Workbook (.xlsx)**—Files are stored as a series of XML objects and then zipped into a single file. This creates significantly smaller file sizes. It also allows other applica-tions (even Notepad!) to edit or create Excel workbooks. Unfortunately, macros cannot be stored in files with an .xlsx extension.

- **Excel Macro-Enabled Workbook (.xlsm)**—This is similar to the default .xlsx format, except macros are allowed. The basic concept is that if someone has an .xlsx file, he will not need to worry about malicious macros. However, if he sees an .xlsm file, he should be concerned that there might be macros attached.

- **Excel Binary Workbook (.xlsb)**—This is a binary format designed to handle the larger 1-million-row grid size introduced in Excel 2007. Legacy versions of Excel stored their files in a proprietary binary format. Although binary formats might load more quickly, they are more prone to corruption, and a few lost bits can destroy the whole file. Macros are allowed in this format.

- **Excel 97-2003 Workbook (.xls)**—This format produces files that can be read by any-one using legacy versions of Excel. Macros are allowed in this binary format; however, when you save in this format, you lose access to any cells outside of A1:IV65536. In addition, if someone opens the file in Excel 2003, she loses access to anything that used features introduced in Excel 2007 or later.

To avoid having to choose a macro-enabled workbook in the Save As dialog, you can customize your copy of Excel to always save new files in the .xlsm format by following these steps:

1. Click the File menu and select Options.
2. In the Excel Options dialog, select the Save category from the left navigation pane.
3. The first drop-down is Save Files in This Format. Open the drop-down and select Excel Macro-Enabled Workbook (*.xlsm). Click OK.

> **NOTE**
>
> Although you and I are not afraid to use macros, I have encountered some people who seem to freak out when they see the .xlsm file type. They actually seem angry that I sent them an .xlsm file that did not have any macros. Their reaction seemed reminiscent of King Arthur's "You got me all worked up!" line in *Monty Python and the Holy Grail*. Google's Gmail has joined this camp, refusing to show a preview of any attachments sent in the .xlsm format.
>
> If you encounter someone who seems to have a fear of the .xlsm file type, remind them of these points:
>
> - Every workbook created in the past 20 years could have had macros, but in fact, most did not.
>
> - If someone is trying to avoid macros, she should use the security settings to prevent macros from running anyway. The person can still open the .xlsm file to get the data in the spreadsheet.
>
> With these arguments, I hope you can overcome any fears of the .xlsm file type so that it can be your default file type.

Macro Security

After a Word VBA macro was used as the delivery method for the Melissa virus, Microsoft changed the default security settings to prevent macros from running. Therefore, before we can begin discussing the recording of a macro, we need to show you how to adjust the default settings.

In Excel 2013, you can either globally adjust the security settings or control macro settings for certain workbooks by saving the workbooks in a trusted location. Any workbook stored in a folder that is marked as a trusted location automatically has its macros enabled.

You can find the macro security settings under the Macro Security icon on the Developer tab. When you click this icon, the Macro Settings category of the Trust Center is displayed. You can use the left navigation bar in the dialog to access the Trusted Locations list.

Adding a Trusted Location

You can choose to store your macro workbooks in a folder that is marked as a trusted location. Any workbook stored in a trusted folder will have its macros enabled. Microsoft suggests that a trusted location should be on your hard drive. The default setting is that you cannot trust a location on a network drive.

To specify a trusted location, follow these steps:

1. Click Macro Security in the Developer tab.

2. Click Trusted Locations in the left navigation pane of the Trust Center.

3. If you want to trust a location on a network drive, select Allow Trusted Locations on My Network.

4. Click the Add New Location button. Excel displays the Microsoft Office Trusted Location dialog (see Figure 1.2).

5. Click the Browse button. Excel displays the Browse dialog.

6. Browse to the parent folder of the folder you want to be a trusted location. Click the trusted folder. Although the folder name does not appear in the Folder Name box, click OK. The correct folder name will appear in the Browse dialog.

7. If you want to trust subfolders of the selected folder, select Subfolders of This Location Are Also Trusted.

8. Click OK to add the folder to the Trusted Locations list.

> **CAUTION**
>
> Use care when selecting a trusted location. When you double-click an Excel attachment in an e-mail, Outlook stores the file in a temporary folder on your C: drive. You will not want to globally add C:\ and all subfolders to the Trusted Locations list.

Figure 1.2
Manage trusted folders in the Trusted Locations category of the Trust Center.

Microsoft Office Trusted Location

Warning: This location will be treated as a trusted source for opening files. If you change or add a location, make sure that the new location is secure.

Path:

C:\Users\Jelen\Documents\ExcelMacros

Browse...

☑ Subfolders of this location are also trusted

Description:

Folder to store trusted macros

Date and Time Created: 7/17/2012 10:32 AM

OK   Cancel

Using Macro Settings to Enable Macros in Workbooks Outside of Trusted Locations

For all macros not stored in a trusted location, Excel relies on the macro settings. The Low, Medium, High, and Very High settings that were familiar in Excel 2003 have been renamed.

To access the macro settings, click Macro Security in the Developer tab. Excel displays the Macro Settings category of the Trust Center dialog. Select the second option, Disable All Macros with Notification. A description of each option follows:

- **Disable All Macros Without Notification**—This setting prevents all macros from running. This setting is for people who never intend to run macros. Because you are currently holding a book that teaches you how to use macros, it is assumed that this setting is not for you. This setting is roughly equivalent to the old Very High Security setting in Excel 2003. With this setting, only macros in the Trusted Locations folders can run.

- **Disable All Macros with Notification**—The operative words in this setting are "with Notification." This means that you see a notification when you open a file with macros and you can choose to enable the content. If you ignore the notification, the macros remain disabled. This setting is similar to Medium security in Excel 2003 and is the recommended setting. In Excel 2013, a message is displayed in the Message Area indicating that macros have been disabled. You can choose to enable the content by clicking that option, as shown in Figure 1.3.

- **Disable All Macros Except Digitally Signed Macros**—This setting requires you to obtain a digital signing tool from VeriSign or another provider. This might be appropriate if you are going to be selling add-ins to others, but a bit of a hassle if you just want to write macros for your own use.

- **Enable All Macros (Not Recommended: Potentially Dangerous Code Can Run)**—This setting is similar to the Low macro security in Excel 2003. Although it requires the least amount of hassle, it also opens your computer to attacks from malicious Melissa-like viruses. Microsoft suggests that you do not use this setting.

Figure 1.3
Open a macro workbook using the Disable All Macros with Notification setting to enable the macros.

Using Disable All Macros with Notification

It is recommended that you set your macro settings to Disable All Macros with Notification. If you use this setting and open a workbook that contains macros, you see a Security Warning in the area just above the formula bar. Assuming you were expecting macros in this workbook, click Enable Content.

1

If you do not want to enable macros for the current workbook, dismiss the Security Warning by clicking the *X* at the far right of the message bar.

If you forget to enable the macros and attempt to run a macro, Excel indicates that you cannot run the macro because all macros have been disabled. If this occurs, close the workbook and reopen it to access the message bar again.

> **CAUTION**
>
> After you enable macros in a workbook stored on a local hard drive and then save the workbook, Excel remembers that you previously enabled macros in this workbook. The next time you open this workbook, macros are automatically enabled.

Overview of Recording, Storing, and Running a Macro

Recording a macro is useful when you do not have experience in writing lines of code in a macro. As you gain more knowledge and experience, you begin to record lines of code less frequently.

To begin recording a macro, select Record Macro from the Developer tab. Before recording begins, Excel displays the Record Macro dialog box, as shown in Figure 1.4.

Figure 1.4
Use the Record Macro dialog box to assign a name and a shortcut key to the macro being recorded.

Filling Out the Record Macro Dialog

In the Macro Name field, type a name for the macro. Be sure to type continuous characters. For example, type `Macro1` without a space, not `Macro 1` with a space. Assuming you will soon be creating many macros, use a meaningful name for the macro. A name such as FormatReport is more useful than one like Macro1.

The second field in the Record Macro dialog box is a shortcut key. If you type a lowercase j in this field, and then press Ctrl+j, this macro runs. Be careful, however, because

Ctrl+a through Ctrl+z (except Ctrl+j) are all already assigned to other tasks in Excel. If you assign a macro to Ctrl+b, you won't be able to use Ctrl+b for Bold anymore. One alternative is to assign the macros to Ctrl+Shift+A through Ctrl+Shift+Z. To assign a macro to a Ctrl+Shift+A, you would type Shift+A in the shortcut key box.

> **CAUTION**
>
> You can reuse a shortcut key for a macro. If you assign a macro to lowercase Ctrl+c, Excel runs your macro instead of doing the normal action of copy.

In the Record Macro dialog box, choose where you want to save a macro when it is recorded: Personal Macro Workbook, New Workbook, This Workbook. It is recommended that you store macros related to a particular workbook in This Workbook.

The Personal Macro Workbook (`Personal.xlsm`) is not a visible workbook; it is created if you choose to save the recording in the Personal Macro Workbook. This workbook is used to save a macro in a workbook that opens automatically when you start Excel, thereby enabling you to use the macro. After Excel is started, the workbook is hidden. If you want to display it, select Unhide from the View tab.

>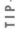
> It is not recommended that you use the personal workbook for every macro you save. Save only those macros that assist you in general tasks—not in tasks that are performed in a specific sheet or workbook.

The fourth box in the Record Macro dialog is for a description. This description is added as a comment to the beginning of your macro. Note that legacy versions of Excel automatically noted the date and username of the person recording the macro. Excel 2013 no longer automatically inserts this information in the Description field.

After you select the location where you want to store the macro, click OK. Record your macro. For this example, type `Hello World` in the active cell and press Ctrl+Enter to accept the entry and stay in the same cell. When you are finished recording the macro, click the Stop Recording icon in the Developer tab.

>
> You can also access a Stop Recording icon in the lower-left corner of the Excel window. Look for a small white square to the right of the word *Ready* in the status bar. Using this Stop button might be more convenient than returning to the Developer tab. After you record your first macro, this area usually has a Record Macro icon, which is a small dot on an Excel worksheet.

Running a Macro

If you assigned a shortcut key to your macro, you can play it by pressing the key combination. You can also assign macros to toolbar buttons, form controls, or drawing objects, or you can run them from the Visual Basic toolbar.

Creating a Macro Button on the Ribbon

You can add an icon to a new group on the Ribbon to run your macro. This is appropriate for macros stored in the Personal Macro Workbook. Icons added to the Ribbon are still enabled even when your macro workbook is not open. If you click the icon when the macro workbook is not open, Excel opens the workbook and runs the macro. Follow these steps to add a macro button to the Ribbon:

1. Click the File menu and select Options from the left navigation bar to open the Excel Options dialog.

2. In the Excel Options dialog, select the Customize Ribbon category from the left-side navigation.

> **TIP**
>
> Note that a shortcut to replace steps 1 and 2 is to right-click the Ribbon and select Customize Ribbon.

3. In the list box on the right, choose the tab name where you want to add an icon.

4. Click the New Group button below the right list box. Excel adds a new entry called New Group (Custom) to the end of the groups in that Ribbon tab.

5. To move the group to the left in the Ribbon tab, click the up-arrow icon on the right side of the dialog several times.

6. To rename the group, click the Rename button. Type a new name, such as Report Macros. Click OK. Excel shows the group in the list box as Report Macros (Custom). Note that the word *Custom* does not appear in the Ribbon.

7. Open the upper-left drop-down and choose Macros from the list. The Macros category is fourth in the list. Excel displays a list of available macros in the left list box.

8. Choose a macro from the left list box. Click the Add button in the center of the dialog. Excel moves the macro to the right list box in the selected group. Excel uses a generic VBA icon for all macros. You can change the icon by following steps 9 and 10.

9. Click the macro in the right list box. Click the Rename button at the bottom of the right list box. Excel displays a list of 180 possible icons. Choose an icon. Alternatively, type a friendly label for the icon, such as Format Report.

10. You can move the Report Macros group to a new location on the Ribbon tab. Click Report Macros (Custom) and use the up- and down-arrow icons on the right of the dialog.

11. Click OK to close Excel options. The new button appears on the selected Ribbon tab.

Creating a Macro Button on the Quick Access Toolbar

You can add an icon to the Quick Access toolbar to run your macro. If your macro is stored in the Personal Macro Workbook, you can have the button permanently displayed in the Quick Access toolbar. If the macro is stored in the current workbook, you can specify that the icon should appear only when the workbook is open. Follow these steps to add a macro button to the Quick Access toolbar:

1. Click the File menu and select Options to open the Excel Options dialog.

2. In the Excel Options dialog select the Quick Access Toolbar category from the left-side navigation.

> **TIP**
> Note that a shortcut to replace steps 1 and 2 is to right-click the Quick Access toolbar and select Customize Quick Access Toolbar.

3. If your macro should be available only when the current workbook is open, open the upper-right drop-down and change For All Documents (Default) to For *FileName.xlsm*. Any icons associated with the current workbook are displayed at the end of the Quick Access toolbar.

4. Open the upper-left drop-down and select Macros from the list. The Macros category is fourth in the list. Excel displays a list of available macros in the left list box.

5. Choose a macro from the left list box. Click the Add button in the center of the dialog. Excel moves the macro to the right list box. Excel uses a generic VBA icon for all macros. You can change the icon by following steps 6 through 8.

6. Click the macro in the right list box. Click the Modify button at the bottom of the right list box. Excel displays a list of 180 possible icons (see Figure 1.5).

> **NOTE**
> Considering that Excel 2003 offered 4,096 possible icons and an icon editor, the list of 180 is a disappointment.

7. Choose an icon from the list. In the Display Name box, replace the macro name with a short name that appears in the ToolTip for the icon.

8. Click OK to close the Modify Button dialog.

9. Click OK to close Excel options. The new button appears on the Quick Access toolbar.

Figure 1.5
Attach a macro to a button on the Quick Access toolbar.

Enter the ToolTip here

Assigning a Macro to a Form Control, Text Box, or Shape

If you want to create a macro specific to a workbook, store the macro in the workbook and attach it to a form control or any object on the sheet.

Follow these steps to attach a macro to a form control on the sheet:

1. On the Developer tab, click the Insert button to open its drop-down list. Excel offers 12 form controls and 12 ActiveX controls in this one drop-down menu. The form controls are at the top and the ActiveX controls are at the bottom. Most icons in the ActiveX section of the drop-down look identical to an icon in the forms control section of the drop-down. Click the Button Form Control icon at the upper-left corner of the Insert drop-down.

2. Move your cursor over the worksheet; the cursor changes to a plus sign.

3. Draw a button on the sheet by clicking and holding the left mouse button while drawing a box shape. Release the button when you have finished.

4. Choose a macro from the Assign Macro dialog box and click OK. The button is created with generic text such as Button 1. To customize the text or the button appearance, follow steps 5 through 7.

5. Type a new label for the button. Note that while you are typing, the selection border around the button changes from dots to diagonal lines to indicate that you are in Text Edit mode. You cannot change the button color while in Text Edit mode. To exit Text Edit mode, either click the diagonal lines to change them to dots or Ctrl-click the button again. Note that if you accidentally click away from the button, you should Ctrl-click the button to select it. Then drag the cursor over the text on the button to select the text.

6. Right-click the dots surrounding the button and select Format Control. Excel displays the Format Control dialog with seven tabs across the top. If your Format Control dialog has only a Font tab, you failed to exit Text Edit mode. If this occurred, close the dialog, Ctrl-click the button, and repeat this step.

7. Use the settings in the Format Control dialog to change the font size, font color, margins, and similar settings for the control. Click OK to close the Format Control dialog when you have finished. Click a cell to deselect the button.

8. Click the button to run the macro.

Macros can be assigned to any worksheet object such as clip art, a shape, SmartArt graphics, or a text box. In Figure 1.6, the top button is a traditional button form control. The other images are clip art, a shape with WordArt, and a SmartArt graphic. To assign a macro to any object, right-click the object, and select Assign Macro.

Figure 1.6

Assigning a macro to a form control or an object is appropriate for macros stored in the same workbook as the control. You can assign a macro to any of these objects.

Understanding the VB Editor

If you want to edit your recorded macro, you do it in the VB Editor. Press Alt+F11 or use the Visual Basic icon in the Developer tab.

Figure 1.7 shows an example of the typical VB Editor screen. You can see three windows: Project Explorer, the Properties window, and the Programming window. Don't worry if your window doesn't look exactly like this because you will see how to display the windows you need in this review of the editor.

Figure 1.7
The VB Editor window.

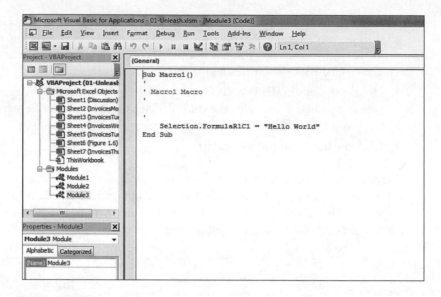

VB Editor Settings

Several settings in the VB Editor enable you to customize this editor and assist you in writing your macros.

Under Tools, Options, Editor, you find several useful settings. All settings except for one are set correctly by default. The remaining setting requires some consideration on your part. This setting is Require Variable Declaration. By default, Excel does not require you to declare variables. I prefer this setting because it can save time when you create a program. My coauthor prefers to change this setting to require variable declaration. This change forces the compiler to stop if it finds a variable that it does not recognize, which reduces misspelled variable names. It is a matter of your personal preference as to whether you turn this setting on or keep it off.

The Project Explorer

The Project Explorer lists any open workbooks and add-ins that are loaded. If you click the + icon next to the VBA Project, you see that there is a folder with Microsoft Excel objects. There can also be folders for forms, class modules, and standard modules. Each folder includes one or more individual components.

Right-clicking a component and selecting View Code or just double-clicking the components brings up any code in the Programming window. The exception is userforms, where double-clicking displays the userform in Design view.

To display the Project Explorer window, select View, Project Explorer from the menu, or press Ctrl+R or locate the bizarre Project Explorer icon just below the Tools menu, sandwiched between Design Mode and Properties Window.

To insert a module, right-click your project, select Insert, and then choose the type of module you want. The available modules are as follows:

- **Microsoft Excel objects**—By default, a project consists of sheet modules for each sheet in the workbook and a single ThisWorkbook module. Code specific to a sheet such as controls or sheet events is placed on the corresponding sheet. Workbook events are placed in the ThisWorkbook module. You'll learn more about events in Chapter 7, "Event Programming."

- **Forms**—Excel enables you to design your own forms to interact with the user. You'll learn more about these forms in Chapter 10.

- **Modules**—When you record a macro, Excel automatically creates a module in which to place the code. Most of your code resides in these types of modules.

- **Class modules**—Class modules are Excel's way of letting you create your own objects. They also allow pieces of code to be shared among programmers without the programmer's needing to understand how it works. You'll learn more about class modules in Chapter 9, "Creating Classes, Records, and Collections."

The Properties Window

The Properties window enables you to edit the properties of various components such as sheets, workbooks, modules, and form controls. The Property list varies according to what component is selected. To display this window, select View, Properties Window from the menu, press F4, or click the Project Properties icon on the toolbar.

Understanding Shortcomings of the Macro Recorder

Suppose you work in an accounting department. Each day you receive a text file from the company system showing all the invoices produced the prior day. This text file has commas separating each field. The columns in the file are InvoiceDate, InvoiceNumber, SalesRepNumber, CustomerNumber, ProductRevenue, ServiceRevenue, and ProductCost (see Figure 1.8).

Figure 1.8
Invoice.txt file.

```
invoice.txt - Notepad
File  Edit  Format  View  Help
InvoiceDate,InvoiceNumber,SalesRepNumber,CustomerNumber,ProductRevenue,ServiceRevenue,ProductCost
06/09/2014,123829,S21,C8754,538400,0,299897
06/09/2014,123830,S45,C4056,588600,0,307563
06/09/2014,123831,S54,C8323,882200,0,521726
06/09/2014,123832,S21,C6026,830900,0,494831
06/09/2014,123833,S45,C3025,673600,0,374953
06/09/2014,123834,S54,C8663,966300,0,528575
06/09/2014,123835,S21,C1508,467100,0,257942
06/09/2014,123836,S45,C7366,658500,10000,308719
06/09/2014,123837,S54,C4533,191700,0,109534
```

Each morning, you manually import this file into Excel. You add a total row to the data, bold the headings, and then print the report for distribution to a few managers.

This seems like a simple process that would be ideally suited to using the macro recorder. However, due to some problems with the macro recorder, your first few attempts might not be successful. The following case study explains how to overcome these problems.

CASE STUDY: PREPARING TO RECORD THE MACRO

The task mentioned in the preceding section is perfect for a macro. However, before you record a macro, think about the steps you will use. In this case, the steps you will use are as follows:

1. Click the File menu and select Open.
2. Navigate to the folder where `Invoice.txt` is stored.
3. Select All Files (*.*) from the Files of Type drop-down list.
4. Select Invoice.txt.
5. Click Open.
6. In the Text Import Wizard—Step 1 of 3, select Delimited from the Original Data Type section.
7. Click Next.
8. In the Text Import Wizard—Step 2 of 3, clear the Tab key and select Comma in the Delimiters section.
9. Click Next.
10. In the Text Import Wizard—Step 3 of 3, select General in the Column Data Format section and change it to `Date: MDY`.
11. Click Finish to import the file.
12. Press the End key followed by the down arrow to move to the last row of data.
13. Press the down arrow one more time to move to the total row.
14. Type the word `Total`.
15. Press the right-arrow key four times to move to Column E of the total row.
16. Click the AutoSum button and press Ctrl+Enter to add a total to the Product Revenue column while remaining in that cell.
17. Click the AutoFill handle and drag it from Column E to Column G to copy the total formula to Columns F and G.
18. Highlight Row 1 and click the Bold icon on the Home tab to set the headings in bold.
19. Highlight the Total row and click the Bold icon on the Home tab to set the totals in bold.
20. Press Ctrl+A to select all cells.
21. From the Home tab, select Format, AutoFit Column Width.

After you have rehearsed these steps in your head, you are ready to record your first macro. Open a blank workbook and save it with a name such as `MacroToImportInvoices.xlsm`. Click the Record Macro button on the Developer tab.

In the Record Macro dialog, the default macro name is Macro1. Change this to something descriptive like `ImportInvoice`. Make sure that the macros will be stored in This Workbook. You might want an easy way to run this macro later, so enter the letter `i` in the Shortcut Key field. In the Description field, add a little descriptive text to tell what the macro is doing (see Figure 1.9). Click OK when you are ready.

Figure 1.9
Before recording your
macro, complete the
Record Macro dialog box.

Recording the Macro

The macro recorder is now recording your every move. For this reason, perform your steps in exact order without extraneous actions. If you accidentally move to Column F, type a value, clear the value, and then move back to E to enter the first total, the recorded macro will blindly make that same mistake day after day after day. Recorded macros move fast, but there is nothing like watching the macro recorder play out your mistakes repeatedly.

Carefully execute all the actions necessary to produce the report. After you have performed the final step, click the Stop button in the lower-left corner of the Excel window or click Stop Recording in the Developer tab.

Now it is time to look at your code. Switch to the VB Editor by selecting Visual Basic from the Developer tab or pressing Alt+F11.

Examining Code in the Programming Window

Let's look at the code you just recorded from the case study. Don't worry if it doesn't make sense yet.

To open the VB Editor, press Alt+F11. In your VBA Project (MacroToImportInvoices.xlsm), find the component Module1, right-click the module, and select View Code. Notice that some lines start with an apostrophe—these are comments and are ignored by the program. The macro recorder starts your macros with a few comments, using the description you entered in the Record Macro dialog. The comment for the Keyboard Shortcut is there to remind you of the shortcut.

> **NOTE** The comment does *not* assign the shortcut. If you change the comment to be Ctrl+J, it does not change the shortcut. You must change the setting in the Macro dialog box in Excel or run this line of code:
>
> ```
> Application.MacroOptions Macro:="ImportInvoice", _
>     Description:="", ShortcutKey:="j"
> ```

Recorded macro code is usually pretty neat (see Figure 1.10). Each noncomment line of code is indented four characters. If a line is longer than 100 characters, the recorder breaks it into multiple lines and indents the lines an additional four characters. To continue a line of code, type a space and an underscore at the end of the first line and then continue the code on the next line. Don't forget the space before the underscore. Using an underscore without the preceding space causes an error.

> **NOTE**
>
> Note that the physical limitations of this book do not allow 100 characters on a single line. Therefore, the lines will be broken at 80 characters so that they fit on a page. For this reason, your recorded macro might look slightly different from the ones that appear in this book.

Figure 1.10
The recorded macro is neat looking and nicely indented.

```
(General)                                                    ▼   ImportInvoices

Sub ImportInvoices()
'
' ImportInvoices Macro
' Imports invoice.txt, add a total row. Does some formatting.
'
' Keyboard Shortcut: Ctrl+i
'
    Workbooks.OpenText Filename:="C:\Users\Jelen\Desktop\2013VBA\invoice.txt", _
        Origin:=437, StartRow:=1, DataType:=xlDelimited, TextQualifier:= _
        xlDoubleQuote, ConsecutiveDelimiter:=False, Tab:=False, Semicolon:=False _
        , Comma:=True, Space:=False, Other:=False, FieldInfo:=Array(Array(1, 3), _
        Array(2, 1), Array(3, 1), Array(4, 1), Array(5, 1), Array(6, 1), Array(7, 1)), _
        TrailingMinusNumbers:=True
    Selection.End(xlDown).Select
    Range("A11").Select
    ActiveCell.FormulaR1C1 = "Total"
    Range("E11").Select
    Selection.FormulaR1C1 = "=SUM(R[-9]C:R[-1]C)"
    Selection.AutoFill Destination:=Range("E11:G11"), Type:=xlFillDefault
    Range("E11:G11").Select
    Rows("1:1").Select
    Selection.Font.Bold = True
    Rows("11:11").Select
    Selection.Font.Bold = True
    Cells.Select
    Range("A11").Activate
    Selection.Columns.AutoFit
End Sub
```

Consider that the following seven lines of recorded code are actually only one line of code that has been broken into seven lines for readability:

```
Workbooks.OpenText Filename:="C:\somepath\invoice.txt", _
    Origin:=437, StartRow:=1, DataType:=xlDelimited, _
    TextQualifier:=xlDoubleQuote, ConsecutiveDelimiter:=False, _
    Tab:=True, Semicolon:=False, Comma:=True, Space:=False, _
    Other:=False, FieldInfo:=Array(Array(1, 3), Array(2, 1), _
    Array(3, 1), Array(4, 1), Array(5, 1), Array(6, 1), _
    Array(7, 1)), TrailingMinusNumbers:=True
```

Counting this as one line, the macro recorder was able to record our 21-step process in 15 lines of code, which is pretty impressive.

> **NOTE** Each action you perform in the Excel user interface might equate to one or more lines of recorded code. Some actions might generate a dozen lines of code.

Test Each Macro

It is always a good idea to test macros. To test your new macro, return to the regular Excel interface by pressing Alt+F11. Close `Invoice.txt` without saving any changes. `MacroToImportInvoices.xls` is still open.

Press Ctrl+I to run the recorded macro. It should work beautifully if you completed the steps correctly. The data is imported, totals are added, bold formatting is applied, and the columns are made wider. This seems like a perfect solution (see Figure 1.11).

Figure 1.11
The macro formats the data in the sheet.

▲	A	B	C	D	E	F	G	H
1	InvoiceDate	InvoiceNumber	SalesRepNumber	CustomerNumber	ProductRevenue	ServiceRevenue	ProductCost	
2	6/9/2014	123829	S21	C8754	538400	0	299897	
3	6/9/2014	123830	S45	C4056	588600	0	307563	
4	6/9/2014	123831	S54	C8323	882200	0	521726	
5	6/9/2014	123832	S21	C6026	830900	0	494831	
6	6/9/2014	123833	S45	C3025	673600	0	374953	
7	6/9/2014	123834	S54	C8663	966300	0	528575	
8	6/9/2014	123835	S21	C1508	467100	0	257942	
9	6/9/2014	123836	S45	C7366	658500	10000	308719	
10	6/9/2014	123837	S54	C4533	191700	0	109534	
11	Total				5797300	10000	3203740	
12								

Running the Macro on Another Day Produces Undesired Results

After testing the macro, be sure to save your macro file to use on another day. But suppose that the next day, after receiving a new `Invoice.txt` file from the system, you open the macro and press Ctrl+I to run it, and disaster strikes. The data for June 9 happened to have 9 invoices, but the data for June 10 now has 17 invoices. The recorded macro blindly added the totals in Row 11 because this was where you put the totals when the macro was recorded (see Figure 1.12).

This problem arises because the macro recorder is recording all your actions in absolute mode by default. As an alternative to using the default state of the macro recorder, the next section discusses relative recording and how this might get you closer to a final solution.

Figure 1.12
The intent of the recorded macro was to add a total at the end of the data, but the recorder made a macro that always adds totals at Row 11.

	A	B	C	D	E	F	G
1	InvoiceDate	InvoiceNumber	SalesRepNumber	CustomerNumber	ProductRevenue	ServiceRevenue	ProductCost
2	6/10/2014	123813	S82	C8754	716100	12000	423986
3	6/10/2014	123814		C4894	224200	0	131243
4	6/10/2014	123815	S43	C7278	277000	0	139208
5	6/10/2014	123816	S54	C6425	746100	15000	350683
6	6/10/2014	123817	S43	C6291	928300	0	488988
7	6/10/2014	123818	S43	C1000	723200	0	383069
8	6/10/2014	123819	S82	C6025	982600	0	544025
9	6/10/2014	123820	S17	C8026	490100	45000	243808
10	6/10/2014	123821	S43	C4244	615800	0	300579
11	Total	123822	S45	C1007	5703400	72000	3005589
12	6/10/2014	123823	S87	C1878	338100	0	165666
13	6/10/2014	123824	S43	C3068	567900	0	265775
14	6/10/2014	123825	S43	C7571	123456	0	55555
15	6/10/2014	123826	S55	C7181	37900	0	19811
16	6/10/2014	123827	S43	C7570	582700	0	292000
17	6/10/2014	123828	S87	C5302	495000	0	241504
18	6/10/2014	123828	S87	C5302	495000	0	241504
19							

Possible Solution: Use Relative References When Recording

By default, the macro recorder records all actions as *absolute* actions. If you navigate to Row 11 when you record the macro, the macro will always go to Row 11 when the macro is run. This is rarely appropriate when dealing with variable numbers of rows of data. The better option is to use relative references when recording.

Macros recorded with absolute references note the actual address of the cell pointer, such as A11. Macros recorded with relative references note that the cell pointer should move a certain number of rows and columns from its current position. For example, if the cell pointer starts in cell A1, the code `ActiveCell.Offset(16, 1).Select` would move the cell pointer to B17, which is the cell 16 rows down and 1 column to the right.

Let's try the same case study again, this time using relative references. The solution will be much closer to working correctly.

CASE STUDY: RECORDING THE MACRO WITH RELATIVE REFERENCES

Let's try to record the macro again, but this time you will use relative references. Close `Invoice.txt` without saving changes. In the workbook `MacroToImportInvoices.xls`, record a new macro by selecting Record Macro from the Developer tab. Give the new macro a name of `ImportInvoicesRelative` and assign a different shortcut key such as Ctrl+Shift+J.

As you start to record the macro, go through the process of opening the `Invoice.txt` file. Before navigating to the last row of data by pressing the End key and then the down-arrow key, click the Use Relative References button on the Developer tab (refer to Figure 1.1).

Repeat steps 1 through 11 in the previous case study to import the file and then follow these steps:

1. Press the End key followed by the down-arrow key to move to the last row of data.

2. Press the down arrow one more time to move to the total row.

3. Type the word **Total**.

4. Press the right-arrow key four times to move to Column E of the Total row.

5. Hold the Shift key while pressing the right arrow twice to select E11:G11.

6. Click the AutoSum button.

7. Press Shift+spacebar to select the entire row. Type Ctrl+b to apply bold formatting to it. At this point, you need to move to Cell A1 to apply bold to the headings. You do not want the macro recorder to record the movement from Row 11 to Row 1 because it would record this as moving 10 rows up, which might not be correct tomorrow. Before moving to A1, toggle the Use Relative Recording button off, and then continue recording the rest of the macro.

8. Highlight Row 1 and click the Bold icon to set the headings in bold.

9. Press Ctrl+A to select all cells.

10. From the Home tab, select Format, AutoFit Column Width.

11. Select cell A1.

12. Stop recording.

Press Alt+F11 to go to the VB Editor to review your code. The new macro appears in Module1 below the previous macro.

If you close Excel between recording the first and second macros, Excel inserts a new module called Module2 for the newly recorded macro.

The following code has been edited with two comments that will help you remember where you turned the relative recording on and then off:

```
Sub ImportInvoicesRelative()
'
' ImportInvoicesRelative Macro
' Use relative references for some of the steps of the macro
' to format the invoice.txt file
'
    Workbooks.OpenText Filename:= _
       "C:\invoice.txt", Origin:=437, StartRow:=1, _
       DataType:=xlDelimited, TextQualifier:=xlDoubleQuote, _
       ConsecutiveDelimiter:=False, Tab:=True, _
       Semicolon:=False, Comma:=True, Space:=False, _
       Other:=False, FieldInfo:=Array(Array(1, 3), Array(2, 1), _
       Array(3, 1), Array(4, 1), Array(5, 1), Array(6, 1), _
       Array(7, 1)), TrailingMinusNumbers:=True

' Turned on relative recording here
    Selection.End(xlDown).Select
    ActiveCell.Offset(1, 0).Range("A1").Select
    ActiveCell.FormulaR1C1 = "'Total"
    ActiveCell.Offset(0, 4).Range("A1:C1").Select
```

```
      Selection.FormulaR1C1 = "=SUM(R[-9]C:R[-1]C)"

' Turned off relative recording here
    ActiveCell.Rows("1:1").EntireRow.Select
    ActiveCell.Activate
    Selection.Font.Bold = True
    Rows("1:1").Select
    Selection.Font.Bold = True
    Cells.Select
    Selection.Columns.AutoFit
    Range("A1").Select
End Sub
```

To test the macro, close `Invoice.txt` without saving, and then run the macro with Ctrl+J. Everything should look good, and you should get the same results.

The next test is to see whether the program works on the next day when you might have more rows. If you are working along with the sample files, rename `invoice.txt` to `Invoice1.txt`. Rename `Invoice2.txt` to `Invoice.txt`.

Open `MacroToImportInvoices.xls` and run the new macro with Ctrl+Shift+J. This time, everything should look good with the totals in the correct places. Look at Figure 1.13—see anything out of the ordinary?

Figure 1.13
The result of running the Relative macro.

	A	B	C	D	E	F	G
1	InvoiceDate	InvoiceNumber	SalesRepNumber	CustomerNumber	ProductRevenue	ServiceRevenue	ProductCost
2	6/10/2014	123813	S82	C8754	716100	12000	423986
3	6/10/2014	123814		C4894	224200	0	131243
4	6/10/2014	123815	S43	C7278	277000	0	139208
5	6/10/2014	123816	S54	C6425	746100	15000	350683
6	6/10/2014	123817	S43	C6291	928300	0	488988
7	6/10/2014	123818	S43	C1000	723200	0	383069
8	6/10/2014	123819	S82	C6025	982600	0	544025
9	6/10/2014	123820	S17	C8026	490100	45000	243808
10	6/10/2014	123821	S43	C4244	615800	0	300579
11	6/10/2014	123822	S45	C1007	271300	0	153253
12	6/10/2014	123823	S87	C1878	338100	0	165666
13	6/10/2014	123824	S43	C3068	567900	0	265775
14	6/10/2014	123825	S43	C7571	123456	0	55555
15	6/10/2014	123826	S55	C7181	37900	0	19811
16	6/10/2014	123827	S43	C7570	582700	0	292000
17	6/10/2014	123828	S87	C5302	495000	0	241504
18	6/10/2014	123828	S87	C5302	495000	0	241504
19	Total				3527156	0	1735647
20							

If you aren't careful, you might print these reports for your manager. If you did, you would be in trouble. When you look in cell E19, you can see that Excel has inserted a green triangle to tell you to look at the cell. If you happened to try this back in Excel 95 or Excel 97 before SmartTags, there would not have been an indicator that anything was wrong.

When you move the cell pointer to E19, an alert indicator pops up near the cell. This indicator tells you that the formula fails to include adjacent cells. If you look in the formula bar, you will see that the macro totaled only from Row 10 to Row 18. Neither the relative recording nor the nonrelative recording is smart enough to replicate the logic of the AutoSum button.

At this point, some people would give up. However, imagine that you had fewer invoice records on this particular day. Excel would have rewarded you with the illogical formula of =SUM(E6:E1048574), as shown in Figure 1.14. Since this formula would be in E7, circular reference warnings will appear in the status bar.

Figure 1.14
The result of running the Relative macro with fewer invoice records.

	A	B	C	D	E	F	G
1	InvoiceDate	InvoiceNumber	SalesRepNumber	CustomerNumber	ProductRevenue	ServiceRevenue	ProductCost
2	6/12/2014	123850		C1654	161000	0	90761
3	6/12/2014	123851		C6460	275500	10000	146341
4	6/12/2014	123852		C5143	925400	0	473515
5	6/12/2014	123853		C7868	148200	0	75700
6	6/12/2014	123854		C3310	890200	0	468333
7	Total				0	0	0
8							

E7 formula: =SUM(E6:E1048574)

If you have tried using the macro recorder, most likely you have run into problems similar to the ones produced in the previous two case studies. Although this is frustrating, you should be happy to know that the macro recorder actually gets you 95 percent of the way to a useful macro.

Your job is to recognize where the macro recorder is likely to fail and then to be able to dive into the VBA code to fix the one or two lines that require adjusting to have a perfect macro. With some added human intelligence, you can produce awesome macros to speed up your daily work.

If you are like me, you are cursing Microsoft about now. We have wasted a good deal of time over a couple of days, and neither macro works. What makes it worse is that this sort of procedure would have been handled perfectly by the old Lotus 1-2-3 macro recorder introduced in 1983. Mitch Kapor solved this problem 30 years ago, and Microsoft still can't get it right.

Did you know that up through Excel 97, Microsoft Excel secretly ran Lotus command-line macros? I found this out right after Microsoft quit supporting Excel 97. At that time, a number of companies upgraded to Excel XP, which no longer supported the Lotus 1-2-3 macros. Many of these companies hired us to convert the old Lotus 1-2-3 macros to Excel VBA. It is interesting that from Excel 5, Excel 95, and Excel 97, Microsoft offered an interpreter that could handle the Lotus macros that solved this problem correctly, yet their own macro recorder couldn't (and still can't!) solve the problem.

Never Use the AutoSum or Quick Analysis While Recording a Macro

There actually is a macro-recorder solution to the current problem. It is important to recognize that the macro recorder will never correctly record the intent of the AutoSum button.

If you are in cell E99 and click the AutoSum button, Excel starts scanning from cell E98 upward until it locates a text cell, a blank cell, or a formula. It then proposes a formula that sums everything between the current cell and the found cell.

However, the macro recorder records the particular result of that search on the day that the macro was recorded. Rather than recording something along the lines of "do the normal AutoSum logic," the macro recorder inserts a single line of code to add up the previous 98 cells.

Excel 2013 added the Quick Analysis feature. Select E2:G99, open the Quick Analysis, choose Totals, Sum at Bottom, and you would get the correct totals in Row 100. The macro recorder hard-codes the formulas to always appear in Row 100 and to always total Row 2 through Row 99.

The somewhat bizarre workaround is to type a SUM function that uses a mix of relative and absolute row references. If you type =SUM(E$2:E10) while the macro recorder is running, Excel correctly adds code that always sums from a fixed row two down to the relative reference that is just above the current cell.

Here is the resulting code with a few comments:

```
Sub FormatInvoice3()
'
' FormatInvoice2 Macro
' Third try. Use relative. Don't touch AutoSum
'
' Keyboard Shortcut: Ctrl+Shift+K
'
    Workbooks.OpenText Filename:="C:\somepath\invoice.txt", _
        Origin:=437, StartRow:=1, DataType:=xlDelimited, _
        TextQualifier:=xlDoubleQuote, ConsecutiveDelimiter:=False, _
        Tab:=False, Semicolon:=False, Comma:=True, _
        Space:=False, Other:=False, FieldInfo:=Array( _
        Array(1, 3), Array(2, 1), Array(3, 1), Array(4, 1), _
        Array(5, 1), Array(6, 1), Array(7, 1)), _
        TrailingMinusNumbers:=True
    ' Relative turned on here
    Selection.End(xlDown).Select
    ActiveCell.Offset(1, 0).Range("A1").Select
    ActiveCell.FormulaR1C1 = "Total"
    ActiveCell.Offset(0, 4).Range("A1").Select
    ' Don't use AutoSum. Type this formula:
    Selection.FormulaR1C1 = "=SUM(R2C:R[-1]C)"
    Selection.AutoFill Destination:=ActiveCell.Range("A1:C1"), _
        Type:= xlFillDefault
    ActiveCell.Range("A1:C1").Select
    ' Relative turned off here
    ActiveCell.Rows("1:1").EntireRow.Select
```

```
    ActiveCell.Activate
    Selection.Font.Bold = True
    Cells.Select
    Selection.Columns.AutoFit
    Range("A1").Select
End Sub
```

This third macro consistently works with any size of dataset.

Three Tips When Using the Macro Recorder

You will rarely be able to record 100 percent of your macros and have them work. However, you will get much closer by using the three tips listed in the following subsections.

Tip 1: The Use Relative References Setting Usually Needs to Be On

Microsoft should have made this setting the default. Unless you specifically need to move to Row 1 from the bottom of a dataset, you should usually leave the Use Relative References button in the Developer tab turned on.

Tip 2: Use Special Navigation Keys to Move to the Bottom of a Dataset

If you are at the top of a dataset and need to move to the last cell with data, you can press Ctrl+down arrow or press the End key and then the down-arrow key.

Similarly, to move to the last column in the current row of the dataset, press Ctrl+right arrow or press End and then press the right-arrow key.

By using these navigation keys, you can jump to the end of the dataset, no matter how many rows or columns you have today.

Tip 3: Never Touch the AutoSum Icon While Recording a Macro

The macro recorder will not record the "essence" of the AutoSum button. Instead, it hardcodes the formula that resulted from pressing the AutoSum button. This formula does not work any time you have more or fewer records in the dataset.

Instead, type a formula with a single dollar sign, such as =SUM(E$2:E10). When this is done, the macro recorder records the first E$2 as a fixed reference and starts the SUM range directly below the Row 1 headings. Provided that the active cell is E11, the macro recorder recognizes E10 as a relative reference pointing directly above the current cell.

Next Steps

Chapter 2, "This Sounds Like BASIC, So Why Doesn't It Look Familiar?" examines the three macros you recorded in this chapter to make more sense out of them. After you know how to decode the VBA code, it will feel natural to either correct the recorded code or simply write code from scratch. Hang on through one more chapter. You'll soon learn that VBA is the solution, and you'll be writing useful code that works consistently.

This Sounds Like BASIC, So Why Doesn't It Look Familiar?

2

I Can't Understand This Code

As mentioned previously, if you have taken a class in a procedural language such as BASIC or COBOL, you might be confused when you look at VBA code. Even though VBA stands for *Visual Basic for Applications*, it is an *object-oriented* version of BASIC. Here is a bit of VBA code:

```
Selection.End(xlDown).Select
Range("A11").Select
ActiveCell.FormulaR1C1 = "Total"
Range("E11").Select
Selection.FormulaR1C1 = "=SUM(R[-9]C:R[-1]C)"
Selection.AutoFill
Destination:=Range("E11:G11"),
Type:=xlFillDefault
```

This code likely makes no sense to anyone who knows only procedural languages. Unfortunately, your first introduction to programming in school (assuming you are over 35 years old) would have been a procedural language.

Here is a section of code written in the BASIC language:

```
For x = 1 to 10
    Print Rpt$(" ",x);
    Print "*"
Next x
```

If you run this code, you get a pyramid of asterisks on your screen:

```
*
 *
  *
   *
    *
     *
      *
       *
        *
         *
```

If you have ever been in a procedural programming class, you can probably look at the code and figure out what is going on because procedural languages are more English-like than object-oriented languages. The statement `Print "Hello World"` follows the verb-object format, which is how you would generally talk. Let's step away from programming for a second and think about a concrete example.

Understanding the Parts of VBA "Speech"

If you were going to write code for instructions to play soccer using BASIC, the instruction to kick a ball would look something like this:

```
"Kick the Ball"
```

Hey—this is how you talk! It makes sense. You have a verb (kick) and then a noun (ball). The BASIC code in the preceding section has a verb (print) and a noun (the asterisk). Life is good.

Here is the problem. VBA doesn't work like this. In fact, no object-oriented language works like this. In an object-oriented language, the objects (nouns) are most important, hence the name: object-oriented. If you were going to write code for instructions to play soccer with VBA, the basic structure would be as follows:

```
Ball.Kick
```

You have a noun (ball), which comes first. In VBA, this is an *object*. Then you have the verb (kick), which comes next. In VBA, this is a *method*.

The basic structure of VBA is a bunch of lines of code in which you have

```
Object.Method
```

Needless to say, this is not English. If you took a romance language in high school, you will remember that those languages use a "noun adjective" construct. However, no one uses "noun verb" to tell someone to do something:

```
Water.Drink
Food.Eat
Girl.Kiss
```

That is why VBA is confusing to someone who previously took a procedural programming class.

Let's carry the analogy a bit further. Imagine that you walk onto a grassy field and there are five balls in front of you. There are a soccer ball, basketball, baseball, bowling ball, and tennis ball. You want to instruct the kid on your soccer team to "kick the soccer ball."

If you tell him to kick the ball (or `ball.kick`), you really aren't sure which one of the five balls he will kick. Maybe he will kick the one closest to him, which could be a problem if he is standing in front of the bowling ball.

For almost any noun, or object in VBA, there is a collection of that object. Think about Excel. If you can have one row, you can have a bunch of rows. If you can have one cell, you can have a bunch of cells. If you can have one worksheet, you can have a bunch of worksheets. The only difference between an object and a collection is that you will add an *s* to the name of the object:

```
Row becomes Rows.
Cell becomes Cells.
Ball becomes Balls.
```

When you refer to something that is a collection, you have to tell the programming language to which item you are referring. There are a couple of ways to do this. You can refer to an item by using a number. For example, if the soccer ball is the second ball, you might say this:

```
Balls(2).Kick
```

This works fine, but it could be a dangerous way to program. For example, it might work on Tuesday. However, if you get to the field on Wednesday and someone has rearranged the balls, `Balls(2).Kick` might be a painful exercise.

A much safer way to go is to use a name for the object in a collection. You can say the following:

```
Balls("Soccer").Kick
```

With this method, you always know that it will be the soccer ball that is being kicked.

So far, so good. You know that a ball will be kicked, and you know that it will be the soccer ball. For most of the verbs, or methods in Excel VBA, there are *parameters* that tell *how* to do the action. These parameters act as adverbs. You might want the soccer ball to be kicked to the left and with a hard force. In this case, the method would have a number of parameters that tell how the program should perform the method:

```
Balls("Soccer").Kick Direction:=Left, Force:=Hard
```

When you are looking at VBA code, the colon–equal sign combination indicates that you are looking at parameters of how the verb should be performed.

Sometimes, a method will have a list of 10 parameters, some of which are optional. For example, if the `Kick` method has an `Elevation` parameter, you would have this line of code:

```
Balls("Soccer").Kick Direction:=Left, Force:=Hard, Elevation:=High
```

Here is the confusing part. Every method has a default order for its parameters. If you are not a conscientious programmer and you happen to know the order of the parameters, you can leave off the parameter names. The following code is equivalent to the previous line of code:

```
Balls("Soccer").Kick Left, Hard, High
```

This throws a monkey wrench into our understanding. Without the colon-equal signs, it is not obvious that you have parameters. Unless you know the parameter order, you might not understand what is being said. It is pretty easy with `Left`, `Hard`, and `High`, but when you have parameters like the following

```
ActiveSheet.Shapes.AddShape type:=1, Left:=10, Top:=20, Width:=100, Height:=200
```

it gets confusing if you instead have this:

```
ActiveSheet.Shapes.AddShape 1, 10, 20, 100, 200
```

The preceding line is valid code. However, unless you know that the default order of the parameters for this Add method is Type, Left, Top, Width, Height, this code does not make sense. The default order for any particular method is the order of the parameters as shown in the help topic for that method.

To make life more confusing, you are allowed to start specifying parameters in their default order without naming them and then switch to naming parameters when you hit one that does not match the default order. If you want to kick the ball to the left and high, but do not care about the force (you are willing to accept the default force), the following two statements are equivalent:

```
Balls("Soccer").Kick Direction:=Left, Elevation:=High
Balls("Soccer").Kick Left, Elevation:=High
```

However, keep in mind that as soon as you start naming parameters, they have to be named for the remainder of that line of code.

Some methods simply act on their own. To simulate pressing the F9 key, you use this code:

```
Application.Calculate
```

Other methods perform an action and create something. For example, you can add a worksheet using the following:

```
Worksheets.Add Before:=Worksheets(1)
```

However, because Worksheets.Add creates a new object, you can assign the results of this method to a variable. In this case, you must surround the parameters with parentheses:

```
Set MyWorksheet = Worksheets.Add(Before:=Worksheets(1))
```

One final bit of grammar is necessary: adjectives. Just as adjectives describe a noun, *properties* describe an object. Because you are Excel fans, let's switch from the soccer analogy to an Excel analogy midstream. There is an object to describe the active cell. Fortunately, it has a very intuitive name:

```
ActiveCell
```

Suppose you want to change the color of the active cell to red. There is a property called Interior.Color for a cell that uses a complex series of codes. However, you can turn a cell to red by using this code:

```
ActiveCell.Interior.Color = 255
```

You can see how this can be confusing. Again, there is the Noun-dot-Something construct, but this time it is Object.Property rather than Object.Method. Telling them apart is quite subtle—there is no colon before the equal sign. A property is almost always being set equal to something, or perhaps the value of a property is being assigned to something else.

To make this cell color the same as cell A1, you might say this:

```
ActiveCell.Interior.Color = Range("A1").Interior.Color
```

Interior.Color is a property. By changing the value of a property, you can make things look different. It is kind of bizarre—change an adjective, and you are actually doing something to the cell. Humans would say, "Color the cell red," whereas VBA says this:

```
ActiveCell.Interior.Color = 255
```

Table 2.1 summarizes the VBA "parts of speech."

Table 2.1   Parts of the VBA Programming Language

VBA Component	Analogous To	Notes
Object	Noun	Examples include cell or sheet
Collection	Plural noun	Usually specifies which object: `Worksheets(1)`.
Method	Verb	`Object.Method.`
Parameter	Adverb	Lists parameters after the method. Separate the parameter name from its value with `:=`.
Property	Adjective	You can set a property (for example, `activecell.height=10`) or store the value of a property (for example, `x = activecell.height`).

VBA Is Not Really Hard

Knowing whether you are dealing with properties or methods helps you set up the correct syntax for your code. Don't worry if it all seems confusing right now. When you are writing VBA code from scratch, it is tough to know whether the process of changing a cell to yellow requires a verb or an adjective. Is it a method or a property?

This is where the beauty of the macro recorder comes in. When you don't know how to code something, you record a short little macro, look at the recorded code, and figure out what is going on.

VBA Help Files: Using F1 to Find Anything

Excel VBA Help is an amazing feature, provided you are connected to the Internet. If you are going to write VBA macros, you absolutely *must* have access to the VBA help topics installed. Here are the steps to see how easy it is to get help in VBA.

1. Open Excel and switch to the VB Editor by pressing Alt+F11. From the Insert menu, select Module (see Figure 2.1).

Figure 2.1
Insert a new module in the blank workbook.

2. Type the three lines of code shown in Figure 2.2. Click inside the word *MsgBox*.

Figure 2.2
Click inside the word
MsgBox and press F1.

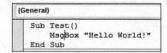

```
(General)

   Sub Test()
       MsgBox "Hello World!"
   End Sub
```

3. With the cursor in the word *MsgBox*, press F1. If you can reach the Internet, you see the help topic shown in Figure 2.3.

Figure 2.3
Provided you are con-
nected to the Internet,
you will see this screen.

MsgBox Function

Other Versions ▾ | This topic has not yet been rated - Rate this topic
This documentation is preliminary and is subject to change.

Displays a message in a dialog box, waits for the user to click a button, and returns an **Integer** indicating which button the user clicked.

Syntax

MsgBox(*prompt*[, *buttons*] [, *title*] [, *helpfile*, *context*])

The **MsgBox** function syntax has these named arguments:

Part	Description
prompt	Required. String expression displayed as the message in the dialog box. The maximum length of *prompt* is approximately 1024 characters, depending on the width of the characters used. If *prompt* consists of more than one line, you can separate the lines using a carriage return character (**Chr(13)**), a linefeed character (**Chr(10)**), or carriage return – linefeed character combination (**Chr(13) & Chr(10)**) between each line.
buttons	Optional. Numeric expression that is the sum of values specifying the number and type of buttons to display, the icon style to use, the identity of the default button, and the modality of

Using Help Topics

If you request help on a function or method, the help topic walks you through the various available arguments. If you browse to the bottom of the help topics, code samples are provided under the Example heading, which is a great resource (see Figure 2.4).

It is possible to select the code, copy it to the Clipboard by pressing Ctrl+C, and then paste it into your module by pressing Ctrl+V.

After you record a macro, if there are objects or methods about which you are unsure, you can get help by inserting the cursor in any keyword and pressing F1.

Figure 2.4
Most help topics include code samples.

◢ Example

This example uses the **MsgBox** function to display a critical-error message in a dialog box with Yes and No buttons. The No button is specified as the default response. The value returned by the **MsgBox** function depends on the button chosen by the user. This example assumes that DEMO.HLP is a Help file that contains a topic with a Help context number equal to is a Help file that contains a topic with a Help context number equal to 1000 .

```vba
VBA

Dim Msg, Style, Title, Help, Ctxt, Response, MyString
Msg = "Do you want to continue ?"    ' Define message.
Style = vbYesNo + vbCritical + vbDefaultButton2    ' Define buttons.
Title = "MsgBox Demonstration"    ' Define title.
Help = "DEMO.HLP"    ' Define Help file.
Ctxt = 1000    ' Define topic
            ' context.
            ' Display message.
Response = MsgBox(Msg, Style, Title, Help, Ctxt)
If Response = vbYes Then    ' User chose Yes.
    MyString = "Yes"    ' Perform some action.
Else    ' User chose No.
    MyString = "No"    ' Perform some action.
End If
```

Examining Recorded Macro Code: Using the VB Editor and Help

Let's take a look at the code you recorded in Chapter 1, "Unleash the Power of Excel with VBA," to see whether it makes more sense now in the context of objects, properties, and methods. You can also see whether it's possible to correct the errors brought about by the macro recorder.

Figure 2.5 shows the first code that Excel recorded in the example from Chapter 1.

Figure 2.5
Recorded code from the example in Chapter 1.

```
(General)

Sub ImportInvoice()
'
' ImportInvoice Macro
' Imports invoice.txt, adds a total row. Does some formatting.
'
' Keyboard Shortcut: Ctrl+i
'
    Workbooks.OpenText Filename:="C:\Users\Owner\Documents\invoice3.txt", Origin _
        :=437, StartRow:=1, DataType:=xlDelimited, TextQualifier:=xlDoubleQuote _
        , ConsecutiveDelimiter:=False, Tab:=False, Semicolon:=False, Comma:= _
        True, Space:=False, Other:=False, FieldInfo:=Array(Array(1, 3), Array(2, 1), _
        Array(3, 1), Array(4, 1), Array(5, 1), Array(6, 1), Array(7, 1)), TrailingMinusNumbers _
        :=True
    Range("A1").Select
    Selection.End(xlDown).Select
    Range("A11").Select
    ActiveCell.FormulaR1C1 = "Total"
    Range("E11").Select
    Selection.FormulaR1C1 = "=SUM(R[-9]C:R[-1]C)"
    Selection.AutoFill Destination:=Range("E11:G11"), Type:=xlFillDefault
    Range("E11:G11").Select
    Rows("1:1").Select
    Selection.Font.Bold = True
    Rows("11:11").Select
    Selection.Font.Bold = True
    Cells.Select
    Selection.Columns.AutoFit
End Sub
```

Now that you understand the concept of Noun.Verb or Object.Method, consider the first line of code that says `Workbooks.OpenText`. In this case, `Workbooks` is an object, and `OpenText` is a method. Click your cursor inside the word `OpenText` and press F1 for an explanation of the `OpenText` method (see Figure 2.6).

The help file confirms that `OpenText` is a method or an action word. The default order for all the arguments that can be used with `OpenText` appears in the gray box. Notice that only one argument is required: `Filename`. All the other arguments are listed as optional.

Figure 2.6
Part of the help topic for the `OpenText` method.

Parameters

Name	Required/Optional	Data Type	Description
Filename	Required	**String**	Specifies the file name of the text file to be opened and parsed.
Origin	Optional	**Variant**	Specifies the origin of the text file. Can be one of the following **XlPlatform** constants: **xlMacintosh, xlWindows,** or **xlMSDOS.** Additionally, this could be an integer representing the code page number of the desired code page. For example, "1256" would specify that the encoding of the source text file is Arabic (Windows). If this argument is omitted, the method uses the current setting of the **File Origin** option in the **Text Import Wizard.**
StartRow	Optional	**Variant**	The row number at which to start parsing text. The default value is 1.
DataType	Optional	**Variant**	Specifies the column format of the data in the file. Can be one of the following **XlTextParsingType** constants: **xlDelimited** or **xlFixedWidth.** If this argument is not specified, Microsoft Excel attempts to determine the column format when it opens the file.
TextQualifier	Optional	**XlTextQualifier**	Specifies the text qualifier.
ConsecutiveDelimiter	Optional	**Variant**	**True** to have consecutive delimiters considered one delimiter. The default is **False.**

Optional Parameters

The help file can tell you if you happen to skip an optional parameter. For `StartRow`, the help file indicates that the default value is 1. If you leave out the `StartRow` parameter, Excel starts importing at Row 1. This is fairly safe.

Now look at the help file note about `Origin`. If this argument is omitted, you inherit whatever value was used for `Origin` the last time someone used this feature in Excel on this computer. That is a recipe for disaster. For example, your code might work 98 percent of the time. However, immediately after someone imports an Arabic file, Excel remembers the setting for Arabic and assumes that this is what your macro wants if you don't explicitly code this parameter.

Defined Constants

Look at the help file entry for DataType in Figure 2.6, which says it can be one of these constants: xlDelimited or xlFixedWidth. The help file says these are the valid xlTextParsing-Type constants that are predefined in Excel VBA. In the VB Editor, press Ctrl+G to bring up the Immediate window. In the Immediate window, type this line and press Enter:

```
Print xlFixedWidth
```

2

The answer appears in the Immediate window. xlFixedWidth is the equivalent of saying "2" (see Figure 2.7). Ask the Immediate window to Print xlDelimited, which is really the same as typing 1. Microsoft correctly assumes that it is easier for someone to read code that uses the somewhat English-like term xlDelimited rather than 1.

Figure 2.7
In the Immediate window of the VB Editor, query to see the true value of constants such as xlFixedWidth.

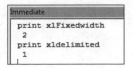

```
Immediate
    print xlFixedwidth
     2
    print xldelimited
     1
```

If you were an evil programmer, you could certainly memorize all these constants and write code using the numeric equivalents of the constants. However, the programming gods (and the next person who has to look at your code) will curse you for this.

In most cases, the help file either specifically calls out the valid values of the constants or offers a hyperlink that opens the help topic showing the complete enumeration and the valid values for the constants (see Figure 2.8).

One complaint with this excellent help system is that it does not identify which parameters are new to a given version. In this particular case, TrailingMinusNumbers was introduced in Excel 2002. If you attempt to give this program to someone who is still using Excel 2000, the code does not run because it does not understand the TrailingMinusNumbers parameter. Sadly, the only way to learn to handle this frustrating problem is through trial and error.

If you read the help topic on OpenText, you can surmise that it is basically the equivalent of opening a file using the Text Import Wizard. In Step 1 of the wizard, you normally choose either Delimited or Fixed Width. You also specify the File Origin and at which row to start (see Figure 2.9). This first step of the wizard is handled by these parameters of the OpenText method:

```
Origin:=437
StartRow:=1
DataType:=xlDelimited
```

Figure 2.8
Click the blue hyperlink to see all the possible constant values. Here, the 10 possible x1Column-DataType constants are revealed in a new help topic.

XlColumnDataType Enumeration (Excel)

Other Versions ▾ | This topic has not yet been rated - Rate this topic
This documentation is preliminary and is subject to change.

Specifies how a column is to be parsed.

▲ Version Information

Version Added: Excel 2007

Name	Value	Description
xlDMYFormat	4	DMY date format.
xlDYMFormat	7	DYM date format.
xlEMDFormat	10	EMD date format.
xlGeneralFormat	1	General.
xlMDYFormat	3	MDY date format.
xlMYDFormat	6	MYD date format.
xlSkipColumn	9	Column is not parsed.
xlTextFormat	2	Text.
xlYDMFormat	8	YDM date format.
xlYMDFormat	5	YMD date format.

Figure 2.9
The first step of the Text Import Wizard in Excel is covered by three parameters of the OpenText method.

Step 2 of the Text Import Wizard enables you to specify that your fields be delimited by a comma. Because we do not want to treat two commas as a single comma, the Treat

Consecutive Delimiters as One check box is not selected. Sometimes, a field may contain a comma, such as "XYZ, Inc." In this case, the field should have quotes around the value, as specified in the Text Qualifier box (see Figure 2.10). This second step of the wizard is handled by the following parameters of the OpenText method:

```
TextQualifier:=xlDoubleQuote
ConsecutiveDelimiter:=False
Tab:=False
Semicolon:=False
Comma:=True
Space:=False
Other:=False
```

Figure 2.10
The second step of the Text Import Wizard is handled by the seven parameters of the OpenText method.

Step 3 of the wizard is where you actually identify the field types. In this case, you leave all fields as General except for the first field, which is marked as a date in MDY (Month, Day, Year) format (see Figure 2.11). This is represented in code by the FieldInfo parameter.

The third step of the Text Import Wizard is fairly complex. The entire FieldInfo parameter of the OpenText method duplicates the choices made on this step of the wizard. If you happen to click the Advanced button on the third step of the wizard, you have an opportunity to specify something other than the default Decimal and Thousands separator, as well as the setting for Trailing Minus for Negative Numbers (see Figure 2.12).

TIP

Note that the macro recorder does not write code for DecimalSeparator or ThousandsSeparator unless you change these from the defaults. The macro recorder does always record the TrailingMinusNumbers parameter.

Figure 2.11
Specify the first column is a date in MDY format.

Figure 2.12
The `Trailing MinusNumbers` parameter comes from the Advanced Text Import Settings. If you change either of the separator fields, new parameters are recorded by the macro recorder.

Every action you perform in Excel while recording a macro gets translated to VBA code. In the case of many dialog boxes, the settings you do not change are often recorded along with the items you do change. When you click OK to close the dialog, the macro recorder often records all the current settings from the dialog in the macro.

Here is another example. The next line of code in the macro is this:

```
Selection.End(xlDown).Select
```

You can click to get help for three topics in this line of code: `Selection`, `End`, and `Select`. Assuming that `Selection` and `Select` are somewhat self-explanatory, click in the word `End` and press F1 for help. A Context Help dialog box appears, saying that there are two possible help topics for `End`—one in the Excel library and one in the VBA library (see Figure 2.13).

If you are new to VBA, you might not know which help library to select. Select one and then click Help. In this case, the End help topic in the VBA library is talking about the `End` statement, which is not what you need.

Figure 2.13
Sometimes you must choose which help library to use.

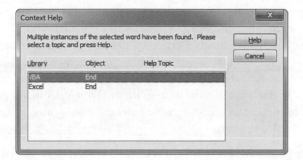

Close Help, press F1 again, and select the End object in the Excel library. This help topic says that End is a property. It returns a Range object that is equivalent to pressing End+Up or End+Down in the Excel interface (see Figure 2.14). If you click the blue hyperlink for xlDirection, you see the valid parameters that can be passed to the End function.

Figure 2.14
The correct help topic for the End property.

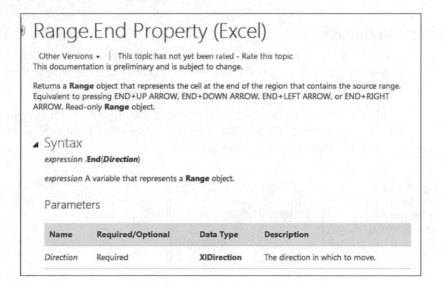

Properties Can Return Objects

Recall that the discussion at the start of this chapter says that the basic syntax of VBA is Object.Method. Consider the line of code currently under examination:

```
Selection.End(xlDown).Select
```

In this particular line of code, the method is Select. The End keyword is a property, but from the help file, you see that it returns a Range object. Because the Select method can apply to a Range object, the method is actually appended to a property.

2

Based on this information, you might assume that `Selection` is the object in this line of code. If you click the mouse in the word `Selection` and press F1, you will see that according to the help topic, `Selection` is actually a property and not an object. In reality, the proper code would be to use `Application.Selection`. However, when you are running within Excel, VBA assumes you are referring to the Excel object model, so you can leave off the `Application` object. If you were to write a program in Word VBA to automate Excel, you would be required to include an object variable before the `Selection` property to qualify to which application you are referring.

In this case, the `Application.Selection` can return several types of objects. If a cell is selected, it returns the `Range` object.

Using Debugging Tools to Figure Out Recorded Code

This section introduces some awesome debugging tools that are featured in VB Editor. These tools are excellent for helping you see what a recorded macro code is doing.

Stepping Through Code

Generally, a macro runs quickly—you start it, and less than a second later, it is done. If something goes wrong, you do not have an opportunity to figure out what it is doing. However, using Excel's Step Into feature makes it possible to run one line of code at a time.

To use this feature, make sure your cursor is in the procedure you want to run, such as the `ImportInvoice` procedure, and then from the menu select Debug, Step Into, as shown in Figure 2.15. Alternatively, you can press F8.

Figure 2.15
Using the Step Into feature enables you to run a single line of code at a time.

The VB Editor is now in Break mode. The line about to be executed is highlighted in yellow with a yellow arrow in the margin before the code (see Figure 2.16).

Figure 2.16
The first line of the macro is about to run.

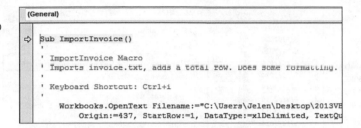

In this case, the next line to be executed is the Sub ImportInvoice() line. This basically says, "You are about to start running this procedure." Press the F8 key to execute the line in yellow and move to the next line of code. The long code for OpenText is then highlighted. Press F8 to run this line of code. When you see that Selection.End(xlDown).Select is highlighted, you know that Visual Basic has finished running the OpenText command. At this point, you can press Alt+Tab to switch to Excel and see that the Invoice.txt file has been parsed into Excel. Note that A1 is selected (see Figure 2.17).

Figure 2.17
The Excel window behind the VBA Editor shows that the Invoice.txt file has been imported.

> **NOTE**
>
> If you have a wide monitor, you can use the Restore Down icon at the top right of the VBA window to arrange the window so that you can see both the VBA window and the Excel window. (Restore Down is the two-tiled-window icon between the Minimize "dash" and the Close Window "x" icon at the top of every window).
>
> This is also a great trick to use while recording new code. You can actually watch the code appear as you do things in Excel.

Switch back to the VB Editor by pressing Alt+Tab. The next line about to be executed is Selection.End(xlDown).Select. Press F8 to run this code. Switch to Excel to see the results. Now A22 is selected (see Figure 2.18).

Press F8 again to run the Range("A11").Select line. If you switch to Excel by pressing Alt+Tab, you see that this is where the macro starts to have problems. Instead of moving to the first blank row, the program moves to the wrong row (see Figure 2.19).

Figure 2.18
Verify that the
End(xlDown).
Select command
worked as expected. This
is equivalent to pressing
the End key and then the
down arrow.

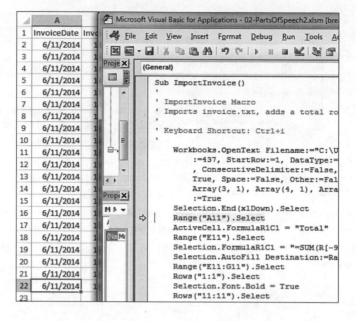

Figure 2.19
The recorded macro code
blindly moves to Row 11
for the Total row.

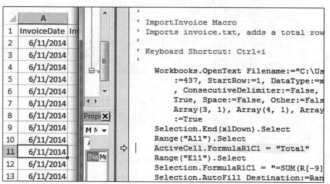

Now that you have identified the problem area, you can stop the code execution by using the Reset command. You can start the Reset command either by selecting Run, Reset or by clicking the Reset button on the toolbar (see Figure 2.20). After clicking Reset, you should return to Excel and undo anything done by the partially completed macro. In this case, you need to close the Invoice.txt file without saving.

Figure 2.20
The Reset button in the
toolbar stops a macro
that is in Break mode.

More Debugging Options: Breakpoints

If you have hundreds of lines of code, you might not want to step through each line one at a time. If you have a general idea that the problem is happening in one particular section of the program, you can set a breakpoint. You can then have the code start to run, but the macro breaks just before it executes the breakpoint line of code.

To set a breakpoint, click in the gray margin area to the left of the line of code on which you want to break. A large brown dot appears next to this code, and the line of code is highlighted in brown (see Figure 2.21). (If you don't see the margin area, go to Tools, Options, Editor Format and choose Margin Indicator Bar.)Or, select a line of code and press F9 to toggle a breakpoint on or off.

Figure 2.21
The large brown dot signifies a breakpoint.

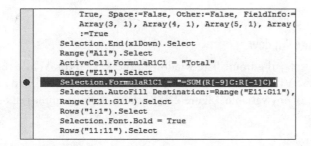

```
          True, Space:=False, Other:=False, FieldInfo:=
          Array(3, 1), Array(4, 1), Array(5, 1), Array(
          :=True
    Selection.End(xlDown).Select
    Range("A11").Select
    ActiveCell.FormulaR1C1 = "Total"
    Range("E11").Select
    Selection.FormulaR1C1 = "=SUM(R[-9]C:R[-1]C)"
    Selection.AutoFill Destination:=Range("E11:G11"),
    Range("E11:G11").Select
    Rows("1:1").Select
    Selection.Font.Bold = True
    Rows("11:11").Select
```

Next, from the Start menu select Run, Run Sub, or press F5. The program executes but stops just before running the line in the breakpoint. The VB Editor shows the breakpoint line highlighted in yellow. You can now press F8 to begin stepping through the code.

After you have finished debugging your code, remove the breakpoints by clicking the dark brown dot in the margin next to each breakpoint to toggle it off. Alternatively, you can select Debug, Clear All Breakpoints or press Ctrl+Shift+F9 to clear all breakpoints that you set in the project.

Backing Up or Moving Forward in Code

When you are stepping through code, you might want to jump over some lines of code, or you might have corrected some lines of code that you want to run again. This is easy to do when you are working in Break mode. One favorite method is to use the mouse to grab the yellow arrow. The cursor changes to a three-arrow icon, which means you can move the next line up or down. Drag the yellow line to whichever line you want to execute next (see Figure 2.22). The other option is to right-click the line to which you want to jump and then select Set Next Statement.

Figure 2.22
The cursor as it appears when you are dragging the yellow line to a different line of code to be executed next.

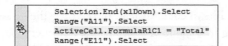

```
    Selection.End(xlDown).Select
    Range("A11").Select
    ActiveCell.FormulaR1C1 = "Total"
    Range("E11").Select
```

Not Stepping Through Each Line of Code

When you are stepping through code, you might want to run a section of code without stepping through each line, such as when you get to a loop. You might want VBA to run through the loop 100 times, so you can step through the lines after the loop. It is particularly monotonous to press the F8 key hundreds of times to step through a loop. Instead, click the cursor on the line you want to step to and then press Ctrl+F8 or select Debug, Run to Cursor. This command is also available in the right-click menu.

Querying Anything While Stepping Through Code

Even though variables have not yet been discussed, you can query the value of anything while in Break mode. However, keep in mind that the macro recorder never records a variable.

Using the Immediate Window

Press Ctrl+G to display the Immediate window in the VB Editor. While the macro is in Break mode, ask the VB Editor to tell you the currently selected cell, the name of the active sheet, or the value of any variable. Figure 2.23 shows several examples of queries typed into the Immediate window.

Figure 2.23
Queries that can be typed into the Immediate window while a macro is in Break mode, shown along with their answers.

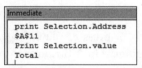

Instead of typing `Print`, you can type a question mark: `? Selection.Address`. Read the question mark as, "What is."

When invoked with Ctrl+G, the Immediate window usually appears at the bottom of the Code window. You can use the resize handle, which is located above the blue Immediate title bar, to make the Immediate window larger or smaller.

There is a scrollbar on the side of the Immediate window that you can use to scroll backward or forward through past entries in the Immediate window.

It is not necessary to run queries only at the bottom of the Immediate window. For example, if you have just run a line of code, in the Immediate window you can ask for the `Selection.Address` to ensure that this line of code worked (see Figure 2.24).

Press the F8 key to run the next line of code. Instead of retyping the same query, click in the Immediate window anywhere in the line containing the last query (see Figure 2.25).

Figure 2.24

The Immediate window shows the results before the current line is executed.

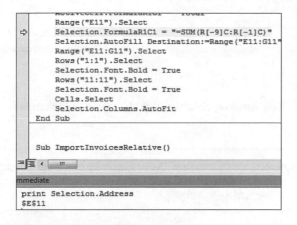

```
         Range("E11").Select
⇨        Selection.FormulaR1C1 = "=SUM(R[-9]C:R[-1]C)"
         Selection.AutoFill Destination:=Range("E11:G11"
         Range("E11:G11").Select
         Rows("1:1").Select
         Selection.Font.Bold = True
         Rows("11:11").Select
         Selection.Font.Bold = True
         Cells.Select
         Selection.Columns.AutoFit
     End Sub


     Sub ImportInvoicesRelative()
```

```
mmediate
   print Selection.Address
   $E$11
```

Figure 2.25

Place the cursor anywhere in the previous command and press Enter to avoid typing the same commands over in the Immediate window.

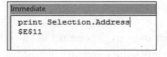

```
Immediate
   print Selection.Address
   $E$11
```

Press Enter, and the Immediate window runs this query again, displaying the results on the next line and pushing the old results farther down the window. In this case, the selected address is $E$11:$G$11. The previous answer, $E$11, is pushed down the window (see Figure 2.26).

Figure 2.26

The prior answer ($E$11) is shifted down, and the current answer ($E$11:$G$11) appears below the query.

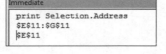

```
Immediate
   print Selection.Address
   $E$11:$G$11
   $E$11
```

You can also use this method to change the query by clicking to the right of the word Address in the Immediate window. Press the Backspace key to erase the word Address and instead type Columns.Count. Press Enter, and the Immediate window shows the number of columns in the selection (see Figure 2.27).

This is an excellent technique to use when you are trying to figure out a sticky bit of code. For example, you can query the name of the active sheet (Print Activesheet.Name), the selection (Print Selection.Address), the active cell (Print ActiveCell.Address), the formula in the active cell (Print ActiveCell.Formula), the value of the active cell (Print ActiveCell.Value, or Print ActiveCell because Value is the default property of a cell), and so on.

2

Figure 2.27
Delete part of a query, type something new, and press Enter. The previous answers are pushed down, and the current answer is displayed.

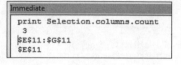

```
Immediate
 print Selection.columns.count
  3
$E$11:$G$11
$E$11
```

To dismiss the Immediate window, click the *X* in the upper-right corner of the Immediate window.

> **NOTE** Ctrl+G does not toggle the window off. Use the *X* at the top right of the Immediate window to close it.

Querying by Hovering

In many instances, you can hover the cursor over an expression in the code and then wait a second for a ToolTip to be displayed that shows the current value of the expression. This is an invaluable tool when you get to looping in Chapter 4, "Looping and Flow Control." It also comes in handy with recorded code. Note that the expression that you hover over does not have to be in the line of code just executed. In Figure 2.28, Visual Basic just selected E1:G1, making E1 the ActiveCell. If you hover the cursor over ActiveCell.FormulaR1C1, you see a ToolTip showing that the formula in the ActiveCell is "=SUM(R[-9]C:R[-1]C)".

Figure 2.28
Hover the mouse cursor over any expression for a few seconds, and a ToolTip shows the current value of the expression.

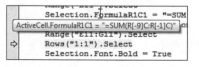

```
            Selection.FormulaR1C1 = "=SUM
ActiveCell.FormulaR1C1 = "=SUM(R[-9]C:R[-1]C)"  o
            Range("E11:G11").Select
⇨           Rows("1:1").Select
            Selection.Font.Bold = True
```

Sometimes the VBA window seems to not respond to hovering. Because some expressions are not supposed to show a value, it is difficult to tell whether VBA is not displaying the value on purpose or whether you are in the buggy "not responding" mode. Try hovering over something that you know should respond, such as a variable. If you get no response, hover, click into the variable, and continue to hover. This tends to wake Excel from its stupor, and hovering works again.

Are you impressed yet? This chapter started by complaining that this didn't seem much like BASIC. However, by now you have to admit that the Visual Basic environment is great to work in and that the debugging tools are excellent.

Querying by Using a Watch Window

In Visual Basic, a watch is not something you wear on your wrist; instead, it allows you to watch the value of any expression while you step through code. Let's say that in the current example, you want to watch to see what is selected as the code runs. You can do this by setting up a watch for `Selection.Address`.

From the VB Editor Debug menu, select Add Watch. In the Add Watch dialog, enter `Selection.Address` in the Expression text box and click OK (see Figure 2.29).

Figure 2.29
Setting up a watch to see the address of the current selection.

A Watches window is added to the busy Visual Basic window, usually at the bottom of the code window. When you start running the macro, import the file and press End+Down to move to the last row with data. Right after selecting E11:G11, the Watches window confirms that `Selection.Address` is `$E$11:$G$11` (see Figure 2.30).

Figure 2.30
Without having to hover or type in the Immediate window, you can always see the value of watched expressions.

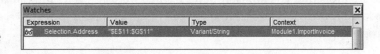

Press the F8 key to run the code `Rows("1:1").Select`. The Watches window is updated to show that the current address of the `Selection` is now `$1:$1`.

In the Watch window, the value column is read/write (where possible)! You can type a new value here and see it change on the worksheet.

Using a Watch to Set a Breakpoint

Right-click any line in the Watches window and select Edit Watch. In the Watch Type section of the Edit Watch dialog, select Break When Value Changes. Click OK.

The glasses icon changes to a hand with triangle icon. You can now press F5 to run the code. The macro starts running lines of code until something new is selected. This is very powerful. Instead of having to step through each line of code, you can now conveniently have the macro stop only when something important has happened. A watch can also be set up to stop when the value of a particular variable changes.

Using a Watch on an Object

In the preceding example, you watched a specific property: `Selection.Address`. It is also possible to watch an object such as `Selection`. In Figure 2.31, when a watch has been set up on `Selection`, you get the glasses icon and a + icon.

Figure 2.31
Setting a watch on an object gives you a + icon next to the glasses.

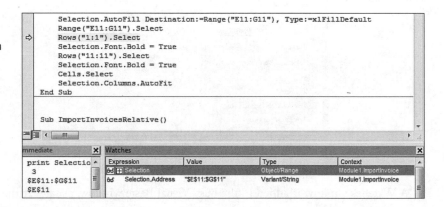

By clicking the + icon, you can see all the properties associated with `Selection`. When you look at Figure 2.32, you can see more than you ever wanted to know about `Selection`! There are properties you probably never realized were available. You can also see that the `AddIndent` property is set to `False` and the `AllowEdit` property is set to `True`. There are useful properties in the list—you can see the `Formula` of the selection.

Figure 2.32
Clicking the + icon shows a plethora of properties and their current values.

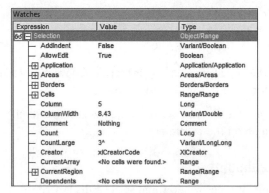

In this Watches window, some entries can be expanded. For example, the Borders collection has a plus next to it, which means that you can click any + icon to see more details.

Object Browser: The Ultimate Reference

In the VB Editor, press F2 to open the Object Browser, which lets you browse and search the entire Excel object library (see Figure 2.33). I've previously owned large Excel books that devoted 400-plus pages to listing every object in the object browser. You can save a tree by learning to use the more-powerful Object Browser. The built-in Object Browser is always available at the touch of F2. The next few pages show you how to use the Object Browser.

Figure 2.33

Press F2 to display the Object Browser. Select a class and then a member. The bottom member shows you Information about the object.

Click X to Close

Press F2 and the Object Browser appears where the code window normally appears. The topmost drop-down currently shows <All Libraries>. There is an entry in this drop-down for Excel, Office, VBA, and each workbook that you have open, plus additional entries for anything you check in Tools, References. For now, go to the drop-down and select only Excel.

In the left window of the Object Browser is a list of all classes available for Excel. Click the Application class in the left window. The right window adjusts to show all properties and methods that apply to the Application object. Click something in the right window, such as ActiveCell. The bottom window of the Object Browser tells you that ActiveCell is a property that returns a range. It also tells you that `ActiveCell` is read-only (an alert that you cannot assign an address to `ActiveCell` to move the cell pointer).

You have learned from the Object Browser that `ActiveCell` returns a range. When you click the green hyperlink for `Range` in the bottom window, you see all the properties and methods that apply to `Range` objects and, hence, to the `ActiveCell` property. Click any property or method and then click the yellow question mark near the top of the Object Browser to go to the help topic for that property or method.

Type any term in the text box next to the binoculars, and click the binoculars to find all matching members of the Excel library.

Methods appear as green books with speed lines. Properties appear as index cards with a hand pointing to them.

The search capabilities and hyperlinks available in the Object Browser make it much more valuable than an alphabetic printed listing of all the information. Learn to make use of the Object Browser in the VBA window by pressing F2. To close the Object Browser and return to your code window, click the lowercase *X* in the upper-right corner.

Seven Tips for Cleaning Up Recorded Code

At this point, you have two tips for recording code from Chapter 1. So far, this chapter has covered how to understand the recorded code, how to access VBA help for any word, and how to use the excellent VBA debugging tools to step through your code. The remainder of this chapter presents seven tips to use when cleaning up recorded code.

Tip 1: Don't Select Anything

Nothing screams "recorded code" more than having code that selects things before acting upon them. This makes sense—in the Excel interface, you have to select Row 1 before you can make it bold.

However, this is done rarely in VBA. There are a couple of exceptions to this rule. For example, you need to select a cell when setting up a formula for conditional formatting. It is possible to directly turn on bold font to Row 1 without selecting it. The following two lines of code turn into one line.

Macro recorder code before it has been streamlined:

```
Cells.Select
Selection.Columns.AutoFit
```

After the recorded code has been streamlined:

```
Cells.Columns.AutoFit
```

There are a couple of advantages to this method. First, there will be half as many lines of code in your program. Second, the program will run faster.

After recording code, highlight literally from before the word Select at the end of one line all the way to the dot after the word Selection on the next line and press Delete (see Figures 2.34 and 2.35).

Figure 2.34
Select from here to here...

```
      Range("E11:G11").Select
      Rows("1:1").Select
      Selection.Font.Bold = True
      Rows("11:11").Select
      Selection.Font.Bold = True
      Cells.Select
      Selection.Columns.AutoFit
End Sub
```

Figure 2.35
...and press the Delete key. This is basic "101" of cleaning up recorded macros.

```
      Selection.End(xlDown).Select
      Range("A11").FormulaR1C1 = "Total"
      Range("E11").FormulaR1C1 = "=SUM(R[-9
      Range("E11").AutoFill Destination:=Ra
      Rows("1:1").Font.Bold = True
      Rows("11:11").Font.Bold = True
      Cells.Columns.AutoFit
End Sub
```

Tip 2: Cells(2,5) **Is More Convenient Than** Range("E2")

The macro recorder uses the Range() property frequently. If you follow the macro recorder's example, you will find yourself building a lot of complicated code. For example, if you have the row number for the total row stored in a variable, you might try to build this code:

```
Range("E" & TotalRow).Formula = "=SUM(E2:E" & TotalRow-1 & ")"
```

In this code, you are using concatenation to join the letter *E* with the current value of the TotalRow variable. This works, but eventually you have to refer to a range where the column is stored in a variable. Say that FinalCol is 10, which indicates Column J. To refer to this column in a Range command, you need to do something like this:

```
FinalColLetter = MID("ABCDEFGHIJKLMNOPQRSTUVWXYZ",FinalCol,1)
Range(FinalColLetter & "2").Select
```

Alternatively, perhaps you could do something like this:

```
FinalColLetter = CHR(64 + FinalCol)
Range(FinalColLetter & "2").Select
```

These approaches work for the first 26 columns but fail for the remaining 99.85 percent of the columns.

You could start to write 10-line functions to calculate that the column letter for column 15896 is WMJ, but it is not necessary. Instead of using Range("WMJ17"), you can use the Cells(Row,Column) syntax.

Chapter 3, "Referring to Ranges," covers this topic in complete detail. However, for now you need to understand that `Range("E10")` and `Cells(10, 5)` both point to the cell at the intersection of the fifth column and the tenth row. Chapter 3 also shows you how to use `.Resize` to point to a rectangular range. `Cells(11, 5).Resize(1, 3)` is E11:G11.

Tip 3: Use More Reliable Ways to Find the Last Row

It is difficult to trust data from just anywhere. If you are analyzing data in Excel, remember that the data can come from "who knows what" system written "who knows how long ago." The universal truth is that eventually some clerk will find a way to break the source system and enter a record without an invoice number. Maybe it will take a power failure to do it, but invariably, you cannot count on having every cell filled in.

This is a problem when you're using the End+Down shortcut. This key combination does not take you to the last row with data in the worksheet. It takes you to the last row with data in the current range. In Figure 2.36, pressing End+Down would move the cursor to cell A7 rather than the true last row with data.

Figure 2.36
End+Down fails in the user interface if a record is missing a value. Similarly, End(xlDown) fails in Excel VBA.

One better solution is to start at the bottom of the worksheet and look for the first non-blank cell with:

```
FinalRow = Cells(Rows.Count, 1).End(xlUp).Row
```

That method could fail if the very last record happens to have the blank row. If the data is non-sparse enough that there will always be a diagonal path of non-blank cells to the last row, you could use:

```
FinalRow = Cells(1,1).CurrentRegion.Rows.Count
```

If you are sure that there are not any notes or stray activated cells below the data set, you might try:

```
FinalRow = Cells(1, 1).SpecialCells(xlLastCell).Row
```

You will have to choose from these various methods based on the nature of your data set. If you are not sure, you could loop through all columns. If you are expecting seven columns of data, you could use this code:

```
FinalRow = 0
For i = 1 to 7
    ThisFinal = Cells(Rows.Count, i).End(xlUp).Row
    If ThisFinal > FinalRow then FinalRow = ThisFinal
Next i
```

Tip 4: Use Variables to Avoid Hard-Coding Rows and Formulas

The macro recorder never records a variable. Variables are easy to use, but just as in BASIC, a variable can remember a value. Variables are discussed in more detail in Chapter 4.

It is recommended that you set the last row with data to a variable. Be sure to use meaningful variable names such as FinalRow:

```
FinalRow = Cells(Rows.Count, 1).End(xlUp).Row
```

Now that you know the row number of the last record, put the word *Total* in Column A of the next row:

```
Cells(FinalRow + 1, 1).Value = "Total"
```

You can even use the variable when building the formula. This formula totals everything from E2 to the FinalRow of E:

```
Cells(FinalRow + 1, 5).Formula = "=SUM(E2:E" & FinalRow & ")"
```

Tip 5: R1C1 Formulas That Make Your Life Easier

The macro recorder often writes formulas in an arcane R1C1 style. However, most people change the code back to use a regular A1-style formula. After reading Chapter 5, "R1C1-Style Formulas," you will understand there are times when you can build an R1C1 formula that is much simpler than the corresponding A1-style formula. By using an R1C1 formula, you can add totals to all three cells in the Total row with the following:

```
Cells(FinalRow+1, 5).Resize(1, 3).FormulaR1C1 = "=SUM(R2C:R[-1]C)"
```

Tip 6: Learn to Copy and Paste in a Single Statement

Recorded code is notorious for copying a range, selecting another range, and then doing an ActiveSheet.Paste. The Copy method as it applies to a range is actually much more powerful. You can specify what to copy and specify the destination in one statement.

Recorded code:

```
Range("E14").Select
Selection.Copy
Range("F14:G14").Select
ActiveSheet.Paste
```

Better code:

```
Range("E14").Copy Destination:=Range("F14:G14")
```

Tip 7: Use With...End With to Perform Multiple Actions

If you were going to make the total row bold, double underline, with a larger font and a special color, you might get recorded code like this:

```
Range("A14:G14").Select
Selection.Font.Bold = True
Selection.Font.Size = 12
Selection.Font.ColorIndex = 5
Selection.Font.Underline = xlUnderlineStyleDoubleAccounting
```

For four of those lines of code, VBA must resolve the expression Selection.Font. Because you have four lines that all refer to the same object, you can name the object once at the top of a With block. Inside the With...End With block, everything that starts with a period is assumed to refer to the With object:

```
With Range("A14:G14").Font
    .Bold = True
    .Size = 12
    .ColorIndex = 5
    .Underline = xlUnderlineStyleDoubleAccounting
End With
```

CASE STUDY: PUTTING IT ALL TOGETHER: FIXING THE RECORDED CODE

Using the seven tips discussed in the preceding section, you can convert the recorded code into efficient, professional-looking code. Here is the code as recorded by the macro recorder at the end of Chapter 1:

```
Sub FormatInvoice3()
'
' FormatInvoice3 Macro
' Third try. Use relative. Don't touch AutoSum
'
' Keyboard Shortcut: Ctrl+Shift+K
'
    Workbooks.OpenText
        Filename:="C:\Users\Owner\Documents\invoice.txt", _
        Origin:=437, StartRow:=1, DataType:=xlDelimited, _
        TextQualifier:=xlDoubleQuote, ConsecutiveDelimiter:=False, _
        Tab:=False, Semicolon:=False, Comma:=True, Space:=False, _
        Other:=False, FieldInfo:=Array(Array(1, 3),Array(2, 1), _
        Array(3, 1), Array(4, 1), Array(5, 1), Array(6, 1), Array(7, 1)), _
TrailingMinusNumbers:=True
    ' Relative turned on here
    Selection.End(xlDown).Select
    ActiveCell.Offset(1, 0).Range("A1").Select
```

```
        ActiveCell.FormulaR1C1 = "Total"
        ActiveCell.Offset(0, 4).Range("A1").Select
        ' Don't use AutoSum. Type this formula:
        Selection.FormulaR1C1 = "=SUM(R2C:R[-1]C)"
        Selection.AutoFill Destination:=ActiveCell.Range("A1:C1"), _
            Type:=xlFillDefault
        ActiveCell.Range("A1:C1").Select
        ' Relative turned off here
        ActiveCell.Rows("1:1").EntireRow.Select
        ActiveCell.Activate
        Selection.Font.Bold = True
        Cells.Select
        Selection.Columns.AutoFit
        Range("A1").Select
End Sub
```

Follow these steps to clean up the macro:

1. The `Workbook.OpenText` lines are fine as recorded.

2. The following lines of code attempt to locate the final row of data so that the program knows where to enter the total row:

   ```
   Selection.End(xlDown).Select
   ```

   You do not need to select anything to find the last row. It also helps to assign the row number of the final row and the total row to a variable so that they can be used later. To handle the unexpected case in which a single cell in Column A is blank, start at the bottom of the worksheet and go up to find the last used row:

   ```
   ' Find the last row with data. This might change every day
   FinalRow = Cells(Rows.Count, 1).End(xlUp).Row
   TotalRow = FinalRow + 1
   ```

3. These lines of code enter the word `Total` in Column A of the Total row:

   ```
   Range("A14").Select
   ActiveCell.FormulaR1C1 = "'Total"
   ```

   The better code uses the `TotalRow` variable to locate where to enter the word `Total`. Again, there is no need to select the cell before entering the label:

   ```
   ' Build a Total row below this
   Cells(TotalRow,1).Value = "Total"
   ```

4. These lines of code enter the `Total` formula in Column E and copy it to the next two columns:

   ```
   Range("E14").Select
   Selection.FormulaR1C1 = "=SUM(R[-12]C:R[-1]C)"
   Selection.AutoFill Destination:=Range("E14:G14"), Type:=xlFillDefault
   Range("E14:G14").Select
   ```

   There is no reason to do all this selecting. The following line enters the formula in three cells. The R1C1 style of formulas is discussed in Chapter 5:

   ```
   Cells(TotalRow,5).Resize(1, 3).FormulaR1C1 = "=SUM(R2C:R[-1]C)"
   ```

5. The macro recorder selects a range and then applies formatting:

   ```
   Rows("1:1").Select
   Selection.Font.Bold = True
   Rows("14:14").Select
   ```

```
Selection.Font.Bold = True
```

There is no reason to select before applying the formatting. These two lines perform the same action and do it much quicker:

```
Rows("1:1").Font.Bold = True
Rows(TotalRow).Font.Bold = True
```

6. The macro recorder selects all cells before doing the AutoFit command:

```
Cells.Select
Selection.Columns.AutoFit
```

There is no need to select the cells before doing the AutoFit:

```
Cells.Columns.AutoFit
```

7. The macro recorder adds a short description to the top of each macro:

```
' ImportInvoice Macro
```

Now that you have changed the recorded macro code into something that will actually work, feel free to add your name as author to the description and mention what the macro will do:

```
' ImportInvoice Macro
'Written by Bill Jelen. This macro will import invoice.txt and add totals.
```

Here is the final macro with the changes:

```
Sub ImportInvoiceFixed()
'
' ImportInvoice Macro
' Written by Bill Jelen. This macro will import invoice.txt and add totals.
'
' Keyboard Shortcut: Ctrl+i
'

    Workbooks.OpenText Filename:= _
        "C:\invoice.txt", Origin _
        :=437, StartRow:=1, DataType:=xlDelimited, _
        TextQualifier:=xlDoubleQuote _
        , ConsecutiveDelimiter:=False, Tab:=True, Semicolon:=False, _
        Comma:=True _
        , Space:=False, Other:=False, FieldInfo:=Array(Array(1, 3), _
        Array(2, 1), _
        Array(3, 1), Array(4, 1), Array(5, 1), Array(6, 1), Array(7, 1)), _
        TrailingMinusNumbers:=True
    ' Find the last row with data. This might change every day
    FinalRow = Cells(Rows.Count, 1).End(xlUp).Row
    TotalRow = FinalRow + 1
    ' Build a Total row below this
    Cells(TotalRow,1).Value = "Total"
    Cells(TotalRow,5).Resize(1, 3).FormulaR1C1 = "=SUM(R2C:R[-1]C)"
    Rows(1).Font.Bold = True
    Rows(TotalRow).Font.Bold = True
    Cells.Columns.AutoFit
End Sub
```

Next Steps

By now, you should know how to record a macro. You should also be able to use help and debugging to figure out how the code works. This chapter provided seven tools for making the recorded code look like professional code.

The next chapters go into more detail about referring to ranges, looping, and the crazy but useful R1C1 style of formulas that the macro recorder loves to use.

2

Referring to Ranges

A *range* can be a cell, a row, a column, or a grouping of any of these. The RANGE object is probably the most frequently used object in Excel VBA—after all, you are manipulating data on a sheet. Although a range can refer to any grouping of cells on a sheet, it can refer to only one sheet at a time. If you want to refer to ranges on multiple sheets, you must refer to each sheet separately.

This chapter shows you different ways of referring to ranges such as specifying a row or column. You also find out how to manipulate cells based on the active cell and how to create a new range from overlapping ranges.

The Range Object

The following is the Excel object hierarchy:

Application > Workbook > Worksheet > Range

The Range object is a property of the Worksheet object. This means it requires that a sheet be active or it must reference a worksheet. Both of the following lines mean the same thing if Worksheets(1) is the active sheet:

```
Range("A1")
Worksheets(1).Range("A1")
```

There are several ways to refer to a Range object. Range("A1") is the most identifiable because that is how the macro recorder refers to it. However, each of the following is equivalent when referring to a range:

```
Range("D5")
[D5]
Range("B3").Range("C3")
Cells(5,4)
Range("A1").Offset(4,3)
Range("MyRange") 'assuming that D5 has a Name
'of MyRange
```

Which format you use depends on your needs. Keep reading—it will all make sense soon!

3

Syntax to Specify a Range

The Range property has two acceptable syntaxes. To specify a rectangular range in the first syntax, specify the complete range reference just as you would in a formula in Excel:

```
Range("A1:B5")
```

In the alternative syntax, specify the upper-left corner and lower-right corner of the desired rectangular range. In this syntax, the equivalent statement might be this:

```
Range("A1", "B5")
```

For either corner, you can substitute a named range, the Cells property, or the ActiveCell property. The following line of code selects the rectangular range from A1 to the active cell:

```
Range("A1", ActiveCell).Select
```

The following statement selects from the active cell to five rows below the active cell and two columns to the right:

```
Range(ActiveCell, ActiveCell.Offset(5, 2)).Select
```

Named Ranges

You probably have already used named ranges on your worksheets and in formulas. You can also use them in VBA.

Use the following code to refer to the range "MyRange" in Sheet1:

```
Worksheets("Sheet1").Range("MyRange")
```

Notice that the name of the range is in quotes—unlike the use of named ranges in formulas on the sheet itself. If you forget to put the name in quotes, Excel thinks you are referring to a variable in the program. One exception is if you use the shortcut syntax discussed in the next section. In this case, quotes are not used.

Shortcut for Referencing Ranges

A shortcut is available when referencing ranges. The shortcut uses square brackets, as shown in Table 3.1.

Table 3.1 Shortcuts for Referencing Ranges

Standard Method	Shortcut
Range("D5")	[D5]
Range("A1:D5")	[A1:D5]
Range("A1:D5, G6:I17")	[A1:D5, G6:I17]
Range("MyRange")	[MyRange]

Referencing Ranges in Other Sheets

Switching between sheets by activating the needed sheet can dramatically slow down your code. To avoid this slowdown, you can refer to a sheet that is not active by first referencing the `Worksheet` object:

```
Worksheets("Sheet1").Range("A1")
```

This line of code references Sheet1 of the active workbook even if Sheet2 is the active sheet.

If you need to reference a range in another workbook, include the `Workbook` object, the `Worksheet` object, and then the `Range` object:

```
Workbooks("InvoiceData.xlsx").Worksheets("Sheet1").Range("A1")
```

Be careful if you use the `Range` property as an argument within another `Range` property. You must identify the range fully each time. For example, suppose that Sheet1 is your active sheet and you need to total data from Sheet2:

```
WorksheetFunction.Sum(Worksheets("Sheet2").Range(Range("A1"), Range("A7")))
```

This line does not work. Why not? Because `Range("A1"), Range("A7")` is meant to refer to the sheet at the beginning of the code line. However, Excel does not assume that you want to carry the `Worksheet` object reference over to these other `Range` objects and assumes they refer to Sheet1. So what do you do? Well, you could write this:

```
WorksheetFunction.Sum(Worksheets("Sheet2").Range(Worksheets("Sheet2"). _
    Range("A1"), Worksheets("Sheet2").Range("A7")))
```

But this not only is a long line of code but also is difficult to read! Thankfully, there is a simpler way, using `With...End With`:

```
With Worksheets("Sheet2")
    WorksheetFunction.Sum(.Range(.Range("A1"), .Range("A7")))
End With
```

Notice now that there is a `.Range` in your code, but without the preceding object reference. That's because `With Worksheets("Sheet2")` implies that the object of the range is the worksheet. Whenever Excel sees a period without an object reference directly to the left of it, it looks up the code for the closest `With` statement and uses that as the object reference.

Referencing a Range Relative to Another Range

Typically, the `RANGE` object is a property of a worksheet. It is also possible to have `RANGE` be the property of another range. In this case, the `Range` property is relative to the original range, which makes for unintuitive code. Consider this example:

```
Range("B5").Range("C3").Select
```

This code actually selects cell D7. Think about cell C3, which is located two rows below and two columns to the right of cell A1. The preceding line of code starts at cell B5. If we assume that B5 is in the A1 position, VBA finds the cell that would be in the C3 position relative to B5. In other words, VBA finds the cell that is two rows below and two columns to the right of B5, which is D7.

Again, I consider this coding style to be very unintuitive. This line of code mentions two addresses, and the actual cell selected is neither of these addresses! It seems misleading when you are trying to read this code.

You might consider using this syntax to refer to a cell relative to the active cell. For example, the following line of code activates the cell three rows down and four columns to the right of the currently active cell:

```
Selection.Range("E4").Select
```

This syntax is mentioned only because the macro recorder uses it. Recall that when you recorded a macro in Chapter 1, "Unleash the Power of Excel with VBA," with Relative References on, the following line was recorded:

```
ActiveCell.Offset(0, 4).Range("A2").Select
```

This line found the cell four columns to the right of the active cell, and from there it selected the cell that would correspond to A2. This is not the easiest way to write code, but that is the way the macro recorder does it.

Although a worksheet is usually the object of the Range property, occasionally, such as during recording, a range may be the property of a range.

Use the `Cells` Property to Select a Range

The Cells property refers to all the cells of the specified range object, which can be a worksheet or a range of cells. For example, this line selects all the cells of the active sheet:

```
Cells.Select
```

Using the Cells property with the Range object might seem redundant:

```
Range("A1:D5").Cells
```

This line refers to the original Range object. However, the Cells property has an Item property that makes the Cells property very useful. The Item property enables you to refer to a specific cell relative to the Range object.

The syntax for using the Item property with the Cells property is as follows:

```
Cells.Item(Row,Column)
```

You must use a numeric value for Row, but you may use the numeric value or string value for Column. Both of the following lines refer to cell C5:

```
Cells.Item(5,"C")
Cells.Item(5,3)
```

Because the Item property is the default property of the RANGE object, you can shorten these lines as follows:

```
Cells(5,"C")
Cells(5,3)
```

The ability to use numeric values for parameters is particularly useful if you need to loop through rows or columns. The macro recorder usually uses something like `Range("A1")`. `Select` for a single cell and `Range("A1:C5").Select` for a range of cells. If you are learning to code only from the recorder, you might be tempted to write code like this:

```
FinalRow = Cells(Rows.Count, 1).End(xlUp).Row
For i = 1 to FinalRow
    Range("A" & i & ":E" & i).Font.Bold = True
Next i
```

This little piece of code, which loops through rows and bolds the cells in Columns A through E, is awkward to read and write. But, how else can you do it?

```
FinalRow = Cells(Rows.Count, 1).End(xlUp).Row
For i = 1 to FinalRow
    Cells(i,"A").Resize(,5).Font.Bold = True
Next i
```

Instead of trying to type the range address, the new code uses the `Cells` and `Resize` properties to find the required cell, based on the active cell. See the "Use the Resize Property to Change the Size of a Range" section later in this chapter for more information on the `Resize` property.

`Cells` properties can be used as parameters in the `Range` property. The following refers to the range A1:E5:

```
Range(Cells(1,1),Cells(5,5))
```

This is particularly useful when you need to specify your variables with a parameter, as in the previous looping example.

Use the `Offset` Property to Refer to a Range

You have already seen a reference to `Offset` when the macro recorder used it when you recorded a relative reference. `Offset` enables you to manipulate a cell based off the location of the active cell. In this way, you do not need to know the address of a cell.

The syntax for the `Offset` property is as follows:

```
Range.Offset(RowOffset, ColumnOffset)
```

The syntax to affect cell F5 from cell A1 is

```
Range("A1").Offset(RowOffset:=4, ColumnOffset:=5)
```

Or, shorter yet, write this:

```
Range("A1").Offset(4,5)
```

The count of the rows and columns starts at A1 but does not include A1.

But what if you need to go over only a row or a column, but not both? You don't have to enter both the row and the column parameter. If you need to refer to a cell one column over, use one of these lines:

```
Range("A1").Offset(ColumnOffset:=1)
Range("A1").Offset(,1)
```

Both lines mean the same, so the choice is yours. Referring to a cell one row up is similar:

```
Range("B2").Offset(RowOffset:=-1)
Range("B2").Offset(-1)
```

Once again, you can choose which one to use. It is a matter of readability of the code.

Suppose you have a list of produce in column A with totals next to them in column B. If you want to find any total equal to zero and place LOW in the cell next to it, do this:

```
Set Rng = Range("B1:B16").Find(What:="0", LookAt:=xlWhole, LookIn:=xlValues)
Rng.Offset(, 1).Value = "LOW"
```

Used in a sub and looping through a table, it would look like this:

```
Sub FindLow()
With Range("B1:B16")
    Set Rng = .Find(What:="0", LookAt:=xlWhole, LookIn:=xlValues)
    If Not Rng Is Nothing Then
        firstAddress = Rng.Address
        Do
            Rng.Offset(, 1).Value = "LOW"
            Set Rng = .FindNext(Rng)
        Loop While Not Rng Is Nothing And Rng.Address <> firstAddress
    End If
End With
End Sub
```

The LOW totals are noted by the program, as shown in Figure 3.1.

Figure 3.1
Find the produce with zero totals.

◢	A	B	C
1	Apples	45	
2	Oranges	12	
3	Grapefruit	86	
4	Lemons	0	LOW

> **NOTE**
> Refer to the section "Object Variables" in Chapter 4 for more information on the Set statement.

Offsetting isn't only for single cells—you can use it with ranges. You can shift the focus of a range over in the same way you can shift the active cell. The following line refers to B2:D4 (see Figure 3.2):

```
Range("A1:C3").Offset(1,1)
```

Figure 3.2
Offsetting a range:
Range("A1:C3").
Offset(1,1).
Select.

Use the `Resize` **Property to Change the Size of a Range**

The `Resize` property enables you to change the size of a range based on the location of the active cell. You can create a new range as needed. The syntax for the `Resize` property is

```
Range.Resize(RowSize, ColumnSize)
```

To create a range B3:D13, use the following:

```
Range("B3").Resize(RowSize:=11, ColumnSize:=3)
```

Or here's a simpler way to create this range:

```
Range("B3").Resize(11, 3)
```

But what if you need to resize by only a row or a column—not both? You do not have to enter both the row and the column parameters.

If you need to expand by two columns, use one of the following:

```
Range("B3").Resize(ColumnSize:=2)
```

or

```
Range("B3").Resize(,2)
```

Both lines mean the same thing. The choice is yours. Resizing just the rows is similar. You can use either of the following:

```
Range("B3").Resize(RowSize:=2)
```

or

```
Range("B3").Resize(2)
```

Once again, the choice is yours. It is a matter of readability of the code.

From the list of produce, find the zero totals and color the cells of the total and corresponding produce (see Figure 3.3):

```
Set Rng = Range("B1:B16").Find(What:="0", LookAt:=xlWhole, LookIn:=xlValues)
Rng.Offset(, -1).Resize(, 2).Interior.ColorIndex = 15
```

Notice that the `Offset` property was used first to move the active cell over. When you are resizing, the upper-left-corner cell must remain the same.

Figure 3.3
Resizing a range to extend the selection.

	A	B
1	Apples	45
2	Oranges	12
3	Grapefruit	0
4	Lemons	0

Resizing isn't only for single cells—you can use it to resize an existing range. For example, if you have a named range but need it and the column next to it, use this:

```
Range("Produce").Resize(,2)
```

Remember, the number you resize by is the total number of rows/columns you want to include.

Use the `Columns` and `Rows` Properties to Specify a Range

The `Columns` and `Rows` properties refer to the columns and rows of a specified `Range` object, which can be a worksheet or a range of cells. They return a `Range` object referencing the rows or columns of the specified object.

You have seen the following line used, but what is it doing?

```
FinalRow = Cells(Rows.Count, 1).End(xlUp).Row
```

This line of code finds the last row in a sheet in which Column A has a value and places the row number of that `Range` object into `FinalRow`. This can be useful when you need to loop through a sheet row by row—you will know exactly how many rows you need to go through.

> **NOTE**
>
> Some properties of columns and rows require contiguous rows and columns to work properly. For example, if you were to use the following line of code, 9 would be the answer because only the first range would be evaluated:
>
> ```
> Range("A1:B9, C10:D19").Rows.Count
> ```
>
> However, if the ranges were grouped separately, the answer would be 19.
>
> ```
> Range("A1:B9", "C10:D19").Rows.Count
> ```

Use the `Union` Method to Join Multiple Ranges

The `Union` method enables you to join two or more noncontiguous ranges. It creates a temporary object of the multiple ranges, which enables you to affect them together:

```
Application.Union(argument1, argument2, etc.)
```

The expression, `Application`, is not required. The following code joins two named ranges on the sheet, inserts the `=RAND()` formula, and bolds them:

```
Set UnionRange = Union(Range("Range1"), Range("Range2"))
With UnionRange
    .Formula = "=RAND()"
    .Font.Bold = True
End With
```

Use the `Intersect` Method to Create a New Range from Overlapping Ranges

The `Intersect` method returns the cells that overlap between two or more ranges:

```
Application.Intersect(argument1, argument2, etc.)
```

The expression, `Application`, is not required. The following code colors the overlapping cells of the two ranges:

```
Set IntersectRange = Intersect(Range("Range1"), Range("Range2"))
IntersectRange.Interior.ColorIndex = 6
```

Use the `ISEMPTY` Function to Check Whether a Cell Is Empty

The `ISEMPTY` function returns a Boolean value that indicates whether a single cell is empty: `True` if empty, `False` if not. The cell must truly be empty for the function to return `True`. Even if it has a space that you cannot see, Excel does not consider the cell to be empty:

```
IsEmpty(Cell)
```

You have several groups of data separated by a blank row. You want to make the separations a little more obvious. The following code goes down the data in Column A. When it finds an empty cell, it colors in the first four cells for that row (see Figure 3.4):

```
LastRow = Cells(Rows.Count, 1).End(xlUp).Row
For i = 1 To LastRow
    If IsEmpty(Cells(i, 1)) Then
        Cells(i, 1).Resize(1, 4).Interior.ColorIndex = 1
    End If
Next i
```

Figure 3.4
Colored rows separating data.

	A	B	C	D
1	Apples	Oranges	Grapefruit	Lemons
2	45	12	86	15
3	83%	19%	6%	58%
4				
5	Tomatoes	Cabbage	Lettuce	Green Peppers
6	58	24	31	0
7	72%	5%	87%	25%
8				
9	Potatoes	Yams	Onions	Garlic
10	10	61	26	29
11	33%	54%	26%	84%

Use the `CurrentRegion` Property to Select a Data Range

`CurrentRegion` returns a Range object representing a set of contiguous data. As long as the data is surrounded by one empty row and one empty column, you can select the table with `CurrentRegion`:

```
RangeObject.CurrentRegion
```

The following line selects A1:D3 because this is the contiguous range of cells around cell A1 (see Figure 3.5):

```
Range("A1").CurrentRegion.Select
```

This is useful if you have a table whose size is in constant flux.

Figure 3.5
Use `CurrentRegion` to select a range of contiguous data around the active cell.

	A	B	C	D
1	Apples	Oranges	Grapefruit	Lemons
2	79	69	16	92
3	9%	44%	19%	16%
4				

CASE STUDY: USING THE SPECIALCELLS METHOD TO SELECT SPECIFIC CELLS

Even Excel power users might not have encountered the Go To Special dialog box. If you press the F5 key in an Excel worksheet, you get the normal Go To dialog box (see Figure 3.6). In the lower-left corner of this dialog is a button labeled Special. Click that button to get to the superpowerful Go To Special dialog box (see Figure 3.7).

Figure 3.6
Although the Go To dialog doesn't seem useful, click the Special button in the lower-left corner.

Figure 3.7
The Go To Special dialog has many incredibly useful selection tools, such as selecting only the formulas on a sheet.

In the Excel interface, the Go To Special dialog enables you to select only cells with formulas, only blank cells, or only the visible cells. Selecting only visible cells is excellent for grabbing the visible results of AutoFiltered data.

To simulate the Go To Special dialog in VBA, use the `SpecialCells` method. This enables you to act on cells that meet a certain criteria:

```
RangeObject.SpecialCells(Type, Value)
```

This method has two parameters: Type and Value. Type is one of the xlCellType constants:

```
xlCellTypeAllFormatConditions
xlCellTypeAllValidation
xlCellTypeBlanks
xlCellTypeComments
xlCellTypeConstants
xlCellTypeFormulas
xlCellTypeLastCell
xlCellTypeSameFormatConditions
xlCellTypeSameValidation
xlCellTypeVisible
```

Value is optional and can be one of the following:

```
xlErrors
xlLogical
xlNumbers
xlTextValues
```

The following code returns all the ranges that have conditional formatting set up. It produces an error if there are no conditional formats and adds a border around each contiguous section it finds:

```
Set rngCond = ActiveSheet.Cells.SpecialCells(xlCellTypeAllFormatConditions)
If Not rngCond Is Nothing Then
    rngCond.BorderAround xlContinuous
End If
```

Have you ever had someone send you a worksheet without all the labels filled in? Some people consider that the data shown in Figure 3.8 looks neat. They enter the Region field only once for each region. This might look aesthetically pleasing, but it is impossible to sort.

Figure 3.8
The blank cells in the Region column make it difficult to sort data tables such as this.

▲	A	B	C
1	Region	Product	Sales
2	North	ABC	766,469
3		DEF	776,996
4		XYZ	832,414
5	East	ABC	703,255
6		DEF	891,799
7		XYZ	897,949

Using the SpecialCells method to select all the blanks in this range is one way to fill in all the blank region cells quickly with the region found above them:

```
Sub FillIn()
    On Error Resume Next 'Need this because if there aren't any blank
'cells, the code will error
    Range("A1").CurrentRegion.SpecialCells(xlCellTypeBlanks).FormulaR1C1 _
    = "=R[-1]C"
    Range("A1").CurrentRegion.Value = Range("A1").CurrentRegion.Value
End Sub
```

In this code, `Range("A1").CurrentRegion` refers to the contiguous range of data in the report. The `SpecialCells` method returns just the blank cells in that range. Although you can read more about R1C1-style formulas in Chapter 5, "R1C1-Style Formulas," this particular formula fills in all the blank cells with a formula that points to the cell above the blank cell. The second line of code is a fast way to simulate doing a Copy and then Paste Special Values. Figure 3.9 shows the results.

Figure 3.9
After the macro runs, the blank cells in the Region column have been filled in with data.

	A	B	C
1	Region	Product	Sales
2	North	ABC	766,469
3	North	DEF	776,996
4	North	XYZ	832,414
5	East	ABC	703,255
6	East	DEF	891,799
7	East	XYZ	897,949

Use the `Areas` Collection to Return a Noncontiguous Range

The `Areas` collection is a collection of noncontiguous ranges within a selection. It consists of individual `Range` objects representing contiguous ranges of cells within the selection. If the selection contains only one area, the `Areas` collection contains a single `Range` object corresponding to that selection.

You might be tempted to loop through the rows in a sheet and check the properties of a cell in a row, such as its formatting (for example, font or fill) or whether the cell contains a formula or value. Then, you could copy the row and paste it to another section. However, there is an easier way. In Figure 3.10, the user enters the values below each fruit and vegetable. The percentages are formulas. The following code selects the cells with numerical constants and copies them to another area:

```
Range("A:D").SpecialCells(xlCellTypeConstants, xlNumbers).Copy Range("I1")
Set NewDestination = Range("I1")
For each Rng in Cells.SpecialCells(xlCellTypeConstants, xlNumbers).Areas
    Rng.Copy Destination:=NewDestinations
    Set NewDestination = NewDestination.Offset(Rng.Rows.Count)
Next Rng
```

Figure 3.10
The `Areas` collection makes it easier to manipulate noncontiguous ranges.

	A	B	C	D	E	F	G	H	I	J	K	L
1	Apples	Oranges	Grapefruit	Lemons					45	12	86	15
2	45	12	86	15					58	24	31	0
3	78%	27%	61%	76%					10	61	26	29
4									46	64	79	95
5	Tomatoes	Cabbage	Lettuce	Green Peppers								
6	58	24	31	0								
7	66%	8%	56%	66%								
8												
9	Potatoes	Yams	Onions	Garlic								
10	10	61	26	29								
11	20%	85%	2%	11%								
12												
13	Green Beans	Broccoli	Peas	Carrots								
14	46	64	79	95								
15	37%	41%	33%	28%								

Referencing Tables

Tables are a special type of range that offers the convenience of referencing named ranges, but they are not created in the same manner. For more information on how to create a named table, see Chapter 6, "Create and Manipulate Names in VBA."

The table itself is referenced using the standard method of referring to a ranged name. To refer to the data in Table1 in Sheet1, do this:

```
Worksheets(1).Range("Table1")
```

This references the data part of the table but does not include the header or total row. To include the header and total row, do this:

```
Worksheets(1).Range("Table1[#All]")
```

What I really like about this feature is the ease of referencing specific columns of a table. You don't have to know how many columns to move in from a starting position or the letter/number of the column, and you don't have to use a FIND function. Instead, you can use the header name of the column. For example, do this to reference the Qty column of the table:

```
Worksheets(1).Range("Table1[Qty]")
```

3

Next Steps

Chapter 4, "Looping and Flow Control," describes a fundamental component of any programming language: loops. If you have taken a programming class, you will be familiar with basic loop structures. VBA supports all the usual loops. In the next chapter, you'll also learn about a special loop, For Each...Next, which is unique to object-oriented programming such as VBA.

Looping and Flow Control

Loops make your life easier. You might have 20 lines of macro code that do something cool one time. Add a line of code above and below and suddenly your macro fixes a million rows instead of one row. Loops are a fundamental component of any programming language. If you've taken any programming classes, even BASIC, you've likely encountered a `For...Next` loop. Fortunately, VBA supports all the usual loops, plus a special loop that is excellent to use with VBA.

This chapter covers the basic loop constructs:

- `For...Next`
- `Do...While`
- `Do...Until`
- `While...Wend`
- `Until...Loop`

This chapter also discusses the useful loop construct that is unique to object-oriented languages:

- `For Each...Next`

For...Next **Loops**

`For` and `Next` are common loop constructs. Everything between `For` and the `Next` is run multiple times. Each time the code runs, a certain counter variable, specified in the `For` statement, has a different value.

Consider this code:

```
For I = 1 to 10
    Cells(I, I).Value = I
Next I
```

As this program starts to run, you need to give the counter variable a name. In this example, the name of the variable is `I`. The first time through the code, the variable `I` is set to 1. The first time that the loop is executed, `I` is equal to 1, so the cell in Row 1, Column 1 is set to 1 (see Figure 4.1).

Figure 4.1

After the first iteration through the loop, the cell in Row 1, Column 1 has the value of 1.

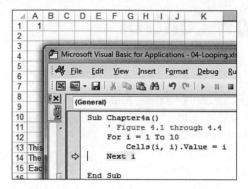

Let's take a close look at what happens as VBA gets to the line that says Next I. Before this line is run, the variable I is equal to 1. During the execution of Next I, VBA must make a decision. VBA adds 1 to the variable I and compares it to the maximum value in the To clause of the For statement. If it is within the limits specified in the To clause, the loop is not finished. In this case, the value of I is incremented to 2. Code execution then moves back to the first line of code after the For statement. Figure 4.2 shows the state of the program before it runs the Next line. Figure 4.3 shows what happens after the Next line is executed.

Figure 4.2

Before the Next I statement is run, I is equal to 1. VBA can safely add 1 to I, and it will be less than or equal to the 10 specified in the To clause of the For statement.

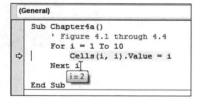

Figure 4.3

After the Next I statement is run, I is incremented to 2. Code execution continues with the line of code immediately following the For statement, which writes a 2 to cell B2.

```
(General)

    Sub Chapter4a()
        ' Figure 4.1 through 4.4
        For i = 1 To 10
            Cells(i, i).Value = i
        Next i
            i = 2
    End Sub
```

The second time through the loop, the value of I is 2. The cell in Row 2, Column 2 (that is, cell B2) gets a value of 2.

As the process continues, the Next I statement advances I up to 3, 4, and so on. On the tenth pass through the loop, the cell in Row 10, Column 10 is assigned a value of 10.

It is interesting to watch what happens to the variable I on the last pass through `Next I`. Before running the `Next I` line, the variable contains a 10. VBA is now at a decision point. It adds 1 to the variable `I`. `I` is now equal to 11, which is greater than the limit in the `For...Next` loop. VBA then moves execution to the next line in the macro after the `Next` statement (see Figure 4.4). In case you are tempted to use the variable `I` later in the macro, it is important to realize that it will be incremented beyond the limit specified in the `To` clause of the `For` statement.

Figure 4.4

After incrementing `I` to 11, code execution moves to the line after the `Next` statement.

The common use for such a loop is to walk through all the rows in a dataset and decide to perform some action based on some criteria. For example, if you want to mark all the rows with positive service revenue in Column F, you could use this loop:

```
For I = 2 to 10
    If Cells(I, 6).Value > 0 Then
        Cells(I, 8).Value = "Service Revenue"
        Cells(I, 1).Resize(1, 8).Interior.ColorIndex = 4
    End If
Next i
```

This loop checks each item of data from Row 2 through Row 10. If there is a positive number in Column F, Column H of that row has a new label, and the cells in Columns A:H of the row are colored using the color index of 4, which is green. After this macro has been run, the results look as shown in Figure 4.5.

Figure 4.5
After the loop completes all nine iterations, any rows with positive values in Column F are colored green and have the label "Service Revenue" added to Column H.

	A	B	C	D	E	F	G	H	I
1	InvoiceDate	InvoiceNumber	SalesRepNumber	CustomerNumber	ProductRevenue	ServiceRevenue	ProductCost		
2	6/8/2015	123829	S21	C8754	21000	0	9875		
3	6/8/2015	123834	S54	C7796	339000	0	195298		
4	6/8/2015	123835	S21	C1654	161000	0	90761		
5	6/8/2015	123836	S45	C6460	275500	10000	146341	Service Revenue	
6	6/8/2015	123837	S54	C5143	925400	0	473515		
7	6/8/2015	123841	S21	C8361	94400	0	53180		
8	6/8/2015	123842	S45	C1842	36500	55000	20696	Service Revenue	
9	6/8/2015	123843	S54	C4107	599700	0	276718		
10	6/8/2015	123844	S21	C5205	244900	0	143393		
11									

Using Variables in the For Statement

The previous example is not very useful in that it works only when there are exactly 10 rows of data. It is possible to use a variable to specify the upper/lower limit of the For statement. This code sample identifies FinalRow with data and then loops from Row 2 to that row:

```
FinalRow = Cells(Rows.Count, 1).End(xlUp).Row
For I = 2 to FinalRow
    If Cells(I, 6).Value > 0 Then
        Cells(I, 8).Value = "Service Revenue"
        Cells(I, 1).Resize(1, 8).Interior.ColorIndex = 4
    End If
Next I
```

> **CAUTION**
>
> Exercise caution when using variables. What if the imported file today is empty and has only a heading row? In this case, the FinalRow variable is equal to 1. This makes the first statement of the loop essentially, say, For I = 2 to 1. Because the start number is higher than the end number, the loop does not execute at all. The variable I is equal to 2, and code execution jumps to the line after Next.

Variations on the For...Next Loop

In a For...Next loop, it is possible to have the loop variable jump up by something other than 1. For example, you might use it to apply green-bar formatting to every other row in a dataset. In this case, you want to have the counter variable I examine every other row in the dataset. Indicate this by adding the Step clause to the end of the For statement:

```
FinalRow = Cells(Rows.Count, 1).End(xlUp).Row
For i = 2 to FinalRow Step 2
    Cells(i, 1).Resize(1, 8).Interior.ColorIndex = 35
Next i
```

While running this code, VBA adds a light green shading to Rows 2, 4, 6, and so on (see Figure 4.6).

Figure 4.6
The Step clause in the
For statement of the
loop causes the action to
occur on every other row.

⊿	A	B	C	D	E
1	InvoiceDate	InvoiceNumber	SalesRepNumber	CustomerNumber	ProductRevenue
2	6/7/2011	123829	S21	C8754	21000
3	6/7/2011	123830	S45	C3390	188100
4	6/7/2011	123831	S54	C2523	510600
5	6/7/2011	123832	S21	C5519	86200
6	6/7/2011	123833	S45	C3245	800100
7	6/7/2011	123834	S54	C7796	339000
8	6/7/2011	123835	S21	C1654	161000
9	6/7/2011	123836	S45	C6460	275500
10	6/7/2011	123837	S54	C5143	925400

The Step clause can be any number. You might want to check every tenth row of a dataset
to extract a random sample. In this case, you would use Step 10:

```
FinalRow = Cells(Rows.Count, 1).End(xlUp).Row
NextRow = FinalRow + 5
Cells(NextRow-1, 1).Value = "Random Sample of Above Data"
For I = 2 to FinalRow Step 10
    Cells(I, 1).Resize(1, 8).Copy Destination:=Cells(NextRow, 1)
    NextRow = NextRow + 1
Next i
```

You can also have a For...Next loop run backward from high to low. This is particularly
useful if you are selectively deleting rows. To do this, reverse the order of the For statement
and have the Step clause specify a negative number:

```
' Delete all rows where column C is the Internal rep - S54
FinalRow = Cells(Rows.Count, 1).End(xlUp).Row
For I = FinalRow to 2 Step -1
    If Cells(I, 3).Value = "S54" Then
        Rows(I).Delete
    End If
Next i
```

4

> **NOTE** There is a faster way to delete the records, which is discussed in the "Replacing a Loop with AutoFilter"
> section of Chapter 11, "Data Mining with Advanced Filter."

Exiting a Loop Early After a Condition Is Met

Sometimes you don't need to execute the whole loop. Perhaps you just need to read
through the dataset until you find one record that meets a certain criteria. In this case, you
want to find the first record and then stop the loop. A statement called Exit For does this.

The following sample macro looks for a row in the dataset where service revenue in
Column F is positive and product revenue in Column E is 0. If such a row is found, you
might indicate a message that the file needs manual processing today and move the cell
pointer to that row:

```
' Are there any special processing situations in the data?
FinalRow = Cells(Rows.Count, 1).End(xlUp).Row
ProblemFound = False
For I = 2 to FinalRow
```

```
    If Cells(I, 6).Value > 0 Then
        If cells(I, 5).Value = 0 Then
            Cells(I, 6).Select

            ProblemFound = True
            Exit For
        End If
    End If
Next I
If ProblemFound Then
    MsgBox "There is a problem at row " & I
    Exit Sub
End If
```

Nesting One Loop Inside Another Loop

It is okay to run a loop inside another loop. The following code has the first loop run through all the rows in a recordset, while the second loop runs through all the columns:

```
' Loop through each row and column
' Add a checkerboard format
FinalRow = Cells(Rows.Count, 1).End(xlUp).Row
FinalCol = Cells(1, Columns.Count).End(xlToLeft).Column
For I = 2 to FinalRow
    ' For even numbered rows, start in column 1
    ' For odd numbered rows, start in column 2
    If I Mod 2 = 1 Then ' Divide I by 2 and keep remainder
        StartCol = 1
    Else
        StartCol = 2
    End If
    For J = StartCol to FinalCol Step 2
        Cells(I, J).Interior.ColorIndex = 35
    Next J
Next I
```

In this code, the outer loop is using the I counter variable to loop through all the rows in the dataset. The inner loop is using the J counter variable to loop through all the columns in that row. Because Figure 4.7 has seven data rows, the code runs through the I loop seven times. Each time through the I loop, the code runs through the J loop six or seven times. This means that the line of code that is inside the J loop ends up being executed several times for each pass through the I loop. Figure 4.7 shows the result.

Figure 4.7
The result of nesting one loop inside the other; VBA can loop through each row and then each column.

⊿	A	B	C	D	E
1	Item	January	February	March	April
2	Hardware Revenue	1,972,637	1,655,321	1,755,234	1,531,060
3	Software Revenue	236,716	198,639	210,628	183,727
4	Service Revenue	473,433	397,277	421,256	367,454
5	Cost of Good Sold	1,084,951	910,427	965,379	842,083
6	Selling Expense	394,527	331,064	351,047	306,212
7	G&A Expense	150,000	150,000	150,000	150,000
8	R&D	125,000	125,000	125,000	125,000
9					

Do **Loops**

There are several variations of the Do loop. The most basic Do loop is useful for doing a bunch of mundane tasks. For example, suppose that someone sends you a list of addresses going down a column, as shown in Figure 4.8.

Figure 4.8

It would be more useful to have these addresses in a database format to use in a mail merge.

6	John Smith
7	123 Main Street
8	Akron OH 44308
9	
10	Jane Doe
11	245 State Street
12	Merritt Island FL 32953
13	
14	Ralph Emerson
15	345 2nd Ave
16	New York NY 10011

In this case, you might need to rearrange these addresses into a database with name in Column B, street in Column C, city and state in Column D. By setting Relative Recording (see Chapter 1, "Unleash the Power of Excel with VBA") and using a hotkey of Ctrl+A, you can record this bit of useful code. The code is designed to copy one single address into database format. The code also navigates the cell pointer to the name of the next address in the list. Each time you press Ctrl+A, one address is reformatted.

```
Sub FixOneRecord()
' Keyboard Shortcut: Ctrl+Shift+A
    ActiveCell.Offset(1, 0).Range("A1").Select
    Selection.Cut
    ActiveCell.Offset(-1, 1).Range("A1").Select
    ActiveSheet.Paste
    ActiveCell.Offset(2, -1).Range("A1").Select
    Selection.Cut
    ActiveCell.Offset(-2, 2).Range("A1").Select
    ActiveSheet.Paste
    ActiveCell.Offset(1, -2).Range("A1:A3").Select
    Selection.EntireRow.Delete
    ActiveCell.Select
End Sub
```

> **NOTE** Do not assume that the preceding code is suitable for a professional application. You don't need to select something before acting on it. However, sometimes macros are written just to automate a one-time mundane task.

Without a macro, a lot of manual copying and pasting would be required. However, with the preceding recorded macro, you can simply place the cell pointer on a name in Column A and press Ctrl+Shift+A. That one address is copied into three columns, and the cell pointer moves to the start of the next address (see Figure 4.9).

4

Figure 4.9

After the macro is run once, one address is moved into the proper format, and the cell pointer is positioned to run the macro again.

6	John Smith		123 Main Street	Akron OH 44308
7	Jane Doe			
8	245 State Street			
9	Merritt Island FL 32953			

When you use this macro, you are able to process an address every second using the hotkey. However, when you need to process 5,000 addresses, you will not want to keep running the same macro over and over.

In this case, you can use a Do...Loop to set up the macro to run continuously. You can have VBA run this code continuously by enclosing the recorded code with Do at the top and Loop at the end. Now you can sit back and watch the code perform this insanely boring task in minutes rather than hours.

Note that this particular Do...Loop will run forever because there is no mechanism to stop it. This works for the task at hand because you can watch the progress on the screen and press Ctrl+Break to stop execution when the program advances past the end of this database.

This code uses a Do loop to fix the addresses:

```
Sub FixAllRecords()
' Figure 4.8 & Figure 4.9
'
    Do
    ActiveCell.Offset(1, 0).Range("A1").Select
    Selection.Cut
    ActiveCell.Offset(-1, 1).Range("A1").Select
    ActiveSheet.Paste
    ActiveCell.Offset(2, -1).Range("A1").Select
    Selection.Cut
    ActiveCell.Offset(-2, 2).Range("A1").Select
    ActiveSheet.Paste
    ActiveCell.Offset(1, -2).Range("A1:A3").Select
    Selection.EntireRow.Delete
    ActiveCell.Select
    Loop
End Sub
```

These examples are "quick and dirty" loops that are great for when you need to accomplish a task quickly. The Do...Loop provides a number of options to enable you to have the program stop automatically when it accomplishes the end of the task.

The first option is to have a line in the Do...Loop that detects the end of the dataset and exits the loop. In the current example, this could be accomplished by using the Exit Do command in an If statement. If the current cell is on a cell that is empty, you can assume that you have reached the end of the data and stopped processing the loop:

```
Do
    If Selection.Value = "" Then Exit Do
    ActiveCell.Offset(1, 0).Range("A1").Select
```

```
        Selection.Cut
        ActiveCell.Offset(-1, 1).Range("A1").Select
        ActiveSheet.Paste
        ActiveCell.Offset(2, -1).Range("A1").Select
        Selection.Cut
        ActiveCell.Offset(-2, 2).Range("A1").Select
        ActiveSheet.Paste
        ActiveCell.Offset(1, -2).Range("A1:A3").Select
        Selection.EntireRow.Delete
        ActiveCell.Select
    Loop
End Sub
```

Using the `While` or `Until` Clause in `Do` Loops

There are four variations of using `While` or `Until`. These clauses can be added to either the `Do` statement or the `Loop` statement. In each case, the `While` or `Until` clause includes some test that evaluates to `True` or `False`.

With a `Do While` *test expression*...`Loop` construct, the loop is never executed if *test expression* is false. If you are reading records from a text file, you cannot assume that the file has one or more records. Instead, you need to test to see whether you are already at the end of file with the `EOF` function before you enter the loop:

```
' Read a text file, skipping the Total lines
    Open "C:\Invoice.txt" For Input As #1
    R = 1
    Do While Not EOF(1)
        Line Input #FileNumber, Data
        If Not Left (Data, 5) = "TOTAL" Then
            ' Import this row
            r = r + 1
            Cells(r, 1).Value = Data
        End If
    Loop
    Close #1
```

In this example, the `Not` keyword `EOF(1)` evaluates to `True` after there are no more records to be read from `Invoice.txt`. Some programmers believe that it is hard to read a program that contains a lot of instances of `Not`. To avoid the use of `Not`, use the `Do Until <test expression>`...`Loop` construct:

```
' Read a text file, skipping the Total lines
    Open "C:\Invoice.txt" For Input As #1
    R = 1
    Do Until EOF(1)
        Line Input #1, Data
        If Not Left(Data, 5) = "TOTAL" Then
            ' Import this row
            r = r + 1
            Cells(r, 1).Value = Data
        End If
    Loop
    Close #1
```

In other examples, you might always want the loop to be executed the first time. In these cases, move the While or Until instruction to the end of the loop. This code sample asks the user to enter sales amounts made that day. It continually asks them for sales amounts until they enter a zero:

```
TotalSales = 0
Do
    x = InputBox( _
        Prompt:="Enter Amount of Next Invoice. Enter 0 when done.", _
        Type:=1)
    TotalSales = TotalSales + x
Loop Until x = 0
MsgBox "The total for today is $" & TotalSales
```

In the following loop, a check amount is entered, and then it looks for open invoices to which the check can be applied. However, it is often the case that a single check is received that covers several invoices. The following program sequentially applies the check to the oldest invoices until 100 percent of the check has been applied:

```
' Ask for the amount of check received. Add zero to convert to numeric.
AmtToApply = InputBox("Enter Amount of Check") + 0
  ' Loop through the list of open invoices.
' Apply the check to the oldest open invoices and Decrement AmtToApply
NextRow = 2
Do While AmtToApply > 0
    OpenAmt = Cells(NextRow, 3)
    If OpenAmt > AmtToApply Then
        ' Apply total check to this invoice
        Cells(NextRow, 4).Value = AmtToApply
        AmtToApply = 0
    Else
        Cells(NextRow, 4).Value = OpenAmt
        AmtToApply = AmtToApply - OpenAmt
    End If
    NextRow = NextRow + 1
Loop
```

Because you can construct the Do...Loop with the While or Until qualifiers at the beginning or end, you have a great deal of subtle control over whether the loop is always executed once, even when the condition is true at the beginning.

While...Wend **Loops**

While...Wend loops are included in VBA for backward compatibility. In the VBA help file, Microsoft suggests that Do...Loops are more flexible. However, because you might encounter While...Wend loops in code written by others, this chapter includes a quick example. In this loop, the first line is always While <condition>. The last line of the loop is always Wend. Note that there is no Exit While statement. In general, these loops are okay, but the Do... Loop construct is more robust and flexible. Because the Do loop offers either the While or Until qualifier, you can use this qualifier at the beginning or end of the loop, and there is the possibility to exit a Do loop early:

```
' Read a text file, adding the amounts
    Open "C:\Invoice.txt" For Input As #1
```

```
    TotalSales = 0
    While Not EOF(1)
        Line Input #1, Data
        TotalSales = TotalSales + Data
    Wend
    MsgBox "Total Sales=" & TotalSales
    Close #1
```

The VBA Loop: For Each

Even though the VBA loop is an excellent loop, the macro recorder never records this type of loop. VBA is an object-oriented language. It is common to have a collection of objects in Excel such as a collection of worksheets in a workbook, cells in a range, pivot tables on a worksheet, or data series on a chart.

This special type of loop is great for looping through all the items in the collection. However, before discussing this loop in detail, you need to understand a special kind of variable called *object variables*.

Object Variables

At this point, you have seen a variable that contains a single value. When you have a variable such as TotalSales = 0, TotalSales is a normal variable and generally contains only a single value. It is also possible to have a more powerful variable called an *object variable* that holds many values. In other words, any property associated with the object is also associated with the object variable.

Generally, developers do not take the time to declare variables. Many books implore you to use the DIM statement to identify all your variables at the top of the procedure. This enables you to specify that a certain variable must be of a certain type, such as Integer or Double. Although this saves a tiny bit of memory, it requires you to know up front which variables you plan on using. However, developers tend to whip up a new variable on the fly as the need arises. Even so, there are great benefits to declaring object variables. For example, the VBA AutoComplete feature turns on if you declare an object variable at the top of your procedure. The following lines of code declare three object variables: a worksheet, range, and a pivot table:

```
Sub Test()
    Dim WSD as Worksheet
    Dim MyCell as Range
    Dim PT as PivotTable
    Set WSD = ThisWorkbook.Worksheets("Data")
    Set MyCell = WSD.Cells(Rows.Count, 1).End(xlUp).Offset(1, 0)
    Set PT = WSD.PivotTables(1)
    ...
```

In this code, you can see that more than an equals statement is used to assign object variables. You also need to use the Set statement to assign a specific object to the object variable.

There are many good reasons to use object variables, not the least of which is the fact that it can be a great shorthand notation. It is easier to have many lines of code refer to WSD rather than ThisWorkbook.Worksheets("Data"). In addition, as mentioned earlier, the object variable inherits all the properties of the object to which it refers.

The For Each...Loop employs an object variable rather than a Counter variable. The following code loops through all the cells in Column A. The code uses the .CurrentRegion property to define the current region and then uses the .Resize property to limit the selected range to a single column. The object variable is called Cell. Any name could be used for the object variable, but Cell seems more appropriate than something arbitrary like Fred.

```
For Each cell in Range("A1").CurrentRegion.Resize(, 1)
    If cell.Value = "Total" Then
        cell.resize(1,8).Font.Bold = True
    End If
Next cell
```

This code sample searches all open workbooks, looking for a workbook in which the first worksheet is called Menu:

```
For Each wb in Workbooks
    If wb.Worksheets(1).Name = "Menu" Then
    WBFound = True
    WBName = wb.Name
    Exit For
End If
Next wb
```

In this code sample, all shapes on the current worksheet are deleted:

```
For Each Sh in ActiveSheet.Shapes
    Sh.Delete
Next Sh
```

This code sample deletes all pivot tables on the current sheet:

```
For Each pt in ActiveSheet.PivotTables
    pt.TableRange2.Clear
Next pt
```

CASE STUDY: LOOPING THROUGH ALL FILES IN A DIRECTORY

This case study includes some useful procedures that make extensive use of loops.

The first procedure uses VBA's Scripting.FileSystemObject to find all JPG picture files in a certain directory. Each file is listed down a column in Excel.

```
Sub FindJPGFilesInAFolder()
    Dim fso As Object
    Dim strName As String
    Dim strArr(1 To 1048576, 1 To 1) As String, i As Long

    ' Enter the folder name here
```

```
     Const strDir As String = "C:\Artwork\"

     strName = Dir$(strDir & "*.jpg")
     Do While strName <> vbNullString
         i = i + 1
         strArr(i, 1) = strDir & strName
         strName = Dir$()
     Loop
     Set fso = CreateObject("Scripting.FileSystemObject")
     Call recurseSubFolders(fso.GetFolder(strDir), strArr(), i)
     Set fso = Nothing
     If i > 0 Then
         Range("A1").Resize(i).Value = strArr
     End If

     ' Next, loop through all found files
     ' and break into path and filename
     FinalRow = Cells(Rows.Count, 1).End(xlUp).Row
     For i = 1 To FinalRow
         ThisEntry = Cells(i, 1)
         For j = Len(ThisEntry) To 1 Step -1
             If Mid(ThisEntry, j, 1) = Application.PathSeparator Then
                 Cells(i, 2) = Left(ThisEntry, j)

                 Cells(i, 3) = Mid(ThisEntry, j + 1)
                 Exit For
             End If
         Next j
     Next i

End Sub
Private Sub recurseSubFolders(ByRef Folder As Object, _
    ByRef strArr() As String, _
    ByRef i As Long)
Dim SubFolder As Object
Dim strName As String
For Each SubFolder In Folder.SubFolders
    strName = Dir$(SubFolder.Path & "*.jpg")
    Do While strName <> vbNullString
        i = i + 1
        strArr(i, 1) = SubFolder.Path & strName
        strName = Dir$()
    Loop
    Call recurseSubFolders(SubFolder, strArr(), i)
Next
End Sub
```

The idea in this situation is to organize the photos into new folders. In Column D, if you want to move a picture to a new folder, type the path of that folder. The following For...Each loop takes care of copying the pictures. Each time through the loop, the object variable named Cell contains a reference to a cell in Column A. You can use Cell.Offset(0, 3) to return the value from the cell three columns to the right of the range represented by the variable Cell:

```
Sub CopyToNewFolder()
    FinalRow = Cells(Rows.Count, 1).End(xlUp).Row
```

```
    For Each Cell In Range("A2:A" & FinalRow)
        OrigFile = Cell.Value
        NewFile = Cell.Offset(0, 3) & Application.PathSeparator & _
            Cell.Offset(0, 2)
        FileCopy OrigFile, NewFile
    Next Cell
End Sub
```

Note that `Application.PathSeparator` is a backslash on Windows computers but might be different if the code is running on a Macintosh.

Flow Control: Using `If...Then...Else` and `Select Case`

Another aspect of programming that will never be recorded by the macro recorder is the concept of flow control. Sometimes you do not want every line of your program to be executed every time you run the macro. VBA offers two excellent choices for flow control: the `If...Then...Else` construct and the `Select Case` construct.

Basic Flow Control: `If...Then...Else`

The most common device for program flow control is the `If` statement. For example, suppose you have a list of products as shown in Figure 4.10. You want to loop through each product in the list and copy it to either a Fruits list or a Vegetables list. Beginning programmers might be tempted to loop through the rows twice—once to look for fruit and a second time to look for vegetables. However, there is no need to loop through twice because you can use an `If...Then...Else` construct on a single loop to copy each row to the correct place.

Figure 4.10
A single loop can look for fruits or vegetables.

▲	A	B	C	D
1	Class	Product	Quantity	
2	Fruit	Apples	1	
3	Fruit	Apricots	3	
4	Vegetable	Asparagus	62	
5	Fruit	Bananas	55	
6	Fruit	Blueberry	17	
7	Vegetable	Broccoli	56	
8	Vegetable	Cabbage	35	
9	Fruit	Cherries	59	
10	Herbs	Dill	91	
11	Vegetable	Eggplant	94	
12	Fruit	Kiwi	86	

Conditions

Any `If` statement needs a condition that is being tested. The condition should always evaluate to TRUE or FALSE. Here are some examples of simple and complex conditions:

- `If Range("A1").Value = "Title" Then`
- `If Not Range("A1").Value = "Title" Then`

- If Range("A1").Value = "Title" And Range("B1").Value = "Fruit" Then
- If Range("A1").Value = "Title" Or Range("B1").Value = "Fruit" Then

If...Then...End If

After the If statement, you can include one or more program lines that will be executed only if the condition is met. You should then close the If block with an End If line. Here is a simple example of an If statement:

```
Sub ColorFruitRedBold()
    FinalRow = Cells(Rows.Count, 1).End(xlUp).Row

    For i = 2 To FinalRow
        If Cells(i, 1).Value = "Fruit" Then
            Cells(i, 1).Resize(1, 3).Font.Bold = True
            Cells(i, 1).Resize(1, 3).Font.ColorIndex = 3
        End If
    Next i

    MsgBox "Fruit is now bold and red"
End Sub
```

Either/Or Decisions: If...Then...Else...End If

Sometimes you will want to do one set of statements if the condition is true, and another set of statements if the condition is not true. To do this with VBA, the second set of conditions would be coded after the Else statement. There is still only one End If statement associated with this construct. For example, you could use the following code if you want to color the fruit red and the vegetables green:

```
Sub FruitRedVegGreen()
    FinalRow = Cells(Rows.Count, 1).End(xlUp).Row

    For i = 2 To FinalRow
        If Cells(i, 1).Value = "Fruit" Then
            Cells(i, 1).Resize(1, 3).Font.ColorIndex = 3
        Else
            Cells(i, 1).Resize(1, 3).Font.ColorIndex = 50
        End If
    Next i

    MsgBox "Fruit is red / Veggies are green"
End Sub
```

Using If...ElseIf...End If for Multiple Conditions

Notice that our product list includes one item that is classified as an herb. You have three conditions that can be used to test items on the list. It is possible to build an If...End If structure with multiple conditions. First, test to see whether the record is a fruit. Next, use an Else If to test whether the record is a vegetable. Then, test to see whether the record is an herb. Finally, if the record is none of those, highlight the record as an error.

```
Sub MultipleIf()
    FinalRow = Cells(Rows.Count, 1).End(xlUp).Row
```

```
    For i = 2 To FinalRow
        If Cells(i, 1).Value = "Fruit" Then
            Cells(i, 1).Resize(1, 3).Font.ColorIndex = 3
        ElseIf Cells(i, 1).Value = "Vegetable" Then
            Cells(i, 1).Resize(1, 3).Font.ColorIndex = 50
        ElseIf Cells(i, 1).Value = "Herbs" Then
            Cells(i, 1).Resize(1, 3).Font.ColorIndex = 5
        Else
            ' This must be a record in error
            Cells(i, 1).Resize(1, 3).Interior.ColorIndex = 6
        End If
    Next i

    MsgBox "Fruit is red / Veggies are green / Herbs are blue"
End Sub
```

Using `Select Case...End Select` for Multiple Conditions

When you have many different conditions, it becomes unwieldy to use many `Else If` statements. For this reason, VBA offers another construct known as the `Select Case` construct. In your running example, always check the value of the Class in column A. This value is called the *test expression*. The basic syntax of this construct starts with the words `Select Case` followed by the test expression:

```
Select Case Cells(i, 1).Value
```

Thinking about this problem in English, you might say, "In cases in which the record is fruit, color the record with red." VBA uses a shorthand version of this. You write the word `Case` followed by the literal `"Fruit"`. Any statements that follow `Case "Fruit"` are executed whenever the test expression is a fruit. After these statements, you have the next `Case` statement: `Case "Vegetables"`. You continue in this fashion, writing a `Case` statement followed by the program lines that are executed if that case is true.

After you have listed all the possible conditions you can think of, you can optionally include a `Case Else` section at the end. The `Case Else` section includes what the program should do if the test expression matches none of your cases. Below, the macro adds a note in column D if an unexpected value is found in A. Finally, close the entire construct with the `End Select` statement.

The following program does the same operation as the previous macro but uses a `Select Case` statement:

```
Sub SelectCase()
    FinalRow = Cells(Rows.Count, 1).End(xlUp).Row

    For i = 2 To FinalRow
        Select Case Cells(i, 1).Value
            Case "Fruit"
                Cells(i, 1).Resize(1, 3).Font.ColorIndex = 3
            Case "Vegetable"
                Cells(i, 1).Resize(1, 3).Font.ColorIndex = 50
            Case "Herbs"
                Cells(i, 1).Resize(1, 3).Font.ColorIndex = 5
            Case Else
```

```
                Cells(i, 4).Value = "Unexpected value!"
        End Select
    Next i

    MsgBox "Fruit is red / Veggies are green / Herbs are blue"
End Sub
```

Complex Expressions in Case **Statements**

It is possible to have fairly complex expressions in Case statements. You might want to perform the same actions for all berry records:

```
Case "Strawberry", "Blueberry", "Raspberry"
    AdCode = 1
```

If it makes sense, you might code a range of values in the Case statement:

```
Case 1 to 20
    Discount = 0.05
Case 21 to 100
    Discount = 0.1
```

You can include the keyword Is and a comparison operator, such as > or <:

```
Case Is < 10
    Discount = 0
Case Is > 100
    Discount = 0.2
Case Else
    Discount = 0.10
```

Nesting If **Statements**

It is not only possible, but also common to nest an If statement inside another If statement. In this situation, it is important to use proper indenting. You will often find that you have several End If lines at the end of the construct. By having proper indenting, it is easier to tell which End If is associated with a particular If.

The final macro has a lot of logic. Our discount rules are as listed here:

- For Fruit, quantities less than 5 cases get no discount.
- Quantities from 5 to 20 cases get a 10 percent discount.
- Quantities greater than 20 cases get a 15 percent discount.
- For Herbs, quantities less than 10 cases get no discount.
- Quantities from 10 cases to 15 cases get a 3 percent discount.
- Quantities greater than 15 cases get a 6 percent discount.
- For Vegetables except Asparagus, quantities of 5 cases and greater earn a 12 percent discount.
- Asparagus requires 20 cases for a discount of 12 percent.
- None of the discounts applies if the product is on sale this week. The sale price is 25 percent off the normal price. This week's sale items are Strawberry, Lettuce, and Tomatoes.

4

The code to execute this logic follows:

```
Sub ComplexIf()
    FinalRow = Cells(Rows.Count, 1).End(xlUp).Row

    For i = 2 To FinalRow
        ThisClass = Cells(i, 1).Value
        ThisProduct = Cells(i, 2).Value
        ThisQty = Cells(i, 3).Value

        ' First, figure out if the item is on sale
        Select Case ThisProduct
            Case "Strawberry", "Lettuce", "Tomatoes"
                Sale = True
            Case Else
                Sale = False
        End Select

        ' Figure out the discount
        If Sale Then
            Discount = 0.25
        Else
            If ThisClass = "Fruit" Then
                Select Case ThisQty
                    Case Is < 5
                        Discount = 0
                    Case 5 To 20
                        Discount = 0.1
                    Case Is > 20
                        Discount = 0.15
                End Select
            ElseIf ThisClass = "Herbs" Then
                Select Case ThisQty
                    Case Is < 10
                        Discount = 0
                    Case 10 To 15
                        Discount = 0.03
                    Case Is > 15
                        Discount = 0.05
                End Select
            ElseIf ThisClass = "Vegetables" Then
                ' There is a special condition for asparagus
                If ThisProduct = "Asparagus" Then
                    If ThisQty < 20 Then
                        Discount = 0
                    Else
                        Discount = 0.12
                    End If
                Else
                    If ThisQty < 5 Then
                        Discount = 0
                    Else
                        Discount = 0.12
                    End If
                End If ' Is the product asparagus or not?
            End If ' Is the product a vegetable?
        End If ' Is the product on sale?
```

```
        Cells(i, 4).Value = Discount

        If Sale Then
            Cells(i, 4).Font.Bold = True
        End If

    Next i

    Range("D1").Value = "Discount"

    MsgBox "Discounts have been applied"

End Sub
```

Next Steps

Loops add a tremendous amount of power to your recorded macros. Anytime you need to repeat a process over all worksheets or all rows in a worksheet, a loop is the way to go. Excel VBA supports the traditional programming loops of For...Next and Do...Loop and the object-oriented loop of For Each...Next. Chapter 5, "R1C1-Style Formulas," discusses the seemingly arcane R1C1 style of formulas and shows why it is important in Excel VBA.

4

R1C1-Style Formulas

Referring to Cells: A1 Versus R1C1 References

Understanding R1C1 formulas will make your job easier in VBA. You could skip this chapter, but your code will be harder to write. Taking 30 minutes to understand R1C1 will make every macro you write for the rest of your life easier to code.

We can trace the A1 style of referencing back to VisiCalc. Dan Bricklin and Bob Frankston used A1 to refer to the cell in the upper-left corner of the spreadsheet. Mitch Kapor used this same addressing scheme in Lotus 1-2-3. Upstart Multiplan from Microsoft attempted to buck the trend and used something called R1C1-style addressing. In R1C1 addressing, the cell known as A1 is referred to as R1C1 because it is in Row 1, Column 1.

With the dominance of Lotus 1-2-3 in the 1980s and early 1990s, the A1 style became the standard. Microsoft realized it was fighting a losing battle and eventually offered either R1C1-style addressing or A1-style addressing in Excel. When you open Excel today, the A1 style is used by default. Officially, however, Microsoft supports both styles of addressing.

You would think that this chapter would be a nonissue. Anyone who uses the Excel interface would agree that the R1C1 style is dead. However, we have what on the face of it seems to be an annoying problem: The macro recorder records formulas in the R1C1 style. So you might be thinking that you just need to learn R1C1 addressing so that you can read the recorded code and switch it back to the familiar A1 style.

I have to give Microsoft credit. After you understand R1C1-style formulas, they are actually more efficient, especially when you are dealing with writing formulas in VBA. Using R1C1-style addressing enables you to write more efficient code. Plus, there are some features such as setting up array formulas that require you to enter the formula in R1C1 style.

I can hear the collective groan from Excel users everywhere. You could skip these pages of this old-fashioned addressing style if it were only an annoyance or an efficiency issue. However, because it is necessary to understand R1C1 addressing to effectively use important features such as array formulas, you have to dive in and learn this style.

Toggling to R1C1-Style References

You don't need to switch to R1C1 style in order to use .FormulaR1C1 in your code. However, while you're learning about R1C1, it will help to temporarily switch to R1C1 style.

To switch to R1C1-style addressing, select Options from the File menu. In the Formulas category, select the R1C1 Reference Style check box (see Figure 5.1).

Figure 5.1
Selecting the R1C1 reference style on the Formulas category of the Excel Options dialog causes Excel to revert to R1C1 style in the Excel user interface.

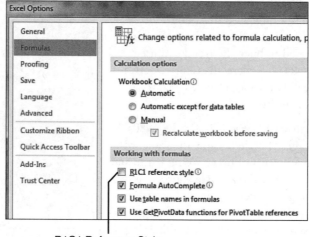

R1C1 Reference Style

After you switch to R1C1 style, the column letters A, B, C across the top of the worksheet are replaced by numbers 1, 2, 3 (see Figure 5.2).

Figure 5.2
In R1C1 style, the column letters are replaced by numbers.

	1	2	3	4
1	Tax	6.25%		
2				
3	SKU	Quantity	Unit Price	Total Price
4	217		12	12.45
5	123		144	1.87

Numbers

In this format, the cell that you know as B5 is called R5C2 because it is in Row 5, Column 2.

Every couple of weeks, someone manages to accidentally turn on this option, and we get an urgent support request at MrExcel. This style is foreign to 99 percent of spreadsheet users.

The Miracle of Excel Formulas

Automatically recalculating thousands of cells is the main benefit of electronic spreadsheets over the green ledger paper used up until 1979. However, a close second-prize award would be that you can enter one formula and copy that formula to thousands of cells.

Enter a Formula Once and Copy 1,000 Times

Consider the simple worksheet shown in Figure 5.3. Enter a simple formula such as =C4*B4 in cell D4, double-click the AutoFill handle, and the formula intelligently changes as it is copied down the range.

Figure 5.3
Double-click the AutoFill handle, and Excel intelligently copies this relative-reference formula down the column.

	A	B	C	D	E
1	Tax	6.25%			
2					
3	SKU	Quantity	Unit Price	Total Price	Taxable?
4	217	12	12.45	149.4	TRUE
5	123	144	1.87		TRUE
6	329	18	19.95		TRUE
7	616	1	642		FALSE
8	909	64	17.5		TRUE
9	527	822	0.12		TRUE
10	Total				

D4 — fx =C4*B4

A formula such as =C4*B4 is rewritten in each row, eventually becoming =C9*B9. It seems intimidating to consider having a macro enter all of these different formulas. Figure 5.4 shows how the formulas change when you copy them down columns D, F, and G.

The formula in cell F4 includes both relative and absolute formulas: =IF(E4,ROUND(D4*$B$1,2),0). Thanks to the dollar signs inserted in cell B1, you can copy down this formula, and it always multiplies the Total Price in this row by the tax rate in cell B1.

Figure 5.4
Press Ctrl+' to switch to showing formulas rather than their results. It is amazing that Excel adjusts the cell references in each formula as you copy down the column.

D	E	F	G
Total Price	Taxable?	Tax	Total
=B4*C4	TRUE	=IF(E4,ROUND(D4*$B$1,2),0)	=F4+D4
=B5*C5	TRUE	=IF(E5,ROUND(D5*$B$1,2),0)	=F5+D5
=B6*C6	TRUE	=IF(E6,ROUND(D6*$B$1,2),0)	=F6+D6
=B7*C7	FALSE	=IF(E7,ROUND(D7*$B$1,2),0)	=F7+D7
=B8*C8	TRUE	=IF(E8,ROUND(D8*$B$1,2),0)	=F8+D8
=B9*C9	TRUE	=IF(E9,ROUND(D9*$B$1,2),0)	=F9+D9
		=SUM(G4:G9)	

5

The Secret: It's Not That Amazing

Remember that Excel does everything in R1C1-style formulas. Excel shows addresses and formulas in A1 style merely because it needs to adhere to the standard made popular by VisiCalc and Lotus.

If you switch the worksheet in Figure 5.4 to use R1C1 notation, you will notice that the "different" formulas in D4:D9 are all actually identical formulas in R1C1 notation. The same is true of F4:F9 and G4:G9.

Use the Options dialog to change the sample worksheet to R1C1-style addresses. If you examine the formulas in Figure 5.5, you will see that in R1C1 language, every formula in Column 4 is identical. Given that Excel is storing the formulas in R1C1 style, copying them, and then merely translating to A1 style for us to understand, it is no longer that amazing that Excel can easily manipulate A1-style formulas as it does.

This is one of the reasons R1C1-style formulas are more efficient in VBA. When you have the same formula being entered in an entire range, it is less confusing.

Figure 5.5
The same formulas in R1C1 style. Note that every formula in Column 4 is the same, and every formula in Column 6 is the same.

4	5	6	7
Total Price	Taxable?	Tax	Total
=RC[-2]*RC[-1]	TRUE	=IF(RC[-1],ROUND(RC[-2]*R1C2,2),0)	=RC[-1]+RC[-3]
=RC[-2]*RC[-1]	TRUE	=IF(RC[-1],ROUND(RC[-2]*R1C2,2),0)	=RC[-1]+RC[-3]
=RC[-2]*RC[-1]	TRUE	=IF(RC[-1],ROUND(RC[-2]*R1C2,2),0)	=RC[-1]+RC[-3]
=RC[-2]*RC[-1]	FALSE	=IF(RC[-1],ROUND(RC[-2]*R1C2,2),0)	=RC[-1]+RC[-3]
=RC[-2]*RC[-1]	TRUE	=IF(RC[-1],ROUND(RC[-2]*R1C2,2),0)	=RC[-1]+RC[-3]
=RC[-2]*RC[-1]	TRUE	=IF(RC[-1],ROUND(RC[-2]*R1C2,2),0)	=RC[-1]+RC[-3]
		=SUM(R[-6]C[1]:R[-1]C[1])	

CASE STUDY: ENTERING A1 VERSUS R1C1 IN VBA

Think about how you would set up this spreadsheet in the Excel interface. First, you enter a formula in cells D4, F4, G4. Next, you copy these cells, and paste them the rest of the way down the column. The code might look something like this:

```
Sub A1Style()
    ' Locate the FinalRow
    FinalRow = Cells(Rows.Count, 2).End(xlUp).Row
    ' Enter the first formula
    Range("""D4").Formula = "=B4*C4"
    Range("F4").Formula = "=IF(E4,ROUND(D4*$B$1,2),0)"
    Range("G4").Formula = "=F4+D4"
    ' Copy the formulas from Row 4 down to the other cells
    Range("D4").Copy Destination:=Range("D5:D" & FinalRow)
    Range("F4:G4").Copy Destination:=Range("F5:G" & FinalRow)
    ' Enter the Total Row
    Cells(FinalRow + 1, 1).Value = "Total"
    Cells(FinalRow + 1, 6).Formula = "=SUM(G4:G" & FinalRow & ")"
End Sub
```

In this code, it takes three lines to enter the formulas at the top of the row and then another two lines to copy the formulas down the column.

The equivalent code in R1C1 style allows the formulas to be entered for the entire column in a single statement. Remember, the advantage of R1C1-style formulas is that all the formulas in Columns D and F, and most of G, are identical:

```
Sub R1C1Style()
    ' Locate the FinalRow
    FinalRow = Cells(Rows.Count, 2).End(xlUp).Row
    ' Enter the first formula
    Range("D4:D" & FinalRow).FormulaR1C1 = "=RC[-1]*RC[-2]"
    Range("F4:F" & FinalRow).FormulaR1C1 = _
        "=IF(RC[-1],ROUND(RC[-2]*R1C2,2),0)"
    Range("G4:G" & FinalRow).FormulaR1C1 = "=RC[-1]+RC[-3]"
    ' Enter the Total Row
    Cells(FinalRow + 1, 1).Value = "Total"
    Cells(FinalRow + 1, 6).FormulaR1C1 = "=SUM(R4C:R[-1]C)"
End Sub
```

In reality, you do not need to enter A1-style formulas in the top row and then copy them down. It seems counterintuitive, but when you specify an A1-style formula, Microsoft internally converts the formula to R1C1 and then enters that formula in the entire range. Thus, you can actually add the "same" A1-style formula to an entire range in a single line of code.

```
Sub A1StyleModified()
    ' Locate the FinalRow
    FinalRow = Cells(Rows.Count, 2).End(xlUp).Row
    ' Enter the first formula
    Range("D4:D" & FinalRow).Formula = "=B4*C4"
    Range("F4:F" & FinalRow).Formula = "=IF(E4,ROUND(D4*$B$1,2),0)"
    Range("G4:G" & FinalRow).Formula = "=F4+D4"
    ' Enter the Total Row
    Cells(FinalRow + 1, 1).Value = "Total"
    Cells(FinalRow + 1, 6).Formula = "=SUM(G4:G" & FinalRow & ")"
End Sub
```

5

NOTE Note that although you are asking for a formula of =B4*C4 to be entered in D4:D1000, Excel enters this formula in Row 4 and appropriately adjusts the formula for the additional rows.

Explanation of R1C1 Reference Style

An R1C1-style reference includes the letter *R* to refer to row and the letter *C* to refer to column. Because the most common reference in a formula is a relative reference, let's look at relative references in R1C1 style first.

Using R1C1 with Relative References

Imagine you are entering a formula in a cell. To point to a cell in a formula, you use the letters *R* and *C*. After each letter, enter the number of rows or columns in square brackets.

The following list explains the "rules" for using R1C1 relative references:

- For columns, a positive number means to move to the right a certain number of columns, and a negative number means to move to the left a certain number of columns. From cell E5, use RC[1] to refer to F5 and RC[-1] to refer to D5.

- For rows, a positive number means to move down the spreadsheet a certain number of rows. A negative number means to move toward the top of the spreadsheet a certain number of rows. From cell E5, use R[1]C to refer to E6 and use cell R[-1]C to refer to E4.

- If you leave off the number for either the R or the C, it means that you are pointing to a cell in the same row or column as the cell with the formula. The "R" in RC[3] means that you are pointing to this row.

- If you enter =R[-1]C[-1] in cell E5, you are referring to a cell one row up and one column to the left. This would be cell D4.

- If you enter =RC[1] in cell E5, you are referring to a cell in the same row, but one column to the right. This would be cell F5.

- If you enter =RC in cell E5, you are referring to a cell in the same row and column, which is cell E5 itself. You would generally not do this because it would create a circular reference.

Figure 5.6 shows how you would enter a reference in cell E5 to point to various cells around E5.

Figure 5.6

Here are various relative references. These would be entered in cell E5 to describe each cell around E5.

◢	3	4	5	6	7
3			R[-2]C		
4		R[-1]C[-1]	R[-1]C	R[-1]C[1]	
5	RC[-2]	RC[-1]		RC[1]	RC[2]
6		R[1]C[-1]	R[1]C	R[1]C[1]	
7			R[2]C		
8					
9					

One row above, same column (points to R[-1]C)

You can use R1C1 style to refer to a range of cells. If you want to add up the 12 cells to the left of the current cell, the formula is this:

```
=SUM(RC[-12]:RC[-1])
```

Using R1C1 with Absolute References

An absolute reference is one in which the row and column remain fixed when the formula is copied to a new location. In A1-style notation, Excel uses a $ before the row number or column letter to keep that row or column absolute as the formula is copied.

To always refer to an absolute row or column number, just leave off the square brackets. This reference refers to cell $B$3 no matter where it is entered:

```
=R3C2
```

Using R1C1 with Mixed References

A mixed reference is one in which the row is fixed and the column is allowed to be relative, or in which the column is fixed and the row is allowed to be relative. This will be useful in many situations.

Imagine you have written a macro to import Invoice.txt into Excel. Using .End(xlUp), you find where the total row should go. As you are entering totals, you know that you want to sum from the row above the formula up to Row 2. The following code would handle that:

```
Sub MixedReference()
    TotalRow = Cells(Rows.Count, 1).End(xlUp).Row + 1
    Cells(TotalRow, 1).Value = "Total"
    Cells(TotalRow, 5).Resize(1, 3).FormulaR1C1 = "=SUM(R2C:R[-1]C)"
End Sub
```

In this code, the reference R2C:R[-1]C indicates that the formula should add from Row 2 in the same column to the row just above the formula in the current column. Do you see the advantage to R1C1 formulas in this case? You can use a single R1C1 formula with a mixed reference to easily enter a formula to handle an indeterminate number of rows of data (see Figure 5.7).

Figure 5.7
After the macro has run, the formulas in Columns 5:7 of the total row will have a reference to a range that is locked to Row 2, but all other aspects are relative.

	1	2	3	4	5	6	7	8
1	InvoiceDa	InvoiceNu	SalesRepN	Customer	ProductRe	ServiceRe	ProductCost	
2	6/9/2014	123829	S21	C8754	538400	0	299897	
3	6/9/2014	123830	S45	C4056	588600	0	307563	
4	6/9/2014	123831	S54	C8323	882200	0	521726	
5	6/9/2014	123832	S21	C6026	830900	0	494831	
6	6/9/2014	123833	S45	C3025	673600	0	374953	
7	6/9/2014	123834	S54	C8663	966300	0	528575	
8	6/9/2014	123835	S21	C1508	467100	0	257942	
9	6/9/2014	123836	S45	C7366	658500	10000	308719	
10	6/9/2014	123837	S54	C4533	191700	0	109534	
11					5797300	10000	=SUM(R2C:R[-1]C)	
12								

Referring to Entire Columns or Rows with R1C1 Style

You will occasionally write a formula that refers to an entire column. For example, you might want to know the maximum value in Column G. If you don't know how many rows you will have in G, you can write =MAX($G:$G) in A1 style or =MAX(C7) in R1C1 style. To find the minimum value in Row 1, use =MIN($1:$1) in A1 style or =MIN(R1) in R1C1 style. You can use relative reference for either rows or columns. To find the average of the row above the current cell, use =AVERAGE(R[-1]).

Replacing Many A1 Formulas with a Single R1C1 Formula

After you get used to R1C1-style formulas, they actually seem a lot more intuitive to build. One classic example to illustrate R1C1-style formulas is building a multiplication table. It is easy to build a multiplication table in Excel using a single mixed-reference formula.

Building the Table

Enter the numbers **1** through **12** going across B1:M1. Copy and transpose these so that the same numbers are going down A2:A13. Now the challenge is to build a single formula that works in all cells of B2:M13 and that shows the multiplication of the number in Row 1 times the number in Column 1. Using A1-style formulas, you must press the F4 key five times to get the dollar signs in the proper locations. The following is a far simpler formula in R1C1 style:

```
Sub MultiplicationTable()
    ' Build a multiplication table using a single formula
    Range("B1:M1").Value = Array(1, 2, 3, 4, 5, 6, 7, 8, 9, 10, 11, 12)
    Range("B1:M1").Font.Bold = True
    Range("B1:M1").Copy
    Range("A2:A13").PasteSpecial Transpose:=True
    Range("B2:M13").FormulaR1C1 = "=RC1*R1C"
    Cells.EntireColumn.AutoFit
End Sub
```

The R1C1-style reference =RC1*R1C could not be simpler. In English, it is saying, "Take this row's Column 1 and multiply it by Row 1 of this column." It works perfectly to build the multiplication table shown in Figure 5.8.

Figure 5.8
The macro creates a multiplication table. The formula in B2 uses two mixed references: =$A2*B$1.

CAUTION

After running the macro and producing the multiplication table shown in Figure 5.8, note that Excel still has the copied range from line 2 of the macro as the active clipboard item. If the user of this macro selects a cell and presses Enter, the contents of those cells copy to the new location. However, this is generally not desirable. To get Excel out of Cut/Copy mode, add this line of code before your programs ends:

```
Application.CutCopyMode = False
```

An Interesting Twist

Try this experiment. Move the cell pointer to F6. Turn on macro recording using the Record Macro button on the Developer tab. Click the Use Relative Reference button on the Developer tab. Enter the formula =A1 and press Ctrl+Enter to stay in F6. Click the Stop Recording button on the floating toolbar.

You get this single-line macro, which enters a formula that points to a cell five rows up and five columns to the left:

```
Sub Macro1()
    ActiveCell.FormulaR1C1 = "=R[-5]C[-5]"
End Sub
```

Now, move the cell pointer to cell A1 and run the macro that you just recorded. You might think that pointing to a cell five rows above A1 would lead to the ubiquitous Run Time Error 1004. But it doesn't! When you run the macro, the formula in cell A1 is pointing to =XFA1048572, as shown in Figure 5.9, meaning that R1C1-style formulas actually wrap from the left side of the workbook to the right side. I cannot think of any instance in which this would be actually useful, but for those of you who rely on Excel to error out when you ask for something that does not make sense, be aware that your macro will happily provide a result and probably not the one that you expected!

Figure 5.9
The formula to point to five rows above B1 wraps around to the bottom of the worksheet.

Remembering Column Numbers Associated with Column Letters

I like these formulas enough to use them regularly in VBA. I don't like them enough to change my Excel interface over to R1C1-style numbers. So I routinely have to know that the cell known as U21 is really R21C21.

Knowing that U is the twenty-first letter of the alphabet is not something that comes naturally. We have 26 letters, so A is 1 and Z is 26. M is the halfway point of the alphabet and is Column 13. The rest of the letters are not particularly intuitive. If you play this little game for a few minutes each day, soon you will memorize the column numbers:

```
Sub QuizColumnNumbers()
    Do
        i = Int(Rnd() * 26) + 1
        Ans = InputBox("What column number is the letter " & _
        Chr(64 + i) & "?")
        If Ans = "" Then Exit Do
        If Not (Ans + 0) = i Then
            MsgBox "Letter " & Chr(64 + i) & " is column # " & i
        End If
    Loop
End Sub
```

If memorizing column numbers doesn't sound fun, or even if you have to figure out the column number of Column DGX someday, there is a straightforward way to do so using the Excel interface. Move the cell pointer to cell A1. Hold down the Shift key and start pressing the right-arrow key. For the first screen of columns, the column number appears in the name box to the left of the formula bar (see Figure 5.10).

Figure 5.10
While you select cells with the keyboard, the Name box displays how many columns are selected for the first screen full of columns.

Name box

F is the sixth column

As you keep pressing the right-arrow key beyond the first screen, a ToolTip box to the right of the current cell tells you how many columns are selected. When you get to Column DGX, it informs you that you are at Column 2910 (see Figure 5.11).

You could also enter =COLUMN() in a cell to find the column number. Or, select any cell in DGX, switch to VBA, press Ctrl+G for the Immediate window and type **? ActiveCell. Column** followed by pressing Enter.

Figure 5.11
After the first screen of columns, a ToolTip bar keeps track of the column number.

Tooltip: column DGX is the 2910th column

Array Formulas Require R1C1 Formulas

Array formulas are powerful "superformulas." At MrExcel.com, we call these CSE formulas because you have to use Ctrl+Shift+Enter to enter them. If you are not familiar with array formulas, they look as though they should not work.

The array formula in E21, shown in Figure 5.12, is a formula that does 19 multiplications and then sums the result. It looks as though this would be an illegal formula. In fact, if you happen to enter it without using Ctrl+Shift+Enter, you get the expected #VALUE! error. However, if you enter it with Ctrl+Shift+Enter, the formula miraculously multiplies row by row and then sums the result.

You do not type the curly braces when entering the formula.

Figure 5.12
The array formula in E21 does 19 multiplications and then sums them. You must use Ctrl+Shift+Enter to enter this formula.

| E21 | | : | × | ✓ | fx | {=SUM(D$2:D20*E$2:E20)} | |

▲	A	B	C	D	E	F
1	Region	Product	Date	Quantity	Unit Price	Unit Cost
2	East	XYZ	1/1/2001	1000	22.81	10.22
3	Central	DEF	1/2/2001	100	22.57	9.84
4	East	ABC	1/2/2001	500	20.49	8.47
5	Central	XYZ	1/3/2001	500	22.48	10.22
6	Central	XYZ	1/4/2001	400	23.01	10.22
7	East	DEF	1/4/2001	800	23.19	9.84
8	East	XYZ	1/4/2001	400	22.88	10.22
9	Central	ABC	1/5/2001	400	17.15	8.47
10	East	ABC	1/7/2001	400	21.14	8.47
11	East	DEF	1/7/2001	1000	21.73	9.84
12	West	XYZ	1/7/2001	600	23.01	10.22
13	Central	ABC	1/9/2001	800	20.52	8.47
14	East	XYZ	1/9/2001	900	23.35	10.22
15	Central	XYZ	1/10/2001	900	23.82	10.22
16	East	XYZ	1/10/2001	900	23.85	10.22
17	Central	ABC	1/12/2001	300	20.89	8.47
18	West	XYZ	1/12/2001	400	22.86	10.22
19	Central	ABC	1/14/2001	100	17.4	8.47
20	East	XYZ	1/14/2001	100	24.01	10.22
21			Total Revenue		234198	

The code to enter these formulas follows. Although the formulas appear in the user interface in A1-style notation, you must use R1C1-style notation for entering array formulas:

```
Sub EnterArrayFormulas()
    ' Add a formula to multiply unit price x quantity
    FinalRow = Cells(Rows.Count, 1).End(xlUp).Row
    Cells(FinalRow + 1, 5).FormulaArray = _
        "=SUM(R2C[-1]:R[-1]C[-1]*R2C:R[-1]C)"
End Sub
```

TIP Use this trick to quickly find the R1C1 formula. Enter a regular A1-style formula or an array formula in any cell in Excel. Select that cell. Switch to the VBA editor. Press Ctrl+G to display the Immediate window. Type **Print ActiveCell.FormulaR1C1** and press Enter. Excel converts the formula in the formula bar to an R1C1-style formula. You also can use a question mark instead of **Print**.

Next Steps

Read Chapter 6, "Create and Manipulate Names in VBA," to learn how to use named ranges in your macros.

Create and Manipulate Names in VBA

6

Excel Names

You have probably named ranges in a worksheet by highlighting a range and typing a name in the Name box to the left of the Formula bar. You also might have created more complicated names containing formulas. For example, perhaps you created a name with a formula that finds the last row in a column. The ability to set a name to a range makes it much easier to write formulas and set tables.

The ability to create and manipulate names is also available in VBA and provides the same benefits as naming ranges in a worksheet. For example, you can store a new range in a name.

This chapter explains different types of names and the various ways you can use them.

Global Versus Local Names

Names can be *global*, which means they are available anywhere in the workbook. Names can also be *local*, which means they are available only on a specific worksheet. With local names, you can have multiple references in the workbook with the same name. Global names must be unique to the workbook.

The Name Manager dialog box (found on the Formulas tab) lists all the names in a workbook, even a name that has been assigned to both the global and the local levels. The Scope column lists the scope of the name, whether it is the workbook or a specific sheet such as Sheet1.

For example, in Figure 6.1 the name "Apples" is assigned to Sheet1, but also to the workbook.

Figure 6.1
The Name Manager lists all local and global names.

Adding Names

If you record the creation of a named range and then view the code, you see something like this:

```
ActiveWorkbook.Names.Add Name:="Fruits", RefersToR1C1:="=Sheet2!R1C1:R6C6"
```

This creates a global name `"Fruits"`, which includes the range A1:F6 (`R1C1:R6C6`). The formula is enclosed in quotes, and the equal sign in the formula must be included. In addition, the range reference must be absolute (include the $ sign) or in R1C1 notation. If the sheet on which the name is created is the active sheet, the sheet reference does not have to be included. However, including the sheet reference can make the code easier to understand.

> **NOTE**
> If the reference is not absolute, the name might be created, but it will not point to the correct range. For example, if you run the following line of code, the name is created in the workbook. However, as you can see in Figure 6.2, it hasn't actually been assigned to the range. The reference will change depending on what the active cell is when the name is viewed.
>
> ```
> ActiveWorkbook.Names.Add Name:="Citrus", _
>     RefersTo:="=Sheet1!A1"
> ```

Figure 6.2
Despite what was coded, because absolute referencing was not used, Citrus refers to the active cell.

To create a local name, include the sheet name with the `Name` parameter:

```
ActiveWorkbook.Names.Add Name:="Sheet2!Fruits", _
    RefersToR1C1:="=Sheet2!R1C1:R6C6"
```

Alternatively, specify that the Names collection belongs to a worksheet:

```
Worksheets("Sheet1").Names.Add Name:="Fruits", _
    RefersToR1C1:="=Sheet1!R1C1:R6C6"
```

The preceding example is what you would learn from the macro recorder. There is a simpler way:

```
Range("A1:F6").Name = "Fruits"
```

Alternatively, for a local variable only, you can use this:

```
Range("A1:F6").Name = "Sheet1!Fruits"
```

When creating names with these methods, absolute referencing is not required.

> **NOTE** You can use Table names like defined names, but you don't create them the same way. See the "Tables" section, later in this chapter, for more information about creating table names.

Although this method is much easier and quicker than what the macro recorder creates, it is limited in that it works only for ranges. Formulas, strings, numbers, and arrays require the use of the `Add` method.

The `Name` property of the name `ObjectName` is an object but still has a `Name` property. The following line renames an existing name:

```
Names("Fruits").Name = "Produce"
```

`Fruits` no longer exists; `Produce` is now the name of the range.

When you are renaming names in which a local reference and a global reference both carry the same name, the previous line renames the local reference first.

Deleting Names

Use the `Delete` method to delete a name:

```
Names("ProduceNum").Delete
```

An error occurs if you attempt to delete a name that does not exist.

> **NOTE** If both local and global references with the same name exist, be more specific as to which name is being deleted because the local reference is deleted first.

6

Adding Comments

You can add comments about names, such as why the name was created or where it is used. To insert a comment for the local name LocalOffice, do this:

```
ActiveWorkbook.Worksheets("Sheet7").Names("LocalOffice").Comment = _
"Holds the name of the current office"
```

The comments appear in a column in the Name Manager, as shown in Figure 6.3.

> **CAUTION**
>
> The name must exist before a comment can be added to it.

Figure 6.3
You can add comments about names to help remember their purpose.

Types of Names

The most common use of names is for storing ranges; however, names can store more than just ranges. After all, that's what they're for: Names store information. Names make it simple to remember and use potentially complex or large amounts of information. In addition, unlike variables, names remember what they store beyond the life of the program.

You have covered creating range names, but you can also assign names to name formulas, strings, numbers, and arrays.

Formulas

The syntax for storing a formula in a name is the same as for a range because the range is essentially a formula:

```
Names.Add Name:="ProductList", _
    RefersTo:="=OFFSET(Sheet2!$A$2,0,0,COUNTA(Sheet2!$A:$A))"
```

The preceding code allows for a dynamic named column with the item listing starting in A2. The code is useful for creating dynamic tables or for referencing any dynamic listing on which calculations may be performed, as shown in Figure 6.4.

Figure 6.4
Dynamic formulas can be
assigned to names.

Strings

When using names to hold strings such as the name of the current fruit producer, enclose
the string value in quotes. Because no formula is involved, an equal sign is not needed.
If you were to include an equal sign, Excel would treat the value as a formula. Let Excel
include the equal sign shown in the Name Manager.

```
Names.Add Name: = "Company", RefersTo:="CompanyA"
```

Figure 6.5 shows how the coded name will appear in the Name Manager window.

Figure 6.5
A string value can be
assigned to a name.

Using Names to Store Values

Because names do not lose their references between sessions, this is a great way to store values as opposed to
storing values in cells from which the information would have to be retrieved. For example, to track the leading producer between seasons, create the name Leader. If the new season's leading producer matches the name reference,
you could create a special report comparing the seasons. The other option is to create a special sheet to track the
values between sessions and then retrieve the values when needed. With Names, the values are readily available.

The following procedure shows how cells in a variable sheet are used to retain information between sessions:

```
Sub NoNames(ByRef CurrentTop As String)
TopSeller = Worksheets("Variables").Range("A1").Value
If CurrentTop = TopSeller Then
    MsgBox "Top Producer is " & TopSeller & " again."
Else
    MsgBox "New Top Producer is " & CurrentTop
End If
End Sub
```

The following procedure shows how names are used to store information between sessions:

```
Sub WithNames()
If Evaluate("Current") = Evaluate("Previous") Then
    MsgBox "Top Producer is " & Evaluate("Previous") & " again."
Else
    MsgBox "New Top Producer is " & Evaluate("Current")
End If
End Sub
```

If Current and Previous are previously declared names, you access them directly rather than create variables in which to pass them. Note the use of the Evaluate method to extract the values in names. The string being stored cannot have more than 255 characters.

Numbers

You can also use names to store numbers between sessions. Use this:

```
NumofSales = 5123
Names.Add Name:="TotalSales", RefersTo:=NumofSales
```

Alternatively, you can use this:

```
Names.Add Name:="TotalSales", RefersTo:=5123
```

Notice the lack of quotes or an equal sign in the RefersTo parameter. Using quotes changes the number to a string. With the addition of an equal sign, the number changes to a formula.

To retrieve the value in the name, you have a longer and a shorter option:

```
NumofSales = Names("TotalSales").Value
```

or

```
NumofSales = [TotalSales]
```

> **NOTE** Keep in mind that someone reading your code might not be familiar with the use of the Evaluate method (square brackets). If you know that someone else will be reading your code, avoid the use of the Evaluate method or add a comment explaining it.

Tables

Excel Tables share some of the properties of defined names, but they also have their own unique methods. Unlike defined names, which are what you are used to dealing with, you cannot manually create Tables. In other words, you cannot select a range on a sheet and type a name in the Name field. However, you can manually create them via VBA.

Tables are not created using the same method as the defined names. Instead of `Range(xx).Add` or `Names.Add`, use `ListObjects.Add`.

To create a Table from cells A1:C26, and assuming that the data table has column headers, as shown in Figure 6.6, do this:

```
ActiveSheet.ListObjects.Add(xlSrcRange, Range("$A$1:$C$26"), , xlYes).Name = _
"Table1"
```

Figure 6.6
You can turn a normal table into an Excel Table by assigning a Name to it using VBA.

#	A Product	B Date	C Qty
1	Product	Date	Qty
2	Apples	1/1/2012	274
3	Bananas	1/1/2012	228
4	Kiwis	1/1/2012	160
5	Lemons	1/1/2012	478
6	Oranges	1/1/2012	513
7	Apples	1/2/2012	412
8	Bananas	1/2/2012	776
9	Kiwis	1/2/2012	183

`xlSrcRange` (the `SourceType`) tells Excel that the source of the data is an Excel range. You then need to specify the range (the source) of the table. If you have headers in the table, include that row when indicating the range. The next argument, which is not used in the preceding example, is the `LinkSource`, a Boolean indicating whether there is an external data source and is not used if the `SourceType` is `xlSrcRange`. `xlYes` lets Excel know that the data table has column headers; otherwise, Excel automatically generates them. The final argument, which is not shown in the preceding example, is the destination. This is used when the `SourceType` is `xlSrcExternal`, indicating the upper-left cell where the table will begin.

Using Arrays in Names

A name can also hold the data stored in an array. The array size is limited by available memory. See Chapter 8, "Arrays," for more information about arrays.

An array reference is stored in a name the same way as a numeric reference:

```
Sub NamedArray()
Dim myArray(10, 5)
Dim i As Integer, j As Integer
'The following For loops fill the array myArray
For i = 0 To 10 'by default arrays start at 0
    For j = 0 To 5
        myArray(i, j) = i + j
    Next j
```

```
Next i
'The following line takes our array and gives it a name
Names.Add Name:="FirstArray", RefersTo:=myArray
End Sub
```

Because the name is referencing a variable, no quotes or equal signs are required.

Reserved Names

Excel uses local names of its own to keep track of information. These local names are considered reserved, and if you use them for your own references, they might cause problems.

Highlight an area on a sheet. Then from the Page Layout tab, select Print Area, Set Print Area.

As shown in Figure 6.7, a `Print_Area` listing is in the Range Name field. Deselect the area and look again in the Range Name field dropdown. The name is still listed there. Select it, and the print area previously set is now highlighted. If you save, close, and reopen the workbook, `Print_Area` is still set to the same range. `Print_Area` is a name reserved by Excel for its own use.

Figure 6.7
Excel creates its own names.

	A	B	C	D	E
1	Apples	Oranges	Lemons	Kiwis	Bananas
2	274	228	160	478	513
3	412	776	183	724	438
4	159	344	502	755	600
5	314	245	583	618	456
6	837	487	100	778	51

> **NOTE** Each sheet has its own print area. In addition, setting a new print area on a sheet with an existing print area overwrites the original print-area name.

Fortunately, Excel does not have a large list of reserved names:

    Criteria

    Database

    Extract

    Print_Area

    Print_Titles

`Criteria` and `Extract` are used when the Advanced Filter (on the Data tab, select Advanced from the Sort & Filter group) is configured to extract the results of the filter to a new location.

`Database` is no longer required in Excel. However, some features, such as Data Form, still recognize it. Legacy versions of Excel used it to identify the data you wanted to manipulate in certain functions.

`Print_Area` is used when a print area is set (from the Page Layout tab, select Print Area, Set Print Area) or when Page Setup options that designate the print area (from the Page Layout tab, Scale) are changed.

`Print_Titles` is used when print titles are set (Page Layout, Print Titles).

These names should be avoided and variations used with caution. For example, if you create a name PrintTitles, you might accidentally code this:

```
Worksheets("Sheet4").Names("Print_Titles").Delete
```

You have just deleted the Excel name rather than your custom name.

Hiding Names

Names are incredibly useful, but you don't necessarily want to see all the names you have created. Like many other objects, names have a `Visible` property. To hide a name, set the `Visible` property to `False`. To unhide a name, set the `Visible` property to `True`:

```
Names.Add Name:="ProduceNum", RefersTo:="=$A$1", Visible:=False
```

> **NOTE** If a user creates a Name object with the same name as your hidden one, the hidden name is overwritten without any warning message. To prevent this, protect the worksheet.

Checking for the Existence of a Name

You can use the following function to check for the existence of a user-defined name, even a hidden one. Keep in mind that this function does not return the existence of Excel's reserved names. Even so, this is a handy addition to your arsenal of "programmer's useful code" (see Chapter 14, "Sample User-Defined Functions," for more information on implementing custom functions):

```
Function NameExists(FindName As String) As Boolean
Dim Rng As Range
Dim myName As String
On Error Resume Next 'skip the error if the name doesn't exist
myName = ActiveWorkbook.Names(FindName).Name
If Err.Number = 0 Then
    NameExists = True
Else
    NameExists = False
End If
End Function
```

The preceding code is also an example of how to use errors to your advantage. If the name for which you are searching does not exist, an error message is generated. By adding the `On Error Resume Next` line at the beginning, you force the code to continue. Then you use `Err.Number` to tell you whether it ran into an error. If it didn't, `Err.Number` is zero, which means the name exists. Otherwise, you had an error and the name does not exist.

6

CASE STUDY: USING NAMED RANGES FOR VLOOKUP

Every day, you import a file of sales data from a chain of retail stores. The file includes the store number but not the store name. You obviously don't want to have to type store names every day, but you would like to have store names appear on all the reports that you run.

Normally, you would enter a table of store numbers and names in an out-of-the way spot on a back worksheet. You can use VBA to help maintain the list of stores each day and then use the VLOOKUP function to get store names from the list into your dataset.

The basic steps are as listed here:

1. Import the data file.

2. Find all the unique store numbers in today's file.

3. See whether any of these store numbers are not in your current table of store names.

4. For any stores that are new, add them to the table and ask the user for a store name.

5. The Store Names table is now larger, so reassign the named range used to describe the store table.

6. Use a VLOOKUP function in the original dataset to add a store name to all records. This VLOOKUP references the named range of the newly expanded Store Names table.

The following code handles these six steps:

```
Sub ImportData()
' This routine imports sales.csv to the data sheet
' Check to see whether any stores in column A are new
' If any are new, then add them to the StoreList table

Dim WSD As Worksheet
Dim WSM As Worksheet
Dim WB As Workbook

Set WB = ThisWorkbook
' Data is stored on the Data worksheet
Set WSD = WB.Worksheets("Data")
' StoreList is stored on a menu worksheet
Set WSM = WB.Worksheets("Menu")

' Open the file. This makes the csv file active
Workbooks.Open Filename:="C:\Sales.csv"
' Copy the data to WSD and close
ActiveWorkbook.Range("A1").CurrentRegion.Copy Destination:=WSD.Range("A1")
ActiveWorkbook.Close SaveChanges:=False

' Find a list of unique stores from column A and place in Z
FinalRow = WSD.Cells(WSD.Rows.Count, 1).End(xlUp).Row
WSD.Range("A1").Resize(FinalRow, 1).AdvancedFilter Action:=xlFilterCopy, _
    CopyToRange:=WSD.Range("Z1"), Unique:=True

' For all the unique stores, see whether they are in the
' current store list using lookup formula in AA
FinalStore = WSD.Range("Z" & WSD.Rows.Count).End(xlUp).Row
WSD.Range("AA1").Value = "There?"
```

```
WSD.Range("AA2:AA" & FinalStore).FormulaR1C1 = _
    "=ISNA(VLOOKUP(RC[-1],StoreList,1,False))"

' Find the next row for a new store. Because StoreList starts in A1
' of the Menu sheet, find the next available row
NextRow = WSM.Range("A" & WSM.Rows.Count).End(xlUp).Row + 1

' Loop through the list of today's stores. If they are shown
' as missing, then add them at the bottom of the StoreList
For i = 2 To FinalStore
    If WSD.Cells(i, 27).Value = True Then
        ThisStore = Cells(i, 26).Value
        WSM.Cells(NextRow, 1).Value = ThisStore
        WSM.Cells(NextRow, 2).Value = _
            InputBox(Prompt:="What is name of store " _
            & ThisStore, Title:="New Store Found")
        NextRow = NextRow + 1
    End If
Next i

' Delete the temporary list of stores in Z & AA
WSD.Range("Z1:AA" & FinalStore).Clear

' In case any stores were added, redefine StoreList name
FinalStore = WSM.Range("A" & WSM.Rows.Count).End(xlUp).Row
WSM.Range("A1:B" & FinalStore).Name = "StoreList"

' Use VLOOKUP to add StoreName to column B of the dataset
WSD.Range("B1").EntireColumn.Insert
WSD.Range("B1").Value = "StoreName"
WSD.Range("B2:B" & FinalRow).FormulaR1C1 = "=VLOOKUP(RC1,StoreList,2,False)"

' Change Formulas to Values
WSD.Range("B2:B" & FinalRow).Value = Range("B2:B" & FinalRow).Value

'Fix columnwidths
WSD.Range("A1").CurrentRegion.EntireColumn.AutoFit

'Release our variables to free system memory
Set WB = Nothing
Set WSD = Nothing
Set WSM = Nothing
End Sub
```

6

Next Steps

In Chapter 7, "Event Programming," you'll find out how you can write code to run automatically based on users' actions such as activating a sheet or selecting a cell. This is done
with events, which are actions in Excel that can be captured and used to your advantage.

Event Programming

Levels of Events

Earlier in the book, you read about workbook events and you have seen examples of worksheet events. *Events* allow you to automatically trigger a program to run based on something a user or another program does in Excel. For example, if a user changes the contents of a cell, after pressing Enter or Tab, the code would run automatically. The event that triggered it is the changing of the contents of the cell.

You can find these events at the following levels:

- **Application level**—Control based on application actions such as `Application_NewWorkbook`
- **Workbook level**—Control based on workbook actions such as `Workbook_Open`
- **Worksheet level**—Control based on worksheet actions such as `Worksheet_SelectionChange`
- **Chart sheet level**—Control based on chart actions such as `Chart_Activate`

Listed here are the places where you should place different types of events:

- Workbook events go into the ThisWorkbook module.
- Worksheet events go into the module of the sheet they affect, such as Sheet1.
- Chart sheet events go into the module of the chart sheet they affect, such as Chart1.
- PivotTable events go into the module of the sheet with the PivotTable, or they can go into the ThisWorkbook module.
- Embedded chart and application events go into class modules.

The events can still make procedure or function calls outside their own modules. Therefore, if you want the same action to take place for two different

7

IN THIS CHAPTER

sheets, you don't have to copy the code. Instead, place the code in a module and have each sheet event call the procedure.

In this chapter, you'll learn about different levels of events, where to find them, and how to use the events.

> **NOTE** Userform and control events are discussed in Chapter 10, "Userforms: An Introduction," and Chapter 22, "Advanced Userform Techniques."

Using Events

Each level consists of several types of events, and memorizing the syntax of them all would be a feat. Excel makes it easy to view and insert the available events in their proper modules right from the VB Editor.

When a ThisWorkbook, Sheet, Chart Sheet, or Class module is active, the corresponding events are available through the Object and Procedure drop-downs, as shown in Figure 7.1.

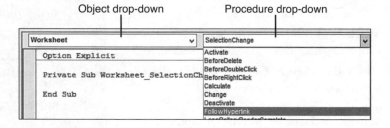

Figure 7.1
The different events are easy to access from the VB Editor Object and Procedure drop-downs.

After the object is selected, the Procedure drop-down updates to list the events available for that object. Selecting a procedure automatically places the procedure header (`Private Sub`) and footer (`End Sub`) in the editor, as shown in Figure 7.2.

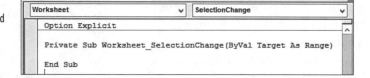

Figure 7.2
The procedure header and footer are automatically placed.

Event Parameters

Some events have parameters, such as `Target` or `Cancel`, that allow values to be passed into the procedure. For example, some procedures are triggered before the actual event, such as

BeforeRightClick. Assigning True to the Cancel parameter prevents the default action from taking place. In this case, the shortcut menu is prevented from appearing:

```
Private Sub Worksheet_BeforeRightClick(ByVal Target As Range, Cancel As Boolean)
Cancel = True
End Sub
```

Enabling Events

Some events can trigger other events including themselves. For example, the Worksheet_Change event is triggered by a change in a cell. If the event is triggered and the procedure itself changes a cell, the event gets triggered again, which changes a cell, triggering the event, and so on. The procedure gets stuck in an endless loop.

To prevent this, disable the events and then reenable them at the end of the procedure:

```
Private Sub Worksheet_Change(ByVal Target As Range)
Application.EnableEvents = False
Range("A1").Value = Target.Value
Application.EnableEvents = True
End Sub
```

> **TIP** To interrupt a macro, press Esc or Ctrl+Break. To restart it, use Run on the toolbar or press F5.

Workbook Events

The following event procedures are available at the workbook level. Some events, such as Workbook_SheetActivate, are sheet events available at the workbook level. This means you don't have to copy and paste the code in each sheet in which you want it to run.

Workbook_Activate()

Workbook_Activate occurs when the workbook containing this event becomes the active workbook.

Workbook_Deactivate()

Workbook_Deactivate occurs when the active workbook is switched from the workbook containing the event to another workbook.

Workbook_Open()

Workbook_Open is the default workbook event. This procedure is activated when a workbook is opened; no user interface is required. The procedure has a variety of uses, such as checking the username and then customizing the user's privileges in the workbook.

7

The following code checks the `UserName`. If it is not Admin, this code protects each sheet from user changes.

```
Private Sub Workbook_Open()
Dim sht As Worksheet
If Application.UserName <> "Admin" Then
    For Each sht In Worksheets
        sht.Protect UserInterfaceOnly:=True
    Next sht
End If
End Sub
```

> **TIP**
> `UserInterfaceOnly` allows macros to make changes on a sheet, but not the user.

Workbook_BeforeSave(ByVal SaveAsUI As Boolean, Cancel As Boolean)

`Workbook_BeforeSave` occurs when the workbook is saved. `SaveAsUI` is set to `True` if the Save As dialog box is to be displayed. `Cancel` set to `True` prevents the workbook from being saved.

Workbook_AfterSave (ByVal Success As Boolean)

`Workbook_AfterSave` occurs after the workbook is saved. `Success` returns `True` if the file saved successfully; `False` is returned if the save was not successful.

Workbook_BeforePrint(Cancel As Boolean)

`Workbook_BeforePrint` occurs when any print command is used, whether it is in the ribbon, keyboard, or macro. `Cancel` set to `True` prevents the workbook from being printed.

The following code tracks each time a sheet is printed. It logs the date, time, username, and sheet printed in a hidden print log (see Figure 7.3):

```
Private Sub Workbook_BeforePrint(Cancel As Boolean)
Dim LastRow As Long
Dim PrintLog As Worksheet
Set PrintLog = Worksheets("PrintLog")
LastRow = PrintLog.Cells(PrintLog.Rows.Count, 1).End(xlUp).Row + 1
With PrintLog
    .Cells(LastRow, 1).Value = Now()
    .Cells(LastRow, 2).Value = Application.UserName
    .Cells(LastRow, 3).Value = ActiveSheet.Name
End With
End Sub
```

Figure 7.3
Use the `BeforePrint` event to keep a hidden print log in a workbook.

	A	B	C
1	Date/Time	Username	Sheet Printed
2	8/5/2012 19:08	Tracy Syrstad	PrintLog
3			

You also can use the `BeforePrint` event to add information to a header or footer before the sheet is printed. Although you can enter the file path into a header or footer through the Page Setup, before Office XP the only way to add the file path was with code. In legacy versions of Office, the following code was commonly used:

```
Private Sub Workbook_BeforePrint(Cancel As Boolean)
    ActiveSheet.PageSetup.RightFooter = ActiveWorkbook.FullName
End Sub
```

Workbook_BeforeClose(Cancel As Boolean)

`Workbook_BeforeClose` occurs when the user closes a workbook. `Cancel` set to `True` prevents the workbook from closing.

Workbook_NewSheet(ByVal Sh As Object)

`Workbook_NewSheet` occurs when a new sheet is added to the active workbook. `Sh` is the new Worksheet or Chart Sheet object.

Workbook_SheetBeforeDelete(ByVal Sh As Object)

`Workbook_SheetBeforeDelete` occurs before any worksheet in the workbook is deleted. `Sh` is the sheet being deleted.

Workbook_NewChart(ByVal Ch As Chart)

`Workbook_NewChart` occurs when the user adds a new chart to the active workbook. `Ch` is the new Chart object. The event is not triggered if a chart is moved from one location to another, unless it is moved between a chart sheet and a chart object. In that case, the event is triggered because a new chart sheet or object is being created.

Workbook_WindowResize(ByVal Wn As Window)

`Workbook_WindowResize` occurs when the user resizes the active workbook. `Wn` is the window.

> **NOTE**
> Only resizing the active workbook window starts this event. Resizing the application window is an application-level event that is not affected by the workbook-level event.

This code disables the resizing of the active workbook:

```
Private Sub Workbook_WindowResize(ByVal Wn As Window)
Wn.EnableResize = False
End Sub
```

7

> **CAUTION**
> If you disable the capability to resize, the minimize and maximize buttons are removed, and the user cannot resize the workbook. To undo this, type `ActiveWindow.EnableResize = True` in the Immediate window.

Workbook_WindowActivate(ByVal Wn As Window)

Workbook_WindowActivate occurs when the user activates any workbook window. Wn is the window. Only activating the workbook window starts this event.

Workbook_WindowDeactivate(ByVal Wn As Window)

Workbook_WindowDeactivate occurs when the user deactivates any workbook window. Wn is the window. Only deactivating the workbook window starts this event.

Workbook_AddInInstall()

Workbook_AddInInstall occurs when the user installs the workbook as an add-in (by selecting File, Options, Add-ins). Double-clicking an XLAM file (an add-in) to open it does not activate the event.

Workbook_AddInUninstall()

Workbook_AddInUninstall occurs when the user uninstalls the workbook (add-in). The add-in is not automatically closed.

Workbook_Sync(ByVal SyncEventType As Office.MsoSyncEventType)

Workbook_Sync occurs when the user synchronizes the local copy of a sheet in a workbook that is part of a Document Workspace with the copy on the server. SyncEventType is the status of the synchronization.

Workbook_PivotTableCloseConnection(ByVal Target As PivotTable)

Workbook_PivotTableCloseConnection occurs when a PivotTable report closes its connection to its data source. Target is the PivotTable that has closed the connection.

Workbook_PivotTableOpenConnection(ByVal Target As PivotTable)

Workbook_PivotTableOpenConnection occurs when a PivotTable report opens a connection to its data source. Target is the PivotTable that has opened the connection.

Workbook_RowsetComplete(ByVal Description As String, ByVal Sheet As String, ByVal Success As Boolean)

Workbook_RowsetComplete occurs when the user drills through a recordset or calls upon the rowset action on an OLAP PivotTable. Description is a description of the event; Sheet is the name of the sheet on which the recordset is created; Success indicates success or failure.

Workbook_BeforeXmlExport(ByVal Map As XmlMap, ByVal Url As String, Cancel As Boolean)

Workbook_BeforeXmlExport occurs when the user exports or saves XML data. Map is the map used to export or save the data; Url is the location of the XML file; Cancel set to True cancels the export operation.

Workbook_AfterXmlExport(ByVal Map As XmlMap, ByVal Url As String, ByVal Result As XlXmlExportResult)

Workbook_AfterXmlExport occurs after the user exports or saves XML data. Map is the map used to export or save the data; Url is the location of the XML file; Result indicates success or failure.

Workbook_BeforeXmlImport(ByVal Map As XmlMap, ByVal Url As String, ByVal IsRefresh As Boolean, Cancel As Boolean)

Workbook_BeforeXmlImport occurs when the user imports or refreshes XML data. Map is the map used to import the data; Url is the location of the XML file; IsRefresh returns True if the event was triggered by refreshing an existing connection and False if triggered by importing from a new data source; Cancel set to True cancels the import or refresh operation.

Workbook_AfterXmlImport(ByVal Map As XmlMap, ByVal IsRefresh As Boolean, ByVal Result As XlXmlImportResult)

Workbook_AfterXmlImport occurs when the user exports or saves XML data. Map is the map used to export or save the data; IsRefresh returns True if the event was triggered by refreshing an existing connection and False if triggered by importing from a new data source; Result indicates success or failure.

Workbook_ModelChange(ByVal Changes As ModelChanges)

Workbook_ModelChange occurs when the user changes a data model. Changes is the type of change, such as columns added, changed, or deleted, that was made to the data model.

Workbook Level Sheet and Chart Events

The following are sheet and chart events available at the workbook level. These events affect all sheets in the workbook. Unless otherwise indicated, to affect a specific sheet, replace the text Workbook_Sheet with Worksheet_ or Chart_ to access the sheet- or chart-level event. For example, if the event is Workbook_SheetSelectionChange, the sheet-level event is Worksheet_SelectionChange.

Workbook_SheetActivate(ByVal Sh As Object)

Workbook_SheetActivate occurs when the user activates any chart sheet or worksheet in the workbook. Sh is the active sheet.

Workbook_SheetBeforeDoubleClick (ByVal Sh As Object, ByVal Target As Range, Cancel As Boolean)

Workbook_SheetBeforeDoubleClick occurs when the user double-clicks any chart sheet or worksheet in the active workbook. Sh is the active sheet; Target is the object double-clicked; Cancel set to True prevents the default action from taking place.

7

`Workbook_SheetBeforeRightClick(ByVal Sh As Object, ByVal Target As Range, Cancel As Boolean)`

`Workbook_SheetBeforeRightClick` occurs when the user right-clicks any worksheet in the active workbook. `Sh` is the active worksheet; `Target` is the object right-clicked; `Cancel` set to `True` prevents the default action from taking place.

`Workbook_SheetCalculate(ByVal Sh As Object)`

`Workbook_SheetCalculate` occurs when any worksheet is recalculated or any updated data is plotted on a chart. `Sh` is the sheet triggering the calculation.

`Workbook_SheetChange (ByVal Sh As Object, ByVal Target As Range)`

`Workbook_SheetChange` occurs when the user changes any range in a worksheet. `Sh` is the worksheet; `Target` is the changed range.

There is no Chart version of this event.

`Workbook_SheetDeactivate (ByVal Sh As Object)`

`Workbook_SheetDeactivate` occurs when the user deactivates any chart sheet or worksheet in the workbook. `Sh` is the sheet being switched from.

`Workbook_SheetFollowHyperlink (ByVal Sh As Object, ByVal Target As Hyperlink)`

`Workbook_SheetFollowHyperlink` occurs when the user clicks any hyperlink in Excel. `Sh` is the active worksheet; `Target` is the hyperlink.

There is no Chart version of this event.

`Workbook_SheetSelectionChange(ByVal Sh As Object, ByVal Target As Range)`

`Workbook_SheetSelectionChange` occurs when the user selects a new range on any sheet. `Sh` is the active sheet; `Target` is the affected range.

There is no Chart version of this event.

`Workbook_SheetTableUpdate(ByVal Sh As Object, ByVal Target As TableObject)`

`Workbook_SheetTableUpdate` occurs when the user changes a table object. `Sh` is the sheet with the table; `Target` is the table object that was updated.

There is no Chart version of this event.

`Workbook_SheetLensGalleryRenderComplete(ByVal Sh As Object)`

`Workbook_SheetLensGalleryRenderComplete` occurs when the user selects the Quick Analysis tool. `Sh` is the active sheet.

There is no Chart version of this event.

Workbook_SheetPivotTableUpdate(ByVal Sh As Object, ByVal Target As PivotTable)

`Workbook_SheetPivotTableUpdate` occurs when the user updates a PivotTable. `Sh` is the sheet with the PivotTable; `Target` is the updated PivotTable.

Workbook_SheetPivotTableAfterValueChange(ByVal Sh As Object, ByVal TargetPivotTable As PivotTable, ByVal TargetRange As Range)

`Workbook_SheetPivotTableAfterValueChange` occurs after the user edits cells inside a PivotTable or the user recalculates them if they contain a formula. `Sh` is the sheet the PivotTable is on; `TargetPivotTable` is the PivotTable with the changed cells; `TargetRange` is the range that was changed.

Workbook_SheetPivotTableBeforeAllocateChanges(ByVal Sh As Object, ByVal TargetPivotTable As PivotTable, ByVal ValueChangeStart As Long, ByVal ValueChangeEnd As Long, Cancel As Boolean)

`Workbook_SheetPivotTableBeforeAllocateChanges` occurs before a PivotTable is updated from its OLAP data source. `Sh` is the sheet the PivotTable is on; `TargetPivotTable` is the updated PivotTable; `ValueChangeStart` is the index number of the first change; `ValueChangeEnd` is the index number of the last change; `Cancel` set to `True` prevents the changes from being applied to the PivotTable.

Workbook_SheetPivotTableBeforeCommitChanges(ByVal Sh As Object, ByVal TargetPivotTable As PivotTable, ByVal ValueChangeStart As Long, ByVal ValueChangeEnd As Long, Cancel As Boolean)

`Workbook_SheetPivotTableBeforeCommitChanges` occurs before an OLAP PivotTable updates its data source. `Sh` is the sheet the PivotTable is on; `TargetPivotTable` is the updated PivotTable; `ValueChangeStart` is the index number of the first change; `ValueChangeEnd` is the index number of the last change; `Cancel` set to `True` prevents the changes from being applied to the data source.

Workbook_SheetPivotTableBeforeDiscardChanges(ByVal Sh As Object, ByVal TargetPivotTable As PivotTable, ByVal ValueChangeStart As Long, ByVal ValueChangeEnd As Long)

`Workbook_SheetPivotTableBeforeDiscardChanges` occurs before an OLAP PivotTable discards changes from its data source. `Sh` is the sheet the PivotTable is on; `TargetPivotTable` is the PivotTable with changes to discard; `ValueChangeStart` is the index number of the first change; `ValueChangeEnd` is the index number of the last change.

7

```
Workbook_SheetPivotTableChangeSync(ByVal Sh As Object, ByVal Target
As PivotTable)
```

Workbook_SheetPivotTableChangeSync occurs after the user changes a PivotTable. Sh is the sheet the PivotTable is on; Target is the PivotTable that has been changed.

Worksheet Events

The following event procedures are available at the worksheet level.

Worksheet_Activate()

Worksheet_Activate occurs when the sheet on which the event is located becomes the active sheet.

Worksheet_Deactivate()

Worksheet_Deactivate occurs when another sheet becomes the active sheet.

> **NOTE** If a Deactivate event is on the active sheet and you switch to a sheet with an Activate event, the Deactivate event runs first, followed by the Activate event.

Worksheet_BeforeDoubleClick(ByVal Target As Range, Cancel As Boolean)

Worksheet_BeforeDoubleClick allows control over what happens when the user double-clicks the sheet. Target is the selected range on the sheet; Cancel is set to False by default, but if set to True, it prevents the default action, such as entering a cell, from happening.

The following code prevents the user from entering a cell with a double-click. In addition, if the formula field is hidden, this code does not allow the user to enter information in the traditional way:

```
Private Sub Worksheet_BeforeDoubleClick(ByVal Target As Range, _
    Cancel As Boolean)
Cancel = True
End Sub
```

> **NOTE** The preceding code does not prevent the user from double-clicking to size a row or column.

Preventing the double-click from entering a cell allows it to be used for something else, such as highlighting a cell. The following code changes a cell's interior color to red when the user double-clicks it:

```
Private Sub Worksheet_BeforeDoubleClick(ByVal Target As Range, _
    Cancel As Boolean)
Target.Interior.ColorIndex = 3
End Sub
```

Worksheet_BeforeRightClick(ByVal Target As Range, Cancel As Boolean)

Worksheet_BeforeRightClick is triggered when the user right-clicks a range. Target is the object right-clicked; Cancel set to True prevents the default action from taking place.

Worksheet_Calculate()

Worksheet_Calculate occurs after a sheet is recalculated.

The following example compares a month's profits between the previous and current year. If profit has fallen, a red down arrow appears below the month; if profit has risen, a green up arrow appears (see Figure 7.4):

```
Private Sub Worksheet_Calculate()
Select Case Range("C3").Value
    Case Is < Range("C4").Value
        SetArrow 10, msoShapeDownArrow
    Case Is > Range("C4").Value
        SetArrow 3, msoShapeUpArrow
End Select
End Sub

Private Sub SetArrow(ByVal ArrowColor As Integer, ByVal ArrowDegree)
' The following code is added to remove the prior shapes
For Each sh In ActiveSheet.Shapes
    If sh.Name Like "*Arrow*" Then
        sh.Delete
    End If
Next sh
ActiveSheet.Shapes.AddShape(ArrowDegree, 22, 40, 5, 10).Select
With Selection.ShapeRange
    With .Fill
        .Visible = msoTrue
        .Solid
        .ForeColor.SchemeColor = ArrowColor
        .Transparency = 0#
    End With
    With .Line
        .Weight = 0.75
        .DashStyle = msoLineSolid
        .Style = msoLineSingle
        .Transparency = 0#
        .Visible = msoTrue
        .ForeColor.SchemeColor = 64
        .BackColor.RGB = RGB(255, 255, 255)
    End With
End With
Range("A3").Select 'Place the selection back on the drop-down
End Sub
```

7

Figure 7.4
Use the `Calculate` event to add graphics that emphasize the change in profits.

1	2010 vs 2011 Profit						
2							
3	June	Current	3307		Month	2010	2011
4	⇑	Previous	1383		January	4000	7258
5					February	9704	3459
6					March	3950	3874
7					April	7518	3907
8					May	4542	9774
9					June	1383	3307
10					July	2888	4741

Worksheet_Change(ByVal Target As Range)

`Worksheet_Change` is triggered by a change to a cell's value, such as when the user enters, edits, or deletes text. `Target` is the cell that has been changed.

> **NOTE**
> The event can also be triggered by pasting values. Recalculation of a value does not trigger the event. Therefore, the `Calculation` event should be used instead.

Worksheet_SelectionChange(ByVal Target As Range)

`Worksheet_SelectionChange` occurs when the user selects a new range. `Target` is the newly selected range.

The following example helps identify a single selected cell by highlighting the row and column:

```
Private Sub Worksheet_SelectionChange(ByVal Target As Range)
Dim iColor As Integer
On Error Resume Next
iColor = Target.Interior.ColorIndex
If iColor < 0 Then
    iColor = 36
Else
    iColor = iColor + 1
End If
If iColor = Target.Font.ColorIndex Then iColor = iColor + 1
Cells.FormatConditions.Delete
With Range("A" & Target.Row, Target.Address)
    .FormatConditions.Add Type:=2, Formula1:="TRUE"
    .FormatConditions(1).Interior.ColorIndex = iColor
End With
With Range(Target.Offset(1 - Target.Row, 0).Address & ":" & _
    Target.Offset(-1, 0).Address)
    .FormatConditions.Add Type:=2, Formula1:="TRUE"
    .FormatConditions(1).Interior.ColorIndex = iColor
End With
End Sub
```

> **CAUTION**
> This example makes use of conditional formatting and overwrites any existing conditional formatting on the sheet. The code might also clear the Clipboard, which makes it difficult to copy and paste on the sheet.

Worksheet_FollowHyperlink(ByVal Target As Hyperlink)

Worksheet_FollowHyperlink occurs when the user clicks a hyperlink. Target is the hyperlink.

Worksheet_LensGalleryRenderComplete

Worksheet_LensGalleryRenderComplete occurs when the user selects the Quick Analysis tool.

Worksheet_PivotTableUpdate(ByVal Target As PivotTable)

Worksheet_PivotTableUpdate occurs when the user updates a PivotTable. Target is the updated PivotTable.

Worksheet_PivotTableAfterValueChange(ByVal TargetPivotTable As PivotTable, ByVal TargetRange As Range)

Worksheet_PivotTableAfterValueChange occurs after the user edits cells inside a PivotTable or the user recalculates them if they contain a formula. TargetPivotTable is the PivotTable with the changed cells; TargetRange is the range that was changed.

Worksheet_PivotTableBeforeAllocateChanges(ByVal TargetPivotTable As PivotTable, ByVal ValueChangeStart As Long, ByVal ValueChangeEnd As Long, Cancel As Boolean)

Worksheet_PivotTableBeforeAllocateChanges occurs before a PivotTable is updated from its OLAP data source. Sh is the sheet the PivotTable is on; TargetPivotTable is the updated PivotTable; ValueChangeStart is the index number of the first change; ValueChangeEnd is the index number of the last change; Cancel set to True prevents the changes from being applied to the PivotTable.

Worksheet_PivotTableBeforeCommitChanges(ByVal TargetPivotTable As PivotTable, ByVal ValueChangeStart As Long, ByVal ValueChangeEnd As Long, Cancel As Boolean)

Worksheet_PivotTableBeforeCommitChanges occurs before an OLAP PivotTable updates its data source. TargetPivotTable is the updated PivotTable; ValueChangeStart is the index number of the first change; ValueChangeEnd is the index number of the last change; Cancel set to True prevents the changes from being applied to the data source.

Worksheet_PivotTableBeforeDiscardChanges(ByVal TargetPivotTable As PivotTable, ByVal ValueChangeStart As Long, ByVal ValueChangeEnd As Long)

Worksheet_PivotTableBeforeDiscardChanges occurs before an OLAP PivotTable discards changes from its data source. TargetPivotTable is the PivotTable with changes to discard;

ValueChangeStart is the index number of the first change; ValueChangeEnd is the index number of the last change.

Worksheet_PivotTableChangeSync(ByVal Target As PivotTable)

Worksheet_PivotTableChangeSync occurs after a PivotTable has been changed. Target is the PivotTable that has been changed.

CASE STUDY: QUICKLY ENTERING MILITARY TIME INTO A CELL

You're entering arrival and departure times and want the times to be formatted with a 24-hour clock, which is also known as *military time*. You have tried formatting the cell, but no matter how you enter the times, they are displayed in the 0:00 hours and minutes format.

The only way to get the time to appear as military time, such as 23:45, is to have the time entered in the cell in this manner. Because typing the colon is time-consuming, it would be more efficient to enter the numbers and let Excel format it for you.

The solution is to use a Change event to take what is in the cell and insert the colon for you:

```
Private Sub Worksheet_Change(ByVal Target As Range)
Dim ThisColumn As Integer
Dim UserInput As String, NewInput As String
ThisColumn = Target.Column
If ThisColumn < 3 Then
  If Target.Count > 1 Then Exit Sub 'check that only 1 cell is selected
  If Len(Target) = 1 Then Exit Sub 'check more than 1 character entered

  UserInput = Target.Value
  If UserInput > 1 Then
      NewInput = Left(UserInput, Len(UserInput) - 2) & ":" & _
      Right(UserInput, 2)
      Application.EnableEvents = False
      Target = NewInput
      Application.EnableEvents = True
  End If
End If
End Sub
```

An entry of 2345 displays as 23:45. Note that the code limits this format change to Columns A and B (If ThisColumn < 3). Without this limitation, entering numbers anywhere on a sheet such as in a totals column would force it to be reformatted.

> **NOTE**
> Use Application.EnableEvents = False to prevent the procedure from calling itself when the value in the target is updated.

Chart Sheet Events

Chart events occur when a chart is changed or activated. Embedded charts require the use of class modules to access the events. For more information about class modules, see Chapter 9, "Creating Classes, Records, and Collections."

Embedded Charts

Because embedded charts do not create chart sheets, the chart events are not as readily available. However, you can make them available by adding a class module, as described here:

1. Insert a class module.
2. Rename the module to something that will make sense to you, such as cl_ChartEvents.
3. Enter the following line of code in the class module:

```
Public WithEvents myChartClass As Chart
```

The chart events are now available to the chart, as shown in Figure 7.5. They are accessed in the class module rather than on a chart sheet.

4. Insert a standard module.
5. Enter the following lines of code in a standard module:

```
Dim myClassModule As New cl_ChartEvents
Sub InitializeChart()
    Set myClassModule.myChartClass = _
        Worksheets(1).ChartObjects(1).Chart
End Sub
```

These lines initialize the embedded chart to be recognized as a Chart object. The procedure must be run once per session.

> **NOTE** You can use Workbook_Open to automatically run the InitializeChart procedure.

Figure 7.5
Embedded chart events are now available in the class module.

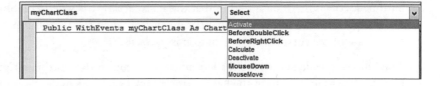

Chart_Activate()

Chart_Activate occurs when a chart sheet is activated or changed.

Chart_BeforeDoubleClick(ByVal ElementID As Long, ByVal Arg1 As Long, ByVal Arg2 As Long, Cancel As Boolean)

Chart_BeforeDoubleClick occurs when any part of a chart is double-clicked. ElementID is the part of the chart that is double-clicked, such as the legend. Arg1 and Arg2 are dependent on the ElementID; Cancel set to True prevents the default double-click action from occurring.

The following sample hides the legend when the user double-clicks it, whereas double-clicking either axis brings back the legend:

```
Private Sub MyChartClass_BeforeDoubleClick(ByVal ElementID As Long, _
    ByVal Arg1 As Long, ByVal Arg2 As Long, Cancel As Boolean)
Select Case ElementID
    Case xlLegend
        Me.HasLegend = False
        Cancel = True
    Case xlAxis
        Me.HasLegend = True
        Cancel = True
End Select
End Sub
```

Chart_BeforeRightClick(Cancel As Boolean)

Chart_BeforeRightClick occurs when the user right-clicks a chart. Cancel set to True prevents the default right-click action from occurring.

Chart_Calculate()

Chart_Calculate occurs when the user changes a chart's data.

Chart_Deactivate()

Chart_Deactivate occurs when the user makes another sheet the active sheet.

Chart_MouseDown(ByVal Button As Long, ByVal Shift As Long, ByVal x As Long, ByVal y As Long)

Chart_MouseDown occurs when the cursor is over the chart and the user presses any mouse button. Button is the mouse button that was clicked; Shift is whether a Shift, Ctrl, or Alt key was pressed; X is the X coordinate of the cursor when the button is pressed; Y is the Y coordinate of the cursor when the button is pressed.

The following code zooms in on a left mouse click and zooms out on a right mouse click. Use the Cancel argument in the BeforeRightClick event to handle the menus that appear when you right-click a chart.

```
Private Sub MyChartClass_MouseDown(ByVal Button As Long, ByVal Shift _
    As Long, ByVal x As Long, ByVal y As Long)
If Button = 1 Then 'left button
    ActiveChart.Axes(xlValue).MaximumScale = _
    ActiveChart.Axes(xlValue).MaximumScale - 50
```

7

```
End If
If Button = 2 Then 'right button
   ActiveChart.Axes(xlValue).MaximumScale = _
   ActiveChart.Axes(xlValue).MaximumScale + 50
End If
End Sub
```

Chart_MouseMove(ByVal Button As Long, ByVal Shift As Long, ByVal x As Long, ByVal y As Long)

Chart_MouseMove occurs as the user moves the cursor over a chart. Button is the mouse button being held down, if any; Shift is whether a Shift, Ctrl, or Alt key was pressed; X is the X coordinate of the cursor on the chart; Y is the Y coordinate of the cursor on the chart.

Chart_MouseUp(ByVal Button As Long, ByVal Shift As Long, ByVal x As Long, ByVal y As Long)

Chart_MouseUp occurs when the user releases any mouse button while the cursor is on the chart. Button is the mouse button that was clicked; Shift is whether a Shift, Ctrl, or Alt key was pressed; X is the X coordinate of the cursor when the button is released; Y is the Y coordinate of the cursor when the button is released.

Chart_Resize()

Chart_Resize occurs when the user resizes a chart using the sizing handles. However, this does not occur when the size is changed using the size control on the Format tab or task pane of the chart tools.

Chart_Select(ByVal ElementID As Long, ByVal Arg1 As Long, ByVal Arg2 As Long)

Chart_Select occurs when the user selects a chart element. ElementID is the part of the chart selected such as the legend. Arg1 and Arg2 are dependent on the ElementID.

The following code highlights the dataset when a point on the chart is selected—assuming that the series starts in A1 and each row is a point to plot—as shown in Figure 7.6:

```
Private Sub MyChartClass_Select(ByVal ElementID As Long, ByVal Arg1 _
    As Long, ByVal Arg2 As Long)
If Arg1 = 0 Then Exit Sub
Sheets("Sheet1").Cells.Interior.ColorIndex = xlNone
If ElementID = 3 Then
   If Arg2 = -1 Then
      ' Selected the entire series in Arg1
      Sheets("Sheet1").Range("A2:A22").Offset(0, Arg1). _
Interior.ColorIndex = 19
   Else
      ' Selected a single point in range Arg1, Point Arg2
      Sheets("Sheet1").Range("A1").Offset(Arg2, Arg1).Interior.ColorIndex = 19
   End If
End If
End Sub
```

7

Figure 7.6
Use the Chart_
Select event to
highlight the data used
to create a point on the
chart.

```
Chart_SeriesChange(ByVal SeriesIndex As Long, ByVal
PointIndex As Long)
```

Chart_SeriesChange occurs when a chart data point is updated. SeriesIndex is the offset in the Series collection of updated series; PointIndex is the offset in the Point collection of updated points.

Application-Level Events

Application-level events affect all open workbooks in an Excel session. They require a class module to access them. This is similar to the class module used to access events for embedded chart events. Follow these steps to create the class module:

1. Insert a class module.

2. Rename the module to something that will make sense to you, such as cl_AppEvents.

3. Enter the following line of code in the class module:
   ```
   Public WithEvents AppEvent As Application
   ```
   The application events are now available to the workbook as shown in Figure 7.7. They are accessed in the class module rather than in a standard module.

4. Insert a standard module.

5. Enter the following lines of code in the standard module:

   ```
   Dim myAppEvent As New cl_AppEvents
   Sub InitializeAppEvent()
       Set myAppEvent.AppEvent = Application
   End Sub
   ```

   These lines initialize the application to recognize application events. The procedure must be run once per session.

You can use `Workbook_Open` to automatically run the `InitializeAppEvent` procedure.

Figure 7.7
Application events are
now available through
the class module.

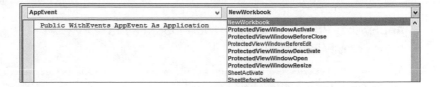

The object in front of the event such as `AppEvent` is dependent on the name given in the class module.

AppEvent_AfterCalculate()

`AppEvent_AfterCalculate` occurs after all calculations are complete and there aren't any outstanding queries or incomplete calculations.

This event occurs after all other `Calculation`, `AfterRefresh`, and `SheetChange` events and after `Application.CalculationState` is set to `xlDone`.

AppEvent_NewWorkbook(ByVal Wb As Workbook)

`AppEvent_NewWorkbook` occurs when the user creates a new workbook. `Wb` is the new workbook. The following code arranges the open workbooks in a tiled configuration:

```
Private Sub AppEvent_NewWorkbook(ByVal Wb As Workbook)
    Application.Windows.Arrange xlArrangeStyleTiled
End Sub
```

AppEvent_ProtectedViewWindowActivate(ByVal Pvw As ProtectedViewWindow)

`AppEvent_ProtectedViewWindowActivate` occurs when the user activates a workbook in Protected View mode. `Pvw` is the workbook being activated.

AppEvent_ProtectedViewWindowBeforeClose(By Val Pvw As ProtectedViewWindow, ByVal Reason As XlProtectedViewCloseReason, Cancel As Boolean)

`AppEvent_ProtectedViewWindowBeforeClose` occurs when the user closes a workbook in Protected View mode. `Pvw` is the workbook being deactivated; `Reason` is why the workbook closed; `Cancel` set to `True` prevents the workbook from closing.

7

AppEvent_ProtectedViewWindowDeactivate(ByVal Pvw As ProtectedViewWindow)

AppEvent_ProtectedViewWindowDeactivate occurs when the user deactivates a workbook in Protected View mode. Pvw is the workbook being deactivated.

AppEvent_ProtectedViewWindowOpen(ByVal Pvw As ProtectedViewWindow)

AppEvent_ProtectedViewWindowOpen occurs when a workbook is open in Protected View mode. Pvw is the workbook being opened.

AppEvent_ProtectedViewWindowResize(ByVal Pvw As ProtectedViewWindow)

AppEvent_ProtectedViewWindowResize occurs when the user resizes the window of the protected workbook. However, this does not occur in the application itself. Pvw is the workbook being resized.

AppEvent_ProtectedViewWindowBeforeEdit(ByVal Pvw As ProtectedViewWindow, Cancel As Boolean)

AppEvent_ProtectedViewWindowBeforeEdit occurs when the user clicks the Enable Editing button of a protected workbook. Pvw is the protected workbook; Cancel set to True prevents the workbook from being enabled.

AppEvent_SheetActivate (ByVal Sh As Object)

AppEvent_SheetActivate occurs when the user activates a sheet. Sh is the worksheet or chart sheet.

AppEvent_SheetBeforeDelete(ByVal Sh As Object)

AppEvent_SheetBeforeDelete occurs before any worksheet in a workbook is deleted. Sh is the sheet being deleted.

AppEvent_SheetBeforeDoubleClick(ByVal Sh As Object, ByVal Target As Range, Cancel As Boolean)

AppEvent_SheetBeforeDoubleClick occurs when the user double-clicks a worksheet. Target is the selected range on the sheet; Cancel is set to False by default. However, when set to True, it prevents the default action such as entering a cell from happening.

AppEvent_SheetBeforeRightClick(ByVal Sh As Object, ByVal Target As Range, Cancel As Boolean)

AppEvent_SheetBeforeRightClick occurs when the user right-clicks any worksheet. Sh is the active worksheet; Target is the object right-clicked; Cancel set to True prevents the default action from taking place.

7

AppEvent_SheetCalculate(ByVal Sh As Object)

AppEvent_SheetCalculate occurs when the user recalculates any worksheet or plots any updated data on a chart. Sh is the active sheet.

AppEvent_SheetChange(ByVal Sh As Object, ByVal Target As Range)

AppEvent_SheetChange occurs when the user changes the value of any cell. Sh is the worksheet; Target is the changed range.

AppEvent_SheetDeactivate(ByVal Sh As Object)

AppEvent_SheetDeactivate occurs when the user deactivates any chart sheet or worksheet in a workbook. Sh is the sheet being deactivated.

AppEvent_SheetFollowHyperlink(ByVal Sh As Object, ByVal Target As Hyperlink)

AppEvent_SheetFollowHyperlink occurs when the user clicks any hyperlink in Excel. Sh is the active worksheet; Target is the hyperlink.

AppEvent_SheetSelectionChange(ByVal Sh As Object, ByVal Target As Range)

AppEvent_SheetSelectionChange occurs when the user selects a new range on any sheet. Sh is the active sheet; Target is the selected range.

AppEvent_SheetTableUpdate(ByVal Sh As Object, ByVal Target As TableObject)

AppEvent_SheetTableUpdate occurs when the user changes a table object. Sh is the active sheet; Target is the table object that was updated.

AppEvent_SheetLensGalleryRenderComplete(ByVal Sh As Object)

AppEvent_SheetLensGalleryRenderComplete occurs when the user selects the Quick Analysis tool. Sh is the active sheet.

AppEvent_SheetPivotTableUpdate(ByVal Sh As Object, ByVal Target As PivotTable)

AppEvent_SheetPivotTableUpdate occurs when the user updates a PivotTable. Sh is the active sheet; Target is the updated PivotTable.

AppEvent_SheetPivotTableAfterValueChange(ByVal Sh As Object, ByVal TargetPivotTable As PivotTable, ByVal TargetRange As Range)

AppEvent_SheetPivotTableAfterValueChange occurs after the user edits cells inside a PivotTable or, if the cells contain a formula, the user recalculates them. Sh is the sheet the

PivotTable is on; `TargetPivotTable` is the PivotTable with the changed cells; `TargetRange` is the range that was changed.

AppEvent_SheetPivotTableBeforeAllocateChanges(ByVal Sh As Object, ByVal TargetPivotTable As PivotTable, ByVal ValueChangeStart As Long, ByVal ValueChangeEnd As Long, Cancel As Boolean)

`AppEvent_SheetPivotTableBeforeAllocateChanges` occurs before a PivotTable is updated from its OLAP data source. `Sh` is the sheet the PivotTable is on; `TargetPivotTable` is the updated PivotTable; `ValueChangeStart` is the index number of the first change; `ValueChangeEnd` is the index number of the last change; `Cancel` set to `True` prevents the changes from being applied to the PivotTable.

AppEvent_SheetPivotTableBeforeCommitChanges(ByVal Sh As Object, ByVal TargetPivotTable As PivotTable, ByVal ValueChangeStart As Long, ByVal ValueChangeEnd As Long, Cancel As Boolean)

`AppEvent_SheetPivotTableBeforeCommitChanges` occurs before an OLAP PivotTable updates its data source. `Sh` is the sheet the PivotTable is on; `TargetPivotTable` is the updated PivotTable; `ValueChangeStart` is the index number of the first change; `ValueChangeEnd` is the index number of the last change; `Cancel` set to `True` prevents the changes from being applied to the data source.

AppEvent_SheetPivotTableBeforeDiscardChanges(ByVal Sh As Object, ByVal TargetPivotTable As PivotTable, ByVal ValueChangeStart As Long, ByVal ValueChangeEnd As Long)

`AppEvent_SheetPivotTableBeforeDiscardChanges` occurs before an OLAP PivotTable discards changes from its data source. `Sh` is the sheet the PivotTable is on; `TargetPivotTable` is the PivotTable with changes to discard; `ValueChangeStart` is the index number of the first change; `ValueChangeEnd` is the index number of the last change.

AppEvent_SheetPivotTableChangeSync(ByVal Sh As Object, ByVal Target As PivotTable)

`AppEvent_SheetPivotTableChangeSync` occurs after the user changes a PivotTable. `Sh` is the sheet the PivotTable is on; `Target` is the PivotTable that has been changed.

AppEvent_WindowActivate(ByVal Wb As Workbook, ByVal Wn As Window)

`AppEvent_WindowActivate` occurs when the user activates any workbook window. `Wb` is the workbook being deactivated; `Wn` is the window. This works only if there are multiple windows.

7

AppEvent_WindowDeactivate(ByVal Wb As Workbook, ByVal Wn As Window)

AppEvent_WindowDeactivate occurs when the user deactivates any workbook window. Wb is the active workbook; Wn is the window. This works only if there are multiple windows.

AppEvent_WindowResize(ByVal Wb As Workbook, ByVal Wn As Window)

AppEvent_WindowResize occurs when the user resizes the active workbook. Wb is the active workbook; Wn is the window. This works only if there are multiple windows.

> **NOTE** If you disable the capability to resize (EnableResize = False), the minimize and maximize buttons are removed, and the user cannot resize the workbook. To undo this, type ActiveWindow. EnableResize = True in the Immediate window.

AppEvent_WorkbookActivate(ByVal Wb As Workbook)

AppEvent_WorkbookActivate occurs when the user activates any workbook. Wb is the workbook being activated. The following sample maximizes any workbook when it is activated:

```
Private Sub AppEvent_WorkbookActivate(ByVal Wb as Workbook)
    Wb.WindowState = xlMaximized
End Sub
```

AppEvent_WorkbookDeactivate(ByVal Wb As Workbook)

AppEvent_WorkbookDeactivate occurs when the user switches between workbooks. Wb is the workbook being switched away from.

AppEvent_WorkbookAddinInstall(ByVal Wb As Workbook)

AppEvent_WorkbookAddinInstall occurs when the user installs a workbook as an add-in (File, Options, Add-ins). Double-clicking an XLAM file to open it does not activate the event. Wb is the workbook being installed.

AppEvent_WorkbookAddinUninstall(ByVal Wb As Workbook)

AppEvent_WorkbookAddinUninstall occurs when the user uninstalls a workbook (add-in). The add-in is not automatically closed. Wb is the workbook being uninstalled.

AppEvent_WorkbookBeforeClose(ByVal Wb As Workbook, Cancel As Boolean)

AppEvent_WorkbookBeforeClose occurs when the user closes a workbook. Wb is the workbook; Cancel set to True prevents the workbook from closing.

7

AppEvent_WorkbookBeforePrint(ByVal Wb As Workbook, Cancel As Boolean)

AppEvent_WorkbookBeforePrint occurs when the user uses any print command (via the ribbon, keyboard, or a macro). Wb is the workbook; Cancel set to True prevents the workbook from being printed.

The following code places the username in the footer of the active sheet printed:

```
Private Sub AppEvent_WorkbookBeforePrint(ByVal Wb As Workbook, _
    Cancel As Boolean)
Wb.ActiveSheet.PageSetup.LeftFooter = Application.UserName
End Sub
```

AppEvent_WorkbookBeforeSave(ByVal Wb As Workbook, ByVal SaveAsUI As Boolean, Cancel As Boolean)

AppEvent_Workbook_BeforeSave occurs when the user saves the workbook. Wb is the workbook; SaveAsUI is set to True if the Save As dialog box is to be displayed; Cancel set to True prevents the workbook from being saved.

AppEvent_WorkbookAfterSave (ByVal Wb As Workbook, ByVal Success As Boolean)

AppEvent_WorkbookAfterSave occurs after the user has saved the workbook. Wb is the workbook; Success returns True if the file saved successfully; False is returned if the save was not successful.

AppEvent_WorkbookNewSheet(ByVal Wb As Workbook, ByVal Sh As Object)

AppEvent_WorkbookNewSheet occurs when the user adds a new sheet to the active workbook. Wb is the workbook; Sh is the new worksheet.

AppEvent_WorkbookNewChart(ByVal Wb As Workbook, ByVal Ch As Chart)

AppEvent_WorkbookNewChart occurs when the user adds a new chart to the active workbook. Wb is the workbook; Ch is the new chart object. The event is not triggered if the user moves a chart from one location to another, unless the user moves it between a chart sheet and a chart object. In that case, the event is triggered because a new chart sheet or object is being created.

AppEvent_WorkbookOpen(ByVal Wb As Workbook)

AppEvent_WorkbookOpen occurs when the user opens a workbook. Wb is the workbook that was just opened.

AppEvent_WorkbookPivotTableCloseConnection(ByVal Wb As Workbook, ByVal Target As PivotTable)

AppEvent_WorkbookPivotTableCloseConnection occurs when a PivotTable report closes its connection to its data source. Wb is the workbook containing the PivotTable that triggered the event; Target is the PivotTable that has closed the connection.

AppEvent_WorkbookPivotTableOpenConnection(ByVal Wb As Workbook, ByVal Target As PivotTable)

AppEvent_WorkbookPivotTableOpenConnection occurs when a PivotTable report opens a connection to its data source. Wb is the workbook containing the PivotTable that triggered the event; Target is the PivotTable that has opened the connection.

AppEvent_WorkbookRowsetComplete(ByVal Wb As Workbook, ByVal Description As String, ByVal Sheet As String, ByVal Success As Boolean)

AppEvent_WorkbookRowsetComplete occurs when the user drills through a recordset or calls upon the rowset action on an OLAP PivotTable. Wb is the workbook that triggered the event; Description is a description of the event; Sheet is the name of the sheet on which the recordset is created; Success indicates success or failure.

AppEvent_WorkbookSync(ByVal Wb As Workbook, ByVal SyncEventType As Office.MsoSyncEventType)

AppEvent_WorkbookSync occurs when the user synchronizes the local copy of a sheet in a workbook that is part of a Document Workspace with the copy on the server. Wb is the workbook that triggered the event; SyncEventType is the status of the synchronization.

AppEvent_WorkbookBeforeXmlExport(ByVal Wb As Workbook, ByVal Map As XmlMap, ByVal Url As String, Cancel As Boolean)

AppEvent_WorkbookBeforeXmlExport occurs when the user exports or saves XML data. Wb is the workbook that triggered the event; Map is the map used to export or save the data; Url is the location of the XML file; Cancel set to True cancels the export operation.

AppEvent_WorkbookAfterXmlExport(ByVal Wb As Workbook, ByVal Map As XmlMap, ByVal Url As String, ByVal Result As XlXmlExportResult)

AppEvent_WorkbookAfterXmlExport occurs after the user exports or saves XML data. Wb is the workbook that triggered the event; Map is the map used to export or save the data; Url is the location of the XML file; Result indicates success or failure.

7

```
AppEvent_WorkbookBeforeXmlImport(ByVal Wb As Workbook, ByVal
Map As XmlMap, ByVal Url As String, ByVal IsRefresh As
Boolean, Cancel As Boolean)
```

AppEvent_WorkbookBeforeXmlImport occurs when the user imports or refreshes XML data. Wb is the workbook that triggered the event; Map is the map used to import the data; Url is the location of the XML file; IsRefresh returns True if the event was triggered by refreshing an existing connection and False if triggered by importing from a new data source; Cancel set to True cancels the import or refresh operation.

```
AppEvent_WorkbookAfterXmlImport(ByVal Wb As Workbook, ByVal
Map As XmlMap, ByVal IsRefresh As Boolean, ByVal Result As
XlXmlImportResult)
```

AppEvent_WorkbookAfterXmlImport occurs when the user exports or saves XML data. Wb is the workbook that triggered the event; Map is the map used to export or save the data; IsRefresh returns True if the event was triggered by refreshing an existing connection and False if triggered by importing from a new data source; Result indicates success or failure.

```
AppEvent_WorkbookModelChange(ByVal Wb As Workbook, ByVal
Changes As ModelChanges)
```

AppEvent_WorkbookModelChange occurs when the user changes a data model. Wb is the workbook that triggered the event; Changes is the type of change, such as columns added, changed, or deleted, that the user made to the data model.

Next Steps

In this chapter, you learned more about interfacing with Excel. In Chapter 8, "Arrays," you find out how to use multidimensional arrays. Reading data into a multidimensional array, performing calculations on the array, and then writing the array back to a range can speed up your macros dramatically.

7

Arrays

An *array* is a type of variable that can be used to hold more than one piece of data. For example, if you have to work with the name and address of a client, your first thought might be to assign one variable for the name and another for the address of the client. Instead, consider using an array, which can hold both pieces of information—and not for just one client, but for hundreds.

Declare an Array

Declare an array by adding parentheses after the array name. The parentheses contain the number of elements in the array:

```
Dim myArray (2)
```

This creates an array, myArray, that contains three elements. Three elements are included because, by default, the index count starts at 0:

```
myArray(0) = 10
myArray(1) = 20
myArray(2) = 30
```

If the index count needs to start on 1, use `Option Base 1`. This forces the count to start at 1. To do this, place the `Option Base` statement in the declarations section of the module:

```
Option Base 1
Dim myArray(2)
```

This now forces the array to have only two elements.

You can also create an array independent of the `Option Base` statement by declaring its lower bound:

```
Dim myArray (1 to 10)
Dim BigArray (100 to 200)
```

Every array has a lower bound (`Lbound`) and an upper bound (`Ubound`). When you declare `Dim myArray (2)`, you are declaring the upper bound and allowing the option base to declare the lower bound.

By declaring `Dim myArray (1 to 10)`, you declare the lower bound, 1, and the upper bound, 10.

Declare a Multidimensional Array

The arrays just discussed are considered *one-dimensional arrays* because only one number designates the location of an element of the array. The array is like a single row of data, but because there can be only one row, you do not have to worry about the row number—only the column number. For example, to retrieve the second element (`Option Base 0`), use `myArray (1)`.

In some cases, a single dimension is not enough. This is where multidimensional arrays come in. Whereas a one-dimensional array is a single row of data, a multidimensional array contains rows *and* columns.

> **NOTE** Another word for array is *matrix*, which is what a spreadsheet is. The `Cells` object refers to elements of a spreadsheet—and a cell consists of a row and a column. You have been using arrays all along!

To declare another dimension to an array, add another argument. The following creates an array of 10 rows and 20 columns:

```
Dim myArray (1 to 10, 1 to 20)
```

This places values in the first two columns of the first row, as shown in Figure 8.1:

```
myArray (1,1) = 10
myArray (1,2) = 20
```

Figure 8.1
The VB Editor Watches window shows the first "row" of the array being filled from the previous lines of code.

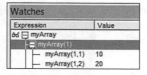

This places values in the first two columns of the second row:

```
myArray (2,1) = 20
myArray (2,2) = 40
```

And so on. Of course, this is time-consuming and can require many lines of code. Other ways to fill an array are discussed in the next section.

Fill an Array

Now that you can declare an array, you need to fill it. One method discussed earlier is to enter a value for each element of the array individually. However, there is a quicker way, as shown in the following sample code and Figure 8.2:

```vba
Option Base 1

Sub ColumnHeaders()
Dim myArray As Variant 'Variants can hold any type of data, including arrays
Dim myCount As Integer

' Fill the variant with array data
myArray = Array("Name", "Address", "Phone", "Email")

' Empty the array
With Worksheets("Sheet2")
    For myCount = 1 To UBound(myArray)
        .Cells(1, myCount).Value = myArray(myCount)
    Next myCount
End With
End Sub
```

Figure 8.2
Use an array to create column headers quickly.

⊿	A	B	C	D
1	Name	Address	Phone	Email

`Variant` variables can hold any type of information. Create a `Variant`-type variable that can be treated like an array. Use the `Array` function to shove the data into the variant, forcing the variant to take on the properties of an array. Notice that you don't declare the size of the array when you fill it as shown in the previous example.

If the information needed in the array is on the sheet already, use the following to fill an array quickly:

```vba
Dim myArray As Variant

myArray = Worksheets("Sheet1").Range("B2:C17")
```

Although these two methods are quick and straightforward, they might not always suit the situation. For example, if you need every other row in the array, use the following code (see Figure 8.3):

```vba
Sub EveryOtherRow()
'there are 16 rows of data, but we are only filling every other row
'half the table size, so our array needs only 8 rows
Dim myArray(1 To 8, 1 To 2)
Dim i As Integer, j As Integer, myCount As Integer

'Fill the array with every other row
For i = 1 To 8
    For j = 1 To 2
'i*2 directs the program to retrieve every other row
```

```
      myArray(i, j) = Worksheets("Sheet1").Cells(i * 2, j + 1).Value
   Next j
Next i

'Calculate contents of array and transfer results to sheet
For myCount = LBound(myArray) To UBound(myArray)
   Worksheets("Sheet1").Cells(myCount * 2, 4) = _
   WorksheetFunction.Sum(myArray(myCount, 1), myArray(myCount, 2))
Next myCount
End Sub
```

Figure 8.3
Fill the array with only the data needed.

◢	A	B	C	D
1		Dec '11	Jan '12	Sum
2	Apples	45	0	45
3	Oranges	12	10	
4	Grapefruit	86	12	98
5	Lemons	15	15	
6	Tomatoes	58	24	82

LBound finds the start location, the lower bound, of the array (myArray). UBound finds the end location, the upper bound, of the array. The program can then loop through the array and sum the information as it writes it to the sheet. How to empty an array is explained in the following section.

Retrieve Data from an Array

After an array is filled, the data needs to be retrieved. However, before you do that, you can manipulate the data or return information about it such as the maximum integer, as shown in the following code (see Figure 8.4):

```
Sub QuickFillMax()
Dim myArray As Variant

myArray = Worksheets("Sheet1").Range("B2:C12")
MsgBox "Maximum Integer is: " & WorksheetFunction.Max(myArray)

End Sub
```

Figure 8.4
Return the Max variable in an array.

◢	A	B	C	D	E
1		Dec '11	Jan '12		
2	Apples	45	0		
3	Oranges	12	10		Microsoft Excel
4	Grapefruit	86	12		
5	Lemons	15	15		
6	Tomatoes	58	24		Maximum Integer is: 95
7	Onions	26	58		
8	Garlic	29	61		
9	Green Beans	46	64		
10	Broccoli	64	79		OK
11	Peas	79	86		
12	Carrots	95	95		

Data can also be manipulated as it is returned to the sheet. In the following example, Lbound and Ubound are used with a For loop to loop through the elements of the array and average each set. The result is placed on the sheet in a new column (see Figure 8.5).

> **NOTE** MyCount + 1 is used to place the results back on the sheet because the Lbound is 1 and the data starts in Row 2.

```
Sub QuickFillAverage()
Dim myArray As Variant
Dim myCount As Integer
'fill the array
myArray = Worksheets("Sheet1").Range("B2:C12")

'Average the data in the array just as it is placed on the sheet
For myCount = LBound(myArray) To UBound(myArray)
'calculate the average and place the result in column E
    Worksheets("Sheet1").Cells(myCount + 1, 5).Value = _
    WorksheetFunction.Average(myArray(myCount, 1), myArray(myCount, 2))
Next myCount

End Sub
```

Figure 8.5
Calculations can be done on the data as it is returned to the sheet.

⊿	A	B	C	D	E
1		Dec '11	Jan '12	Sum	Average
2	Apples	45	0	45	22.5
3	Oranges	12	10		11
4	Grapefruit	86	12	98	49
5	Lemons	15	15		15
6	Tomatoes	58	24	82	41
7	Cabbage	24	26		25
8	Garlic	29	61	90	45
9	Green Beans	46	64		55
10	Broccoli	64	79	143	71.5
11	Peas	79	86		82.5
12	Carrots	95	95	190	95

Use Arrays to Speed Up Code

So far you have learned that arrays can make it easier to manipulate data and get information from it—but is that all they are good for? No, arrays are so powerful because they can actually make the code run faster!

Typically, when there are columns of data to average such as in the preceding example, your first thought might be the following:

```
Sub SlowAverage()
Dim myCount As Integer, LastRow As Integer

LastRow = Worksheets("Sheet1").Cells(Worksheets("Sheet1").Rows.Count, 1). _
    End(xlUp).Row

For myCount = 2 To LastRow
```

8

```
With Worksheets("Sheet1")
    .Cells(myCount, 6).Value = _
    WorksheetFunction.Average(Cells(myCount, 2), Cells(myCount, 3))
End With
Next myCount

End Sub
```

Although this works fine, the program has to look at each row of the sheet individually, get the data, do the calculation, and then place the result in the correct column. Wouldn't it be easier to grab all the data at one time, and then do the calculations and place the result back on the sheet? Also, with the slower version of the code, you need to know which columns on the sheet to manipulate, which in this example are Columns 2 and 3. With an array, you need to know only what element of the array you want to manipulate.

To make arrays even more useful, instead of using an address range to fill the array, you can use a named range. With a named range in an array, it does not matter where on the sheet the range is.

For example, instead of

```
myArray = Range("B2:C12")
```

use this:

```
myArray = Range("myData")
```

With the slow method, you need to know where myData is so that you can return the correct columns. However, with an array all you need to know is that you want the first and second columns.

NOTE You can make your array even faster! Technically, if you place a column of data into an array, it is a two-dimensional array. If you want to process it, you must process the row and column.

However, you can process the column more quickly if it is just a single row, as long as it does not exceed 16,384 columns. To do this, use the Transpose function to turn the one column into one row (see Figure 8.6):

```
Sub TransposeArray()
Dim myArray As Variant
'place myTran, a single column of data, into array
myArray = WorksheetFunction.Transpose(Range("myTran"))

'return the 5th element of the array
MsgBox "The 5th element of the Transposed Array is: " & myArray(5)
End Sub
```

Figure 8.6
Use the `Transpose`
function to turn a two-
dimensional array into a
one-dimensional array.

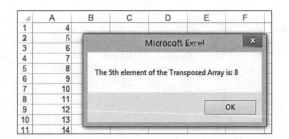

Use Dynamic Arrays

You cannot always know how big of an array you will need. You could create an array based on how big it could ever need to be, but that's a waste of memory—and what if it turns out it needs to be even bigger? To avoid this problem, you can use a *dynamic array*.

A dynamic array is an array that does not have a set size. In other words, you declare the array but leave the parentheses empty:

```
Dim myArray ()
```

Later, as the program needs to use the array, `Redim` is used to set the size of the array. The following program, which returns the names of all the sheets in the workbook, first creates a boundless array, and then it sets the upper bound after it knows how many sheets are in the workbook:

```
Option Base 1
Sub MySheets()
Dim myArray() As String
Dim myCount As Integer, NumShts As Integer

NumShts = ActiveWorkbook.Worksheets.Count

' Size the array
ReDim myArray(1 To NumShts)

For myCount = 1 To NumShts
    myArray(myCount) = ActiveWorkbook.Sheets(myCount).Name
Next myCount

End Sub
```

Using `Redim` reinitializes the array. Therefore, if you were to use it many times such as in a loop, you would lose all the data it holds. To prevent this from happening, you need to use `Preserve`. The `Preserve` keyword enables you to resize the last array dimension, but you cannot use it to change the number of dimensions.

The following example looks for all the Excel files in a directory and puts the results in an array. Because you do not know how many files there will be until you actually look at them, you can't size the array before the program is run:

```
Sub XLFiles()
Dim FName As String
Dim arNames() As String
Dim myCount As Integer

FName = Dir("C:\Excel VBA 2013 by Jelen & Syrstad\*.xls*")
Do Until FName = ""
    myCount = myCount + 1
    ReDim Preserve arNames(1 To myCount)
    arNames(myCount) = FName
    FName = Dir
Loop

End Sub
```

> **NOTE** Using `Preserve` with large amounts of data in a loop can slow down the program. If possible, use code to figure out the maximum size of the array.

Passing an Array

Just like strings, integers, and other variables, arrays can be passed into other procedures. This makes for more efficient and easier-to-read code. The following sub, `PassAnArray`, passes the array, `myArray`, into the function `RegionSales`. The data in the array is summed for the specified region and the result is returned to the sub. Refer to Chapter 14, "User-Defined Functions," to learn more about using functions.

```
Sub PassAnArray()
Dim myArray() As Variant
Dim myRegion As String

myArray = Range("mySalesData") 'named range containing all the data
myRegion = InputBox("Enter Region - Central, East, West")
MsgBox myRegion & " Sales are: " & Format(RegionSales(myArray, _
    myRegion), "$#,#00.00")

End Sub

Function RegionSales(ByRef BigArray As Variant, sRegion As String) As Long
Dim myCount As Integer

RegionSales = 0
For myCount = LBound(BigArray) To UBound(BigArray)
'The regions are listed in column 1 of the data, hence the 1st column of the array
    If BigArray(myCount, 1) = sRegion Then
'The data to sum is the 6th column in the data
        RegionSales = BigArray(myCount, 6) + RegionSales
    End If
Next myCount

End Function
```

Next Steps

Arrays are a type of variable used for holding more than one piece of data. In Chapter 9, "Creating Classes, Records, and Collections," you'll learn about the powerful technique of setting up your own Class module. With this technique, you can set up your own object with its own methods and properties.

8

Creating Classes, Records, and Collections

Excel already has many objects available, but there are times when a custom object would be better suited for the job at hand. You can create custom objects that you use in the same way as Excel's built-in objects. These special objects are created in *class modules*.

Class modules are used to create custom objects with custom properties and methods. They can trap application events, embedded chart events, ActiveX control events, and more.

9

Inserting a Class Module

From the VB Editor, select Insert, Class Module. A new module, Class1, is added to the VBAProject workbook and is visible in the Project Explorer window (see Figure 9.1). Two things to keep in mind concerning class modules:

- Each custom object must have its own module. (Event trapping can share a module.)
- The class module should be renamed to reflect the custom object.

Figure 9.1
Custom objects are created in class modules.

Trapping Application and Embedded Chart Events

Chapter 7, "Event Programming," showed you how certain actions in workbooks, worksheets, and nonembedded charts could be trapped and used to activate code. Briefly, it reviewed how to set up a class module to trap application and chart events. The following text goes into more detail about what was shown in that chapter.

Application Events

The `Workbook_BeforePrint` event is triggered when the workbook in which it resides is printed. If you want to run the same code in every workbook available, you have to copy the code to each workbook. Alternatively, you can use an application event, `Workbook_BeforePrint`, which is triggered when any workbook is printed.

The application events already exist, but a class module must be set up first so that they can be seen. To create a class module, follow these steps:

1. Insert a class module into the project. Rename it to something that makes sense to you such as `clsAppEvents`. Select View, Properties Window to rename a module.

2. Enter the following into the class module:

```
Public WithEvents xlApp As Application
```

The name of the variable, `xlApp`, can be any variable name. The `WithEvents` keyword exposes the events associated with the `Application` object.

3. `xlApp` is now available from that class module's Object drop-down list. Select it from the drop-down, and then click the Procedure drop-down menu to its right to view the list of events that are available for the `xlApp`'s object type (`Application`), as shown in Figure 9.2.

→ For a review of the various application events, **see** the "Application-Level Events" section in Chapter 7, **p. 140**.

Figure 9.2
Events are made available after the object is created.

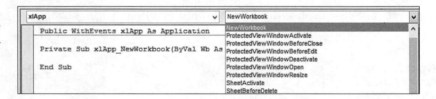

Any of the events listed can be captured, just as workbook and worksheet events were captured in an earlier chapter. The following example uses the `NewWorkbook` event to set up footer information automatically. This code is placed in the class module, below the `xlApp` declaration line you just added:

```
Private Sub xlApp_NewWorkbook(ByVal Wb As Workbook)
Dim wks As Worksheet

With Wb
```

```
    For Each wks In .Worksheets
        wks.PageSetup.LeftFooter = "Created by: " & .Application.UserName
        wks.PageSetup.RightFooter = Now
    Next wks
End With

End Sub
```

The procedure placed in a class module does not run automatically as events in workbook or worksheet modules would. An instance of the class module must be created and the Application object assigned to the xlApp property. After that is complete, the TrapAppEvent procedure needs to run. As long as the procedure is running, the footer is created on each sheet every time a new workbook is added. Place the following in a standard module:

```
Public myAppEvent As New clsAppEvents

Sub TrapAppEvent()

Set myAppEvent.xlApp = Application

End Sub
```

> **NOTE** The application event trapping can be terminated by any action that resets the module level or public variables including editing code in the VB Editor. To restart, run the procedure that creates the object (TrapAppEvent).

In this example, the public myAppEvent declaration was placed in a standard module with the TrapAppEvent procedure. To automate the running of the entire event trapping, all the modules could be transferred to the Personal.xlsb and the procedure transferred to a Workbook_Open event. In any case, the Public declaration of myAppEvent *must* remain in a standard module so that it can be shared among modules.

Embedded Chart Events

Preparing to trap embedded chart events is the same as preparing for trapping application events. Create a class module, insert the public declaration for a chart type, create a procedure for the desired event, and then add a standard module procedure to initiate the trapping. The same class module used for the application event can be used for the embedded chart event.

Place the following line in the declaration section of the class module. The available chart events are now viewable (see Figure 9.3):

```
Public WithEvents xlChart As Chart
```

➜ For a review of the various charts events, **see** "Chart Sheet Events" in Chapter 7 on **p. 137**.

Figure 9.3
The chart events are available after the chart type variable has been declared.

Let's create a program to change the chart scale. Three events are set up. The primary event, MouseDown, changes the chart scale with a right-click or double-click. Because these actions also have actions associated with them, you need two more events: BeforeRightClick and BeforeDoubleClick, which prevent the usual action from taking place.

The following BeforeDoubleClick event prevents the normal result of a double-click from taking place:

```
Private Sub xlChart_BeforeDoubleClick(ByVal ElementID As Long, _
    ByVal Arg1 As Long, ByVal Arg2 As Long, Cancel As Boolean)
Cancel = True
End Sub
```

The following BeforeRightClick event prevents the normal result of a right-click from taking place:

```
Private Sub xlChart_BeforeRightClick(Cancel As Boolean)
Cancel = True
End Sub
```

Now that the normal actions of the double-click and right-click have been controlled, ChartMouseDown rewrites the actions initiated by a right-click and double-click:

```
Private Sub xlChart_MouseDown(ByVal Button As Long, ByVal Shift As Long, _
    ByVal x As Long, ByVal y As Long)
    If Button = 1 Then 'left mouse button
        xlChart.Axes(xlValue).MaximumScale = _
    xlChart.Axes(xlValue).MaximumScale - 50
    End If

    If Button = 2 Then 'right mouse button
        xlChart.Axes(xlValue).MaximumScale = _
    xlChart.Axes(xlValue).MaximumScale + 50
    End If

End Sub
```

After the events are set in the class module, all that is left to do is declare the variable in a standard module, as follows:

```
Public myChartEvent As New clsEvents
```

Then create a procedure that captures the events on the embedded chart:

```
Sub TrapChartEvent()

Set myChartEvent.xlChart = Worksheets("EmbedChart"). _
    ChartObjects("Chart 2").Chart

End Sub
```

NOTE The `BeforeDoubleClick` and `BeforeRightClick` events are triggered only when the user clicks the plot area itself. The area around the plot area does not trigger the events. However, the `MouseDown` event is triggered from anywhere on the chart.

Creating a Custom Object

Class modules are useful for trapping events, but they are also valuable because they can be used to create custom objects. When you are creating a custom object, the class module becomes a template of the object's properties and methods. To help you understand this better, the following example creates an employee object to track employee name, ID, hourly wage rate, and hours worked.

Insert a class module and rename it to `clsEmployee`. The `clsEmployee` object has four properties:

- `EmpName`—Employee name
- `EmpID`—Employee ID
- `EmpRate`—Hourly wage rate
- `EmpWeeklyHrs`—Hours worked

Properties are variables that you can declare `Private` or `Public`. If they are declared `Private`, you can access the properties only within the module in which you declared them. These properties need to be accessible to the standard module, so they will be declared `Public`. Place the following lines at the top of the class module:

```
Public EmpName As String
Public EmpID As String
Public EmpRate As Double
Public EmpWeeklyHrs As Double
```

Methods are actions that the object can take. In the class module, these actions take shape as procedures and functions. The following code creates a method, `EmpWeeklyPay()`, for the object that calculates weekly pay:

```
Public Function EmpWeeklyPay() As Double
EmpWeeklyPay = EmpRate * EmpWeeklyHrs
End Function
```

The object is now complete. It has four properties and one method. The next step is using the object in an actual program.

Using a Custom Object

After a custom object is properly configured in a class module, it can be referenced from another module. Declare a variable as the custom object type in the declarations section:

```
Dim Employee As clsEmployee
```

In the procedure, set the variable to be a New object:

```
Set Employee = New clsEmployee
```

Continue entering the rest of the procedure. As you refer to the properties and method of the custom object, a screen tip appears, just as with Excel's standard objects (see Figure 9.4).

Figure 9.4
The properties and method of the custom object are just as easily accessible as they are for standard objects.

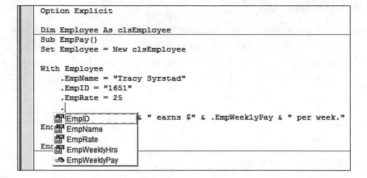

```
Dim Employee As clsEmployee

Sub EmpPay()

Set Employee = New clsEmployee

With Employee
    .EmpName = "Tracy Syrstad"
    .EmpID = "1651"
    .EmpRate = 25
    .EmpWeeklyHrs = 40
    MsgBox .EmpName & " earns $" & .EmpWeeklyPay & " per week."
End With

End Sub
```

The procedure declares an object Employee as a new instance of clsEmployee. It then assigns values to the four properties of the object and generates a message box displaying the employee name and weekly pay (see Figure 9.5). The object's method, EmpWeeklyPay, is used to generate the displayed pay.

Figure 9.5
Create custom objects to make code more efficient.

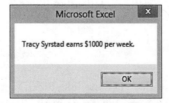

Using `Property Let` and `Property Get` to Control How Users Utilize Custom Objects

As declared in the earlier example, public variables have read/write properties. When they are used in a program, the values of the variables can be retrieved or changed. To assign read/write limitations, use `Property Let` and `Property Get` procedures.

`Property Let` procedures give you control of how properties can be assigned values. `Property Get` procedures give you control of how the properties are accessed. In the custom object example, there is a public variable for weekly hours. This variable is used in a method for calculating pay for the week but doesn't consider overtime pay. Variables for normal hours and overtime hours are needed, but the variables must be read-only.

To accomplish this, the class module must be reconstructed. It needs two new properties, `EmpNormalHrs` and `EmpOverTimeHrs`. However, because these two properties are to be confined to read-only, they are not declared as variables. `Property Get` procedures are used to create them.

If `EmpNormalHrs` and `EmpOverTimeHrs` are going to be read-only, they must have values assigned somehow. Their values are a calculation of the `EmpWeeklyHrs`. Because `EmpWeeklyHrs` will be used to set the property values of these two object properties, it can no longer be a public variable. There are two private variables, `NormalHrs` and `OverHrs`, which are used within the confines of the class module:

```
Public EmpName As String
Public EmpID As String
Public EmpRate As Double

Private NormalHrs As Double
Private OverHrs As Double
```

A `Property Let` procedure is created for `EmpWeeklyHrs` to break down the hours into normal and overtime hours:

```
Property Let EmpWeeklyHrs(Hrs As Double)

NormalHrs = WorksheetFunction.Min(40, Hrs)
OverHrs = WorksheetFunction.Max(0, Hrs - 40)

End Property
```

The `Property Get EmpWeeklyHrs` totals these hours and returns a value to this property. Without it, a value cannot be retrieved from `EmpWeeklyHrs`:

```
Property Get EmpWeeklyHrs() As Double

EmpWeeklyHrs = NormalHrs + OverHrs

End Property
```

`Property Get` procedures are created for `EmpNormalHrs` and `EmpOverTimeHrs` to set their values. If you use `Property Get` procedures only, the values of these two properties are read-only. They can be assigned values only through the `EmpWeeklyHrs` property:

9

```
Property Get EmpNormalHrs() As Double

EmpNormalHrs = NormalHrs

End Property


Property Get EmpOverTimeHrs() As Double

EmpOverTimeHrs = OverHrs

End Property
```

Finally, the method EmpWeeklyPay is updated to reflect the changes in the properties and goal:

```
Public Function EmpWeeklyPay() As Double

EmpWeeklyPay = (EmpNormalHrs * EmpRate) + (EmpOverTimeHrs * EmpRate * 1.5)

End Function
```

Update the procedure in the standard module to take advantage of the changes in the class module. Figure 9.6 shows the new message box resulting from this updated procedure:

```
Sub EmpPayOverTime()
Dim Employee As New clsEmployee

With Employee
    .EmpName = "Tracy Syrstad"
    .EmpID = "1651"
    .EmpRate = 25
    .EmpWeeklyHrs = 45
    MsgBox .EmpName & Chr(10) & Chr(9) & _
    "Normal Hours: " & .EmpNormalHrs & Chr(10) & Chr(9) & _
    "OverTime Hours: " & .EmpOverTimeHrs & Chr(10) & Chr(9) & _
    "Weekly Pay : $" & .EmpWeeklyPay
End With

End Sub
```

Figure 9.6
Use Property Let and Property Get procedures for more control over custom object properties.

Using Collections to Hold Multiple Records

Up to now, you have been able to have only one record at a time of the custom object. To create more, a *collection* that allows more than a single record to exist at a time is needed. For example, `Worksheet` is a member of the `Worksheets` collection. You can add, remove, count, and refer to each worksheet in a workbook by item. This functionality is also available to your custom object.

Creating a Collection in a Standard Module

The quickest way to create a collection is to use the built-in `Collection` method. By setting up a collection in a standard module, you can access the four default collection methods: `Add`, `Remove`, `Count`, and `Item`.

The following example reads a list of employees from a sheet and into an array. It then processes the array, supplying each property of the object with a value, and places each record in the collection:

```
Sub EmpPayCollection()
Dim colEmployees As New Collection
Dim recEmployee As New clsEmployee
Dim LastRow As Integer, myCount As Integer
Dim EmpArray As Variant

LastRow = ActiveSheet.Cells(ActiveSheet.Rows.Count, 1).End(xlUp).Row
EmpArray = ActiveSheet.Range(Cells(1, 1), Cells(LastRow, 4))

For myCount = 1 To UBound(EmpArray)
    Set recEmployee = New clsEmployee
    With recEmployee
        .EmpName = EmpArray(myCount, 1)
        .EmpID = EmpArray(myCount, 2)
        .EmpRate = EmpArray(myCount, 3)
        .EmpWeeklyHrs = EmpArray(myCount, 4)
        colEmployees.Add recEmployee, .EmpID
    End With
Next myCount

MsgBox "Number of Employees: " & colEmployees.Count & Chr(10) & _
    "Employee(2) Name: " & colEmployees(2).EmpName
MsgBox "Tracy's Weekly Pay: $" & colEmployees("1651").EmpWeeklyPay

Set recEmployee = Nothing

End Sub
```

The collection, `colEmployees`, is declared as a new collection and the record, `recEmployee`, as a new variable of the custom object type.

After the object's properties are given values, the record, `recEmployee`, is added to the collection. The second parameter of the `Add` method applies a unique key to the record, which, in this case, is the employee ID number. This allows a specific record to be accessed quickly, as shown by the second message box (`colEmployees("1651").EmpWeeklyPay`) (see Figure 9.7).

Figure 9.7
Individual records in a collection can be easily accessed.

The unique key is an optional parameter. An error message appears if a duplicate key is entered.

Creating a Collection in a Class Module

Collections can be created in a class module. In this case, the innate methods of the collection (Add, Remove, Count, Item) are not available; they need to be created in the class module. These are the advantages of creating a collection in a class module:

- The entire code is in one module.
- You have more control over what is done with the collection.
- You can prevent access to the collection.

Insert a new class module for the collection and rename it clsEmployees. Declare a private collection to be used within the class module:

```
Private AllEmployees As New Collection
```

Add the new properties and methods required to make the collection work. The innate methods of the collection are available within the class module and can be used to create the custom methods and properties.

Insert an Add method for adding new items to the collection:

```
Public Sub Add(recEmployee As clsEmployee)

AllEmployees.Add recEmployee, recEmployee.EmpID

End Sub
```

Insert a Count property to return the number of items in the collection:

```
Public Property Get Count() As Long

Count = AllEmployees.Count

End Property
```

Insert an Items property to return the entire collection:

```
Public Property Get Items() As Collection

Set Items = AllEmployees

End Property
```

Insert an `Item` property to return a specific item from the collection:

```
Public Property Get Item(myItem As Variant) As clsEmployee

Set Item = AllEmployees(myItem)

End Property
```

Insert a `Remove` property to remove a specific item from the collection:

```
Public Sub Remove(myItem As Variant)

AllEmployees.Remove (myItem)

End Sub
```

Property `Get` is used with `Count`, `Item`, and `Items` because these are read-only properties. `Item` returns a reference to a single member of the collection, whereas `Items` returns the entire collection so that it can be used in `For Each Next` loops.

After the collection is configured in the class module, you can write a procedure in a standard module to use it:

```
Sub EmpAddCollection()
Dim colEmployees As New clsEmployees
Dim recEmployee As New clsEmployee
Dim LastRow As Integer, myCount As Integer
Dim EmpArray As Variant

LastRow = ActiveSheet.Cells(ActiveSheet.Rows.Count, 1).End(xlUp).Row
EmpArray = ActiveSheet.Range(Cells(1, 1), Cells(LastRow, 4))

For myCount = 1 To UBound(EmpArray)
    Set recEmployee = New clsEmployee
    With recEmployee
        .EmpName = EmpArray(myCount, 1)
        .EmpID = EmpArray(myCount, 2)
        .EmpRate = EmpArray(myCount, 3)
        .EmpWeeklyHrs = EmpArray(myCount, 4)
        colEmployees.Add recEmployee
    End With
Next myCount

MsgBox "Number of Employees: " & colEmployees.Count & Chr(10) & _
    "Employee(2) Name: " & colEmployees.Item(2).EmpName
MsgBox "Tracy's Weekly Pay: $" & colEmployees.Item("1651").EmpWeeklyPay

For Each recEmployee In colEmployees.Items
    recEmployee.EmpRate = recEmployee.EmpRate * 1.5
Next recEmployee

MsgBox "Tracy's Weekly Pay (after Bonus): $" & colEmployees.Item("1651"). _
    EmpWeeklyPay

Set recEmployee = Nothing

End Sub
```

This program is not that different from the one used with the standard collection, but there are a few key differences:

- Instead of declaring `colEmployees` as Collection, declare it as type `clsEmployees`, the new class module collection.

- The array and collection are filled the same way, but the way the records in the collection are referenced has changed. When a member of the collection, such as employee record 2, is referenced, the `Item` property must be used.

Compare the syntax of the message boxes in this program to the previous program. The `For Each Next` loop goes through each record in the collection and multiplies the `EmpRate` by 1.5, changing its value. The result of this "bonus" is shown in a message box similar to the one shown previously in Figure 9.7.

CASE STUDY: HELP BUTTONS

You have a complex sheet that requires a way for the user to get help. You can place the information in comment boxes, but they are not very obvious, especially to the novice Excel user. Another option is to create help buttons.

To do this, create small ActiveX labels with a question mark in each one on the worksheet. To get the button-like appearance shown in Figure 9.8, set the `SpecialEffect` property of the labels to `Raised` and darken the `BackColor`. Place one label per row. Two columns over from the button, enter the help text you want to appear when the label is clicked. Hide this help text column.

Figure 9.8
Attach help buttons to the sheet and enter help text.

◢	A	B	C	D	E	F	G
1							
2							
3		?		You can create a collection of custom help buttons.			
4							
5							
6		?		It makes it much easier for someone to update the help text			
7							
8							
9		?		And the buttons are easy to see.			
10							

Create a simple userform with a label and a Close button (see Chapter 10, "Userforms—An Introduction" for more information on userforms). Rename the form `HelpForm`, the button `CloseHelp`, and the label `HelpText`. Size the label large enough to hold the help text. Add a macro, `CloseHelp_Click` (shown below), behind the form to hide it when the button is clicked. At this point, you could program each button separately. If you have many buttons, this would be tedious. If you ever need to add more buttons, you also will have to update the code. Or you could create a class module and a collection that will automatically include all the help buttons on the sheet, now and in the future.

```
Private Sub CloseHelp_Click()
Unload Me
End Sub
```

Insert a class module named clsLabel. You need a variable, Lbl, to capture the control events:

```
Public WithEvents Lbl As MSForms.Label
```

In addition, you need a method of finding and displaying the corresponding help text:

```
Private Sub Lbl_Click()
Dim Rng As Range

Set Rng = Lbl.TopLeftCell

If Lbl.Caption = "?" Then
    HelpForm.Caption = "Label in cell " & Rng.Address(0, 0)
    HelpForm.HelpText.Caption = Rng.Offset(, 2).Value
    HelpForm.Show
End If

End Sub
```

In the ThisWorkbook module, create a Workbook_Open procedure to create a collection of the labels in the workbook:

```
Option Explicit
Option Base 1
Dim col As Collection
Sub Workbook_Open()
Dim WS As Worksheet
Dim cLbl As clsLabel
Dim OleObj As OLEObject

Set col = New Collection

For Each WS In ThisWorkbook.Worksheets
    For Each OleObj In WS.OLEObjects
        If OleObj.OLEType = xlOLEControl Then
'in case you have other controls on the sheet, include only the labels
            If TypeName(OleObj.Object) = "Label" Then
                Set cLbl = New clsLabel
                Set cLbl.Lbl = OleObj.Object
                col.Add cLbl
            End If
        End If
    Next OleObj
Next WS

End Sub
```

Run Workbook_Open to create the collection. Click a label on the worksheet. The corresponding help text appears in the help form, as shown in Figure 9.9.

Figure 9.9
Help text is only a click away.

Using User-Defined Types to Create Custom Properties

User-defined types (UDTs) provide some of the power of a custom object, but without the need of a class module. A class module allows the creation of custom properties and methods, whereas a UDT allows only custom properties. However, sometimes that is all you need.

A UDT is declared with a `Type...End Type` statement. It can be `Public` or `Private`. A name that is treated like an object is given to the UDT. Within the `Type`, individual variables are declared that become the properties of the UDT.

Within an actual procedure, a variable is defined of the custom type. When that variable is used, the properties are available, just as they are in a custom object (see Figure 9.10).

Figure 9.10
The properties of a UDT are available as they are in a custom object.

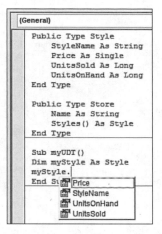

The following example uses two UDTs to summarize a report of product styles in various stores. The first UDT consists of properties for each product style:

```
Public Type Style
    StyleName As String
    Price As Single
    UnitsSold As Long
    UnitsOnHand As Long
End Type
```

The second UDT consists of the store name and an array whose type is the first UDT:

```
Public Type Store
    Name As String
    Styles() As Style
End Type
```

After the UDTs are established, the main program is written. Only a variable of the second UDT type, `Store`, is needed because that type contains the first type, `Style` (see Figure 9.11). However, all the properties of the UDTs are easily available. In addition, with the use of the UDT, the various variables are easy to remember—they are only a dot (.) away:

```
Sub UDTMain()
Dim FinalRow As Integer, ThisRow As Integer, ThisStore As Integer
Dim CurrRow As Integer, TotalDollarsSold As Integer, TotalUnitsSold As Integer
Dim TotalDollarsOnHand As Integer, TotalUnitsOnHand As Integer
Dim ThisStyle As Integer
Dim StoreName As String

ReDim Stores(0 To 0) As Store ' The UDT is declared

FinalRow = Cells(Rows.Count, 1).End(xlUp).Row

' The following For loop fills both arrays. The outer array is filled with the
' store name and an array consisting of product details.
' To accomplish this, the store name is tracked and when it changes,
' the outer array is expanded.
' The inner array for each outer array expands with each new product
For ThisRow = 2 To FinalRow
    StoreName = Range("A" & ThisRow).Value
' Checks whether this is the first entry in the outer array
    If LBound(Stores) = 0 Then
        ThisStore = 1
        ReDim Stores(1 To 1) As Store
        Stores(1).Name = StoreName
        ReDim Stores(1).Styles(0 To 0) As Style
    Else
        For ThisStore = LBound(Stores) To UBound(Stores)
            If Stores(ThisStore).Name = StoreName Then Exit For
        Next ThisStore
        If ThisStore > UBound(Stores) Then
            ReDim Preserve Stores(LBound(Stores) To UBound(Stores) + 1) As _
                Store
            Stores(ThisStore).Name = StoreName
            ReDim Stores(ThisStore).Styles(0 To 0) As Style
        End If
    End If
    With Stores(ThisStore)
        If LBound(.Styles) = 0 Then
            ReDim .Styles(1 To 1) As Style
        Else
            ReDim Preserve .Styles(LBound(.Styles) To _
        UBound(.Styles) + 1) As Style
        End If
        With .Styles(UBound(.Styles))
            .StyleName = Range("B" & ThisRow).Value
            .Price = Range("C" & ThisRow).Value
            .UnitsSold = Range("D" & ThisRow).Value
            .UnitsOnHand = Range("E" & ThisRow).Value
        End With
    End With
Next ThisRow

' Create a report on a new sheet
Sheets.Add
Range("A1:E1").Value = Array("Store Name", "Units Sold", _
    "Dollars Sold", "Units On Hand", "Dollars On Hand")
CurrRow = 2

For ThisStore = LBound(Stores) To UBound(Stores)
```

```
    With Stores(ThisStore)
        TotalDollarsSold = 0
        TotalUnitsSold = 0
        TotalDollarsOnHand = 0
        TotalUnitsOnHand = 0
' Go through the array of product styles within the array
' of stores to summarize information
        For ThisStyle = LBound(.Styles) To UBound(.Styles)
            With .Styles(ThisStyle)
                TotalDollarsSold = TotalDollarsSold + .UnitsSold * .Price
                TotalUnitsSold = TotalUnitsSold + .UnitsSold
                TotalDollarsOnHand = TotalDollarsOnHand + .UnitsOnHand * .Price
                TotalUnitsOnHand = TotalUnitsOnHand + .UnitsOnHand
            End With
        Next ThisStyle
        Range("A" & CurrRow & ":E" & CurrRow).Value = _
        Array(.Name, TotalUnitsSold, TotalDollarsSold, _
        TotalUnitsOnHand, TotalDollarsOnHand)
    End With
    CurrRow = CurrRow + 1
Next ThisStore

End Sub
```

Figure 9.11
UDTs can make a potentially confusing multivariable program easier to write.

⏴	A	B	C	D	E
1	Store	Style	Price	Units Sold	Units On Hand
2	Store A	Style C	96.87	16	45
3	Store A	Style A	38.43	7	94
4	Store A	Style B	91.24	5	18
5	Store A	Style E	19.89	0	96
6	Store A	Style D	2.45	20	66
7	Store B	Style B	92.59	4	83
8	Store B	Style A	15.75	9	66
9	Store B	Style F	13.12	2	35
10	Store B	Style G	30.86	22	37
11	Store B	Style H	37.38	21	77
12					
13	Store Name	Units Sold	Dollars Sold	Units On Hand	Dollars On Hand
14	Store A	48	2324	319	11684
15	Store B	58	2002	298	13203

The results of this program have been combined with the raw data for convenience.

Next Steps

Chapter 10, "Userforms—An Introduction," introduces the tools you can use to interact with users. You'll learn how to prompt users for information to use in your code, warn them of illegal actions, or provide them with an interface to work with other than the spreadsheet.

Userforms: An Introduction

10

User Interaction Methods

Userforms enable you to display information and allow the user to input information. InputBox and MsgBox controls are simple ways of doing this. You can use the userform controls in the VB Editor to create forms that are more complex.

This chapter covers simple user interfaces using input boxes and message boxes and the basics of creating userforms in the VB Editor.

→ To learn more about advanced userform programming, **see** Chapter 22, "Advanced Userform Techniques."

Input Boxes

The InputBox function is used to create a basic interface element that requests input from the user before the program can continue. You can configure the prompt, the title for the window, a default value, the window position, and user help files. The only two buttons provided are the OK and Cancel buttons. The returned value is a string.

The following code asks the user for the number of months to be averaged. Figure 10.1 shows the resulting InputBox.

```
AveMos = InputBox(Prompt:="Enter the number " & _
" of months to average", Title:="Enter Months", _
Default:="3")
```

Figure 10.1
A simple but effective input box.

Message Boxes

The MsgBox function creates a message box that displays information and waits for the user to click a button before continuing. Whereas InputBox has only OK and Cancel buttons, the MsgBox function enables you to choose from several configurations of buttons, including Yes, No, OK, and Cancel. You can also configure the prompt, the window title, and help files. The following code produces a prompt to find out whether the user wants to continue. A Select Case statement is then used to continue the program with the appropriate action. Figure 10.2 shows the resulting customized message box.

```
myTitle = "Sample Message"
MyMsg = "Do you want to Continue?"
Response = MsgBox(myMsg, vbExclamation + vbYesNoCancel, myTitle)
Select Case Response
    Case Is = vbYes
        ActiveWorkbook.Close SaveChanges:=False

    Case Is = vbNo
        ActiveWorkbook.Close SaveChanges:=True
    Case Is = vbCancel
        Exit Sub
End Select
```

Figure 10.2
The MsgBox function is used to display information and obtain a basic response from the user.

Creating a Userform

Userforms combine the capabilities of InputBox and MsgBox to create a more efficient way of interacting with the user. For example, rather than have the user fill out personal information on a sheet, you can create a userform that prompts for the required data (see Figure 10.3).

Figure 10.3
Create a custom userform
to get more information
from the user.

Insert a userform in the VB Editor by selecting Insert, UserForm from the main menu. When a UserForm module is added to the Project Explorer, a blank form appears in the window where your code usually is, and the Controls toolbox appears.

You can resize the form by grabbing and dragging the handles on the right side, bottom edge, or lower-right corner of the userform. To add controls to the form, click the desired control in the toolbox and draw it on the form. You can move and resize controls at any time.

> **NOTE** By default, the toolbox displays the most common controls. To access more controls, right-click the toolbox and select Additional Controls. However, be careful; other users might not have the same additional controls as you do. If you send these users a form with a control they do not have installed, the program generates an error.

After you add a control to a form, you can change its properties from the Properties window. These properties can be set manually now or set later programmatically. If the Properties window is not visible, you can bring it up by selecting View, Properties Window. Figure 10.4 shows the Properties window for a text box.

Figure 10.4
Use the Properties
window to change the
properties of a control.

Calling and Hiding a Userform

A userform can be called from any module. `FormName.Show` causes a form for the user to pop up:

```
frm_AddEmp.Show
```

The Load method can also be used to call a userform. This allows a form to be loaded but remain hidden:

```
Load frm_AddEmp
```

To hide a userform, use the Hide method. The form is still active but is hidden from the user. However, the controls on the form can still be accessed programmatically:

```
Frm_AddEmp.Hide
```

The Unload method unloads the form from memory and removes it from the user's view, which means the form cannot be accessed by the user or programmatically:

```
Unload Me
```

> **TIP**
> Me is a keyword that can be used to refer to the userform itself. It can be used in the code of any control to refer to itself.

Programming the Userform

The code for a control goes in the Forms module. Unlike the other modules, double-clicking the Forms module opens up the form in Design view. To view the code, you can right-click either the module or the userform in Design mode and select View Code.

Userform Events

Just like a worksheet, a userform has events triggered by actions. After the userform has been added to the project, the events are available in the Properties drop-down list at the top right of the code window (see Figure 10.5); to access them, select UserForm from the Objects drop-down on the left.

Figure 10.5
Various events for the userform can be selected from the drop-down list at the top of the code window.

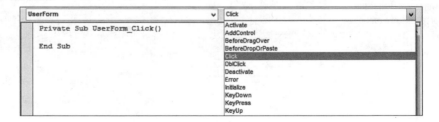

The available events for userforms are described in Table 10.1.

Table 10.1   The Events for Userforms

Event	Description
Activate	Occurs when a userform is shown from being either loaded or shown. This event is triggered after the Initialize event.
AddControl	Occurs when a control is added to a userform at runtime. Does not run at design time or upon userform initialization.
BeforeDragOver	Occurs while the user does a drag and drop onto the userform.
BeforeDropOrPaste	Occurs right before the user is about to drop or paste data into the userform.
Click	Occurs when the user clicks the userform with the mouse.
DblClick	Occurs when the user double-clicks the userform with the mouse. If a click event is also in use, the double-click event will not work.
Deactivate	Occurs when a userform is deactivated.
Error	Occurs when the userform runs into an error and cannot return the error information.
Initialize	Occurs when the userform is first loaded, before the Activate event. If you hide and then show a form, Initialize will not trigger.
KeyDown	Occurs when the user presses a key on the keyboard.
KeyPress	Occurs when the user presses an ANSI key. An ANSI key is a typable character such as the letter *A*. An example of a nontypable character is the Tab key.
KeyUp	Occurs when the user releases a key on the keyboard.
Layout	Occurs when the control changes size.
MouseDown	Occurs when the user presses the mouse button within the borders of the userform.
MouseMove	Occurs when the user moves the mouse within the borders of the userform.
MouseUp	Occurs when the user releases the mouse button within the borders of the userform.
QueryClose	Occurs before a userform closes. It allows you to recognize the method used to close a form and have code respond accordingly.
RemoveControl	Occurs when a control is deleted from within the userform.
Resize	Occurs when the userform is resized.
Scroll	Occurs when a visible scrollbar box is repositioned.
Terminate	Occurs after the userform has been unloaded. This is triggered after QueryClose.
Zoom	Occurs when the zoom value is changed.

10

Programming Controls

To program a control, highlight the control and select View, Code. The footer, header, and default action for the control are entered in the programming field automatically. To see the other actions that are available for a control, select the control from the Object drop-down and view the actions in the Properties drop-down, as shown in Figure 10.6.

Figure 10.6
You can select various actions for a control from the VB Editor drop-downs.

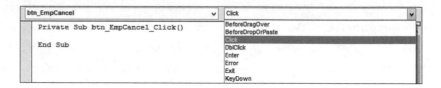

10

The controls are objects, like ActiveWorkbook. They have properties and methods, dependent on the type of control. Most of the programming for the controls is done in the form's module. However, if another module needs to refer to a control, the parent, which is the form, needs to be included with the object. Here's how this is done:

```
Private Sub btn_EmpCancel_Click()
Unload Me
End Sub
```

The preceding code can be broken down into three sections:

- btn_EmpCancel—Name given to the control
- Click—Action of the control
- Unload Me—Code behind the control, which, in this case, is unloading the form

> **TIP**
> Change the (Name) property in the control's Properties window to rename a control from the default assigned by the editor.

CASE STUDY: BUG FIX WHEN ADDING CONTROLS TO AN EXISTING FORM

If you have been using a userform for some time and later try to add a new control, you might find that Excel seems to get confused about the control. You will see that the control is added to the form, but when you right-click the control and select View Code, the code module does not seem to acknowledge that the control exists. The control name will not be available in the left drop-down at the top of the code module.

To work around this situation, follow these steps:

1. Add all the controls you need to add to the existing userform.
2. In the Project Explorer, right-click the userform and select Export File. Select Save to save the file in the default location.

3. In the Project Explorer, right-click the userform and select Remove. Because you just exported the userform, click No to the question about exporting.

4. Right-click anywhere in the Project Explorer and select Import File. Select the filename that you saved in step 2.

The new controls are now available in the code pane of the userform.

Using Basic Form Controls

Each control has different events associated with it, which enables you to code what happens based on the user's actions. A table reviewing the control events is available at the end of each of the sections that follow.

   Using Labels, Text Boxes, and Command Buttons

The basic form shown in Figure 10.7 consists of labels, text boxes, and command buttons. It is a simple yet effective method of requesting information from the user. After the text boxes have been filled in, the user clicks OK, and your code adds the information to a sheet (see Figure 10.8), as shown in the following code.

Figure 10.7
A simple form to collect information from the user.

Figure 10.8
The information is added to the sheet.

⯅	A	B	C
1	Add	View	
2	Name	Position	Hire Date
3	Tracy Syrstad	Project Consultant	20-Jul-03
4	Cort Chilldon_Hoff	CEO	6-Aug-03
5	Bill Jelen	Owner	1-Sep-00
6			

```
Private Sub btn_EmpOK_Click()
Dim LastRow As Long
LastRow = Worksheets("Employee").Cells(Worksheets("Employee").Rows.Count, 1) _
.End(xlUp).Row + 1
Cells(LastRow, 1).Value = tb_EmpName.Value
Cells(LastRow, 2).Value = tb_EmpPosition.Value
Cells(LastRow, 3).Value = tb_EmpHireDate.Value
End Sub
```

With a change in the code shown in the following sample, the same form design can be used to retrieve information. The following code retrieves the position and hire date after the employee's name is entered:

```
Private Sub btn_EmpOK_Click()
Dim EmpFound As Range
With Range("EmpList") 'a named range on a sheet listing the employee names
    Set EmpFound = .Find(tb_EmpName.Value)
    If EmpFound Is Nothing Then
        MsgBox "Employee not found!"
        tb_EmpName.Value = ""

    Else
        With Range(EmpFound.Address)
            tb_EmpPosition = .Offset(0, 1)
            tb_HireDate = .Offset(0, 2)
        End With
    End If
End With
Set EmpFound = Nothing
End Sub
```

The available events for Label, TextBox, and CommandButton controls are described in Table 10.2.

Table 10.2   The Events for Label, TextBox, **and** CommandButton **Controls**

Event	Description
AfterUpdate[2]	Occurs after the control's data has been changed by the user.
BeforeDragOver	Occurs while the user drags and drops data onto the control.
BeforeDropOrPaste	Occurs right before the user is about to drop or paste data into the control.
BeforeUpdate[2]	Occurs before the data in the control is changed.
Change[2]	Occurs when the value of the control is changed.
Click[1]	Occurs when the user clicks the control with the mouse.
DblClick	Occurs when the user double-clicks the control with the mouse.
DropButtonClick[2]	Occurs when the user presses F4 on the keyboard. This is similar to the drop-down control on the combo box, but there is no drop-down on a text box.
Enter[3]	Occurs right before the control receives the focus from another control on the same userform.
Error	Occurs when the control runs into an error and cannot return the error information.
Exit[3]	Occurs right after the control loses focus to another control on the same userform.
KeyDown[3]	Occurs when the user presses a key on the keyboard.
KeyPress[3]	Occurs when the user presses an ANSI key. An ANSI key is a typable character such as the letter *A*. An example of a nontypable character is the Tab key.
KeyUp[3]	Occurs when the user releases a key on the keyboard.

Event	Description
MouseDown	Occurs when the user presses the mouse button within the borders of the control.
MouseMove	Occurs when the user moves the mouse within the borders of the control.
MouseUp	Occurs when the user releases the mouse button within the borders of the control.

[1] Label *and* CommandButton *controls*

[2] TextBox *control only*

[3] TextBox *and* CommandButton *controls*

Deciding Whether to Use List Boxes or Combo Boxes in Forms

You can let users type in an employee name to search for, but what if they misspell the name? You need a way to make sure that the name is typed correctly. Which do you use: a list box or a combo box?

■ A list box displays a list of values from which the user can choose.

■ A combo box displays a list of values from which the user can choose and allows the user to enter a new value.

In this case, when you want to limit user options, you should use a list box to list the employee names, as shown in Figure 10.9.

Figure 10.9
Use a list box to control user input.

In the RowSource property of the list box, enter the range from which the control should draw its data. Use a dynamic named range to keep the list updated if employees are added, as shown in the following code:

```
Private Sub btn_EmpOK_Click()
Dim EmpFound As Range
With Range("EmpList")
    Set EmpFound = .Find(lb_EmpName.Value)
    If EmpFound Is Nothing Then
```

```
            MsgBox ("Employee not found!")
            lb_EmpName.Value = ""
            Exit Sub
        Else
            With Range(EmpFound.Address)
                tb_EmpPosition = .Offset(0, 1)
                tb_HireDate = .Offset(0, 2)
            End With
        End If
    End With
End Sub
```

Using the `MultiSelect` Property of a List Box

List boxes have a `MultiSelect` property, which enables the user to select multiple items from the choices in the list box, as shown in Figure 10.10:

- `fmMultiSelectSingle`—The default setting allows only a single item selection at a time.

- `fmMultiSelectMulti`—This allows an item to be deselected when it is clicked again; multiple items can also be selected.

- `fmMultiSelectExtended`—This allows the Ctrl and Shift keys to be used to select multiple items.

Figure 10.10
`MultiSelect` enables the user to select multiple items from a list box.

If multiple items are selected, the `Value` property cannot be used to retrieve the items. Instead, check to see whether the item is selected, and then manipulate it as needed using the following code:

```
Private Sub btn_EmpOK_Click()
Dim LastRow As Long, i As Integer
LastRow = Worksheets("Sheet2").Cells(Worksheets("Sheet2").Rows.Count, 1) _
.End(xlUp).Row + 1
Cells(LastRow, 1).Value = tb_EmpName.Value
'check the selection status of the items in the ListBox
For i = 0 To lb_EmpPosition.ListCount - 1
'if the item is selected, add it to the sheet
    If lb_EmpPosition.Selected(i) = True Then
        Cells(LastRow, 2).Value = Cells(LastRow, 2).Value & _
        lb_EmpPosition.List(i) & ","
    End If
Next i
```

```
Cells(LastRow, 2).Value = Left(Cells(LastRow, 2).Value, _
Len(Cells(LastRow, 2).Value) - 1) 'remove last comma from string
Cells(LastRow, 3).Value = tb_HireDate.Value
End Sub
```

The items in a list box start counting at zero. For this reason, if you use the ListCount property, you must subtract one from the result:

```
For i = 0 To lb_EmpPosition.ListCount - 1
```

The available events for ListBox controls and ComboBox controls are described in Table 10.3.

Table 10.3   Events for ListBox **and** ComboBox **Controls**

Event	Description
AfterUpdate	Occurs after the control's data has been changed by the user.
BeforeDragOver	Occurs while the user drags and drops data onto the control.
BeforeDropOrPaste	Occurs right before the user is about to drop or paste data into the control.
BeforeUpdate	Occurs before the data in the control is changed.
Change	Occurs when the value of the control is changed.
Click	Occurs when the user selects a value from the list box or combo box.
DblClick	Occurs when the user double-clicks the control with the mouse.
DropButtonClick[1]	Occurs when the drop-down list appears after the user clicks the drop-down arrow of the combo box or presses F4 on the keyboard.
Enter	Occurs right before the control receives the focus from another control on the same userform.
Error	Occurs when the control runs into an error and can't return the error information.
Exit	Occurs right after the control loses focus to another control on the same userform.
KeyDown	Occurs when the user presses a key on the keyboard.
KeyPress	Occurs when the user presses an ANSI key. An ANSI key is a typable character such as the letter A. An example of a nontypable character is the Tab key.
KeyUp	Occurs when the user releases a key on the keyboard.
MouseDown	Occurs when the user presses the mouse button within the borders of the control.
MouseMove	Occurs when the user moves the mouse within the borders of the control.
MouseUp	Occurs when the user releases the mouse button within the borders of the control.

[1] ComboBox *control only*

10

Adding Option Buttons to a Userform

Option buttons are similar to check boxes in that they can be used to make a selection. However, unlike check boxes, option buttons can be configured to allow only one selection out of a group.

Using the Frame tool, draw a frame to separate the next set of controls from the other controls on the userform. The frame is used to group option buttons together, as shown in Figure 10.11.

Figure 10.11
Use a frame to group option buttons together.

Option buttons have a `GroupName` property. If you assign the same group name, Buildings, to a set of option buttons, you force them to act collectively, as a toggle, so that only one button in the set can be selected. Selecting an option button automatically deselects the other buttons in the same group or frame. To prevent this behavior, either leave the `GroupName` property blank or enter another name.

> **NOTE**
> For users who prefer to select the option button's label rather than the button itself, create a separate label and add code to the label to trigger the option button.
>
> ```
> Private Sub Lbl_Bldg1_Click()
> Obtn_Bldg1.Value = True
> End Sub
> ```

The available events for `OptionButton` controls and `Frame` controls are described in Table 10.4.

Table 10.4   Events for OptionButton **and** Frame **Controls**

Event	Description
AfterUpdate[1]	Occurs after the control's data has been changed by the user.
AddControl[2]	Occurs when a control is added to a frame on a form at runtime. Does not run at design time or upon userform initialization.
BeforeDragOver	Occurs while the user does a drag and drop onto the control.
BeforeDropOrPaste	Occurs right before the user is about to drop or paste data into the control.
BeforeUpdate[1]	Occurs before the data in the control is changed.
Change[1]	Occurs when the value of the control is changed.
Click	Occurs when the user clicks the control with the mouse.
DblClick	Occurs when the user double-clicks the control with the mouse.
Enter	Occurs right before the control receives the focus from another control on the same userform.
Error	Occurs when the control runs into an error and cannot return the error information.
Exit	Occurs right after the control loses focus to another control on the same userform.
KeyDown	Occurs when the user presses a key on the keyboard.
KeyPress	Occurs when the user presses an ANSI key. An ANSI key is a typable character such as the letter *A*. An example of a nontypable character is the Tab key.
KeyUp	Occurs when the user releases a key on the keyboard.
Layout[2]	Occurs when the frame changes size.
MouseDown	Occurs when the user presses the mouse button within the borders of the control.
MouseMove	Occurs when the user moves the mouse within the borders of the control.
MouseUp	Occurs when the user releases the mouse button within the borders of the control.
RemoveControl[2]	Occurs when a control is deleted from within the frame control.
Scroll[2]	Occurs when the scrollbar box, if visible, is repositioned.
Zoom[2]	Occurs when the zoom value is changed.

[1] OptionButton *control only*

[2] Frame *control only*

Adding Graphics to a Userform

A listing on a form can be even more helpful if a corresponding graphic is added to the form. The following code displays the photograph corresponding to the selected employee from the list box:

```
Private Sub lb_EmpName_Change()
Dim EmpFound As Range
With Range("EmpList")
    Set EmpFound = .Find(lb_EmpName.Value)
    If EmpFound Is Nothing Then
        MsgBox "Employee not found!"
        lb_EmpName.Value = ""
    Else
        With Range(EmpFound.Address)
            tb_EmpPosition = .Offset(0, 1)
            tb_HireDate = .Offset(0, 2)
            On Error Resume Next
            Img_Employee.Picture = LoadPicture _
    ("C:\Excel VBA 2013 by Jelen & Syrstad\" & EmpFound & ".bmp")
            On Error GoTo 0
        End With
    End If
End With
Set EmpFound = Nothing
Exit Sub
```

The available events for Graphic controls are described in Table 10.5.

Table 10.5   Events for Graphic Controls

Event	Description
BeforeDragOver	Occurs while the user drags and drops data onto the control.
BeforeDropOrPaste	Occurs right before the user is about to drop or paste data into the control.
Click	Occurs when the user clicks the image with the mouse.
DblClick	Occurs when the user double-clicks the image with the mouse.
Error	Occurs when the control runs into an error and can't return the error information.
MouseDown	Occurs when the user presses the mouse button within the borders of the image.
MouseMove	Occurs when the user moves the mouse within the borders of the image.
MouseUp	Occurs when the user releases the mouse button within the borders of the control.

Using a Spin Button on a Userform

As it is, the Hire Date field allows the user to enter the date in any format, including 1/1/1 or January 1, 2001. This possible inconsistency can create problems later if you need to use or search for dates. The solution? Force users to enter dates in a unified manner.

Spin buttons allow the user to increment/decrement through a series of numbers. In this way, the user is forced to enter numbers rather than text.

Draw a spin button for a Month entry on the form. In the Properties, set the Min to 1 for January and the Max to 12 for December. In the Value property, enter 1, the first month. Next, draw a text box next to the spin button. This text box reflects the value of the spin button. In addition, you can use labels.

```
Private Sub SpBtn_Month_Change()
tb_Month.Value = SpBtn_Month.Value
End Sub
```

Finish building the form. Use a Min of 1 and Max of 31 for Day, or a Min of 1900 and a Max of 2100 for Year:

```
Private Sub btn_EmpOK_Click()
Dim LastRow As Long, i As Integer
LastRow = Worksheets("Sheet2").Cells(Worksheets("Sheet2").Rows.Count, 1) _
.End(xlUp).Row + 1
Cells(LastRow, 1).Value = tb_EmpName.Value
For i = 0 To lb_EmpPosition.ListCount - 1
    If lb_EmpPosition.Selected(i) = True Then
        Cells(LastRow, 2).Value = Cells(LastRow, 2).Value & _
        lb_EmpPosition.List(i) & ","
    End If
Next i
'Concatenate the values from the textboxes to create the date
Cells(LastRow, 3).Value = tb_Month.Value & "/" & tb_Day.Value & _
    "/" & tb_Year.Value
Cells(LastRow, 2).Value = Left(Cells(LastRow, 2).Value, _
Len(Cells(LastRow, 2).Value) - 1) 'remove trailing comma
End Sub
```

The available events for SpinButton controls are described in Table 10.6.

Table 10.6   Events for SpinButton Controls

Event	Description
AfterUpdate	Occurs after the control's data has been changed by the user.
BeforeDragOver	Occurs while the user drags and drops data onto the control.
BeforeDropOrPaste	Occurs right before the user is about to drop or paste data into the control.
BeforeUpdate	Occurs before the data in the control is changed.
Change	Occurs when the value of the control is changed.
Enter	Occurs right before the control receives the focus from another control on the same userform.
Error	Occurs when the control runs into an error and cannot return the error information.
Exit	Occurs right after the control loses focus to another control on the same userform.
KeyDown	Occurs when the user presses a key on the keyboard.
KeyPress	Occurs when the user presses an ANSI key. An ANSI key is a typable character such as the letter *A*. An example of a nontypable character is the Tab key.

10

Event	Description
KeyUp	Occurs when the user releases a key on the keyboard.
SpinDown	Occurs when the user clicks the lower or left spin button, decreasing the value.
SpinUp	Occurs when the user clicks the upper or right spin button, increasing the value.

 ## Using the MultiPage Control to Combine Forms

The MultiPage control provides a neat way of organizing multiple forms. Instead of having one form for personal employee information and one for on-the-job information, combine the information into one multipage form, as shown in Figures 10.12 and 10.13.

Figure 10.12
Use the MultiPage control to combine multiple forms. This is the first page of the form.

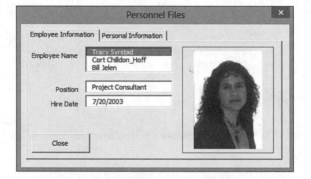

Figure 10.13
This is the second page of the form.

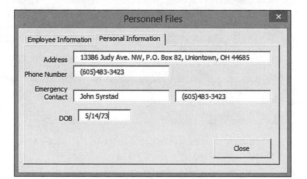

> **TIP**
> Adding multipage forms after the rest of the form has been created is not an easy task. Therefore, plan multipage forms from the beginning. If you decide later that you need a multipage form, insert a new form, draw the multipage, and copy/paste the controls from the other forms to the new form.

> **NOTE** Do not right-click in the tab area to view the MultiPage code. Instead, right-click in the MultiPage's main area to get the View Code option.

You can modify a page by right-clicking the tab of the page, which displays the following menu of options: New Page, Delete Page, Rename, and Move.

Unlike many of the other controls in which the Value property holds a user-entered or selected value, the MultiPage control uses the Value property to hold the number of the active page, starting at zero. For example, if you have a five-page form and want to activate the fourth page, do this:

```
MultiPage1.Value = 3
```

If you have a control you want all the pages to share, such as the Save, Cancel, or Close buttons, place the control on the main userform rather than on the individual pages, as shown in Figure 10.14.

Figure 10.14
Place common controls such as the Close button on the main userform.

The available events for MultiPage controls are described in Table 10.7.

Table 10.7 Events for the MultiPage **Control**

Event	Description
AddControl	Occurs when a control is added to a page of the MultiPage control. Does not run at design time or upon userform initialization.
BeforeDragOver	Occurs while the user drags and drops data onto a page of the MultiPage control.
BeforeDropOrPaste	Occurs right before the user is about to drop or paste data onto a page of the MultiPage control.
Change	Occurs when the user changes pages of a MultiPage control.
Click	Occurs when the user clicks on a page of the MultiPage control.

Event	Description
DblClick	Occurs when the user double-clicks a page of the MultiPage control with the mouse.
Enter	Occurs right before the MultiPage control receives the focus from another control on the same userform.
Error	Occurs when the MultiPage control runs into an error and cannot return the error information.
Exit	Occurs right after the MultiPage control loses focus to another control on the same userform.
KeyDown	Occurs when the user presses a key on the keyboard.
KeyPress	Occurs when the user presses an ANSI key. An ANSI key is a typable character, such as the letter *A*. An example of a nontypable character is the Tab key.
KeyUp	Occurs when the user releases a key on the keyboard.
Layout	Occurs when the MultiPage control changes size.
MouseDown	Occurs when the user presses the mouse button within the borders of the control.
MouseMove	Occurs when the user moves the mouse within the borders of the control.
MouseUp	Occurs when the user releases the mouse button within the borders of the control.
RemoveControl	Occurs when a control is removed from a page of the MultiPage control.
Scroll	Occurs when the scrollbar box, if visible, is repositioned.
Zoom	Occurs when the zoom value is changed.

Verifying Field Entry

Even if users are told to fill in all the fields, there is no way to force them to do so—except with an electronic form. As a programmer, you can ensure that all required fields are filled in by not allowing the user to continue until all requirements are met. Here's how to do this:

```
If tb_EmpName.Value = "" Then
    frm_AddEmp.Hide
    MsgBox ("Please enter an Employee Name")
    frm_AddEmp.Show
    Exit Sub
End If
```

Illegal Window Closing

The userforms created in the VB Editor are not that different from normal windows; they also include the *X* close button in the upper-right corner. Although using the button is not wrong, it can cause problems, depending on the objective of the userform. In cases like this, you might want to control what happens if the user presses the button. Use the `QueryClose` event of the userform to find out what method is used to close the form and code an appropriate action:

```
Private Sub UserForm_QueryClose(Cancel As Integer, CloseMode As Integer)
If CloseMode = vbFormControlMenu Then
    MsgBox "Please use the OK or Cancel buttons to close the form", vbCritical
    Cancel = True 'prevent the form from closing
End If
End Sub
```

After you know which method the user used to try to close the form, you can create a message box similar to the one shown in Figure 10.15 to warn the user that the method was illegal.

Figure 10.15
Control what happens when the user clicks the X button.

The `QueryClose` event can be triggered in four ways:

- `vbFormControlMenu`—The user either right-clicks on the form's title bar and selects the Close command, or clicks the X in the upper-right corner of the form.
- `vbFormCode`—The `Unload` statement is used.
- `vbAppWindows`—Windows shuts down.
- `vbAppTaskManager`—The application is shut down by the Task Manager.

Getting a Filename

One of the most common client interactions is when you need the client to specify a path and filename. Excel VBA has a built-in function to display the File Open dialog box, as shown in Figure 10.16. The client browses to and selects a file. When the client clicks the Open button, instead of opening the file Excel VBA returns the full path and filename to the code.

```
Sub SelectFile()
' Ask which file to copy
```

```
x = Application.GetOpenFilename( _
    FileFilter:="Excel Files (*.xls*), *.xls*", _
    Title:="Choose File to Copy", MultiSelect:=False)

' check in case no files were selected
If x = "False" Then Exit Sub

MsgBox "You selected " & x
End Sub
```

Figure 10.16
Use the File Open dialog box to allow the user to select a file.

The preceding code allows the client to select one file. If you want him to specify multiple files, use this code:

```
Sub ManyFiles()
Dim x As Variant

x = Application.GetOpenFilename( _
    FileFilter:="Excel Files (*.xls*), *.xls*", _
    Title:="Choose Files", MultiSelect:=True)

On Error Resume Next
If Ubound(x) > 0 Then
    For i = 1 To UBound(x)
        MsgBox "You selected " & x(i)
    Next i
ElseIf x = "False" Then Exit Sub
End If
On Error GoTo 0

End Sub
```

In a similar fashion, you can use `Application.GetSaveAsFileName` to find the path and file-name that should be used to save a file.

Next Steps

Userforms allow you to get information from the users and guide them on how they provide the program with that information. In Chapter 11, "Data Mining with Advanced Filter," you'll find out about using the Advanced Filter tools to produce reports quickly.

10

Data Mining with Advanced Filter

Read this chapter.

Although very few people use Advanced Filter in Excel, it is a workhorse in Excel VBA.

I will estimate that I end up using one of these filtering techniques as the core of a macro in 80 percent of the macros I develop for clients. Given that Advanced Filter is used in less than 1 percent of Excel sessions, this is a dramatic statistic.

So even if you hardly ever use Advanced Filter in regular Excel, you should study this chapter for powerful VBA techniques.

Replacing a Loop with AutoFilter

In Chapter 4, "Looping and Flow Control," you read about several ways to loop through a dataset to format records that match certain criteria. By using the Filter, you can achieve the same result much faster. Although Microsoft changed the name of AutoFilter to Filter in Excel 2007, the VBA code still refers to AutoFilter.

When the AutoFilter was added to Excel, the team at Microsoft added extra care and attention to the AutoFilter. Items hidden because of an AutoFilter are not simply treated like other hidden rows. AutoFilter gets special treatment. You've likely run into the frustrating situation in the past where you have applied formatting to visible rows and the formatting gets applied to the hidden rows. This is certainly a problem when you've hidden rows by clicking the #2 Group and Outline button after using the Subtotal command. This is always a problem when you manually hide rows. But it is never a problem when the rows are hidden because of the AutoFilter.

Once you've applied an AutoFilter to hide rows, any action performed on the CurrentRegion is only applied to the visible rows. You can apply bold. You can change the font to red. You can even CurrentRegion.EntireRow.Delete to delete the visible rows and the rows hidden by the filter are not impacted.

Let's say that you have a dataset as shown in Figure 11.1, and you want to perform some action on all the records that match a certain criteria, such as all Ford records.

Figure 11.1
Find all Ford records and mark them.

	A	B	C	D	E	F	G	H
1	Region	Product	Date	Customer	Quantity	Revenue	COGS	Profit
82	Central	W435	9-Sep-14	Trustworthy Flagpole Partners	600	12282	6494	5788
83	Central	R537	10-Sep-14	Magnificent Eggbeater Corporation	500	11525	5621	5904
84	East	R537	11-Sep-14	Mouthwatering Notebook Inc.	1000	20940	11242	9698
85	East	R537	12-Sep-14	Trustworthy Flagpole Partners	100	2257	1082	1175
86	Central	W435	13-Sep-14	Ford	900	20610	9742	10868
87	Central	R537	13-Sep-14	Distinctive Wax Company	700	17367	7869	9498
88	West	M556	13-Sep-14	Guarded Aerobic Corporation	700	12145	6522	5623

In Chapter 5, "R1C1-Style Formulas," you learned to write code like this, which we could use to color all the Ford records green:

```
Sub OldLoop()
    FinalRow = Cells(Rows.Count, 1).End(xlUp).Row
    For i = 2 To FinalRow
        If Cells(i, 4) = "Ford" Then
            Cells(i, 1).Resize(1, 8).Interior.Color = RGB(0,255,0)
        End If
    Next i
End Sub
```

If you needed to delete records, you had to be careful to run the loop from the bottom of the dataset to the top using code like this:

```
Sub OldLoopToDelete()
    FinalRow = Cells(Rows.Count, 1).End(xlUp).Row
    For i = FinalRow To 2 Step -1
        If Cells(i, 4) = "Ford" Then
            Rows(i).Delete
        End If
    Next i
End Sub
```

The AutoFilter method, however, enables you to isolate all the Ford records in a single line of code:

```
Range("A1").AutoFilter Field:=4, Criteria1:= "Ford"
```

After isolating the matching records, you do not need to use the VisibleCellsOnly setting to format the matching records. Instead, the following line of code will format all the matching records to be green:

```
Range("A1").CurrentRegion.Interior.Color = RGB(0,255,00)
```

> **NOTE**
> Note that the .CurrentRegion property extends the A1 reference to include the entire dataset.

There are two problems with the current two-line macro. First, the program leaves the AutoFilter drop-downs in the dataset. Second, the heading row is also formatted in green.

If you want to turn off the AutoFilter drop-downs and clear the filter, this single line of code will work:

```
Range("A1").AutoFilter
```

If you want to leave the AutoFilter drop-downs on but clear the Column D drop-down from showing Ford, you can use this line of code:

```
ActiveSheet.ShowAllData
```

The second problem is a bit more difficult. After you apply the filter and select `Range("A1").CurrentRegion`, the selection includes the headers automatically in the selection. Any formatting is also applied to the header row.

If you did not care about the first blank row below the data, you could simply add an `OFFSET(1)` to move the current region down to start in A2. This would be fine if your goal were to delete all the Ford records:

```
Sub DeleteFord()
    ' skips header, but also deletes blank row below
    Range("A1").AutoFilter Field:=4, Criteria1:="Ford"
    Range("A1").CurrentRegion.Offset(1).EntireRow.Delete
    Range("A1").AutoFilter

End Sub
```

11

> **NOTE** The OFFSET property usually requires the number of rows and the number of columns. Using `.OFFSET(-2, 5)` moves two rows up and five columns right. If you do not want to adjust by any columns, you can leave off the column parameter. Using `.OFFSET(1)` means one row down and zero columns over.

The preceding code works because you do not mind if the first blank row below the data is deleted. However, if you are applying a green format to those rows, the code will apply the green format to the blank row below the dataset, which would not look right.

If you will be doing some formatting, you can determine the height of the dataset and use `.Resize` to reduce the height of the current region while you use `OFFSET`:

```
Sub ColorFord()
    DataHt = Range("A1").CurrentRegion.Rows.Count
    Range("A1").AutoFilter Field:=4, Criteria1:="Ford"

    With Range("A1").CurrentRegion.Offset(1).Resize(DataHt - 1)
    ' No need to use VisibleCellsOnly for formatting
        .Interior.Color = RGB(0,255,0)
        .Font.Bold = True
    End With
    ' Clear the AutoFilter & remove drop-downs
    Range("A1").AutoFilter

End Sub
```

Using New AutoFilter Techniques

Excel 2007 introduced the possibility of selecting multiple items from a filter, filtering by color, filtering by icon, filtering by top 10, and filtering to virtual date filters. Excel 2010 introduces the new search box in the filter drop-down. All these new filters have VBA equivalents, although some of them are implemented in VBA using legacy filtering methods.

Selecting Multiple Items

Legacy versions of Excel allowed you to select two values, joined by AND or OR. In this case, you would specify xlAnd or xlOr as the operator:

```
Range("A1").AutoFilter Field:=4, _
    Criteria1:="Ford", _
    Operator:=xlOr, _
    Criteria2:="General Motors"
```

As the AutoFilter command became more flexible, Microsoft continued to use the same three parameters, even if they didn't quite make sense. For example, Excel lets you filter a field by asking for the top five items or the bottom 8 percent of records. To use this type of filter, specify either "5" or "8" as the Criteria1 argument, and then specify xlTop10Items, xlTop10Percent, xlBottom10Items, or xlBottom10Percent as the operator. The following code produces the top 12 revenue records:

```
Sub Top10Filter()
    ' Top 12 Revenue Records
    Range("A1").AutoFilter Field:=6, _
        Criteria1:="12", _
        Operator:=xlTop10Items
End Sub
```

There are a lot of numbers (6, 12, 10) in the code for this AutoFilter. Field 6 indicates that you are looking at the sixth column. xlTop10Items is the name of the filter, but the filter is not limited to 10 items. The criteria of 12 indicates the number of items that you want the filter to return.

Excel offers several new filter options. It continues to force these filter options to fit in the old object model where the filter command must fit in an operator and up to two criteria fields.

If you want to choose three or more items, change the operator to Operator:=xlFilterValues and specify the list of items as an array in the Criteria1 argument:

```
Range("A1").AutoFilter Field:=4, _
    Criteria1:=Array("General Motors", "Ford", "Fiat"), _
    Operator:=xlFilterValues
```

Selecting Using the Search Box

Excel 2010 introduced the new Search box in the AutoFilter drop-down. After typing something in the Search box, you can use the Select All Search Results item.

The macro recorder does a poor job of recording the Search box. The macro recorder hard-codes a list of customers who matched the search at the time you ran the macro.

Think about the Search box. It is really a shortcut way of selecting Text Filters, Contains. In addition, the Contains filter is actually a shortcut way of specifying the search string surrounded by asterisks. Therefore, to filter to all the records that contain "AT," use this:

```
Range("A1").AutoFilter, Field:=4, Criteria1:="*at*"
```

Filtering by Color

To find records that have a particular font color, use an operator of xlFilterFontColor and specify a particular RGB value as the criteria. This code finds all cells with a red font in Column F:

```
Sub FilterByFontColor()
    Range("A1").AutoFilter Field:=6, _
        Criteria1:=RGB(255, 0, 0), Operator:=xlFilterFontColor
End Sub
```

To find records that have no particular font color, use an operator of xlFilterAutomatic-FillColor and do not specify any criteria.

```
Sub FilterNoFontColor()
    Range("A1").AutoFilter Field:=6, _
        Operator:=xlFilterAutomaticFontColor
End Sub
```

To find records that have a particular fill color, use an operator of xlFilterCellColor and specify a particular RGB value as the criteria. This code finds all red cells in Column F:

```
Sub FilterByFillColor()
    Range("A1").AutoFilter Field:=6, _
        Criteria1:=RGB(255, 0, 0), Operator:=xlFilterCellColor
End Sub
```

To find records that have no fill color, use an operator of xlFilterNoFill and do not specify any criteria.

Filtering by Icon

If you are expecting the dataset to have an icon set applied, you can filter to show only records with one particular icon by using the xlFilterIcon operator.

For the criteria, you have to know which icon set has been applied and which icon within the set. The icon sets are identified using the names shown in Column A of Figure 11.2. The items range from 1 through 5. The following code filters the Revenue column to show the rows containing an upward-pointing arrow in the 5 Arrows Gray icon set:

```
Sub FilterByIcon()
    Range("A1").AutoFilter Field:=6, _
        Criteria1:=ActiveWorkbook.IconSets(xl5ArrowsGray).Item(5), _
        Operator:=xlFilterIcon
End Sub
```

To find records that have no conditional formatting icon, use an operator of xlFilterNo Icon and do not specify any criteria.

11

Figure 11.2
To search for a particular icon, you need to know the icon set from Column A and the item number from Row 1.

Selecting a Dynamic Date Range Using AutoFilters

Perhaps the most powerful feature in Excel filters is the dynamic filters. These filters enable you to choose records that are above average or with a date field to select virtual periods, such as Next Week or Last Year.

To use a dynamic filter, specify xlFilterDynamic as the operator and then use one of 34 values as Criteria1. The following code finds all dates that are in the next year:

```
Sub DynamicAutoFilter()
    Range("A1").AutoFilter Field:=3, _
        Criteria1:=xlFilterNextYear, _
        Operator:=xlFilterDynamic
End Sub
```

The following lists all the dynamic filter criteria options. Specify these values as Criteria1 in the AutoFilter method:

- **Criteria for values**—Use xlFilterAboveAverage or xlFilterBelowAverage to find all the rows that are above or below average. Note that in Lake Wobegon, using xlFilter-BelowAverage will likely return no records.

- **Criteria for future periods**—Use xlFilterTomorrow, xlFilterNextWeek, xlFil-terNextMonth, xlFilterNextQuarter, or xlFilterNextYear to find rows that fall in a certain future period. Note that "next week" starts on Sunday and ends on Saturday.

- **Criteria for current periods**—Use xlFilterToday, xlFilterThisWeek, xlFilterThis-Month, xlFilterThisQuarter, or xlFilterThisYear to find rows that fall within the current period. Excel will use the system clock to find the current day.

- **Criteria for past periods**—Use xlFilterYesterday, xlFilterLastWeek, xlFilterLast-Month, xlFilterLastQuarter, xlFilterLastYear, or xlFilterYearToDate to find rows that fall within a previous period.

- **Criteria for specific quarters**—Use xlFilterDatesInPeriodQuarter1, xlFilter DatesInPeriodQuarter2, xlFilterDatesInPeriodQuarter3, or xlFilterDatesInPeriod- Quarter4 to filter to rows that fall within a specific quarter. Note that these filters do not differentiate based on a year. If you ask for quarter 1, you might get records from this January, last February, and next March.

- **Criteria for specific months**—Use xlFilterDatesInPeriodJanuary through xlFilter- DatesInPeriodDecember to filter to records that fall during a certain month. Like the quarters, the filter does not filter to any particular year.

Unfortunately, you cannot combine criteria. You might think that you can specify xlFilter- DatesInPeriodJanuary as Criteria1 and xlFilterDatesNextYear as Criteria2. Even though this is a brilliant thought, Microsoft does not support this syntax (yet).

Selecting Visible Cells Only

After you apply a filter, most commands operate only on the visible rows in the selection. If you need to delete the records, format the records, or apply a conditional format to the records, you can simply refer to the .CurrentRegion of the first heading cell and perform the command.

However, if you have a dataset in which the rows have been hidden using the Hide Rows command, any formatting applied to the .CurrentRegion will apply to the hidden rows, too. In these cases, you should use the Visible Cells Only option of the Go To Special dialog, as shown in Figure 11.3.

11

Figure 11.3
If rows have been manually hidden, use Visible Cells Only in the Go To Special dialog.

To use Visible Cells Only in code, use the SpecialCells property:

```
Range("A1").CurrentRegion.SpecialCells(xlCellTypeVisible)
```

CASE STUDY: GO TO SPECIAL INSTEAD OF LOOPING

The Go To Special dialog also plays a role in the following case study.

At a Data Analyst Boot Camp, one of the attendees had a macro that was taking a long time to run. The workbook had a number of selection controls. A complex IF function in cells H10:H750 was choosing which records should be included in a report. While that IF statement had many nested conditions, the formula was inserting either KEEP or HIDE in each cell:

```
=IF(logical_test,"KEEP","HIDE")
```

The following section of code was hiding individual rows:

```
For Each cell In Range("H10:H750")
    If cell.Value = "HIDE" Then
        cell.EntireRow.Hidden = True
    End If
Next cell
```

The macro was taking several minutes to run. SUBTOTAL formulas that excluded hidden rows were recalculating after each pass through the loop. The first attempts to speed up the macro involved turning off screen updating and calculation:

```
Application.ScreenUpdating = False
Application.Calculation = xlCalculationManual
For Each cell In Range("H10:H750")
    If cell.Value = "HIDE" Then
        cell.EntireRow.Hidden = True
    End If
Next cell
Application.Calculation = xlCalculationAutomatic
Application.ScreenUpdating = True
```

For some reason, it was still taking too long to loop through all the records. We tried using AutoFilter to isolate the HIDE records, then hiding those rows, but you lose the manual row hiding after turning off AutoFilter.

The solution was to make use of the Go To Special dialog's ability to limit the selection to text results of formulas. First, the formula in Column H was changed to return either HIDE or a number:

```
=IF(logical_test,"KEEP",1)
```

Then, the following single line of code was able to hide the rows that evaluated to a text value in Column H:

```
Range("H10:H750") _
    .SpecialCells(xlCellTypeFormulas, xlTextValues) _
    .EntireRow.Hidden = True
```

Because all the rows were hidden in a single command, that section of the macro ran in seconds rather than minutes.

Advanced Filter Is Easier in VBA Than in Excel

Using the arcane Advanced Filter command is so difficult in the Excel user interface that it is pretty rare to find someone who enjoys using it regularly.

However, in VBA, advanced filters are a joy to use. With a single line of code, you can rapidly extract a subset of records from a database or quickly get a unique list of values in any column. This is critical when you want to run reports for a specific region or customer. Two advanced filters are used most often in the same procedure—one to get a unique list of customers and a second to filter to each individual customer, as shown in Figure 11.4. The rest of this chapter builds toward such a routine.

Figure 11.4
A typical macro uses two advanced filters.

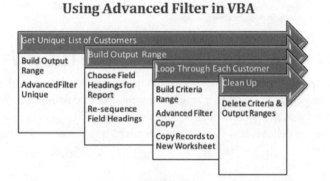

Using Advanced Filter in VBA

Using the Excel Interface to Build an Advanced Filter

Because not many people use the Advanced Filter feature, this section walks you through examples using the user interface to build an advanced filter and then shows you the analogous code. You will be amazed at how complex the user interface seems and yet how easy it is to program a powerful advanced filter to extract records.

One reason Advanced Filter is hard to use is that you can use the filter in several different ways. You must make three basic choices in the Advanced Filter dialog box. Because each choice has two options, there are eight (2 × 2 × 2) possible combinations of these choices. The three basic choices are shown in Figure 11.5 and described here:

- **Action**—You can select Filter the List, In-Place or you can select Copy to Another Location. If you choose to filter the records in place, the nonmatching rows are hidden. Choosing to copy to a new location copies the records that match the filter to a new range.

- **Criteria**—You can filter with or without criteria. Filtering with criteria is appropriate for getting a subset of rows. Filtering without criteria is still useful when you want a subset of columns or when you are using the Unique Records Only option.

- **Unique**—You can choose to request Unique Records Only or request all matching records. The Unique option makes the Advanced Filter command one of the fastest ways to find a unique list of values in one field. By placing the "Customer" heading in the output range, you will get a unique list of values for that one column.

11

Figure 11.5
The Advanced Filter dialog is complicated to use in the Excel user interface. Fortunately, it is much easier in VBA.

Using Advanced Filter to Extract a Unique List of Values

One of the simplest uses of Advanced Filter is to extract a unique list of a single field from a dataset. In this example, you want to get a unique list of customers from a sales report. You know that Customer is in Column D of the dataset. You have an unknown number of records starting in cell A2, and Row 1 is the header row. There is nothing located to the right of the dataset.

Extracting a Unique List of Values with the User Interface

To extract a unique list of values, follow these steps:

1. With the cursor anywhere in the data range, select Advanced from the Sort & Filter group on the Data tab. The first time you use the Advanced Filter command on a worksheet, Excel automatically populates the List Range text box with the entire range of your dataset. On subsequent uses of the Advanced Filter command, this dialog box remembers the settings from the prior advanced filter.

2. Select the Unique Records Only check box at the bottom of the dialog.

3. In the Action section, select Copy to Another Location.

4. Type J1 in the Copy To text box.

By default, Excel copies all the columns in the dataset. You can filter just the Customer column either by limiting the List Range to include only Column D or by specifying one or more headings in the Copy To range. Either method has its own drawbacks.

Change the List Range to a Single Column

Edit the List Range to point to the Customer column. In this case, it means changing the default $A$1:$H$1127 to $D$1:$D$1127. The Advanced Filter dialog should appear.

> **NOTE** When you initially edit any range in the dialog box, Excel might be in Point mode. In this mode, pressing a left- or right-arrow key inserts a cell reference in the text box. If you see the word *Point* in the lower-left corner of your Excel window, press the F2 key to change from Point mode to Edit mode.

The drawback of this method is that Excel remembers the list range on subsequent uses of the Advanced Filter command. If you later want to get a unique list of regions, you will be constantly specifying the list range.

Copy the Customer Heading Before Filtering

With a little forethought before invoking the Advanced Filter command, you can allow Excel to keep the default list range of $A$1:$H$1127. In cell J1, type the **Customer** heading as shown in Figure 11.6. You leave the List Range field pointing to Columns A through H. Because the Copy To range of J1 already contains a valid heading from the list range, Excel copies data only from the Customer column. This is the preferred method, particularly if you will be doing multiple advanced filters. Because Excel remembers the prior settings from the preceding advanced filter, it is more convenient to always filter the entire columns of the list range and limit the columns by setting up headings in the Copy To range.

After you use either of these methods to perform the advanced filter, a concise list of the unique customers appears in Column J (see Figure 11.6).

Figure 11.6
The advanced filter extracted a unique list of customers from the dataset and copied it to Column J.

J	K	L	N
Customer			
Amazing Shoe Company			
Mouthwatering Notebook Inc.			
Cool Saddle Traders			
Tasty Shovel Company			
Distinctive Wax Company			

Extracting a Unique List of Values with VBA Code

In VBA, you use the AdvancedFilter method to carry out the Advanced Filter command. Again, you have three choices to make:

- **Action**—Choose to either filter in place with the parameter Action:=xlFilterInPlace or copy with Action:=xlFilterCopy. If you want to copy, you also have to specify the parameter CopyToRange:=Range("J1").

- **Criteria**—To filter with criteria, include the parameter CriteriaRange:=Range("L 1:L2"). To filter without criteria, omit this optional parameter.

- **Unique**—To return only unique records, specify the parameter Unique:=True.

The following code sets up a single-column output range two columns to the right of the last-used column in the data range:

```
Sub GetUniqueCustomers()
    Dim IRange As Range
    Dim ORange As Range

    ' Find the size of today's dataset
    FinalRow = Cells(Rows.Count, 1).End(xlUp).Row
    NextCol = Cells(1, Columns.Count).End(xlToLeft).Column + 2
```

```
    ' Set up output range. Copy heading from D1 there
    Range("D1").Copy Destination:=Cells(1, NextCol)
    Set ORange = Cells(1, NextCol)

    ' Define the Input Range
    Set IRange = Range("A1").Resize(FinalRow, NextCol - 2)

    ' Do the Advanced Filter to get unique list of customers
    IRange.AdvancedFilter Action:=xlFilterCopy, CopyToRange:=ORange, _
        Unique:=True

End Sub
```

By default, an advanced filter copies all columns. If you just want one particular column, use that column heading as the heading in the output range.

The first bit of code finds the final row and column in the dataset. Although it is not necessary to do so, you can define an object variable for the output range (ORange) and for the input range (IRange).

This code is generic enough that it will not have to be rewritten if new columns are added to the dataset later. Setting up the object variables for the input and output range is done for readability rather than out of necessity. The previous code could be written just as easily like this shortened version:

```
Sub UniqueCustomerRedux()
    ' Copy a heading to create an output range
    Range("J1").Value = Range("D1").Value
    ' Do the Advanced Filter
    Range("A1").CurrentRegion.AdvancedFilter xlFilterCopy, _
        CopyToRange:=Range("J1"), Unique:=True
End Sub
```

When you run either of the previous blocks of code on the sample dataset, you get a unique list of customers off to the right of the data. The key to getting a unique list of customers is copying the header from the Customer field to a blank cell and specifying this cell as the output range.

After you have the unique list of customers, you can sort the list and add a SUMIF formula to get total revenue by customer. The following code gets the unique list of customers, sorts it, and then builds a formula to total revenue by customer. Figure 11.7 shows the results:

```
Sub RevenueByCustomers()
    Dim IRange As Range
    Dim ORange As Range

    ' Find the size of today's in
    FinalRow = Cells(Rows.Count, 1).End(xlUp).Row
    NextCol = Cells(1, Columns.Count).End(xlToLeft).Column + 2

    ' Set up output range. Copy heading from D1 there
    Range("D1").Copy Destination:=Cells(1, NextCol)
    Set ORange = Cells(1, NextCol)

    ' Define the Input Range
```

```
Set IRange = Range("A1").Resize(FinalRow, NextCol - 2)

' Do the Advanced Filter to get unique list of customers
IRange.AdvancedFilter Action:=xlFilterCopy, _
    CopyToRange:=ORange, Unique:=True

' Determine how many unique customers we have
LastRow = Cells(Rows.Count, NextCol).End(xlUp).Row

' Sort the data
Cells(1, NextCol).Resize(LastRow, 1).Sort Key1:=Cells(1, NextCol), _
    Order1:=xlAscending, Header:=xlYes

' Add a SUMIF formula to get totals
Cells(1, NextCol + 1).Value = "Revenue"
Cells(2, NextCol + 1).Resize(LastRow - 1).FormulaR1C1 = _
    "=SUMIF(R2C4:R" & FinalRow & _
    "C4,RC[-1],R2C6:R" & FinalRow & "C6)"

End Sub
```

Figure 11.7
This macro produced a summary report by customer from a lengthy dataset. Using AdvancedFilter is the key to powerful macros such as these.

=SUMIF($D$2:$D$1127,J2,$F$2:$F$1127)		
J	K	L
Customer	Revenue	
Agile Aquarium Ind	97107	
Amazing Shoe Co	820384	
Appealing Eggbeat	92544	
Cool Saddle Trade	53170	
Distinctive Wax Co	947025	
Enhanced Eggbea	1543677	
First-Rate Glass C	106442	

Another use of a unique list of values is to quickly populate a list box or a combo box on a userform. For example, suppose that you have a macro that can run a report for any one specific customer. To allow your clients to choose which customers to report, create a simple userform. Add a list box to the userform and set the list box's MultiSelect property to 1-fmMultiSelectMulti. In this case, the form is named frmReport. In addition to the list box, there are four command buttons: OK, Cancel, Mark All, and Clear All. The code to run the form follows. Note that the Userform_Initialize procedure includes an advanced filter to get the unique list of customers from the dataset:

```
Private Sub CancelButton_Click()
    Unload Me
End Sub

Private Sub cbSubAll_Click()
    For i = 0 To lbCust.ListCount - 1
        Me.lbCust.Selected(i) = True
    Next i
End Sub

Private Sub cbSubClear_Click()
    For i = 0 To lbCust.ListCount - 1
```

```
            Me.lbCust.Selected(i) = False
        Next i
    End Sub

    Private Sub OKButton_Click()
        For i = 0 To lbCust.ListCount - 1
            If Me.lbCust.Selected(i) = True Then
                ' Call a routine to produce this report
                RunCustReport WhichCust:=Me.lbCust.List(i)
            End If
        Next i
        Unload Me
    End Sub

    Private Sub UserForm_Initialize()
        Dim IRange As Range
        Dim ORange As Range

        ' Find the size of today's dataset
        FinalRow = Cells(Rows.Count, 1).End(xlUp).Row
        NextCol = Cells(1, Columns.Count).End(xlToLeft).Column + 2

        ' Set up output range. Copy heading from D1 there
        Range("D1").Copy Destination:=Cells(1, NextCol)
        Set ORange = Cells(1, NextCol)

        ' Define the Input Range
        Set IRange = Range("A1").Resize(FinalRow, NextCol - 2)

        ' Do the Advanced Filter to get unique list of customers
        IRange.AdvancedFilter Action:=xlFilterCopy, _
            CopyToRange:=ORange, Unique:=True

        ' Determine how many unique customers we have
        LastRow = Cells(Rows.Count, NextCol).End(xlUp).Row

        ' Sort the data
        Cells(1, NextCol).Resize(LastRow, 1).Sort Key1:=Cells(1, NextCol), _
            Order1:=xlAscending, Header:=xlYes

With Me.lbCust
    .RowSource = ""
    .List = Cells(2, NextCol).Resize(LastRow - 1, 1).Value
End With

        ' Erase the temporary list of customers
        Cells(1, NextCol).Resize(LastRow, 1).Clear
    End Sub
```

Launch this form with a simple module such as this:

```
Sub ShowCustForm()
    frmReport.Show
End Sub
```

Your clients are presented with a list of all valid customers from the dataset. Because the list box's MultiSelect property is set to allow it, they can select any number of customers.

Getting Unique Combinations of Two or More Fields

To get all unique combinations of two or more fields, build the output range to include the additional fields. This code sample builds a list of unique combinations of two fields, Customer and Product:

```
Sub UniqueCustomerProduct()
    Dim IRange As Range
    Dim ORange As Range

    ' Find the size of today's dataset
    FinalRow = Cells(Rows.Count, 1).End(xlUp).Row
    NextCol = Cells(1, Columns.Count).End(xlToLeft).Column + 2

    ' Set up output range. Copy headings from D1 & B1
    Range("D1").Copy Destination:=Cells(1, NextCol)
    Range("B1").Copy Destination:=Cells(1, NextCol + 1)
    Set ORange = Cells(1, NextCol).Resize(1, 2)

    ' Define the Input Range
    Set IRange = Range("A1").Resize(FinalRow, NextCol - 2)

    ' Do the Advanced Filter to get unique list of customers & product
    IRange.AdvancedFilter Action:=xlFilterCopy, _
        CopyToRange:=ORange, Unique:=True

    ' Determine how many unique rows we have
    LastRow = Cells(Rows.Count, NextCol).End(xlUp).Row

    ' Sort the data
    Cells(1, NextCol).Resize(LastRow, 2).Sort Key1:=Cells(1, NextCol), _
        Order1:=xlAscending, Key2:=Cells(1, NextCol + 1), _
        Order2:=xlAscending, Header:=xlYes

End Sub
```

In the result shown in Figure 11.8, you can see that Enhanced Eggbeater buys only one product, and Agile Aquarium buys three products. This might be useful as a guide in running reports on either customer by product or product by customer.

Figure 11.8

By including two columns in the output range on a Unique Values query, we get every combination of Customer and Product.

Customer	Product
Agile Aquarium Inc.	M556
Agile Aquarium Inc.	R537
Agile Aquarium Inc.	W435
Amazing Shoe Comp	M556
Amazing Shoe Comp	R537
Amazing Shoe Comp	W435
Appealing Eggbeater	M556
Appealing Eggbeater	R537
Appealing Eggbeater	W435
Cool Saddle Traders	M556
Cool Saddle Traders	R537
Cool Saddle Traders	W435
Distinctive Wax Com	M556
Distinctive Wax Com	R537
Distinctive Wax Com	W435
Enhanced Eggbeater	R537
First-Rate Glass Cor	M556
First-Rate Glass Cor	R537

11

Using Advanced Filter with Criteria Ranges

As the name implies, Advanced Filter is usually used to filter records—in other words, to get a subset of data. You specify the subset by setting up a criteria range. Even if you are familiar with criteria, be sure to check out using the powerful Boolean formula in criteria ranges later in this chapter, in the section "The Most Complex Criteria: Replacing the List of Values with a Condition Created as the Result of a Formula."

Set up a criteria range in a blank area of the worksheet. A criteria range always includes two or more rows. The first row of the criteria range contains one or more field header values to match the one(s) in the data range you want to filter. The second row contains a value showing which records to extract. In Figure 11.9, Range J1:J2 is the criteria range, and Range L1 is the output range.

In the Excel user interface, to extract a unique list of products that were purchased by a particular customer, select Advanced Filter and set up the Advanced Filter dialog, as shown in Figure 11.9. Figure 11.10 shows the results.

Figure 11.9
To learn a unique list of products purchased by Cool Saddle Traders, set up the criteria range shown in J1:J2.

Figure 11.10
The results of the advanced filter that uses a criteria range and asks for a unique list of products. Of course, more complex and interesting criteria can be built.

	J	K	L
	Customer		Product
	Cool Saddle Traders		R537
			M556
			W435

In VBA, you use the following code to perform an equivalent advanced filter:

```
Sub UniqueProductsOneCustomer()
    Dim IRange As Range
    Dim ORange As Range
    Dim CRange As Range
```

```
' Find the size of today's dataset
FinalRow = Cells(Rows.Count, 1).End(xlUp).Row
NextCol = Cells(1, Columns.Count).End(xlToLeft).Column + 2

' Set up the Output Range with one customer
Cells(1, NextCol).Value = Range("D1").Value
' In reality, this value should be passed from the userform
Cells(2, NextCol).Value = Range("D2").Value
Set CRange = Cells(1, NextCol).Resize(2, 1)

' Set up output range. Copy heading from B1 there
Range("B1").Copy Destination:=Cells(1, NextCol + 2)
Set ORange = Cells(1, NextCol + 2)

' Define the Input Range
Set IRange = Range("A1").Resize(FinalRow, NextCol - 2)

' Do the Advanced Filter to get unique list of customers & product
IRange.AdvancedFilter Action:=xlFilterCopy, _
    CriteriaRange:=CRange, CopyToRange:=ORange, Unique:=True
' The above could also be written as:
'IRange.AdvancedFilter xlFilterCopy, CRange, ORange, True

' Determine how many unique rows we have
LastRow = Cells(Rows.Count, NextCol + 2).End(xlUp).Row

' Sort the data
Cells(1, NextCol + 2).Resize(LastRow, 1).Sort Key1:=Cells(1, _
    NextCol + 2), Order1:=xlAscending, Header:=xlYes

End Sub
```

Joining Multiple Criteria with a Logical OR

You might want to filter records that match one criteria or another. For example, you can extract customers who purchased either product M556 or product R537. This is called a *logical OR* criteria.

When your criteria should be joined by a logical OR, place the criteria on subsequent rows of the criteria range. For example, the criteria range shown in J1:J3 of Figure 11.11 tells you which customers order product M556 or product W435.

Figure 11.11
Place criteria on successive rows to join them with an OR. This criteria range gets customers who ordered either product M556 or W435.

Joining Two Criteria with a Logical AND

Other times, you will want to filter records that match one criterion and another criterion. For example, you might want to extract records in which the product sold was W435 and the region was the West region. This is called a *logical AND*.

To join two criteria by AND, put both criteria on the same row of the criteria range. For example, the criteria range shown in J1:K2 of Figure 11.12 gets the customers who ordered product W435 in the West region.

Figure 11.12
Place criteria on the same row to join them with an AND. The criteria range in J1:K2 gets customers from the West region who ordered product W435.

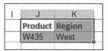

Other Slightly Complex Criteria Ranges

The criteria range shown in Figure 11.13 is based on two different fields that are joined with an OR. The query finds all records that either are from the West region or in which the product is W435.

Figure 11.13
The criteria range in J1:K3 returns records in which either the Region is West or the Product is W435.

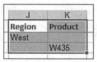

The Most Complex Criteria: Replacing the List of Values with a Condition Created as the Result of a Formula

It is possible to have a criteria range with multiple logical AND and logical OR criteria joined together. Although this might work in some situations, in other scenarios it quickly gets out of hand. Fortunately, Excel allows for criteria in which the records are selected as the result of a formula to handle this situation.

CASE STUDY: WORKING WITH VERY COMPLEX CRITERIA

Your clients so loved the "Create a Customer" report that they hired you to write a new report. In this case, they could select any customer, any product, any region, or any combination of them. You can quickly adapt the `frmReport` user-form to show three list boxes, as shown in Figure 11.14.

In your first test, imagine that you select two customers and two products. In this case, your program has to build a five-row criteria range, as shown in Figure 11.15. This isn't too bad.

Figure 11.14
This super-flexible form lets clients run any types of reports that they can imagine. It creates some nightmarish criteria ranges, unless you know the way out.

Figure 11.15
This criteria range returns any records for which the two selected customers ordered any of the two selected products.

J	K
Customer	**Product**
First-Rate Glass Corporation	M556
First-Rate Glass Corporation	R537
Guarded Aerobic Corporation	M556
Guarded Aerobic Corporation	R537

This gets crazy if someone selects 10 products, all regions but the house region, and all customers except the internal customer. Your criteria range would need unique combinations of the selected fields. This could easily be 10 products times 9 regions times 499 customers, or more than 44,000 rows of criteria range. You can quickly end up with a criteria range that spans thousands of rows and three columns. I was once foolish enough to actually try running an advanced filter with such a criteria range. It would still be trying to compute if I hadn't rebooted the computer.

The solution for this report is to replace the lists of values with a formula-based condition.

Setting Up a Condition as the Result of a Formula

Amazingly, there is an incredibly obscure version of Advanced Filter criteria that can replace the 44,000-row criteria range in the previous case study. In the alternative form of criteria range, the top row is left blank. There is no heading above the criteria. The criterion set up in Row 2 is a formula that results in True or False. If the formula contains any relative references to Row 2 of the data range, Excel compares that formula to every row of the data range, one by one.

For example, if you want all records in which the Gross Profit Percentage is below 53 percent, the formula built in J2 will reference the Profit in H2 and the Revenue in F2. To do this, leave J1 blank to tell Excel that you are using a computed criterion. Cell J2 contains the formula =(H2/F2)<0.53. The criteria range for the advanced filter would be specified as J1:J2.

As Excel performs the advanced filter, it logically copies the formula and applies it to all rows in the database. Anywhere that the formula evaluates to True, the record is included in the output range.

This is incredibly powerful and runs remarkably fast. You can combine multiple formulas in adjacent columns or rows to join the formula criteria with AND or OR, just as you do with regular criteria.

> **NOTE** Row 1 of the criteria range doesn't have to be blank, but it cannot contain any words that are headings in the data range. You could perhaps use that row to explain that someone should look to this page in this book for an explanation of these computed criteria.

CASE STUDY: USING FORMULA-BASED CONDITIONS IN THE EXCEL USER INTERFACE

11

You can use formula-based conditions to solve the report introduced in the previous case study. Figure 11.16 shows the flow of setting up a formula-based criterion.

Figure 11.16
Here are the logical steps in using formula-based conditions to solve the problem.

1. Write Customer Choices to a Range in O
2. Assign Name MyCust to Range
3. Criteria Formula in J2: =NOT(ISNA(MATCH(D2,MyCust
4. Write Product Choices to column P
5. Assign Name MyProd to Range
6. Criteria Formula in K2: =NOT(ISNA(MATCH(B2,MyProd
7. Write Region Choices in Q
8. Assign Name MyReg to Range
9. Criteria Formula in L2: =NOT(ISNA(MATCH(B2,MyReg
10. Advanced Filter using J1:L1 as Criteria

To illustrate, off to the right of the criteria range, set up a column of cells with the list of selected customers. Assign a name to the range, such as MyCust. In cell J2 of the criteria range, enter a formula such as =NOT(ISNA(Match(D2, MyCust,0))).

To the right of the MyCust range, set up a range with a list of selected products. Assign this range the name of MyProd. In K2 of the criteria range, add a formula to check products, =NOT(ISNA(Match(B2,MyProd,0))).

To the right of the MyProd range, set up a range with a list of selected regions. Assign this range the name of MyRegion. In L2 of the criteria range, add a formula to check for selected regions, =NOT(ISNA(Match(A2, MyRegion,0))).

Now, with a criteria range of J1:L2, you can effectively retrieve the records matching any combination of selections from the userform.

Using Formula-Based Conditions with VBA

Referring back to the userform shown in Figure 11.14, you can use formula-based conditions to filter the report using the userform. The following is the code for this userform. Note the logic in OKButton_Click that builds the formula. Figure 11.17 shows the Excel sheet just before the advanced filter is run.

Figure 11.17
The worksheet just before the macro runs the advanced filter.

The following code initializes the user form. Three advanced filters find the unique list of customers, products, and regions:

```
Private Sub UserForm_Initialize()
    Dim IRange As Range
    Dim ORange As Range

    ' Find the size of today's dataset
    FinalRow = Cells(Rows.Count, 1).End(xlUp).Row
    NextCol = Cells(1, Columns.Count).End(xlToLeft).Column + 2

    ' Define the input range
    Set IRange = Range("A1").Resize(FinalRow, NextCol - 2)
```

```
' Set up output range for Customer. Copy heading from D1 there
Range("D1").Copy Destination:=Cells(1, NextCol)
Set ORange = Cells(1, NextCol)

' Do the Advanced Filter to get unique list of customers
IRange.AdvancedFilter Action:=xlFilterCopy, CriteriaRange:="", _
    CopyToRange:=ORange, Unique:=True

' Determine how many unique customers we have
LastRow = Cells(Rows.Count, NextCol).End(xlUp).Row

' Sort the data
Cells(1, NextCol).Resize(LastRow, 1).Sort Key1:=Cells(1, NextCol), _
    Order1:=xlAscending, Header:=xlYes

With Me.lbCust
    .RowSource = ""
    .List = Application.Transpose(Cells(2,NextCol).Resize(LastRow-1,1))
End With

' Erase the temporary list of customers
Cells(1, NextCol).Resize(LastRow, 1).Clear

' Set up output range for product. Copy heading from D1 there
Range("B1").Copy Destination:=Cells(1, NextCol)
Set ORange = Cells(1, NextCol)

' Do the Advanced Filter to get unique list of customers
IRange.AdvancedFilter Action:=xlFilterCopy, _
    CopyToRange:=ORange, Unique:=True

' Determine how many unique customers we have
LastRow = Cells(Rows.Count, NextCol).End(xlUp).Row

' Sort the data
Cells(1, NextCol).Resize(LastRow, 1).Sort Key1:=Cells(1, NextCol), _
    Order1:=xlAscending, Header:=xlYes

With Me.lbProduct
    .RowSource = ""
    .List = Application.Transpose(Cells(2,NextCol).Resize(LastRow-1,1))
End With

' Erase the temporary list of customers
Cells(1, NextCol).Resize(LastRow, 1).Clear

' Set up output range for Region. Copy heading from A1 there
Range("A1").Copy Destination:=Cells(1, NextCol)
Set ORange = Cells(1, NextCol)

' Do the Advanced Filter to get unique list of customers
IRange.AdvancedFilter Action:=xlFilterCopy, CopyToRange:=ORange, _
    Unique:=True

' Determine how many unique customers we have
LastRow = Cells(Rows.Count, NextCol).End(xlUp).Row
```

11

```
' Sort the data
Cells(1, NextCol).Resize(LastRow, 1).Sort Key1:=Cells(1, NextCol), _
    Order1:=xlAscending, Header:=xlYes

With Me.lbRegion
    .RowSource = ""
    .List = Application.Transpose(Cells(2,NextCol).Resize(LastRow-1,1))
End With

' Erase the temporary list of customers
Cells(1, NextCol).Resize(LastRow, 1).Clear

End Sub
```

These tiny procedures run when someone clicks Mark All or Clear All in the userform in Figure 11.14:

```
Private Sub CancelButton_Click()
    Unload Me
End Sub

Private Sub cbSubAll_Click()
    For i = 0 To lbCust.ListCount - 1
        Me.lbCust.Selected(i) = True
    Next i
End Sub

Private Sub cbSubClear_Click()
    For i = 0 To lbCust.ListCount - 1
        Me.lbCust.Selected(i) = False
    Next i
End Sub

Private Sub CommandButton1_Click()
    ' Clear all products
    For i = 0 To lbProduct.ListCount - 1
        Me.lbProduct.Selected(i) = False
    Next i
End Sub

Private Sub CommandButton2_Click()
    ' Mark all products
    For i = 0 To lbProduct.ListCount - 1
        Me.lbProduct.Selected(i) = True
    Next i
End Sub

Private Sub CommandButton3_Click()
    ' Clear all regions
    For i = 0 To lbRegion.ListCount - 1
        Me.lbRegion.Selected(i) = False
    Next i
End Sub

Private Sub CommandButton4_Click()
    ' Mark all regions
    For i = 0 To lbRegion.ListCount - 1
```

```
                Me.lbRegion.Selected(i) = True
        Next i
    End Sub
```

The following code is attached to the OK button. This code builds three ranges in O, P, and Q that list the selected customers, products, and regions. The actual criteria range is composed of three blank cells in J1:L1 and then three formulas in J2:L2.

```
Private Sub OKButton_Click()
    Dim CRange As Range, IRange As Range, ORange As Range
    ' Build a complex criteria that ANDs all choices together
    NextCCol = 10
    NextTCol = 15

    For j = 1 To 3
        Select Case j
            Case 1
                MyControl = "lbCust"
                MyColumn = 4
            Case 2
                MyControl = "lbProduct"
                MyColumn = 2
            Case 3
                MyControl = "lbRegion"
                MyColumn = 1
        End Select
        NextRow = 2
        ' Check to see what was selected.
        For i = 0 To Me.Controls(MyControl).ListCount - 1
            If Me.Controls(MyControl).Selected(i) = True Then
                Cells(NextRow, NextTCol).Value = _
                    Me.Controls(MyControl).List(i)
                NextRow = NextRow + 1
            End If
        Next i
        ' If anything was selected, build a new criteria formula
        If NextRow > 2 Then
            ' the reference to Row 2 must be relative in order to work
            MyFormula = "=NOT(ISNA(MATCH(RC" & MyColumn & ",R2C" & _
                NextTCol & ":R" & NextRow - 1 & "C" & NextTCol & ",0)))"
            Cells(2, NextCCol).FormulaR1C1 = MyFormula
            NextTCol = NextTCol + 1
            NextCCol = NextCCol + 1
        End If
    Next j
    Unload Me

    ' Figure 11.19 shows the worksheet at this point
    ' If we built any criteria, define the criteria range
    If NextCCol > 10 Then
        Set CRange = Range(Cells(1, 10), Cells(2, NextCCol - 1))
        Set IRange = Range("A1").CurrentRegion
        Set ORange = Cells(1, 20)
        IRange.AdvancedFilter xlFilterCopy, CRange, ORange

        ' Clear out the criteria
        Cells(1, 10).Resize(1, 10).EntireColumn.Clear
```

```
    End If

    ' At this point, the matching records are in T1

End Sub
```

Figure 11.17 shows the worksheet just before the `AdvancedFilter` method is called. The user has selected customers, products, and regions. The macro has built temporary tables in Columns O, P, and Q to show which values the user selected. The criteria range is J1:L2. That criteria formula in J2 looks to see whether the value in $D2 is in the list of selected customers in O. The formulas in K2 and L2 compare $B2 to Column P and $A2 to Column Q.

> **NOTE** Excel VBA Help says that if you do not specify a criteria range, no criteria are used. This is not true in Excel 2013. If no criteria range is specified in Excel 2013, the advanced filter inherits the criteria range from the prior advanced filter. You should include `CriteriaRange:=""` to clear the prior value.

Using Formula-Based Conditions to Return Above-Average Records

The formula-based conditions formula criteria are cool but are a rarely used feature in a rarely used function. Some interesting business applications use this technique. For example, this criteria formula would find all the above-average rows in the dataset:

```
=$A2>Average($A$2:$A$1048576)
```

Using Filter in Place in Advanced Filter

It is possible to filter a large dataset in place. In this case, you do not need an output range. You would normally specify a criteria range—otherwise, you return 100 percent of the records and there is no need to do the advanced filter!

In the user interface of Excel, running a Filter in Place makes sense: You can easily peruse the filtered list looking for something in particular.

Running a Filter in Place in VBA is a little less convenient. The only good way to programmatically peruse the filtered records is to use the `xlCellTypeVisible` option of the `SpecialCells` method. In the Excel user interface, the equivalent action is to select Find & Select, Go to Special from the Home tab. In the Go to Special dialog, select Visible Cells Only.

To run a Filter in Place, use the constant `XLFilterInPlace` as the Action parameter in the `AdvancedFilter` command and remove the `CopyToRange` from the command:

```
IRange.AdvancedFilter Action:=xlFilterInPlace, CriteriaRange:=CRange, _
    Unique:=False
```

Then, the programmatic equivalent to loop through Visible Cells Only is this code:

```
For Each cell In Range("A2:A" & FinalRow).SpecialCells(xlCellTypeVisible)
    Ctr = Ctr + 1
Next cell
```

11

```
MsgBox Ctr & " cells match the criteria"
```

If you know that there would be no blanks in the visible cells, you could eliminate the loop with

```
Ctr = Application.Counta(Range("A2:A" & _
FinalRow).SpecialCells(xlCellTypeVisible))
```

Catching No Records When Using Filter in Place

Just as when using Copy, you have to watch out for the possibility of having no records match the criteria. However, in this case it is more difficult to realize that nothing is returned. You generally find out when the .SpecialCells method returns a Runtime Error 1004—no cells were found.

To catch this condition, you have to set up an error trap to anticipate the 1004 error with the SpecialCells method.

→ **See** Chapter 24, "Handling Errors," for more information on catching errors.

```
On Error GoTo NoRecs
    For Each cell In Range("A2:A" & FinalRow).SpecialCells(xlCellTypeVisible)
        Ctr = Ctr + 1
    Next cell
    On Error GoTo 0
    MsgBox Ctr & " cells match the criteria"
    Exit Sub
NoRecs:
    MsgBox "No records match the criteria"
End Sub
```

This error trap works because it specifically excludes the header row from the SpecialCells range. The header row is always visible after an advanced filter. Including it in the range would prevent the 1004 error from being raised.

Showing All Records After Filter in Place

After doing a Filter in Place, you can get all records to show again by using the ShowAllData method:

```
ActiveSheet.ShowAllData
```

The Real Workhorse: xlFilterCopy with All Records Rather Than Unique Records Only

The examples at the beginning of this chapter talked about using xlFilterCopy to get a unique list of values in a field. You used unique lists of customer, region, and product to populate the list boxes in your report-specific userforms.

However, a more common scenario is to use an advanced filter to return all records that match the criteria. After the client selects which customer to report, an advanced filter can extract all records for that customer.

In all the examples in the following sections, you want to keep the Unique Records Only check box cleared. You do this in VBA by specifying `Unique:=False` as a parameter to the `AdvancedFilter` method.

This is not difficult to do, and you have some powerful options. If you need only a subset of fields for a report, copy only those field headings to the output range. If you want to resequence the fields to appear exactly as you need them in the report, you can do this by changing the sequence of the headings in the output range.

The next sections walk you through three quick examples to show the options available.

Copying All Columns

To copy all columns, specify a single blank cell as the output range. You will get all columns for those records that match the criteria, as shown in Figure 11.18:

```
Sub AllColumnsOneCustomer()
    Dim IRange As Range
    Dim ORange As Range
    Dim CRange As Range

    ' Find the size of today's dataset
    FinalRow = Cells(Rows.Count, 1).End(xlUp).Row
    NextCol = Cells(1, Columns.Count).End(xlToLeft).Column + 2

    ' Set up the criteria range with one customer
    Cells(1, NextCol).Value = Range("D1").Value
    ' In reality, this value should be passed from the userform
    Cells(2, NextCol).Value = Range("D2").Value
    Set CRange = Cells(1, NextCol).Resize(2, 1)

    ' Set up output range. It is a single blank cell
    Set ORange = Cells(1, NextCol + 2)

    ' Define the Input Range
    Set IRange = Range("A1").Resize(FinalRow, NextCol - 2)

    ' Do the Advanced Filter to get unique list of customers & product
    IRange.AdvancedFilter Action:=xlFilterCopy, _
        CriteriaRange:=CRange, CopyToRange:=ORange

End Sub
```

Figure 11.18

When using `xlFilterCopy` with a blank output range, you get all columns in the same order as they appear in the original list range.

D		E	F	G	H
Customer		Region	Product	Date	
Trustworthy Flagpole Partners		East	R537	19-Jul-14	
		East	W435	3-Sep-14	
		West	M556	7-Sep-14	
		Central	W435	9-Sep-14	

Copying a Subset of Columns and Reordering

If you are doing the advanced filter to send records to a report, it is likely that you might need only a subset of columns and you might need them in a different sequence.

This example finishes the frmReport example that was presented earlier in this chapter. As you recall, frmReport allows the client to select a customer. The OK button then calls the RunCustReport routine, passing a parameter to identify for which customer to prepare a report.

Imagine this is a report being sent to the customer. The customer really does not care about the surrounding region, and you do not want to reveal your cost of goods sold or profit. Assuming that you will put the customer's name in the title of the report, the fields that you need in order to produce the report are Date, Quantity, Product, and Revenue.

The following code copies those headings to the output range. The advanced filter produces data, as shown in Figure 11.19. The program then goes on to copy the matching records to a new workbook. A title and a total row are added, and the report is saved with the customer's name. Figure 11.20 shows the final report.

```
Sub RunCustReport(WhichCust As Variant)
    Dim IRange As Range
    Dim ORange As Range
    Dim CRange As Range
    Dim WBN As Workbook
    Dim WSN As Worksheet
    Dim WSO As Worksheet

    Set WSO = ActiveSheet
    ' Find the size of today's dataset
    FinalRow = Cells(Rows.Count, 1).End(xlUp).Row
    NextCol = Cells(1, Columns.Count).End(xlToLeft).Column + 2

    ' Set up the criteria range with one customer
    Cells(1, NextCol).Value = Range("D1").Value
    Cells(2, NextCol).Value = WhichCust
    Set CRange = Cells(1, NextCol).Resize(2, 1)

    ' Set up output range. We want Date, Quantity, Product, Revenue
    ' These columns are in C, E, B, and F
    Cells(1, NextCol + 2).Resize(1, 4).Value = _
        Array(Cells(1, 3), Cells(1, 5), Cells(1, 2), Cells(1, 6))
    Set ORange = Cells(1, NextCol + 2).Resize(1, 4)

    ' Define the Input Range
    Set IRange = Range("A1").Resize(FinalRow, NextCol - 2)

    ' Do the Advanced Filter to get unique list of customers & products
    IRange.AdvancedFilter Action:=xlFilterCopy, _
        CriteriaRange:=CRange, CopyToRange:=ORange

    ' Create a new workbook with one blank sheet to hold the output
    ' xlWBATWorksheet is the template name for a single worksheet
```

```
Set WBN = Workbooks.Add(xlWBATWorksheet)
Set WSN = WBN.Worksheets(1)

' Set up a title on WSN
WSN.Cells(1, 1).Value = "Report of Sales to " & WhichCust

' Copy data from WSO to WSN
WSO.Cells(1, NextCol + 2).CurrentRegion.Copy Destination:=WSN.Cells(3, 1)
TotalRow = WSN.Cells(Rows.Count, 1).End(xlUp).Row + 1
WSN.Cells(TotalRow, 1).Value = "Total"
WSN.Cells(TotalRow, 2).FormulaR1C1 = "=SUM(R2C:R[-1]C)"
WSN.Cells(TotalRow, 4).FormulaR1C1 = "=SUM(R2C:R[-1]C)"

' Format the new report with bold
WSN.Cells(3, 1).Resize(1, 4).Font.Bold = True
WSN.Cells(TotalRow, 1).Resize(1, 4).Font.Bold = True
WSN.Cells(1, 1).Font.Size = 18

WBN.SaveAs ThisWorkbook.Path & Application.PathSeparator & _
    WhichCust & ".xlsx"
WBN.Close SaveChanges:=False

WSO.Select

' clear the output range, etc.
Range("J:Z").Clear


End Sub
```

11

Figure 11.19
Immediately after the advanced filter, you have just the columns and records needed for the report.

	J	K	L	M	N	O
	Customer		Date	Quantity	Product	Revenue
	Cool Saddle Traders		22-Jul-14	400	R537	9152
			25-Jul-14	600	R537	13806
			16-Aug-14	400	M556	7136
			23-Sep-14	100	R537	2358
			29-Sep-14	100	R537	1819
			21-Oct-14	100	R537	2484
			3-Mar-15	200	W435	4270
			18-Aug-15	700	W435	12145

Figure 11.20
After copying the filtered data to a new sheet and applying some formatting, you have a good-looking report to send to each customer.

	A	B	C	D	E	F
1	Report of Sales to Cool Saddle Traders					
2						
3	Date	Quantity	Product	Revenue		
4	22-Jul-14	400	R537	9152		
5	25-Jul-14	600	R537	13806		
6	16-Aug-14	400	M556	7136		
7	23-Sep-14	100	R537	2358		
8	29-Sep-14	100	R537	1819		
9	21-Oct-14	100	R537	2484		
10	3-Mar-15	200	W435	4270		
11	18-Aug-15	700	W435	12145		
12	Total	2600		53170		

CASE STUDY: UTILIZING TWO KINDS OF ADVANCED FILTERS TO CREATE A REPORT FOR EACH CUSTOMER

The final advanced filter example for this chapter uses several advanced filter techniques. Let's say that after importing invoice records, you want to send a purchase summary to each customer. The process would be as follows:

1. Run an advanced filter requesting unique values to get a list of customers in J. This `AdvancedFilter` specifies the `Unique:=True` parameter and uses a `CopyToRange` that includes a single heading for Customer:

```
' Set up output range. Copy heading from D1 there
Range("D1").Copy Destination:=Cells(1, NextCol)
Set ORange = Cells(1, NextCol)

' Define the Input Range
Set IRange = Range("A1").Resize(FinalRow, NextCol - 2)

' Do the Advanced Filter to get unique list of customers
IRange.AdvancedFilter Action:=xlFilterCopy, CriteriaRange:="", _
    CopyToRange:=ORange, Unique:=True
```

2. For each customer in the list of unique customers in Column J, perform steps 3 through 7. Find the number of customers in the output range from step 1. Then, use a `For Each Cell` loop to loop through the customers:

```
' Loop through each customer
FinalCust = Cells(Rows.Count, NextCol).End(xlUp).Row
For Each cell In Cells(2, NextCol).Resize(FinalCust - 1, 1)
    ThisCust = cell.Value
    ' ... Steps 3 through 7 here
Next Cell
```

3. Build a criteria range in L1:L2 to be used in a new advanced filter. The criteria range would include a heading of Customer in L1 and the customer name from this iteration of the loop in cell L2:

```
' Set up the Criteria Range with one customer
Cells(1, NextCol + 2).Value = Range("D1").Value
Cells(2, NextCol + 2).Value = ThisCust
Set CRange = Cells(1, NextCol + 2).Resize(2, 1)
```

4. Do an advanced filter to copy matching records for this customer to Column N. This `Advanced Filter` statement specifies the `Unique:=False` parameter. Because you want only the columns for Date, Quantity, Product, and Revenue, the `CopyToRange` specifies a four-column range with those headings copied in the proper order:

```
' Set up output range. We want Date, Quantity, Product, Revenue
' These columns are in C, E, B, and F
Cells(1, NextCol + 4).Resize(1, 4).Value = _
    Array(Cells(1, 3), Cells(1, 5), Cells(1, 2), Cells(1, 6))
Set ORange = Cells(1, NextCol + 4).Resize(1, 4)

' Do the Advanced Filter to get unique list of customers & product
IRange.AdvancedFilter Action:=xlFilterCopy, CriteriaRange:=CRange, _
    CopyToRange:=Orange
```

5. Copy the customer records to a report sheet in a new workbook. The VBA code uses the `Workbooks.Add` method to create a new blank workbook. The template name of xlWBATWorksheet is the way to specify that you want a workbook with a single worksheet. The extracted records from step 4 are copied to cell A3 of the new workbook:

```
' Create a new workbook with one blank sheet to hold the output
Set WBN = Workbooks.Add(xlWBATWorksheet)
Set WSN = WBN.Worksheets(1)
```

```
' Copy data from WSO to WSN
WSO.Cells(1, NextCol + 4).CurrentRegion.Copy _
    Destination:=WSN.Cells(3, 1)
```

6. Format the report with a title and totals. In VBA, add a title that reflects the customer's name in cell A1. Make the headings bold and add a total below the final row:

```
' Set up a title on WSN
WSN.Cells(1, 1).Value = "Report of Sales to " & ThisCust

TotalRow = WSN.Cells(Rows.Count, 1).End(xlUp).Row + 1
WSN.Cells(TotalRow, 1).Value = "Total"
WSN.Cells(TotalRow, 2).FormulaR1C1 = "=SUM(R2C:R[-1]C)"
WSN.Cells(TotalRow, 4).FormulaR1C1 = "=SUM(R2C:R[-1]C)"

' Format the new report with bold
WSN.Cells(3, 1).Resize(1, 4).Font.Bold = True
WSN.Cells(TotalRow, 1).Resize(1, 4).Font.Bold = True
WSN.Cells(1, 1).Font.Size = 18
```

7. Use SaveAs to save the workbook based on customer name. After the workbook is saved, close the new workbook. Return to the original workbook and clear the output range to prepare for the next pass through the loop:

```
WBN.SaveAs ThisWorkbook.Path & Application.PathSeparator & _
        WhichCust & ".xlsx"
WBN.Close SaveChanges:=False

WSO.Select
' Free up memory by setting object variables to nothing
Set WSN = Nothing
Set WBN = Nothing
' clear the output range, etc.
Cells(1, NextCol + 2).Resize(1, 10).EntireColumn.Clear
```

The complete code is as follows:

```
Sub RunReportForEachCustomer()
    Dim IRange As Range
    Dim ORange As Range
    Dim CRange As Range
    Dim WBN As Workbook
    Dim WSN As Worksheet
    Dim WSO As Worksheet

    Set WSO = ActiveSheet
    ' Find the size of today's dataset
    FinalRow = Cells(Rows.Count, 1).End(xlUp).Row
    NextCol = Cells(1, Columns.Count).End(xlToLeft).Column + 2
    ' First - get a unique list of customers in J
    ' Set up output range. Copy heading from D1 there

    Range("D1").Copy Destination:=Cells(1, NextCol)
    Set ORange = Cells(1, NextCol)

    ' Define the Input Range
```

11

```vba
Set IRange = Range("A1").Resize(FinalRow, NextCol - 2)

' Do the Advanced Filter to get unique list of customers
IRange.AdvancedFilter Action:=xlFilterCopy, CriteriaRange:="", _
    CopyToRange:=ORange, Unique:=True

' Loop through each customer
FinalCust = Cells(Rows.Count, NextCol).End(xlUp).Row
For Each cell In Cells(2, NextCol).Resize(FinalCust - 1, 1)
    ThisCust = cell.Value

    ' Set up the Criteria Range with one customer
    Cells(1, NextCol + 2).Value = Range("D1").Value
    Cells(2, NextCol + 2).Value = ThisCust
    Set CRange = Cells(1, NextCol + 2).Resize(2, 1)

    ' Set up output range. We want Date, Quantity, Product, Revenue
    ' These columns are in C, E, B, and F
    Cells(1, NextCol + 4).Resize(1, 4).Value = _
        Array(Cells(1, 3), Cells(1, 5), Cells(1, 2), Cells(1, 6))
    Set ORange = Cells(1, NextCol + 4).Resize(1, 4)

    ' Do the Advanced Filter to get unique list of customers & product
    IRange.AdvancedFilter Action:=xlFilterCopy, CriteriaRange:=CRange, _
        CopyToRange:=Orange

    ' Create a new workbook with one blank sheet to hold the output
    Set WBN = Workbooks.Add(xlWBATWorksheet)
    Set WSN = WBN.Worksheets(1)
    ' Copy data from WSO to WSN
    WSO.Cells(1, NextCol + 4).CurrentRegion.Copy _
        Destination:=WSN.Cells(3, 1)

    ' Set up a title on WSN
    WSN.Cells(1, 1).Value = "Report of Sales to " & ThisCust

    TotalRow = WSN.Cells(Rows.Count, 1).End(xlUp).Row + 1
    WSN.Cells(TotalRow, 1).Value = "Total"
    WSN.Cells(TotalRow, 2).FormulaR1C1 = "=SUM(R2C:R[-1]C)"
    WSN.Cells(TotalRow, 4).FormulaR1C1 = "=SUM(R2C:R[-1]C)"

    ' Format the new report with bold
    WSN.Cells(3, 1).Resize(1, 4).Font.Bold = True
    WSN.Cells(TotalRow, 1).Resize(1, 4).Font.Bold = True
    WSN.Cells(1, 1).Font.Size = 18

    WBN.SaveAs ThisWorkbook.Path & Application.PathSeparator & _
        WhichCust & ".xlsx"
    WBN.Close SaveChanges:=False
    WSO.Select
    Set WSN = Nothing

    Set WBN = Nothing

    ' clear the output range, etc.
    Cells(1, NextCol + 2).Resize(1, 10).EntireColumn.Clear
```

```
    Next cell

    Cells(1, NextCol).EntireColumn.Clear
    MsgBox FinalCust - 1 & " Reports have been created!"
End Sub
```

This is a remarkable 45 lines of code. Incorporating a couple of advanced filters and not much else, you have managed to produce a tool that created 27 reports in less than 1 minute. Even an Excel power user would normally take 2 to 3 minutes per report to create these manually. In less than 60 seconds, this code will save someone a few hours every time these reports need to be created. Imagine the real scenario in which there are hundreds of customers. Undoubtedly, there are people in every city who are manually creating these reports in Excel because they simply don't realize the power of Excel VBA.

Excel in Practice: Turning Off a Few Drop-Downs in the AutoFilter

One cool feature is available only in Excel VBA. When you AutoFilter a list in the Excel user interface, every column in the dataset gets a field drop-down in the heading row. Sometimes you have a field that does not make a lot of sense to AutoFilter. For example, in your current dataset, you might want to provide AutoFilter drop-downs for Region, Product, and Customer, but not the numeric or date fields. After setting up the AutoFilter, you need one line of code to turn off each drop-down that you do not want to appear. The following code turns off the drop-downs for Columns C, E, F, G, and H:

```
Sub AutoFilterCustom()
    Range("A1").AutoFilter Field:=3, VisibleDropDown:=False
    Range("A1").AutoFilter Field:=5, VisibleDropDown:=False
    Range("A1").AutoFilter Field:=6, VisibleDropDown:=False
    Range("A1").AutoFilter Field:=7, VisibleDropDown:=False
    Range("A1").AutoFilter Field:=8, VisibleDropDown:=False
End Sub
```

Using this tool is a fairly rare treat. Most of the time, Excel VBA lets you do things that are possible in the user interface—and lets you do them very rapidly. The `VisibleDropDown` parameter actually enables you to do something in VBA that is generally not available in the Excel user interface. Your knowledgeable clients will be scratching their heads trying to figure out how you set up the cool auto filter with only a few filterable columns (see Figure 11.21).

Figure 11.21
Using VBA, you can set up an auto filter where only certain columns have the AutoFilter drop-down.

	A	B	C	D	E	F
1	Region ▼	Product ▼	Date	Customer ▼	Quantity	Revenue
2	East	R537	19-Jul-14	Trustworthy Flagpole Partners	1000	22810
3	East	M556	20-Jul-14	Amazing Shoe Company	500	10245

To clear the filter from the customer column, use this code:

```
Sub SimpleFilter()
    Worksheets("SalesReport").Select
    Range("A1").AutoFilter
    Range("A1").AutoFilter Field:=4
End Sub
```

Next Steps

Using techniques from this chapter, you have many reporting techniques available via the arcane Advanced Filter tool. Chapter 12, "Using VBA to Create Pivot Tables," introduces the most powerful feature in Excel: the pivot table. The combination of advanced filters and pivot tables creates reporting tools that enable amazing applications.

11

Using VBA to Create Pivot Tables

12

Introducing Pivot Tables

Pivot tables are the most powerful tools that Excel has to offer. The concept was first put into practice by Lotus with its Improv product.

I love pivot tables because they are a fast way to summarize massive amounts of data. The name *pivot table* comes from the ability you have to drag fields in the drop zones and have them recalculate. You can use the basic vanilla pivot table to produce a concise summary in seconds. However, pivot tables come in so many flavors that they can be the tools of choice for many different uses. You can build pivot tables to act as the calculation engine to produce reports by store or by style, or to quickly find the top 5 or bottom 10 of anything.

I am not suggesting you use VBA to build pivot tables to give to your user. I am suggesting you use pivot tables as a means to an end—use a pivot table to extract a summary of data and then take this summary on to better uses.

Understanding Versions

As Microsoft invests in making Excel the premier choice in business intelligence, pivot tables continue to evolve. They were introduced in Excel 5 and perfected in Excel 97. In Excel 2000, pivot table creation in VBA was dramatically altered. Some new parameters were added in Excel 2002. A few new properties such as PivotFilters and TableStyle2 were added in Excel 2007. Slicers and new choices for Show Values As were added in Excel 2010. Timelines and the PowerPivot Data Model have been added in Excel 2013. Therefore, you need to be extremely careful when writing code in Excel 2013 that might be run in legacy versions.

Much of the code in this chapter is backward-compatible all the way to Excel 2000. Pivot table creation in Excel 97 required using the `PivotTableWizard` method. Although this book does not include code for Excel 97, one example has been included in the sample file for this chapter.

Each of the previous three versions of Excel offered many new features in pivot tables. If you use code for a new feature, the code works in the current version, but it crashes in previous versions of Excel.

- Excel 2013 introduced the PowerPivot Data Model. You can add tables to the Data Model, create a relationship, and produce a pivot table. This code does not run in Excel 2010 or earlier. The function `xlDistinctCount` is new. Timelines are new.

- Excel 2010 introduced slicers, Repeat All Item Labels, Named Sets, and several new calculation options: `xlPercentOfParentColumn`, `xlPercentOfParentRow`, `xlPercentRunningTotal`, `xlRankAscending`, and `xlRankDescending`. These do not work in Excel 2007.

- Excel 2007 introduced `ConvertToFormulas`, `xlCompactRow` layout, `xlAtTop` for the subtotal location, `TableStyles`, and `SortUsingCustomLists`. Macros that include this code fail in previous versions.

Building a Pivot Table in Excel VBA

This chapter does not mean to imply that you should use VBA to build pivot tables to give to your clients. Instead, the purpose of this chapter is to remind you that you can use pivot tables as a means to an end; you can use a pivot table to extract a summary of data and then use that summary elsewhere.

> **NOTE**
> The code listings from this chapter are available for download at `http://www.MrExcel.com/getcode2013.html`.

> **NOTE**
> Although the Excel user interface has new names for the various sections of a pivot table, VBA code continues to refer to the old names. Microsoft had to use this choice; otherwise, millions of lines of code would stop working in Excel 2007 when they referred to a page field rather than a filter field. Although the four sections of a pivot table in the Excel user interface are Filter, Columns, Rows, and Values, VBA continues to use the old terms of Page fields, Column fields, Row fields, and Data fields.

Defining the Pivot Cache

In this first part of this chapter, the dataset is an eight-column by 5,000-row dataset as shown in Figure 12.1. The macros create a regular pivot table from the worksheet data.

Near the end of the chapter, an example shows how to build a pivot table based on the Data Model and PowerPivot.

Figure 12.1
Create summary reports from this dataset.

	A	B	C	D	E	F	G	H
1	Region	Product	Date	Customer	Quantity	Revenue	COGS	Profit
2	West	D625	1/4/2014	Guarded Kettle Corporatio	430	10937	6248	4689
3	Central	A292	1/4/2014	Mouthwatering Jewelry Co	400	8517	4564	3953
4	West	B722	1/4/2014	Agile Glass Supply	940	23188	11703	11485
5	Central	E438	1/4/2014	Persuasive Kettle Inc.	190	5520	2958	2562
6	East	E438	1/4/2014	Safe Saddle Corporation	130	3933	2024	1909
7	West	C409	1/4/2014	Agile Glass Supply	440	11304	5936	5368
8	West	C409	1/4/2014	Guarded Kettle Corporatio	770	20382	10387	9995
9	Central	E438	1/4/2014	Matchless Yardstick Inc.	570	17584	8875	8709
10	East	D625	1/4/2014	Unique Marble Company	380	10196	5521	4675
11	Central	D625	1/4/2014	Inventive Clipboard Corpor	690	18322	10026	8296
12	West	E438	1/4/2014	Agile Glass Supply	580	16850	9031	7819

In Excel 2000 and later, you first build a pivot cache object to describe the input area of the data:

```
Dim WSD As Worksheet
Dim PTCache As PivotCache
Dim PT As PivotTable
Dim PRange As Range
Dim FinalRow As Long
Dim FinalCol As Long
Set WSD = Worksheets("PivotTable")

' Delete any prior pivot tables
For Each PT In WSD.PivotTables
    PT.TableRange2.Clear
Next PT

' Define input area and set up a Pivot Cache
FinalRow = WSD.Cells(Rows.Count, 1).End(xlUp).Row
FinalCol = WSD.Cells(1, Columns.Count).End(xlToLeft).Column
Set PRange = WSD.Cells(1, 1).Resize(FinalRow, FinalCol)
Set PTCache = ActiveWorkbook.PivotCaches.Add(SourceType:=xlDatabase, _
    SourceData:=PRange)
```

Creating and Configuring the Pivot Table

After defining the pivot cache, use the `CreatePivotTable` method to create a blank pivot table based on the defined pivot cache:

```
Set PT = PTCache.CreatePivotTable(TableDestination:=WSD.Cells(2, _
FinalCol + 2), TableName:="PivotTable1")
```

In the `CreatePivotTable` method, you specify the output location and optionally give the table a name. After running this line of code, you have a strange-looking blank pivot table, like the one shown in Figure 12.2. You now have to use code to drop fields onto the table.

If you choose the Defer Layout Update setting in the user interface to build the pivot table, Excel does not recalculate the pivot table after you drop each field onto the table. By default in VBA, Excel calculates the pivot table as you execute each step of building the table. This could require the pivot table to be executed a half-dozen times before you get the final result. To speed up your code execution, you can temporarily turn off calculation of the pivot table by using the `ManualUpdate` property:

```
PT.ManualUpdate = True
```

Figure 12.2
When you use the `CreatePivotTable` method, Excel gives you a four-cell blank pivot table that is not very useful.

You can now run through the steps needed to lay out the pivot table. In the `.AddFields` method, you can specify one or more fields that should be in the row, column, or filter area of the pivot table.

The `RowFields` parameter enables you to define fields that appear in the Rows drop zone of the PivotTable Field List. The `ColumnFields` parameter corresponds to the Columns drop zone. The `PageFields` parameter corresponds to the Filter drop zone.

The following line of code populates a pivot table with two fields in the row area and one field in the column area:

```
' Set up the row & column fields
PT.AddFields RowFields:=Array("Region", "Customer"), _
    ColumnFields:="Product"
```

To add a field such as Revenue to the values area of the table, you change the `Orientation` property of the field to be `xlDataField`.

Adding Fields to the Data Area

When you are adding fields to the Data area of the pivot table, there are many settings you should control instead of letting Excel's IntelliSense decide.

For example, say you are building a report with revenue in which you will likely want to sum the revenue. If you don't explicitly specify the calculation, Excel scans through the data in the underlying data. If 100 percent of the revenue columns are numeric, Excel sums those columns. If one cell is blank or contains text, Excel decides on that day to count the revenue, which produces confusing results.

Because of this possible variability, you should never use the DataFields argument in the AddFields method. Instead, change the property of the field to xlDataField. You can then specify the Function to be xlSum.

While you are setting up the data field, you can change several other properties within the same With...End With block.

The Position property is useful when you are adding multiple fields to the data area. Specify 1 for the first field, 2 for the second field, and so on.

By default, Excel renames a Revenue field to have a strange name like Sum of Revenue. You can use the .Name property to change that heading back to something normal.

> **NOTE** Note that you cannot reuse the word "Revenue" as a name. Instead, you should use "Revenue " (with a space).

You are not required to specify a number format, but it can make the resulting pivot table easier to understand, and takes only one extra line of code:

```
' Set up the data fields
With PT.PivotFields("Revenue")
    .Orientation = xlDataField
    .Function = xlSum
    .Position = 1
    .NumberFormat = "#,##0"
    .Name = "Revenue "
End With
```

At this point, you have given VBA all the settings required to generate the pivot table correctly. If you set ManualUpdate to False, Excel calculates and draws the pivot table. You can immediately thereafter set this back to True:

```
' Calc the pivot table
PT.ManualUpdate = False
PT.ManualUpdate = True
```

Your pivot table inherits the table style settings selected as the default on whatever computer happens to run the code. If you want control over the final format, you can explicitly choose a table style. The following code applies banded rows and a medium table style:

```
' Format the pivot table
PT.ShowTableStyleRowStripes = True
PT.TableStyle2 = "PivotStyleMedium10"
```

If you want to reuse the data from the pivot table, turn off the grand totals and subtotals and fill in the labels along the left column. The fastest way to suppress the 11 possible subtotals is to turn Subtotals(1) to True and then to False:

```
With PT
    .ColumnGrand = False
    .RowGrand = False
    .RepeatAllLabels xlRepeatLabels ' New in Excel 2010
```

12

```
End With
PT.PivotFields("Region").Subtotals(1) = True
PT.PivotFields("Region").Subtotals(1) = False
```

At this point, you have a complete pivot table like the one shown in Figure 12.3.

Figure 12.3
Fewer than 50 lines of code created this pivot table in less than a second.

Region	Customer	A292	B722	C409	D625	E438
Central	Enhanced Toothpick Corporation	293,017	403,764	364,357	602,380	635,402
Central	Inventive Clipboard Corporation	410,968	440,937	422,647	292,109	346,605
Central	Matchless Yardstick Inc.	476,223	352,550	260,833	392,890	578,970
Central	Mouthwatering Jewelry Company	374,000	446,290	471,812	291,793	522,434
Central	Persuasive Kettle Inc.	1,565,368	1,385,296	1,443,434	1,584,759	2,030,578
Central	Remarkable Umbrella Company	362,851	425,325	469,054	653,531	645,140
Central	Tremendous Bobsled Corporation	560,759	711,826	877,247	802,303	1,095,329
East	Excellent Glass Traders	447,771	386,804	723,888	522,227	454,540
East	Magnificent Patio Traders	395,186	483,856	484,067	430,971	539,616
East	Mouthwatering Tripod Corporation	337,100	310,841	422,036	511,184	519,701
East	Safe Saddle Corporation	646,559	857,573	730,463	1,038,371	1,053,369
East	Unique Marble Company	1,600,347	1,581,665	1,765,305	1,707,140	2,179,242
East	Unique Saddle Inc.	408,114	311,970	543,737	458,428	460,826
East	Vibrant Tripod Corporation	317,953	368,601	313,807	499,055	519,112
West	Agile Glass Supply	628,204	652,845	905,059	712,285	978,745
West	Functional Shingle Corporation	504,818	289,670	408,567	505,071	484,777
West	Guarded Kettle Corporation	1,450,110	1,404,742	1,889,149	1,842,751	2,302,023
West	Innovative Oven Corporation	452,320	364,200	420,624	539,300	582,773
West	Persuasive Yardstick Corporation	268,394	426,882	441,914	257,998	402,987
West	Tremendous Flagpole Traders	446,799	557,376	237,439	554,595	564,562
West	Trouble-Free Eggbeater Inc.	390,917	520,048	506,324	370,819	515,235

Listing 12.1 shows the complete code used to generate the pivot table.

Listing 12.1   Code to Generate a Pivot Table

```
Sub CreatePivot()
    Dim WSD As Worksheet
    Dim PTCache As PivotCache
    Dim PT As PivotTable
    Dim PRange As Range
    Dim FinalRow As Long
    Set WSD = Worksheets("PivotTable")

    ' Delete any prior pivot tables
    For Each PT In WSD.PivotTables
        PT.TableRange2.Clear
    Next PT

    ' Define input area and set up a Pivot Cache
    FinalRow = WSD.Cells(Application.Rows.Count, 1).End(xlUp).Row
    FinalCol = WSD.Cells(1, Application.Columns.Count). _
        End(xlToLeft).Column
    Set PRange = WSD.Cells(1, 1).Resize(FinalRow, FinalCol)
    Set PTCache = ActiveWorkbook.PivotCaches.Add(SourceType:= _
        xlDatabase, SourceData:=PRange.Address)

    ' Create the Pivot Table from the Pivot Cache
    Set PT = PTCache.CreatePivotTable(TableDestination:=WSD. _
        Cells(2, FinalCol + 2), TableName:="PivotTable1")

    ' Turn off updating while building the table
    PT.ManualUpdate = True
```

12

```
' Set up the row & column fields
PT.AddFields RowFields:=Array("Region", "Customer"), _
    ColumnFields:="Product"

' Set up the data fields
With PT.PivotFields("Revenue")
    .Orientation = xlDataField
    .Function = xlSum
    .Position = 1
    .NumberFormat = "#,##0"
    .Name = "Revenue "
End With

' Calc the pivot table
PT.ManualUpdate = False
PT.ManualUpdate = True

'Format the pivot table
PT.ShowTableStyleRowStripes = True
PT.TableStyle2 = "PivotStyleMedium10"
With PT
    .ColumnGrand = False
    .RowGrand = False
    .RepeatAllLabels xlRepeatLabels ' New in Excel 2010
End With
PT.PivotFields("Region").Subtotals(1) = True
PT.PivotFields("Region").Subtotals(1) = False
WSD.Activate
Range("J2").Select

End Sub
```

Learning Why You Cannot Move or Change Part of a Pivot Report

Although pivot tables are incredible, they have annoying limitations; for example, you cannot move or change just part of a pivot table. Try to run a macro that clears row 2. The macro comes to a screeching halt with the error 1004, as shown in Figure 12.4. To get around this limitation, you can copy the pivot table and paste as values.

Figure 12.4
You cannot delete just part of a pivot table.

12

Determining the Size of a Finished Pivot Table to Convert the Pivot Table to Values

Knowing the size of a pivot table in advance is difficult. If you run a report of transactional data on one day, you might or might not have sales from the West region, for example. This could cause your table to be either six or seven columns wide. Therefore, you should use the special property `TableRange2` to refer to the entire resultant pivot table.

`PT.TableRange2` includes the entire pivot table. In Figure 12.5, `TableRange2` includes the extra row at the top with the field heading of Revenue. To eliminate that row, the code copies `PT.TableRange2` but offsets this selection by one row by using `.Offset(1, 0)`. Depending on the nature of your pivot table, you might need to use an offset of two or more rows to get rid of extraneous information at the top of the pivot table.

Figure 12.5

This figure shows an intermediate result of the macro. Only the summary in J12:M17 will remain after the macro finishes.

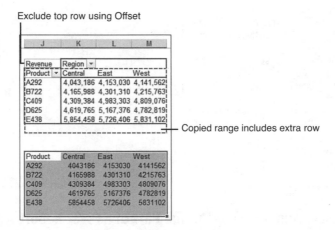

The code copies `PT.TableRange2` and uses `PasteSpecial` on a cell five rows below the current pivot table. At that point in the code, your worksheet appears as shown in Figure 12.5. The table in J2 is a live pivot table, and the table in J12 is just the copied results.

You can then eliminate the pivot table by applying the `Clear` method to the entire table. If your code is then going on to do additional formatting, you should remove the pivot cache from memory by setting `PTCache` equal to `Nothing`.

The code in Listing 12.2 uses a pivot table to produce a summary from the underlying data. At the end of the code, the pivot table is copied to static values and the pivot table is cleared.

Listing 12.2   Code to Produce a Static Summary from a Pivot Table

```
Sub CreateSummaryReportUsingPivot()
    ' Use a Pivot Table to create a static summary report
    ' with product going down the rows and regions across
    Dim WSD As Worksheet
    Dim PTCache As PivotCache
```

```vba
Dim PT As PivotTable
Dim PRange As Range
Dim FinalRow As Long
Set WSD = Worksheets("PivotTable")

' Delete any prior pivot tables
For Each PT In WSD.PivotTables
    PT.TableRange2.Clear
Next PT
WSD.Range("J1:Z1").EntireColumn.Clear

' Define input area and set up a Pivot Cache
FinalRow = WSD.Cells(Application.Rows.Count, 1).End(xlUp).Row
FinalCol = WSD.Cells(1, Application.Columns.Count). _
    End(xlToLeft).Column
Set PRange = WSD.Cells(1, 1).Resize(FinalRow, FinalCol)
Set PTCache = ActiveWorkbook.PivotCaches.Add(SourceType:= _
    xlDatabase, SourceData:=PRange.Address)

' Create the Pivot Table from the Pivot Cache
Set PT = PTCache.CreatePivotTable(TableDestination:=WSD. _
    Cells(2, FinalCol + 2), TableName:="PivotTable1")

' Turn off updating while building the table
PT.ManualUpdate = True

' Set up the row fields
PT.AddFields RowFields:="Product", ColumnFields:="Region"

' Set up the data fields
With PT.PivotFields("Revenue")
    .Orientation = xlDataField
    .Function = xlSum
    .Position = 1
    .NumberFormat = "#,##0"
    .Name = "Revenue "
End With

With PT
    .ColumnGrand = False
    .RowGrand = False
    .NullString = "0"
End With

' Calc the pivot table
PT.ManualUpdate = False
PT.ManualUpdate = True

' PT.TableRange2 contains the results. Move these to J12
' as just values and not a real pivot table.
PT.TableRange2.Offset(1, 0).Copy
WSD.Cells(5 + PT.TableRange2.Rows.Count, FinalCol + 2). _
    PasteSpecial xlPasteValues

' At this point, the worksheet looks like Figure 12.5
' Stop

' Delete the original Pivot Table & the Pivot Cache
PT.TableRange2.Clear
```

12

```
    Set PTCache = Nothing

    WSD.Activate
    Range("J12").Select
End Sub
```

The code in Listing 12.2 creates the pivot table. It then copies the results and pastes them as values in J12:M13. Figure 12.5, which was shown previously, includes an intermediate result just before the original pivot table is cleared.

So far, this chapter has walked you through building the simplest of pivot table reports. Pivot tables offer far more flexibility. The sections that follow present more complex reporting examples.

Using Advanced Pivot Table Features

In this section, you take the detailed transactional data and produce a series of reports for each product line manager. This section covers the following advanced pivot table steps that are required in these reports:

1. Group the daily dates up to yearly dates.

2. Add multiple fields to the value area.

3. Control the sort order so the largest customers are listed first.

4. Use the ShowPages feature to replicate the report for each product line manager.

5. After producing the pivot tables, convert the pivot table to values and do some basic formatting.

Figure 12.6 shows the report for one product line manager so that you can understand the final goal.

Figure 12.6
Using pivot tables simplifies the creation of the report.

	A	B	C	D	E
1	Product report for A292				
2					
3					
4		2014			2015
5	Customer	# of Orders	Revenue	% of Total	# of Orders
6	Unique Marble Company	59	716,631	12.4%	70
7	Persuasive Kettle Inc.	64	860,540	14.9%	54
8	Guarded Kettle Corporation	63	710,732	12.3%	56
9	Safe Saddle Corporation	15	184,144	3.2%	37
10	Agile Glass Supply	31	353,678	6.1%	24
11	Tremendous Bobsled Corporation	28	304,831	5.3%	23
12	Functional Shingle Corporation	0	0	0.0%	40
13	Matchless Yardstick Inc.	18	263,819	4.6%	17

Using Multiple Value Fields

The report has three fields in the values area: Count of Orders, Revenue, and % of Total Revenue. Anytime you have two or more fields in the values area, a new virtual field named Data becomes available in your pivot table.

In Excel 2013, this field appears as sigma values in the drop zone of the Pivot Table Field List. When creating your pivot table, you can specify Data as one of the column fields or row fields.

The position of the Data field is important. It usually works best as the innermost column field.

When you define your pivot table in VBA, you have two columns fields: the Date field and the Data field. To specify two or more fields in the AddFields method, you wrap those fields in an array function.

Use this code to define the pivot table:

```
' Set up the row fields
PT.AddFields RowFields:="Customer", _
    ColumnFields:=Array("Date", "Data"), _
    PageFields:="Product"
```

This is the first time you have seen the PageFields parameter in this chapter. If you were creating a pivot table for someone to use, the fields in the PageField allow for easy ad hoc analysis. In this case, the value in the PageField is going to make it easy to replicate the report for every product-line manager.

Counting the Number of Records

So far, the .Function property of the data fields has always been xlSum. A total of 11 functions are available: xlSum, xlCount, xlAverage, xlStdDev, xlMin, xlMax, and so on.

Count is the only function that works for text fields. To count the number of records, and hence the number of orders, add a text field to the data area and choose xlCount as the function:

```
With PT.PivotFields("Region")
    .Orientation = xlDataField
    .Function = xlCount
    .Position = 1
    .NumberFormat = "#,##0"
    .Name = "# of Orders "
End With
```

> **NOTE**
> This is a count of the number of records. It is not a count of the distinct values in a field. This was previously difficult to do in a pivot table. It is now possible using the Data Model. See the "Using the Data Model in Excel 2013" section later in this chapter for details.

Grouping Daily Dates to Months, Quarters, or Years

Pivot tables have the amazing capability to group daily dates up to months, quarters, and/or years. In VBA, this feature is a bit annoying because you must select a date cell before

12

issuing the command. As you saw in Figure 12.2, your pivot table usually stays as four blank cells until the end of the macro, so there really is not a date field to select.

However, if you need to group a date field, you have to let the pivot table redraw. To do this, use this code:

```
' Pause here to group daily dates up to years
' Need to draw the pivot table so you can select date heading
PT.ManualUpdate = False
PT.ManualUpdate = True
```

> **NOTE** I used to go through all sorts of gyrations to figure out where the first date field was. In fact, you can simply refer to PT.PivotFields("Date").LabelRange to point to the date heading.

There are seven ways to group times or dates: Seconds, Minutes, Hours, Days, Months, Quarters, and Years. Note that you can group a field by multiple items. You specify a series of seven True/False values corresponding to Seconds, Minutes, and so on.

For example, to group by Months, Quarters, and Years, you would use the following:

```
PT.PivotFields("Date").LabelRange.Group , Periods:= _
    Array(False, False, False, False, True, True, True)
```

> **NOTE** Never choose to group by only months without including years. If you do this, Excel combines January from all years in the data into a single item called January. Although this is great for seasonality analyses, it is rarely what you want in a summary. Always choose Years and Months in the Grouping dialog.

If you want to group by week, you group only by day and use 7 as the value for the By parameter:

```
PT.PivotFields("Date").LabelRange.Group _
    Start:=True, End:=True, By:=7, _
    Periods:=Array(False, False, False, True, False, False, False)
```

Specifying True for Start and End starts the first week at the earliest date in the data. If you want to show only the weeks from Monday December 30, 2013, to Sunday, January 3, 2016, use this code:

```
With PT.PivotFields("Date")
    .LabelRange.Group _
        Start:=DateSerial(2013, 12, 30), _
        End:=DateSerial(2016, 1, 3), _
        By:=7, _
        Periods:=Array(False, False, False, True, False, False, False)
    On Error Resume Next
    .PivotItems("<12/30/2013").Visible = False
    .PivotItems(">1/3/2016").Visible = False
    On Error Goto 0
End With
```

> **NOTE** There is one limitation to grouping by week. When you group by week, you cannot also group by any other measure. For example, grouping by both week and quarter is not valid.

For this report, you need to group only by year, so the code is as follows:

```
' Group daily dates up to years
PT.PivotFields("Date").LabelRange.Group , Periods:= _
    Array(False, False, False, False, False, False, True)
```

> **TIP** Before grouping the daily dates up to years, you had about 500 date columns across this report. After grouping, you have two date columns plus a total. I prefer to group the dates as soon as possible in the macro. If you added the other two data fields to the report before grouping, your report would be 1,500 columns wide. Although this is not a problem since Excel 2007 increased the column limit from 256 to 16,384, it still creates an unusually large report when you ultimately need only a few columns. Allowing the pivot table to grow to 1,500 columns, even for a few lines of code, would make the worksheet's last cell be column BER.

After you group daily dates to years, the new Year field is still called Date. This might not always be true. If you roll daily dates up to months and to years, the Date field contains months, and a new Year field is added to the field list to hold years.

Changing the Calculation to Show Percentages

Excel 2013 offers 15 choices on the Show Values As tab of the Value Field Settings dialog.

These calculations enable you to change how a field is displayed in the report. Instead of showing sales, you could show the sales as a percentage of the total sales. You could show a running total. You could show each day's sales as a percentage of the previous day's sales.

All these settings are controlled through the .Calculation property of the pivot field. Each calculation has its own unique set of rules. Some, such as % of Column, work without any further settings. Others, such as Running Total In, require a base field. Others, such as Running Total, require a base field and a base item.

To get the percentage of the total, specify xlPercentOfTotal as the .Calculation property for the page field:

```
.Calculation = xlPercentOfTotal
```

To set up a running total, you have to specify a BaseField. Say that you need a running total along a date column:

```
' Set up Running Total
    .Calculation = xlRunningTotal
    .BaseField = "Date"
```

With ship months going down the columns, you might want to see the percentage of revenue growth from month to month. You can set up this arrangement with the xlPercent-DifferenceFrom setting. In this case, you must specify that the BaseField is "Date" and that the BaseItem is something called (previous):

```
' Set up % change from prior month
With PT.PivotFields("Revenue")
    .Orientation = xlDataField
    .Function = xlSum
    .Caption = "%Change"
    .Calculation = xlPercentDifferenceFrom
    .BaseField = "Date"
    .BaseItem = "(previous)"
    .NumberFormat = "#0.0%"
End With
```

Note that with positional calculations, you cannot use the AutoShow or AutoSort method. This is too bad; it would be interesting to sort the customers high to low and to see their sizes in relation to each other.

You can use the xlPercentDifferenceFrom setting to express revenues as a percentage of the West region sales:

```
' Show revenue as a percentage of California
With PT.PivotFields("Revenue")
    .Orientation = xlDataField
    .Function = xlSum
    .Caption = "% of West"
    .Calculation = xlPercentDifferenceFrom
    .BaseField = "State"
    .BaseItem = "California"
    .Position = 3
    .NumberFormat = "#0.0%"
End With
```

Table 12.1 shows the complete list of .Calculation options. The second column indicates whether the calculation is compatible with earlier versions of Excel. The third column indicates whether you need a base field and base item.

Table 12.1   Complete List of .Calculation **Options**

Calculation	Version	BaseField/BaseItem
xlDifferenceFrom	All	Both required
xlIndex	All	Neither
xlNoAdditionalCalculation	All	Neither
xlPercentDifferenceFrom	All	Both required
xlPercentOf	All	Both required
xlPercentOfColumn	All	Neither
xlPercentOfParent	2010/2013 only	BaseField only

Calculation	Version	BaseField/BaseItem
`xlPercentOfParentColumn`	2010/2013 only	Both required
`xlPercentOfParentRow`	2010/2013 only	Both required
`xlPercentOfRow`	All	Neither
`xlPercentOfTotal`	All	Neither
`xlPercentRunningTotal`	2010/2013 only	BaseField only
`xlRankAscending`	2010/2013 only	BaseField only
`xlRankDescending`	2010/2013 only	BaseField only
`xlRunningTotal`	All	BaseField only

After that long explanation of the `.Calculation` property, you can build the other two pivot table fields for the product line report.

Add `Revenue` to the report twice. The first time, there is no calculation. The second time, calculate the percentage of total:

```
' Set up the data fields - Revenue
With PT.PivotFields("Revenue")
    .Orientation = xlDataField
    .Function = xlSum
    .Position = 2
    .NumberFormat = "#,##0"
    .Name = "Revenue "
End With

' Set up the data fields - % of total Revenue
With PT.PivotFields("Revenue")
    .Orientation = xlDataField
    .Function = xlSum
    .Position = 3
    .NumberFormat = "0.0%"
    .Name = "% of Total "
    .Calculation = xlPercentOfColumn
End With
```

> **NOTE** Take careful note of the name of the first field in the preceding code. By default, Excel would use Sum of Revenue. If you think this is a goofy title (as I do), you can change it. However, you cannot change it to Revenue because there is already a field in the pivot table field list with that name.
>
> In the preceding code, I use the name "Revenue " (with a trailing space). This works fine, and no one notices the extra space. However, in the rest of the macro, when you refer to this field, remember to refer to it as "Revenue " (with a trailing space).

12

Eliminating Blank Cells in the Values Area

If you have some customers who were new in year 2, their sales will appear blank in year 1. Anyone using Excel 97 or later can replace blank cells with zeros. In the Excel interface, you can find the setting on the Layout & Format tab of the PivotTable Options dialog box. Select the For Empty Cells, Show option and type 0 in the box.

The equivalent operation in VBA is to set the `NullString` property for the pivot table to "0":

```
PT.NullString = "0"
```

> **NOTE**   Although the proper code is to set this value to a text zero, Excel actually puts a real zero in the empty cells.

Controlling the Sort Order with AutoSort

The Excel interface offers an AutoSort option that enables you to show customers in descending order based on revenue. The equivalent code in VBA to sort the product field by descending revenue uses the `AutoSort` method:

```
PT.PivotFields("Customer").AutoSort Order:=xlDescending, _
    Field:="Revenue "
```

After applying some formatting in the macro, you now have one report with totals for all products, as shown in Figure 12.7.

Figure 12.7
The Product drop-down in column K enables you to filter the report to certain products.

J	K	L	M	N
Product	(All) ▾			
	Date ▾	Data		
	2014			2015
Customer	▾↓ # of Orders	Revenue	% of Total	# of Orders
Guarded Kettle Corporation	316	4,501,310	13.2%	290
Unique Marble Company	307	4,418,324	13.0%	316
Persuasive Kettle Inc.	268	3,870,414	11.4%	295
Safe Saddle Corporation	135	1,979,144	5.8%	160
Tremendous Bobsled Corporation	146	1,991,712	5.8%	148
Agile Glass Supply	148	2,128,660	6.2%	130

Replicating the Report for Every Product

As long as your pivot table was not built on an OLAP data source, you now have access to one of the most powerful, but least well-known, features in pivot tables. The command is called Show Report Filter Pages, and it takes your pivot table and replicates it for every item in one of the fields in the Filters area.

Because you built the report with Product as a filter field, it takes only one line of code to replicate the pivot table for every product:

```
' Replicate the pivot table for each product
```

```
PT.ShowPages PageField:="Product"
```

After running this line of code, you have a new worksheet for every product in the dataset. Starting in Excel 2013, the new product pivot tables inherit the `.ManualUpdate` setting from the original pivot table. Be sure to set the original pivot table to `.ManualUpdate = False` before using the command; otherwise, the new pivot tables do not draw correctly.

From there, you have some simple formatting and calculations. Check the end of the macro for these techniques, which should be second nature by this point in the book.

Listing 12.3 shows the complete macro.

Listing 12.3   Produce Report per Product

```
Sub CustomerByProductReport()
    ' Use a Pivot Table to create a report for each product
    ' with customers in rows and years in columns
    Dim WSD As Worksheet
    Dim PTCache As PivotCache
    Dim PT As PivotTable
    Dim PT2 As PivotTable
    Dim WS As Worksheet
    Dim WSF As Worksheet
    Dim PRange As Range
    Dim FinalRow As Long
    Set WSD = Worksheets("PivotTable")

    ' Delete any prior pivot tables
    For Each PT In WSD.PivotTables
        PT.TableRange2.Clear
    Next PT
    WSD.Range("J1:Z1").EntireColumn.Clear

    ' Define input area and set up a Pivot Cache
    FinalRow = WSD.Cells(Application.Rows.Count, 1).End(xlUp).Row
    FinalCol = WSD.Cells(1, Application.Columns.Count). _
        End(xlToLeft).Column
    Set PRange = WSD.Cells(1, 1).Resize(FinalRow, FinalCol)
    Set PTCache = ActiveWorkbook.PivotCaches.Add(SourceType:= _
        xlDatabase, SourceData:=PRange.Address)

    ' Create the Pivot Table from the Pivot Cache
    Set PT = PTCache.CreatePivotTable(TableDestination:=WSD. _
        Cells(2, FinalCol + 2), TableName:="PivotTable1")

    ' Turn off updating while building the table
    PT.ManualUpdate = True

    ' Set up the row fields
    PT.AddFields RowFields:="Customer", _
        ColumnFields:=Array("Date", "Data"), _
        PageFields:="Product"

    ' Set up the data fields - count of orders
    With PT.PivotFields("Region")
        .Orientation = xlDataField
```

12

```
        .Function = xlCount
        .Position = 1
        .NumberFormat = "#,##0"
        .Name = "# of Orders "
    End With

    ' Pause here to group daily dates up to years
    ' Need to draw the pivot table so you can select date heading
    PT.ManualUpdate = False
    PT.ManualUpdate = True

    ' Group daily dates up to years
    PT.PivotFields("Date").LabelRange.Group , Periods:= _
        Array(False, False, False, False, False, False, True)

    ' Set up the data fields - Revenue
    With PT.PivotFields("Revenue")
        .Orientation = xlDataField
        .Function = xlSum
        .Position = 2
        .NumberFormat = "#,##0"
        .Name = "Revenue "
    End With

    ' Set up the data fields - % of total Revenue
    With PT.PivotFields("Revenue")
        .Orientation = xlDataField
        .Function = xlSum
        .Position = 3
        .NumberFormat = "0.0%"
        .Name = "% of Total "
        .Calculation = xlPercentOfColumn
    End With

    ' Sort the customers so the largest is at the top
    PT.PivotFields("Customer").AutoSort Order:=xlDescending, _
        Field:="Revenue "

    With PT
        .ShowTableStyleColumnStripes = True
        .ShowTableStyleRowStripes = True
        .TableStyle2 = "PivotStyleMedium10"
        .NullString = "0"
    End With

    ' Calc the pivot table
    PT.ManualUpdate = False

    ' Replicate the pivot table for each product
    PT.ShowPages PageField:="Product"

    Ctr = 0
    For Each WS In ActiveWorkbook.Worksheets
        If WS.PivotTables.Count > 0 Then
            If WS.Cells(1, 1).Value = "Product" Then
                ' Save some info
                WS.Select
```

```
            ThisProduct = Cells(1, 2).Value
            Ctr = Ctr + 1
            If Ctr = 1 Then
                Set WSF = ActiveSheet
            End If
            Set PT2 = WS.PivotTables(1)
            CalcRows = PT2.TableRange1.Rows.Count - 3

            PT2.TableRange2.Copy
            PT2.TableRange2.PasteSpecial xlPasteValues

            Range("A1:C3").ClearContents
            Range("A1:B2").Clear
            Range("A1").Value = "Product report for " & ThisProduct
            Range("A1").Style = "Title"

            ' Fix some headings
            Range("b5:d5").Copy Destination:=Range("H5:J5")
            Range("H4").Value = "Total"
            Range("I4:J4").Clear

            ' Copy the format
            Range("J1").Resize(CalcRows + 5, 1).Copy
            Range("K1").Resize(CalcRows + 5, 1). _
                PasteSpecial xlPasteFormats
            Range("K5").Value = "% Rev Growth"
            Range("K6").Resize(CalcRows, 1).FormulaR1C1 = _
                "=IFERROR(RC6/RC3-1,1)"

            Range("A2:K5").Style = "Heading 4"
            Range("A2").Resize(CalcRows + 10, 11).Columns.AutoFit

        End If
    End If
Next WS

WSD.Select
PT.TableRange2.Clear
Set PTCache = Nothing

WSF.Select
MsgBox Ctr & " product reports created."

End Sub
```

Filtering a Dataset

There are many ways to filter a pivot table, from the new slicers, to the conceptual filters, to simply selecting and clearing items from one of the many field drop-downs.

Manually Filtering Two or More Items in a Pivot Field

When you open a field heading drop-down and select or clear items from the list, you are applying a manual filter. (See Figure 12.8.)

Figure 12.8
This filter drop-down offers manual filters, a search box, and conceptual filters.

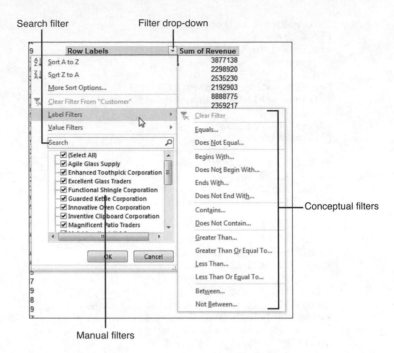

Search filter

Filter drop-down

Conceptual filters

Manual filters

For example, you have one client who sells shoes. In the report showing sales of sandals, he wants to see just the stores that are in warm-weather states. The code to hide a particular store is as follows:

```
PT.PivotFields("Store").PivotItems("Minneapolis").Visible = False
```

This process is easy in VBA. After building the table with Product in the page field, loop through to change the Visible property to show only the total of certain products:

```
' Make sure all PivotItems along line are visible
For Each PivItem In _
    PT.PivotFields("Product").PivotItems
    PivItem.Visible = True
Next PivItem

' Now - loop through and keep only certain items visible
For Each PivItem In _
    PT.PivotFields("Product").PivotItems
    Select Case PivItem.Name
        Case "Landscaping/Grounds Care", _
            "Green Plants and Foliage Care"
            PivItem.Visible = True
        Case Else
            PivItem.Visible = False
    End Select
Next PivItem
```

Using the Conceptual Filters

Excel 2007 introduced new conceptual filters for date fields, numeric fields, and text fields. Open the drop-down for any field label in the pivot table. In the drop-down that appears, you can choose Label Filters, Date Filters, or Value Filters. The date filters offer the capability to filter to a conceptual period such as last month or next year (see Figure 12.9).

Figure 12.9
These date filters were introduced in Excel 2007.

To apply a label filter in VBA, use the `PivotFilters.Add` method. The following code filters to the customers that start with the letter *E*:

```
PT.PivotFields("Customer").PivotFilters.Add _
    Type:=xlCaptionBeginsWith, Value1:="E"
```

To clear the filter from the Customer field, use the `ClearAllFilters` method:

```
PT.PivotFields("Customer").ClearAllFilters
```

To apply a date filter to the date field to find records from this week, use this code:

```
PT.PivotFields("Date").PivotFilters.Add Type:=xlThisWeek
```

The value filters enable you to filter one field based on the value of another field. For example, to find all the markets where the total revenue is more than $100,000, use this code:

```
PT.PivotFields("Market").PivotFilters.Add _
    Type:=xlValueIsGreaterThan, _
    DataField:=PT.PivotFields("Sum of Revenue"), _
    Value1:=100000
```

Other value filters might enable you to specify that you want branches where the revenue is between $50,000 and $100,000. In this case, you specify one limit as `Value1` and the second limit as `Value2`:

```
PT.PivotFields("Market").PivotFilters.Add _
    Type:=xlValueIsBetween, _
    DataField:=PT.PivotFields("Sum of Revenue"), _
    Value1:=50000, Value2:=100000
```

Table 12.2 lists all the possible filter types.

12

Table 12.2   Filter Types

Filter Type	Description
xlBefore	Filters for all dates before a specified date
xlBeforeOrEqualTo	Filters for all dates on or before a specified date
xlAfter	Filters for all dates after a specified date
xlAfterOrEqualTo	Filters for all dates on or after a specified date
xlAllDatesInPeriodJanuary	Filters for all dates in January
xlAllDatesInPeriodFebruary	Filters for all dates in February
xlAllDatesInPeriodMarch	Filters for all dates in March
xlAllDatesInPeriodApril	Filters for all dates in April
xlAllDatesInPeriodMay	Filters for all dates in May
xlAllDatesInPeriodJune	Filters for all dates in June
xlAllDatesInPeriodJuly	Filters for all dates in July
xlAllDatesInPeriodAugust	Filters for all dates in August
xlAllDatesInPeriodSeptember	Filters for all dates in September
xlAllDatesInPeriodOctober	Filters for all dates in October
xlAllDatesInPeriodNovember	Filters for all dates in November
xlAllDatesInPeriodDecember	Filters for all dates in December
xlAllDatesInPeriodQuarter1	Filters for all dates in Quarter 1
xlAllDatesInPeriodQuarter2	Filters for all dates in Quarter 2
xlAllDatesInPeriodQuarter3	Filters for all dates in Quarter 3
xlAllDatesInPeriodQuarter4	Filters for all dates in Quarter 4
xlBottomCount	Filters for the specified number of values from the bottom of a list
xlBottomPercent	Filters for the specified percentage of values from the bottom of a list
xlBottomSum	Sums the values from the bottom of the list
xlCaptionBeginsWith	Filters for all captions beginning with the specified string
xlCaptionContains	Filters for all captions that contain the specified string
xlCaptionDoesNotBeginWith	Filters for all captions that do not begin with the specified string
xlCaptionDoesNotContain	Filters for all captions that do not contain the specified string
xlCaptionDoesNotEndWith	Filters for all captions that do not end with the specified string
xlCaptionDoesNotEqual	Filters for all captions that do not match the specified string
xlCaptionEndsWith	Filters for all captions that end with the specified string

12

Filter Type	Description
xlCaptionEquals	Filters for all captions that match the specified string
xlCaptionIsBetween	Filters for all captions that are between a specified range of values
xlCaptionIsGreaterThan	Filters for all captions that are greater than the specified value
xlCaptionIsGreaterThanOrEqualTo	Filters for all captions that are greater than or match the specified value
xlCaptionIsLessThan	Filters for all captions that are less than the specified value
xlCaptionIsLessThanOrEqualTo	Filters for all captions that are less than or match the specified value
xlCaptionIsNotBetween	Filters for all captions that are not between a specified range of values
xlDateBetween	Filters for all dates that are between a specified range of dates
xlDateLastMonth	Filters for all dates that apply to the previous month
xlDateLastQuarter	Filters for all dates that apply to the previous quarter
xlDateLastWeek	Filters for all dates that apply to the previous week
xlDateLastYear	Filters for all dates that apply to the previous year
xlDateNextMonth	Filters for all dates that apply to the next month
xlDateNextQuarter	Filters for all dates that apply to the next quarter
xlDateNextWeek	Filters for all dates that apply to the next week
xlDateNextYear	Filters for all dates that apply to the next year
xlDateThisMonth	Filters for all dates that apply to the current month
xlDateThisQuarter	Filters for all dates that apply to the current quarter
xlDateThisWeek	Filters for all dates that apply to the current week
xlDateThisYear	Filters for all dates that apply to the current year
xlDateToday	Filters for all dates that apply to the current date
xlDateTomorrow	Filters for all dates that apply to the next day
xlDateYesterday	Filters for all dates that apply to the previous day
xlNotSpecificDate	Filters for all dates that do not match a specified date
xlSpecificDate	Filters for all dates that match a specified date
xlTopCount	Filters for the specified number of values from the top of a list
xlTopPercent	Filters for the specified percentage of values from the top of a list
xlTopSum	Sums the values from the top of the list
xlValueDoesNotEqual	Filters for all values that do not match the specified value

12

Filter Type	Description
xlValueEquals	Filters for all values that match the specified value
xlValueIsBetween	Filters for all values that are between a specified range of values
xlValueIsGreaterThan	Filters for all values that are greater than the specified value
xlValueIsGreaterThanOrEqualTo	Filters for all values that are greater than or match the specified value
xlValueIsLessThan	Filters for all values that are less than the specified value
xlValueIsLessThanOrEqualTo	Filters for all values that are less than or match the specified value
xlValueIsNotBetween	Filters for all values that are not between a specified range of values
xlYearToDate	Filters for all values that are within 1 year of a specified date

Using the Search Filter

Excel 2010 added a Search box to the filter drop-down. Although this is a slick feature in the Excel interface, there is no equivalent magic in VBA. Whereas the drop-down offers the Select All Search Results check box, the equivalent VBA just lists all the items that match the selection.

There is nothing new in Excel 2013 VBA to emulate the search box. To achieve the same results in VBA, use the xlCaptionContains filter described in the code that precedes Table 12.2.

CASE STUDY: FILTERING TO THE TOP 5 OR TOP 10 USING A FILTER

If you are designing an executive dashboard utility, you might want to spotlight the top five customers. As with the AutoSort option, you could be a pivot table pro and never have stumbled across the Top 10 AutoShow feature in Excel. This setting enables you to select either the top or the bottom *n* records based on any Data field in the report.

The code to use AutoShow in VBA uses the .AutoShow method:

```
' Show only the top 5 Customers
PT.PivotFields("Customer").AutoShow Top:=xlAutomatic, Range:=xlTop, _
    Count:=5, Field:= "Sum of Revenue"
```

When you create a report using the .AutoShow method, it is often helpful to copy the data and then go back to the original pivot report to get the totals for all markets. In the code, this is achieved by removing the Customer field from the pivot table and copying the grand total to the report. The code that follows produces the report shown in Figure 12.10.

Figure 12.10
The Top 5 Customers report contains two pivot tables.

	A	B	C	D	E	F	G
1	Top 5 Customers						
2							
3	Customer	A292	B733	C409	D625	E438	Grand Total
4	Guarded Kettle Corporation	1,450,110	1,404,742	1,889,149	1,842,751	2,302,023	8,888,775
5	Unique Marble Company	1,600,347	1,581,665	1,765,305	1,707,140	2,179,242	8,833,699
6	Persuasive Kettle Inc.	1,565,368	1,385,296	1,443,434	1,584,759	2,030,578	8,009,435
7	Safe Saddle Corporation	646,559	857,573	730,463	1,038,371	1,053,369	4,326,335
8	Tremendous Bobsled Corporation	560,759	711,826	877,247	802,303	1,095,329	4,047,464
9	Top 5 Total	5,823,143	5,941,102	6,705,598	6,975,324	8,660,541	34,105,708
10							
11	Total Company	12,337,778	12,683,061	14,101,763	14,569,960	17,411,966	71,104,528

```
Sub Top5Customers()
    ' Produce a report of the top 5 customers
    Dim WSD As Worksheet
    Dim WSR As Worksheet
    Dim WBN As Workbook
    Dim PTCache As PivotCache
    Dim PT As PivotTable
    Dim PRange As Range
    Dim FinalRow As Long
    Set WSD = Worksheets("PivotTable")

    ' Delete any prior pivot tables
    For Each PT In WSD.PivotTables
        PT.TableRange2.Clear
    Next PT
    WSD.Range("J1:Z1").EntireColumn.Clear

    ' Define input area and set up a Pivot Cache
    FinalRow = WSD.Cells(Application.Rows.Count, 1).End(xlUp).Row

    FinalCol = WSD.Cells(1, Application.Columns.Count). _
        End(xlToLeft).Column
    Set PRange = WSD.Cells(1, 1).Resize(FinalRow, FinalCol)
    Set PTCache = ActiveWorkbook.PivotCaches.Add(SourceType:= _
        xlDatabase, SourceData:=PRange.Address)

    ' Create the Pivot Table from the Pivot Cache
    Set PT = PTCache.CreatePivotTable(TableDestination:=WSD. _
        Cells(2, FinalCol + 2), TableName:="PivotTable1")

    ' Turn off updating while building the table
    PT.ManualUpdate = True

    ' Set up the row fields
    PT.AddFields RowFields:="Customer", ColumnFields:="Product"

    ' Set up the data fields
    With PT.PivotFields("Revenue")
        .Orientation = xlDataField
        .Function = xlSum
        .Position = 1
```

12

```
        .NumberFormat = "#,##0"
        .Name = "Total Revenue"
End With

' Ensure that we get zeros instead of blanks in the data area
PT.NullString = "0"

' Sort customers descending by sum of revenue
PT.PivotFields("Customer").AutoSort Order:=xlDescending, _
    Field:="Total Revenue"

' Show only the top 5 customers
PT.PivotFields("Customer").AutoShow Type:=xlAutomatic, Range:=xlTop, _
    Count:=5, Field:="Total Revenue"

' Calc the pivot table to allow the date label to be drawn
PT.ManualUpdate = False
PT.ManualUpdate = True

' Create a new blank workbook with one worksheet
Set WBN = Workbooks.Add(xlWBATWorksheet)
Set WSR = WBN.Worksheets(1)
WSR.Name = "Report"
' Set up title for report
With WSR.[A1]
    .Value = "Top 5 Customers"
    .Font.Size = 14
End With

' Copy the pivot table data to row 3 of the report sheet
' Use offset to eliminate the title row of the pivot table

PT.TableRange2.Offset(1, 0).Copy
WSR.[A3].PasteSpecial Paste:=xlPasteValuesAndNumberFormats
LastRow = WSR.Cells(Rows.Count, 1).End(xlUp).Row
WSR.Cells(LastRow, 1).Value = "Top 5 Total"

' Go back to the pivot table to get totals without the AutoShow
PT.PivotFields("Customer").Orientation = xlHidden
PT.ManualUpdate = False
PT.ManualUpdate = True
PT.TableRange2.Offset(2, 0).Copy
WSR.Cells(LastRow + 2, 1).PasteSpecial Paste:= _
    xlPasteValuesAndNumberFormats
WSR.Cells(LastRow + 2, 1).Value = "Total Company"

' Clear the pivot table
PT.TableRange2.Clear
Set PTCache = Nothing

' Do some basic formatting

' Autofit columns, bold the headings, right-align
WSR.Range(WSR.Range("A3"), WSR.Cells(LastRow + 2, 6)).Columns.AutoFit
Range("A3").EntireRow.Font.Bold = True
```

```
        Range("A3").EntireRow.HorizontalAlignment = xlRight
        Range("A3").HorizontalAlignment = xlLeft

        Range("A2").Select
        MsgBox "CEO Report has been Created"
End Sub
```

The Top 5 Customers report actually contains two snapshots of a pivot table. After using the AutoShow feature to grab the top five markets with their totals, the macro went back to the pivot table, removed the AutoShow option, and grabbed the total of all customers to produce the Total Company row.

Setting Up Slicers to Filter a Pivot Table

Excel 2010 introduced the concept of slicers to filter a pivot table. A *slicer* is a visual filter. You can resize and reposition slicers. You can control the color of the slicer and control the number of columns in a slicer. You can also select or unselect items from a slicer using VBA.

Figure 12.11 shows a pivot table with five slicers. Three of the slicers are modified to show multiple columns.

Figure 12.11

Slicers provide a visual filter of several fields.

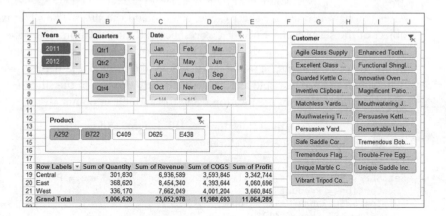

Slicers were new in Excel 2010 and work only with pivot tables designed to be used by Excel 2010 or newer. That introduces some changes to the previous code in this chapter.

All the previous examples created the PivotCache using the `PivotCaches.Add` method. This method works from Excel 2000 through the current version. The method is not documented, but it works. Starting in Excel 2007, Microsoft replaced the `PivotCaches.Add` method with `PivotCaches.Create`. When you switch from using `.Add` to using `.Create`, your code causes an error in Excel 2003. Because Excel 2003 is still a supported product, it seems dangerous to switch over to `PivotCaches.Create`.

However, if you want to use a slicer or a timeline, you are forced to switch over to `PivotCaches.Create` and then specify that you explicitly understand that the workbook works only in Excel 2010 or newer using the `xlPivotTableVersion14` argument.

Here is the code for creating the PivotCache and the pivot table when you plan on using a slicer:

```
Set PTCache = ActiveWorkbook.PivotCaches.Create( _
    SourceType:=xlDatabase, _
    SourceData:=PRange.Address, _
    Version:=xlPivotTableVersion14)
Set PT = PTCache.CreatePivotTable( _
    TableDestination:=Cells(6, FinalCol + 2), _
    TableName:="PivotTable1", _
    DefaultVersion:=xlPivotTableVersion14)
```

A slicer consists of a slicer cache and a slicer. To define a slicer cache, you need to specify a pivot table as the source and a field name as the `SourceField`. The slicer cache is defined at the workbook level. This would enable you to have the slicer on a different worksheet than the actual pivot table:

```
Dim SCP as SlicerCache
Dim SCR as SlicerCache
Set SCP = ActiveWorkbook.SlicerCaches.Add(Source:=PT, SourceField:="Product")
Set SCR = ActiveWorkbook.SlicerCaches.Add(Source:=PT, SourceField:="Region")
```

After you have defined the slicer cache, you can add the slicer. The slicer is defined as an object of the slicer cache. Specify a worksheet as the destination. The `name` argument controls the internal name for the slicer. The `Caption` argument is the heading that is visible in the slicer. This might be useful if you would like to show the name Region, but the IT department defined the field as IDKRegn. Specify the size of the slicer using height and width in points. Specify the location using top and left in points.

In the following code, the values for top, left, height, and width are assigned to be equal to the location or size of certain cell ranges:

```
Dim SLP as Slicer
Set SLP = SCP.Slicers.Add(SlicerDestination:=WSD, Name:="Product", _
    Caption:="Product", _
    Top:=WSD.Range("A12").Top, _
    Left:=WSD.Range("A12").Left + 10, _
    Width:=WSR.Range("A12:C12").Width, _
    Height:=WSD.Range("A12:A16").Height)
```

All slicers start out as one column. You can change the style and number of columns with this code:

```
' Format the color and number of columns
With SLP
    .Style = "SlicerStyleLight6"
    .NumberOfColumns = 5
End With
```

After the slicer is defined, you can actually use VBA to choose which items are activated in the slicer. It seems counterintuitive, but to choose items in the slicer, you have to change the `SlicerItem`, which is a member of the `SlicerCache`, not a member of the `Slicer`:

```
With SCP
    .SlicerItems("A292").Selected = True
    .SlicerItems("B722").Selected = True
    .SlicerItems("C409").Selected = False
    .SlicerItems("D625").Selected = False
    .SlicerItems("F438").Selected = False
End With
```

You might need to deal with slicers that already exist. If a slicer is created for the product field, the name of the SlicerCache is "Slicer_Product". The following code formats existing slicers:

```
Sub MoveAndFormatSlicer()
    Dim SCP As SlicerCache
    Dim SLP as Slicer
    Dim WSD As Worksheet
    Set WSD = ActiveSheet
    Set SCP = ActiveWorkbook.SlicerCaches("Slicer_Product")
    Set SLP = SCS.Slicers("Product")
    With SLP
        .Style = "SlicerStyleLight6"
        .NumberOfColumns = 5
        .Top = WSD.Range("A1").Top + 5
        .Left = WSD.Range("A1").Left + 5
        .Width = WSD.Range("A1:B14").Width - 60
        .Height = WSD.Range("A1:B14").Height
    End With
End Sub
```

Setting Up a Timeline to Filter an Excel 2013 Pivot Table

Microsoft introduced the timeline slicer in Excel 2013. This is a special type of slicer. It is not compatible with Excel 2010 or earlier. In the language of VBA, the marketing name of Excel 2013 is really called Version 15.

Whereas the other examples in this chapter use the .Add method for adding a pivot cache, this example must use the .Create method for defining the pivot table cache. The difference? The .Create method enables you to specify DefaultVersion:=xlPivotTable Version15, whereas the .Add method does not. If you do not define the pivot cache and pivot table as destined for version 15, the Insert Timeline icon is grayed out.

Here is the code to set up a pivot cache and a pivot table that allows a timeline control:

```
' Define the pivot table cache
Set PTCache = ActiveWorkbook.PivotCaches.Create( _
    SourceType:=xlDatabase, _
    SourceData:=PRange.Address, _
    Version:=xlPivotTableVersion15)

' Create the Pivot Table from the Pivot Cache
Set PT = PTCache.CreatePivotTable( _
    TableDestination:=Cells(10, FinalCol + 2), _
    TableName:="PivotTable1", _
    DefaultVersion:=xlPivotTableVersion15)
```

12

Later, after adding fields to your pivot table, you define a slicer cache and specify the type as xlTimeLine:

```
' Define the Slicer Cache
' First two arguments are Source and SourceField
' Third argument, Name should be skipped
Set SC = WBD.SlicerCaches.Add(PT, "ShipDate", , _
    SlicerCacheType:=xlTimeline)
```

The slicer is then added to the Slicer Cache:

```
' Define the timeline as a slicer
Set SL = SC.Slicers.Add(WSD, , _
    Name:="ShipDate", _
    Caption:="Year", _
    Top:=WSD.Range("J1").Top, _
    Left:=WSD.Range("J1").Left, _
    Width:=262.5, Height:=108)
```

Timelines can exist at the day, month, quarter, or year level. To change the level of the timeline, use the TimelineViewState.Level property:

```
SL.TimelineViewState.Level = xlTimelineLevelYears
```

To actually filter the timeline to certain dates, you have to use the TimelineState.SetFilterDataRange property, which applies to the Slicer Cache:

```
SC.TimelineState.SetFilterDateRange "1/1/2014", "12/31/2015"
```

Listing 12.4 shows the complete macro to build a version 15 pivot table and add a timeline slicer.

Listing 12.4 Pivot with Timeline

```
Sub PivotWithYearSlicer()
Dim SC As SlicerCache
Dim SL As Slicer
Dim WSD As Worksheet
Dim WSR As Worksheet
Dim WBD As Workbook
Dim PT As PivotTable
Dim PTCache As PivotCache
Dim PRange As Range
Dim FinalRow As Long
Set WBD = ActiveWorkbook
Set WSD = Worksheets("Data")

' Delete any prior pivot tables
For Each PT In WSD.PivotTables
    PT.TableRange2.Clear
Next PT

' Delete any prior slicer cache
For Each SC In ActiveWorkbook.SlicerCaches
    SC.Delete
Next SC

' Define input area and set up a Pivot Cache
```

```
    WSD.Select
    FinalRow = WSD.Cells(Rows.Count, 1).End(xlUp).Row
    FinalCol = WSD.Cells(1, Columns.Count). _
        End(xlToLeft).Column
    Set PRange = WSD.Cells(1, 1).Resize(FinalRow, FinalCol)

    ' Define the pivot table cache
    Set PTCache = ActiveWorkbook.PivotCaches.Create( _
        SourceType:=xlDatabase, _
        SourceData:=PRange.Address, _
        Version:=xlPivotTableVersion15)

    ' Create the Pivot Table from the Pivot Cache
    Set PT = PTCache.CreatePivotTable( _
        TableDestination:=Cells(10, FinalCol + 2), _
        TableName:="PivotTable1", _
        DefaultVersion:=xlPivotTableVersion15)

    ' Turn off updating while building the table
    PT.ManualUpdate = True

    ' Set up the row & column fields
    PT.AddFields RowFields:=Array("Customer")

    ' Set up the data fields
    With PT.PivotFields("Revenue")
        .Orientation = xlDataField
        .Function = xlSum
        .Position = 1
        .NumberFormat = "#,##0"
        .Name = "Revenue "
    End With

    PT.ManualUpdate = False

    ' Define the Slicer Cache
    ' First two arguments are Source and SourceField
    ' Third argument, Name should be skipped
    Set SC = WBD.SlicerCaches.Add(PT, "ShipDate", , _
        SlicerCacheType:=xlTimeline)

    ' Define the timeline as a slicer
    Set SL = SC.Slicers.Add(WSD, , _
        Name:="ShipDate", _
        Caption:="Year", _
        Top:=WSD.Range("J1").Top, _
        Left:=WSD.Range("J1").Left, _
        Width:=262.5, Height:=108)

    ' Set the timeline to show years
    SL.TimelineViewState.Level = xlTimelineLevelYears

    ' Set the dates for the timeline
    SC.TimelineState.SetFilterDateRange "1/1/2014", "12/31/2014"
End Sub
```

Figure 12.12 shows the timeline slicer.

Figure 12.12
Timelines are new in Excel 2013 and require special pivot table code to exist.

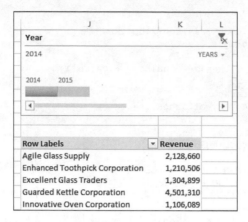

Row Labels	Revenue
Agile Glass Supply	2,128,660
Enhanced Toothpick Corporation	1,210,506
Excellent Glass Traders	1,304,899
Guarded Kettle Corporation	4,501,310
Innovative Oven Corporation	1,106,089

Using the Data Model in Excel 2013

Excel 2013 incorporates parts of PowerPivot into the core Excel product. Items in the Excel ribbon are incorporated into the Data Model. Items in the PowerPivot ribbon are not. This means you can add two tables to the Data Model, create a relationship, and then build a pivot table from the Data Model.

To follow along with this example, open the 12-BeforeDataModel.xlsm file from the sample download files. This workbook has two tables: Sales and Sector. Sector is a lookup table that is related to the Sales table via a customer field. To build the pivot table, follow these general steps in the macro:

1. Add the main table to the model.
2. Add the lookup table to the model.
3. Link the two tables with a relationship.
4. Create a pivot cache from ThisWorkbookDataModel.
5. Create a pivot table from the cache.
6. Add row fields.
7. Define a measure. Add the measure to the pivot table.

Adding Both Tables to the Data Model

You should already have a dataset in the workbook that has been converted to a table using the Ctrl+T shortcut. On the Table Tools Design tab, change the table name to Sales. To link this table to the Data Model, use this code:

```
' Build Connection to the main Sales table
Set WBT = ActiveWorkbook
TableName = "Sales"
WBT.Connections.Add Name:="LinkedTable_" & TableName, _
    Description:="", _
    ConnectionString:="WORKSHEET;" & WBT.FullName, _
```

```
CommandText:=WBT.Name & "!" & TableName, _
    lCmdType:=7, _
    CreateModelConnection:=True, _
    ImportRelationships:=False
```

There are several variables in that code that use the table name, the workbook path, and/or the workbook name. By storing the table name in a variable at the top of the code, you can build the connection name, connection string, and command text using the variables.

Adapting the preceding code to link to the lookup table then requires only changing the TableName variable:

```
TableName = "Sector"
WBT.Connections.Add Name:="LinkedTable_" & TableName, _
    Description:="", _
    ConnectionString:="WORKSHEET;" & WBT.FullName, _
    CommandText:=WBT.Name & "!" & TableName, _
    lCmdType:=7, _
    CreateModelConnection:=True, _
    ImportRelationships:=False
```

Creating a Relationship Between the Two Tables

When you create a relationship in the Excel interface, you specify four items in the Create Relationship dialog box. (See Figure 12.13.)

Figure 12.13
To create a relationship, specify a field in both tables.

The code to create the relationship is more streamlined. There can be only one Data Model per workbook. Set an object variable MO to refer to the model in this workbook. Use the ModelRelationships.Add method, specifying the two fields that are linked:

```
' Relate the two tables
Dim MO As Model
Set MO = ActiveWorkbook.Model
MO.ModelRelationships.Add _
    ForeignKeyColumn:=MO.ModelTables("Sales").ModelTableColumns("Customer"), _
    PrimaryKeyColumn:=MO.ModelTables("Sector").ModelTableColumns("Customer")
```

Defining the PivotCache and Building the Pivot Table

The code to define the pivot cache specifies that the data is external. Even though the linked tables are in your workbook, and even though the Data Model is stored as a binary large object within the workbook, this is still considered an external data connection. The connection is always called ThisWorkbookDataModel.

12

```
' Define the PivotCache
Set PTCache = WBT.PivotCaches.Create(SourceType:=xlExternal, _
    SourceData:=WBT.Connections("ThisWorkbookDataModel"), _
    Version:=xlPivotTableVersion15)

' Create the Pivot Table from the Pivot Cache
Set PT = PTCache.CreatePivotTable( _
    TableDestination:=WSD.Cells(1, 1), TableName:="PivotTable1")
```

Adding Model Fields to the Pivot Table

There are really two types of fields you will add to the pivot table. Text fields such as Customer, Sector, or Product are simply fields that can be added to the row or column area of the pivot table. No calculation has to happen to these fields. The code for adding text fields is shown in this section. When you add a numeric field to the values area in the Excel interface, you are actually implicitly defining a new calculated field. To do this in VBA, you have to explicitly define the field and then add it.

First, the simpler example of adding a text field to the row area. The VBA code generically looks like this:

```
With PT.CubeFields("[TableName].[FieldName]")
    .Orientation = xlRowField
    .Position = 1
End With
```

In the current example, add the Sector field from the Sector table using this code:

```
With PT.CubeFields("[Sector].[Sector]")
    .Orientation = xlRowField
    .Position = 1
End With
```

Adding Numeric Fields to the Values Area

In Excel 2010, PowerPivot Calculated Fields were called Measures. In Excel 2013, the Excel interface calls them Calculations. However, the underlying VBA code still calls them Measures.

If you have a Data Model pivot table and you check the Revenue field, you see the Revenue Field move to the Values area. Behind the scenes, though, Excel is implicitly defining a new measure called Sum of Revenue. (You can see the implicit measures in the PowerPivot window if you have Excel 2013 Pro Plus.) In VBA, your first step is to define a new measure for Sum of Revenue. To make it easier to refer to this measure later, assign the new measure to an object variable:

```
' Before you can add Revenue to the pivot table,
' you have to define the measure.
' This happens using the GetMeasure method.
' Assign the cube field to CFRevenue object
Dim CFRevenue As CubeField
Set CFRevenue = PT.CubeFields.GetMeasure( _
    AttributeHierarchy:="[Sales].[Revenue]", _
    Function:=xlSum, _
    Caption:="Sum of Revenue")
```

```
' Add the newly created cube field to the pivot table
PT.AddDataField Field:=CFRevenue, _
    Caption:="Total Revenue"
PT.PivotFields("Total Revenue").NumberFormat = "$#,##0,K"
```

You can use the preceding sample to create a new measure. The following measure uses the new Distinct Count function to count the number of unique customers in each sector:

```
' Add Distinct Count of Customer as a Cube Field
Dim CFCustCount As CubeField
Set CFCustCount = PT.CubeFields.GetMeasure( _
    AttributeHierarchy:="[Sales].[Customer]", _
    Function:=xlDistinctCount, _
    Caption:="Customer Count")
' Add the newly created cube field to the pivot table
PT.AddDataField Field:=CFCustCount, _
    Caption:="Customer Count"
```

Caution: Before you get too excited, the Excel team drew an interesting line in the sand with regard to what parts of PowerPivot are available via VBA. Any functionality that is available in Office 2013 Standard is available in VBA. If you try to define a new calculated field that uses the PowerPivot DAX formula language, it will not work in VBA.

Putting It All Together

Figure 12.14 shows the Data Model pivot table created using the code in Listing 12.5.

Figure 12.14
Two tables linked with a pivot table and two measures via a macro.

	A	B	C
1	Row Labels ▾	Total Revenue	Customer Count
2	Apparel	$758,407	2
3	Chemical	$568,851	1
4	Consumer	$2,194,976	7
5	Electronics	$222,022	4
6	Food	$750,163	1
7	Hardware	$2,178,683	11
8	Textiles	$34,710	1
9	Grand Total	$6,707,812	27
10			

Listing 12.5   Code to Create a Data Model Pivot Table

```
Sub BuildModelPivotTable()
    Dim WBT As Workbook
    Dim WC As WorkbookConnection
    Dim MO As Model
    Dim PTCache As PivotCache
    Dim PT As PivotTable
    Dim WSD As Worksheet
    Dim CFRevenue As CubeField
    Dim CFCustCount As CubeField

    Set WBT = ActiveWorkbook
    Set WSD = WBT.Worksheets("Report")

    ' Build Connection to the main Sales table
```

12

```
TableName = "Sales"
WBT.Connections.Add Name:="LinkedTable_" & TableName, _
    Description:="MainTable", _
    ConnectionString:="WORKSHEET;" & WBT.FullName, _
    CommandText:=WBT.Name & "!" & TableName, _
    lCmdType:=7, _
    CreateModelConnection:=True, _
    ImportRelationships:=False

' Build Connection to the Sector lookup table
TableName = "Sector"
WBT.Connections.Add Name:="LinkedTable_" & TableName, _
    Description:="LookupTable", _
    ConnectionString:="WORKSHEET;" & WBT.FullName, _
    CommandText:=WBT.Name & "!" & TableName, _
    lCmdType:=7, _
    CreateModelConnection:=True, _
    ImportRelationships:=False

' Relate the two tables
Set MO = ActiveWorkbook.Model
MO.ModelRelationships.Add _
    ForeignKeyColumn:=MO.ModelTables("Sales").ModelTableColumns("Customer"), _
    PrimaryKeyColumn:=MO.ModelTables("Sector").ModelTableColumns("Customer")

' Delete any prior pivot tables
For Each PT In WSD.PivotTables
    PT.TableRange2.Clear
Next PT

' Define the PivotCache
Set PTCache = WBT.PivotCaches.Create(SourceType:=xlExternal, _
    SourceData:=WBT.Connections("ThisWorkbookDataModel"), _
    Version:=xlPivotTableVersion15)

' Create the Pivot Table from the Pivot Cache
Set PT = PTCache.CreatePivotTable( _
    TableDestination:=WSD.Cells(1, 1), TableName:="PivotTable1")

' Add the Sector field from the Sector table to the Row areas
With PT.CubeFields("[Sector].[Sector]")
    .Orientation = xlRowField
    .Position = 1
End With

' Before you can add Revenue to the pivot table,
' you have to define the measure.
' This happens using the GetMeasure method
' Assign the cube field to CFRevenue object
Set CFRevenue = PT.CubeFields.GetMeasure( _
    AttributeHierarchy:="[Sales].[Revenue]", _
    Function:=xlSum, _
    Caption:="Sum of Revenue")
' Add the newly created cube field to the pivot table
PT.AddDataField Field:=CFRevenue, _
    Caption:="Total Revenue"
PT.PivotFields("Total Revenue").NumberFormat = "$#,##0,K"
```

```
' Add Distinct Count of Customer as a Cube Field
Set CFCustCount = PT.CubeFields.GetMeasure( _
    AttributeHierarchy:="[Sales].[Customer]", _
    Function:=xlDistinctCount, _
    Caption:="Customer Count")
' Add the newly created cube field to the pivot table
PT.AddDataField Field:=CFCustCount, _
    Caption:="Customer Count"

End Sub
```

Using Other Pivot Table Features

This section covers a few additional features in pivot tables that you might need to code with VBA.

Calculated Data Fields

Pivot tables offer two types of formulas. The most useful type defines a formula for a calculated field. This adds a new field to the pivot table. Calculations for calculated fields are always done at the summary level. If you define a calculated field for average price as revenue divided by units sold, Excel first adds the total revenue and total quantity, and then it does the division of these totals to get the result. In many cases, this is exactly what you need. If your calculation does not follow the associative law of mathematics, it might not work as you expect.

To set up a Calculated field, use the Add method with the CalculatedFields object. You have to specify a field name and a formula.

> **NOTE** Note that if you create a field called Profit Percent, the default pivot table produces a field called Sum of Profit Percent. This title is misleading and downright silly. The solution is to use the Name property when defining the Data field to replace Sum of Profit Percent with something such as GP Pct. Keep in mind that this name must differ from the name for the Calculated field.

12

```
' Define Calculated Fields
    PT.CalculatedFields.Add Name:="ProfitPercent", Formula:="=Profit/Revenue"
    With PT.PivotFields("ProfitPercent")
        .Orientation = xlDataField
        .Function = xlSum
        .Position = 3
        .NumberFormat = "#0.0%"
        .Name = "GP Pct"
    End With
```

Calculated Items

Suppose you have a Measure field with two items: Budget and Actual. You would like to add a new position to calculate Variance as Actual-Budget. You can do this with a calculated item by using this code:

```
' Define calculated item along the product dimension
PT.PivotFields("Measure").CalculatedItems _
    .Add "Variance", "='Actual'-'Budget'"
```

Using `ShowDetail` to Filter a Recordset

When you take any pivot table in the Excel user interface and then double-click any number in the table, Excel inserts a new sheet in the workbook and copies all the source records that represent that number. In the Excel user interface, this is a great way to perform a drill-down query into a dataset.

The equivalent VBA property is `ShowDetail`. By setting this property to `True` for any cell in the pivot table, you generate a new worksheet with all the records that make up that cell:

```
PT.TableRange2.Offset(2, 1).Resize(1, 1).ShowDetail = True
```

Changing the Layout from the Design Tab

The Layout group of the Design tab contains four drop-downs that control the following:

- Location of subtotals (top or bottom)
- Presence of grand totals
- Report layout including whether outer row labels are repeated
- Presence of blank rows

Subtotals can appear either at the top or at the bottom of a group of pivot items. The `SubtotalLocation` property applies to the entire pivot table; valid values are `xlAtBottom` or `xlAtTop`:

```
PT.SubtotalLocation:=xlAtTop
```

Grand totals can be turned on or off for rows or columns. Because these two settings can be confusing, remember that at the bottom of a report, there is a total line that most people would call the Grand Total Row. To turn off that row, you have to use the following:

```
PT.ColumnGrand = False
```

You need to turn off the `ColumnGrand` when you want to suppress the total row because Microsoft calls that row the "grand total for columns." Get it? In other words, they are saying that the row at the bottom contains the total of the columns above it. I finally started doing better when I would decide which one to turn off, and then turn off the opposite one.

To suppress what you would call the Grand Total Column along the right side of the report, you have to suppress what Microsoft calls the Total for Rows with the following code:

```
PT.RowGrand = False
```

Settings for the Report Layout

There are three settings for the report layout:

- **Tabular layout**— Similar to the default layout in Excel 2003
- **Outline layout** — Optionally available in Excel 2003
- **Compact layout**— Introduced in Excel 2007

When you create a pivot table in the Excel interface, you get the compact layout. When you build a pivot table in VBA, you get the tabular layout. You can change to one of the other layouts with one of these lines:

```
PT.RowAxisLayout xlTabularRow
PT.RowAxisLayout xlOutlineRow
PT.RowAxisLayout xlCompactRow
```

Starting in Excel 2007, you can add a blank line to the layout after each group of pivot items. Although the Design tab offers a single setting to affect the entire pivot table, the setting is actually applied individually to each pivot field. The macro recorder responds by recording a dozen lines of code for a pivot table with 12 fields. You can intelligently add a single line of code for the outer Row fields:

```
PT.PivotFields("Region").LayoutBlankLine = True
```

Suppressing Subtotals for Multiple Row Fields

As soon as you have more than one row field, Excel automatically adds subtotals for all but the innermost row field. That extra row field can get in the way if you plan to reuse the results of the pivot table as a new dataset for some other purpose. Although accomplishing this task manually can be relatively simple, the VBA code to suppress subtotals is surprisingly complex.

Most people do not realize that it is possible to show multiple types of subtotals. For example, you can choose to show Total, Average, Min, and Max in the same pivot table.

To suppress subtotals for a field, you must set the Subtotals property equal to an array of 12 False values. The first False turns off automatic subtotals, the second False turns off the Sum subtotal, the third False turns off the Count subtotal, and so on. This line of code suppresses the Region subtotal:

```
PT.PivotFields("Region").Subtotals = Array(False, False, False, False, _
    False, False, False, False, False, False, False, False)
```

A different technique is to turn on the first subtotal. This method automatically turns off the other 11 subtotals. You can then turn off the first subtotal to make sure that all subtotals are suppressed:

```
PT.PivotFields("Region").Subtotals(1) = True
PT.PivotFields("Region").Subtotals(1) = False
```

12

CASE STUDY: APPLYING A DATA VISUALIZATION

Beginning with Excel 2007, fantastic data visualizations such as icon sets, color gradients, and in-cell data bars are offered. When you apply visualization to a pivot table, you should exclude the total rows from the visualization.

If you have 20 customers that average $3 million in revenue each, the total for the 20 customers is $60 million. If you include the total in the data visualization, the total gets the largest bar, and all the customer records have tiny bars.

In the Excel user interface, you always want to use the Add Rule or Edit Rule choice to select the option All Cells Showing "Sum of Revenue" for "Customer."

The code to add a data bar to the Revenue field is as follows:

```
' Apply a Databar
PT.TableRange2.Cells(3, 2).Select
Selection.FormatConditions.AddDatabar
Selection.FormatConditions(1).ShowValue = True
Selection.FormatConditions(1).SetFirstPriority
With Selection.FormatConditions(1)
    .MinPoint.Modify newtype:=xlConditionValueLowestValue
    .MaxPoint.Modify newtype:=xlConditionValueHighestValue
End With
With Selection.FormatConditions(1).BarColor
    .ThemeColor = xlThemeColorAccent3
    .TintAndShade = -0.5
End With
Selection.FormatConditions(1).ScopeType = xlFieldsScope
```

Next Steps

12

If you cannot already tell, pivot tables are my favorite feature in Excel. They are incredibly powerful and flexible. Combined with VBA, they provide an excellent calculation engine and power many of the reports I build for clients. In Chapter 13, "Excel Power," you'll learn multiple techniques for handling various tasks in VBA.

Excel Power

13

A major secret of successful programmers is to never waste time writing the same code twice. They all have little bits—or even big bits—of code that they use over and over again. Another big secret is to never take 8 hours doing something that can be done in 10 minutes—which is what this book is about!

This chapter contains programs donated by several Excel power programmers. These are programs they have found useful, and they hope these will help you too. Not only can these programs save you time, but they also can teach you new ways of solving common problems.

Different programmers have different programming styles, and we did not rewrite the submissions. As you review the lines of code, you will notice different ways of doing the same task, such as referring to ranges.

File Operations

The following utilities deal with handling files in folders. Being able to loop through a list of files in a folder is a useful task.

List Files in a Directory

Submitted by our good friend Nathan P. Oliver of Minneapolis, Minnesota.

This program returns the filename, size, and date modified of all specified file types in the selected directory and its subfolders:

```
Sub ExcelFileSearch()
Dim srchExt As Variant, srchDir As Variant
Dim i As Long, j As Long, strName As String
Dim varArr(1 To 1048576, 1 To 3) As Variant
Dim strFileFullName As String
Dim ws As Worksheet
Dim fso As Object
```

```vba
Let srchExt = Application.InputBox("Please Enter File Extension", "Info Request")
If srchExt = False And Not TypeName(srchExt) = "String" Then
    Exit Sub
End If

Let srchDir = BrowseForFolderShell
If srchDir = False And Not TypeName(srchDir) = "String" Then
    Exit Sub
End If

Application.ScreenUpdating = False

Set ws = ThisWorkbook.Worksheets.Add(Sheets(1))
On Error Resume Next
Application.DisplayAlerts = False
ThisWorkbook.Worksheets("FileSearch Results").Delete
Application.DisplayAlerts = True
On Error GoTo 0
ws.Name = "FileSearch Results"

Let strName = Dir$(srchDir & "\*" & srchExt)
Do While strName <> vbNullString
    Let i = i + 1
    Let strFileFullName = srchDir & strName
    Let varArr(i, 1) = strFileFullName
    Let varArr(i, 2) = FileLen(strFileFullName) \ 1024
    Let varArr(i, 3) = FileDateTime(strFileFullName)
    Let strName = Dir$()
Loop

Set fso = CreateObject("Scripting.FileSystemObject")
Call recurseSubFolders(fso.GetFolder(srchDir), varArr(), i, CStr(srchExt))
Set fso = Nothing

ThisWorkbook.Windows(1).DisplayHeadings = False
With ws
    If i > 0 Then
        .Range("A2").Resize(i, UBound(varArr, 2)).Value = varArr
        For j = 1 To i
            .Hyperlinks.Add anchor:=.Cells(j + 1, 1), Address:=varArr(j, 1)
        Next
    End If
    .Range(.Cells(1, 4), .Cells(1, .Columns.Count)).EntireColumn.Hidden = True
    .Range(.Cells(.Rows.Count, 1).End(xlUp)(2), _
        .Cells(.Rows.Count, 1)).EntireRow.Hidden = True
    With .Range("A1:C1")
        .Value = Array("Full Name", "Kilobytes", "Last Modified")
        .Font.Underline = xlUnderlineStyleSingle
        .EntireColumn.AutoFit
        .HorizontalAlignment = xlCenter
    End With
End With
Application.ScreenUpdating = True
End Sub

Private Sub recurseSubFolders(ByRef Folder As Object, _
    ByRef varArr() As Variant, _
    ByRef i As Long, _
```

```
        ByRef srchExt As String)
Dim SubFolder As Object
Dim strName As String, strFileFullName As String
For Each SubFolder In Folder.SubFolders
    Let strName = Dir$(SubFolder.Path & "\*" & srchExt)
    Do While strName <> vbNullString
        Let i = i + 1
        Let strFileFullName = SubFolder.Path & "\" & strName
        Let varArr(i, 1) = strFileFullName
        Let varArr(i, 2) = FileLen(strFileFullName) \ 1024
        Let varArr(i, 3) = FileDateTime(strFileFullName)
        Let strName = Dir$()
    Loop
    If i > 1048576 Then Exit Sub
    Call recurseSubFolders(SubFolder, varArr(), i, srchExt)
Next
End Sub

Private Function BrowseForFolderShell() As Variant
Dim objShell As Object, objFolder As Object
Set objShell = CreateObject("Shell.Application")
Set objFolder = objShell.BrowseForFolder(0, "Please select a folder", 0, "C:\")
If Not objFolder Is Nothing Then
    On Error Resume Next
    If IsError(objFolder.Items.Item.Path) Then
        BrowseForFolderShell = CStr(objFolder)
    Else
        On Error GoTo 0
        If Len(objFolder.Items.Item.Path) > 3 Then
            BrowseForFolderShell = objFolder.Items.Item.Path & _
                Application.PathSeparator
        Else
            BrowseForFolderShell = objFolder.Items.Item.Path
        End If
    End If
Else
    BrowseForFolderShell = False
End If
Set objFolder = Nothing: Set objShell = Nothing
End Function
```

Import CSV

Submitted by Masaru Kaji of Kobe-City, Japan. Masaru is a computer system's
administrator. He maintains an Excel VBA tip site, Colo's Excel Junk Room, at
excel.toypark.in/tips.shtml

If you find yourself importing a lot of comma-separated variable (CSV) files and then having to go back and delete them, this program is for you. It quickly opens a CSV in Excel
and permanently deletes the original file.

```
Option Base 1

Sub OpenLargeCSVFast()
    Dim buf(1 To 16384) As Variant
    Dim i As Long
```

13

```
'Change the file location and name here
Const strFilePath As String = "C:\temp\Sales.CSV"

Dim strRenamedPath As String
strRenamedPath = Split(strFilePath, ".")(0) & "txt"

With Application
    .ScreenUpdating = False
    .DisplayAlerts = False
End With
'Setting an array for FieldInfo to open CSV
For i = 1 To 16384
    buf(i) = Array(i, 2)
Next
Name strFilePath As strRenamedPath
Workbooks.OpenText Filename:=strRenamedPath, DataType:=xlDelimited, _
                Comma:=True, FieldInfo:=buf
Erase buf
ActiveSheet.UsedRange.Copy ThisWorkbook.Sheets(1).Range("A1")
ActiveWorkbook.Close False
Kill strRenamedPath
With Application
    .ScreenUpdating = True
    .DisplayAlerts = True
End With
End Sub
```

Read Entire TXT to Memory and Parse

Submitted by Suat Mehmet Ozgur of Istanbul, Turkey. Suat develops applications in Excel, Access, and Visual Basic.

This sample takes a different approach to reading a text file. Instead of reading one record at a time, the macro loads the entire text file into memory in a single string variable. The macro then parses the string into individual records. The advantage of this method is that you access the file on disk only one time. All subsequent processing occurs in memory and is very fast.

```
Sub ReadTxtLines()
'No need to install Scripting Runtime library since we used late binding
Dim sht As Worksheet
Dim fso As Object
Dim fil As Object
Dim txt As Object
Dim strtxt As String
Dim tmpLoc As Long

    'Working on active sheet
    Set sht = ActiveSheet
    'Clear data in the sheet
    sht.UsedRange.ClearContents

    'File system object that we need to manage files
    Set fso = CreateObject("Scripting.FileSystemObject")
```

```
    'File that we like to open and read
    Set fil = fso.GetFile("c:\temp\Sales.txt")

    'Opening file as a TextStream
    Set txt = fil.OpenAsTextStream(1)

    'Reading entire file into a string variable at once
    strtxt = txt.ReadAll

    'Close textstream and free the file. We don't need it anymore.
    txt.Close

    'Find the first placement of new line char
    tmpLoc = InStr(1, strtxt, vbCrLf)

    'Loop until no more new line
    Do Until tmpLoc = 0
        'Use A column and next empty cell to write the text file line
        sht.Cells(sht.Rows.Count, 1).End(xlUp).Offset(1).Value = _
            Left(strtxt, tmpLoc - 1)

        'Remove the parsed line from the variable where we stored the entire file
        strtxt = Right(strtxt, Len(strtxt) - tmpLoc - 1)

        'Find the next placement of new line char
        tmpLoc = InStr(1, strtxt, vbCrLf)
    Loop

    'Last line that has data but no new line char
    sht.Cells(sht.Rows.Count, 1).End(xlUp).Offset(1).Value = strtxt

    'It will be already released by the ending of this procedure but
    ' as a good habit, set the object as nothing.
    Set fso = Nothing
End Sub
```

Combining and Separating Workbooks

The next four utilities demonstrate how to combine worksheets into a single workbook or separate a single workbook into individual worksheets or Word documents.

Separate Worksheets into Workbooks

Submitted by Tommy Miles of Houston, Texas.

This sample goes through the active workbook and saves each sheet as its own workbook in the same path as the original workbook. It names the new workbooks based on the sheet name, and it overwrites files without prompting. You will also notice that you need to choose whether you save the file as XLSM (macro-enabled) or XLSX (macros will be stripped). In the following code, both lines are included—xlsm and xlsx—but the xlsx lines are commented out, making them inactive:

13

```
Sub SplitWorkbook()

Dim ws As Worksheet
Dim DisplayStatusBar As Boolean

DisplayStatusBar = Application.DisplayStatusBar
Application.DisplayStatusBar = True
Application.ScreenUpdating = False
Application.DisplayAlerts = False

For Each ws In ThisWorkbook.Sheets
    Dim NewFileName As String
    Application.StatusBar = ThisWorkbook.Sheets.Count & " Remaining Sheets"
    If ThisWorkbook.Sheets.Count <> 1 Then
        NewFileName = ThisWorkbook.Path & "\" & ws.Name & ".xlsm" 'Macro-Enabled
'       NewFileName = ThisWorkbook.Path & "\" & ws.Name & ".xlsx" _
            'Not Macro-Enabled
        ws.Copy
        ActiveWorkbook.Sheets(1).Name = "Sheet1"
        ActiveWorkbook.SaveAs Filename:=NewFileName, _
            FileFormat:=xlOpenXMLWorkbookMacroEnabled
'        ActiveWorkbook.SaveAs Filename:=NewFileName, _
            FileFormat:=xlOpenXMLWorkbook
        ActiveWorkbook.Close SaveChanges:=False
    Else
        NewFileName = ThisWorkbook.Path & "\" & ws.Name & ".xlsm"
'        NewFileName = ThisWorkbook.Path & "\" & ws.Name & ".xlsx"
        ws.Name = "Sheet1"
    End If
Next

Application.DisplayAlerts = True
Application.StatusBar = False
Application.DisplayStatusBar = DisplayStatusBar
Application.ScreenUpdating = True
End Sub
```

Combine Workbooks

Submitted by Tommy Miles.

This sample goes through all the Excel files in a specified directory and combines them into a single workbook. It renames the sheets based on the name of the original workbook.

```
Sub CombineWorkbooks()
    Dim CurFile As String, DirLoc As String
    Dim DestWB As Workbook
    Dim ws As Object 'allows for different sheet types

    DirLoc = ThisWorkbook.Path & "\tst\" 'location of files
    CurFile = Dir(DirLoc & "*.xls*")

    Application.ScreenUpdating = False
    Application.EnableEvents = False

    Set DestWB = Workbooks.Add(xlWorksheet)
```

```
        Do While CurFile <> vbNullString
            Dim OrigWB As Workbook
            Set OrigWB = Workbooks.Open(Filename:=DirLoc & CurFile, ReadOnly:=True)

            ' Limit to valid sheet names and removes .xls*
            CurFile = Left(Left(CurFile, Len(CurFile) - 5), 29)

            For Each ws In OrigWB.Sheets
                ws.Copy After:=DestWB.Sheets(DestWB.Sheets.Count)

                If OrigWB.Sheets.Count > 1 Then
                    DestWB.Sheets(DestWB.Sheets.Count).Name = CurFile & ws.Index
                Else
                    DestWB.Sheets(DestWB.Sheets.Count).Name = CurFile
                End If
            Next

            OrigWB.Close SaveChanges:=False
            CurFile = Dir
        Loop

        Application.DisplayAlerts = False
        DestWB.Sheets(1).Delete
        Application.DisplayAlerts = True

        Application.ScreenUpdating = True
        Application.EnableEvents = True

        Set DestWB = Nothing
End Sub
```

Filter and Copy Data to Separate Worksheets

Submitted by Dennis Wallentin of Ostersund, Sweden. Dennis provides Excel tips and tricks at http://xldennis.wordpress.com/.

This sample uses a specified column to filter data and copies the results to new worksheets in the active workbook:

```
Sub Filter_NewSheet()
Dim wbBook As Workbook
Dim wsSheet As Worksheet
Dim rnStart As Range, rnData As Range
Dim i As Long

Set wbBook = ThisWorkbook
Set wsSheet = wbBook.Worksheets("Sheet1")

With wsSheet
    'Make sure that the first row contains headings.
    Set rnStart = .Range("A2")
    Set rnData = .Range(.Range("A2"), .Cells(.Rows.Count, 3).End(xlUp))
End With

Application.ScreenUpdating = True
```

13

```
For i = 1 To 5
    'Here we filter the data with the first criterion.
    rnStart.AutoFilter Field:=1, Criteria1:="AA" & i
    'Copy the filtered list
    rnData.SpecialCells(xlCellTypeVisible).Copy
    'Add a new worksheet to the active workbook.
    Worksheets.Add Before:=wsSheet
    'Name the added new worksheets.
    ActiveSheet.Name = "AA" & i
    'Paste the filtered list.
    Range("A2").PasteSpecial xlPasteValues
Next i

'Reset the list to its original status.
rnStart.AutoFilter Field:=1

With Application
    'Reset the clipboard.
    .CutCopyMode = False
    .ScreenUpdating = False
End With

End Sub
```

Export Data to Word

Submitted by Dennis Wallentin.

This program transfers data from Excel to the first table found in a Word document. It uses early binding, so a reference must be established in the VB Editor using Tools, References to the Microsoft Word object library.

```
Sub Export_Data_Word_Table()
Dim wdApp As Word.Application
Dim wdDoc As Word.Document
Dim wdCell As Word.Cell
Dim i As Long
Dim wbBook As Workbook
Dim wsSheet As Worksheet
Dim rnData As Range
Dim vaData As Variant

Set wbBook = ThisWorkbook
Set wsSheet = wbBook.Worksheets("Sheet1")

With wsSheet
    Set rnData = .Range("A1:A10")
End With

'Add the values in the range to a one-dimensional variant-array.
vaData = rnData.Value

'Here we instantiate the new object.
Set wdApp = New Word.Application
'Here the target document resides in the same folder as the workbook.
Set wdDoc = wdApp.Documents.Open(ThisWorkbook.Path & "\Test.docx")
```

```
'Import data to the first table and in the first column of a ten-row table.
For Each wdCell In wdDoc.Tables(1).Columns(1).Cells
    i = i + 1
    wdCell.Range.Text = vaData(i, 1)
Next wdCell

'Save and close the document.
With wdDoc
    .Save
    .Close
End With

'Close the hidden instance of Microsoft Word.
wdApp.Quit
'Release the external variables from the memory
Set wdDoc = Nothing
Set wdApp = Nothing

MsgBox "The data has been transferred to Test.docx.", vbInformation

End Sub
```

Working with Cell Comments

Cell comments are often underused features of Excel. The following three utilities help you get the most out of cell comments.

List Comments

Submitted by Tommy Miles.

Excel allows the user to print the comments in a workbook; however, it does not specify the workbook or worksheet on which the comments appear, but only the cell, as shown in Figure 13.1.

Figure 13.1
Excel prints only the origin cell address and its comment.

```
        Cell: C5
Comment: Bill Jelen:
            Does not include the special sale.

        Cell: D14
Comment: Bill Jelen:
            Thanks for downloading our project files.

        Cell: A27
Comment: Bill Jelen:
            Visit MrExcel.com for over 70,000 articles on Microsoft Excel.
```

13

The following sample places comments, author, and location of each comment on a new sheet for easy viewing, saving, or printing. Figure 13.2 shows a sample result.

Figure 13.2
Easily list all the information pertaining to comments.

⊿	A	B	C	D	E	F	G	H	I	J
1	Author	Book	Sheet	Range	Comment					
2	Bill Jelen	Comment	ListComm	$C$5	Does not include the special sale.					
3	Bill Jelen	Comment	ListComm	$D$14	Thanks for downloading our project files.					
4	Bill Jelen	Comment	ListComm	$A$27	Visit MrExcel.com for over 70,000 articles on Microsoft Excel.					

```
Sub ListComments()
    Dim wb As Workbook
    Dim ws As Worksheet

    Dim cmt As Comment

    Dim cmtCount As Long

    cmtCount = 2

    On Error Resume Next
        Set ws = ActiveSheet
            If ws Is Nothing Then Exit Sub
    On Error GoTo 0

    Application.ScreenUpdating = False

    Set wb = Workbooks.Add(xlWorksheet)

    With wb.Sheets(1)
        .Range("$A$1") = "Author"
        .Range("$B$1") = "Book"
        .Range("$C$1") = "Sheet"
        .Range("$D$1") = "Range"
        .Range("$E$1") = "Comment"
    End With

    For Each cmt In ws.Comments
        With wb.Sheets(1)
            .Cells(cmtCount, 1) = cmt.author
'Parent is the object to which another object belongs.
'For example, the parent of a comment is the cell in which it resides.
'The parent of the cell is the sheet on which it resides.
'So if you have Comment.Parent.Parent.Name, you are returning the sheet name.
            .Cells(cmtCount, 2) = cmt.Parent.Parent.Parent.Name
            .Cells(cmtCount, 3) = cmt.Parent.Parent.Name
            .Cells(cmtCount, 4) = cmt.Parent.Address
            .Cells(cmtCount, 5) = CleanComment(cmt.author, cmt.Text)
        End With

        cmtCount = cmtCount + 1
    Next

    wb.Sheets(1).UsedRange.WrapText = False

    Application.ScreenUpdating = True

    Set ws = Nothing
    Set wb = Nothing
End Sub
```

13

```
Private Function CleanComment(author As String, cmt As String) As String
    Dim tmp As String

    tmp = Application.WorksheetFunction.Substitute(cmt, author & ":", "")
    tmp = Application.WorksheetFunction.Substitute(tmp, Chr(10), "")

    CleanComment = tmp
End Function
```

Resize Comments

Submitted by Tom Urtis of San Francisco, California. Tom is the principal owner of Atlas Programming Management, an Excel consulting firm in the Bay Area.

Excel doesn't automatically resize cell comments. In addition, if you have several on a sheet, as shown in Figure 13.3, it can be a hassle to resize them one at a time. The following sample code resizes all the comment boxes on a sheet so that, when selected, the entire comment is easily viewable, as shown in Figure 13.4.

Figure 13.3
By default, Excel doesn't size the comment boxes to show all the entered text.

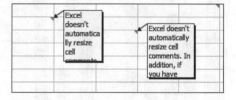

Figure 13.4
Resize the comment boxes to fit all the text.

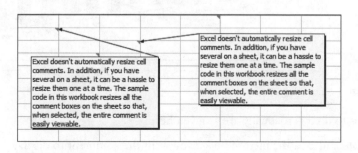

13

```
Sub CommentFitter1()
Application.ScreenUpdating = False
Dim x As Range, y As Long

For Each x In Cells.SpecialCells(xlCellTypeComments)
    Select Case True
        Case Len(x.NoteText) <> 0
            With x.Comment
                .Shape.TextFrame.AutoSize = True
                If .Shape.Width > 250 Then
                    y = .Shape.Width * .Shape.Height
                    .Shape.Width = 150
                    .Shape.Height = (y / 200) * 1.3
```

```
                     End If
              End With
        End Select
Next x
Application.ScreenUpdating = True
End Sub
```

Place a Chart in a Comment

Submitted by Tom Urtis.

A live chart cannot exist in a shape, but you can take a picture of the chart and load it into the comment shape, as shown in Figure 13.5.

Figure 13.5
Place a chart in a cell
comment.

The steps to do this manually are as given here:

1. Create and save the picture image you want the comment to display.

2. If you have not already done so, create the comment and select the cell in which the comment is located.

3. From the Review tab, select Edit Comment, or right-click the cell and select Edit Comment.

4. Right-click the comment border and select Format Comment.

5. Select the Colors and Lines tab, and click the down arrow belonging to the Color field of the Fill section.

6. Select Fill Effects, select the Picture tab, and then click the Select Picture button.

7. Navigate to your desired image, select the image, and click OK twice.

13

The effect of having a "live chart" in a comment can be achieved if, for example, the code is part of a SheetChange event when the chart's source data is being changed. In addition, business charts are updated often, so you might want a macro to keep the comment updated and to avoid repeating the same steps.

The following macro does just that—just modify the macro for file pathname, chart name, destination sheet, cell, and size of comment shape, depending on the size of the chart:

```
Sub PlaceGraph()
Dim x As String, z As Range

Application.ScreenUpdating = False

'assign a temporary location to hold the image
x = "C:\temp\XWMJGraph.gif"

'assign the cell to hold the comment
Set z = Worksheets("ChartInComment").Range("A3")

'delete any existing comment in the cell
On Error Resume Next
z.Comment.Delete
On Error GoTo 0

'select and export the chart
ActiveSheet.ChartObjects("Chart 1").Activate
ActiveChart.Export x

'add a new comment to the cell, set the size and insert the chart
With z.AddComment
    With .Shape
        .Height = 322
        .Width = 465
        .Fill.UserPicture x
    End With
End With

'delete the temporary image
Kill x

Range("A1").Activate
Application.ScreenUpdating = True

Set z = Nothing
End Sub
```

Utilities to Wow Your Clients

The next four utilities will amaze and impress your clients.

Using Conditional Formatting to Highlight Selected Cell

Submitted by Ivan F. Moala of Auckland, New Zealand. Ivan is the site author of The XcelFiles (www.xcelfiles.com), where you can find out how to do things you thought you could not do in Excel.

Conditional formatting is used to highlight the row and column of the active cell to help you visually locate it, as shown in Figure 13.6.

Figure 13.6
Use conditional formatting to highlight the selected cell in a table.

◢	A	B	C	D	E	F	G	H
1	Region	Product	Date	Customer	Quantity	Revenue	COGS	Profit
2	Central	Laser Prii	1/2/2011	Alluring Shoe Company	500	11240	5110	6130
3	Central	Laser Prii	1/3/2011	Alluring Shoe Company	400	9204	4088	5116
4	East	Laser Prii	1/9/2011	Alluring Shoe Company	900	21465	9198	12267
5	West	Laser Prii	1/11/2011	Alluring Shoe Company	400	9144	4088	5056
6	Central	Multi-Fur	1/26/2011	Alluring Shoe Company	500	10445	4235	6210

> **NOTE**
> Do *not* use this method if you already have conditional formats on the worksheet. Any existing conditional formats will be overwritten. In addition, this program clears the Clipboard. Therefore, it is not possible to use this method while doing copy, cut, or paste.

```
Const iInternational As Integer = Not (0)

Private Sub Worksheet_SelectionChange(ByVal Target As Range)
Dim iColor As Integer
'// On error resume in case
'// user selects a range of cells
On Error Resume Next
iColor = Target.Interior.ColorIndex
'// Leave On Error ON for Row offset errors

If iColor < 0 Then
    iColor = 36
Else
    iColor = iColor + 1
End If

'// Need this test in case font color is the same
If iColor = Target.Font.ColorIndex Then iColor = iColor + 1

Cells.FormatConditions.Delete

'// Horizontal color banding
With Range("A" & Target.Row, Target.Address) 'Rows(Target.Row)
    .FormatConditions.Add Type:=2, Formula1:=iInternational 'Or just 1 '"TRUE"
    .FormatConditions(1).Interior.ColorIndex = iColor
End With

'// Vertical color banding
With Range(Target.Offset(1 - Target.Row, 0).Address & ":" & _
    Target.Offset(-1, 0).Address)
    .FormatConditions.Add Type:=2, Formula1:=iInternational 'Or just 1 '"TRUE"
    .FormatConditions(1).Interior.ColorIndex = iColor
End With

End Sub
```

13

Highlight Selected Cell Without Using Conditional Formatting

Submitted by Ivan F. Moala.

This example visually highlights the active cell without using conditional formatting when the keyboard arrow keys are used to move around the sheet.

Place the following in a standard module:

```
Dim strCol As String
Dim iCol As Integer
Dim dblRow As Double

Sub HighlightRight()
    HighLight 0, 1
End Sub

Sub HighlightLeft()
    HighLight 0, -1
End Sub

Sub HighlightUp()
    HighLight -1, 0, -1
End Sub

Sub HighlightDown()
    HighLight 1, 0, 1
End Sub

Sub HighLight(dblxRow As Double, iyCol As Integer, Optional dblZ As Double = 0)
On Error GoTo NoGo
strCol = Mid(ActiveCell.Offset(dblxRow, iyCol).Address, _
        InStr(ActiveCell.Offset(dblxRow, iyCol).Address, "$") + 1, _
        InStr(2, ActiveCell.Offset(dblxRow, iyCol).Address, "$") - 2)
iCol = ActiveCell.Column
dblRow = ActiveCell.Row

Application.ScreenUpdating = False

With Range(strCol & ":" & strCol & "," & dblRow + dblZ & ":" & dblRow + dblZ)
    .Select
    Application.ScreenUpdating = True
    .Item(dblRow + dblxRow).Activate
End With

NoGo:
End Sub

Sub ReSet() 'manual reset
    Application.OnKey "{RIGHT}"
    Application.OnKey "{LEFT}"
    Application.OnKey "{UP}"
    Application.OnKey "{DOWN}"
End Sub
```

Place the following in the ThisWorkbook module:

13

```
Private Sub Workbook_Open()
    Application.OnKey "{RIGHT}", "HighlightRight"
    Application.OnKey "{LEFT}", "HighlightLeft"
    Application.OnKey "{UP}", "HighlightUp"
    Application.OnKey "{DOWN}", "HighlightDown"
    Application.OnKey "{DEL}", "DisableDelete"
End Sub

Private Sub Workbook_BeforeClose(Cancel As Boolean)
    Application.OnKey "{RIGHT}"
    Application.OnKey "{LEFT}"
    Application.OnKey "{UP}"
    Application.OnKey "{DOWN}"
    Application.OnKey "{DEL}"
End Sub
```

Custom Transpose Data

Submitted by Masaru Kaji.

You have a report where the data is set up in rows (see Figure 13.7). However, you need the data formatted such that each date and batch is in a single row, with the Value and Finish Position going across. Note that the Finish Position is not shown in Figure 13.8. The following program does a customized data transposition based on the specified column, as shown in Figure 13.8.

Figure 13.7
The original data has similar records in separate rows.

	A	B	C	D	E
1	ItemName	ItemDate	Batch#	FinishPosition	Value
2	Thermal	10/23/2012	1	8	2.15
3	Thermal	10/23/2012	1	3	3.2
4	Thermal	10/23/2012	1	2	4.9
5	Thermal	10/23/2012	1	1	6.1
6	Thermal	10/23/2012	1	7	6.2
7	Thermal	10/23/2012	1	4	12.9
8	Thermal	10/23/2012	1	9	23
9	Thermal	10/23/2012	1	5	36
10	Thermal	10/23/2012	1	6	36.25
11	Thermal	10/23/2012	2	2	1.05
12	Thermal	10/23/2012	2	1	2.5
13	Thermal	10/23/2012	2	8	7.3

Figure 13.8
The formatted data transposes the data so that identical dates and batches are merged into a single row.

	A	B	C	D	E	F	G	H	I	J	K	L	M	N
1	ItemName	ItemDate	Batch#	V1	V2	V3	V4	V5	V6	V7	V8	V9	V10	V11	V
2	Thermal	10/23/2012	1	2.15	3.2	4.9	6.1	6.2	12.9	23	36	36.25		
3	Thermal	10/23/2012	2	1.05	2.5	7.3	10.9	12.1	21.7	33.25	43	43.25		
4	Thermal	10/23/2012	3	1.65	3.1	3.1	3.75	7.1	7.1	7.7	18.7	34	55.5	
5	Thermal	10/23/2012	4	1.1	2.75	4	9.5	14.3	25	37.75				
6	Thermal	10/23/2012	5	0.9	3.75	7.1	9	16	18.1	19.5	22.5	74.75		
7	Thermal	10/23/2012	6	1.6	3.4	5.2	7.8	8.2	9.4	11.5				
8	Thermal	10/23/2012	7	0.8	4.2	4.9	9.6	15	21.2	24.75	63.25			
9	Thermal	10/23/2012	8	0.7	6.2	8.4	10.3	10.6	12.3	28.75	31.75	52	76.75	

```
Sub TransposeData()
Dim shOrg As Worksheet, shRes As Worksheet
Dim rngStart As Range, rngPaste As Range
Dim lngData As Long
```

```
Application.ScreenUpdating = False
On Error Resume Next
Application.DisplayAlerts = False
Sheets("TransposeResult").Delete
Application.DisplayAlerts = True
On Error GoTo 0

On Error GoTo terminate

Set shOrg = Sheets("TransposeData")
Set shRes = Sheets.Add(After:=shOrg)
shRes.Name = "TransposeResult"
With shOrg
    '--Sort
    .Cells.CurrentRegion.Sort Key1:=.[B2], Order1:=1, Key2:=.[C2], _
        Order2:=1, Key3:=.[E2], Order3:=1, Header:=xlYes
    '--Copy title
    .Rows(1).Copy shRes.Rows(1)
    '--Set start range
    Set rngStart = .[C2]
    Do Until IsEmpty(rngStart)
        Set rngPaste = shRes.Cells(shRes.Rows.Count, 1).End(xlUp).Offset(1)
        lngData = GetNextRange(rngStart)
        rngStart.Offset(, -2).Resize(, 5).Copy rngPaste

        'Copy to V1 to V14
        rngStart.Offset(, 2).Resize(lngData).Copy
        rngPaste.Offset(, 5).PasteSpecial Paste:=xlAll, Operation:=xlNone, _
         SkipBlanks:=False, Transpose:=True
        'Copy to V1FP to V14FP
        rngStart.Offset(, 1).Resize(lngData).Copy
        rngPaste.Offset(, 19).PasteSpecial Paste:=xlAll, Operation:=xlNone, _
         SkipBlanks:=False, Transpose:=True
        Set rngStart = rngStart.Offset(lngData)
    Loop
End With

Application.Goto shRes.[A1]
With shRes
    .Cells.Columns.AutoFit
    .Columns("D:E").Delete shift:=xlToLeft
End With

Application.ScreenUpdating = True
Application.CutCopyMode = False

If MsgBox("Do you want to delete the original worksheet?", 36) = 6 Then
'6 is the numerical value of vbYes
    Application.DisplayAlerts = False
    Sheets("TransposeData").Delete
    Application.DisplayAlerts = True
End If

Set rngPaste = Nothing
Set rngStart = Nothing
Set shRes = Nothing

Exit Sub
```

13

```
terminate:
End Sub

Function GetNextRange(ByVal rngSt As Range) As Long
    Dim i As Long
    i = 0

    Do Until rngSt.Value <> rngSt.Offset(i).Value
        i = i + 1
    Loop

    GetNextRange = i
End Function
```

Select/Deselect Noncontiguous Cells

Submitted by Tom Urtis.

Ordinarily, to deselect a single cell or range on a sheet, you must click an unselected cell to deselect all cells and then start over by reselecting all the correct cells. This is inconvenient if you need to reselect a lot of noncontiguous cells.

This sample adds two new options to the contextual menu of a selection: Deselect ActiveCell and Deselect ActiveArea. With the noncontiguous cells selected, hold down the Ctrl key, click the cell you want to deselect to make it active, release the Ctrl key, and then right-click the cell you want to deselect. The contextual menu shown in Figure 13.9 appears. Click the menu item that deselects either that one active cell or the contiguously selected area of which it is a part.

Figure 13.9
The Modify
RightClick proce-
dure provides a custom
contextual menu for
deselecting noncontigu-
ous cells.

Enter the following procedures in a standard module:

```
Sub ModifyRightClick()
'add the new options to the right-click menu
Dim O1 As Object, O2 As Object
```

```
'delete the options if they exist already
On Error Resume Next
With CommandBars("Cell")
    .Controls("Deselect ActiveCell").Delete
    .Controls("Deselect ActiveArea").Delete
End With
On Error GoTo 0

'add the new options
Set O1 = CommandBars("Cell").Controls.Add

With O1
    .Caption = "Deselect ActiveCell"
    .OnAction = "DeselectActiveCell"
End With

Set O2 = CommandBars("Cell").Controls.Add

With O2
    .Caption = "Deselect ActiveArea"
    .OnAction = "DeselectActiveArea"
End With
End Sub

Sub DeselectActiveCell()
Dim x As Range, y As Range

If Selection.Cells.Count > 1 Then
    For Each y In Selection.Cells
        If y.Address <> ActiveCell.Address Then
            If x Is Nothing Then
                Set x = y
            Else
                Set x = Application.Union(x, y)
            End If
        End If
    Next y
    If x.Cells.Count > 0 Then
        x.Select
    End If
End If
End Sub

Sub DeselectActiveArea()
Dim x As Range, y As Range

If Selection.Areas.Count > 1 Then
    For Each y In Selection.Areas
        If Application.Intersect(ActiveCell, y) Is Nothing Then
            If x Is Nothing Then
                Set x = y
            Else
                Set x = Application.Union(x, y)
            End If
        End If
    Next y
```

13

```
    x.Select
End If
End Sub
```

Add the following procedures to the ThisWorkbook module:

```
Private Sub Workbook_Activate()
ModifyRightClick
End Sub

Private Sub Workbook_Deactivate()
Application.CommandBars("Cell").Reset
End Sub
```

Techniques for VBA Pros

The next eight utilities amaze me. In the various message board communities on the Internet, VBA programmers are constantly coming up with new ways to do something faster or better. When someone posts some new code that obviously runs circles around the prior generally accepted best code, everyone benefits.

Excel State Class Module

Submitted by Juan Pablo Gonzàlez Ruiz of Bogotà, Colombia. Juan Pablo is an Excel consultant and runs his photography business at www.juanpg.com.

The following class module is one of my favorites and I use it in almost every project I create. Before Juan shared the module with me, I used to enter the four lines of code to turn off and back on screen updating, events, alerts, and calculations. At the beginning of a sub I would turn them off, and at the end I would turn them back on. That was quite a bit of typing. Now, I just place the class module in a new workbook I create and call it as needed.

Insert a class module named CAppState and place the following code in it:

```
Private m_su As Boolean
Private m_ee As Boolean
Private m_da As Boolean
Private m_calc As Long
Private m_cursor As Long

Private m_except As StateEnum

Public Enum StateEnum
    None = 0
    ScreenUpdating = 1
    EnableEvents = 2
    DisplayAlerts = 4
    Calculation = 8
    Cursor = 16
End Enum

Public Sub SetState(Optional ByVal except As StateEnum = StateEnum.None)
    m_except = except
    With Application
        If Not m_except And StateEnum.ScreenUpdating Then
```

```
                .ScreenUpdating = False
        End If

        If Not m_except And StateEnum.EnableEvents Then
            .EnableEvents = False
        End If

        If Not m_except And StateEnum.DisplayAlerts Then
            .DisplayAlerts = False
        End If

        If Not m_except And StateEnum.Calculation Then
            .Calculation = xlCalculationManual
        End If

        If Not m_except And StateEnum.Cursor Then
            .Cursor = xlWait
        End If
    End With
End Sub

Private Sub Class_Initialize()
    With Application
        m_su = .ScreenUpdating
        m_ee = .EnableEvents
        m_da = .DisplayAlerts
        m_calc = .Calculation
        m_cursor = .Cursor
    End With
End Sub

Private Sub Class_Terminate()
    With Application
        If Not m_except And StateEnum.ScreenUpdating Then
            .ScreenUpdating = m_su
        End If

        If Not m_except And StateEnum.EnableEvents Then
            .EnableEvents = m_ee
        End If

        If Not m_except And StateEnum.DisplayAlerts Then
            .DisplayAlerts = m_da
        End If

        If Not m_except And StateEnum.Calculation Then
            .Calculation = m_calc
        End If

        If Not m_except And StateEnum.Cursor Then
            .Cursor = m_cursor
        End If
    End With
End Sub
```

The following code is an example of calling the class module to turn off the various states, running your code, and then setting the states back.

13

```
Sub RunFasterCode
Dim appState As CAppState
Set appState = New CAppState
appState.SetState None
'run your code
'if you have any formulas that need to update, use
'Application.Calculate
'to force the workbook to calculate
Set appState = Nothing
End Sub
```

Pivot Table Drill-Down

Submitted by Tom Urtis.

When you are double-clicking the data section, a pivot table's default behavior is to insert a new worksheet and display that drill-down information on the new sheet. The following example serves as an option for convenience, to keep the drilled-down recordsets on the same sheet as the pivot table (see Figure 13.10) so that you can delete them as you want.

Figure 13.10
Show the drill-down recordset on the same sheet as the pivot table.

26	⊟ Zelda	Q4	86	1803	5037		69
27	Zelda Total		86	1803	5037		69
28	Grand Total		48780	20396	38672	11738	1195
29							
30	**Name**	**Region**	**Quarter**	**Item**	**Color**	**Sales**	
31	Jim	South	Q3	Hats	Yellow	1941	
32	Jim	South	Q3	Hats	Yellow	7400	
33							

To use this macro, double-click the data section or the Totals section to create stacked drill-down recordsets in the next available row of the sheet. To delete any drill-down recordsets you have created, double-click anywhere in their respective current region.

```
Private Sub Worksheet_BeforeDoubleClick(ByVal Target As Range, Cancel As Boolean)
Application.ScreenUpdating = False
Dim LPTR&

With ActiveSheet.PivotTables(1).DataBodyRange
    LPTR = .Rows.Count + .Row - 1
End With

Dim PTT As Integer
On Error Resume Next
PTT = Target.PivotCell.PivotCellType
If Err.Number = 1004 Then
    Err.Clear
    If Not IsEmpty(Target) Then
        If Target.Row > Range("A1").CurrentRegion.Rows.Count + 1 Then
            Cancel = True
            With Target.CurrentRegion
                .Resize(.Rows.Count + 1).EntireRow.Delete
            End With
        End If
    Else
        Cancel = True
```

```
        End If
    Else
        CS = ActiveSheet.Name
    End If
    Application.ScreenUpdating = True
    End Sub
```

Custom Sort Order

Submitted by Wei Jiang of Wuhan City, China. Jiang is a consultant for MrExcel.com.

By default, Excel enables you to sort lists numerically or alphabetically, but sometimes that is not what is needed. For example, a client might need each day's sales data sorted by the default division order of belts, handbags, watches, wallets, and everything else. Although you can manually set up a custom series and sort using it, if you're creating an automated workbook for other users, this might not be an option. This sample uses a custom sort order list to sort a range of data into default division order and then deletes the custom sort order. Figure 13.11 shows the results.

Figure 13.11

When you use the macro, the list in A:C is sorted first by date and then by the custom sort list in Column I.

	A	B	C	D	E	F	G	H	I	
1	Date	Category	# sold						Belts	
2	1/1/2009	Belts	15						Handbags	
3	1/1/2009	Handbags	23						Watches	
4	1/1/2009	Watches	42						Wallets	
5	1/1/2009	Wallets	17						Everything Else	
6	1/1/2009	Everything Else	36							
7	1/2/2009	Belts	17							
8	1/2/2009	Handbags	21							

```
Sub CustomSort()
    ' add the custom list to Custom Lists
    Application.AddCustomList ListArray:=Range("I1:I5")

    ' get the list number
    nIndex = Application.GetCustomListNum(Range("I1:I5").Value)

    ' Now, we could sort a range with the custom list.
    ' Note, we should use nIndex + 1 as the custom list number here,
    ' for the first one is Normal order
    Range("A2:C16").Sort Key1:=Range("B2"), Order1:=xlAscending, _
                         Header:=xlNo, Orientation:=xlSortColumns, _
                         OrderCustom:=nIndex + 1
    Range("A2:C16").Sort Key1:=Range("A2"), Order1:=xlAscending, _
                         Header:=xlNo, Orientation:=xlSortColumns

    ' At the end, we should remove this custom list...
    Application.DeleteCustomList nIndex
End Sub
```

13

Cell Progress Indicator

Submitted by Tom Urtis.

I have to admit, the conditional formatting options in Excel, such as data bars, are fantastic. However, there still isn't an option for a visual like that shown in Figure 13.12. The following example builds a progress indicator in Column C based on entries in Columns A and B.

Figure 13.12
Use indicators in cells to show progress.

	A	B	C
	Progress made	Progress required	Visual representation of progress made vs progress completed
1			
2	11	15	■■■■■■■■■■■□□□□
3	14	20	■■■■■■■■■■■■■■□□□□□□
4	1	5	■□□□□
5	4	10	■■■■□□□□□□
6	4	10	■■■■□□□□□□
7	10	10	■■■■■■■■■■
8	8	10	■■■■■■■■□□
9	0	10	□□□□□□□□□□
10		10	□□□□□□□□□□
11		10	□□□□□□□□□□

```
Private Sub Worksheet_Change(ByVal Target As Range)
If Target.Column > 2 Or Target.Cells.Count > 1 Then Exit Sub
If Application.IsNumber(Target.Value) = False Then
    Application.EnableEvents = False
    Application.Undo
    Application.EnableEvents = True
    MsgBox "Numbers only please."
    Exit Sub
End If
Select Case Target.Column
    Case 1
        If Target.Value > Target.Offset(0, 1).Value Then
            Application.EnableEvents = False
            Application.Undo
            Application.EnableEvents = True
            MsgBox "Value in column A may not be larger than value in column B."
            Exit Sub
        End If
    Case 2
        If Target.Value < Target.Offset(0, -1).Value Then
            Application.EnableEvents = False
            Application.Undo
            Application.EnableEvents = True
            MsgBox "Value in column B may not be smaller " & _
                "than value in column A."
            Exit Sub
        End If
End Select
Dim x As Long
x = Target.Row
Dim z As String
z = Range("B" & x).Value - Range("A" & x).Value
```

```
With Range("C" & x)
    .Formula = "=IF(RC[-1]<=RC[-2],REPT(""n"",RC[-1]) _
        &REPT(""n"",RC[-2]-RC[-1]),REPT(""n"",RC[-2]) _
        &REPT(""o"",RC[-1]-RC[-2]))"
    .Value = .Value
    .Font.Name = "Wingdings"
    .Font.ColorIndex = 1
    .Font.Size = 10
    If Len(Range("A" & x)) <> 0 Then
        .Characters(1, (.Characters.Count - z)).Font.ColorIndex = 3
        .Characters(1, (.Characters.Count - z)).Font.Size = 12
    End If
End With
End Sub
```

Protected Password Box

Submitted by Daniel Klann of Sydney, Australia. Daniel works mainly with VBA in Excel and Access, but dabbles in all sorts of languages.

Using an input box for password protection has a major security flaw: The characters being entered are easily viewable. This program changes the characters to asterisks as they are entered—just like a real password field (see Figure 13.13). Note that the code that follows does not work in 64-bit Excel. Refer to Chapter 23, "Windows Application Programming Interface (API)," for information on modifying the code for 64-bit Excel.

Figure 13.13
Use an input box as a
secure password field.

```
Private Declare Function CallNextHookEx Lib "user32" (ByVal hHook As Long, _
ByVal ncode As Long, ByVal wParam As Long, lParam As Any) As Long

Private Declare Function GetModuleHandle Lib "kernel32" _
    Alias "GetModuleHandleA" (ByVal lpModuleName As String) As Long

Private Declare Function SetWindowsHookEx Lib "user32" _
    Alias "SetWindowsHookExA" _
    (ByVal idHook As Long, ByVal lpfn As Long, _
    ByVal hmod As Long,ByVal dwThreadId As Long) As Long

Private Declare Function UnhookWindowsHookEx Lib "user32" _
    (ByVal hHook As Long) As Long

Private Declare Function SendDlgItemMessage Lib "user32" _
    Alias "SendDlgItemMessageA" _
    (ByVal hDlg As Long, _
    ByVal nIDDlgItem As Long, ByVal wMsg As Long, _
```

13

```
            ByVal wParam As Long, ByVal lParam As Long) As Long

    Private Declare Function GetClassName Lib "user32" _
        Alias "GetClassNameA" (ByVal hwnd As Long, _
        ByVal lpClassName As String, _
        ByVal nMaxCount As Long) As Long

    Private Declare Function GetCurrentThreadId _
        Lib "kernel32" () As Long

    'Constants to be used in our API functions
    Private Const EM_SETPASSWORDCHAR = &HCC
    Private Const WH_CBT = 5
    Private Const HCBT_ACTIVATE = 5
    Private Const HC_ACTION = 0

    Private hHook As Long

    Public Function NewProc(ByVal lngCode As Long, _
        ByVal wParam As Long, ByVal lParam As Long) As Long
        Dim RetVal
        Dim strClassName As String, lngBuffer As Long

        If lngCode < HC_ACTION Then
            NewProc = CallNextHookEx(hHook, lngCode, wParam, lParam)
            Exit Function
        End If

        strClassName = String$(256, " ")
        lngBuffer = 255

        If lngCode = HCBT_ACTIVATE Then       'A window has been activated

            RetVal = GetClassName(wParam, strClassName, lngBuffer)

            'Check for class name of the Inputbox
            If Left$(strClassName, RetVal) = "#32770" Then
                'Change the edit control to display the password character *.
                'You can change the Asc("*") as you please.
                SendDlgItemMessage wParam, &H1324, EM_SETPASSWORDCHAR, Asc("*"), &H0
            End If

        End If

        'This line will ensure that any other hooks that may be in place are
        'called correctly.
        CallNextHookEx hHook, lngCode, wParam, lParam
    End Function

    Public Function InputBoxDK(Prompt, Optional Title, _
        Optional Default, Optional XPos, _
        Optional YPos, Optional HelpFile, Optional Context) As String
        Dim lngModHwnd As Long, lngThreadID As Long

        lngThreadID = GetCurrentThreadId
        lngModHwnd = GetModuleHandle(vbNullString)
```

```
      hHook = SetWindowsHookEx(WH_CBT, AddressOf NewProc, lngModHwnd, lngThreadID)
      On Error Resume Next
      InputBoxDK = InputBox(Prompt, Title, Default, XPos, YPos, HelpFile, Context)
      UnhookWindowsHookEx hHook
End Function

Sub PasswordBox()
If InputBoxDK("Please enter password", "Password Required") <> "password" Then

      MsgBox "Sorry, that was not a correct password."
   Else
      MsgBox "Correct Password!  Come on in."
   End If
End Sub
```

Change Case

Submitted by Ivan F. Moala.

Word can change the case of selected text, but that capability is notably lacking in Excel. This program enables the Excel user to change the case of text in any selected range, as shown in Figure 13.14.

Figure 13.14
You can now change the case of words, just like in Word.

```
Sub TextCaseChange()
Dim RgText As Range
Dim oCell As Range
Dim Ans As String
Dim strTest As String
Dim sCap As Integer, _
    lCap As Integer, _
    i As Integer

'// You need to select a range to alter first!

Again:
Ans = Application.InputBox("[L]owercase" & vbCr & "[U]ppercase" & vbCr & _
        "[S]entence" & vbCr & "[T]itles" & vbCr & "[C]apsSmall", _
        "Type in a Letter", Type:=2)
```

13

```
    If Ans = "False" Then Exit Sub
    If InStr(1, "LUSTC", UCase(Ans), vbTextCompare) = 0 _
        Or Len(Ans) > 1 Then GoTo Again

    On Error GoTo NoText
    If Selection.Count = 1 Then
        Set RgText = Selection
    Else
        Set RgText = Selection.SpecialCells(xlCellTypeConstants, 2)
    End If
    On Error GoTo 0

    For Each oCell In RgText
        Select Case UCase(Ans)
            Case "L": oCell = LCase(oCell.Text)
            Case "U": oCell = UCase(oCell.Text)
            Case "S": oCell = UCase(Left(oCell.Text, 1)) & _
                LCase(Right(oCell.Text, Len(oCell.Text) - 1))
            Case "T": oCell = Application.WorksheetFunction.Proper(oCell.Text)
            Case "C"
                    lCap = oCell.Characters(1, 1).Font.Size
                    sCap = Int(lCap * 0.85)
                    'Small caps for everything.
                    oCell.Font.Size = sCap
                    oCell.Value = UCase(oCell.Text)
                    strTest = oCell.Value
                    'Large caps for 1st letter of words.
                    strTest = Application.Proper(strTest)
                    For i = 1 To Len(strTest)
                        If Mid(strTest, i, 1) = UCase(Mid(strTest, i, 1)) Then
                            oCell.Characters(i, 1).Font.Size = lCap
                        End If
                    Next i
        End Select
    Next

    Exit Sub
NoText:
    MsgBox "No text in your selection @ " & Selection.Address

End Sub
```

Selecting with SpecialCells

Submitted by Ivan F. Moala.

Typically, when you want to find certain values, text, or formulas in a range, the range is selected and each cell is tested. The following example shows how `SpecialCells` can be used to select only the desired cells. Having fewer cells to check speeds up your code.

The following code ran in the blink of an eye on my machine. However, the version that checked each cell in the range (A1:Z20000) took 14 seconds—an eternity in the automation world!

```
Sub SpecialRange()
Dim TheRange As Range
Dim oCell As Range
```

```
    Set TheRange = Range("A1:Z20000").SpecialCells(__
    xlCellTypeConstants, xlTextValues)

    For Each oCell In TheRange
        If oCell.Text = "Your Text" Then
            MsgBox oCell.Address
            MsgBox TheRange.Cells.Count
        End If
    Next oCell

End Sub
```

ActiveX Right-Click Menu

Submitted by Tom Urtis.

There is no built-in menu for the right-click event of ActiveX objects on a sheet. This is a utility for that, using a command button for the example in Figure 13.15. Set the Take Focus on Click property of the command button to False.

Figure 13.15
Customize the contextual (right-click) menu of an ActiveX control.

Place the following in the ThisWorkbook module:

```
Private Sub Workbook_Open()
With Application
    .CommandBars("Cell").Reset
    .WindowState = xlMaximized
    .Goto Sheet1.Range("A1"), True
End With
End Sub

Private Sub Workbook_Activate()
Application.CommandBars("Cell").Reset
End Sub

Private Sub Workbook_SheetBeforeRightClick(ByVal Sh As Object, _
    ByVal Target As Range, Cancel As Boolean)
Application.CommandBars("Cell").Reset
End Sub

Private Sub Workbook_Deactivate()
Application.CommandBars("Cell").Reset
End Sub

Private Sub Workbook_BeforeClose(Cancel As Boolean)
With Application
    .CommandBars("Cell").Reset
    .WindowState = xlMaximized
```

13

```
    .Goto Sheet1.Range("A1"), True
End With
ThisWorkbook.Save
End Sub
```

Place the following in the control's sheet module, such as Sheet1:

```
Private Sub CommandButton1_Click()
MsgBox "You left-clicked the command button." & vbCrLf & _
"Right-click the button for a custom menu demonstration.", 64, "FYI..."
End Sub


Private Sub CommandButton1_MouseDown ()
If Button = 2 Then Run "MyRightClickMenu"
End Sub
```

Place the following in a standard module:

```
Sub MyRightClickMenu()
Application.CommandBars("Cell").Reset
Dim cbc As CommandBarControl
  For Each cbc In Application.CommandBars("cell").Controls
      cbc.Visible = False
  Next cbc
With Application.CommandBars("Cell").Controls.Add(temporary:=True)
   .Caption = "My Macro 1"
   .OnAction = "Test1"
   End With
With Application.CommandBars("Cell").Controls.Add(temporary:=True)
   .Caption = "My Macro 2"
   .OnAction = "Test2"
   End With
With Application.CommandBars("Cell").Controls.Add(temporary:=True)
   .Caption = "My Macro 3"
   .OnAction = "Test3"
   End With
Application.CommandBars("Cell").ShowPopup
End Sub


Sub Test1()
MsgBox "This is the Test1 macro from the ActiveX object's custom " & _
    "right-click event menu.", , "''My Macro 1'' menu item."
End Sub


Sub Test2()
MsgBox "This is the Test2 macro from the ActiveX object's custom " & _
    "right-click event menu.", , "''My Macro 2'' menu item."
End Sub


Sub Test3()
MsgBox "This is the Test3 macro from the ActiveX object's custom " & _
    "right-click event menu.", , "''My Macro 3'' menu item."
End Sub
```

Cool Applications

These last samples are interesting applications that you might be able to incorporate into your own projects.

Historical Stock/Fund Quotes

Submitted by Nathan P. Oliver.

The following code retrieves the average of a valid stock ticker or the close of a fund for the specified date:

```
Private Sub GetQuote()
Dim ie As Object, lCharPos As Long, sHTML As String
Dim HistDate As Date, HighVal As String, LowVal As String
Dim cl As Range

Set cl = ActiveCell
HistDate = cl(, 0)

If Intersect(cl, Range("C2:C" & Cells.Rows.Count)) Is Nothing Then
    MsgBox "You must select a cell in column C."
    Exit Sub
End If

If Not CBool(Len(cl(, -1))) Or Not CBool(Len(cl(, 0))) Then
    MsgBox "You must enter a symbol and date."
    Exit Sub
End If

Set ie = CreateObject("InternetExplorer.Application")

With ie
    .Navigate _
        "http://bigcharts.marketwatch.com/historical" & _
        "/default.asp?detect=1&symb=" _
        & cl(, -1) & "&closedate=" & Month(HistDate) & "%2F" & _
        Day(HistDate) & "%2F" & Year(HistDate) & "&x=0&y=0"
    Do While .Busy And .ReadyState <> 4
        DoEvents
    Loop
    sHTML = .Document.body.innertext
    .Quit
End With

Set ie = Nothing

lCharPos = InStr(1, sHTML, "High:", vbTextCompare)
If lCharPos Then HighVal = Mid$(sHTML, lCharPos + 5, 15)

If Not Left$(HighVal, 3) = "n/a" Then
    lCharPos = InStr(1, sHTML, "Low:", vbTextCompare)
    If lCharPos Then LowVal = Mid$(sHTML, lCharPos + 4, 15)
    cl.Value = (Val(LowVal) + Val(HighVal)) / 2
Else: lCharPos = InStr(1, sHTML, "Closing Price:", vbTextCompare)
    cl.Value = Val(Mid$(sHTML, lCharPos + 14, 15))
End If

Set cl = Nothing
End Sub
```

13

Using VBA Extensibility to Add Code to New Workbooks

You have a macro that moves data to a new workbook for the regional managers. What if you need to also copy macros to the new workbook? You can use Visual Basic for Application Extensibility to import modules to a workbook or to actually write lines of code to the workbook.

To use any of these examples, you must first open VB Editor, select References from the Tools menu, and select the reference for Microsoft Visual Basic for Applications Extensibility 5.3. You must also trust access to VBA by going to the Developer tab, choosing Macro Security, and checking Trust Access to the VBA Project Object Model.

The easiest way to use VBA Extensibility is to export a complete module or userform from the current project and import it to the new workbook. Perhaps you have an application with thousands of lines of code. You want to create a new workbook with data for the regional manager and give her three macros to enable custom formatting and printing. Place all of these macros in a module called modToRegion. Macros in this module also call the frmRegion userform. The following code transfers this code from the current workbook to the new workbook:

```
Sub MoveDataAndMacro()
    Dim WSD as worksheet
    Set WSD = Worksheets("Report")
    ' Copy Report to a new workbook
    WSD.Copy
    ' The active workbook is now the new workbook
    ' Delete any old copy of the module from C
    On Error Resume Next
    ' Delete any stray copies from hard drive
    Kill ("C:\temp\ModToRegion.bas")
    Kill ("C:\temp\frmRegion.frm")
    On Error GoTo 0
    ' Export module & form from this workbook
    ThisWorkbook.VBProject.VBComponents("ModToRegion").Export _
        ("C:\temp\ModToRegion.bas")
    ThisWorkbook.VBProject.VBComponents("frmRegion").Export _
        ("C:\temp\frmRegion. frm")
    ' Import to new workbook
    ActiveWorkbook.VBProject.VBComponents.Import ("C:\temp\ModToRegion.bas")
    ActiveWorkbook.VBProject.VBComponents.Import ("C:\temp\frmRegion.frm")
    On Error Resume Next
    Kill ("C:\temp\ModToRegion.bas")
    Kill ("C:\temp\frmRegion.bas")
    On Error GoTo 0
End Sub
```

The preceding method works if you need to move modules or userforms to a new workbook. However, what if you need to write some code to the Workbook_Open macro in the ThisWorkbook module? There are two tools to use. The Lines method enables you to return a particular set of code lines from a given module. The InsertLines method enables you to insert code lines to a new module.

> **NOTE**
> With each call to InsertLines, you must insert a complete macro. Excel attempts to compile the code after each call to InsertLines. If you insert lines that do not completely compile, Excel might crash with a general protection fault (GPF).

```
Sub MoveDataAndMacro()
    Dim WSD as worksheet
    Dim WBN as Workbook
    Dim WBCodeMod1 As Object, WBCodeMod2 As Object
    Set WSD = Worksheets("Report")
    ' Copy Report to a new workbook
    WSD.Copy
    ' The active workbook is now the new workbook
    Set WBN = ActiveWorkbook
    ' Copy the Workbook level Event handlers
    Set WBCodeMod1 = ThisWorkbook.VBProject.VBComponents("ThisWorkbook") _
        .CodeModule
    Set WBCodeMod2 = WBN.VBProject.VBComponents("ThisWorkbook").CodeModule
    WBCodeMod2.insertlines 1, WBCodeMod1.Lines(1, WBCodeMod1.countoflines)
End Sub
```

Next Steps

The utilities in this chapter aren't Excel's only source of programming power. User-defined functions (UDFs) enable you to create complex custom formulas to cover what Excel's functions don't. In Chapter 14, "Sample User-Defined Functions," you'll find out how to create and share your own functions.

13

Sample User-Defined Functions

Creating User-Defined Functions

Excel provides many built-in functions. However, sometimes you need a complex custom function not offered, such as a function that sums a range of cells based on their interior color.

So, what do you do? You could go down your list and copy the colored cells to another section.
Or perhaps you have a calculator next to you as you work your way down your list—beware you don't enter the same number twice! Both methods are time-consuming and prone to accidents. What to do?

You could write a procedure to solve this problem—after all, that's what this book is about. However, you have another option: *user-defined functions* (UDFs).

Functions can be created in VBA and can be used just like Excel's built-in functions, such as SUM. After the custom function is created, a user needs to know only the function name and its arguments.

> **NOTE**
>
> You can enter UDFs only into standard modules. Sheet and ThisWorkbook modules are a special type of module. If you enter the function there, Excel does not recognize that you are creating a UDF.

14

CASE STUDY: CUSTOM FUNCTIONS: EXAMPLE AND EXPLANATION

Let's build a custom function to add two values. After you have created it, you will use it on a worksheet.

Insert a new module in the VB Editor. Type the following function into the module. It is a function called ADD that totals two numbers in different cells. The function has two arguments:

```
Add(Number1,Number2)
```

Number1 is the first number to add; Number2 is the second number to add:

```
Function Add(Number1 As Integer, Number2 As Integer) As Integer
Add = Number1 + Number2
End Function
```

Let's break this down:

- Function name: ADD.

- Arguments are placed in parentheses after the name of the function. This example has two arguments: Number1 and Number2.

- As Integer defines the variable type of the result as a whole number.

- ADD =Number1 + Number2: The result of the function is returned.

Here is how to use the function on a worksheet:

1. Type numbers into cells A1 and A2.

2. Select cell A3.

3. Press Shift+F3 to open the Insert Function dialog box, or from the Formulas tab choose Insert Function.

4. Select the User Defined category (see Figure 14.1).

Figure 14.1
You can find your UDFs under the User Defined category of the Insert Function dialog box.

5. Select the Add function.

6. In the first argument box, select cell A1 (see Figure 14.2).

Figure 14.2
Use the Function
Arguments dialog to
enter your arguments.

```
Function Arguments                                    ?  ☒

Add
   Number1  A1              [▦]  =  5
   Number2  A2|             [▦]  =  74
                                 =  79
No help available.

                     Number2


Formula result =  79
Help on this function                    OK        Cancel
```

7. In the second argument box, select cell A2.

8. Click OK.

Congratulations! You have created your first custom function.

NOTE

You can easily share custom functions because the users are not required to know how the function works. See the section "Sharing UDFs," later in this chapter, for more information.

Most of the functions used on sheets can also be used in VBA and vice versa. However, in VBA you call the UDF (ADD) from a procedure (Addition):

```
Sub Addition ()
Dim Total as Integer
Total = Add (1,10) 'we use a user-defined function Add
MsgBox "The answer is: " & Total
End Sub
```

Sharing UDFs

Where you store a UDF affects how you can share it:

- **Personal.xlsb**—Store the UDF in Personal.xlsb if it is just for your use and won't be used in a workbook opened on another computer.
- **Workbook**—Store the UDF in the workbook in which it is being used if it needs to be distributed to many people.

14

■ **Add-in**—Distribute the UDF via an add-in if the workbook is to be shared among a select group of people. See Chapter 26, "Creating Add-Ins," for information on how to create an add-in.

■ **Template**—Store the UDF in a template if it needs to be used to create several workbooks and the workbooks are distributed to many people.

Useful Custom Excel Functions

The sections that follow include a sampling of functions that can prove useful in the everyday Excel world.

> **NOTE**
>
> This chapter contains functions donated by several Excel programmers. These are functions that they have found useful and that they hope will also be of help to you.
>
> Different programmers have different programming styles. We did not rewrite the submissions. As you review the lines of code, you might notice different ways of doing the same task, such as referring to ranges.

Set the Current Workbook's Name in a Cell

The following function sets the name of the active workbook in a cell, as shown in Figure 14.3:

```
MyName()
```

Figure 14.3
Use a UDF to show the filename or the filename with directory path.

| ProjectFilesChapter14.xlsm | =MyName() |
| C:\Chapter 14 - Sample User-Defined Functions\ProjectFilesChapter14.xlsm | =MyFullName() |

No arguments are used with this function:

```
Function MyName() As String
    MyName = ThisWorkbook.Name
End Function
```

Set the Current Workbook's Name and File Path in a Cell

A variation of the preceding function, the following function sets the file path and name of the active workbook in a cell, as shown previously in Figure 14.3:

```
MyFullName()
```

No arguments are used with this function:

```
Function MyFullName() As String
    MyFullName = ThisWorkbook.FullName
End Function
```

Check Whether a Workbook Is Open

There might be times when you need to check whether a workbook is open. The following function returns True if the workbook is open and False if it is not:

```
BookOpen(Bk)
```

The argument is Bk, which is the name of the workbook being checked:

```
Function BookOpen(Bk As String) As Boolean
Dim T As Excel.Workbook
Err.Clear 'clears any errors
On Error Resume Next 'if the code runs into an error, it skips it and continues
Set T = Application.Workbooks(Bk)
BookOpen = Not T Is Nothing
'If the workbook is open, then T will hold the workbook object and therefore
 'will NOT be Nothing
Err.Clear
On Error GoTo 0
End Function
```

Here is an example of using the function:

```
Sub OpenAWorkbook()
Dim IsOpen As Boolean
Dim BookName As String
BookName = "ProjectFilesChapter14.xlsm"
IsOpen = BookOpen(BookName) 'calling our function - don't forget the parameter
If IsOpen Then
    MsgBox BookName & " is already open!"
Else
    Workbooks.Open (BookName)
End If
End Sub
```

Check Whether a Sheet in an Open Workbook Exists

This function requires that the workbook(s) it checks be open. It returns True if the sheet is found and False if it is not.

```
SheetExists(SName, WBName)
```

The arguments are as shown here:

- SName—The name of the sheet being searched
- WBName—(Optional) The name of the workbook containing the sheet

```
Function SheetExists(SName As String, Optional WB As Workbook) As Boolean
    Dim WS As Worksheet

    ' Use active workbook by default
    If WB Is Nothing Then
        Set WB = ActiveWorkbook
    End If

    On Error Resume Next
        SheetExists = CBool(Not WB.Sheets(SName) Is Nothing)
    On Error GoTo 0

End Function
```

14

CBool is a function that converts the expression between the parentheses to a Boolean value.

Here is an example of using this function:

```
Sub CheckForSheet()
Dim ShtExists As Boolean
ShtExists = SheetExists("Sheet9")
'notice that only one parameter was passed; the workbook name is optional
If ShtExists Then
    MsgBox "The worksheet exists!"
Else
    MsgBox "The worksheet does NOT exist!"
End If
End Sub
```

Count the Number of Workbooks in a Directory

This function searches the current directory, and its subfolders if you want, counting all Excel macro workbook files (XLSM), including hidden files, or just the ones starting with a string of letters:

```
NumFilesInCurDir (LikeText, Subfolders)
```

The arguments are as listed here:

- LikeText—(Optional) A string value to search for; must include an asterisk (*), such as Mr*

- Subfolders—(Optional) True to search subfolders, False (default) not to

FileSystemObject requires the Microsoft Scripting Runtime reference library. To enable this setting, go to Tools, References, and check Microsoft Scripting Runtime.

This function is a recursive function—it calls itself until a specific condition is met; in this case, until all subfolders are processed:

```
Function NumFilesInCurDir(Optional strInclude As String = "", _
Optional blnSubDirs As Boolean = False)
Dim fso As FileSystemObject
Dim fld As Folder
Dim fil As File
Dim subfld As Folder
Dim intFileCount As Integer
Dim strExtension As String
  strExtension = "XLSM"
  Set fso = New FileSystemObject
  Set fld = fso.GetFolder(ThisWorkbook.Path)
  For Each fil In fld.Files
    If UCase(fil.Name) Like "*" & UCase(strInclude) & "*." & _
        UCase(strExtension) Then
```

```
      intFileCount = intFileCount + 1
    End If
  Next fil
  If blnSubDirs Then
    For Each subfld In fld.Subfolders
      intFileCount = intFileCount + NumFilesInCurDir(strInclude, True)
    Next subfld
  End If
  NumFilesInCurDir = intFileCount
  Set fso = Nothing
End Function
```

Here is an example of using this function:

```
Sub CountMyWkbks()
Dim MyFiles As Integer
MyFiles = NumFilesInCurDir("MrE*", True)
MsgBox MyFiles & " file(s) found"
End Sub
```

Retrieve USERID

Ever need to keep a record of who saves changes to a workbook? With the USERID function, you can retrieve the name of the user logged in to a computer. Combine it with the function discussed in the "Retrieve Permanent Date and Time" section, later in this chapter, and you have a nice log file. You can also use the USERID function to set up user rights to a workbook.

```
WinUserName ()
```

No arguments are used with this function.

> **NOTE**
> The USERID function is an advanced function that uses the *application programming interface* (API), which is reviewed in Chapter 23, "Windows Application Programming Interface (API)." The code is specific to 32-bit Excel. If you are running 64-bit Excel, refer to Chapter 23 for changes to make it work.

This first section (Private declarations) must be at the top of the module:

```
Private Declare Function WNetGetUser Lib "mpr.dll" Alias "WNetGetUserA" _
    (ByVal lpName As String, ByVal lpUserName As String, _
    lpnLength As Long) As Long
Private Const NO_ERROR = 0
Private Const ERROR_NOT_CONNECTED = 2250&
Private Const ERROR_MORE_DATA = 234
Private Const ERROR_NO_NETWORK = 1222&
Private Const ERROR_EXTENDED_ERROR = 1208&
Private Const ERROR_NO_NET_OR_BAD_PATH = 1203&
```

You can place the following section of code anywhere in the module as long as it is below the preceding section:

```
Function WinUsername() As String
    'variables
    Dim strBuf As String, lngUser As Long, strUn As String
    'clear buffer for user name from api func
```

14

```
strBuf = Space$(255)
'use api func WNetGetUser to assign user value to lngUser
'will have lots of blank space
lngUser = WNetGetUser("", strBuf, 255)
'if no error from function call
If lngUser = NO_ERROR Then
    'clear out blank space in strBuf and assign val to function
    strUn = Left(strBuf, InStr(strBuf, vbNullChar) - 1)
    WinUsername = strUn
Else
'error, give up
    WinUsername = "Error :" & lngUser
End If
End Function
```

Function example:

```
Sub CheckUserRights()
Dim UserName As String
UserName = WinUsername
Select Case UserName
    Case "Administrator"
        MsgBox "Full Rights"
    Case "Guest"
        MsgBox "You cannot make changes"
    Case Else
        MsgBox "Limited Rights"
End Select
End Sub
```

Retrieve Date and Time of Last Save

This function retrieves the saved date and time of any workbook, including the current one:

```
LastSaved(FullPath)
```

> **NOTE** The cell must be formatted for date and time to display the date/time correctly.

The argument is FullPath, a string showing the full path and filename of the file in question:

```
Function LastSaved(FullPath As String) As Date
LastSaved = FileDateTime(FullPath)
End Function
```

Retrieve Permanent Date and Time

Because of the volatility of the NOW function, it isn't very useful for stamping a worksheet with the creation or editing date. Every time the workbook is opened or recalculated, the result of the NOW function is updated. The following function uses the NOW function.

14

However, because you need to reenter the cell to update the function, it is much less volatile (see Figure 14.4).

```
DateTime()
```

Figure 14.4
Even after forcing a recalculation, the DateTime() cell shows the time when it was originally placed in the cell, whereas NOW() shows the current system time.

9/16/2012 13.02	=NOW()
9/16/2012 12:41	=DateTime()

No arguments are used with this function:

```
DateTime()
```

> **NOTE**
> The cell must be formatted properly to display the date/time.

Function example:

```
Function DateTime()
    DateTime = Now
End Function
```

Validate an Email Address

If you manage an email subscription list, you might receive invalid email addresses, such as addresses with a space before the "at" symbol (@). The ISEMAILVALID function can check addresses and confirm that they are proper email addresses (see Figure 14.5).

```
IsEmailValid (strEmail)
```

Figure 14.5
Validating email addresses.

Tracy@ MrExcel.com	FALSE	<-a space after @
Bill@MrExcel.com	TRUE	
consult?@MrExcel/com	FALSE	<-invalid characters

> **NOTE**
> This function cannot verify that an email address is an existing one. It only checks the syntax to verify that the address might be legitimate.

14

The argument is strEmail, an email address:

```
Function IsEmailValid(strEmail As String) As Boolean
Dim strArray As Variant
Dim strItem As Variant
Dim i As Long
Dim c As String
Dim blnIsItValid As Boolean
blnIsItValid = True
'count the @ in the string
i = Len(strEmail) - Len(Application.Substitute(strEmail, "@", ""))
'if there is more than one @, invalid email
If i <> 1 Then IsEmailValid = False: Exit Function
ReDim strArray(1 To 2)
'the following two lines place the text to the left and right
'of the @ in their own variables
strArray(1) = Left(strEmail, InStr(1, strEmail, "@", 1) - 1)
strArray(2) = Application.Substitute(Right(strEmail, Len(strEmail) - _
    Len(strArray(1))), "@", "")

For Each strItem In strArray
    'verify there is something in the variable.
'If there isn't, then part of the email is missing
    If Len(strItem) <= 0 Then
        blnIsItValid = False
        IsEmailValid = blnIsItValid
        Exit Function
    End If
    'verify only valid characters in the email
    For i = 1 To Len(strItem)
'lowercases all letters for easier checking
        c = LCase(Mid(strItem, i, 1))
        If InStr("abcdefghijklmnopqrstuvwxyz_-.", c) <= 0 _
            And Not IsNumeric(c) Then
            blnIsItValid = False
            IsEmailValid = blnIsItValid
            Exit Function
        End If
    Next i
'verify that the first character of the left and right aren't periods
    If Left(strItem, 1) = "." Or Right(strItem, 1) = "." Then
        blnIsItValid = False
        IsEmailValid = blnIsItValid
        Exit Function
    End If
Next strItem
'verify there is a period in the right half of the address
If InStr(strArray(2), ".") <= 0 Then
    blnIsItValid = False
    IsEmailValid = blnIsItValid
    Exit Function
End If
i = Len(strArray(2)) - InStrRev(strArray(2), ".") 'locate the period
'verify that the number of letters corresponds to a valid domain extension
If i <> 2 And i <> 3 And i <> 4 Then
    blnIsItValid = False
    IsEmailValid = blnIsItValid
    Exit Function
End If
```

```
'verify that there aren't two periods together in the email
If InStr(strEmail, "..") > 0 Then
    blnIsItValid = False
    IsEmailValid = blnIsItValid
    Exit Function
End If
IsEmailValid = blnIsItValid
End Function
```

Sum Cells Based on Interior Color

Let's say you have created a list of how much each of your clients owes. From this list, you want to sum just those cells to which you have applied a cell fill to indicate clients who are 30 days past due. This function will sum cells based on their fill color.

```
SumColor(CellColor, SumRange)
```

> **NOTE**
> Cells colored by conditional formatting will not work; the cells must have an interior color.

The arguments are as given here:

- CellColor—The address of a cell with the target color
- SumRange—The range of cells to be searched

```
Function SumByColor(CellColor As Range, SumRange As Range)
Dim myCell As Range
Dim iCol As Integer
Dim myTotal
iCol = CellColor.Interior.ColorIndex 'get the target color
For Each myCell In SumRange 'look at each cell in the designated range
'if the cell color matches the target color
If myCell.Interior.ColorIndex = iCol Then
'add the value in the cell to the total
myTotal = WorksheetFunction.Sum(myCell) + myTotal
End If
Next myCell
SumByColor = myTotal
End Function
```

Figure 14.6 shows a sample worksheet using this function.

Figure 14.6
Sum cells based on interior color.

	A	B	C
1	11		
2	6		
3	10		31
4	15		=SumByColor(C2,A1:A10)
5	19		
6	18		
7	20		
8	2		
9	3		
10	1		

14

Count Unique Values

How many times have you had a long list of values and needed to know how many were unique values? This function goes through a range and provides that information, as shown in Figure 14.7:

```
NumUniqueValues(Rng)
```

Figure 14.7
Count the number of unique values in a range.

▲	A	B	C	D
1	A	EE		11
2	R	1		=NumUniqueValues(A1:B8)
3	T	19		
4	A	V		
5	V	Q		
6	F	V		
7	123	GE		
8	1	V		

The argument is Rng, the range to search unique values.

Function example:

```
Function NumUniqueValues(Rng As Range) As Long
Dim myCell As Range
Dim UniqueVals As New Collection
Application.Volatile 'forces the function to recalculate when the range changes
On Error Resume Next
'the following places each value from the range into a collection
'because a collection, with a key parameter, can contain only unique values,
'there will be no duplicates. The error statements force the program to
'continue when the error messages appear for duplicate items in the collection
For Each myCell In Rng
    UniqueVals.Add myCell.Value, CStr(myCell.Value)
Next myCell
On Error GoTo 0
'returns the number of items in the collection
NumUniqueValues = UniqueVals.Count
End Function
```

Remove Duplicates from a Range

No doubt, you have also had a list of items and needed to list only the unique values. The following function goes through a range and stores only the unique values:

```
UniqueValues (OrigArray)
```

The argument is OrigArray, an array from which the duplicates will be removed.

This first section (Const declarations) must be at the top of the module:

```
Const ERR_BAD_PARAMETER = "Array parameter required"
Const ERR_BAD_TYPE = "Invalid Type"
Const ERR_BP_NUMBER = 20000
Const ERR_BT_NUMBER = 20001
```

You can place the following section of code anywhere in the module as long as it is below the preceding section:

```
Public Function UniqueValues(ByVal OrigArray As Variant) As Variant
    Dim vAns() As Variant
    Dim lStartPoint As Long
    Dim lEndPoint As Long
    Dim lCtr As Long, lCount As Long
    Dim iCtr As Integer
    Dim col As New Collection
    Dim sIndex As String
    Dim vTest As Variant, vItem As Variant
    Dim iBadVarTypes(4) As Integer
    'Function does not work if array element is one of the
    'following types
    iBadVarTypes(0) = vbObject
    iBadVarTypes(1) = vbError
    iBadVarTypes(2) = vbDataObject
    iBadVarTypes(3) = vbUserDefinedType
    iBadVarTypes(4) = vbArray
    'Check to see whether the parameter is an array
    If Not IsArray(OrigArray) Then
        Err.Raise ERR_BP_NUMBER, , ERR_BAD_PARAMETER
        Exit Function
    End If
    lStartPoint = LBound(OrigArray)
    lEndPoint = UBound(OrigArray)
    For lCtr = lStartPoint To lEndPoint
        vItem = OrigArray(lCtr)
        'First check to see whether variable type is acceptable
        For iCtr = 0 To UBound(iBadVarTypes)
            If VarType(vItem) = iBadVarTypes(iCtr) Or _
                VarType(vItem) = iBadVarTypes(iCtr) + vbVariant Then
                Err.Raise ERR_BT_NUMBER, , ERR_BAD_TYPE
                Exit Function
            End If
        Next iCtr
        'Add element to a collection, using it as the index
        'if an error occurs, the element already exists
        sIndex = CStr(vItem)
        'first element, add automatically
        If lCtr = lStartPoint Then
            col.Add vItem, sIndex
            ReDim vAns(lStartPoint To lStartPoint) As Variant
            vAns(lStartPoint) = vItem
        Else
            On Error Resume Next
            col.Add vItem, sIndex
            If Err.Number = 0 Then
                lCount = UBound(vAns) + 1
                ReDim Preserve vAns(lStartPoint To lCount)
                vAns(lCount) = vItem
            End If
        End If
        Err.Clear
    Next lCtr
    UniqueValues = vAns
End Function
```

Here is an example of using this function:

```
Function nodupsArray(rng As Range) As Variant
    Dim arr1() As Variant
    If rng.Columns.Count > 1 Then Exit Function
    arr1 = Application.Transpose(rng)
    arr1 = UniqueValues(arr1)
    nodupsArray = Application.Transpose(arr1)
End Function
```

Find the First Nonzero-Length Cell in a Range

Suppose you imported a large list of data with many empty cells. Here is a function that evaluates a range of cells and returns the value of the first nonzero-length cell:

```
FirstNonZeroLength(Rng)
```

The argument is Rng, the range to search.

Function example:

```
Function FirstNonZeroLength(Rng As Range)
Dim myCell As Range
FirstNonZeroLength = 0#
For Each myCell In Rng
    If Not IsNull(myCell) And myCell <> "" Then
        FirstNonZeroLength = myCell.Value
        Exit Function
    End If
Next myCell
FirstNonZeroLength = myCell.Value
End Function
```

Figure 14.8 shows the function on a sample worksheet.

Figure 14.8
Find the value of the first nonzero-length cell in a range.

◢	A	B	C	D
1		2		
2		=FirstNonZeroLength(A1:A7)		
3	2			
4				
5	7			
6	8			
7	9			

Substitute Multiple Characters

Excel has a substitute function, but it is a value-for-value substitution. What if you have several characters you need to substitute? Figure 14.9 shows several examples of how this function works.

```
MSubstitute(trStr, frStr, toStr)
```

Figure 14.9
Substitute multiple characters in a cell.

◢	A	B	C
1	1 Introduction	Introduction	=msubstitute(A1,"1","")
2	This warn a test	This was a test	=msubstitute(A2,"warn", "was")
3	123abc456	abc	=msubstitute(A3,"1234567890","")
4	Adnothyer Tuiest	Another Test	=msubstitute(A4,"dyui","")
5			

The arguments are as listed here:

- trStr—The string to be searched
- frStr—The text being searched for
- toStr—The replacement text

Function example:

```
Function MSubsitute(ByVal trStr As Variant, frStr As String, _
        toStr As String) As Variant
Dim iCol As Integer
Dim j As Integer
Dim Ar As Variant
Dim vfr() As String
Dim vto() As String
ReDim vfr(1 To Len(frStr))
ReDim vto(1 To Len(frStr))
'place the strings into an array
For j = 1 To Len(frStr)
    vfr(j) = Mid(frStr, j, 1)
    If Mid(toStr, j, 1) <> "" Then
        vto(j) = Mid(toStr, j, 1)
    Else
        vto(j) = ""
    End If
Next j
'compare each character and substitute if needed
If IsArray(trStr) Then
    Ar = trStr
    For iRow = LBound(Ar, 1) To UBound(Ar, 1)
        For iCol = LBound(Ar, 2) To UBound(Ar, 2)
            For j = 1 To Len(frStr)
                Ar(iRow, iCol) = Application.Substitute(Ar(iRow, iCol), _
                    vfr(j), vto(j))
            Next j
        Next iCol
    Next iRow
Else
    Ar = trStr
    For j = 1 To Len(frStr)
        Ar = Application.Substitute(Ar, vfr(j), vto(j))
    Next j
End If
MSUBSTITUTE = Ar
End Function
```

> **NOTE**
>
> The toStr argument is assumed to be the same length as frStr. If it isn't, the remaining characters are considered null (""). The function is case sensitive. To replace all instances of a, use a and A. You cannot replace one character with two characters. For example,
>
> =MSUBSTITUTE("This is a test","i","$@")
>
> results in this:
>
> "Th$s $s a test"

Retrieve Numbers from Mixed Text

This function extracts and returns numbers from text that is a mix of numbers and letters:

```
RetrieveNumbers (myString)
```

The argument is myString, the text containing the numbers to be extracted.

Function example:

```
Function RetrieveNumbers(myString As String)
Dim i As Integer, j As Integer
Dim OnlyNums As String
'starting at the END of the string and moving backwards (Step -1)
For i = Len(myString) To 1 Step -1
'IsNumeric is a VBA function that returns True if a variable is a number
'When a number is found, it is added to the OnlyNums string
    If IsNumeric(Mid(myString, i, 1)) Then
        j = j + 1
        OnlyNums = Mid(myString, i, 1) & OnlyNums
    End If
    If j = 1 Then OnlyNums = CInt(Mid(OnlyNums, 1, 1))
Next i
RetrieveNumbers = CLng(OnlyNums)
End Function
```

Convert Week Number into Date

Have you ever received a spreadsheet report in which all the headers showed the week number? This can be confusing because you probably don't know what Week 15 actually is. You would have to get out your calendar and count the weeks. This problem is exacerbated if you need to count weeks in a previous year. What you need is a nice little function that converts Week ## Year into the date of a particular day in a given week, as shown in Figure 14.10:

```
Weekday(Str)
```

Figure 14.10
Convert a week number into a date more easily referenced.

=convertWEEKDAY(E1)	
E	F
Week 15 2012	Monday, April 9, 2012
Week 26 2011	Monday, June 27, 2011
Week 51 2012	Monday, December 17, 2012
Week 8 1965	Monday, February 15, 1965

> **NOTE** The result must be formatted as a date.

The argument is Str, the week to be converted in "Week ##, YYYY" format.

Function example:

```
Function ConvertWeekDay(Str As String) As Date
Dim Week As Long
```

```
Dim FirstMon As Date
Dim TStr As String
FirstMon = DateSerial(Right(Str, 4), 1, 1)
FirstMon = FirstMon - FirstMon Mod 7 + 2
TStr = Right(Str, Len(Str) - 5)
Week = Left(TStr, InStr(1, TStr, " ", 1)) + 0
ConvertWeekDay = FirstMon + (Week - 1) * 7
End Function
```

Separate Delimited String

In this example, you need to paste a column of delimited data. You could use Excel's Text to Columns, but you need only an element or two from each cell. Text to Columns parses the entire thing. What you need is a function that lets you specify the number of the element in a string that you need, as shown in Figure 14.11:

```
StringElement(str,chr,ind)
```

Figure 14.11

Extracting a single element from delimited text.

⊿	A	B	C	D	E	F	G	H	I
1					ind				
2	str	chr	1	2	3	4	5	6	
3	A|B|C|D|E|F	|	A	B	C	D	E	F	
4			=StringElement($A$3,$B$3,C2)						
5									
6									
7									
8									
9									
10									

The arguments are as listed here:

- str—The string to be parsed
- chr—The delimiter
- ind—The position of the element to be returned

Function example:

```
Function StringElement(str As String, chr As String, ind As Integer)
Dim arr_str As Variant
arr_str = Split(str, chr) 'Not compatible with XL97
StringElement = arr_str(ind - 1)
End Function
```

Sort and Concatenate

The following function enables you to take a column of data, sort it by numbers and then by letters, and concatenate it using a comma (,) as the delimiter (see Figure 14.12):

```
SortConcat(Rng)
```

14

Figure 14.12
Sort and concatenate a
range of variables.

	A	B
1	**Unsorted List**	**Sorted String**
2	q	1,9,14,50,A,a,f,g,q,r,rrrr
3	r	=sortConcat(A2:A12)
4	a	
5	f	
6	g	
7	1	
8	9	
9	50	
10	14	
11	A	
12	rrrr	

The argument is Rng, the range of data to be sorted and concatenated. SortConcat calls
another procedure, BubbleSort, that must be included.

Function example:

```
Function SortConcat(Rng As Range) As Variant
Dim MySum As String, arr1() As String
Dim j As Integer, i As Integer
Dim cl As Range
Dim concat As Variant
On Error GoTo FuncFail:
'initialize output
SortConcat = 0#
'avoid user issues
If Rng.Count = 0 Then Exit Function
'get range into variant variable holding array
ReDim arr1(1 To Rng.Count)
'fill array
i = 1
For Each cl In Rng
    arr1(i) = cl.Value
    i = i + 1
Next
'sort array elements
Call BubbleSort(arr1)
'create string from array elements
For j = UBound(arr1) To 1 Step -1
    If Not IsEmpty(arr1(j)) Then
        MySum = arr1(j) & ", " & MySum
    End If
Next j
'assign value to function
SortConcat = Left(MySum, Len(MySum) - 1)
'exit point
concat_exit:
Exit Function
'display error in cell
FuncFail:
SortConcat = Err.Number & " - " & Err.Description
Resume concat_exit
End Function
```

14

The following function is the ever-popular `BubbleSort`. Many developers use this program to do a simple sort of data.

```
Sub BubbleSort(List() As String)
'    Sorts the List array in ascending order
Dim First As Integer, Last As Integer
Dim i As Integer, j As Integer
Dim Temp
First = LBound(List)
Last = UBound(List)
For i = First To Last - 1
    For j = i + 1 To Last
        If List(i) > List(j) Then
            Temp = List(j)
            List(j) = List(i)
            List(i) = Temp
        End If
    Next j
Next i
End Sub
```

Sort Numeric and Alpha Characters

This function takes a mixed range of numeric and alpha characters and sorts them—first numerically and then alphabetically. The result is placed in an array that can be displayed on a worksheet by using an array formula, as shown in Figure 14.13.

```
sorter(Rng)
```

Figure 14.13
Sort a mixed alphanumeric list.

{=Sorter($E$2:$E$14)}	
E	F
start data	data sorted
E	2
B	3
Y	6
T	9
R	9d
F	B
SS	DD
DD	E
9	F
3	R
2	SS
6	T
9d	Y

The argument is `Rng`, the range to be sorted.

Function example:

```
Function sorter(Rng As Range) As Variant
'returns an array
Dim arr1() As Variant
If Rng.Columns.Count > 1 Then Exit Function
arr1 = Application.Transpose(Rng)
QuickSort arr1
```

14

```
sorter = Application.Transpose(arr1)
End Function
```

The function uses the following two procedures to sort the data in the range:

```
Public Sub QuickSort(ByRef vntArr As Variant,
    Optional ByVal lngLeft As Long = -2, _
    Optional ByVal lngRight As Long = -2)
Dim i, j, lngMid As Long
Dim vntTestVal As Variant
If lngLeft = -2 Then lngLeft = LBound(vntArr)
If lngRight = -2 Then lngRight = UBound(vntArr)
If lngLeft < lngRight Then
    lngMid = (lngLeft + lngRight) \ 2
    vntTestVal = vntArr(lngMid)
    i = lngLeft
    j = lngRight
    Do
        Do While vntArr(i) < vntTestVal
            i = i + 1
        Loop
        Do While vntArr(j) > vntTestVal
            j = j - 1
        Loop
        If i <= j Then
            Call SwapElements(vntArr, i, j)
            i = i + 1
            j = j - 1
        End If
    Loop Until i > j
    If j <= lngMid Then
        Call QuickSort(vntArr, lngLeft, j)
        Call QuickSort(vntArr, i, lngRight)
    Else
        Call QuickSort(vntArr, i, lngRight)
        Call QuickSort(vntArr, lngLeft, j)
    End If
End If
End Sub

Private Sub SwapElements(ByRef vntItems As Variant, _
    ByVal lngItem1 As Long, _
    ByVal lngItem2 As Long)
Dim vntTemp As Variant
vntTemp = vntItems(lngItem2)
vntItems(lngItem2) = vntItems(lngItem1)
vntItems(lngItem1) = vntTemp
End Sub
```

Search for a String Within Text

Ever needed to find out which cells contain a specific string of text? This function can search strings in a range, looking for specified text. It returns a result identifying which cells contain the text, as shown in Figure 14.14.

```
ContainsText(Rng,Text)
```

Figure 14.14
Return a result identifying which cells contain a specified string.

◢	A	B	C
1	This is an apple	A3	=ContainsText(A1:A3,"banana")
2	This is an orange	A1,A2	=ContainsText(A1:A3,"This is")
3	Here is a banana		
4			

The arguments are as listed here:

- `Rng`—The range in which to search
- `Text`—The text for which to search

Function example:

```
Function ContainsText(Rng As Range, Text As String) As String
Dim T As String
Dim myCell As Range
For Each myCell In Rng 'look in each cell
    If InStr(myCell.Text, Text) > 0 Then 'look in the string for the text
        If Len(T) = 0 Then 'if the text is found, add the address to my result
            T = myCell.Address(False, False)
        Else
            T = T & "," & myCell.Address(False, False)
        End If
    End If
Next myCell
ContainsText = T
End Function
```

Reverse the Contents of a Cell

This function is mostly fun, but you might find it useful—it reverses the contents of a cell:

```
ReverseContents(myCell, IsText)
```

The arguments are as given here:

- `myCell`—The specified cell
- `IsText`—(Optional) Whether the cell value should be treated as text (default) or a number

Function example:

```
Function ReverseContents(myCell As Range, Optional IsText As Boolean = True)
Dim i As Integer
Dim OrigString As String, NewString As String
OrigString = Trim(myCell) 'remove leading and trailing spaces
For i = 1 To Len(OrigString)
'by adding the variable NewString to the character,
'instead of adding the character to NewString the string is reversed
    NewString = Mid(OrigString, i, 1) & NewString
Next i
If IsText = False Then
    ReverseContents = CLng(NewString)
Else
    ReverseContents = NewString
End If
End Function
```

14

Multiple Max

MAX finds and returns the maximum value in a range, but it doesn't tell you whether there is more than one maximum value. This function returns the addresses of the maximum values in a range, as shown in Figure 14.15:

```
ReturnMaxs(Rng)
```

Figure 14.15
Return the addresses of all maximum values in a range.

The argument is Rng, the range to search for the maximum values.

Function example:

```
Function ReturnMaxs(Rng As Range) As String
Dim Mx As Double
Dim myCell As Range
'if there is only one cell in the range, then exit
If Rng.Count = 1 Then ReturnMaxs = Rng.Address(False, False): Exit Function
Mx = Application.Max(Rng) 'uses Excel's Max to find the max in the range
'Because you now know what the max value is,
'search the range to find matches and return the address
For Each myCell In Rng
    If myCell = Mx Then
        If Len(ReturnMaxs) = 0 Then
            ReturnMaxs = myCell.Address(False, False)
        Else
            ReturnMaxs = ReturnMaxs & ", " & myCell.Address(False, False)
        End If
    End If
Next myCell
End Function
```

Return Hyperlink Address

Let's say that you've received a spreadsheet with a list of hyperlinked information. You want to see the actual links, not the descriptive text. You could just right-click the hyperlink and select Edit Hyperlink, but you want something more permanent. This function extracts the hyperlink address, as shown in Figure 14.16:

```
GetAddress(HyperlinkCell)
```

The argument is HyperlinkCell, the hyperlinked cell from which you want the address extracted.

Figure 14.16
Extract the hyperlink
address from behind a
hyperlink.

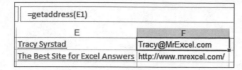

Function example:

```
Function GetAddress(HyperlinkCell As Range)
    GetAddress = Replace(HyperlinkCell.Hyperlinks(1).Address, "mailto:", "")
End Function
```

Return the Column Letter of a Cell Address

You can use CELL("Col") to return a column number; but what if you need the column letter? This function extracts the column letter from a cell address, as shown in Figure 14.17:

```
ColName(Rng)
```

Figure 14.17
Return the column letter
of a cell address.

◢	A	B
1	A	=ColName(A1)
2	XFD	=ColName(XFD1048576)
3		

The argument is Rng, the cell for which you want the column letter.

Function example:

```
Function ColName(Rng As Range) As String
ColName = Left(Rng.Range("A1").Address(True, False), _
    InStr(1, Rng.Range("A1").Address(True, False), "$", 1) - 1)
End Function
```

Static Random

The function =RAND() can prove very useful for creating random numbers, but it constantly recalculates. What if you need random numbers but don't want them to change constantly? The following function places a random number, but the number changes only if you force the cell to recalculate, as shown in Figure 14.18:

```
StaticRAND()
```

Figure 14.18
Produce random numbers
that are not quite so
volatile.

◢	A	B
1	0.709677	=StaticRAND()
2	10.1967	=StaticRAND()*100
3	1.782848	=SUM(A1:A2)*StaticRAND()

14

There are no arguments for this function.

Function example:

```
Function StaticRAND() As Double
Randomize
STATICRAND = Rnd
End Function
```

Using Select Case on a Worksheet

At some point, you have probably nested an If...Then...Else on a worksheet to return a value. The Select...Case statement available in VBA makes this a lot easier, but you can't use Select...Case statements in a worksheet formula. Instead, you can create a UDF (see Figure 14.19).

Figure 14.19
Example of using a Select...Case structure in a UDF rather than nested If... Then statements.

This example takes the user input, calculates the BMI (body mass index), and then compares that calculated value to various ranges to return a BMI descriptive, as shown in Figure 14.19. When creating a UDF, think of the formula in the same way you would write it down, because this is very similar to how you enter it in the UDF. The formula for calculating BMI is as follows:

```
BMI=(weight in pounds*703)/height in inches(squared)
```

The table for returning the BMI descriptive is as follows:

> Below 18.5 = underweight
>
> 18.5–24.9 = normal
>
> 25–29.9 = overweight
>
> 30 & above = obese

The code for calculating the BMI and then returning the descriptive is the following:

```
Function BMI(Height As Long, Weight As Long) As String
'Do the initial BMI calculation to get the numerical value
calcBMI = (Weight / (Height ^ 2)) * 703
Select Case calcBMI 'evaluate the calculated BMI to get a string value
    Case Is <=18.5 'if the calcBMI is less than 18.5
        BMI = "Underweight"
    Case 18.5 To 24.9 'if the calcBMI is a value between 18.5 and 24.9
        BMI = "Normal"
    Case 24.9 To 29.9
        BMI = "Overweight"
    Case Is >= 30 'if the calcBMI is greater than 30
        BMI = "Obese"
End Select
End Function
```

14

Next Steps

In Chapter 15, "Creating Charts," you'll find out how spreadsheet charting has become a highly customizable resource capable of handling large amounts of data.

14

Creating Charts

15

Charting in Excel 2013

Charting gets a major makeover in Excel 2013, and this creates a host of new charting methods and properties in Excel 2013 VBA.

The process of creating a chart introduces a streamlined `.AddChart2` method. With this method, you can specify a chart style, a chart type, and a new property: `NewLayout:=True`. When you choose `NewLayout`, you will finally avoid a legend for single-series charts.

After you select a chart, three icons appear to the right of the chart. (See Figure 15.1.)

Two of the three icons lead to new methods or properties:

- The first icon is a plus sign. It offers a new way to change old settings. Rather than using the Layout tab or Format dialog box as you did with Excel 2010, you can, with the plus sign, access all of those settings from a small fly-out menu and a task pane. Other than some data label improvements, all the VBA to control the settings under the plus sign icon remain the same as in Excel 2010.

- The second icon is the paintbrush icon. This leads to a menu for Style and Color. You get two new VBA properties here. The `.ChartStyle` property supports new values from 201 to 353 to correspond to the options available in the Style menu. The `.ChartColor` property is new. It supports values from 1 to 26, which correspond to various combinations from the Theme colors. The `.ChartStyle` property enables you to select a professionally designed chart template. Everything in that template was available in Excel 2010; now, one line of code in Excel 2013 replaces 35 individual settings required in Excel 2010.

15

■ The third icon is the funnel. You can use this to filter rows or columns from the chart source data out of the chart. A new `.IsFiltered` property is added to replicate changes made in the funnel icon.

Figure 15.1
Three new icons appear to the right of the chart.

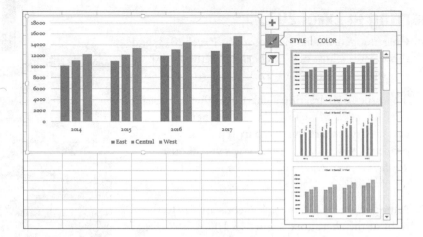

Excel 2007 had introduced a series of `.SetElement` values to replicate choices on the old Layout tab of the ribbon. A new `msoElementDataLabelCallout` value enables you to specify that the data labels should appear in a callout balloon.

The final new trick in Excel 2013 is getting the text for data labels from a range of cells. A new `.InsertChartField` method enables you to specify a formula that points to a range of cells that contain the data labels.

Considering Backward Compatibility

These new chart methods are great if you have Excel 2013 and everyone who uses your macro also has Excel 2013. Because it generally takes two years for a majority of people to upgrade to a new version of Office, you will most likely have to code for Excel 2010 until sometime in 2015. That means using the `.AddChart` method instead of the `.AddChart2` method. There is even a chance you will run into someone using Excel 2003, in which charts were created using `Charts.Add`.

This chapter includes examples of creating charts for Excel 2003, Excel 2007–2010, and Excel 2013.

Referencing the Chart Container

If you go back far enough in Excel history, you will find that all charts used to be created as their own chart sheets. VBA was less complex then. To reference a chart, you simply referred to the chart sheet name:

```
Sheets("Chart1").ChartArea.Interior.ColorIndex = 4
```

Then, in the mid-1990s, Excel added the amazing capability to embed a chart right onto an existing worksheet. This allowed a report to be created with tables of numbers and charts all on the same page, something we take for granted today. Up through Excel 2003, a macro would use the `.ChartObjects` as a container for a chart. Here is code to change the color of the chart area in Excel 2003:

```
Worksheets("Jan").ChartObjects("Chart 1"). _
    Chart.ChartArea.Interior.ColorIndex = 4
```

In Excel 2007 through Excel 2013, a chart is a member of the Shapes collection. The equivalent code for referencing a chart in Excel 2013 is as follows:

```
Worksheets("Jan").Shapes("Chart 1"). _
    Chart.ChartArea.Interior.ColorIndex = 4
```

Although it is less common to see standalone chart sheets today, you need to understand that you have a different way of referring to a chart depending on whether the chart is embedded or standalone, and whether the code is running in a version of Excel before Excel 2007.

Understanding the Global Settings

Although the charting interface has changed in Excel 2007 and Excel 2013, there are a few major concepts that have applied to every chart since Excel 97. It does not matter whether you are writing code for Excel 2003, Excel 2007, or Excel 2013; you need to understand the 73 chart types, size, position, and how to refer to a chart.

Specifying a Built-in Chart Type

Although the charting interface has evolved over the years, Excel has offered the same 73 chart types ever since Excel 97. Each method for creating a chart includes a `ChartType` property. You use one of the constant values shown in the second column of Table 15.1.

What if you need to mix a column chart and a line chart? This is more complicated. See the "Creating a Combo Chart" section, later in this chapter.

Table 15.1 lists the 73 chart type constants that you can use to create various charts. The sequence of the table matches the sequence of the charts in the All Charts tab of the Insert Chart dialog.

Table 15.1   Chart Types for Use in VBA

Chart Type	Constant
Clustered Column	xlColumnClustered
Stacked Column	xlColumnStacked
100% Stacked Column	xlColumnStacked100
3-D Clustered Column	xl3DColumnClustered

Chart Type	Constant
Stacked Column in 3-D	xl3DColumnStacked
100% Stacked Column in 3-D	xl3DColumnStacked100
3-D Column	xl3DColumn
Clustered Cylinder	xlCylinderColClustered
Stacked Cylinder	xlCylinderColStacked
100% Stacked Cylinder	xlCylinderColStacked100
3-D Cylinder	xlCylinderCol
Clustered Cone	xlConeColClustered
Stacked Cone	xlConeColStacked
100% Stacked Cone	xlConeColStacked100
3-D Cone	xlConeCol
Clustered Pyramid	xlPyramidColClustered
Stacked Pyramid	xlPyramidColStacked
100% Stacked Pyramid	xlPyramidColStacked100
3-D Pyramid	xlPyramidCol
Line	xlLine
Stacked Line	xlLineStacked
100% Stacked Line	xlLineStacked100
Line with Markers	xlLineMarkers
Stacked Line with Markers	xlLineMarkersStacked
100% Stacked Line with Markers	xlLineMarkersStacked100
3-D Line	xl3DLine
Pie	xlPie
Pie in 3-D	xl3DPie
Pie of Pie	xlPieOfPie
Exploded Pie	xlPieExploded
Exploded Pie in 3-D	xl3DPieExploded
Bar of Pie	xlBarOfPie
Clustered Bar	xlBarClustered
Stacked Bar	xlBarStacked
100% Stacked Bar	xlBarStacked100
Clustered Bar in 3-D	xl3DBarClustered
Stacked Bar in 3-D	xl3DBarStacked
100% Stacked Bar in 3-D	xl3DBarStacked100
Clustered Horizontal Cylinder	xlCylinderBarClustered

15

Chart Type	Constant
Stacked Horizontal Cylinder	xlCylinderBarStacked
100% Stacked Horizontal Cylinder	xlCylinderBarStacked100
Clustered Horizontal Cone	xlConeBarClustered
Stacked Horizontal Cone	xlConeBarStacked
100% Stacked Horizontal Cone	xlConeBarStacked100
Clustered Horizontal Pyramid	xlPyramidBarClustered
Stacked Horizontal Pyramid	xlPyramidBarStacked
100% Stacked Horizontal Pyramid	xlPyramidBarStacked100
Area	xlArea
Stacked Area	xlAreaStacked
100% Stacked Area	xlAreaStacked100
3-D Area	xl3DArea
Stacked Area in 3-D	xl3DAreaStacked
100% Stacked Area in 3-D	xl3DAreaStacked100
Scatter with Only Markers	xlXYScatter
Scatter with Smooth Lines and Markers	xlXYScatterSmooth
Scatter with Smooth Lines	xlXYScatterSmoothNoMarkers
Scatter with Straight Lines and Markers	xlXYScatterLines
Scatter with Straight Lines	xlXYScatterLinesNoMarkers
High-Low-Close	xlStockHLC
Open-High-Low-Close	xlStockOHLC
Volume-High-Low-Close	xlStockVHLC
Volume-Open-High-Low-Close	xlStockVOHLC
3-D Surface	xlSurface
Wireframe 3-D Surface	xlSurfaceWireframe
Contour	xlSurfaceTopView
Wireframe Contour	xlSurfaceTopViewWireframe
Doughnut	xlDoughnut
Exploded Doughnut	xlDoughnutExploded
Bubble	xlBubble
Bubble with a 3-D Effect	xlBubble3DEffect
Radar	xlRadar
Radar with Markers	xlRadarMarkers
Filled Radar	xlRadarFilled

15

Specifying Location and Size of the Chart

For each method, you have an opportunity to specify the chart type, chart location, and size of the chart.

Chart location is controlled by specifying the .Top and .Left of the top-left corner of the chart *in pixels*. This is admittedly a really strange measurement. I can look at a cell and guess inches, but I can never remember how many pixels per inch or the dot pitch. Plus, if I want the chart to appear in cell S17, how do I even begin estimating the number? One approach is to randomly guess.

Figure 15.2 shows a chart created by a macro in which I randomly guessed the .Top at 170 and the .Width at 1400. I was shooting for S17 and I ended up in AA12. With a little more research, I discovered that a default row is 15 pixels tall and the default width is 71 pixels. Perhaps a better estimate would have been 16*15+1 for the top and 18 columns * 71 pixels + 1 to arrive in Column S.

Figure 15.2
Guessing the number of pixels to arrive at S17 Is an imperfect science.

But wait. Before you even type =16*15+1 into a cell in Excel to calculate the .Top and .Left, this estimate fails if someone has specified a different theme or different default font, or if they have changed any column widths from A:R.

The better solution is to set the .Top and .Left of the chart to the .Top and .Left of the cell where you want the chart to appear. If you want the chart to appear in cell S17, then specify this:

```
.Top = Range("S17").Top, .Left = Range("S17").Left
```

You can shorten this code by using [S17] as a shorter way to refer to Range("S17").

```
.Top = [S17].Top, .Left = [S17].Left
```

How about the length and width of the chart? Again, you could guess for .Height and .Width, or you can set these properties to the .Height and .Width of a known range. If you want the chart to fill S17:Y32, you could use

```
.Height = [A17:A32].Height, .Width = [S1:Y1].Left
```

Referring to a Specific Chart

The macro recorder has an unsatisfactory way of writing code for the chart creation. The macro recorder uses the `.AddChart2` method and adds a `.Select` to the end of the line in order to select the chart. The rest of the chart settings then apply to the `ActiveChart` object. This approach is a bit frustrating, because you are required to do all the chart formatting before you select anything else in the worksheet.

The macro recorder does this because chart names are unpredictable. The first time you run a macro, the chart might be called Chart 1. But if you run the macro on another day or on a different worksheet, the chart might be called Chart 3 or Chart 5.

For the most flexibility, you should assign each new chart to a `Chart` object. This is a bit strange to do. Remember that a chart exists inside a container. Starting in Excel 2007, that container is a `Shape` object. You cannot simply refer to `Worksheets("Sheet1")`. `Charts("Chart 1")`. This results in an error.

Ignoring the specifics of the `AddChart2` method for a moment, you could use this coding approach, which captures the `Shape` object in the `SH` object variable and then assigns the `Sh`. `Chart` to the `CH` object variable:

```
Dim WS as Worksheet
Dim SH as Shape
Dim CH as Chart
Set WS = ActiveSheet
Set SH = WS.Shapes.AddChart2(...)
Set CH = SH.Chart
```

You can simplify the preceding code by appending `.Chart` to the end of the `AddChart2` method. The following code has one less object variable:

```
Dim WS as Worksheet
Dim CH as Chart
Set WS = ActiveSheet
Set CH = WS.Shapes.AddChart2(...).Chart
```

If you need to modify a preexisting chart—such as a chart that you did not create—and there is only one shape on the worksheet, you can use this line of code:

```
WS.Shapes(1).Chart.Interior.Color = RGB(0,0,255)
```

If there are many charts, and you need to find the one with the upper-left corner located in cell A4, you can loop through all the `Shape` objects until you find one in the correct location, like this:

```
For each Sh in ActiveSheet.Shapes
    If Sh.TopLeftCell.Address = "$A$4" then
        Sh.Chart.Interior.Color = RGB(0,255,0)
    End If
Next Sh
```

15

Creating a Chart in Various Excel Versions

The following sections show the code for creating a chart. All the code samples work in Excel 2013. If your code needs to run in Excel 2010 or even Excel 2003, you need to change the method used for creating the chart.

Using .AddChart2 Method in Excel 2013

Excel 2013 introduces the new .AddChart2 method. This method is very flexible and easy to use. But it does not work in Excel 2010.

When you select a chart in Excel, three icons appear to the right of the chart. The paint-brush icon leads to a variety of professionally designed chart styles. For a clustered column chart, there are a total of 15 chart styles defined in Excel 2013. The various styles offer a mix of effects. The effects range from rotated data labels to gradients, dark backgrounds, patterns, and more. Figure 15.3 shows the 15 chart styles designed for clustered column charts.

Figure 15.3
These professionally designed templates combine as many as 20 adjustments to formatting in a chart.

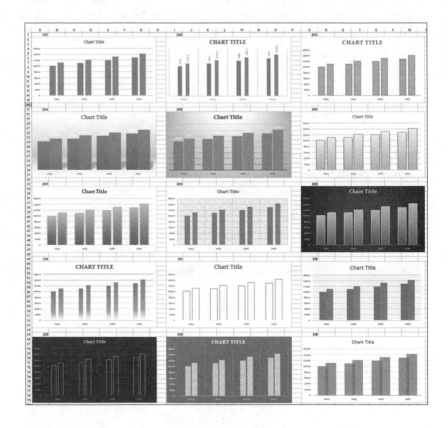

The .AddChart2 method lets you specify a ChartStyle. The valid values for ChartStyle are 201 through 353. Although only chart styles 201 through 215 were designed with the Clustered Column chart in mind, you can actually apply any of the 153 styles to any chart.

The easiest way to discover the correct chart style number is to turn on the macro recorder, select a chart, and then choose the desired style from the paintbrush icon.

The .AddChart2 method requires you to specify a .ChartStyle (201 through 353), a chart type from Table 15.1, the location and size for the chart, and then an interesting parameter called NewLayout.

People using Excel have long complained about this typical chart in Excel 2010. In prior versions of Excel, a default chart always had a legend. The default chart has a title only when there is a single data series. The title repeats the single legend entry as the title, leading to the redundant title and legend in a single-series chart. (See Figure 15.4.)

Figure 15.4
Do you think this chart is about the East region?

If you specify NewLayout:=False, you continue to get the chart with a legend and title for a single series chart. When you instead specify NewLayout:=True, your single-series chart does not have a legend. All charts have a title, even if that title is the useless "Chart Title." The theory is that when people see "Chart Title," they are forced to click the title and change it. Of course, with VBA, you can change the chart title.

The following code produces the chart shown in Figure 15.5:

```
Sub CreateChartExcel2013()
    Dim WS As Worksheet
    Dim ch As Chart
    Set WS = ActiveSheet

    ' Select the data for the chart
    Range("A1:E4").Select

    ' Define the chart,
    ' use style 202 for rotated data labels
    Set ch = WS.Shapes.AddChart2( _
        Style:=202, _
        XlChartType:=xlColumnClustered, _
        Left:=[A6].Left, _
        Top:=[A6].Top, _
        Width:=[A6:G6].Width, _
        Height:=[A6:A20].Height, _
```

```
        NewLayout:=True).Chart
    ' Adjust the title
    ch.ChartTitle.Text = "2015 Sales by Region"

End Sub
```

Figure 15.5
Chart style 202 provides the rotated data labels in lieu of vertical axis labels.

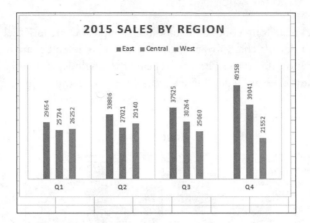

The preceding code required you to select the chart data before creating the chart. Good VBA code avoids selecting anything. You can avoid selecting the data by letting VBA create a blank chart and then specifying the source data with this code:

```
ch.SetSourceData Source:=Range("Data!$A$1:$E$4")
```

Two other features introduced in Excel 2013 are the 26 .ChartColor values and the capability to get chart data labels from a range of cells, as discussed later in the chapter.

Creating Charts in Excel 2007–2013

The AddChart2 method works only in Excel 2013. If you need to have your code work in Excel 2010 or Excel 2007, you have to use the AddChart method instead. This method enables you to specify a chart type, location, and size. You don't have access to chart styles or the NewLayout setting.

The following code works in Excel 2007 and newer. It creates the bar chart shown in Figure 15.6.

```
Sub CreateChartExcel2007()
    ' Works in Excel 2007 & Newer
    Dim WS As Worksheet
    Dim ch As Chart
    Set WS = ActiveSheet

    ' Define the chart,
    Set ch = WS.Shapes.AddChart( _
        XlChartType:=xlBarClustered, _
        Left:=[A6].Left, _
        Top:=[A6].Top, _
        Width:=[A6:G6].Width, _
```

```
        Height:=[A6:A20].Height).Chart
    ch.SetSourceData Source:=Range("Data!$A$1:$E$4")

End Sub
```

Figure 15.6
After using the older
.AddChart method,
you usually have to cus-
tomize the chart.

Creating Charts in Excel 2003–2013

Prior to Excel 2007, you needed to use Charts.Add to create a chart. This resulting chart is a new chart on a standalone chart sheet. Just as you can refer to the active worksheet with ActiveSheet, you can refer to the active chart sheet as ActiveChart. After specifying the chart type and source data, you move the ActiveChart to a worksheet, creating an embedded chart.

At this point, you cannot refer to ActiveChart anymore, but the newly created chart is still selected. The Excel 2003 code to assign the chart to an object variable requires you to Set CH = Selection.Parent.

Use this macro to create a chart if that chart has to be compatible with Excel 2003:

```
Sub Chart2003()
    Dim CH As Chart
    ' Add a chart as a ChartSheet
    Charts.Add
    ActiveChart.SetSourceData Source:=Worksheets("Sheet1").Range("A1:E4")
    ActiveChart.ChartType = xlColumnClustered
    ' Move the chart to a worksheet
    ActiveChart.Location Where:=xlLocationAsObject, Name:="Sheet1"
    ' You cannot refer to ActiveChart anymore
    ' The chart is still selected
```

15

```
        Set CH = Selection.Parent
        CH.Top = Range("B6").Top
        CH.Left = Range("B6").Left
End Sub
```

Customizing a Chart

The `AddChart` and `AddChart2` methods enable you to specify a chart type, location, and size for your chart. You will probably need to customize additional items in the chart. The chart customizations fall into three broad categories:

- Customizing a global chart, such as changing the chart style or color theme in the chart. In the Excel Interface, these are changes on the Design tab of the ribbon or in the paintbrush icon to the right of the selected chart.

- Adding or moving a chart element, such as adding a chart title or moving the legend to a new location. In the Excel interface, the first and second-level fly-out menus from the Plus icon to the right of the chart control the chart elements.

- Micro-managing the formatting for one specific series, point, or chart element. These are settings from the Format tab of the ribbon or the Format task pane.

However, given that the new charting interface is going to be creating a lot of charts with the unhelpful words "Chart Title" at the top of every chart, you should start with the code for changing the chart title to something useful.

Specifying a Chart Title

Every chart created with `NewLayout:=True` has a chart title. When the chart has two or more series, that title is "Chart Title." You are going to have to plan on changing the chart title to something useful.

To specify a chart title in VBA, use this code:

```
ActiveChart.ChartTitle.Caption = "Sales by Region"
```

Assuming that you are changing the chart title of a newly created chart that is assigned to the `CH` object variable, you can use this:

```
CH.ChartTitle.Caption = "Sales by Region"
```

This code works if your chart already has a title. If you are not sure that the selected chart style has a title, you can ensure that the title is present first with

```
CH.SetElement msoElementChartTitleAboveChart
```

Although it is relatively easy to add a chart title and specify the words in the title, it becomes increasingly complex to change the formatting of the chart title. The following code changes the font, size, and color of the title:

```
With CH.ChartTitle.Format.TextFrame2.TextRange.Font
    .Name = "Rockwell"
    .Fill.ForeColor.ObjectThemeColor = msoThemeColorAccent2
    .Size = 14
End With
```

The two axis titles operate the same as the chart title. To change the words, use the
`.Caption` property. To format the words, you use the `Format` property. Similarly, you can
specify the axis titles by using the `Caption` property. The following code changes the axis
title along the category axis:

```
CH.SetElement msoFlementPrimaryCategoryAxisTitleHorizontal
CH.Axes(xlCategory, xlPrimary).AxisTitle.Caption = "Months"
CH.Axes(xlCategory, xlPrimary).AxisTitle. _
    Format.TextFrame2.TextRange.Font.Fill. _
    ForeColor.ObjectThemeColor = msoThemeColorAccent2
```

Quickly Formatting a Chart Using New Excel 2013 Features

Excel 2013 offers new chart styles, color settings, filtering, and the capability to create data
labels as captions that come from selected cells. All of these features are excellent additions,
but the code works only in Excel 2013 and is not backward compatible with Excel 2010 or
older.

Specifying a Chart Style

Excel 2013 introduces new chart styles that quickly apply professional formatting to a chart.
You can see the chart styles in the large Chart Style gallery on the Design tab.

The chart style concept is not new in Excel 2013. Excel 2007 offered 48 chart styles. The
difference is that the chart styles in Excel 2013 are interesting and offer variability between
the styles. In Excel 2007–2010, the 48 chart styles were boring variations on four styles:
monochrome, colorful, single-color, and dark background.

If you create your chart using the `AddChart2` method, you can specify a chart style as the
first parameter of that method. If you do not specify a chart style or later want to change a
chart style, use this code:

```
ch.ClearToMatchStyle
ch.ChartStyle = 339
```

Valid chart styles are 201 through 353. The fastest way to learn the chart style is to select
a chart, turn on the macro recorder, select a style from the gallery on the Design tab, and
then stop recording.

CAUTION ──────────────────────────────

The ToolTip that appears in the Chart Styles gallery does not convert to the chart style value.

As an experiment, create a clustered column chart. Copy that chart and paste it three times, changing
the chart type to a line, stacked area, and stacked bar. Turn on the macro recorder. Select each chart
and choose the last dark style from the Chart Styles gallery. You might notice that the ToolTip is different when you select the style. When you look at the recorded code, the `.ChartStyle` value is
dramatically different for each chart. See the ToolTip and the `ChartStyle` value in the title of each
chart in Figure 15.7.

15

Although the chart styles look alike in the various Chart Style galleries, they are really different chart styles.

Using VBA, you are able to apply any of the 153 new chart styles to any type of chart. Although it works, it might not look as good as if you applied the style designed for that type of chart.

Rather than randomly selecting a chart style, use the macro recorder to learn the correct style.

Figure 15.7
The ToolTip says Style 8, but the .ChartStyle varies.

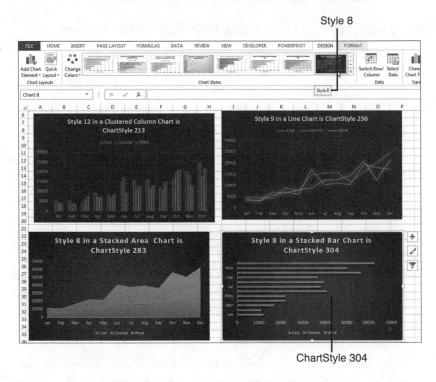

Style 8

ChartStyle 304

TIP

Choose a chart type before choosing a chart style.

Say that you create an area chart and apply Style 8 from the Chart Styles gallery. In the background, Excel applies .ChartStyle =283 to the chart. If you later change the chart type to a clustered column chart, Excel does not convert the .ChartStyle back to the correct value of 213. The chart style stays as 283.

Figure 15.8 shows the four charts from Figure 15.7 after they were converted back to a clustered column chart. Each chart looks a little different. Vertical gridlines do not appear on some charts. The legend moves from the top to the bottom. Glow, Fill, and Overlap are different in the various charts.

When you open the Chart Styles gallery, none of the thumbnails appears as the chosen style. This is because the current ChartStyle of 304 is no longer shown in the gallery.

Figure 15.8
If you change the chart type after choosing a style, you see subtle differences.

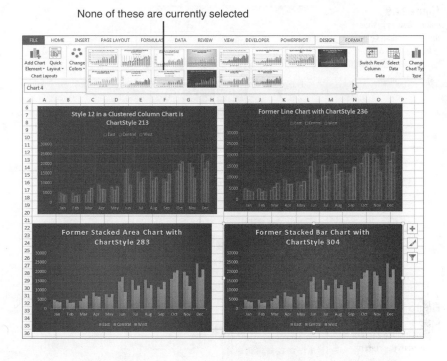

The old chart style values of 1 through 48 continue to work. Try 1 for Monochrome, 2 for colorful, 3 for shades of blue, and 42 for a dark background that works well with PowerPoint.

In the sample files for this book, open 15-TestAllStyles.xlsm to see a clustered column chart represented in all 153 styles.

Applying a Chart Color

Excel 2013 also introduces a ch.ChartColor property that assigns one of 26 color themes to a chart. Assign a value from 1 to 26, but be aware that the order of the colors in the Chart Styles fly-out menu (see Figure 15.9) has nothing to do with the 26 values.

To understand the ChartColor values, consider the color drop-down shown in Figure 15.10. This drop-down offers 10 columns of colors: Background 1, Text 1, Background 2, Text 2, and then Theme 1 through Theme 6.

Here is a synopsis of the 26 values you can use for ChartColor:

- ChartColor 1, 9, and 20 use grayscale colors from column 3. A ChartColor value of 1 starts with a dark gray, then a light gray, then medium gray. A ChartColor value of 9 starts with light gray and moves to darker grays. A ChartColor value of 20 starts with three medium grays, then black, very light gray, then medium gray.
- Value 2 uses the six theme colors in the top row from left to right.

Figure 15.9
Color schemes in the menu are called Color 1, Color 2, and so on, but have nothing to do with the VBA settings.

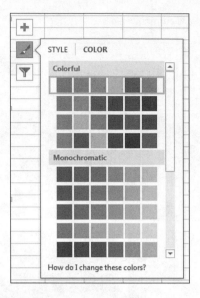

Figure 15.10
ChartColor combinations include a mix of colors from the current theme.

- Values 3 through 8 use a single column of colors. For example, `ChartColor = 3` uses the six colors in Theme 1, from dark to light. `ChartColor` values of 4 through 8 correspond to Themes 2 through 6.

- Value 10 repeats value 2 but adds a light border around the chart element.

- Values 11 through 13 are the most inventive. They use three theme colors from the top row combined with the same three theme colors from the bottom row. This produces light and dark versions of three different colors. `ChartColor 11` uses the odd-numbered themes (1, 3, and 5). `ChartColor 12` uses the even-numbered themes. `ChartColor 13` uses Themes 6, 5, and 4.

- Values 14 through 19 repeat values 3 through 8, but add a light border.

- Values 21 through 26 are similar to values 3 through 8, but the colors progress from light to dark.

The following code changes the chart to use varying shades of Themes 6, 5, and 4:

```
ch.ChartColor = 13
```

In Excel 2007 and 2010, the `ChartColor` property causes an error. For backward compatibility, use a `.ChartStyle` value from 1 to 48. These correspond to the order of the colors in the old Chart Styles gallery in Excel 2007 and Excel 2010.

Filtering a Chart in Excel 2013

In real life, creating charts from tables of data is not always simple. Tables frequently have totals or subtotals. The table in Figure 15.11 has quarterly total columns intermixed with the monthly values. Rows 5, 9, and 10 contain totals of various regions. When you create a chart from this data, the total columns and rows create a bad chart. The scale of the chart is wrong because of the $5.3 million grand total cell.

Figure 15.11
The subtotals in this table cause a bad-looking chart.

	A	B	C	D	E	F	G	H	I	J	K	L	M	N	O	P	Q	R
1		Jan	Feb	Mar	Q1	Apr	May	Jun	Q2	Jul	Aug	Sep	Q3	Oct	Nov	Dec	Q4	Total
2	Southeast	30K	33K	38K	102K	40K	44K	49K	134K	54K	58K	62K	173K	68K	79K	90K	237K	646K
3	Mid Atlantic	44K	43K	42K	129K	43K	44K	44K	130K	44K	44K	44K	131K	44K	46K	45K	135K	526K
4	Northeast	48K	55K	61K	164K	70K	80K	90K	241K	101K	113K	124K	338K	132K	141K	159K	431K	1,174K
5	Total East	123K	131K	142K	396K	153K	169K	182K	504K	198K	215K	229K	642K	244K	265K	295K	804K	2,346K
6	Seattle	37K	43K	49K	130K	55K	64K	73K	192K	86K	99K	111K	296K	130K	144K	166K	440K	1,059K
7	San Francisco	50K	57K	65K	172K	74K	80K	92K	247K	101K	106K	118K	324K	130K	149K	159K	438K	1,181K
8	Los Angeles	34K	38K	41K	114K	44K	50K	55K	149K	62K	67K	70K	199K	80K	91K	105K	276K	737K
9	Total West	121K	138K	156K	416K	174K	194K	219K	587K	249K	272K	299K	819K	341K	384K	430K	1,155K	2,977K
10	Total	244K	270K	297K	811K	327K	363K	402K	1,092K	447K	487K	528K	1,461K	585K	649K	724K	1,958K	5,32_K

In previous versions of Excel, you could attempt to select the eight noncontiguous regions before creating the chart. For example, A1:D4, F1:H4, ..., N6:P8.

The new paradigm in Excel 2013 is to select the whole range, create the horrible-looking chart, and then use the Funnel icon to the right of the chart to remove the total rows and total columns.

To filter a row or column in VBA, you set the new .IsFiltered property to True. The following code removes the total columns and total rows to produce the chart shown in Figure 15.12:

```
Sub FilterChart()
    Dim CH As Chart
    Dim WS As Worksheet
    Set WS = ActiveSheet

    Set CH = WS.Shapes.AddChart2(Style:=239, _
        XlChartType:=xlLine, _
        Left:=[B12].Left, _
        Top:=[B12].Top, _
        NewLayout:=False).Chart
    CH.SetSourceData Source:=Range("Sheet1!$A$1:$R$10")
```

15

```
' Hide the rows containing totals from row 5, 9, 10
CH.FullSeriesCollection(4).IsFiltered = True
CH.FullSeriesCollection(8).IsFiltered = True
CH.FullSeriesCollection(9).IsFiltered = True
' Hide the columns containing quarters and total
CH.ChartGroups(1).FullCategoryCollection(4).IsFiltered = True
CH.ChartGroups(1).FullCategoryCollection(8).IsFiltered = True
CH.ChartGroups(1).FullCategoryCollection(12).IsFiltered = True
CH.ChartGroups(1).FullCategoryCollection(16).IsFiltered = True
CH.ChartGroups(1).FullCategoryCollection(17).IsFiltered = True
' Reapply style 239; it applies markers with <7 series
CH.ChartStyle = 239
End Sub
```

Figure 15.12
Filter the total rows and columns to have monthly data by region on the chart.

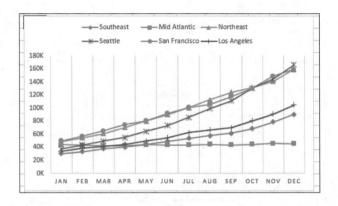

CAUTION

The `.IsFiltered` property is not backward compatible with Excel 2010 or earlier.

Note: Chart Style 239 is supposed to include markers on the line. When the original chart contained nine series, the markers were deleted. Reapplying the chart style 239 at the end of the macro brings the markers back to the resulting six-series chart.

Using Cell Formulas as Data Label Captions in Excel 2013

Excel 2013 introduces the capability to caption a data point using a callout that is based on a cell in the worksheet. You now have the flexibility to calculate data captions on the fly.

In Figure 15.13, the sales figures in Row 2 are random numbers that change every time the worksheet is calculated. You never know which month is going to be the best or the worst month.

Row 5 contains a somewhat complex formula to build a dynamic caption for the month. If the sales for the month match the maximum sales for all the months, the caption reads "Best month with $x." If the sales match the minimum sales, the caption says it was the worst month. For all the other months, the caption is blank. The formula in B5 is

```
=IF(B2=MAX($B2:$M2),"Best month with $"&B2,"")&
    IF(B2=MIN($B2:$M2),"Worst month with $"&B2,"")
```

Figure 15.13
A formula generates the
caption that displays on
the chart.

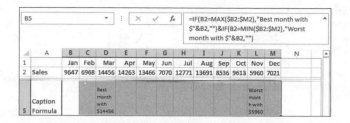

To specify that the data labels should appear as a callout, use this new argument in Excel
2013:

```
CH.SetElement (msoElementDataLabelCallout)
```

You can then specify the range that contains the labels for an individual series. The
InsertChartField method is applied to the TextRange property of the TextFrame2.

```
' Specify a range for the data labels for Series 1
Dim Ser as Series
Dim TF as TextFrame2
Set Ser = CH.SeriesCollection(1)
Set TF = Ser.DataLabels.Format.TextFrame2
TF.TextRange.InsertChartField _
    ChartFieldType:=msoChartFieldFormula, _
    Formula:="=Sheet1!$B$5:$M$5", _
    Position:=xlLabelPositionAbove
Ser.DataLabels.ShowRange = True
```

The chart in Figure 15.14 is created with the following code.

```
Sub LabelCaptionsFromRange()
    Dim WS As Worksheet
    Dim CH As Chart
    Dim Ser As Series
    Dim TF As TextFrame2

    Set WS = ActiveSheet
    Set CH = WS.Shapes.AddChart2(Style:=201, _
        XlChartType:=xlColumnClustered, _
        Left:=[B7].Left, _
        Top:=[B7].Top, _
        NewLayout:=True).Chart
    CH.SetSourceData Source:=Range("Sheet1!$A$1:$M$2")
    ' Apply Labels as a Callout
    CH.SetElement (msoElementDataLabelCallout)
    ' Specify a range for the data labels for Series 1
    Set Ser = CH.SeriesCollection(1)
    Set TF = Ser.DataLabels.Format.TextFrame2
    TF.TextRange.InsertChartField _
        ChartFieldType:=msoChartFieldFormula, _
        Formula:="=Sheet1!$B$5:$M$5", _
        Position:=xlLabelPositionAbove
    ' New in Excel 2013
    Ser.DataLabels.ShowRange = True
    ' Turn off the category name and value
    ' This has to be done after ShowRange = True
    ' If you turn off all first, the label is deleted
```

```
        Ser.DataLabels.ShowValue = False
        Ser.DataLabels.ShowCategoryName = False
        ' Vary colors by points
        CH.ChartGroups(1).VaryByCategories = True
        ' Make columns wider by making gaps narrower
        CH.ChartGroups(1).GapWidth = 77
    End Sub
```

Figure 15.14
The callouts dynamically appear on the largest and smallest points.

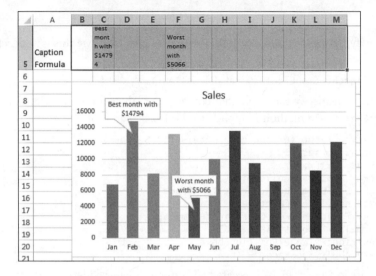

Using `SetElement` to Emulate Changes from the Plus Icon

When you select a chart, three icons appear to the right of the chart. The top icon is a plus sign. All the choices in the first- and second-level fly-out menus use the `SetElement` method in VBA. Note that the Add Chart Element drop-down on the Design tab includes all of these settings, plus Lines and Up/Down Bars.

> **NOTE**
> `SetElement` does not cover the choices in the Format task pane that often appears. See the "Using the Format Method to Micromanage Formatting Options" section later in this chapter to change those settings.

If you do not feel like looking up the proper constant in this book, you can always quickly record a macro.

The `SetElement` method is followed by a constant that specifies which menu item to select. For example, if you want to choose Show Legend at Left, you can use this code:

```
ActiveChart.SetElement msoElementLegendLeft
```

Table 15.2 shows all the available constants you can use with the SetElement method. These constants are in roughly the same order in which they appear in the Add Chart Element drop-down.

Table 15.2   Constants Available with SetElement

Element Group	Chart Element Constant
Axes	msoElementPrimaryCategoryAxisNone
Axes	msoElementPrimaryCategoryAxisShow
Axes	msoElementPrimaryCategoryAxisWithoutLabels
Axes	msoElementPrimaryCategoryAxisReverse
Axes	msoElementPrimaryCategoryAxisThousands
Axes	msoElementPrimaryCategoryAxisMillions
Axes	msoElementPrimaryCategoryAxisBillions
Axes	msoElementPrimaryCategoryAxisLogScale
Axes	msoElementSecondaryCategoryAxisNone
Axes	msoElementSecondaryCategoryAxisShow
Axes	msoElementSecondaryCategoryAxisWithoutLabels
Axes	msoElementSecondaryCategoryAxisReverse
Axes	msoElementSecondaryCategoryAxisThousands
Axes	msoElementSecondaryCategoryAxisMillions
Axes	msoElementSecondaryCategoryAxisBillions
Axes	msoElementSecondaryCategoryAxisLogScaIe
Axes	msoElementPrimaryValueAxisNone
Axes	msoElementPrimaryValueAxisShow
Axes	msoElementPrimaryValueAxisThousands
Axes	msoElementPrimaryValueAxisMillions
Axes	msoElementPrimaryValueAxisBillions
Axes	msoElementPrimaryValueAxisLogScale
Axes	msoElementSecondaryValueAxisNone
Axes	msoElementSecondaryValueAxisShow
Axes	msoElementSecondaryValueAxisThousands
Axes	msoElementSecondaryValueAxisMillions
Axes	msoElementSecondaryValueAxisBillions
Axes	msoElementSecondaryValueAxisLogScale

15

Element Group	Chart Element Constant
Axes	`msoElementSeriesAxisNone`
Axes	`msoElementSeriesAxisShow`
Axes	`msoElementSeriesAxisReverse`
Axes	`msoElementSeriesAxisWithoutLabeling`
Axis Titles	`msoElementPrimaryCategoryAxisTitleNone`
Axis Titles	`msoElementPrimaryCategoryAxisTitleBelowAxis`
Axis Titles	`msoElementPrimaryCategoryAxisTitleAdjacentToAxis`
Axis Titles	`msoElementPrimaryCategoryAxisTitleHorizontal`
Axis Titles	`msoEIementPrimaryCategoryAxisTitleVertical`
Axis Titles	`msoElementPrimaryCategoryAxisTitleRotated`
Axis Titles	`msoElementSecondaryCategoryAxisTitleAdjacentToAxis`
Axis Titles	`msoElementSecondaryCategoryAxisTitleBelowAxis`
Axis Titles	`msoElementSecondaryCategoryAxisTitleHorizontal`
Axis Titles	`msoElementSecondaryCategoryAxisTitleNone`
Axis Titles	`msoElementSecondaryCategoryAxisTitleRotated`
Axis Titles	`msoElementSecondaryCategoryAxisTitleVertical`
Axis Titles	`msoElementPrimaryValueAxisTitleAdjacentToAxis`
Axis Titles	`msoElementPrimaryValueAxisTitleBelowAxis`
Axis Titles	`msoElementPrimaryValueAxisTitleHorizontal`
Axis Titles	`msoElementPrimaryValueAxisTitleNone`
Axis Titles	`msoElementPrimaryValueAxisTitleRotated`
Axis Titles	`msoElementPrimaryValueAxisTitleVertical`
Axis Titles	`msoElementSecondaryValueAxisTitleBelowAxis`
Axis Titles	`msoElementSecondaryValueAxisTitleHorizontal`
Axis Titles	`msoElementSecondaryValueAxisTitleNone`
Axis Titles	`msoElementSecondaryValueAxisTitleRotated`
Axis Titles	`msoElementSecondaryValueAxisTitleVertical`
Axis Titles	`msoElementSeriesAxisTitleHorizontal`
Axis Titles	`msoElementSeriesAxisTitleNone`
Axis Titles	`msoElementSeriesAxisTitleRotated`
Axis Titles	`msoElementSeriesAxisTitleVertical`
Axis Titles	`msoElementSecondaryValueAxisTitleAdjacentToAxis`
Chart Title	`msoElementChartTitleNone`

Element Group	Chart Element Constant
Chart Title	`msoElementChartTitleCenteredOverlay`
Chart Title	`msoElementChartTitleAboveChart`
Data Labels	`msoElementDataLabelCallout` (new in Excel 2013)
Data Labels	`msoElementDataLabelCenter`
Data Labels	`msoElementDataLabelInsideEnd`
Data Labels	`msoElementDataLabelNone`
Data Labels	`msoElementDataLabelInsideBase`
Data Labels	`msoElementDataLabelOutSideEnd`
Data Labels	`msoElementDataLabelTop`
Data Labels	`msoElementDataLabelBottom`
Data Labels	`msoElementDataLabelRight`
Data Labels	`msoElementDataLabelLeft`
Data Labels	`msoElementDataLabelShow`
Data Labels	`msoElementDataLabelBestFit`
Data Table	`msoElementDataTableNone`
Data Table	`msoElementDataTableShow`
Data Table	`msoElementDataTableWithLegendKeys`
Error Bars	`msoElementErrorBarNone`
Error Bars	`msoElementErrorBarStandardError`
Error Bars	`msoElementErrorBarPercentage`
Error Bars	`msoElementErrorBarStandardDeviation`
GridLines	`msoElementPrimaryCategoryGridLinesNone`
GridLines	`msoElementPrimaryCategoryGridLinesMajor`
GridLines	`msoElementPrimaryCategoryGridLinesMinor`
GridLines	`msoElementPrimaryCategoryGridLinesMinorMajor`
GridLines	`msoElementSecondaryCategoryGridLinesNone`
GridLines	`msoElementSecondaryCategoryGridLinesMajor`
GridLines	`msoElementSecondaryCategoryGridLinesMinor`
GridLines	`msoElementSecondaryCategoryGridLinesMinorMajor`
GridLines	`msoElementPrimaryValueGridLinesNone`
GridLines	`msoElementPrimaryValueGridLinesMajor`
GridLines	`msoElementPrimaryValueGridLinesMinor`
GridLines	`msoElementPrimaryValueGridLinesMinorMajor`

15

15

Element Group	Chart Element Constant
GridLines	`msoElementSecondaryValueGridLinesNone`
GridLines	`msoElementSecondaryValueGridLinesMajor`
GridLines	`msoElementSecondaryValueGridLinesMinor`
GridLines	`msoElementSecondaryValueGridLinesMinorMajor`
GridLines	`msoElementSeriesAxisGridLinesNone`
GridLines	`msoElementSeriesAxisGridLinesMajor`
GridLines	`msoElementSeriesAxisGridLinesMinor`
GridLines	`msoElementSeriesAxisGridLinesMinorMajor`
Legend	`msoElementLegendNone`
Legend	`msoElementLegendRight`
Legend	`msoElementLegendTop`
Legend	`msoElementLegendLeft`
Legend	`msoElementLegendBottom`
Legend	`msoElementLegendRightOverlay`
Legend	`msoElementLegendLeftOverlay`
Lines	`msoElementLineNone`
Lines	`msoElementLineDropLine`
Lines	`msoElementLineHiLoLine`
Lines	`msoElementLineDropHiLoLine`
Lines	`msoElementLineSeriesLine`
Trendline	`msoElementTrendlineNone`
Trendline	`msoElementTrendlineAddLinear`
Trendline	`msoElementTrendlineAddExponential`
Trendline	`msoElementTrendlineAddLinearForecast`
Trendline	`msoElementTrendlineAddTwoPeriodMovingAverage`
Up/Down Bars	`msoElementUpDownBarsNone`
Up/Down Bars	`msoElementUpDownBarsShow`
Plot Area	`msoElementPlotAreaNone`
Plot Area	`msoElementPlotAreaShow`
Chart Wall	`msoElementChartWallNone`
Chart Wall	`msoElementChartWallShow`
Chart Floor	`msoElementChartFloorNone`
Chart Floor	`msoElementChartFloorShow`

> **NOTE** If you attempt to format an element that is not present, Excel will return a -2147467259 `Method Failed` error.

Using SetElement enables you to change chart elements quickly. As an example, charting gurus say that the legend should always appear to the left or above the chart. Few of the built-in styles show the legend above the chart. I also prefer to show the values along the axis in thousands or millions when appropriate. This is better than displaying three or six zeros on every line.

Two lines of code handle these settings after creating the chart:

```
Sub UseSetElement()
    Dim WS As Worksheet
    Dim CH As Chart

    Set WS = ActiveSheet
    Set CH = WS.Shapes.AddChart2(Style:=201, _
        XlChartType:=xlColumnClustered, _
        Left:=[B6].Left, _
        Top:=[B6].Top, _
        NewLayout:=False).Chart
    CH.SetSourceData Source:=Range("Sheet1!$A$1:$M$4")

    ' Set value axis to display thousands
    CH.SetElement msoElementPrimaryValueAxisThousands

    ' move the legend to the top
    CH.SetElement msoElementLegendTop
End Sub
```

Using the Format **Method to Micromanage Formatting Options**

The Format tab offers icons for changing colors and effects for individual chart elements. Although many people call the Shadow, Glow, Bevel, and Material settings "chart junk," there are ways in VBA to apply these formats.

Excel 2013 includes an object called the ChartFormat object that contains the settings for Fill, Glow, Line, PictureFormat, Shadow, SoftEdge, TextFrame2, and ThreeD. You can access the ChartFormat object by using the Format method on many chart elements. Table 15.3 lists a sampling of chart elements you can format using the Format method.

Table 15.3   Chart Elements to Which Formatting Applies

Chart Element	VBA to Refer to This Chart
Chart Title	ChartTitle
Axis Title–Category	Axes(xlCategory, xlPrimary).AxisTitle
Axis Title–Value	Axes(xlValue, xlPrimary).AxisTitle

Chart Element	VBA to Refer to This Chart
Legend	Legend
Data Labels for Series 1	SeriesCollection(1).DataLabels
Data Labels for Point 2	SeriesCollection(1).DataLabels(2) or SeriesCollection(1).Points(2).DataLabel
Data Table	DataTable
Axes–Horizontal	Axes(xlCategory, xlPrimary)
Axes–Vertical	Axes(xlValue, xlPrimary)
Axis–Series (Surface Charts Only)	Axes(xlSeries, xlPrimary)
Major Gridlines	Axes(xlValue, xlPrimary).MajorGridlines
Minor Gridlines	Axes(xlValue, xlPrimary).MinorGridlines
Plot Area	PlotArea
Chart Area	ChartArea
Chart Wall	Walls
Chart Back Wall	BackWall
Chart Side Wall	SideWall
Chart Floor	Floor
Trendline for Series 1	SeriesCollection(1).TrendLines(1)
Droplines	ChartGroups(1).DropLines
Up/Down Bars	ChartGroups(1).UpBars
Error Bars	SeriesCollection(1).ErrorBars
Series(1)	SeriesCollection(1)
Series(1) DataPoint	SeriesCollection(1).Points(3)

The Format method is the gateway to settings for Fill, Glow, and so on. Each of those objects has different options. The following sections provide examples of how to set up each type of format.

Changing an Object's Fill

The Shape Fill drop-down on the Format tab enables you to choose a single color, a gradient, a picture, or a texture for the fill.

To apply a specific color, you can use the RGB (red, green, blue) setting. To create a color, you specify a value from 0 to 255 for levels of red, green, and blue. The following code applies a simple blue fill:

```
Dim cht As Chart
Dim upb As UpBars
Set cht = ActiveChart
```

```
Set upb = cht.ChartGroups(1).UpBars
upb.Format.Fill.ForeColor.RGB = RGB(0, 0, 255)
```

If you would like an object to pick up the color from a specific theme accent color, you use the `ObjectThemeColor` property. The following code changes the bar color of the first series to accent color 6, which is an orange color in the Office theme. However, this might be another color if the workbook is using a different theme.

```
Sub ApplyThemeColor()
    Dim cht As Chart
    Dim ser As Series
    Set cht = ActiveChart
    Set ser = cht.SeriesCollection(1)
    ser.Format.Fill.ForeColor.ObjectThemeColor = msoThemeColorAccent6
End Sub
```

To apply a built-in texture, you use the `PresetTextured` method. The following code applies a green marble texture to the second series. However, you can apply any of the 20 textures:

```
Sub ApplyTexture()
    Dim cht As Chart
    Dim ser As Series
    Set cht = ActiveChart
    Set ser = cht.SeriesCollection(2)
    ser.Format.Fill.PresetTextured msoTextureGreenMarble
End Sub
```

> **NOTE** When you type `PresetTextured` followed by a space, the VB Editor offers a complete list of possible texture values.

To fill the bars of a data series with a picture, you use the `UserPicture` method and specify the path and filename of an image on the computer, as in the following example:

```
Sub FormatWithPicture()
    Dim cht As Chart
    Dim ser As Series
    Set cht = ActiveChart
    Set ser = cht.SeriesCollection(1)
    MyPic = "C:\PodCastTitle1.jpg"
    ser.Format.Fill.UserPicture MyPic
End Sub
```

Microsoft removed patterns as fills from Excel 2007. However, this method was restored in Excel 2010 because of the outcry from customers who used patterns to differentiate columns printed on monochrome printers.

In Excel 2013, you can apply a pattern using the `.Patterned` method. Patterns have a type such as `msoPatternPlain`, as well as a foreground and background color. The following code creates dark red vertical lines on a white background:

```
Sub FormatWithPicture()
    Dim cht As Chart
    Dim ser As Series
```

15

```
    Set cht = ActiveChart
    Set ser = cht.SeriesCollection(1)
    With ser.Format.Fill
        .Patterned msoPatternDarkVertical
        .BackColor.RGB = RGB(255,255,255)
        .ForeColor.RGB = RGB(255,0,0)
    End With
End Sub
```

> **NOTE** Code that uses patterns works in every version of Excel except Excel 2007. Therefore, do not use this code if you will be sharing the macro with co-workers who use Excel 2007.

Gradients are more difficult to specify than fills. Excel 2013 provides three methods that help you set up the common gradients. The OneColorGradient and TwoColorGradient methods require that you specify a gradient direction such as msoGradientFromCorner. You can then specify one of four styles, numbered 1 through 4, depending on whether you want the gradient to start at the top left, top right, bottom left, or bottom right. After using a gradient method, you need to specify the ForeColor and the BackColor settings for the object. The following macro sets up a two-color gradient using two theme colors:

```
Sub TwoColorGradient()
    Dim cht As Chart
    Dim ser As Series
    Set cht = ActiveChart
    Set ser = cht.SeriesCollection(1)
    ser.Format.Fill.TwoColorGradient msoGradientFromCorner, 3
    ser.Format.Fill.ForeColor.ObjectThemeColor = msoThemeColorAccent6
    ser.Format.Fill.BackColor.ObjectThemeColor = msoThemeColorAccent2
End Sub
```

When using the OneColorGradient method, you specify a direction, a style (1 through 4), and a darkness value between 0 and 1 (0 for darker gradients or 1 for lighter gradients).

When using the PresetGradient method, you specify a direction, a style (1 through 4), and the type of gradient such as msoGradientBrass, msoGradientLateSunset, or msoGradient-Rainbow. Again, as you are typing this code in the VB Editor, the AutoComplete tool provides a complete list of the available preset gradient types.

Formatting Line Settings

The LineFormat object formats either a line or the border around an object. You can change numerous properties for a line, such as the color, arrows, and dash style.

The following macro formats the trendline for the first series in a chart:

```
Sub FormatLineOrBorders()
    Dim cht As Chart
    Set cht = ActiveChart
    With cht.SeriesCollection(1).Trendlines(1).Format.Line
        .DashStyle = msoLineLongDashDotDot
        .ForeColor.RGB = RGB(50, 0, 128)
```

```
        .BeginArrowheadLength = msoArrowheadShort
        .BeginArrowheadStyle = msoArrowheadOval
        .BeginArrowheadWidth = msoArrowheadNarrow
        .EndArrowheadLength = msoArrowheadLong
        .EndArrowheadStyle = msoArrowheadTriangle
        .EndArrowheadWidth = msoArrowheadWide
    End With
End Sub
```

When you are formatting a border, the arrow settings are not relevant, so the code is shorter than the code for formatting a line. The following macro formats the border around a chart:

```
Sub FormatBorder()
    Dim cht As Chart
    Set cht = ActiveChart
    With cht.ChartArea.Format.Line
        .DashStyle = msoLineLongDashDotDot
        .ForeColor.RGB = RGB(50, 0, 128)
    End With
End Sub
```

Creating a Combo Chart

Sometimes you need to chart series of data that are of differing orders of magnitude. Normal charts do a lousy job of showing the smaller series. Combo charts can save the day.

Consider the data and chart in Figure 15.15. You want to plot the number of sales per month and also show two quality ratings. Perhaps this is a fictitious car dealer where they sell 80 to 100 cars a month and the customer satisfaction is represented and usually runs in the 80% to 90% range. When you try to plot this data on a chart, the columns for 90 cars sold dwarfs the column for 80% customer satisfaction. (I won't insult you by reminding you that 90 is 112.5 times larger than 80%!)

Figure 15.15
The values for two series are too small to be visible.

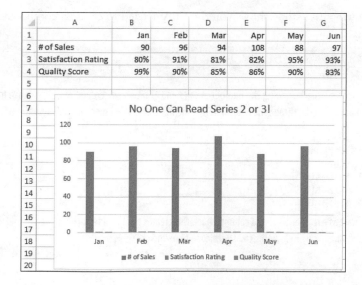

15

The solution in the Excel interface is to use the new interface for creating a combo chart. You move the two small series to the secondary axis and change their chart type to a line chart. (See Figure 15.16.)

Figure 15.16
A combo chart solves the problem.

The following case study shows you the VBA needed to create a combo chart.

CASE STUDY: CREATING A COMBO CHART

You want to create a chart showing the number of sales and also two percentage measurements. In this process, you have to format each of the three series. At the top of the macro, declare object variables for the worksheet, the chart, and each of the series:

```
Dim WS As Worksheet
Dim CH As Chart
Dim Ser1 As Series
Dim Ser2 As Series
Dim Ser3 As Series
```

Create the chart as a regular clustered column chart. This creates the horrible-looking chart from Figure 15.15. That's okay, because you quickly follow this code with code to fix the chart:

```
Set WS = ActiveSheet
 Set CH = WS.Shapes.AddChart2(Style:=201, _
     XlChartType:=xlColumnClustered, _
     Left:=[B6].Left, _
     Top:=[B6].Top, _
     NewLayout:=False).Chart
 CH.SetSourceData Source:=Range("Sheet1!$A$1:$G$4")
```

To work with a series, assign the `FullSeriesCollection` to an object variable such as Ser2. You could get away with a single object variable called Ser that you use over and over. This code enables you to come back later in the macro to refer to any of the three series.

After you have the Ser2 object variable defined, assign the series to the secondary axis group and change the chart type of just that series to a line; then repeat the code for Series 3:

```
' Move Series 2 to secondary axis as line
 Set Ser2 = CH.FullSeriesCollection(2)
 With Ser2
     .AxisGroup = xlSecondary
     .ChartType = xlLine
 End With

 ' Move Series 3 to secondary axis as line
 Set Ser3 = CH.FullSeriesCollection(3)
 With Ser3
     .AxisGroup = xlSecondary
     .ChartType = xlLine
 End With
```

You now have something close to what you see in the top of Figure 15.16.

Note that, at this point, you did not have to touch Series 1. Series 1 is fine as a column chart on the primary axis. You'll come back to Series 1 later in the macro.

Because too many of the data points in Series 3 were close to 100%, the Excel charting engine decided to make the right axis span all the way up to 120%. This is silly because no one can get a rating higher than 100%. You can override the automatic settings and choose a scale for the right axis. The following code uses 60% as the minimum and 100% as the maximum. Note that 0.6 is the same as 60% and 1 is the same as 100%.

```
' Set the secondary axis to go from 60% to 100%
CH.Axes(xlValue, xlSecondary).MinimumScale = 0.6
CH.Axes(xlValue, xlSecondary).MaximumScale = 1
```

When you override the scale values, Excel automatically guesses where you want the gridlines and axis labels. Rather than leaving this to chance, you can use the `MajorUnit` and `MinorUnit`. Axis labels and major gridlines appear at the increment specified by `MajorUnit`. The `MinorUnit` is important only if you plan on showing minor gridlines.

```
' Labels every 10%, secondary gridline at 5%
CH.Axes(xlValue, xlSecondary).MajorUnit = 0.1
CH.Axes(xlValue, xlSecondary).MinorUnit = 0.05
CH.Axes(xlValue, xlSecondary).TickLabels.NumberFormat = "0%"
```

At this point, take a look at the chart in Figure 15.17. It probably makes sense to you because you created the

15

chart. But imagine someone who is not familiar with the chart and not familiar with all the hoops you had to jump through to get here. There are numbers on the left axis and numbers on the right axis. I instantly went to the percentages on the right side and tried to follow the gridlines across. But this doesn't work because the gridlines don't line up with the numbers on the right side. They line up with the numbers on the left side. You can't really tell this for sure, though, because the gridlines coincidentally happen to line up with 100%, 80%, and 60%.

Figure 15.17
Close, but the gridlines are annoying when compared to the right axis.

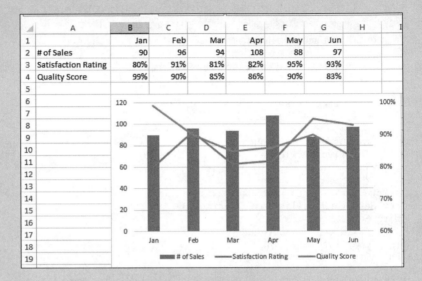

At this point, you might decide to get creative. Delete the gridlines for the left axis. Add major and minor gridlines for the right axis. Even better, delete the numbers along the left axis. Replace the numbers on the axis with a data label in the center of each column.

```
' Turn off the gridlines for left axis
CH.Axes(xlValue).HasMajorGridlines = False
' Add gridlines for right axis
CH.SetElement (msoElementSecondaryValueGridLinesMajor)
CH.SetElement (msoElementSecondaryValueGridLinesMinorMajor)

' Hide the labels on the primary axis
CH.Axes(xlValue).TickLabelPosition = xlNone
' Replace axis labels with a data label on the column
Set Ser1 = CH.FullSeriesCollection(1)
Ser1.ApplyDataLabels
Ser1.DataLabels.Position = xlLabelPositionCenter
```

Now you almost have it. Because the book is printed in monochrome, change the color of the Series 1 data label to white:

```
' Data Labels in white
With Ser1.DataLabels.Format.TextFrame2.TextRange.Font.Fill
    .Visible = msoTrue
    .ForeColor.ObjectThemeColor = msoThemeColorBackground1
```

```
    .Solid
End With
```

And because my charting mentors drilled it into my head, the legend has to be at the top or the left. Move it to the top.

```
' Legend at the top, per Gene Z.
CH.SetElement msoElementLegendTop
```

The resulting chart is shown in Figure 15.18. Thanks to the minor gridlines, you can easily tell if each rating was in the 80%–85%, 85%–90%, or 90%–95% range. The columns show the sales and the labels stay out of the way, but they are still readable.

Figure 15.18
The final chart conveys information about three series.

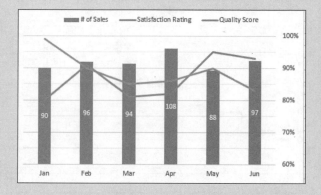

I am actually studying the chart and considering what grade Professor Edward Tufte would assign to this chart. Will it pass Kathy Villella's requirement that every bit of ink left on the chart is necessary? Would Gene Zelazny from McKinsey and Company approve? I hope for a B from Professor Tufte....

Creating Advanced Charts

In *Charts & Graphs for Microsoft Excel 2013* (Que, ISBN 07897486621), I include some amazing charts that do not look as though they can possibly be created using Excel. Building these charts usually involves adding a rogue data series that appears in the chart as an XY series to complete some effect.

The process of creating these charts manually is very tedious, which ensures that most people never resort to creating such charts. However, if the process is automated, the creation of the charts starts to become feasible.

The next sections explain how to use VBA to automate the process of creating these rather complex charts.

Creating True Open-High-Low-Close Stock Charts

If you are a fan of stock charts in the *Wall Street Journal* or finance.yahoo.com, you will recognize the chart type known as Open-High-Low-Close (OHLC) chart. Excel does not offer such a chart. Its High-Low-Close (HLC) chart is missing the left-facing dash that represents the opening for each period. You might think that HLC charts are close enough to OHLC charts. However, one of my personal pet peeves is that the *WSJ* can create better-looking charts than Excel can.

In Figure 15.19, you can see a true OHLC chart.

Figure 15.19
Excel's built-in High-Low-Close chart leaves out the Open mark for each data point.

> **NOTE**
> In Excel 2013, you can specify a custom picture that you can use as the marker in a chart. Given that Excel has a right-facing dash but not a left-facing dash, you need to use Photoshop to create a left-facing dash as a GIF file. This tiny graphic makes up for the fundamental flaw in Excel's chart marker selection.

> **NOTE**
> You can also download a LeftDash.gif file from http://www.mrexcel.com/get-code2013.html.

In the Excel user interface, you indicate that the Open series should have a custom picture and then specify LeftDash.gif as the picture. In VBA code, you use the UserPicture method, as shown here:

```
ActiveChart Cht.SeriesCollection(1).Fill.UserPicture "C:\leftdash.gif"
```

To create a true OHLC chart, follow these steps:

1. Create a line chart from four series; Open, High, Low, Close.
2. Change the line style to none for all four series.
3. Eliminate the marker for the High and Low series.

4. Add a High-Low line to the chart.

5. Change the marker for Close to a right-facing dash, which is called a dot in VBA, with a size of 9.

6. Change the marker for Open to a custom picture and load LeftDash.gif as the fill for the series.

The following code creates the chart in Figure 15.19:

```
Sub CreateOHCLChart()
    ' Download leftdash.gif from the sample files for this book
    ' and save it in the same folder as this workbook
    Dim Cht As Chart
    Dim Ser As Series

    ActiveSheet.Shapes.AddChart(xlLineMarkers).Select
    Set Cht = ActiveChart
    Cht.SetSourceData Source:=Range("Sheet1!$A$1:$E$33")
    ' Format the Open Series
    With Cht.SeriesCollection(1)
        .MarkerStyle = xlMarkerStylePicture
        .Fill.UserPicture ("C:\leftdash.gif")
        .Border.LineStyle = xlNone
        .MarkerForegroundColorIndex = xlColorIndexNone
    End With
    ' Format High & Low Series
    With Cht.SeriesCollection(2)
        .MarkerStyle = xlMarkerStyleNone
        .Border.LineStyle = xlNone
    End With
    With Cht.SeriesCollection(3)
        .MarkerStyle = xlMarkerStyleNone
        .Border.LineStyle = xlNone
    End With
    ' Format the Close series
    Set Ser = Cht.SeriesCollection(4)
    With Ser
        .MarkerBackgroundColorIndex = 1
        .MarkerForegroundColorIndex = 1
        .MarkerStyle = xlDot
        .MarkerSize = 9
        .Border.LineStyle = xlNone
    End With
    ' Add High-Low Lines
    Cht.SetElement (msoElementLineHiLoLine)
    Cht.SetElement (msoElementLegendNone)

End Sub
```

Creating Bins for a Frequency Chart

Suppose that you have results from 3,000 scientific trials. There must be a good way to produce a chart of those results. However, if you just select the results and create a chart, you end up with chaos (see Figure 15.20).

Figure 15.20
Try to chart the results from 3,000 trials and you have a jumbled mess.

The trick to creating an effective frequency distribution is to define a series of categories, or *bins*. A FREQUENCY array function counts the number of items from the 3,000 results that fall within each bin.

The process of creating bins manually is rather tedious and requires knowledge of array formulas. It is better to use a macro to perform all the tedious calculations.

The macro in this section requires you to specify a bin size and a starting bin. If you expect results in the 0 to 100 range, you might specify bins of 10 each, starting at 1. This would create bins of 1–10, 11–20, 21–30, and so on. If you specify bin sizes of 15 with a starting bin of 5, the macro creates bins of 5–20, 21–35, 36–50, and so on.

To use the following macro, your trial results should start in Row 2 and should be in the rightmost column of a dataset. Three variables near the top of the macro define the starting bin, the ending bin, and the bin size:

```
' Define Bins
BinSize = 10
FirstBin = 1
LastBin = 100
```

After that, the macro skips a column and then builds a range of starting bins. In cell D4 in Figure 15.21, the 10 is used to tell Excel that you are looking for the number of values larger than the 0 in D3, but equal to or less than the 10 in D4.

Although the bins extend from D3:D13, the FREQUENCY function entered in Column E needs to include one extra cell, in case any results are larger than the last bin. This single formula returns many results. Formulas that return more than one answer are called *array formulas*. In the Excel user interface, you specify an array formula by holding down Ctrl+Shift while pressing Enter to finish the formula. In Excel VBA, you need to use the FormulaArray property. The following lines of the macro set up the array formula in Column E:

```
' Enter the Frequency Formula
Form = "=FREQUENCY(R2C" & FinalCol & ":R" & FinalRow & "C" & FinalCol & _
    ",R3C" & NextCol & ":R" & _
    LastRow & "C" & NextCol & ")"
Range(Cells(FirstRow, NextCol + 1), Cells(LastRow, NextCol + 1)). _
    FormulaArray = Form
```

Figure 15.21
The macro summarizes the results into bins and provides a meaningful chart of the data.

It is not evident to the reader whether the bin indicated in Column D is the upper or lower limit. The macro builds readable labels in Column G and then copies the frequency results over to Column H.

After the macro builds a simple column chart, the following line eliminates the gap between columns, creating the traditional histogram view of the data:

```
Cht.ChartGroups(1).GapWidth = 0
```

The macro to create the chart in Figure 15.21 follows:

```
Sub CreateFrequencyChart()
    ' Find the last column
    FinalCol = Cells(1, Columns.Count).End(xlToLeft).Column
    ' Find the FinalRow
    FinalRow = Cells(Rows.Count, FinalCol).End(xlUp).Row

    ' Define Bins
    BinSize = 10
    FirstBin = 0
    LastBin = 100

    'The bins will go in row 3, two columns after FinalCol
    NextCol = FinalCol + 2
    FirstRow = 3
    NextRow = FirstRow - 1

    ' Set up the bins for the Frequency function
    For i = FirstBin To LastBin Step BinSize
        NextRow = NextRow + 1
        Cells(NextRow, NextCol).Value = i
    Next i
```

```
' The Frequency function has to be one row larger than the bins
LastRow = NextRow + 1

' Enter the Frequency Formula
Form = "=FREQUENCY(R2C" & FinalCol & ":R" & FinalRow & "C" & FinalCol & _
    ",R3C" & NextCol & ":R" & _
    LastRow & "C" & NextCol & ")"
Range(Cells(FirstRow, NextCol + 1), Cells(LastRow, NextCol + 1)). _
    FormulaArray = Form

' Build a range suitable for a chart source data
LabelCol = NextCol + 3
Form = "=R[-1]C[-3]&""-""&RC[-3]"
Range(Cells(4, LabelCol), Cells(LastRow - 1, LabelCol)).FormulaR1C1 = _
    Form
' Enter the > Last formula
Cells(LastRow, LabelCol).FormulaR1C1 = "="">""&R[-1]C[-3]"
' Enter the < first formula
Cells(3, LabelCol).FormulaR1C1 = "=""<""&RC[-3]"

' Enter the formula to copy the frequency results
Range(Cells(3, LabelCol + 1), Cells(LastRow, LabelCol + 1)).FormulaR1C1 = _
    "=RC[-3]"
' Add a heading
Cells(2, LabelCol + 1).Value = "Frequency"

' Create a column chart
Dim Cht As Chart
ActiveSheet.Shapes.AddChart(xlColumnClustered).Select
Set Cht = ActiveChart
Cht.SetSourceData Source:=Range(Cells(2, LabelCol), _
    Cells(LastRow, LabelCol + 1))
Cht.SetElement (msoElementLegendNone)
Cht.ChartGroups(1).GapWidth = 0
Cht.SetElement (msoElementDataLabelOutSideEnd)

End Sub
```

Creating a Stacked Area Chart

The stacked area chart shown in Figure 15.22 is incredibly difficult to create in the Excel user interface. Although the chart appears to contain four independent charts, this chart actually contains nine series:

- The first series contains the values for the East region.

- The second series contains 1,000 minus the East values. This series is formatted with a transparent fill.

- Series 3, 5, and 7 contain values for Central, Northwest, and Southwest.

- Series 4, 6, and 8 contain 1,000 minus the preceding series.

- The final series is an XY series used to add labels for the left axis. There is one point for each gridline. The markers are positioned at an X position of 0. Custom data labels are added next to invisible markers to force the labels along the axis to start again at 0 for each region.

Figure 15.22
A single chart appears to
hold four different charts.

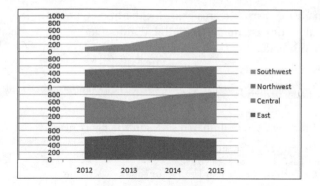

To use the macro provided here, your data should begin in Cell A1.

The macro adds new columns to the right of the data and new rows below the data, so the
rest of the worksheet should be blank.

Two variables at the top of the macro define the height of each chart. In the current example, leaving a height of 1000 allows the sales for each region to fit comfortably. The LabSize
value should indicate how frequently labels should appear along the left axis. This number
must be evenly divisible into the chart height. In this example, values of 500, 250, 200, 125,
or 100 would work:

```
' Define the height of each area chart
ChtHeight = 1000
' Define Tick Mark Size
' ChtHeight should be an even multiple of LabSize
LabSize = 200
```

The macro builds a copy of the data to the right of the original data. New "dummy" series
are added to the right of each region to calculate 1,000 minus the data point. In Figure
15.23, this series is shown in G1:O5.

Figure 15.23
Extra data to the right
and below the original
data are created by the
macro to create the chart.

The macro then creates a stacked area chart for the first eight series. The legend for this chart indicates values of East, dummy, Central, dummy, and so on. To delete every other legend entry, use this code:

```
' Delete series from legend
For i = FinalSeriesCount To 2 Step -2
    Cht.Legend.LegendEntries(i).Delete
Next i
```

Similarly, the fill for each even numbered series in the chart needs to be set to transparent:

```
' Fill the dummy series with no fill
For i = FinalSeriesCount To 2 Step -2
    Cht.SeriesCollection(i).Interior.ColorIndex = xlNone
Next i
```

The trickiest part of the process is adding a new final series to the chart. This series will have far more data points than the other series. Range B8:C28 contains the X and Y values for the new series. You will see that each point has an X value of 0 to ensure that it appears along the left side of the plot area. The Y values increase steadily by the value indicated in the LabSize variable. In Column A next to the X and Y points are the actual labels that will be plotted next to each marker. These labels give the illusion that the chart starts over with a value of 0 for each region.

The process of adding the new series is actually much easier in VBA than in the Excel user interface. The following code identifies each component of the series and specifies that it should be plotted as an XY chart:

```
' Add the new series to the chart
Set Ser = Cht.SeriesCollection.NewSeries
With Ser
    .Name = "Y"
    .Values = Range(Cells(AxisRow + 1, 3), Cells(NewFinal, 3))
    .XValues = Range(Cells(AxisRow + 1, 2), Cells(NewFinal, 2))
    .ChartType = xlXYScatter
    .MarkerStyle = xlMarkerStyleNone
End With
```

Finally, code applies a data label from Column A to each point in the final series:

```
' Label each point in the series
' This code actually adds fake labels along left axis
For i = 1 To TickMarkCount
    Ser.Points(i).HasDataLabel = True
    Ser.Points(i).DataLabel.Text = Cells(AxisRow + i, 1).Value
Next i
```

The complete code to create the stacked chart in Figure 15.23 is shown here:

```
Sub CreatedStackedChart()
    Dim Cht As Chart
    Dim Ser As Series
    FinalRow = Cells(Rows.Count, 1).End(xlUp).Row
    FinalCol = Cells(1, Columns.Count).End(xlToLeft).Column
    OrigSeriesCount = FinalCol - 1
    FinalSeriesCount = OrigSeriesCount * 2

    ' Define the height of each area chart
```

```
ChtHeight = 1000
' Define Tick Mark Size
' ChtHeight should be an even multiple of LabSize
LabSize = 200

' Make a copy of the data
NextCol = FinalCol + 2
Cells(1, 1).Resize(FinalRow, FinalCol).Copy _
    Destination:=Cells(1, NextCol)
FinalCol = Cells(1, Columns.Count).End(xlToLeft).Column

' Add in new columns to serve as dummy series
MyFormula = "=" & ChtHeight & "-RC[-1]"
For i = FinalCol + 1 To NextCol + 2 Step -1
    Cells(1, i).EntireColumn.Insert
    Cells(1, i).Value = "dummy"
    Cells(2, i).Resize(FinalRow - 1, 1).FormulaR1C1 = MyFormula
Next i

' Figure out the new Final Column
FinalCol = Cells(1, Columns.Count).End(xlToLeft).Column

' Build the Chart
ActiveSheet.Shapes.AddChart(xlAreaStacked).Select
Set Cht = ActiveChart
Cht.SetSourceData Source:=Range(Cells(1, NextCol), Cells(FinalRow, _
    FinalCol))
Cht.PlotBy = xlColumns

' Clear out the even number series from the Legend
For i = FinalSeriesCount - 1 To 1 Step -2
    Cht.Legend.LegendEntries(i).Delete
Next i

' Set the axis Maximum Scale & Gridlines
TopScale = OrigSeriesCount * ChtHeight
With Cht.Axes(xlValue)
    .MaximumScale = TopScale
    .MinorUnit = LabSize
    .MajorUnit = ChtHeight
End With
Cht.SetElement (msoElementPrimaryValueGridLinesMinorMajor)

' Fill the dummy series with no fill
For i = FinalSeriesCount To 2 Step -2
    Cht.SeriesCollection(i).Interior.ColorIndex = xlNone
Next i

' Hide the original axis labels
Cht.Axes(xlValue).TickLabelPosition = xlNone

' Build a new range to hold a rogue XY series that will
' be used to create left axis labels
AxisRow = FinalRow + 2
Cells(AxisRow, 1).Resize(1, 3).Value = Array("Label", "X", "Y")
TickMarkCount = OrigSeriesCount * (ChtHeight / LabSize) + 1
' Column B contains the X values. These are all zero
Cells(AxisRow + 1, 2).Resize(TickMarkCount, 1).Value = 0
```

```
' Column C contains the Y values.
Cells(AxisRow + 1, 3).Resize(TickMarkCount, 1).FormulaR1C1 = _
    "=R[-1]C+" & LabSize
Cells(AxisRow + 1, 3).Value = 0
' Column A contains the labels to be used for each point
Cells(AxisRow + 1, 1).Value = 0
Cells(AxisRow + 2, 1).Resize(TickMarkCount - 1, 1).FormulaR1C1 = _
    "=IF(R[-1]C+" & LabSize & ">=" & ChtHeight & _
    ",0,R[-1]C+" & LabSize & ")"
NewFinal = Cells(Rows.Count, 1).End(xlUp).Row
Cells(NewFinal, 1).Value = ChtHeight

' Add the new series to the chart
Set Ser = Cht.SeriesCollection.NewSeries
With Ser
    .Name = "Y"
    .Values = Range(Cells(AxisRow + 1, 3), Cells(NewFinal, 3))
    .XValues = Range(Cells(AxisRow + 1, 2), Cells(NewFinal, 2))
    .ChartType = xlXYScatter
    .MarkerStyle = xlMarkerStyleNone
End With

' Label each point in the series
' This code actually adds fake labels along left axis
For i = 1 To TickMarkCount
    Ser.Points(i).HasDataLabel = True
    Ser.Points(i).DataLabel.Text = Cells(AxisRow + i, 1).Value
Next i

' Hide the Y label in the legend
Cht.Legend.LegendEntries(Cht.Legend.LegendEntries.Count).Delete
End Sub
```

> **NOTE** The websites of Andy Pope (http://www.andypope.info) and Jon Peltier (http://pelti-ertech.com) are filled with examples of unusual charts that require extraordinary effort. If you find that you will regularly be creating stacked charts or any other chart like those on their websites, taking the time to write the VBA eases the pain of creating the charts in the Excel user interface.

Exporting a Chart as a Graphic

You can export any chart to an image file on your hard drive. The ExportChart method requires you to specify a filename and a graphic type. The available graphic types depend on graphic file filters installed in your Registry. It is a safe bet that JPG, BMP, PNG, and GIF work on most computers.

For example, the following code exports the active chart as a GIF file:

```
Sub ExportChart()
    Dim cht As Chart
    Set cht = ActiveChart
    cht.Export Filename:="C:\Chart.gif", Filtername:="GIF"
End Sub
```

Since Excel 2003, Microsoft has supported an `Interactive` argument in the `Export` method. Excel Help indicates that if you set `Interactive` to TRUE, Excel asks for additional settings depending on the file type. However, the dialog that asks for additional settings never appears—at least not for the four standard types of JPG, GIF, BMP, and PNG. To prevent any questions from popping up in the middle of your macro, set `Interactive:=False`.

Creating Pivot Charts

A *pivot chart* is a chart that uses a pivot table as the underlying data source. Unfortunately, pivot charts do not have the cool "show pages" functionality that regular pivot tables have. You can overcome this problem with a quick VBA macro that creates a pivot table and then a pivot chart based on the pivot table. The macro then adds the customer field to the filters area of the pivot table. It then loops through each customer and exports the chart for each customer.

In Excel 2013, you first create a pivot cache by using the `PivotCache.Create` method. You can then define a pivot table based on the pivot cache. The usual procedure is to turn off pivot table updating while you add fields to the pivot table. Then you update the pivot table to have Excel perform the calculations.

It takes a bit of finesse to figure out the final range of the pivot table. If you have turned off the column and row totals, the chartable area of the pivot table starts one row below the `PivotTableRange1` area. You have to resize the area to include one fewer row to make your chart appear correctly.

After the pivot table is created, you can switch back to the `Charts.Add` code discussed earlier in this chapter. You can use any formatting code to get the chart formatted as you desire.

The following code creates a pivot table and a single pivot chart that summarizes revenue by region and product:

```
Sub CreateSummaryReportUsingPivot()
    Dim WSD As Worksheet
    Dim PTCache As PivotCache
    Dim PT As PivotTable
    Dim PRange As Range
    Dim FinalRow As Long
    Dim ChartDataRange As Range
    Dim Cht As Chart
    Set WSD = Worksheets("Data")

    ' Delete any prior pivot tables
    For Each PT In WSD.PivotTables
        PT.TableRange2.Clear
    Next PT
    WSD.Range("I1:Z1").EntireColumn.Clear

    ' Define input area and set up a Pivot Cache
    FinalRow = WSD.Cells(Application.Rows.Count, 1).End(xlUp).Row
    FinalCol = WSD.Cells(1, Application.Columns.Count). _
```

```
        End(xlToLeft).Column
    Set PRange = WSD.Cells(1, 1).Resize(FinalRow, FinalCol)

    Set PTCache = ActiveWorkbook.PivotCaches.Create(SourceType:= _
        xlDatabase, SourceData:=PRange.Address)

    ' Create the Pivot Table from the Pivot Cache
    Set PT = PTCache.CreatePivotTable(TableDestination:=WSD. _
        Cells(2, FinalCol + 2), TableName:="PivotTable1")

    ' Turn off updating while building the table
    PT.ManualUpdate = True

    ' Set up the row fields
    PT.AddFields RowFields:="Region", ColumnFields:="Product", _
        PageFields:="Customer"

    ' Set up the data fields
    With PT.PivotFields("Revenue")
        .Orientation = xlDataField
        .Function = xlSum
        .Position = 1
    End With

    With PT
        .ColumnGrand = False
        .RowGrand = False
        .NullString = "0"
    End With

    ' Calc the pivot table
    PT.ManualUpdate = False
    PT.ManualUpdate = True

    ' Define the Chart Data Range
    Set ChartDataRange = _
        PT.TableRange1.Offset(1, 0).Resize(PT.TableRange1.Rows.Count - 1)

    ' Add the Chart
    WSD.Shapes.AddChart.Select
    Set Cht = ActiveChart
    Cht.SetSourceData Source:=ChartDataRange
    ' Format the Chart
    Cht.ChartType = xlColumnClustered
    Cht.SetElement (msoElementChartTitleAboveChart)
    Cht.ChartTitle.Caption = "All Customers"
    Cht.SetElement msoElementPrimaryValueAxisThousands
    ' Excel 2010 only. Next line will not work in 2007
    Cht.ShowAllFieldButtons = False
End Sub
```

Figure 15.24 shows the resulting chart and pivot table.

Figure 15.24
VBA creates a pivot table and then a chart from the pivot table. Excel automatically displays the PivotChart Filter window in response.

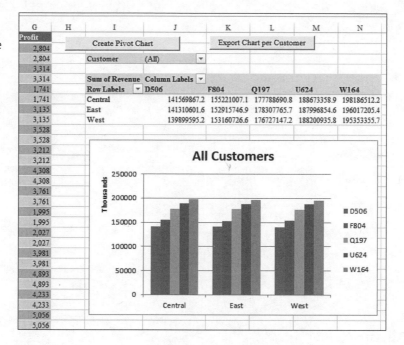

Next Steps

In Chapter 16, you find out how to automate the data visualization tools such as icon sets, color scales, and data bars.

Data Visualizations and Conditional Formatting

16

Introduction to Data Visualizations

The data visualization tools were introduced in Excel 2007 and improved in Excel 2010. Data visualizations appear on a drawing layer that can hold icon sets, data bars, color scales, and now sparklines. Unlike SmartArt graphics, Microsoft exposed the entire object model for the data visualization tools, so you can use VBA to add data visualizations to your reports.

→ **See** Chapter 17, "Dashboarding with Sparklines in Excel 2013," for more information about sparklines.

Excel 2013 provides a variety of data visualizations. A description of each appears here, with an example shown in Figure 16.1:

- **Data bars**—The data bar adds an in-cell bar chart to each cell in a range. The largest numbers have the largest bars, and the smallest numbers have the smallest bars. You can control the bar color as well as the values that should receive the smallest and largest bar. Data bars can be solid or a gradient. The gradient bars can have a border.

- **Color scales**—Excel applies a color to each cell from among a two- or three-color gradient. The two-color gradients are best for reports that are presented in monochrome. The three-color gradients require a presentation in color, but can represent a report in a traditional traffic light color combination of red-yellow-green. You can control the points along the continuum where each color begins, and you can control the two or three colors.

- **Icon sets**—Excel assigns an icon to each number. Icon sets can contain three icons such as the red, yellow, green traffic lights; four icons; or five icons such as the cellphone power bars. With icon sets, you can control the numeric limits for each icon, reverse the order of the icons, or choose to show only the icons.

- **Above/below average**—Found under the top/bottom rules fly-out menu, these rules make it easy to highlight all the cells that are above or below average. You can choose the formatting to apply to the cells. Note in Column G of Figure 16.1 that only 30 percent of the cells are above average. Contrast this with the top 50 percent in Column K.

- **Duplicate values**—Excel highlights any values that are repeated within a dataset. Because the Delete Duplicates command on the Data tab of the Ribbon is so destructive, you might prefer to highlight the duplicates and then intelligently decide which records to delete.

- **Top/bottom rules**—Excel highlights the top or bottom *n* percent of cells or highlights the top or bottom *n* cells in a range.

- **Highlight cells**—The legacy conditional formatting rules such as greater than, less than, between, and text that contains are still available in Excel 2013. The powerful Formula conditions are also available, although you might need to use these less frequently with the addition of the average and top/bottom rules.

Figure 16.1

Visualizations such as data bars, color scales, icon sets, and top/bottom rules are controlled in the Excel user interface from the Conditional Formatting drop-down on the Home tab of the Ribbon.

	A	B	C	D	E	F	G	H	I	J	K	L	M	N
1	Data Bar		Color Scale		Icon Set		Above Average		Duplicates		Top 50%			
2	46		39		41		70		65		70			
3	37		74		62		26		73		26			
4	67		20		33		83		10		83			
5	32		60		63		23		80		23			
6	43		79		26		19		38		19			
7	50		10		72		10		81		10			
8	38		27		73		34		71		34			
9	36		43		31		17		81		17			
10	56		63		70		12		86		12			
11	12		88		17		88		78		88			

VBA Methods and Properties for Data Visualizations

All the data visualization settings are managed in VBA with the FormatConditions collection. Conditional formatting has been in Excel since Excel 97. In Excel 2007, Microsoft expanded the FormatConditions object to handle the new visualizations. Whereas legacy versions of Excel would use the FormatConditions.Add method, Excel 2007–2013 offers additional methods such as AddDataBar, AddIconSetCondition, AddColorScale, AddTop10, AddAboveAverage, and AddUniqueValues.

It is possible to apply several different conditional formatting conditions to the same range. For example, you can apply a two-color color scale, an icon set, and a data bar to the same range. Excel includes a Priority property to specify which conditions should be calculated first. Methods such as SetFirstPriority and SetLastPriority ensure that a new format condition is executed before or after all others.

The StopIfTrue property works in conjunction with the Priority property. Say that you are highlighting duplicates but only want to check text cells. Create a new formula-based condition that use =ISNUMBER() to find numeric values. Make the ISNUMBER condition have a higher priority and apply StopIfTrue to prevent Excel from ever reaching the duplicates condition for numeric cells.

Beginning with Excel 2007, the Type property was expanded dramatically. This property was formerly a toggle between CellValue and Expression, but 13 new types were added in Excel 2007. Table 16.1 shows the valid values for the Type property. Items 3 and above were introduced in Excel 2007. The Excel team must have had plans for mode conditions; items 7, 14, and 15 do not exist, indicating they must have been on the drawing board at one time but then removed in the final version of Excel 2007. One of these was likely the ill-fated "highlight entire table row" feature that was in the Excel 2007 beta but removed in the final version.

Table 16.1   Valid Types for a Format Condition

Value	Description	VBA Constant
1	Cell value	xlCellValue
2	Expression	xlExpression
3	Color scale	xlColorScale
4	Data bar	xlDatabar
5	Top 10 values	xlTop10
6	Icon set	xlIconSet
8	Unique values	xlUniqueValues
9	Text string	xlTextString
10	Blanks condition	xlBlanksCondition
11	Time period	xlTimePeriod
12	Above average condition	xlAboveAverageCondition
13	No blanks condition	xlNoBlanksCondition
16	Errors condition	xlErrorsCondition
17	No errors condition	xlNoErrorsCondition

Adding Data Bars to a Range

The Data Bar command adds an in-cell bar chart to each cell in a range. Many charting experts complained to Microsoft about problems in the Excel 2007 data bars. For this reason, Microsoft changed the data bars in Excel 2013 to address these problems.

In Figure 16.2, Cell C37 reflects changes introduced in Excel 2010. Notice that this cell, which has a value of 0, has no data bar at all. In Excel 2007, the smallest value receives a four-pixel data bar, even if that smallest value is 0. In addition, in Excel 2013 the largest bar in the dataset typically takes up the entire width of the cell.

Figure 16.2
Excel 2013 offers many variations on data bars.

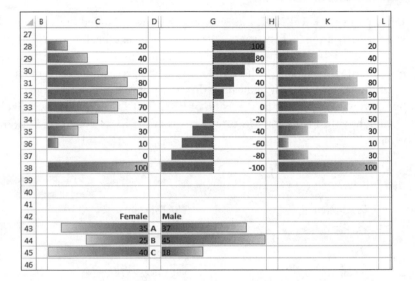

In Excel 2007, the data bars would end in a gradient that made it difficult to tell where the bar ended. Excel 2010–2013 offers a border around the bar. You can choose to change the color of the border or even to remove the border, as shown in Column K of the figure.

Excel 2010–2013 also offers support for negative data bars, as shown in Column G and the data bars that run right to left as shown in Cells C43:C45 of Figure 16.2. These allow comparative histograms.

> **NOTE**
> Although all of these are fine improvements, they add complexity to the VBA that is required to create data bars. In addition, you run the risk that your code will use new properties that will be incompatible with Excel 2007.

To add a data bar, you apply the `.FormatConditions.AddDataBar` method to a range containing your numbers. This method requires no arguments, and it returns an object of the `DataBar` type.

After you add the data bar, you will most likely need to change some of its properties. One method of referring to the data bar is to assume that the recently added data bar is the last item in the collection of format conditions. This code would add a data bar, identify the data bar by counting the conditions, and then change the color:

```
Range("A2:A11").FormatConditions.AddDatabar
ThisCond = Range("A2:A11").FormatConditions.Count
With Range("A2:A11").FormatConditions(ThisCond).BarColor
    .Color = RGB(255, 0, 0) ' Red
    .TintAndShade = -0.5 ' Darker than normal
End With
```

A safer way to go is to define an object variable of type `DataBar`. You can then assign the newly created data bar to the variable:

```
Dim DB As Databar
' Add the data bars
Set DB = Range("A2:A11").FormatConditions.AddDatabar
' Use a red that is 25% darker
With DB.BarColor
    .Color = RGB(255, 0, 0)
    .TintAndShade = -0.25
End With
```

When specifying colors for the data bar or the border, you should use the RGB function to assign a color. You can modify the color by making it darker or lighter using the `TintAndShade` property. Valid values are from -1 to 1. A value of 0 means no modification. Positive values make the color lighter. Negative values make the color darker.

By default, Excel assigns the shortest data bar to the minimum value and the longest data bar to the maximum value. If you want to override the defaults, use the `Modify` method for either the `MinPoint` or the `MaxPoint` properties. Specify a type from those shown in Table 16.2. Types 0, 3, 4, and 5 require a value. Table 16.2 shows valid types.

Table 16.2 `MinPoint` **and** `MaxPoint` **Types**

Value	Description	VBA Constant
0	Number is used	`xlConditionNumber`
1	Lowest value from the list of values	`xlConditionValueLowestValue`
2	Highest value from the list of values	`xlConditionValueHighestValue`
3	Percentage is used	`xlConditionValuePercent`
4	Formula is used	`xlConditionValueFormula`
5	Percentile is used	`xlConditionValuePercentile`
-1	No conditional value	`xlConditionValueNone`

Use the following code to have the smallest bar assigned to values of 0 and below:

```
DB.MinPoint.Modify _
    Newtype:=xlConditionValueNumber, NewValue:=0
```

To have the top 20 percent of the bars have the largest bar, use this code:

```
DB.MaxPoint.Modify _
    Newtype:=xlConditionValuePercent, NewValue:=80
```

An interesting alternative is to show only the data bars and not the value. To do this, use this code:

```
DB.ShowValue = False
```

To show negative data bars in Excel 2013, use this line:

```
DB.AxisPosition = xlDataBarAxisAutomatic
```

When you allow negative data bars, you can specify an axis color, a negative bar color, and a negative bar border color. Samples of how to change the various colors are shown in the following code that creates the data bars shown in Column C of Figure 16.3:

```
Sub DataBar2()
' Add a Data bar
' Include negative data bars
' Control the min and max point
'
    Dim DB As Databar
    With Range("C2:C11")
        .FormatConditions.Delete
        ' Add the data bars
        Set DB = .FormatConditions.AddDatabar()
    End With

    ' Set the lower limit
    DB.MinPoint.Modify newtype:=xlConditionFormula, NewValue:="-600"
    DB.MaxPoint.Modify newtype:=xlConditionValueFormula, NewValue:="600"

    ' Change the data bar to Green
    With DB.BarColor
        .Color = RGB(0, 255, 0)
        .TintAndShade = -0.15
    End With

    ' All of this is new in Excel 2010
    With DB
        ' Use a gradient
        .BarFillType = xlDataBarFillGradient
        ' Left to Right for direction of bars
        .Direction = xlLTR
        ' Assign a different color to negative bars
        .NegativeBarFormat.ColorType = xlDataBarColor
        ' Use a border around the bars
        .BarBorder.Type = xlDataBarBorderSolid
        ' Assign a different border color to negative
        .NegativeBarFormat.BorderColorType = xlDataBarSameAsPositive
        ' All borders are solid black
        With .BarBorder.Color
            .Color = RGB(0, 0, 0)
        End With
```

```
        ' Axis where it naturally would fall, in black
        .AxisPosition = xlDataBarAxisAutomatic
        With .AxisColor
            .Color = 0
            .TintAndShade = 0
        End With
        ' Negative bars in red
        With .NegativeBarFormat.Color
            .Color = 255
            .TintAndShade = 0
        End With
        ' Negative borders in red
    End With

End Sub
```

In Excel 2013, you have a choice of showing a gradient or a solid bar. To show a solid bar, use the following:

```
DB.BarFillType = xlDataBarFillSolid
```

The following code sample produces the solid bars shown in Column E of Figure 16.3:

```
Sub DataBar3()
' Add a Data bar
' Show solid bars
' Allow negative bars
' hide the numbers, show only the data bars
'
    Dim DB As Databar
    With Range("E2:E11")
        .FormatConditions.Delete
        ' Add the data bars
        Set DB = .FormatConditions.AddDatabar()
    End With

    With DB.BarColor
        .Color = RGB(0, 0, 255)
        .TintAndShade = 0.1
    End With
    ' Hide the numbers
    DB.ShowValue = False

    ' New in Excel 2013
    DB.BarFillType = xlDataBarFillSolid
    DB.NegativeBarFormat.ColorType = xlDataBarColor
    With DB.NegativeBarFormat.Color
        .Color = 255
        .TintAndShade = 0
    End With
    ' Allow negatives
    DB.AxisPosition = xlDataBarAxisAutomatic
    ' Negative border color is different
    DB.NegativeBarFormat.BorderColorType = xlDataBarColor
    With DB.NegativeBarFormat.BorderColor
        .Color = RGB(127, 127, 0)
        .TintAndShade = 0
    End With

End Sub
```

To allow the bars to go right to left, use this code:

```
DB.Direction = xlRTL ' Right to Left
```

Figure 16.3
Data bars created by the
macros in this section.

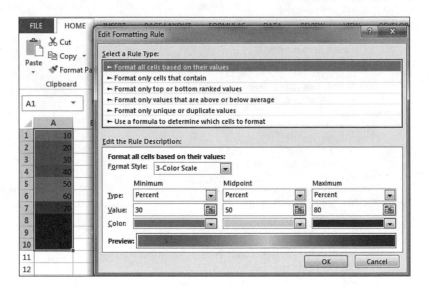

Adding Color Scales to a Range

You can add color scales in either two-color or three-color scale varieties. Figure 16.4
shows the available settings in the Excel user interface for a color scale using three colors.

Figure 16.4
Color scales enable you
to show hot spots in your
dataset.

Like the data bar, you apply a color scale to a range object using the `AddColorScale`
method. You should specify a `ColorScaleType` of either 2 or 3 as the only argument of the
`AddColorScale` method.

Next, you can indicate a color and tint for both or all three of the color scale criteria. You can also specify whether the shade is applied to the lowest value, the highest value, a particular value, a percentage, or at a percentile using the values shown previously in Table 16.2.

The following code generates a three-color color scale in Range A1:A10:

```
Sub Add3ColorScale()
    Dim CS As ColorScale

    With Range("A1:A10")
        .FormatConditions.Delete
        ' Add the Color Scale as a 3-color scale
        Set CS = .FormatConditions.AddColorScale(ColorScaleType:=3)
    End With

    ' Format the first color as light red
    CS.ColorScaleCriteria(1).Type = xlConditionValuePercent
    CS.ColorScaleCriteria(1).Value = 30
    CS.ColorScaleCriteria(1).FormatColor.Color = RGB(255, 0, 0)
    CS.ColorScaleCriteria(1).FormatColor.TintAndShade = 0.25

    ' Format the second color as green at 50%
    CS.ColorScaleCriteria(2).Type = xlConditionValuePercent
    CS.ColorScaleCriteria(2).Value = 50
    CS.ColorScaleCriteria(2).FormatColor.Color = RGB(0, 255, 0)
    CS.ColorScaleCriteria(2).FormatColor.TintAndShade = 0

    ' Format the third color as dark blue
    CS.ColorScaleCriteria(3).Type = xlConditionValuePercent
    CS.ColorScaleCriteria(3).Value = 80
    CS.ColorScaleCriteria(3).FormatColor.Color = RGB(0, 0, 255)
    CS.ColorScaleCriteria(3).FormatColor.TintAndShade = -0.25
End Sub
```

Adding Icon Sets to a Range

Icon sets in Excel come with three, four, or five different icons in the set. Figure 16.5 shows the settings for an icon set with five different icons.

To add an icon set to a range, use the AddIconSet method. No arguments are required. You can then adjust three properties that apply to the icon set. You then use several additional lines of code to specify the icon set in use and the limits for each icon.

Figure 16.5
With additional icons, the complexity of the code increases.

Specifying an Icon Set

After adding the icon set, you can control whether the icon order is reversed, and whether Excel shows only the icons, and then specify one of the 20 built-in icon sets:

```
Dim ICS As IconSetCondition
With Range("A1:C10")
    .FormatConditions.Delete
    Set ICS = .FormatConditions.AddIconSetCondition()
End With

' Global settings for the icon set
With ICS
    .ReverseOrder = False
    .ShowIconOnly = False
    .IconSet = ActiveWorkbook.IconSets(xl5CRV)
End With
```

> **NOTE**
> It is somewhat curious that the `IconSets` collection is a property of the active workbook. This seems to indicate that in future versions of Excel, new icon sets might be available.

Table 16.3 shows the complete list of icon sets.

Table 16.3   Available Icon Sets and Their VBA Constants

Icon	Value	Description	Constant
	1	3 arrows	xl3Arrows
	2	3 arrows gray	xl3ArrowsGray
	3	3 flags	xl3Flags
	4	3 traffic lights 1	xl3TrafficLights1
	5	3 traffic lights 2	xl3TrafficLights2
	6	3 signs	xl3Signs
	7	3 symbols	xl3Symbols
	8	3 symbols 2	xl3Symbols2
	9	4 arrows	xl4Arrows
	10	4 arrows gray	xl4ArrowsGray
	11	4 red to black	xl4RedToBlack
	12	4 power bars	xl4CRV
	13	4 traffic lights	xl4TrafficLights
	14	5 arrows	xl5Arrows
	15	5 arrows gray	xl5ArrowsGray
	16	5 power bars	xl5CRV
	17	5 quarters	xl5Quarters
	18	3 stars	xl3Stars
	19	3 triangles	xl3Triangles
	20	5 boxes	xl5Boxes

16

Specifying Ranges for Each Icon

After specifying the type of icon set, you can specify ranges for each icon within the set. By default, the first icon starts at the lowest value. You can adjust the settings for each of the additional icons in the set:

```
' The first icon always starts at 0

' Settings for the second icon - start at 50%
With ICS.IconCriteria(2)
    .Type = xlConditionValuePercent
    .Value = 50
    .Operator = xlGreaterEqual
End With
With ICS.IconCriteria(3)
    .Type = xlConditionValuePercent
    .Value = 60
    .Operator = xlGreaterEqual
End With
With ICS.IconCriteria(4)
    .Type = xlConditionValuePercent
    .Value = 80
    .Operator = xlGreaterEqual
End With
With ICS.IconCriteria(5)
    .Type = xlConditionValuePercent
    .Value = 90
    .Operator = xlGreaterEqual
End With
```

Valid values for the Operator property are XlGreater or xlGreaterEqual.

> **CAUTION**
>
> With VBA, it is easy to create overlapping ranges such as icon 1 from 0 to 50 and icon 2 from 30 to 90. Even though the Edit Formatting Rule dialog box prevents overlapping ranges, VBA allows them. However, keep in mind that your icon set will display unpredictably if you create invalid ranges.

Using Visualization Tricks

If you use an icon set or a color scale, Excel applies a color to all cells in the dataset. Two tricks in this section enable you to apply an icon set to only a subset of the cells or to apply two different color data bars to the same range. The first trick is available in the user interface, but the second trick is available only in VBA.

Creating an Icon Set for a Subset of a Range

Sometimes, you might want to apply only a red X to the bad cells in a range. This is tricky to do in the user interface.

In the user interface, follow these steps to apply a red X to values greater than or equal to 80:

1. Add a three-symbols icon set to the range.

2. Specify that the symbols should be reversed.

3. Indicate that the red *X* icon appears for values greater than 80 (see Figure 16.6).

Figure 16.6
Add a three-icon set, paying particular attention to the value for the red *X*.

4. Open the drop-down next to the second icon. Choose No Cell Icon.

5. Open the drop-down next to the third icon. Choose No Cell Icon (see Figure 16.7).

Figure 16.7
Change the second and third rule to No Cell Icon.

The code to create this effect in VBA is straightforward. A great deal of the code is spent making sure that the icon set has the red *X* symbols on the cells greater than or equal to 80. To hide the icons for rules two and three, set the `.Icon` property to `xlIconNoCellIcon`.

The code to highlight values greater than or equal to 80 with a red *X* is shown here:

```
Sub TrickyFormatting()
    ' mark the bad cells
    Dim ICS As IconSetCondition
    Dim FC As FormatCondition
    With Range("A1:D9")
        .FormatConditions.Delete
        Set ICS = .FormatConditions.AddIconSetCondition()
    End With
    With ICS
        .ReverseOrder = True
        .ShowIconOnly = False
        .IconSet = ActiveWorkbook.IconSets(xl3Symbols2)
    End With
    ' The threshhold for this icon doesn't really matter,
    ' but you have to make sure that it does not overlap the 3rd icon
```

16

```
With ICS.IconCriteria(2)
    .Type = xlConditionValue
    .Value = 66
    .Operator = xlGreater
    .Icon = xlIconNoCellIcon
End With
' Make sure the red X appears for cells 80 and above
With ICS.IconCriteria(3)
    .Type = xlConditionValue
    .Value = 80
    .Operator = xlGreaterEqual
    .Icon = xlIconNoCellIcon
End With

End Sub
```

Using Two Colors of Data Bars in a Range

This trick is particularly cool because it can be achieved only with VBA. Say that values greater than 90 are acceptable and those 90 and below indicate trouble. You would like acceptable values to have a green bar and others to have a red bar.

Using VBA, you first add the green data bars. Then, without deleting the format condition, you add red data bars.

In VBA, every format condition has a Formula property that defines whether the condition is displayed for a given cell. Therefore, the trick is to write a formula that defines when the green bars are displayed. When the formula is not True, the red bars are allowed to show through.

In Figure 16.8, the effect is being applied to Range A1:D10. You need to write the formula in A1 style, as if it applies to the top-left corner of the selection. The formula needs to evaluate to True or False. Excel automatically copies the formula to all the cells in the range. The formula for this condition is =IF(A1>90,True,False).

> **NOTE** The formula is evaluated relative to the current cell pointer location. Even though it is not usually necessary to select cells before adding a FormatCondition, in this case, selecting the range ensures that the formula will work.

Figure 16.8
The dark bars are red, and the lighter bars are green. VBA was used to create two overlapping data bars, and then the Formula property hid the top bars for cells 90 and below.

	A	B	C	D
1	92	96	81	88
2	88	84	82	99
3	99	85	92	88
4	84	84	82	84
5	90	90	82	99
6	90	80	98	88
7	81	97	81	85
8	89	89	91	93
9	81	94	88	83
10	87	82	86	85
11				

The following code creates the two-color data bars:

```
Sub AddTwoDataBars()
    ' passing values in green, failing in red
    Dim DB As Databar
    Dim DB2 As Databar
    With Range("A1:D10")
        .FormatConditions.Delete
        ' Add a Light Green Data Bar
        Set DB = .FormatConditions.AddDatabar()

        DB.BarColor.Color = RGB(0, 255, 0)
        DB.BarColor.TintAndShade = 0.25
        ' Add a Red Data Bar
        Set DB2 = .FormatConditions.AddDatabar()
        DB2.BarColor.Color = RGB(255, 0, 0)
        ' Make the green bars only
        .Select ' Required to make the next line work
        .FormatConditions(1).Formula = "=IF(A1>90,True,False)"
        DB.Formula = "=IF(A1>90,True,False)"
        DB.MinPoint.Modify newtype:=xlConditionFormula, NewValue:="60"
        DB.MaxPoint.Modify newtype:=xlConditionValueFormula, NewValue:="100"
        DB2.MinPoint.Modify newtype:=xlConditionFormula, NewValue:="60"
        DB2.MaxPoint.Modify newtype:=xlConditionValueFormula, NewValue:="100"
    End With
End Sub
```

The Formula property works for all the conditional formats, which means you could potentially create some obnoxious combinations of data visualizations. In Figure 16.9, five different icon sets are combined in a single range. No one will be able to figure out whether a red flag is worse than a gray down arrow. Even so, this ability opens interesting combinations for those with a little creativity.

Figure 16.9
VBA created this mixture of five different icon sets in a single range. The Formula property in VBA is the key to combining icon sets.

```
Sub AddCrazyIcons()
    With Range("A1:C10")
        .Select ' The .Formula lines below require .Select here
        .FormatConditions.Delete

        ' First icon set
        .FormatConditions.AddIconSetCondition
        .FormatConditions(1).IconSet = ActiveWorkbook.IconSets(xl3Flags)
        .FormatConditions(1).Formula = "=IF(A1<5,TRUE,FALSE)"
```

```
        ' Next icon set
        .FormatConditions.AddIconSetCondition
        .FormatConditions(2).IconSet = ActiveWorkbook.IconSets(xl3ArrowsGray)
        .FormatConditions(2).Formula = "=IF(A1<12,TRUE,FALSE)"

        ' Next icon set
        .FormatConditions.AddIconSetCondition
        .FormatConditions(3).IconSet = ActiveWorkbook.IconSets(xl3Symbols2)
        .FormatConditions(3).Formula = "=IF(A1<22,TRUE,FALSE)"

        ' Next icon set
        .FormatConditions.AddIconSetCondition
        .FormatConditions(4).IconSet = ActiveWorkbook.IconSets(xl4CRV)
        .FormatConditions(4).Formula = "=IF(A1<27,TRUE,FALSE)"

        ' Next icon set
        .FormatConditions.AddIconSetCondition
        .FormatConditions(5).IconSet = ActiveWorkbook.IconSets(xl5CRV)
    End With
End Sub
```

Using Other Conditional Formatting Methods

Although the icon sets, data bars, and color scales get most of the attention, there are still plenty of other uses for conditional formatting.

The remaining examples in this chapter show some of the prior conditional formatting rules and some of the new methods available.

Formatting Cells That Are Above or Below Average

Use the AddAboveAverage method to format cells that are above or below average. After adding the conditional format, specify whether the AboveBelow property is xlAboveAverage or xlBelowAverage.

The following two macros highlight cells above and below average:

```
Sub FormatAboveAverage()
    With Selection
        .FormatConditions.Delete
        .FormatConditions.AddAboveAverage
        .FormatConditions(1).AboveBelow = xlAboveAverage
        .FormatConditions(1).Interior.Color = RGB(255, 0, 0)
    End With
End Sub

Sub FormatBelowAverage()
    With Selection
        .FormatConditions.Delete
        .FormatConditions.AddAboveAverage
        .FormatConditions(1).AboveBelow = xlBelowAverage
        .FormatConditions(1).Interior.Color = RGB(255, 0, 0)
    End With
End Sub
```

Formatting Cells in the Top 10 or Bottom 5

Four of the choices on the Top/Bottom Rules fly-out menu are controlled with the AddTop10 method. After you add the format condition, you need to set three properties that control how the condition is calculated:

- TopBottom—Set this to either xlTop10Top or xlTop10Bottom.
- Rank—Set this to 5 for the top 5, 6 for the top 6, and so on.
- Percent—Set this to False if you want the top 10 items. Set this to True if you want the top 10 percent of the items.

The following code highlights top or bottom cells:

```
Sub FormatTop10Items()
    With Selection
        .FormatConditions.Delete
        .FormatConditions.AddTop10
        .FormatConditions(1).TopBottom = xlTop10Top
        .FormatConditions(1).Rank = 10
        .FormatConditions(1).Percent = False
        .FormatConditions(1).Interior.Color = RGB(255, 0, 0)
    End With
End Sub

Sub FormatBottom5Items()
    With Selection
        .FormatConditions.Delete
        .FormatConditions.AddTop10
        .FormatConditions(1).TopBottom = xlTop10Bottom
        .FormatConditions(1).Rank = 5
        .FormatConditions(1).Percent = False
        .FormatConditions(1).Interior.Color = RGB(255, 0, 0)
    End With
End Sub

Sub FormatTop12Percent()
    With Selection
        .FormatConditions.Delete
        .FormatConditions.AddTop10
        .FormatConditions(1).TopBottom = xlTop10Top
        .FormatConditions(1).Rank = 12
        .FormatConditions(1).Percent = True
        .FormatConditions(1).Interior.Color = RGB(255, 0, 0)
    End With
End Sub
```

Formatting Unique or Duplicate Cells

The Remove Duplicates command on the Data tab of the Ribbon is a destructive command. You might want to mark the duplicates without removing them. If so, the AddUniqueValues method marks the duplicate or unique cells.

After calling the method, set the DupeUnique property to either xlUnique or xlDuplicate.

16

As I rant about in *Excel 2013 In Depth* (Que, ISBN 978-0-7897-4857-7), I do not really like either of these options. Choosing duplicate values marks both cells that contain the duplicate, as shown in Column A of Figure 16.10. For example, both A2 and A8 are marked, when A8 is really the only duplicate value.

Choosing unique values marks only the cells that do not have a duplicate, as shown in Column C of Figure 16.10. This leaves several cells unmarked. For example, none of the cells containing 17 is marked.

Figure 16.10

The AddUnique Values method can mark cells such as those in Columns A and C. Unfortunately, it cannot mark the truly useful pattern in Column E.

As any data analyst knows, the truly useful option would have been to mark the first unique value. In this wishful state, Excel would mark one instance of each unique value. In this case, the 17 in E2 would be marked, but any subsequent cells that contain 17, such as E8, would remain unmarked.

The code to mark duplicates or unique values is shown here:

```
Sub FormatDuplicate()
    With Selection
        .FormatConditions.Delete
        .FormatConditions.AddUniqueValues
        .FormatConditions(1).DupeUnique = xlDuplicate
        .FormatConditions(1).Interior.Color = RGB(255, 0, 0)
    End With
End Sub

Sub FormatUnique()
    With Selection
        .FormatConditions.Delete
        .FormatConditions.AddUniqueValues
        .FormatConditions(1).DupeUnique = xlUnique
        .FormatConditions(1).Interior.Color = RGB(255, 0, 0)
    End With
End Sub

Sub HighlightFirstUnique()
```

```
    With Range("E2:E16")
        .Select
        .FormatConditions.Delete
        .FormatConditions.Add Type:=xlExpression, _
            Formula1:="=COUNTIF(E$2:E2,E2)=1"
        .FormatConditions(1).Interior.Color = RGB(255, 0, 0)
    End With
End Sub
```

Formatting Cells Based on Their Value

The value conditional formats have been around for several versions of Excel. Use the `Add` method with the following arguments:

- `Type`—In this section, the type is `xlCellValue`.

- `Operator`—This can be `xlBetween`, `xlEqual`, `xlGreater`, `xlGreaterEqual`, `xlLess`, `xlLessEqual`, `xlNotBetween`, or `xlNotEqual`.

- `Formula1`—Formula1 is used with each of the operators specified to provide a numeric value.

- `Formula2`—This is used for `xlBetween` and `xlNotBetween`.

The following code sample highlights cells based on their values:

```
Sub FormatBetween10And20()
    With Selection
        .FormatConditions.Delete
        .FormatConditions.Add Type:=xlCellValue, Operator:=xlBetween, _
            Formula1:="=10", Formula2:="=20"
        .FormatConditions(1).Interior.Color = RGB(255, 0, 0)
    End With
End Sub

Sub FormatLessThan15()
    With Selection
        .FormatConditions.Delete
        .FormatConditions.Add Type:=xlCellValue, Operator:=xlLess, _
            Formula1:="=15"
        .FormatConditions(1).Interior.Color = RGB(255, 0, 0)
    End With
End Sub
```

Formatting Cells That Contain Text

When you are trying to highlight cells that contain a certain bit of text, you use the `Add` method, the `xlTextString` type, and an operator of `xlBeginsWith`, `xlContains`, `xlDoesNotContain`, or `xlEndsWith`.

The following code highlights all cells that contain a capital or lower case letter *A*:

```
Sub FormatContainsA()
    With Selection
        .FormatConditions.Delete
        .FormatConditions.Add Type:=xlTextString, String:="A", _
            TextOperator:=xlContains
        ' other choices: xlBeginsWith, xlDoesNotContain, xlEndsWith
```

```
        .FormatConditions(1).Interior.Color = RGB(255, 0, 0)
    End With
End Sub
```

Formatting Cells That Contain Dates

The date conditional formats were new in Excel 2007. The list of available date operators is a subset of the date operators available in the new pivot table filters. Use the Add method, the xlTimePeriod type, and one of these DateOperator values: xlYesterday, xlToday, xlTomorrow, xlLastWeek, xlLast7Days, xlThisWeek, xlNextWeek, xlLastMonth, xlThisMonth, or xlNextMonth.

The following code highlights all dates in the past week:

```
Sub FormatDatesLastWeek()
    With Selection
        .FormatConditions.Delete
        ' DateOperator choices include xlYesterday, xlToday, xlTomorrow,
        ' xlLastWeek, xlThisWeek, xlNextWeek, xlLast7Days
        ' xlLastMonth, xlThisMonth, xlNextMonth,
        .FormatConditions.Add Type:=xlTimePeriod, DateOperator:=xlLastWeek
        .FormatConditions(1).Interior.Color = RGB(255, 0, 0)
    End With
End Sub
```

Formatting Cells That Contain Blanks or Errors

Buried deep within the Excel interface are options to format cells that contain blanks, contain errors, do not contain blanks, or do not contain errors. If you use the macro recorder, Excel uses the complicated xlExpression version of conditional formatting. For example, to look for a blank, Excel tests to see whether the =LEN(TRIM(A1))=0. Instead, you can use any of these four self-explanatory types. You are not required to use any other arguments with these new types:

```
.FormatConditions.Add Type:=xlBlanksCondition
.FormatConditions.Add Type:=xlErrorsCondition
.FormatConditions.Add Type:=xlNoBlanksCondition
.FormatConditions.Add Type:=xlNoErrorsCondition
```

Using a Formula to Determine Which Cells to Format

The most powerful conditional format is still the xlExpression type. In this type, you provide a formula for the active cell that evaluates to True or False. Make sure to write the formula with relative or absolute references so that the formula is correct when Excel copies the formula to the remaining cells in the selection.

An infinite number of conditions can be identified with a formula. Two popular conditions are shown here.

Highlight the First Unique Occurrence of Each Value in a Range

In Column A of Figure 16.11, you would like to highlight the first occurrence of each value in the column. The highlighted cells will then contain a complete list of the unique numbers found in the column.

Figure 16.11
A formula-based condition can mark the first unique occurrence of each value, as shown in Column A, or the entire row with the largest sales, as shown in D:F.

	A	B	C	D	E	F
1	17			Region	Invoice	Sales
2	11			West	1001	112
3	7			East	1002	321
4	7	7 is duplicate of A3		Central	1003	332
5	10			West	1004	596
6	10	10 Is duplicate of A5		East	1005	642
7	17	17 appears in A1		West	1006	700
8	11	11 appears in A2		West	1007	253
9	14			Central	1008	529
10	10	10 is duplicate		East	1009	122
11	12			West	1010	601
12	14	Duplicate of A9		Central	1011	460
13	2			East	1012	878
14	18			West	1013	763
15	4			Central	1014	193
16						

16

The macro should select Cells A1:A15. The formula should be written to return a True or False value for Cell A1. Because Excel logically copies this formula to the entire range, you should use a careful combination of relative and absolute references.

The formula can use the COUNTIF function. Check to see how many times the range from A$1 to A1 contains the value A1. If the result is equal to 1, the condition is True and the cell is highlighted. The first formula is =COUNTIF(A$1:A1,A1)=1. As the formula is copied down to, say A12, the formula changes to =COUNTIF(A$1:A12,A12)=1.

The following macro creates the formatting shown in Column A of Figure 16.11:

```
Sub HighlightFirstUnique()
    With Range("A1:A15")
        .Select
        .FormatConditions.Delete
        .FormatConditions.Add Type:=xlExpression, _
            Formula1:="=COUNTIF(A$1:A1,A1)=1"
        .FormatConditions(1).Interior.Color = RGB(255, 0, 0)
    End With
End Sub
```

Highlight the Entire Row for the Largest Sales Value

Another example of a formula-based condition is when you want to highlight the entire row of a dataset in response to a value in one column. Consider the dataset in Cells D2:F15 of Figure 16.11. If you want to highlight the entire row that contains the largest sale, you select Cells D2:F15 and write a formula that works for Cell D2: =$F2=MAX($F$2:$F$15). The code required to format the row with the largest sales value is as follows:

```
Sub HighlightWholeRow()
    With Range("D2:F15")
        .Select
        .FormatConditions.Delete
        .FormatConditions.Add Type:=xlExpression, _
            Formula1:="=$F2=MAX($F$2:$F$15)"
        .FormatConditions(1).Interior.Color = RGB(255, 0, 0)
    End With
End Sub
```

Using the New NumberFormat Property

In legacy versions of Excel, a cell that matched a conditional format could have a particular font, font color, border, or fill pattern. As of Excel 2007, you can also specify a number format. This can prove useful for selectively changing the number format used to display the values.

For example, you might want to display numbers greater than 999 in thousands, numbers greater than 999,999 in hundred thousands, and numbers greater than 9 million in millions.

If you turn on the macro recorder and attempt to record setting the conditional format to a custom number format, the Excel 2013 VBA macro recorder actually records the action of executing an XL4 macro! Skip the recorded code and use the NumberFormat property as shown here:

```
Sub NumberFormat()
    With Range("E1:G26")
        .FormatConditions.Delete
        .FormatConditions.Add Type:=xlCellValue, Operator:=xlGreater, _
            Formula1:="=9999999"
        .FormatConditions(1).NumberFormat = "$#,##0,""M"""
        .FormatConditions.Add Type:=xlCellValue, Operator:=xlGreater,
            Formula1:="=999999"
        .FormatConditions(2).NumberFormat = "$#,##0.0,""M"""
        .FormatConditions.Add Type:=xlCellValue, Operator:=xlGreater,
            Formula1:="=999"
        .FormatConditions(3).NumberFormat = "$#,##0,K"
    End With
End Sub
```

Figure 16.12 shows the original numbers in Columns A:C. The results of running the macro are shown in Columns E:G. The dialog box shows the resulting conditional format rules.

Figure 16.12
Since Excel 2007, conditional formats have been able to specify a specific number format.

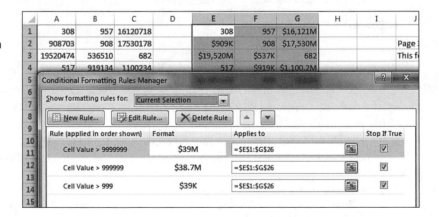

Next Steps

In Chapter 17, you'll find out how to create dashboards from tiny charts called sparklines.

Dashboarding with Sparklines in Excel 2013

One of the new features in Excel 2013 is the ability to create tiny, word-size charts, called sparklines. If you are creating dashboards, you will want to leverage these charts.

The concept of sparklines was first introduced by Professor Edward Tufte. Tufte promoted sparklines as way to show a maximum amount of information with a minimal amount of ink.

Microsoft supports three types of sparklines:

- **Line**—A sparkline shows a single series on a line chart within a single cell. On a sparkline, you can add markers for the highest point, the lowest point, the first point, and the last point. Each of those points can have a different color. You can also choose to mark all the negative points or even all points.

- **Column**—A spark column shows a single series on a column chart. You can choose to show a different color for the first bar, the last bar, the lowest bar, the highest bar, and/or all negative points.

- **Win/Loss**—This is a special type of column chart in which every positive point is plotted at a 100% height and every negative point is plotted as –100% height. The theory is that positive columns represent wins and negative columns represent losses. With these charts you will always want to change the color of the negative columns. It is possible to highlight the highest/lowest point based on the underlying data.

Creating Sparklines

Microsoft figures that you will usually be creating a group of sparklines. The main VBA object for sparklines is the `SparklineGroup`. To create sparklines,

17

you apply the `SparklineGroups.Add` method to the range where you want the sparklines to appear.

In the `Add` method, you specify a type for the sparkline and the location of the source data.

Say that you apply the `Add` method to a three-cell range of B2:D2. Then the source must be a range that is either three columns wide or three rows tall.

The `Type` parameter can be `xlSparkLine` for a line, `xlSparkColumn` for a column, or `xlSpark-Column100` for win/loss.

If the `SourceData` parameter is referring to ranges on the current worksheet, it can be as simple as `"D3:F100"`. If it is pointing to another worksheet, use `"Data!D3:F100"` or `"'My Data'!D3:F100"`. If you've defined a named range, you can specify the name of the range as the source data.

Figure 17.1 shows a table of NASDAQ closing prices for three years. Notice that the actual data for the sparklines is in three contiguous columns, D, E, and F.

Figure 17.1

Arrange the data for the sparklines in a contiguous range.

⊿	A	B	C	D	E	F
1	Date 2009	Date 2010	Date 2011	Close 2009	Close 2010	Close 2011
2	1/2/2009	1/4/2010	1/3/2011	1632.21	2308.42	2691.52
3	1/5/2009	1/5/2010	1/4/2011	1628.03	2308.71	2681.25
4	1/6/2009	1/6/2010	1/5/2011	1652.38	2301.09	2702.2
5	1/7/2009	1/7/2010	1/6/2011	1599.06	2300.05	2709.89
6	1/8/2009	1/8/2010	1/7/2011	1617.01	2317.17	2703.17
7	1/9/2009	1/11/2010	1/10/2011	1571.59	2312.41	2707.8
8	1/12/2009	1/12/2010	1/11/2011	1538.79	2282.31	2716.83

In this example, the data is on the Data worksheet and the sparklines are created on the Dashboard worksheet. The WSD object variable is used for the Data worksheet. WSL is used for the Dashboard worksheet.

Because each column might have one or two extra points, the code to find the final row is slightly different than usual:

```
FinalRow = WSD.[A1].CurrentRegion.Rows.Count
```

The `.CurrentRegion` property starts from Cell A1 and extends in all directions until it hits the edge of the worksheet or the edge of the data.

In this case, the `CurrentRegion` reports that row 253 is the final row.

For this example, the sparklines are created in a row of three cells. Because each cell is showing 252 points, I am going with fairly large sparklines. The sparkline grows to the size of the cell, so this code makes each cell fairly wide and tall:

```
With WSL.Range("B1:D1")
    .Value = array(2009,2010,2011)
    .HorizontalAlignment = xlCenter
    .Style = "Title"
    .ColumnWidth = 39
```

```
    .Offset(1, 0).RowHeight = 100
End With
```

The following code creates three default sparklines. These won't be perfect, but the next section shows how to format them.

```
Dim SG as SparklineGroup
Set SG = WSL.Range("B2:D2").SparklineGroups.Add( _
    Type:=xlSparkLine, _
    SourceData:="Data!D2:F" & FinalRow)
```

The three sparklines are shown in Figure 17.2. There are a number of problems with the default sparklines. Think about the vertical axis of a chart. Sparklines always default to have the scale automatically selected. Because you never really get to see what the scale is, you cannot tell the range of the chart.

Figure 17.2
Three default sparklines.

Gaps because vertical scales are different

Figure 17.3 shows the min and max for each year. From this data, you can guess that the sparkline for 2009 probably goes from about 1250 to 2300. The sparkline for 2010 probably goes from 2075 to 2675. The sparkline for 2011 probably goes from 2325 to 2875.

Figure 17.3
Each sparkline assigns the minimum and maximum scale to be just outside of these limits.

	A	B	C	D	E	F
1	Date 2009	Date 2010	Date 2011	Close 2009	Close 2010	Close 2011
253	12/31/2009	12/31/2010	12/30/2011	2269.15	2652.87	2605.15
254						
255			Min	1,269	2,092	2,336
256			Max	2,291	2,671	2,874
257						

Scaling Sparklines

The default choice for the sparkline vertical axis is that each sparkline has a different minimum and maximum. There are two other choices available.

One choice is to group all the sparklines together, but to continue to allow Excel to choose the minimum and maximum scale. You still won't know exactly what values are chosen for the minimum and maximum.

To force the sparklines to have the same automatic scale, use this code:

```
' Allow automatic axis scale, but all three of them the same
```

```
With SG.Axes.Vertical
    .MinScaleType = xlSparkScaleGroup
    .MaxScaleType = xlSparkScaleGroup
End With
```

Note that `.Axes` belongs to the sparkline group, not to the individual sparklines themselves. In fact, almost all the good properties are applied at the `SparklineGroup` level. This has some interesting ramifications. If you wanted one sparkline to have automatic scale and another sparkline to have a fixed scale, you would have to create each of those sparklines separately, or at least ungroup them.

Figure 17.4 shows the sparklines when both the minimum and the maximum scales are set to act as a group. All three lines nearly meet now, which is a good sign. You can guess that the scale runs from about 1250 up to perhaps 2900. Again, there is no way to tell. The solution is to use the Custom Value for both the Minimum and Maximum axis.

Figure 17.4

All three sparklines have the same minimum and maximum scale, but we don't know what it is.

Another choice is to take absolute control and assign a minimum and maximum for the vertical axis scale. The following code forces the sparklines to run from a minimum of 0 up to a maximum that rounds up to the next 100 above the largest value:

```
Set AF = Application.WorksheetFunction
AllMin = AF.Min(WSD.Range("D2:F" & FinalRow))
AllMax = AF.Max(WSD.Range("D2:F" & FinalRow))
AllMin = Int(AllMin)
AllMax = Int(AllMax + 0.9)
With SG.Axes.Vertical
    .MinScaleType = xlSparkScaleCustom
    .MaxScaleType = xlSparkScaleCustom
    .CustomMinScaleValue = AllMin
    .CustomMaxScaleValue = AllMax
End With
```

Figure 17.5 shows the resulting sparklines. Now, *you* know the minimum and the maximum, but you need a way to communicate this to the reader.

Figure 17.5

You've manually assigned a min and max scale, but it does not appear on the chart.

One method is to put the minimum and maximum value in A2. With 8-point bold Calibri, a row height of 113 allows 10 rows of wrapped text in the cell. So you could put the max value, then `vbLf` eight times, then the min value. (`vbLf` is the equivalent of pressing Alt+Enter when you are entering values in a cell.)

On the right side, you can put the final point's value and attempt to position it within the cell so that it falls roughly at the same height as the final point.

Figure 17.6 shows this option.

Figure 17.6
Labels on the left show the min and max. Labels on the right show the final value.

The code to produce Figure 17.6 is shown here:

```
Sub NASDAQMacro()
' NASDAQMacro Macro
'
Dim SG As SparklineGroup
Dim SL As Sparkline
Dim WSD As Worksheet ' Data worksheet
Dim WSL As Worksheet ' Dashboard

    On Error Resume Next
    Application.DisplayAlerts = False
    Worksheets("Dashboard").Delete
    On Error GoTo 0

    Set WSD = Worksheets("Data")
    Set WSL = ActiveWorkbook.Worksheets.Add
    WSL.Name = "Dashboard"

    FinalRow = WSD.Cells(1, 1).CurrentRegion.Rows.Count
    WSD.Cells(2, 4).Resize(FinalRow - 1, 3).Name = "MyData"

    WSL.Select
    ' Set up Headings
    With WSL.Range("B1:D1")
        .Value = Array(2009, 2010, 2011)
        .HorizontalAlignment = xlCenter
        .Style = "Title"
        .ColumnWidth = 39
        .Offset(1, 0).RowHeight = 100
    End With
```

```vba
    Set SG = WSL.Range("B2:D2").SparklineGroups.Add( _
        Type:=xlSparkLine, _
        SourceData:="Data!D2:F250")

    Set SL = SG.Item(1)

    Set AF = Application.WorksheetFunction
    AllMin = AF.Min(WSD.Range("D2:F" & FinalRow))
    AllMax = AF.Max(WSD.Range("D2:F" & FinalRow))
    AllMin = Int(AllMin)
    AllMax = Int(AllMax + 0.9)


    ' Allow automatic axis scale, but all three of them the same
    With SG.Axes.Vertical
        .MinScaleType = xlSparkScaleCustom
        .MaxScaleType = xlSparkScaleCustom
        .CustomMinScaleValue = AllMin
        .CustomMaxScaleValue = AllMax
    End With

    ' Add two labels to show minimum and maximum
    With WSL.Range("A2")
        .Value = AllMax & vbLf & vbLf & vbLf & vbLf _
            & vbLf & vbLf & vbLf & vbLf & AllMin
        .HorizontalAlignment = xlRight
        .VerticalAlignment = xlTop
        .Font.Size = 8
        .Font.Bold = True
        .WrapText = True
    End With

    ' Put the final value on the right
    FinalVal = Round(WSD.Cells(Rows.Count, 6).End(xlUp).Value, 0)
    Rg = AllMax - AllMin
    RgTenth = Rg / 10
    FromTop = AllMax - FinalVal
    FromTop = Round(FromTop / RgTenth, 0) - 1
    If FromTop < 0 Then FromTop = 0

    Select Case FromTop
        Case 0
            RtLabel = FinalVal
        Case Is > 0
            RtLabel = Application.WorksheetFunction. _
                Rept(vbLf, FromTop) & FinalVal
    End Select

    With WSL.Range("E2")
        .Value = RtLabel
        .HorizontalAlignment = xlLeft
        .VerticalAlignment = xlTop
        .Font.Size = 8
        .Font.Bold = True
    End With
End Sub
```

Formatting Sparklines

Most of the formatting available with sparklines involves setting the color of various elements of the sparkline.

There are a few methods for assigning colors in Excel 2013. Before diving into the sparkline properties, you can read about the two methods of assigning colors in Excel VBA.

Using Theme Colors

Excel 2007 introduced the concept of a theme for a workbook. A theme is composed of a body font, a headline font, a series of effects, and then a series of colors.

The first four colors are used for text and backgrounds. The next six colors are the accent colors. The 20-plus built-in themes include colors that work well together. There are also two colors used for hyperlinks and followed hyperlinks. For now, focus on the accent colors.

Go to Page Layout, Themes, and choose a theme. Next to the theme drop-down is a Colors drop-down. Open that drop-down and select Create New Theme Colors from the bottom of the drop-down. Excel shows the Create New Theme Colors dialog, as shown in Figure 17.7. This gives you a good picture of the 12 colors associated with the theme.

17

Figure 17.7
The current theme includes 12 colors.

Throughout Excel, there are many color chooser drop-downs (see Figure 17.8). There is a section of the drop-down called Theme Colors. The top row under Theme Colors shows the four font and six accent colors.

Figure 17.8
All but the hyperlink colors from the theme appear across the top row.

If you want to choose the last color in the first row, the VBA is as follows:

```
ActiveCell.Font.ThemeColor = xlThemeColorAccent6
```

Going across that top row of Figure 17.8, the 10 colors are as follows:

```
xlThemeColorDark1
xlThemeColorLight1
xlThemeColorDark2
xlThemeColorLight2
xlThemeColorAccent1
xlThemeColorAccent2
xlThemeColorAccent3
xlThemeColorAccent4
xlThemeColorAccent5
xlThemeColorAccent6
```

> **CAUTION**
>
> Note that the first four colors seem to be reversed. xlThemeColorDark1 is a white color. This is because the VBA constants were written from the point of view of the font color to use when the cell contains a dark or light background. If you have a cell filled with a dark color, you would want to display a white font. Hence, xlThemeColorDark1 is white and xlThemeColorLight1 is black.

On your computer, open the Fill drop-down on the Home tab and look at it in color. If you are using the Office theme, the last column is various shades of green. The top row is the actual color from the theme.

There are then five rows that go from a light green to a very dark green.

Excel lets you modify the theme color by lightening or darkening it. The values range from –1, which is very dark, to +1, which is very light. If you look at the very light green in Row 2 of Figure 17.8, that has a tint and shade value of 0.8, which is almost completely light. The next row has a tint and shade level of 0.6. The next row has a tint and shade level of 0.4. That gives you three choices that are lighter than the theme color.

The next two rows are darker than the theme color. Because there are only two darker rows, they have values of –.25 and –.5.

If you turn on the macro recorder and choose one of these colors, it looks like a confusing bunch of code.

```
.Pattern = xlSolid
.PatternColorIndex = xlAutomatic
.ThemeColor = xlThemeColorAccent6
.TintAndShade = 0.799981688894314
.PatternTintAndShade = 0
```

If you are using a solid fill, you can leave out the first, second, and fifth lines of code. The .TintAndShade looks confusing because computers cannot round decimal tenths very well. Remember that computers store numbers in binary. In binary, a simple number like 0.1 is a repeating decimal. As the macro recorder tries to convert 0.8 from binary to decimal, it "misses" by a bit and comes up with a very close number: 0.7998168894314. This is really saying that it should be 80 percent lighter than the base number.

If you are writing code by hand, you only have to assign two values to use a theme color. Assign the .ThemeColor property to one of the six xlThemeColorAccent1 through xlTheme ColorAccent6 values. If you want to use a theme color from the top row of the drop-down, the .TintAndShade should be 0 and can be omitted. If you want to lighten the color, use a positive decimal for .TintAndShade. If you want to darken the color, use a negative decimal.

> **TIP**
> Note that the five shades in the color palette drop-downs are not the complete set of variations. In VBA, you can assign any two-digit decimal value from -1.00 to +1.00. Figure 17.9 shows 201 variations of one theme color created using the .TintAndShade property in VBA.

Figure 17.9
Two hundred shades of one theme color.

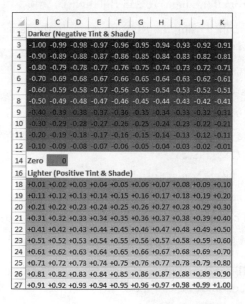

	B	C	D	E	F	G	H	I	J	K
1	Darker (Negative Tint & Shade)									
3	-1.00	-0.99	-0.98	-0.97	-0.96	-0.95	-0.94	-0.93	-0.92	-0.91
4	-0.90	-0.89	-0.88	-0.87	-0.86	-0.85	-0.84	-0.83	-0.82	-0.81
5	-0.80	-0.79	-0.78	-0.77	-0.76	-0.75	-0.74	-0.73	-0.72	-0.71
6	-0.70	-0.69	-0.68	-0.67	-0.66	-0.65	-0.64	-0.63	-0.62	-0.61
7	-0.60	-0.59	-0.58	-0.57	-0.56	-0.55	-0.54	-0.53	-0.52	-0.51
8	-0.50	-0.49	-0.48	-0.47	-0.46	-0.45	-0.44	-0.43	-0.42	-0.41
9	-0.40	-0.39	-0.38	-0.37	-0.36	-0.35	-0.34	-0.33	-0.32	-0.31
10	-0.30	-0.29	-0.28	-0.27	-0.26	-0.25	-0.24	-0.23	-0.22	-0.21
11	-0.20	-0.19	-0.18	-0.17	-0.16	-0.15	-0.14	-0.13	-0.12	-0.11
12	-0.10	-0.09	-0.08	-0.07	-0.06	-0.05	-0.04	-0.03	-0.02	-0.01
14	Zero		0							
16	Lighter (Positive Tint & Shade)									
18	+0.01	+0.02	+0.03	+0.04	+0.05	+0.06	+0.07	+0.08	+0.09	+0.10
19	+0.11	+0.12	+0.13	+0.14	+0.15	+0.16	+0.17	+0.18	+0.19	+0.20
20	+0.21	+0.22	+0.23	+0.24	+0.25	+0.26	+0.27	+0.28	+0.29	+0.30
21	+0.31	+0.32	+0.33	+0.34	+0.35	+0.36	+0.37	+0.38	+0.39	+0.40
22	+0.41	+0.42	+0.43	+0.44	+0.45	+0.46	+0.47	+0.48	+0.49	+0.50
23	+0.51	+0.52	+0.53	+0.54	+0.55	+0.56	+0.57	+0.58	+0.59	+0.60
24	+0.61	+0.62	+0.63	+0.64	+0.65	+0.66	+0.67	+0.68	+0.69	+0.70
25	+0.71	+0.72	+0.73	+0.74	+0.75	+0.76	+0.77	+0.78	+0.79	+0.80
26	+0.81	+0.82	+0.83	+0.84	+0.85	+0.86	+0.87	+0.88	+0.89	+0.90
27	+0.91	+0.92	+0.93	+0.94	+0.95	+0.96	+0.97	+0.98	+0.99	+1.00

17

To recap, if you want to work with theme colors, you generally change two properties: the theme color, in order to choose one of the six accent colors, and then tint and shade, to lighten or darken the base color:

```
.ThemeColor = xlThemeColorAccent6
.TintAndShade = 0.4
```

> **NOTE** Note that one advantage of using theme colors is that your sparklines change color based on the theme. If you later decide to switch from the Office theme to the Metro theme, the colors change to match the theme.

Using RGB Colors

For the past decade, computers have offered a palette of 16 million colors. These colors derive from adjusting the amount of red, green, and blue light in a cell.

Do you remember back in art class in elementary school? You probably learned that the three primary colors were red, yellow, and blue. You could make green by mixing some yellow and blue paint. You could make purple by mixing some red and blue paint. You could make orange by mixing some yellow and red paint. As all of my male classmates and I soon discovered, you could make black by mixing all the paint colors. Those rules all work with pigments in paint, but they don't work with light.

Those pixels on your computer screen are made of up light. In the light spectrum, the three primary colors are red, green, and blue. You can make the 16 million colors of the RGB color palette by mixing various amounts of red, green, and blue light. Each of the three colors is assigned an intensity from 0 (no light) to 255 (full light).

You will often see a color described using the RGB function. In the function, the first value is the amount of red, then green, then blue.

- To make red, you use =RGB(255,0,0).
- To make green, use =RGB(0,255,0).
- To make blue, use =RGB(0,0,255).
- What happens if you mix 100% of all three colors of light? You get white!
- To make white, use =RGB(255,255,255).
- If you shine no light in a pixel? You get black: =RGB(0,0,0).
- To make purple, it is some red, a little green, and some blue: RGB(139,65,123).
- To make yellow, use full red and green and no blue: =RGB(255,255,0).
- To make orange, use less green than the yellow: =RGB(255,153,0).

In VBA, you can use the RGB function just as it is shown here. The macro recorder is not a big fan of using the RGB function. It instead shows the result of the RGB function.

You can assign a number to each of the 16,777,216 colors by doing this math with the three RGB values:

- Take the red value times 1.
- Add the green value times 256.
- Add the blue value times 65,536.

> **NOTE**
>
> In case you were wondering, 65,536 is 256 raised to the second power.

If you choose a red for your sparkline, you frequently see the macro recorder assign a `.Color = 255`. This is because `=RGB(255,0,0)` is 255.

When the macro recorder assigns a value of 5287936, it is pretty tough to figure out that color. Here are the steps I use:

1. In Excel, enter **=Dec2Hex(5287936)**. You get an answer of 50B000. This is the color that web designers refer to as #50B000.

2. Go to your favorite search engine and search for "color chooser." You can find many utilities where you can type in the hex color code and see the color. Type in **50B000**.

In Figure 17.10, ColorSchemer.com shows that #50B000 is RGB(80,176,0). This is a somewhat dark green color.

Figure 17.10
Convert hex to RGB.

17

While you are at the web page, you can click around to find other shades of colors and see the RGB values for those.

To recap, to skip theme colors and use RGB colors, you set the `.Color` property to the result of an RGB function.

Formatting Sparkline Elements

Figure 17.11 shows a plain sparkline. The data is created from 12 points that show performance versus a budget. You really have no idea about the scale from this sparkline.

Figure 17.11
A default sparkline.

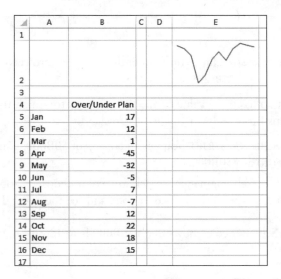

	A	B	C	D	E
1					
2					
3					
4		Over/Under Plan			
5	Jan	17			
6	Feb	12			
7	Mar	1			
8	Apr	-45			
9	May	-32			
10	Jun	-5			
11	Jul	7			
12	Aug	-7			
13	Sep	12			
14	Oct	22			
15	Nov	18			
16	Dec	15			
17					

If your sparkline includes both positive and negative numbers, it helps to show the horizontal axis so that you can figure out which points are above budget and which points are below budget.

To show the axis, use the following:

```
SG.Axes.Horizontal.Axis.Visible = True
```

Figure 17.12 shows the horizontal axis. This helps to show which months were above or below budget.

Figure 17.12
Add the horizontal axis to show which months were above or below budget.

Using code from "Scaling Sparklines," you can add high and low labels to the cell to the left of the sparkline:

```
Set AF = Application.WorksheetFunction
MyMax = AF.Max(Range("B5:B16"))
MyMin = AF.Min(Range("B5:B16"))
LabelStr = MyMax & vbLf & vbLf & vbLf & vbLf & MyMin

With SG.Axes.Vertical
    .MinScaleType = xlSparkScaleCustom
    .MaxScaleType = xlSparkScaleCustom
    .CustomMinScaleValue = MyMin
    .CustomMaxScaleValue = MyMax
End With

With Range("D2")
    .WrapText = True
    .Font.Size = 8
    .HorizontalAlignment = xlRight
    .VerticalAlignment = xlTop
    .Value = LabelStr
    .RowHeight = 56.25
End With
```

The result of this macro is shown in Figure 17.13.

Figure 17.13
Use a nonsparkline feature to label the vertical axis.

To change the color of the sparkline, use this:

```
SG.SeriesColor.Color = RGB(255, 191, 0)
```

The Show group of the Sparkline Tools Design tab offers six options. You can further modify those elements by using the Marker Color drop-down.

You can choose to turn on a marker for every point in the data set, as shown in Figure 17.14.

Figure 17.14
Show All Markers.

The code to show a black marker at every point is as follows:

```
With SG.Points
    .Markers.Color.Color = RGB(0, 0, 0) ' black
    .Markers.Visible = True
End With
```

Instead, you can use the markers to show only the minimum, maximum, first, and last points. The following code shows the minimum in red, maximum in green, first and last in blue:

```
With SG.Points
    .Lowpoint.Color.Color = RGB(255, 0, 0) ' red
    .Highpoint.Color.Color = RGB(51, 204, 77) ' Green
    .Firstpoint.Color.Color = RGB(0, 0, 255) ' Blue
    .Lastpoint.Color.Color = RGB(0, 0, 255) ' blue
    .Negative.Color.Color = RGB(127, 0, 0) ' pink
    .Markers.Color.Color = RGB(0, 0, 0) ' black
    ' Choose Which points to Show
    .Highpoint.Visible = True
    .Lowpoint.Visible = True
    .Firstpoint.Visible = True
    .Lowpoint.Visible = True
    .Negative.Visible = False
    .Markers.Visible = False
End With
```

Figure 17.15 shows the sparkline with the only the high, low, first, and last chosen.

17

Figure 17.15
Show only key markers.

One other element is the negative markers. These are particularly handy when you are formatting win/loss charts.

Formatting Win/Loss Charts

Win/loss charts are a special type of sparkline for tracking binary events. The win/loss chart shows an upward-facing marker for a positive value and a downward-facing marker for any negative value. For a zero, no marker is shown.

You can use these charts to track proposal wins versus losses. In Figure 17.16, a win/loss chart shows the last 25 regular-season baseball games of the famed 1951 pennant race between the Brooklyn Dodgers and the New York Giants. This chart shows how the Giants went on a seven-game winning streak to finish the regular season. The Dodgers went 3–4 during this period and ended in a tie with the Giants, forcing a three-game playoff. The Giants won the first game, lost the second, and then advanced to the World Series by winning the third playoff game. The Giants leapt out to a 2–1 lead over the Yankees but then lost three straight.

Figure 17.16
This win/loss chart documents the most famous pennant race in history.

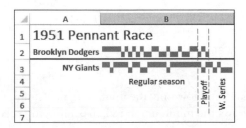

NOTE The words *Regular season*, *Playoff*, and *W. Series*, as well as the two dotted lines, are not part of the sparkline. The lines are drawing objects manually added with Insert, Shapes.

To create the chart, you use .Add a SparkLineGroup with a type of xlSparkColumnStacked100:

```
Set SG = Range("B2:B3").SparklineGroups.Add( _
    Type:=xlSparkColumnStacked100, _
    SourceData:="C2:AD3")
```

You generally show the wins and losses as different colors. One obvious color scheme is red for losses and green for wins.

There is no specific way to change only the "up" markers, so change the color of all markers to be green:

```
' Show all points as green
SG.SeriesColor.Color = 5287936
```

Then change the color of the negative markers to red:

```
'Show losses as red
With SG.Points.Negative
    .Visible = True
    .Color.Color = 255
End With
```

It is easier to create the up/down charts. You don't have to worry about setting the line color. The vertical axis is always fixed.

Creating a Dashboard

Sparklines have the benefit of communicating a lot of information in a very tiny space. In this section, you'll see how to fit 130 charts on one page.

Figure 17.17 shows a data set that summarizes a 1.8-million-row dataset. I used the PowerPivot add-in for Excel to import the records and then calculated three new measures:

- YTD sales by month by store
- YTD sales by month for the previous year
- % increase of YTD sales versus the previous year

This is a key statistic in retail stores—how are you doing now versus the same time last year? Also, this analysis has the benefit of being cumulative. The final number for December represents whether the store was up or down versus the previous year.

Figure 17.17
This summary of 1.8 million records is a sea of numbers.

	A	B	C	D	E	F	G	H	I	J	K	L	M
1	YTD Sales – % Change from Previous Year												
2													
3	Store	Jan	Feb	Mar	Apr	May	Jun	Jul	Aug	Sep	Oct	Nov	Dec
4	Sherman (	1.9%	-1.3%	-0.8%	-0.2%	-0.1%	-0.1%	0.2%	-0.1%	0.0%	0.7%	0.4%	1.1%
5	Brea Mall	6.3%	-0.5%	-0.2%	0.1%	0.1%	-0.8%	-0.1%	-0.7%	-0.5%	-0.3%	-0.5%	0.1%
6	Park Place	4.4%	-0.8%	-0.4%	-0.5%	-0.4%	-0.4%	-0.3%	-0.8%	-0.9%	-0.6%	-1.1%	-1.5%
7	Galleria at	-0.3%	-3.5%	-3.2%	-1.8%	-1.0%	-0.8%	-0.5%	-0.4%	-0.5%	-0.2%	-0.8%	-1.4%
8	Mission V	7.3%	-0.1%	-1.2%	-0.8%	-0.2%	-0.3%	0.0%	0.0%	-0.2%	-0.3%	0.1%	0.1%

Observations About Sparklines

After working with sparklines for a while, some observations come to mind:

■ Sparklines are transparent. You can see through to the underlying cell. This means that the fill color of the underlying cell shows through and the text in the underlying cell shows through.

■ If you make the font really small and align the text with the edge of the cell, you can make the text look like a title or a legend.

■ If you turn on wrap text and make the cell tall enough for 5 or 10 lines of text in the cell, you can control the position of the text in the cell by using vbLf characters in VBA.

■ Sparklines work better when they are bigger than a typical cell. All the examples in this chapter made the column wider, the height taller, or both.

■ Sparklines created together are grouped. Changes made to one sparkline are made to all sparklines.

■ Sparklines can be created on a worksheet separate from the data.

■ Sparklines look better when there is some white space around the cells. This would be tough to do manually because you would have to create each sparkline one at a time. It is easy to do here because you can leverage VBA.

Creating Hundreds of Individual Sparklines in a Dashboard

All those issues can be taken into account when you are creating this dashboard. The plan is to create each store's sparkline individually. This allows a blank row and column to appear between every sparkline.

After inserting a new worksheet for the dashboard, you can format the cells with this code:

```
' Set up the dashboard as alternating cells for sparkline then blank
For c = 1 To 11 Step 2
    WSL.Cells(1, c).ColumnWidth = 15
    WSL.Cells(1, c + 1).ColumnWidth = 0.6
Next c
For r = 1 To 45 Step 2
    WSL.Cells(r, 1).RowHeight = 38
    WSL.Cells(r + 1, 1).RowHeight = 3
Next r
```

Keep track of which cell contains the next sparkline with two variables:

```
NextRow = 1
NextCol = 1
```

Figure out how many rows of data there are on the Data worksheet. Loop from row 4 to the final row. For each row, you make a sparkline.

Build a text string that points back to the correct row on the data sheet using this code. Use that source when defining the sparkline:

```
ThisSource = "Data!B" & i & ":M" & i
Set SG = WSL.Cells(NextRow, NextCol).SparklineGroups.Add( _
    Type:=xlSparkColumn, _
    SourceData:=ThisSource)
```

You want to show a horizontal axis at the zero location. The range of values for all stores was –5 percent to +10 percent. The maximum scale value here is being set to 0.15 (which is equivalent to 15 percent) to allow extra room for the "title" in the cell:

```
SG.Axes.Horizontal.Axis.Visible = True
With SG.Axes.Vertical
    .MinScaleType = xlSparkScaleCustom
    .MaxScaleType = xlSparkScaleCustom
    .CustomMinScaleValue = -0.05
    .CustomMaxScaleValue = 0.15
End With
```

As in the previous example with the win/loss chart, you want the positive columns to be green and the negative columns to be red:

```
' All columns green
SG.SeriesColor.Color = RGB(0, 176, 80)
' Negative columns red
SG.Points.Negative.Visible = True
SG.Points.Negative.Color.Color = RGB(255, 0, 0)
```

Remember that the sparkline has a transparent background. Thus, you can write really small text to the cell, and it behaves almost like chart labels.

The following code joins the store name and the final percentage change for the year into a title for the chart. The program writes this title to the cell but makes it small, centered, and vertically aligned.

```
ThisStore = WSD.Cells(i, 1).Value & " " & _
    Format(WSD.Cells(i, 13), "+0.0%;-0.0%;0%")
' Add a label
With WSL.Cells(NextRow, NextCol)
    .Value = ThisStore
    .HorizontalAlignment = xlCenter
    .VerticalAlignment = xlTop
    .Font.Size = 8
    .WrapText = True
End With
```

The final element is to change the background color of the cell based on the final percentage. If it is up, the background is light green; if it is down, the background is light red:

```
FinalVal = WSD.Cells(i, 13)
```

17

```
' Color the cell light red for negative, light green for positive
With WSL.Cells(NextRow, NextCol).Interior
    If FinalVal <= 0 Then
        .Color = 255
        .TintAndShade = 0.9
    Else
        .Color = 14743493
        .TintAndShade = 0.7
    End If
End With
```

After that sparkline is done, the column and/or row positions are incremented to prepare for the next chart:

```
NextCol = NextCol + 2
If NextCol > 11 Then
    NextCol = 1
    NextRow = NextRow + 2
End If
```

After this, the loop continues with the next store.

The complete code is shown here:

```
Sub StoreDashboard()
Dim SG As SparklineGroup
Dim SL As Sparkline
Dim WSD As Worksheet ' Data worksheet
Dim WSL As Worksheet ' Dashboard

    On Error Resume Next
    Application.DisplayAlerts = False
    Worksheets("Dashboard").Delete
    On Error GoTo 0

    Set WSD = Worksheets("Data")
    Set WSL = ActiveWorkbook.Worksheets.Add
    WSL.Name = "Dashboard"

    ' Set up the dashboard as alternating cells for sparkline then blank
    For c = 1 To 11 Step 2
        WSL.Cells(1, c).ColumnWidth = 15
        WSL.Cells(1, c + 1).ColumnWidth = 0.6
    Next c
    For r = 1 To 45 Step 2
        WSL.Cells(r, 1).RowHeight = 38
        WSL.Cells(r + 1, 1).RowHeight = 3
    Next r

    NextRow = 1
    NextCol = 1

    FinalRow = WSD.Cells(Rows.Count, 1).End(xlUp).Row
```

```
    For i = 4 To FinalRow
        ThisStore = WSD.Cells(i, 1).Value & " " & _
            Format(WSD.Cells(i, 13), "+0.0%;-0.0%;0%")
        ThisSource = "Data!B" & i & ":M" & i
        FinalVal = WSD.Cells(i, 13)

        Set SG = WSL.Cells(NextRow, NextCol).SparklineGroups.Add( _
            Type:=xlSparkColumn, _
            SourceData:=ThisSource)

        SG.Axes.Horizontal.Axis.Visible = True
        With SG.Axes.Vertical
            .MinScaleType = xlSparkScaleCustom
            .MaxScaleType = xlSparkScaleCustom
            .CustomMinScaleValue = -0.05
            .CustomMaxScaleValue = 0.15
        End With

        ' All columns green
        SG.SeriesColor.Color = RGB(0, 176, 80)
        ' Negative columns red
        SG.Points.Negative.Visible = True
        SG.Points.Negative.Color.Color = RGB(255, 0, 0)

        ' Add a label
        With WSL.Cells(NextRow, NextCol)
            .Value = ThisStore
            .HorizontalAlignment = xlCenter
            .VerticalAlignment = xlTop
            .Font.Size = 8
            .WrapText = True
        End With

        ' Color the cell light red for negative, light green for positive
        With WSL.Cells(NextRow, NextCol).Interior
            If FinalVal <= 0 Then
                .Color = 255
                .TintAndShade = 0.9
            Else
                .Color = 14743493
                .TintAndShade = 0.7
            End If
        End With

        NextCol = NextCol + 2
        If NextCol > 11 Then
            NextCol = 1
            NextRow = NextRow + 2
        End If
    Next i
End Sub
```

Figure 17.18 shows the final dashboard. This prints on a single page and summarizes 1.8 million rows of data.

Figure 17.18
One page summarizes the sales from hundreds of stores.

	A	B	C	D	E	F	G	H	I	J	K	L
1	Sherman Oaks Fashion Square +1.1%		Brea Mall +0.1%		Park Place -1.5%		Galleria at Roseville - 1.4%		Mission Viejo Mall +0.1%		Corona Del Mar Plaza +0.4%	
3	San Francisco Center - 0.5%		Kierland Commons - 0.1%		Scottsdale Fashion Square -1.2%		Valley Fair -0.5%		Bellevue Square -0.3%		Perimeter Mall +0.3%	
5	Paseo Nuevo +0.6%		Topanga Plaza -0.2%		Broadway Plaza +0.2%		The Promenade Westlake -0.1%		Keystone -0.5%		Woodfield Mall -0.8%	
7	Country Club Plaza - 0.4%		Kenwood Towne Centre +0.1%		Easton Town Center +0.2%		International Plaza +1.0%		Paseo -1.2%		The Wellington Green -0.8%	

If you zoom in, you can see that every cell tells a story. In Figure 17.19, Park Meadows had a great January, managed to stay ahead of last year through the entire year, and finished up 0.8 percent. Lakeside also had a positive January, but then a bad February and a worse March. They struggled back toward 0 percent for the rest of the year but ended up down seven-tenths of a percent.

> **NOTE**
> The report is addictive. I find myself studying all sorts of trends, but then I have to remind myself that I created the 1.8-million-row dataset using RandBetween just a few weeks ago! The report is so compelling that I am getting drawn into studying fictional data.

Figure 17.19
Detail of two sparkline charts.

Park Meadows +0.8%

Lakeside -0.7%

Next Steps

In Chapter 18, "Reading from and Writing to the Web," you'll learn how to use web queries to import data from the Internet to your Excel applications automatically.

Reading from and Writing to the Web

The Internet has become pervasive and has changed our lives. From your desktop, millions of answers are available at your fingertips. In addition, publishing a report on the Web enables millions of others to instantly access your information.

This chapter discusses automated ways to pull data from the Web into spreadsheets, using web queries. You'll find out how to use VBA to call a website repeatedly to gather information for many data points. It also shows how to save data from your spreadsheet directly to the Web.

Getting Data from the Web

There is an endless variety of data on the Internet. You can gather stock quotes from Quotes.com. You can download historical temperatures from Weather Underground. You can get fantasy football stats from NFL.com. Whatever your interest, there is probably a website somewhere with that information online.

Sometimes the websites make it difficult by putting the information on many different pages. You can use VBA to automate the process of visiting all those pages and collecting the data.

Instead of manually downloading data from a website every day and then importing it into Excel, you can use the Web Query feature in Excel to allow it to automatically retrieve the data from a web page.

You can set up web queries to refresh the data from the Web every day or even every minute. Although they were originally fairly hard to define, the Excel user interface now includes a web browser you can use to build the web query.

As Web 2.0 evolves, there are some sites that are not suitable for web queries. You want to look for web

18

pages where the URL tells you about the selections that you made while getting to that page.

For example, I searched for NFL stats. In the process of getting to an interesting page, I had asked for 2011 regular-season data. I had asked for passing stats and then the complete list. I ended up at a page with a very long URL: `http://www.nfl.com/stats/categorystats ?tabSeq=0&statisticCategory=PASSING&conference=null&season=2011&seasonType=REG&d-447263-s=PASSING_YARDS&d-447263-o=2&d-447263-n=1`.

This looks like an excellent candidate for web queries because all of my choices are embedded in that URL. I can see 2011, REG, PASSING, and YARDS in the URL.

Go to the address bar, change 2011 to 2010, and press Enter. If the correct page comes up with 2010 passing yards, you know that you have a winner.

Another example: Suppose you want currency exchange rates from XE.com. On the XE.com page, you specify 100, CAD for Canadian dollars and USD for U.S. dollars. Click Go. The URL of the returned page is `http://www.xe.com/ucc/convert.cgi?Amount=100&From=CAD&To=USD`. You can see how you can alter this URL by changing USD to GBP to get British pounds.

In contrast, take a look at `http://www.Easy-XL.com`. There are several videos you can watch there. As you navigate to each video, the URL stays exactly the same: `http://www.easy-xl.com/iaplayer.cgi?v=Query&x=play&p=ez%2Fvideos&i=ezVideos.csv`.

There is nothing in that URL that tells you which video you chose. The site is using some Web 2.0 magic via Java to serve up the correct video. A site built like this is not ideal for web queries.

Manually Creating a Web Query and Refreshing with VBA

The easiest way to get started with web queries is to create your first one manually while the macro recorder is running.

Excel 2013 includes the PowerPivot add-in that allows you to mash up disparate datasets. One of the favorite demo applications mashes up daily sales data from a store with daily weather for that city. You probably already have daily sales data for your stores. The hard part is finding daily weather data.

The Weather Underground website has a historical weather query. After browsing to find the data for the Akron Canton airport (code = CAK) for February 17, 2010, you will have this URL: `http://www.wunderground.com/history/airport/KCAK/2010/2/17/DailyHistory.html`.

You can see all the variables in the URL—the airport code of CAK and the date from which you need the weather, albeit in a bizarre format of YYYY/M/D.

Open Excel. Go to a blank worksheet. Rather than leave the cell pointer in A1, move down to about Cell A9 to leave room for some work variables later.

Turn on the macro recorder. Record a new macro called WeatherQuery. From the Data tab of the ribbon, select Get External Data, From Web. Excel shows the New Web Query dialog with your Internet Explorer home page displayed.

Using the browser, go to your desired website. Make the selections necessary to get the data. In the case of Weather Underground, select history, the city, and the date, and click Go. In a moment, the desired web page displays in the dialog box.

Note that in addition to the web page there are a number of yellow squares with a black arrow. These squares are in the upper-left corner of various tables on the web page. Click the square that contains the data you want to import to Excel. If there is no square for your table, import the entire page, as shown in Figure 18.1. While you are clicking, a blue border confirms the table that will be imported. After you click, the yellow arrow changes to a green check mark.

Figure 18.1
Use the New Web Query dialog to browse to a web page. Highlight the table you want to import to Excel by clicking a yellow arrow adjacent to the table.

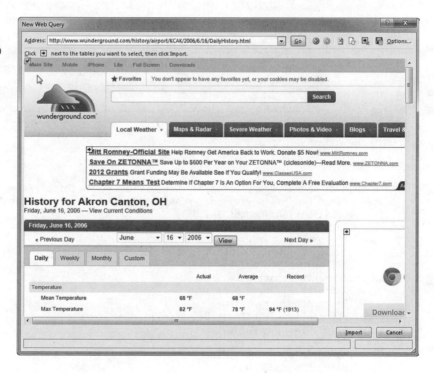

Click the Import button on the New Web Query dialog. Click OK on the Import Data dialog. In a few seconds, you see the live data imported into a range on your spreadsheet. Because you import the entire section of the web page, there will be the data that you want as well as extraneous data. In Figure 18.2, you see that I've manually highlighted the statistics that I think would be relevant in northeastern Ohio. If you live in Maui or Trinidad, you might not care about snowfall. Figure 18.2 shows the returned web query.

Figure 18.2
Data from the web page is automatically copied to your worksheet. You can now use VBA to automatically refresh this data at your command or periodically.

	A	B	C	D
109	History for Akron Canton, OH			
110	Friday, June 16, 2006 — View Current Conditions			
111	Friday, June 16, 2006			
112	« Previous Day		Next Day »	
113	Daily Weekly Monthly Custom			
114		Actual	Average	Record
115	Temperature			
116	Mean Temperature	68 °F	68 °F	
117	Max Temperature	82 °F	78 °F	94 °F (1913)
118	Min Temperature	53 °F	58 °F	39 °F (1908)
119	Degree Days			
120	Heating Degree Days	0	1	
121	Month to date heating degree days		39	
122	Since 1 June heating degree days		39	
123	Since 1 July heating degree days		6140	
124	Cooling Degree Days	2	5	
125	Month to date cooling degree days		54	
126	Year to date cooling degree days		96	
127	Since 1 June cooling degree days		54	
128	Growing Degree Days	18 (Base 50)		
129	Moisture			
130	Dew Point	46 °F		
131	Average Humidity	46		
132	Maximum Humidity	74		
133	Minimum Humidity	30		
134	Precipitation			
135	Precipitation	0.00 in	0.12 in	2.44 in (1953)
136	Month to date precipitation		2.03	
137	Year to date precipitation		17.76	
138	Snow			
139	Snow	0.00 in	0.00 in	- ()
140	Month to date snowfall		0	
141	Since 1 June snowfall		0	

Here's the recorded macro:

```
Sub WeatherQuery()
'
    With ActiveSheet.QueryTables.Add(Connection:= "URL;http://www" & _
".wunderground.com/history/airport/KCAK/2010/2/17/DailyHistory.html" _
        , Destination:=Range("$A$10"))
        .Name = "DailyHistory"
        .FieldNames = True
        .RowNumbers = False
        .FillAdjacentFormulas = False
        .PreserveFormatting = True
        .RefreshOnFileOpen = False
        .BackgroundQuery = True
        .RefreshStyle = xlInsertDeleteCells
        .SavePassword = False
        .SaveData = True
        .AdjustColumnWidth = True
        .RefreshPeriod = 0
        .WebSelectionType = xlEntirePage
        .WebFormatting = xlWebFormattingNone
        .WebPreFormattedTextToColumns = True
        .WebConsecutiveDelimitersAsOne = True
        .WebSingleBlockTextImport = False
        .WebDisableDateRecognition = False
        .WebDisableRedirections = False
        .Refresh BackgroundQuery:=False
    End With
End Sub
```

The important parts of this macro are the connect string, the location of the data returned from the web query, the web table, and the `Refresh BackgroundQuery:=False`.

The connect string is the URL that you found in the address bar of Internet Explorer (preceded by URL:).

The output location for the web query is specified in the destination property.

Setting `BackgroundQuery` to `False` means that the macro does not proceed until the data comes back from the web page. This is the appropriate setting. Your macro might go on to pull certain pieces of data from the results. If you allowed the query to run in the background, the macro would be pulling from a blank web page.

This example loaded the entire web page. If you had specified one table, you would see a line identifying which `.WebTable` to import. The best way to figure out this table number is to record a macro and have the macro recorder tell you the table number that corresponds to the check box that you selected.

> **NOTE** If web query macros are going to break over time, it will be because of a website redesign. If the web owner decides to add a new advertising box at the top of the website, it might move the good data from table #11 to table #12. If you are designing a web query that will be run once a day for the next five years, you should add some code to make sure that you are actually getting the correct data.

In this example, if the word *Actual* does not appear in column B, stop the macro and alert someone:

```
    Dim FoundCell As Range
    Set FoundCell = Columns("B:B").Find(What:="Actual", _
        After:=Range("B1"), LookIn:=xlFormulas, _
        LookAt:=xlPart, SearchOrder:=xlByRows, _
        SearchDirection:=xlNext, MatchCase:=False, _
        SearchFormat:=False)
    If FoundCell Is Nothing Then
        MsgBox "It looks like the website changed. Actual not found in column B."
        Exit Sub
    End If
End Sub
```

Using VBA to Update an Existing Web Query

To update all web queries on the current sheet, use this code:

```
Sub RefreshAllWebQueries()
    Dim QT As QueryTable
    For Each QT In ActiveSheet.QueryTables
        Application.StatusBar = "Refreshing " & QT.Connection
        QT.Refresh
    Next QT
    Application.StatusBar = False
End Sub
```

18

You can assign this macro to a hotkey or to a macro button and refresh all queries on demand.

Building Many Web Queries with VBA

To gather weather data for 24 months, you have to repeat the web query process more than 700 times. This would be tedious to do manually.

Instead, you can use VBA to build and execute the web queries. It is fairly simple to build a web query on the fly. The connect string to get weather for any airport for any day can be broken down into four parts.

The first part can be hard-coded because it never changes:

`"URL;http://www.wunderground.com/history/airport/K"`

The next part is the three-letter airport code. If you are retrieving data for many cities, this part will change:

`CAK`

The third part is a slash, the date in YYYY/M/D format and a slash:

`/2010/2/17/`

The final part can be hard-coded:

`"DailyHistory.html"`

Insert a new worksheet and build an output table. In Cell A2, enter the first date for which you have sales history. Use the fill handle to drag the dates down to the current date.

The formula in B2 is `="/"&Text(A2,"YYYY/M/D")&"/"`.

Add friendly headings across Row 1 for the statistics you will collect.

The data worksheet is shown in Figure 18.3.

Figure 18.3
Build a data worksheet to hold the results of the web query.

	A	B	C	D	E	F	G	H
1	Date	Format	High	Low	Rain	Snow		
2	10/7/2012	/2012/10/7/						
3	10/6/2012	/2012/10/6/						
4	10/5/2012	/2012/10/5/						
5	10/4/2012	/2012/10/4/						
6	10/3/2012	/2012/10/3/						
7	10/2/2012	/2012/10/2/						
8	10/1/2012	/2012/10/1/						
9	9/30/2012	/2012/9/30/						
10	9/29/2012	/2012/9/29/						

B2 cell formula: `="/"&TEXT(A2,"YYYY/M/D")&"/"`

Finding Results from Retrieved Data

Next, you have a decision to make. It looks as though the weather underground website is fairly static. The snow statistic even shows up if I ask for JHM airport in Maui. If you are positive that rainfall is always going to appear in Cell B28 of your results sheet, you could write the macro to get data from there.

However, to be safe, you can build some lookup formulas at the top of the worksheet to look for certain row labels and to pull that data. In Figure 18.4, eight INDEX and MATCH formulas find the statistics for High, Low, Rain, and Snow from the web query.

Figure 18.4
VLOOKUPs at the top of the web worksheet find and pull the relevant data from a web page.

B3		▾	:	×	✓	fx	=MATCH(B2,$A:$A,0)		
⊿	A			B		C		D	E
1			High		Low		Rain		Snow
2	Words in web page results:	Max Temperature		Min Temperature		Precipitation		Snow
3	Row number below:		117		118		134		138
4	Result:	82 °F		53 °F		0.00 in		0.00 in
5	Formula:	=INDEX($B:$B,B3)		=INDEX($B:$B,C3)		=INDEX($B:$B,D3+1)		=INDEX($B:$B,E3+1)
6								

> **NOTE**
> The variable web location of the web data happens more often than you might think. If you are pulling name and address information, some addresses have three lines and some have four lines. Anything that appears after that address might be off by a row. Some stock-quote sites show a different version of the data depending on whether the market is open or closed. If you kick off a series of web queries at 3:45 p.m., the macro might work until 4:00 p.m. and then stop working. For these reasons, it is often safer to take the extra steps of retrieving the correct data from the web query using VLOOKUP statements.

To build the macro, you add some code before the recorded code:

```
Dim WSD as worksheet
Dim WSW as worksheet
Set WSD = Worksheets("Data")
Set WSW = Worksheets("Web")
FinalRow = WSD.Cells(Rows.Count, 1).End(xlUp).Row
```

Then add a loop to go through all the dates in the data worksheet:

```
For I = 2 to FinalRow
    ThisDate = WSD.Cells(I, 2).value
    ' Build the ConnectString
    CS = "URL: URL;http://www.wunderground.com/history/airport/KCAK"
    CS = CS & ThisDate & "DailyHistory.html"
```

If a web query is about to overwrite existing data on the worksheet, it moves that data to the right. You want to clear the previous web query and all the contents:

```
For Each qt In WSD.QueryTables
    qt.Delete
Next qt
WSD.Range("A10:A300").EntireRow.Clear
```

You can now go into the recorded code. Change the `QueryTables.Add` line to the following:

```
With WSD.QueryTables.Add(Connection:= CS, Destination:=WSW.Range("A10"))
```

After the recorded code, add some lines to calculate the VLOOKUPs, copy the results, and finish the loop:

```
WSW.Calculate
WSD.Cells(i, 3).Resize(1, 4).Value = WSW.Range("B4:E4").Value
Next i
```

Step through the code as it goes through the first loop to make sure that everything is working. You should notice that the actual .Refresh line takes about 5 to 10 seconds. To gather two or three years' worth of web pages, it requires more than an hour of processing time. Run the macro, head to lunch, and then come back to a good dataset.

Putting It All Together

In the final macro here, I turned off screen updating and showed the row number that the macro is processing in the status bar. I also deleted some unnecessary properties from the recorded code:

```
Sub GetData()
    Dim WSD As Worksheet
    Dim WSW As Worksheet
    Set WSD = Worksheets("Data")
    Set WSW = Worksheets("Web")
    FinalRow = WSD.Cells(Rows.Count, 1).End(xlUp).Row

    For i = 1 To FinalRow
        ThisDate = WSD.Cells(i, 2).Value
        ' Build the ConnectString
        CS = "URL;http://www.wunderground.com/history/airport/KCAK/"
        CS = CS & ThisDate
        CS = CS & "DailyHistory.html"
        ' Clear results of last web query
        For Each qt In WSW.QueryTables
            qt.Delete
        Next qt
        WSD.Range("A10:A300").EntireRow.Clear

        With WSW.QueryTables.Add(Connection:=CS, Destination:=Range("$A$10"))
            .Name = "DailyHistory"
            .FieldNames = True
            .RowNumbers = False
            .FillAdjacentFormulas = False
            .PreserveFormatting = True
            .RefreshOnFileOpen = False
            .BackgroundQuery = True
            .RefreshStyle = xlInsertDeleteCells
            .SavePassword = False
            .SaveData = True
            .AdjustColumnWidth = True
            .RefreshPeriod = 0
            .WebSelectionType = xlEntirePage
            .WebFormatting = xlWebFormattingNone
            .WebPreFormattedTextToColumns = True
            .WebConsecutiveDelimitersAsOne = True
            .WebSingleBlockTextImport = False
            .WebDisableDateRecognition = False
            .WebDisableRedirections = False
            .Refresh BackgroundQuery:=False
        End With
```

```
        WSW.Calculate
        WSD.Cells(i, 3).Resize(1, 4).Value = WSW.Range("B4:E4").Value
    Next i

End Sub
```

After an hour, you have data retrieved from hundreds of web pages (see Figure 18.5).

Figure 18.5
The results of running the web query hundreds of times.

⟋	A	B	C	D	E	F
1	Date	Format	High	Low	Rain	Snow
2	10/7/2012	/2012/10/7/	48 °F	36 °F	0.02 in	0.00 in
3	10/6/2012	/2012/10/6/	55 °F	41 °F	0.34 in	0.00 in
4	10/5/2012	/2012/10/5/	70 °F	49 °F	0.28 in	0.00 in
5	10/4/2012	/2012/10/4/	73 °F	55 °F	0.00 in	0.00 in
6	10/3/2012	/2012/10/3/	72 °F	58 °F	0.00 in	0.00 in
7	10/2/2012	/2012/10/2/	72 °F	54 °F	0.17 in	0.00 in
8	10/1/2012	/2012/10/1/	63 °F	42 °F	0.15 in	0.00 in

Examples of Scraping Websites Using Web Queries

Over the years, I have used the web query trick many times. Examples include the following:

- Names and company address for all Fortune 1000 CFOs so that I could pitch my Power Excel seminars to them.

- The complete membership roster for a publishing association of which I am a member. (I already had the printed roster, but with an electronic database, I could filter to find publishers in certain cities.)

- A mailing address for every public library in the United States.

- The complete list of Chipotle restaurants (which later ended up in my GPS, but that is a story for the [yet unwritten] Microsoft MapPoint book).

18

Using Application.OnTime to Periodically Analyze Data

VBA offers the OnTime method for running any VBA procedure at a specific time of day or after a specific amount of time has passed.

You can write a macro that would capture data every hour throughout the day. This macro would have times hard-coded. The following code will, theoretically, capture data from a website every hour throughout the day:

```
Sub ScheduleTheDay()
    Application.OnTime EarliestTime:=TimeValue("8:00 AM"), _
        Procedure:=CaptureData
    Application.OnTime EarliestTime:=TimeValue("9:00 AM"), _
        Procedure:=CaptureData
    Application.OnTime EarliestTime:=TimeValue("10:00 AM"), _
```

```
            Procedure:=CaptureData
        Application.OnTime EarliestTime:=TimeValue("11:00 AM"), _
            Procedure:=CaptureData
        Application.OnTime EarliestTime:=TimeValue("12:00 AM"), _
            Procedure:=CaptureData
        Application.OnTime EarliestTime:=TimeValue("1:00 PM"), _
            Procedure:=CaptureData
        Application.OnTime EarliestTime:=TimeValue("2:00 PM"), _
            Procedure:=CaptureData
        Application.OnTime EarliestTime:=TimeValue("3:00 PM"), _
            Procedure:=CaptureData
        Application.OnTime EarliestTime:=TimeValue("4:00 PM"), _
            Procedure:=CaptureData
        Application.OnTime EarliestTime:=TimeValue("5:00 PM"), _
            Procedure:=CaptureData
    End Sub

    Sub CaptureData()
        Dim WSQ As Worksheet
        Dim NextRow As Long
        Set WSQ = Worksheets("MyQuery")
        ' Refresh the web query
        WSQ.Range("A2").QueryTable.Refresh BackgroundQuery:=False
        ' Make sure the data is updated
        Application.Wait (Now + TimeValue("0:00:10"))
        ' Copy the web query results to a new row
        NextRow = WSQ.Cells(Rows.Count, 1).End(xlUp).Row + 1
        WSQ.Range("A2:B2").Copy WSQ.Cells(NextRow, 1)
    End Sub
```

Scheduled Procedures Require Ready Mode

The OnTime method will run provided only that Excel is in Ready, Copy, Cut, or Find mode at the prescribed time. If you start to edit a cell at 7:59:55 a.m. and keep that cell in Edit mode, Excel cannot run the CaptureData macro at 8:00 a.m. as directed.

In the preceding code example, I specified only the start time for the procedure to run. Excel waits anxiously until the spreadsheet is returned to Ready mode and then runs the scheduled program as soon as it can.

The classic example is that you start to edit a cell at 7:59 a.m., and then your manager walks in and asks you to attend a surprise staff meeting down the hall. If you leave your spreadsheet in Edit mode and attend the staff meeting until 10:30 a.m., the program cannot run the first three scheduled hours of updates. As soon as you return to your desk and press Enter to exit Edit mode, the program runs all previously scheduled tasks. In the preceding code, you find that the first three scheduled updates of the program all happen between 10:30 and 10:31 a.m.

Specifying a Window of Time for an Update

One alternative is to provide Excel with a window of time within which to make the update. The following code tells Excel to run the update at any time between 8:00 a.m. and

8:05 a.m. If the Excel session remains in Edit mode for the entire five minutes, the scheduled task is skipped.

```
Application.OnTime EarliestTime:=TimeValue("8:00 AM"), Procedure:=CaptureData,
 LatestTime:=TimeValue("8:05 AM")
```

Canceling a Previously Scheduled Macro

It is fairly difficult to cancel a previously scheduled macro. You must know the exact time that the macro is scheduled to run. To cancel a pending operation, call the OnTime method again, using the Schedule:=False parameter to unschedule the event. The following code cancels the 11:00 a.m. run of CaptureData:

```
Sub CancelEleven()
Application.OnTime EarliestTime:=TimeValue("11:00 AM"), _
    Procedure:=CaptureData, Schedule:=False
End Sub
```

It is interesting to note that the OnTime schedules are remembered by a running instance of Excel. If you keep Excel open but close the workbook with the scheduled procedure, it still runs. Consider this hypothetical series of events:

1. Open Excel at 7:30 a.m.
2. Open Schedule.xls and run a macro to schedule a procedure at 8:00 a.m.
3. Close Schedule.xls but keep Excel open.
4. Open a new workbook and begin entering data.

At 8:00 a.m., Excel reopens Schedule.xls and runs the scheduled macro. Excel doesn't close Schedule.xls. As you can imagine, this is fairly annoying and alarming if you are not expecting it. If you are going to make extensive use of Application.Ontime, you might want to have it running in one instance of Excel while you work in a second instance of Excel.

> **NOTE**
> If you are using a macro to schedule a macro a certain amount of time later, you could remember the time in an out-of-the way cell to be able to cancel the update. See an example in the "Scheduling a Macro to Run x Minutes in the Future" section of this chapter.

Closing Excel Cancels All Pending Scheduled Macros

If you close Excel with File, Exit, all future scheduled macros are automatically canceled. When you have a macro that has scheduled a bunch of macros at indeterminate times, closing Excel is the only way to prevent the macros from running.

Scheduling a Macro to Run x Minutes in the Future

You can schedule a macro to run at a certain time in the future. The macro uses the TIME function to return the current time and adds 2 minutes and 30 seconds to the time. The following macro runs something 2 minutes and 30 seconds from now:

```
Sub ScheduleAnything()
    ' This macro can be used to schedule anything
    WaitHours = 0
    WaitMin = 2
    WaitSec = 30
    NameOfScheduledProc = "CaptureData"
    ' --- End of Input Section -------

    ' Determine the next time this should run
    NextTime = Time + TimeSerial(WaitHours, WaitMin, WaitSec)

    ' Schedule ThisProcedure to run then
    Application.OnTime EarliestTime:=NextTime, Procedure:=NameOfScheduledProc

End Sub
```

Later, if you need to cancel this scheduled event, it would be nearly impossible. You won't know the exact time that the macro grabbed the TIME function. You might try to save this value in an out-of-the-way cell:

```
Sub ScheduleWithCancelOption
    NameOfScheduledProc = "CaptureData"

    ' Determine the next time this should run
    NextTime = Time + TimeSerial(0,2,30)
    Range("ZZ1").Value = NextTime

    ' Schedule ThisProcedure to run then
    Application.OnTime EarliestTime:=NextTime, Procedure:=NameOfScheduledProc

End Sub

Sub CancelLater()
        NextTime = Range("ZZ1").value
        Application.OnTime EarliestTime:=NextTime, _
    Procedure:=CaptureData, Schedule:=False
End Sub
```

Scheduling a Verbal Reminder

The text-to-speech tools in Excel can be fun. The following macro sets up a schedule that reminds you when it is time to go to the staff meeting:

```
Sub ScheduleSpeak()
    Application.OnTime EarliestTime:=TimeValue("9:14 AM"), _
        Procedure:="RemindMe"
End Sub

Sub RemindMe()
    Application.Speech.Speak _
        Text:="Bill. It is time for the staff meeting."
End Sub
```

If you want to pull a prank on your manager, you can schedule Excel to automatically turn on the Speak on Enter feature. Follow this scenario:

1. Tell your manager that you are taking him out to lunch to celebrate April 1.

2. At some point in the morning, while your manager is getting coffee, run the ScheduleSpeech macro. Design the macro to run 15 minutes after your lunch starts.

3. Take your manager to lunch.

4. While the manager is away, the scheduled macro will run.

5. When the manager returns and starts typing data in Excel, the computer will repeat the cells as they are entered. This is slightly reminiscent of the computer on *Star Trek* that repeated everything Lieutenant Uhura said.

After this starts happening, you can pretend to be innocent; after all, you have a firm alibi for when the prank began to happen:

```
Sub ScheduleSpeech()
    Application.OnTime EarliestTime:=TimeValue("12:15 PM"), _
        Procedure:="SetUpSpeech"
End Sub

Sub SetupSpeech())
    Application.Speech.SpeakCellOnEnter = True
End Sub
```

> **NOTE**
> To turn off Speak on Enter, you can either dig out the button from the QAT Customization panel (look in the category called Commands Not on the Ribbon) or, if you can run some VBA, change the SetupSpeech macro to change the True to False.

18

Scheduling a Macro to Run Every Two Minutes

My favorite method is to ask Excel to run a certain macro every two minutes. However, I realize that if a macro gets delayed because I accidentally left the workbook in Edit mode while going to the staff meeting, I don't want dozens of updates to happen in a matter of seconds.

The easy solution is to have the ScheduleAnything procedure recursively schedule itself to run again in two minutes. The following code schedules a run in two minutes and then performs CaptureData:

```
Sub ScheduleAnything()
    ' This macro can be used to schedule anything
    ' Enter how often you want to run the macro in hours and minutes
    WaitHours = 0
    WaitMin = 2
    WaitSec = 0
    NameOfThisProcedure = "ScheduleAnything"
    NameOfScheduledProc = "CaptureData"
    ' --- End of Input Section -------

    ' Determine the next time this should run
    NextTime = Time + TimeSerial(WaitHours, WaitMin, WaitSec)
```

```
' Schedule ThisProcedure to run then
Application.OnTime EarliestTime:=NextTime, Procedure:=NameOfThisProcedure

' Get the Data
Application.Run NameOfScheduledProc
```

```
End Sub
```

This method has some advantages. I have not scheduled a million updates in the future. I have only one future update scheduled at any given time. Therefore, if I decide that I am tired of seeing the national debt every 15 seconds, I only need to comment out the Application.OnTime line of code and wait 15 seconds for the last update to happen.

Publishing Data to a Web Page

This chapter highlights many ways to capture data from the Web. It is also useful for publishing Excel data back to the Web.

The RunReportForEachCustomer macro shown in Chapter 11, "Data Mining with Advanced Filter," produces reports for each customer in a company. Instead of printing and faxing the report, it would be cool to save the Excel file as HTML and post the results on a company intranet so that the customer service reps could instantly access the latest version of the report.

Consider a report like the one shown in Figure 18.6. With the Excel user interface, it is easy to save the report as a web page to create an HTML view of the data.

Figure 18.6

A macro from Chapter 13 was used to automatically generate this Excel workbook. Rather than e-mail the report, we could save it as a web page and post it on the company intranet.

	A	B	C	D	E	F	G	H
1	Report of Sales to Trustworthy Flagpole Partners							
2								
3	Date	Quantity	Product	Revenue				
4	19-Jul-14	1000	R537	22810				
5	3-Sep-14	200	W435	4742				
6	7-Sep-14	300	M556	5700				
7	9-Sep-14	600	W435	12282				
8	12-Sep-14	100	R537	2257				
9	13-Sep-14	1000	R537	22680				
10	13-Sep-14	600	W435	13206				
11	14-Sep-14	900	M556	16209				

In Excel 2013, use File, Save As. Select Web Page (*.htm, *html) in the Save as Type dropdown (see Figure 18.7).

You have control over the title that appears in the window title bar. This title also gets written to the top center of your web page.

Click the Change Title button to change the <Title> tag for the web page. Type a name that ends in either .htm or .html and click Publish.

Figure 18.7
When saving as a web page, you can control the filename and title.

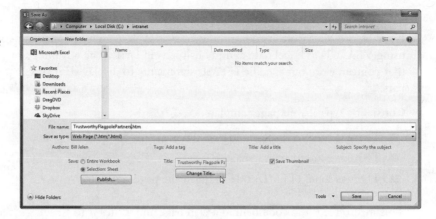

The result is a file that can be viewed in any web browser. The web page accurately shows our number formats and font sizes (see Figure 18.8).

Figure 18.8
The formatting is close to the original worksheet.

18

Whereas the macro from Chapter 11 did WBN.SaveAs, the new macro uses this code to write out each web page:

```
HTMLFN = "C:\Intranet\" & ThisCust & ".html"
On Error Resume Next
Kill HTMLFN
On Error GoTo 0
With WBN.PublishObjects.Add( _
    SourceType:=xlSourceSheet, _
    Filename:=HTMLFN, _
    Sheet:="Sheet1", _
    Source:="", _
    HtmlType:=xlHtmlStatic, _
    DivID:="A", _
    Title:="Sales to " & ThisCust)
    .Publish True
    .AutoRepublish = False
End With
```

Although the data is accurately presented in Figure 18.8, it is not extremely fancy. We don't have a company logo or navigation bar to examine other reports.

Using VBA to Create Custom Web Pages

Long before Microsoft introduced the Save as Web Page functionality, people had been using VBA to take Excel data and publish it as HTML. The advantage of this method is that you can write out specific HTML statements to display company logos and navigation bars.

Consider a typical web page template:

- There is code to display a logo and navigation bar at the top/side.
- There is content for the page.
- There is some HTML code to finish the page.

This macro reads the code behind a web page and writes it to Excel:

```
Sub ImportHTML()
    ThisFile = "C:\Intranet\schedule.html"
    Open ThisFile For Input As #1
    Ctr = 2
    Do
        Line Input #1, Data
        Worksheets("HTML").Cells(Ctr, 2).Value = Data
        Ctr = Ctr + 1
    Loop While EOF(1) = False
    Close #1
End Sub
```

If you import the text of a web page into Excel, even if you don't understand the HTML involved, you can probably find the first lines that contain your page content.

Examine the HTML code in Excel. Copy the lines needed to draw the top part of the web page to a worksheet called Top. Copy the lines of code needed to close the web page to a worksheet called Bottom.

You can use VBA to write out the top, generate content from your worksheet, and then write out the bottom.

Using Excel as a Content Management System

Five hundred million people are proficient in Excel. Companies everywhere have data in Excel, and many staffers who are comfortable in maintaining that data. Rather than force these people to learn how to create HTML pages, why not build a content management system to take their Excel data and write out custom web pages?

You probably already have data for the web page in Excel. Using the ImportHTML routine to read the HTML into Excel, you know the top and bottom portions of the HTML needed to render the web page.

Building a content management system with these tools is simple. To the existing Excel data, I added two worksheets. In the worksheet called Top, I copied the HTML needed to generate the navigation bar of the website. To the worksheet called Bottom, I copied the HTML needed to generate the end of the HTML page. Figure 18.9 shows the simple Bottom worksheet.

Figure 18.9
Companies everywhere are maintaining all sorts of data in Excel and are comfortable updating the data in Excel. Why not marry Excel with a simple bit of VBA so that custom HTML can be produced from Excel?

	A	B	C	D	E	F	G	H	I
	Sequence	**Content**							
1		</UL></p>							
2									
3									
4		Contact: Bill Jelen P.O. Box 82, Uniontown, OH 44685; 							
5		online at: www.mrexcel.com ; and by email at Bill@mrexcel.com 							
6		</p>							
7									
8		<center>####</center> 							
9									
10									
11									
12		</p>							
13		</font>							
14		<p></td>							
15		</tr>							
16		</table>							
17		</td>							
18		</tr>							
19		</table>							
20									
21		<p align="center"><font size="1" color="#1E2463">Excel is a registered tradem							
22		of the Microsoft® Corporation. MrExcel is a registered trademark of Tickli							
23		<p align="center"><font size="1" color="#1E2463">All contents Copyright							
24									
25		1998-2015 by MrExcel Consulting.</font></p>							
26		</font></p>							
27									
28		</body>							
29									
30		</html>							

The macro code opens a text file called `directory.html` for output. First, all the HTML code from the Top worksheet is written to the file.

Then the macro loops through each row in the membership directory, writing data to the file.

After completing this loop, the macro writes out the HTML code from the Bottom worksheet to finish the file:

```
Sub WriteMembershipHTML()
    ' Write web pages
    Dim WST As Worksheet
    Dim WSB As Worksheet
    Dim WSM As Worksheet
    Set WSB = Worksheets("Bottom")
    Set WST = Worksheets("Top")
    Set WSM = Worksheets("Membership")

    ' Figure out the path
    MyPath = ThisWorkbook.Path

    LineCtr = 0

    FinalT = WST.Cells(Rows.Count, 1).End(xlUp).Row
    FinalB = WSB.Cells(Rows.Count, 1).End(xlUp).Row
    FinalM = WSM.Cells(Rows.Count, 1).End(xlUp).Row
```

```
MyFile = "sampleschedule.html"

ThisFile = MyPath & Application.PathSeparator & MyFile
ThisHostFile = MyFile

' Delete the old HTML page
On Error Resume Next
Kill (ThisFile)
On Error GoTo 0

' Build the title
ThisTitle = "<Title>LTCC Membership Directory</Title>"
WST.Cells(3, 2).Value = ThisTitle

' Open the file for output
Open ThisFile For Output As #1

' Write out the top part of the HTML
For j = 2 To FinalT
    Print #1, WST.Cells(j, 2).Value
Next j

' For each row in Membership, write out lines of data to HTML file
For j = 2 To FinalM
    ' Surround Member name with bold tags
    Print #1, "<li>" & WSM.Cells(j, 1).Value
Next j

' Close old file
Print #1, "This page current as of " & Format(Date, "mmmm dd, yyyy") & _
    " " & Format(Time, "h:mm AM/PM")

' Write out HTML code from Bottom worksheet
For j = 2 To FinalB
    Print #1, WSB.Cells(j, 2).Value
Next j
Close #1

Application.StatusBar = False
Application.CutCopyMode = False
MsgBox "web pages updated"

End Sub
```

Figure 18.10 shows the finished web page. This web page looks a lot better than the generic page created by Excel's Save as Web Page option. It maintains the look and feel of the rest of the site.

This system has many advantages. The person who maintains the schedule data is comfortable working in Excel. She has already been maintaining the data in Excel on a regular basis. Now, after updating some records, she presses a button to produce a new version of the web page.

Of course, the web designer is clueless about Excel. However, if he ever wants to change the web design, it is a simple matter to open his new sample.html file in Notepad and copy the new code to the Top and Bottom worksheet.

Figure 18.10
A simple content-management system in Excel was used to generate this web page. The look and feel matches the rest of the website. Excel achieved it without any expensive web database coding.

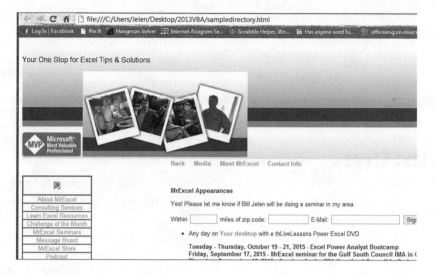

The resulting web page has a small file size—about one-sixth the size of the equivalent page created by Excel's Save as Web Page.

> **NOTE** In real life, the content management system in this example was extended to allow easy maintenance of the organization's calendar, board members, and so on. The resulting workbook made it possible to maintain 41 web pages at the click of a button.

18

Bonus: FTP from Excel

After you are able to update web pages from Excel, you still have the hassle of using an FTP program to upload the pages from your hard drive to the Internet. Again, we have lots of people proficient in Excel, but not so many comfortable with using an FTP client.

Ken Anderson has written a cool command-line FTP freeware utility. Download WCL_FTP from http://www.softlookup.com/display.asp?id=20483. Save WCL_FTP.exe to the root directory of your hard drive and then use this code to automatically upload your recently created HTML files to your web server:

```
Sub DoFTP(fname, pathfname)
' To have this work, copy wcl_ftp.exe to the C:\ root directory
' Download from http://www.softlookup.com/display.asp?id=20483

' Build a string to FTP. The syntax is
' WCL_FTP.exe "Caption" hostname username password host-directory _
' host-filename local-filename get-or-put 0Ascii1Binanry 0NoLog _
' 0Background 1CloseWhenDone 1PassiveMode  1ErrorsText

If Not Worksheets("Menu").Range("I1").Value = True Then Exit Sub

s = """c:\wcl_ftp.exe "" " _
```

```
          & """Upload File to website"" " _
          & "ftp.MySite.com FTPUser FTPPassword www " _
          & fname & " " _
          & """" & pathfname & """ " _
          & "put " _
          & "0 0 0 1 1 1"

    Shell s, vbMinimizedNoFocus
    End Sub
```

Next Steps

Chapter 19, "Text File Processing," covers importing from a text file and writing to a text file. Being able to write to a text file is useful when you need to write out data for another system to read.

Text File Processing

VBA simplifies both reading and writing from text files. This chapter covers importing from a text file and writing to a text file. Being able to write to a text file proves useful when you need to write out data for another system to read, or even when you need to produce HTML files.

Importing from Text Files

There are two basic scenarios when reading from text files. If the file contains fewer than 1,048,576 records, it is not difficult to import the file using the Workbooks.OpenText method. If the file contains more than 1,048,576 records, you have to read the file one record at a time.

Importing Text Files with Fewer Than 1,048,576 Rows

Text files typically come in one of two formats. In one format, the fields in each record are separated by some delimiter such as a comma, pipe, or tab. In the second format, each field takes a particular number of character positions. This is called a *fixed-width file* and it was very popular in the days of COBOL.

Excel can import either type of file. You can also open both types using the OpenText method. In both cases, it is best to record the process of opening the file and then use the recorded snippet of code.

Opening a Fixed-Width File

Figure 19.1 shows a text file in which each field takes up a certain amount of space in the record. Writing the code to open this type of file is slightly arduous because you need to specify the length of each field. In my collection of antiques, I still have the metal ruler used by COBOL programmers to measure the number of characters in a field printed on a green-bar printer. In theory, you could change

19

the font of your file to a monospace font and use this same method. However, using the macro recorder is a slightly more up-to-date method.

Figure 19.1
This file is fixed width. Because you must specify the exact length of each field in the file, opening this file is quite involved.

Region	Product	Date	Customer	Quantity	Revenue	COGS	Profit
East	XYZ	7/24/15	QRS INC.	1000	22810	1022012590	
Central	DEF	7/25/15	JKL, CO	100	2257	984	1273
East	ABC	7/25/15	JKL, CO	500	10245	4235	6010
Central	XYZ	7/26/15	WXY, CO	500	11240	5110	6130
East	XYZ	7/27/15	FGH, CO	400	9152	4088	5064
Central	XYZ	7/27/15	WXY, CO	400	9204	4088	5116
East	DEF	7/27/15	RST INC.	800	18552	787210680	
Central	ABC	7/28/15	EFG S.A.	400	6860	3388	3472
East	DEF	7/30/15	UVW, INC.	1000	21730	984011890	

Turn on the macro recorder by selecting Record Macro from the Developer tab. From the File menu, select Open. Change the Files of Type to All Files and find your text file.

In the Text Import Wizard's step 1, specify that the data is Fixed Width and click Next.

Excel then looks at your data and attempts to figure out where each field begins and ends. Figure 19.2 shows Excel's guess on this particular file. Because the Date field is too close to the Customer field, Excel missed drawing that line.

Figure 19.2
Excel guesses at where each field starts. In this case, it guessed incorrectly for two of the fields.

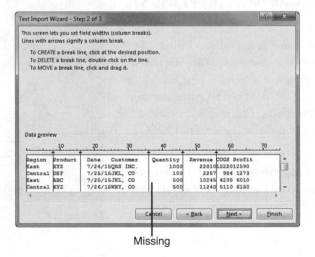

Missing

To add a new field indicator in step 2 of the wizard, click in the appropriate place in the Data Preview window. If you click in the wrong column, click the line and drag it to the right place. If Excel inadvertently put in an extra field line, double-click the line to remove it. Figure 19.3 shows the data preview after the appropriate changes have been made. Note the little ruler above the data. When you click to add a field marker, Excel is actually handling the tedious work of figuring out that the Customer field starts in position 25 for a length of 12.

Figure 19.3
After you add a new field marker and adjust the marker between Customer and Quantity to the right place, Excel can build the code that gives you an idea of the start position and length of each field.

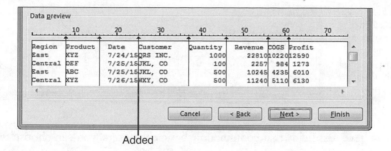

Added

In step 3 of the wizard, Excel always assumes that every field is in General format.

Change the format of any fields that require special handling. Click the third column and choose the appropriate format from the Column Data Format section of the dialog box. Figure 19.4 shows the selections for this file.

Figure 19.4
The third column is a date, and you do not want to import the Cost and Profit columns.

Advanced

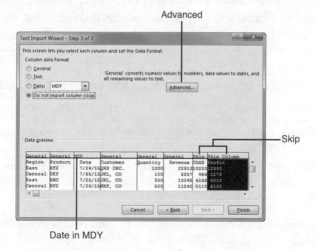

Skip

Date in MDY

19

If you have date fields, click the heading above that column, and change the column data format choice to a date. If you have a file with dates in year-month-day format or day-month-year format, select the drop-down next to Date and choose the appropriate date sequence.

If you prefer to skip some fields, click that column and select Do Not Import Column (Skip) from the Column Data Format selection. There are a couple of instances when this is useful. If the file includes sensitive data that you do not want to show to the client, you can leave it out of the import. For example, perhaps this report is for a customer to whom you do not want to show the cost of goods sold or profit. In this case, you can choose to skip these fields in the import. In addition, occasionally you will encounter a text file that is both fixed width and delimited by a character such as the pipe character. Setting the 1-character-wide pipe columns as "do not import," as shown in Figure 19.5, is a great way to get rid of the pipe characters.

Figure 19.5
This file is both fixed width and pipe delimited. Liberal use of the Do Not Import Column setting for each pipe column eliminates the pipe characters from the file.

If you have text fields that contain alphabetic characters, you can choose the General format. The only time you should choose the Text format is if you have a numeric field that you explicitly need imported as text. One example of this is an account number with leading zeros or a column of ZIP Codes. In this case, change the field to Text format to ensure that ZIP Code 01234 does not lose the leading zero.

> **NOTE**
> After you import a text file and specify that one field is text, that field exhibits seemingly bizarre behavior. Try inserting a new row and entering a formula in the middle of a column imported as text. Instead of getting the results of the formula, Excel enters the formula as text. The solution is to delete the formula, format the entire column as General, and then enter the formula again.

After opening the file, turn off the macro recorder and examine the recorded code:

```
Workbooks.OpenText Filename:="C:\sales.prn", Origin:=437, StartRow:=1, _
DataType:=xlFixedWidth, FieldInfo:=Array(Array(0, 1), Array(8, 1), _
Array(17, 3), Array(27, 1), Array(54, 1), Array(62, 1), Array(71, 9), _
Array(79, 9)), TrailingMinusNumbers:=True
```

The most confusing part of this code is the FieldInfo parameter. You are supposed to code an array of two-element arrays. Each field in the file gets a two-element array to identify both where the field starts and what type of field it is.

The field start position is zero-based. Because the Region field is in the first character position, its start position is listed as zero.

The field type is a numeric code. If you were coding this by hand, you would use the xlColumnDataType constant names; but for some reason, the macro recorder uses the harder-to-understand numeric equivalents.

With Table 19.1, you can decode the meaning of the individual arrays in the FieldInfo array. Array(0, 1) means that this field starts zero characters from the left edge of the file and is a general format. Array(8, 1) indicates that the next field starts eight characters from the left edge of the file and is General format. Array(17, 3) indicates that the next field starts 17 characters from the left edge of the file and is a date format in month-day-year sequence.

Table 19.1 `xlColumnDataType` **Values**

Value	Constant	Used For
1	`xlGeneralFormat`	General
2	`xlTextFormat`	Text
3	`xlMDYFormat`	MDY date
4	`xlDMYFormat`	DMY date
5	`xlYMDFormat`	YMD date
6	`xlMYDFormat`	MYD date
7	`xlDYMFormat`	DYM date
8	`xlYDMFormat`	YDM date
9	`xlSkipColumn`	Skip Column
10	`xlEMDFormat`	EMD date (for use in Taiwan)

As you can see, the `FieldInfo` parameter for fixed-width files is arduous to code and confusing to look at. This is one situation in which it is easier to record the macro and copy the code snippet.

> **NOTE**
> The `xlTrailingMinusNumbers` parameter was new in Excel 2002. If you have any clients who might be using Excel 97 or Excel 2000, take out the recorded parameter. The code runs fine without the parameter in newer versions. However, if left in, it leads to a compile error on older versions. In my experience, this is the number one cause for code to crash on earlier versions of Excel.

Opening a Delimited File

Figure 19.6 shows a text file in which each field is comma separated. The main task in opening such a file is to tell Excel that the delimiter in the file is a comma and then identify any special processing for each field. In this case, we definitely want to identify the third column as being a date in MDY format.

Figure 19.6

This file is comma delimited. Opening this file involves telling Excel to look for a comma as the delimiter and then identifying any special handling, such as treating the third column as a date. This is much easier than handling fixed-width files.

```
Region,Product,Date,Customer,Quantity,Revenue,COGS,Profit
East,XYZ,7/24/2015,QRS INC.,1000,22810,10220,12590
Central,DEF,7/25/2015,"JKL, CO",100,2257,984,1273
East,ABC,7/25/2015,"JKL, CO",500,10245,4235,6010
Central,XYZ,7/26/2015,"WXY, CO",500,11240,5110,6130
East,XYZ,7/27/2015,"FGH, CO",400,9152,4088,5064
Central,XYZ,7/27/2015,"WXY, CO",400,9204,4088,5116
```

> **NOTE**
>
> If you try to record the process of opening a comma-delimited file whose filename ends in .csv, Excel records the Workbooks.Open method rather than Workbooks.OpenText. If you need to control the formatting of certain columns, rename the file to have a .txt extension before recording the macro.

Turn on the macro recorder and record the process of opening the text file. In step 1 of the wizard, specify that the file is delimited.

In the Text Import Wizard–Step 2 of 3 dialog, the data preview might initially look horrible. This is because Excel defaults to assuming that each field is separated by a tab character (see Figure 19.7).

After you've cleared the Tab check box and selected the proper delimiter choice, which in this case is a comma, the data preview in step 2 looks perfect, as shown in Figure 19.8.

Figure 19.7
Before you import a delimited text file, the initial data preview looks like a confusing mess of data because Excel is looking for tab characters between each field when a comma is actually the delimiter in this file.

Figure 19.8
After the delimiter field has been changed from a tab to a comma, the data preview looks perfect. This is certainly easier than the cumbersome process in step 2 for a fixed-width file.

Step 3 of the wizard is identical to step 3 for a fixed-width file. In this case, specify that the third column has a date format. Click Finish, and you have this code in the macro recorder:

```
Workbooks.OpenText Filename:="C:\sales.txt", Origin:=437, _
    StartRow:=1, DataType:=xlDelimited, TextQualifier:=xlDoubleQuote, _
    ConsecutiveDelimiter:=False, Tab:=False, Semicolon:=False, _
    Comma:=True, Space:=False, Other:=False, _
    FieldInfo:=Array(Array(1, 1), Array(2, 1), _
    Array(3, 3), Array(4, 1), Array(5, 1), Array(6, 1), _
    Array(7, 1), Array(8, 1)), TrailingMinusNumbers:=True
```

Although this code appears longer, it is actually simpler. In the `FieldInfo` parameter, the two element arrays consist of a sequence number, starting at 1 for the first field, and then an `xlColumnDataType` from Table 19.1. In this example, `Array(2, 1)` is saying "the second field is of general type." `Array(3, 3)` is saying "the third field is a date in M-D-Y format." The code is longer because it explicitly specifies that each possible delimiter is set to `False`. Because `False` is the default for all delimiters, you really need only the one you will use. The following code is equivalent:

```
Workbooks.OpenText Filename:= "C:\sales.txt", _
    DataType:=xlDelimited, Comma:=True, _
    FieldInfo:=Array(Array(1, 1), Array(2, 1), Array(3, 3), _
    Array(4, 1), Array(5, 1), Array(6, 1), _
    Array(7, 1), Array(8, 1))
```

Finally, to make the code more readable, you can use the constant names rather than the code numbers:

```
Workbooks.OpenText Filename:="C:\sales.txt", _
    DataType:=xlDelimited, _Comma:=True, _
    FieldInfo:=Array(Array(1, xlGeneralFormat), _
    Array(2, xlGeneralFormat), _
    Array(3, xlMDYFormat), Array(4, xlGeneralFormat), _
    Array(5, xlGeneralFormat), Array(6, xlGeneralFormat), _
    Array(7, xlGeneralFormat), Array(8, xlGeneralFormat))
```

Excel has built-in options to read files in which fields are delimited by tabs, semicolons, commas, or spaces. Excel can actually handle anything as a delimiter. If someone sends pipe-delimited text, you would set the `Other` parameter to `True` and specify an `OtherChar` parameter:

```
Workbooks.OpenText Filename:= "C:\sales.txt", Origin:=437, _
    DataType:=xlDelimited, Other:=True, OtherChar:= "|", FieldInfo:=...
```

Reading Text Files One Row at a Time

If you use the Text Import Wizard to read a file with more than 1,048,576 rows of data, you get an error saying, "File not loaded completely." The first 1,048,576 rows of the file load correctly.

If you use `Workbooks.OpenText` to open a file with more than 1,048,576 rows of data, you are given no indication that the file did not load completely. Excel 2013 loads the first 1,048,576 rows and allows macro execution to continue. Your only indication that there is a problem is if someone notices that the reports are not reporting all the sales. If you think that your files will ever get this large, it would be good to check to see whether cell

A1048576 is nonblank after an import. If it is, the odds are that the entire file was not loaded.

Reading Text Files One Row at a Time

You might run into a text file with more than 1,048,576 rows. When this happens, the alternative is to read the text file one row at a time. The code for doing this is the same code you might remember in your first high-school BASIC class.

You need to open the file for INPUT as #1. You use #1 to indicate that this is the first file you are opening. If you had to open two files, you could open the second file as #2. You can then use the Line Input #1 statement to read a line of the file into a variable. The following code opens sales.txt, reads 10 lines of the file into the first 10 cells of the worksheet, and closes the file:

```
Sub Import10()
    ThisFile = "C\sales.txt"
    Open ThisFile For Input As #1
    For i = 1 To 10
        Line Input #1, Data
        Cells(i, 1).Value = Data
    Next i
    Close #1
End Sub
```

Rather than read only 10 records, you want to read until you get to the end of the file. A variable called EOF is updated by Excel automatically. If you open a file for input as #1, checking EOF(1) tells you whether you have read the last record.

Use a Do...While loop to keep reading records until you have reached the end of the file:

```
Sub ImportAll()
    ThisFile = "C:\sales.txt"
    Open ThisFile For Input As #1
    Ctr = 0
    Do
        Line Input #1, Data
        Ctr = Ctr + 1
        Cells(Ctr, 1).Value = Data
    Loop While EOF(1) = False
    Close #1
End Sub
```

After reading records with code such as this, note in Figure 19.9 that the data is not parsed into columns. All the fields are in Column A of the file.

Use the TextToColumns method to parse the records into columns. The parameters for TextToColumns are nearly identical to those for the OpenText method:

```
Cells(1, 1).Resize(Ctr, 1).TextToColumns Destination:=Range("A1"), _
DataType:=xlDelimited, Comma:=True, FieldInfo:=Array(Array(1, _
xlGeneralFormat), Array(2, xlMDYFormat), Array(3, xlGeneralFormat), _
Array(4, xlGeneralFormat), Array(5, xlGeneralFormat), Array(6, _
xlGeneralFormat), Array(7,xlGeneralFormat), Array(8, xlGeneralFormat), _
Array(9, xlGeneralFormat), Array(10,xlGeneralFormat), Array(11, _
xlGeneralFormat))
```

Figure 19.9
When you are reading a text file one row at a time, all the data fields end up in one long entry in Column A.

Cell A1 contains data for eight columns

> **NOTE**
>
> For the remainder of your Excel session, Excel remembers the delimiter settings. There is an annoying bug (feature?) in Excel. After Excel remembers that you are using a comma or a tab as a delimiter, any time that you attempt to paste data from the Clipboard to Excel, the data is parsed automatically by the delimiters specified in the OpenText method. Therefore, if you attempt to paste some text that includes the customer ABC, Inc., the text is parsed automatically into two columns, with text up to ABC in one column and Inc. in the next column.

Rather than hard-code that you are using the #1 designator to open the text file, it is safer to use the FreeFile function. This returns an integer representing the next file number available for use by the Open statement. The complete code to read a text file smaller than 1,048,576 rows is as follows:

```
Sub ImportAll()
    ThisFile = "C:\sales.txt"
    FileNumber = FreeFile
    Open ThisFile For Input As #FileNumber
    Ctr = 0
    Do
        Line Input #FileNumber, Data
        Ctr = Ctr + 1
        Cells(Ctr, 1).Value = Data
    Loop While EOF(FileNumber) = False
    Close #FileNumber
    Cells(1, 1).Resize(Ctr, 1).TextToColumns Destination:=Range("A1"), _
        DataType:=xlDelimited, Comma:=True, _
        FieldInfo:=Array(Array(1, xlGeneralFormat), _
        Array(2, xlMDYFormat), Array(3, xlGeneralFormat), _
        Array(4, xlGeneralFormat), Array(5, xlGeneralFormat), _
        Array(5, xlGeneralFormat), Array(6, xlGeneralFormat), _
        Array(7, xlGeneralFormat), Array(8, xlGeneralFormat), _
        Array(9, xlGeneralFormat), Array(10, xlGeneralFormat), _
        Array(10, xlGeneralFormat), Array(11, xlGeneralFormat))
End Sub
```

Reading Text Files with More Than 1,048,576 Rows

You can use the Line Input method for reading a large text file. A good strategy is to read rows into cells A1:A1048575, and then begin reading additional rows into cell AA2. You can start in Row 2 on the second set so that the headings can be copied from Row 1 of the first dataset. If the file is large enough that it fills up Column AA, move to BA2, CA2, and so on.

Also, you should stop writing columns when you get to Row 1048574, leaving two blank rows at the bottom. This ensures that the code `Cells(Rows.Count, 1).End(xlup).Row` finds the final row. The following code reads a large text file into several sets of columns:

```
Sub ReadLargeFile()
    ThisFile = "C:\sales.txt"
    FileNumber = FreeFile
    Open ThisFile For Input As #FileNumber

    NextRow = 1
    NextCol = 1
    Do While Not EOF(1)
        Line Input #FileNumber, Data
        Cells(NextRow, NextCol).Value = Data
        NextRow = NextRow + 1
        If NextRow = (Rows.Count -2)  Then
            ' Parse these records
            Range(Cells(1, NextCol), Cells(Rows.Count, NextCol)) _
                TextToColumns _
                Destination:=Cells(1, NextCol), DataType:=xlDelimited, _
                Comma:=True, FieldInfo:=Array(Array(1, xlGeneralFormat), _
                Array(2, xlMDYFormat), Array(3, xlGeneralFormat), _
                Array(4, xlGeneralFormat), Array(5, xlGeneralFormat), _
                Array(6, xlGeneralFormat), Array(7, xlGeneralFormat), _
                Array(8, xlGeneralFormat), Array(9, xlGeneralFormat), _
                Array(10, xlGeneralFormat), Array(11, xlGeneralFormat))
            ' Copy the headings from section 1
            If NextCol > 1 Then
                Range("A1:K1").Copy Destination:=Cells(1, NextCol)
            End If
            ' Set up the next section
            NextCol = NextCol + 26
            NextRow = 2
        End If
    Loop
    Close #FileNumber
    ' Parse the final Section of records
    FinalRow = NextRow - 1
    If FinalRow = 1 Then
        ' Handle if the file coincidentally had 1084574 rows exactly
        NextCol = NextCol - 26
    Else
        Range(Cells(2, NextCol), Cells(FinalRow, NextCol)).TextToColumns _
                Destination:=Cells(1, NextCol), DataType:=xlDelimited, _
                Comma:=True, FieldInfo:=Array(Array(1, xlGeneralFormat), _
                Array(2, xlMDYFormat), Array(3, xlGeneralFormat), _
                Array(4, xlGeneralFormat), Array(5, xlGeneralFormat), _
                Array(6, xlGeneralFormat), Array(7, xlGeneralFormat), _
                Array(8, xlGeneralFormat), Array(9, xlGeneralFormat), _
                Array(10, xlGeneralFormat), Array(11, xlGeneralFormat))
        If NextCol > 1 Then
            Range("A1:K1").Copy Destination:=Cells(1, NextCol)
        End If
    End If

    DataSets = (NextCol - 1) / 26 + 1

End Sub
```

Usually you should write the `DataSets` variable to a named cell somewhere in the workbook so that you know how many datasets you have in the worksheet later.

As you can imagine, using this method, it is possible to read 660,601,620 rows of data into a single worksheet. The code you formerly used to filter and report the data now becomes more complex. You might find yourself creating pivot tables from each set of columns to create a dataset summary, and then finally summarizing all the summary tables with a final pivot table. At some point, you need to consider whether the application really belongs in Access. You can also consider whether the data should be stored in Access with an Excel front end, which is discussed in Chapter 21, "Using Access as a Back End to Enhance Multiuser Access to Data."

Writing Text Files

The code for writing text files is similar to that for reading text files. You need to open a specific file for output as `#1`. Then, as you loop through various records, you write them to the file using the `Print #1` statement.

Before you open a file for output, make sure that any prior examples of the file have been deleted. You can use the `Kill` statement to delete a file. `Kill` returns an error if the file was not there in the first place. In this case, you want to use `On Error Resume Next` to prevent an error.

The following code writes out a text file for use by another application:

```
Sub WriteFile()
    ThisFile = "C:\Results.txt"

    ' Delete yesterday's copy of the file
    On Error Resume Next
    Kill ThisFile
    On Error GoTo 0

    ' Open the file
    Open ThisFile For Output As #1
    FinalRow = Cells(Rows.Count, 1).End(xlUp).Row
    ' Write out the file
    For j = 1 To FinalRow
        Print #1, Cells(j, 1).Value
    Next j
End Sub
```

This is a somewhat trivial example. You can use this method to write out any type of text-based file. The code at the end of Chapter 18, "Reading from and Writing to the Web," uses the same concept to write out HTML files.

Next Steps

The next chapter steps outside of the world of Excel to talk about how to transfer Excel data into Microsoft Word documents. Chapter 20, "Automating Word," looks at using Excel VBA to automate and control Microsoft Word.

19

Automating Word

Word, Excel, PowerPoint, Outlook, and Access all use the same VBA language. The only difference is their object models. For example, Excel has a `Workbooks` object and Word has `Documents`. Any one of these applications can access another application's object model as long as the second application is installed.

To access Word's object library, Excel must establish a link to it by using either early binding or late binding. With *early binding*, the reference to the application object is created when the program is compiled. With *late binding*, the reference is created when the program is run.

This chapter is an introduction to accessing Word from Excel.

20

> **NOTE**
>
> Because this chapter does not review Word's entire object model or the object models of other applications, refer to the VBA Object Browser in the appropriate application to learn about other object models.

Using Early Binding to Reference the Word Object

Code written with early binding executes faster than code with late binding. A reference is made to Word's object library before the code is written so that Word's objects, properties, and methods are available in the Object Browser. Tips such as a list of members of an object also appear, as shown in Figure 20.1.

The disadvantage of early binding is that the referenced object library must exist on the system. For example, if you write a macro referencing Word 2013's object library and someone with Word 2007 attempts to run the code, the program fails because the program cannot find the Word 2013 object library.

Figure 20.1
Early binding allows
access to the Word
object's syntax.

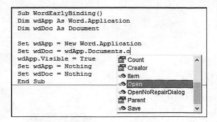

The object library is added through the VB Editor, as described here:

1. Select Tools, References.

2. Check Microsoft Word 15.0 Object Library in the Available References list (see Figure 20.2). If the object library is not found, Word is not installed. If another version is found in the list, such as 12.0, another version of Word is installed.

3. Click OK.

Figure 20.2
Select the object library
from the Available
References list.

After the reference is set, Word variables can be declared with the correct Word variable type, such as Document. However, if the object variable is declared As Object, this forces the program to use late binding. The following example creates a new instance of Word and opens an existing Word document from Excel. The declared variables, wdApp and wdDoc, are Word object types. wdApp is used to create a reference to the Word application in the same way the Application object is used in Excel. New Word.Application is used to create a new instance of Word. If you are opening a document in a new instance of Word, Word is not visible. If the application needs to be shown, it must be unhidden (wdApp.Visible = True). When the program is done, release the connection to Word by setting the object, wdApp, to Nothing.

```
Sub WordEarlyBinding()
Dim wdApp As Word.Application
Dim wdDoc As Document
Set wdApp = New Word.Application
Set wdDoc = wdApp.Documents.Open(ThisWorkbook.Path & _
    "\Automating Word.docx")
```

```
wdApp.Visible = True
Set wdApp = Nothing
Set wdDoc = Nothing
End Sub
```

> **TIP**
> Excel searches through the selected libraries to find the reference for the object type. If the type is found in more than one library, the first reference is selected. You can influence which library is chosen by changing the priority of the reference in the listing.

When the process is finished, it's a good idea to set the object variables to Nothing and release the memory being used by the application, as shown here:

```
Set wdApp = Nothing
Set wdDoc = Nothing
```

If the referenced version of Word does not exist on the system, an error message appears when the code is compiled. View the References list; the missing object is highlighted with the word *MISSING* (see Figure 20.3).

Figure 20.3
Excel won't find the expected Word 2013 object library if the workbook is opened in Excel 2010.

If a previous version of Word is available, you can try running the program with that version referenced. Many objects are the same between versions.

Using Late Binding to Reference the Word Object

When using late binding, you are creating an object that refers to the Word application before linking to the Word library. Because you do not set up a reference beforehand, the only constraint on the Word version is that the objects, properties, and methods must exist. In the case where there are differences between versions of Word, the version can be verified and the correct object used accordingly.

The disadvantage of late binding is that because Excel does not know what is going on, it does not understand that you are referring to Word. This prevents the tips from appearing when referencing Word objects. In addition, built-in constants are not available. This means that when Excel is compiling, it cannot verify that the references to Word are correct. After the program is executed, the links to Word begin to build, and any coding errors are detected at that point.

The following example creates a new instance of Word, and then opens and makes visible an existing Word document. An object variable (wdApp) is declared and set to reference the application (CreateObject("Word.Application")). Other required variables are then declared (wdDoc), and the application object is used to refer these variables to Word's object model. Declaring wdApp and wdDoc as objects forces the use of late binding. The program cannot create the required links to the Word object model until it executes the CreateObject function.

```
Sub WordLateBinding()
Dim wdApp As Object, wdDoc As Object
Set wdApp = CreateObject("Word.Application")
Set wdDoc = wdApp.Documents.Open(ThisWorkbook.Path & _
"\Automating Word.docx")
wdApp.Visible = True
Set wdApp = Nothing
Set wdDoc = Nothing
End Sub
```

Using the New Keyword to Reference the Word Application

In the early-binding example, the keyword New was used to reference the Word application. The New keyword can be used only with early binding; it does not work with late binding. CreateObject or GetObject would also work, but New is best for this example. If an instance of the application is running and you want to use it, use the GetObject function instead.

> **CAUTION**
>
> If your code to open Word runs smoothly but you don't see an instance of Word (and should because you code it to be Visible), open your Task Manager and look for the process WinWord.exe. If it exists, from the Immediate window in Excel's VB Editor, type the following (which uses early binding):
>
> Word.Application.Visible = True
>
> If multiple instances of WinWord.exe are found, you need to make each instance visible and close the extra instance(s) of WinWord.exe.

Using the CreateObject Function to Create a New Instance of an Object

The CreateObject function was used in the late-binding example. However, this function can also be used in early binding. It is used to create a new instance of an object, in this case the Word application. CreateObject has a class parameter consisting of the name and type of the object to be created (Name.Type). For example, the examples in this chapter have shown you (Word.Application), in which Word is the Name and Application is the Type.

Using the `GetObject` **Function to Reference an Existing Instance of Word**

The `GetObject` function can be used to reference an instance of Word that is already running. It creates an error if no instance can be found.

`GetObject`'s two parameters are optional. The first parameter specifies the full path and filename to open, and the second parameter specifies the application program. The following example leaves off the application, allowing the default program, which is Word, to open the document:

```
Sub UseGetObject()
Dim wdDoc As Object
Set wdDoc = GetObject(ThisWorkbook.Path & "\Automating Word.docx")
wdDoc.Application.Visible = True
'more code interacting with the Word document
Set wdDoc = Nothing
End Sub
```

This example opens a document in an existing instance of Word and ensures that the Word application's `Visible` property is set to `True`. Note that to make the document visible, you have to refer to the application object (`wdDoc.Application.Visible`) because `wdDoc` is referencing a document rather than the application.

> **NOTE** Although the Word application's `Visible` property is set to `True`, this code does not make the Word application the active application. In most cases, the Word application icon stays in the taskbar, and Excel remains the active application on the user's screen.

The following example uses errors to learn whether Word is already open before pasting a chart at the end of a document. If Word is not open, it opens Word and creates a new document:

```
Sub IsWordOpen()
Dim wdApp As Word.Application 'early binding

ActiveChart.ChartArea.Copy

On Error Resume Next 'returns Nothing if Word isn't open
Set wdApp = GetObject(, "Word.Application")
If wdApp Is Nothing Then
    'since Word isn't open, open it
    Set wdApp = GetObject("", "Word.Application")
    With wdApp
        .Documents.Add
        .Visible = True
    End With
End If
On Error GoTo 0

With wdApp.Selection
    .EndKey Unit:=wdStory
```

20

```
        .TypeParagraph
        .PasteSpecial Link:=False, DataType:=wdPasteOLEObject, _
            Placement:=wdInLine, DisplayAsIcon:=False
    End With

    Set wdApp = Nothing
    End Sub
```

Using On Error Resume Next forces the program to continue even if it runs into an error. In this case, an error occurs when we attempt to link wdApp to an object that does not exist. wdApp will have no value. The next line, If wdApp Is Nothing Then, takes advantage of this and opens an instance of Word, adding an empty document and making the application visible. Use On Error Goto 0 to return to normal VBA error-handling behavior.

> **TIP**
>
> Note the use of empty quotes for the first parameter in GetObject("", "Word. Application"). This is how to use the GetObject function to open a new instance of Word.

Using Constant Values

The preceding example used constants that are specific to Word such as wdPasteOLEObject and wdInLine. When you are programming using early binding, Excel helps by showing these constants in the tip window.

With late binding, these tips will not appear. So what can you do? You might write your program using early binding, and then change it to late binding after you compile and test the program. The problem with this method is that the program will not compile because Excel does not recognize the Word constants.

The words wdPasteOLEObject and wdInLine are for your convenience as a programmer. Behind each of these text constants is the real value that VBA understands. The solution to this is to retrieve and use these real values with your late binding program.

Using the Watch Window to Retrieve the Real Value of a Constant

One way to retrieve the value is to add a watch for the constants. Then, step through your code and check the value of the constant as it appears in the Watch window, as shown in Figure 20.4.

Figure 20.4
Use the Watch window to get the real value behind a Word constant.

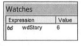

> **NOTE**
>
> See "Querying by Using a Watch Window" in Chapter 2, "This Sounds Like BASIC, so Why Doesn't It Look Familiar?" for more information on using the Watch window.

Using the Object Browser to Retrieve the Real Value of a Constant

Another way to retrieve the value is to look up the constant in the Object Browser. However, you need the Word library set up as a reference to use this method. To set up the Word library, right-click the constant and select Definition. The Object Browser opens to the constant and shows the value in the bottom window, as shown in Figure 20.5.

Figure 20.5
Use the Object Browser to get the real value behind a Word constant.

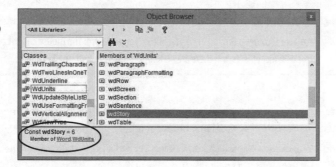

> **TIP**
> You can set up the Word reference library to be accessed from the Object Browser. However, you do not have to set up your code with early binding. In this way, the reference is at your fingertips, but your code is still late binding. Turning off the reference library is just a few clicks away.

Replacing the constants in the earlier code example with their real values would look like this:

```
With wdApp.Selection
    .EndKey Unit:=6
    .TypeParagraph
    .PasteSpecial Link:=False, DataType:=0, Placement:=0, DisplayAsIcon:=False
End With
```

However, what happens a month from now when you return to the code and you try to remember what those numbers mean? The solution is up to you. Some programmers add comments to the code referencing the Word constant. Other programmers create their own variables to hold the real value and use those variables in place of the constants, like this:

```
Const xwdStory As Long = 6
Const xwdPasteOLEObject As Long = 0
Const xwdInLine As Long = 0

With wdApp.Selection
    .EndKey Unit:=xwdStory
    .TypeParagraph
    .PasteSpecial Link:=False, DataType:=xwdPasteOLEObject, _
        Placement:=xwdInLine, DisplayAsIcon:=False
End With
```

20

Understanding Word's Objects

Word's macro recorder can be used to get a preliminary understanding of the Word object model. However, much as with Excel's macro recorder, the results will be long-winded. Keep this in mind and use the recorder to lead you toward the objects, properties, and methods in Word.

> **CAUTION**
>
> The macro recorder is limited in what it allows you to record. The mouse cannot be used to move the cursor or select objects, but there are no limits in doing so with the keyboard.

The following example is what the Word macro recorder produces when adding a new, blank document from File, New, Blank Document:

```
Documents.Add Template:="Normal", NewTemplate:=False, DocumentType:=0
```

Making this more efficient in Word produces this:

```
Documents.Add
```

`Template`, `NewTemplate`, and `DocumentType` are all optional properties that the recorder includes but that are not required unless you need to change a default property or ensure that a property is what you require.

To use the same line of code in Excel, a link to the Word object library is required, as you learned earlier. After that link is established, an understanding of Word's objects is all you need. The next section is a review of *some* of Word's objects—enough to get you off the ground. For a more detailed listing, refer to the object model in Word's VB Editor.

Document **Object**

Word's `Document` object is equivalent to Excel's `Workbook` object. It consists of characters, words, sentences, paragraphs, sections, and headers/footers. It is through the `Document` object that methods and properties affecting the entire document, such as printing, closing, searching, and reviewing, are accomplished.

Create a New Blank Document

To create a blank document in an existing instance of Word, use the `Add` method as shown next. We already learned how to create a new document when Word is closed—refer to `GetObject` and `CreateObject`.

```
Sub NewDocument()
Dim wdApp As Word.Application

Set wdApp = GetObject(, "Word.Application")
```

20

```
wdApp.Documents.Add
'any other Word code you need here

Set wdApp = Nothing
End Sub
```

This example opens a new, blank document that uses the default template. To create a new document that uses a specific template, use this:

```
wdApp.Documents.Add Template:="Memo (Contemporary design).dotx"
```

This creates a new document that uses the Contemporary Memo template. `Template` can be either the name of a template from the default template location or the file path and name.

Open an Existing Document

To open an existing document, use the `Open` method. Several parameters are available, including `Read Only` and `AddtoRecentFiles`. The following example opens an existing document as `Read Only`, and prevents the file from being added to the Recent File List under the File menu:

```
wdApp.Documents.Open _
    Filename:="C:\Excel VBA 2013 by Jelen & Syrstad\Chapter 8 - Arrays.docx", _
    ReadOnly:=True, AddtoRecentFiles:=False
```

Save Changes to a Document

After you have made changes to a document, most likely you will want to save it. To save a document with its existing name, use this:

```
wdApp.Documents.Save
```

If you use the `Save` command with a new document without a name, nothing will happen. To save a document with a new name, you must use the `SaveAs` method instead:

```
wdApp.ActiveDocument.SaveAs _
    "C:\Excel VBA 2013 by Jelen & Syrstad\MemoTest.docx"
```

`SaveAs` requires the use of members of the `Document` object, such as `ActiveDocument`.

Close an Open Document

Use the `Close` method to close a specified document or all open documents. By default, a Save dialog appears for any documents with unsaved changes. You can use the `SaveChanges` argument to change this. To close all open documents without saving changes, use this code:

```
wdApp.Documents.Close SaveChanges:=wdDoNotSaveChanges
```

To close a specific document, you can close the active document or you can specify a document name:

```
wdApp.ActiveDocument.Close
```

or

```
wdApp.Documents("Chapter 8 - Arrays.docx").Close
```

20

Print a Document

Use the `PrintOut` method to print part or all of a document. To print a document with all the default print settings, use this:

```
wdApp.ActiveDocument.PrintOut
```

By default, the print range is the entire document, but you can change this by setting the `Range` and `Pages` arguments of the `PrintOut` method. For example, to print only page 2 of the active document, use this:

```
wdApp.ActiveDocument.PrintOut Range:=wdPrintRangeOfPages, Pages:="2"
```

Selection **Object**

The `Selection` object represents what is selected in the document, such as a word, a sentence, or the insertion point. It also has a `Type` property that returns the type that is selected, such as `wdSelectionIP`, `wdSelectionColumn`, and `wdSelectionShape`.

Navigating with `HomeKey` **and** `EndKey`

The `HomeKey` and `EndKey` methods are used to change the selection; they correspond to using the Home and End keys, respectively, on the keyboard. They have two parameters: `Unit` and `Extend`. `Unit` is the range of movement to make, to either the beginning (`Home`) or end (`End`) of a line (`wdLine`), document (`wdStory`), column (`wdColumn`), or row (`wdRow`). `Extend` is the type of movement: `wdMove` moves the selection, and `wdExtend` extends the selection from the original insertion point to the new insertion point.

To move the cursor to the beginning of the document, use this code:

```
wdApp.Selection.HomeKey Unit:=wdStory, Extend:=wdMove
```

To select the document from the insertion point to the end of the document, use this code:

```
wdApp.Selection.EndKey Unit:=wdStory, Extend:=wdExtend
```

Inserting Text with `TypeText`

The `TypeText` method is used to insert text into a Word document. User settings, such as the `ReplaceSelection` setting, can affect what happens when text is typed into the document when text is selected. The following example first makes sure that the setting for overwriting selected text is turned on. Then it selects the second paragraph (using the `Range` object described in the next section) and overwrites it.

```
Sub InsertText()
Dim wdApp As Word.Application
Dim wdDoc As Document
Dim wdSln As Selection

Set wdApp = GetObject(, "Word.Application")
Set wdDoc = wdApp.ActiveDocument

wdDoc.Application.Options.ReplaceSelection = True
wdDoc.Paragraphs(2).Range.Select
wdApp.Selection.TypeText "Overwriting the selected paragraph."
```

20

```
Set wdApp = Nothing
Set wdDoc = Nothing
End Sub
```

Range **Object**

The Range object uses the following syntax:

```
Range(StartPosition, EndPosition)
```

The Range object represents a contiguous area or areas in the document. It has a starting character position and an ending character position. The object can be the insertion point, a range of text, or the entire document including nonprinting characters such as spaces or paragraph marks.

The Range object is similar to the Selection object, but in some ways it is better. For example, the Range object requires less code to accomplish the same tasks, and it has more capabilities. In addition, it saves time and memory because the Range object does not require Word to move the cursor or highlight objects in the document to manipulate them.

Define a Range

To define a range, enter a starting and ending position, as shown in this code segment:

```
Sub RangeText()
Dim wdApp As Word.Application
Dim wdDoc As Document
Dim wdRng As Word.Range

Set wdApp = GetObject(, "Word.Application")
Set wdDoc = wdApp.ActiveDocument

Set wdRng = wdDoc.Range(0, 50)
wdRng.Select

Set wdApp = Nothing
Set wdDoc = Nothing
Set wdRng = Nothing
End Sub
```

Figure 20.6 shows the results of running this code. The first 50 characters are selected, including nonprinting characters such as paragraph returns.

Figure 20.6
The Range object selects everything in its path.

20

> **NOTE**
>
> The range was selected (wdRng.Select) for easier viewing. It is not required that the range be selected to be manipulated. For example, to delete the range, do this:
>
> wdRng.Delete

The first character position in a document is always zero, and the last is equivalent to the number of characters in the document.

The Range object also selects paragraphs. The following example copies the third paragraph in the active document and pastes it in Excel. Depending on how the paste is done, the text can be pasted into a text box (see Figure 20.7) or into a cell:

```
Sub SelectSentence()
Dim wdApp As Word.Application
Dim wdRng As Word.Range

Set wdApp = GetObject(, "Word.Application")

With wdApp.ActiveDocument
    If .Paragraphs.Count >= 3 Then
        Set wdRng = .Paragraphs(3).Range
        wdRng.Copy
    End If
End With

'This line pastes the copied text into a text box
'because that is the default PasteSpecial method for Word text
Worksheets("Sheet2").PasteSpecial

'This line pastes the copied text in cell A1
Worksheets("Sheet2").Paste Destination:=Worksheets("Sheet2").Range("A1")

Set wdApp = Nothing
Set wdRng = Nothing
End Sub
```

Figure 20.7
Paste Word text into an Excel text box.

Format a Range

After a range is selected, formatting can be applied to it (see Figure 20.8). The following program loops through all the paragraphs of the active document and applies bold to the first word of each paragraph:

```
Sub ChangeFormat()
Dim wdApp As Word.Application
```

```
Dim wdRng As Word.Range
Dim count As Integer

Set wdApp = GetObject(, "Word.Application")

With wdApp.ActiveDocument
    For count = 1 To .Paragraphs.Count
        Set wdRng = .Paragraphs(count).Range
        With wdRng
            .Words(1).Font.Bold = True
            .Collapse
        End With
    Next count
End With

Set wdApp = Nothing
Set wdRng = Nothing
End Sub
```

Figure 20.8
Format the first word of each paragraph in a document.

Word, Excel, PowerPoint, Outlook, and Access all use the same VBA language; the only difference between them is their object models (for example, Excel has a Workbooks object, Word has Documents). Any one of these applications can access another application's object model as long as the second application is installed.

To access Word's object library, Excel must establish a link to it. There are two ways of doing this: early binding or late binding. With early binding, the reference to the application object is created when the program is compiled; with late binding, it is created when the program is run.

This chapter is an introduction to accessing Word from Excel; we will not be reviewing Word's entire object model or the object models of other applications. Refer to the VBA Object Browser in the appropriate application to learn about other object models.

A quick way of changing the formatting of entire paragraphs is to change the style (see Figures 20.9 and 20.10). The following program finds the paragraph with the Normal style and changes it to HA:

```
Sub ChangeStyle()
Dim wdApp As Word.Application
Dim wdRng As Word.Range
Dim count As Integer

Set wdApp = GetObject(, "Word.Application")

With wdApp.ActiveDocument
    For count = 1 To .Paragraphs.Count
        Set wdRng = .Paragraphs(count).Range
        With wdRng
            If .Style = "Normal" Then
                .Style = "HA"
            End If
        End With
    Next count
End With

Set wdApp = Nothing
```

20

```
Set wdRng = Nothing
End Sub
```

Figure 20.9

Before: A paragraph with the Normal style needs to be changed to the HA style.

Word, Excel, PowerPoint, Outlook, and Access all use the same VBA language; the only difference between them is their object models (for example, Excel has a Workbooks object, Word has Documents). Any one of these applications can access another application's object model as long as the second application is installed.	Normal ¶
	NOX ¶
	NX ¶

Figure 20.10

After: Apply styles with code to change paragraph formatting quickly.

Word, Excel, PowerPoint, Outlook, and Access all use the same VBA language; the only difference between them is their object models (for example, Excel has a Workbooks object, Word has Documents). Any one of these applications can access another application's object model as long as the second application is installed.	FTN ¶
	HA ¶
	HA + Underlir

Bookmarks

Bookmarks are members of the Document, Selection, and Range objects. They can help make it easier to navigate around Word. Instead of having to choose words, sentences, or paragraphs, use bookmarks to manipulate sections of a document swiftly.

> **NOTE** You are not limited to using only existing bookmarks. Instead, you can create bookmarks using code.

Bookmarks appear as gray I-bars in Word documents. In Word, go to File, Options, Advanced, Show Document Contents and select Show Bookmarks to turn on bookmarks.

After you have set up bookmarks in a document, you can use the bookmarks to move quickly to a range to insert text or other items, such as charts. The following code automatically inserts text and a chart after bookmarks that were previously set up in the document. Figure 20.11 shows the results.

```
Sub FillInMemo()
Dim myArray()
Dim wdBkmk As String

Dim wdApp As Word.Application
Dim wdRng As Word.Range

myArray = Array("To", "CC", "From", "Subject", "Chart")
Set wdApp = GetObject(, "Word.Application")

'insert text
Set wdRng = wdApp.ActiveDocument.Bookmarks(myArray(0)).Range
wdRng.InsertBefore ("Bill Jelen")
Set wdRng = wdApp.ActiveDocument.Bookmarks(myArray(1)).Range
wdRng.InsertBefore ("Tracy Syrstad")
Set wdRng = wdApp.ActiveDocument.Bookmarks(myArray(2)).Range
```

20

```
wdRng.InsertBefore ("MrExcel")
Set wdRng = wdApp.ActiveDocument.Bookmarks(myArray(3)).Range
wdRng.InsertBefore ("Fruit & Vegetable Sales")

'insert chart
Set wdRng = wdApp.ActiveDocument.Bookmarks(myArray(4)).Range
Worksheets("Fruit Sales").ChartObjects("Chart 1").Copy
wdRng.PasteAndFormat Type:=wdPasteOLEObject

wdApp.Activate
Set wdApp = Nothing
Set wdRng = Nothing

End Sub
```

Figure 20.11
Use bookmarks to enter text or charts into a Word document.

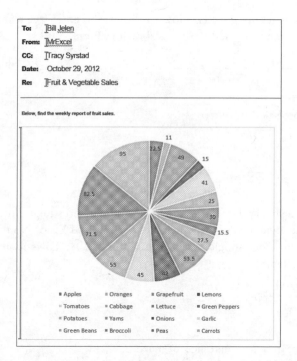

Controlling Form Fields in Word

You have seen how to modify a document by inserting charts and text, modifying formatting, and deleting text. However, a document might contain other items such as controls that you can modify.

For the following example, a template, New Client.dotx, was created consisting of text and bookmarks. The bookmarks are placed after the Name and Date fields. Form Field check boxes were also added. The controls are found under Legacy forms in the Controls section of the Developer tab in Word, as shown in Figure 20.12. Notice in the code sample that follows that the check boxes have all been renamed so they make more sense. For example, one bookmark was renamed chk401k from Checkbox5. To rename a bookmark, right-click the check box, select Properties, and type a new name in the Bookmark field.

Figure 20.12
You can use the Form Fields found under the Legacy Tools to add check boxes to a document.

The questionnaire was set up in Excel, allowing the user to enter free text in B1 and B2, but setting up data validation in B3 and B5:B8, as shown in Figure 20.13.

Figure 20.13
Create an Excel sheet to collect your data.

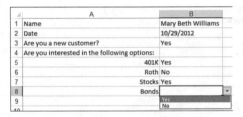

The code goes into a standard module. The name and date go straight into the document. The check boxes use logic to verify whether the user selected Yes or No to confirm whether the corresponding check box should be checked. Figure 20.14 shows a sample document that has been completed.

```
Sub FillOutWordForm()
Dim TemplatePath As String
Dim wdApp As Object
Dim wdDoc As Object

'Open the template in a new instance of Word
TemplatePath = ThisWorkbook.Path & "\New Client.dotx"
Set wdApp = CreateObject("Word.Application")
Set wdDoc = wdApp.documents.Add(Template:=TemplatePath)

'Place our text values in document
With wdApp.ActiveDocument
    .Bookmarks("Name").Range.InsertBefore Range("B1").Text
    .Bookmarks("Date").Range.InsertBefore Range("B2").Text
End With

'Using basic logic, select the correct form object
If Range("B3").Value = "Yes" Then
    wdDoc.formfields("chkCustYes").CheckBox.Value = True
Else
    wdDoc.formfields("chkCustNo").CheckBox.Value = True
End If
```

```
With wdDoc
    If Range("B5").Value = "Yes" Then .Formfields("chk401k").CheckBox.Value = _
        True
    If Range("B6").Value = "Yes" Then .Formfields("chkRoth").CheckBox.Value _
        = True
    If Range("B7").Value = "Yes" Then .Formfields("chkStocks"). _
        CheckBox.Value = True
    If Range("B8").Value = "Yes" Then .Formfields("chkBonds"). _
        CheckBox.Value = True
End With

wdApp.Visible = True

ExitSub:

    Set wdDoc = Nothing
    Set wdApp = Nothing

End Sub
```

Figure 20.14
Excel can control Word's form fields and help automate filling out documents.

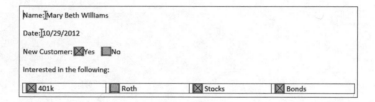

Next Steps

Chapter 19, "Text File Processing," showed you how to read from a text file to import data from another system. In this chapter, you learned how to connect to another Office program and access its object module. In Chapter 21, "Using Access as a Back End to Enhance Multiuser Access to Data," you connect to an Access database and learn about writing to Access Multidimensional Database (MDB) files. Compared to text files, Access files are faster, indexable, and allow multiuser access to data.

20

Using Access as a Back End to Enhance Multiuser Access to Data

21

The example near the end of Chapter 19, "Text File Processing," proposed a method for storing 683 million records in an Excel worksheet. At some point, you need to admit that even though Excel is the greatest product in the world, there is a time to move to Access and take advantage of the Access Multidimensional Database (MDB) files.

Even before you have more than one million rows, another compelling reason to use MDB data files is to allow multiuser access to data without the headaches associated with shared workbooks.

Microsoft Excel offers an option to share a workbook, but you automatically lose a number of important Excel features when you share one. After you share a workbook, you cannot use automatic subtotals, pivot tables, Group and Outline mode, scenarios, protection, Styles, Pictures, Add Charts, or Insert Worksheets.

By using an Excel VBA front end and storing data in an MDB database, you have the best of both worlds. You have the power and flexibility of Excel and the multiuser access capability available in Access.

> **TIP**
>
> MDB is the official file format of both Microsoft Access and Microsoft Visual Basic. This means that you can deploy an Excel solution that reads and writes from an MDB to customers who do not have Microsoft Access. Of course, it helps if you as the developer have a copy of Access because you can use the Access front end to set up tables and queries.

T I P

The examples in this chapter make use of the Microsoft Jet Database Engine for reading from and writing to the Access database. The Jet engine works with access data stored in Access 97 through 2013. If you are sure that all the people running the macro will have Office 2007 or newer, you could instead use the ACE engine. Microsoft now offers a 64-bit version of the ACE engine, but not the Jet engine.

ADO Versus DAO

For several years, Microsoft recommended data access objects (DAO) for accessing data in an external database. DAO became very popular, and a great deal of code was written for it. When Microsoft released Excel 2000, it started pushing ActiveX data objects (ADO). The concepts are similar, and the syntax differs only slightly. I use ADO in this chapter. Realize that if you start going through code written a decade ago, you might run into DAO code. Other than a few syntax changes, the code for both ADO and DAO looks similar.

If you discover that you have to debug some old code using DAO, check out the Microsoft Knowledge Base articles that discuss the differences. You can find them at http://support.microsoft.com/kb/225048.

The following two articles provide the Rosetta Stone between DAO and ADO. The DAO code is shown at http://support.microsoft.com/kb/q146607. The equivalent ADO code is shown at http://support.microsoft.com/kb/q142938.

To use any code in this chapter, open the VB Editor. Select Tools, References from the main menu and then select Microsoft ActiveX Data Objects Library from the Available References list, as shown in Figure 21.1.

Figure 21.1
To read or write from an Access MDB file, add the reference for Microsoft ActiveX Data Objects Library or higher.

NOTE

If you have Windows 7 or newer, you have access to version 6.1 of this library. Windows Vista offered Version 6.0 of the library. If you will be distributing the application to anyone who is still on Windows XP, you should choose version 2.8 instead.

CASE STUDY: CREATING A SHARED ACCESS DATABASE

Linda and Janine are two buyers for a retail chain of stores. Each morning, they import data from the cash registers to get current information on sales and inventory for 2,000 styles. Throughout the day, either buyer may enter transfers of inventory from one store to another. It would be ideal if Linda could see the pending transfers entered by Janine and vice versa.

Each buyer has an Excel application with VBA running on her desktop. They each import the cash register data and have VBA routines that facilitate the creation of pivot table reports to help them make buying decisions.

Attempting to store the transfer data in a common Excel file causes problems. When either buyer attempts to write to the Excel file, the entire file becomes read-only for the other buyer. With a shared workbook, Excel turns off the capability to create pivot tables, and this is required in their application.

Neither Linda nor Janine has the professional version of Office, so they do not have Access running on their desktop PCs.

The solution is to produce an Access database on a network drive that both Linda and Janine can see:

1. Using Access on another PC, produce a new database called `transfers.mdb` and add a table called `tblTransfer`, as shown in Figure 21.2.

Figure 21.2
Multiple people using their own Excel workbooks will read and write to this table inside an MDB file on a network drive.

Field Name	Data Type
ID	AutoNumber
Style	Short Text
FromStore	Number
ToStore	Number
Qty	Number
TDate	Date/Time
Sent	Yes/No
Receive	Yes/No

2. Move the `Transfers.mdb` file to a network drive. You might find that this common folder uses different drive-letter mappings on each machine. It might be H:\Common\ on Linda's machine and I:\Common\ on Janine's machine.

3. On both machines, go to the VB Editor and under Tools, References, add a reference to ActiveX Data Objects Library.

4. In both of their applications, find an out-of-the-way cell in which to store the path to `transfers.mdb`. Name this cell `TPath`.

The application provides nearly seamless multiuser access to both buyers. Both Linda and Janine can read or write to the table at the same time. The only time a conflict would occur is if they both happened to try to update the same record at the same time.

Other than the out-of-the-way cell reference to the path to `transfers.mdb`, neither buyer is aware that her data is being stored in a shared Access table, and neither computer needs to have Access installed.

21

The remainder of this chapter gives you the code necessary to allow the application included in the preceding case study to read or write data from the `tblTransfer` table.

The Tools of ADO

You encounter several terms when using ADO to connect to an external data source.

- **Recordset**—When connecting to an Access database, the recordset is either a table in the database or a query in the database. Most of the ADO methods reference the recordset. You might also want to create your own query on the fly. In this case, you write a SQL statement to extract only a subset of records from a table.

- **Connection**—Defines the path to the database and the type of database. In the case of Access databases, you specify that the connection is using the Microsoft Jet Engine.

- **Cursor**—Think of the cursor as a pointer that keeps track of which record you are using in the database. There are several types of cursors and two places for the cursor to be located (described in the following bullets).

- **Cursor type**—A dynamic cursor is the most flexible cursor. If you define a record-set and someone else updates a row in the table while a dynamic cursor is active, the dynamic cursor knows about the updated record. Although this is the most flexible, it requires the most overhead. If your database doesn't have a lot of transactions, you might specify a static cursor—this type of cursor returns a snapshot of the data at the time the cursor is established.

- **Cursor location**—The cursor can be located either on the client or on the server. For an Access database residing on your hard drive, a server location for the cursor means that the Access Jet Engine on your computer is controlling the cursor. When you specify a client location for the cursor, your Excel session is controlling the cursor. On a very large external dataset, it would be better to allow the server to control the cursor. For small datasets, a client cursor is faster.

- **Lock type**—The point of this entire chapter is to allow multiple people to access a dataset at the same time. The lock type defines how ADO will prevent crashes when two people try to update the record at the same time. With an optimistic lock type, an individual record is locked only when you attempt to update the record. If your application will be doing 90 percent reads and only occasionally updating, then an optimistic lock is perfect. However, if you know that every time you read a record you will soon update the record, then you would use a pessimistic lock type. With pessimistic locks, the record is locked as soon as you read it. If you know that you will never write back to the database, you can use a read-only lock. This enables you to read the records without preventing others from writing to the records.

The primary objects needed to access data in an MDB file are an ADO connection and an ADO recordset.

The ADO connection defines the path to the database and specifies that the connection is based on the Microsoft Jet Engine.

After you have established the connection to the database, you usually use that connection to define a recordset. A recordset can be a table or a subset of records in the table or a predefined query in the Access database. To open a recordset, you have to specify the connection and the values for the CursorType, CursorLocation, LockType, and Options parameters.

Assuming that you have only two users trying to access the table at a time, I generally use a dynamic cursor and an optimistic lock type. For large datasets, the adUseServer value of the CursorLocation property allows the database server to process records without using up RAM on the client machine. If you have a small dataset, it might be faster to use adUseClient for the CursorLocation. When the recordset is opened, all the records are transferred to memory of the client machine. This allows faster navigation from record to record.

Reading data from the Access database is easy provided you have less than 1048576 records. You can use the CopyFromRecordset method to copy all selected records from the recordset to a blank area of the worksheet.

To add a record to the Access table, use the AddNew method for the recordset. You then specify the value for each field in the table and use the Update method to commit the changes to the database.

To delete a record from the table, you can use a pass-through query to delete records that match a certain criteria.

NOTE If you ever find yourself frustrated with ADO and think, "If I could just open Access, I could knock out a quick SQL statement that will do exactly what I need," then the pass-through query is for you. Rather than use ADO to read through the records, the pass-through query sends a request to the database to run the SQL statement that your program builds. This effectively enables you to handle any tasks that your database might support but that are not handled by ADO. The types of SQL statements handled by the pass-through query are dependent on which database type you are connecting to.

Other tools are available that let you make sure that a table exists or that a particular field exists in a table. You can also use VBA to add new fields to a table definition on the fly.

Adding a Record to the Database

Going back to our case study earlier in the chapter, the application we are creating has a userform where buyers can enter transfers. To make the calls to the Access database as simple as possible, a series of utility modules handles the ADO connection to the database. This way, the userform code can simply call AddTransfer(Style, FromStore, ToStore, Qty).

The technique for adding records after the connection is defined is as follows:

1. Open a recordset that points to the table. In the code that follows, see the sections commented Open the Connection, Define the Recordset, and Open the Table.

2. Use AddNew to add a new record.

21

3. Update each field in the new record.

4. Use Update to update the recordset.

5. Close the recordset and then close the connection.

The following code adds a new record to the tblTransfer table:

```
Sub AddTransfer(Style As Variant, FromStore As Variant, _
    ToStore As Variant, Qty As Integer)
    Dim cnn As ADODB.Connection
    Dim rst As ADODB.Recordset

    MyConn = "J:\transfers.mdb"

    ' Open the Connection
    Set cnn = New ADODB.Connection
    With cnn
        .Provider = "Microsoft.Jet.OLEDB.4.0"
        .Open MyConn
    End With

    ' Define the Recordset
    Set rst = New ADODB.Recordset
    rst.CursorLocation = adUseServer

    ' Open the Table
    rst.Open Source:="tblTransfer", _
        ActiveConnection:=cnn, _
        CursorType:=adOpenDynamic, _
        LockType:=adLockOptimistic, _
        Options:=adCmdTable

    ' Add a record
    rst.AddNew

    ' Set up the values for the fields. The first four fields
    ' are passed from the calling userform. The date field
    ' is filled with the current date.
    rst("Style") = Style
    rst("FromStore") = FromStore
    rst("ToStore") = ToStore
    rst("Qty") = Qty
    rst("tDate") = Date
    rst("Sent") = False
    rst("Receive") = False

    ' Write the values to this record
    rst.Update

    ' Close
    rst.Close
    cnn.Close

End Sub
```

Retrieving Records from the Database

Reading records from the Access database is easy. As you define the recordset, you pass a SQL string to return the records in which you are interested.

> **NOTE** A great way to generate the SQL is to design a query in Access that retrieves the records. While viewing the query in Access, select SQL View from the View drop-down on the Query Tools Design tab of the ribbon. Access shows you the proper SQL statement required to execute that query. You can use this SQL statement as a model for building the SQL string in your VBA code.

After the recordset is defined, use the `CopyFromRecordSet` method to copy all the matching records from Access to a specific area of the worksheet.

The following routine queries the `Transfer` table to find all records in which the `Sent` flag is not yet set to `True`. The results are placed on a blank worksheet. The final few lines display the results in a userform to illustrate how to update a record in the next section.

```
Sub GetUnsentTransfers()
    Dim cnn As ADODB.Connection
    Dim rst As ADODB.Recordset
    Dim WSOrig As Worksheet
    Dim WSTemp As Worksheet
    Dim sSQL as String
    Dim FinalRow as Long

    Set WSOrig = ActiveSheet

    'Build a SQL String to get all fields for unsent transfers
    sSQL = "SELECT ID, Style, FromStore, ToStore, Qty, tDate FROM tblTransfer"
    sSQL = sSQL & " WHERE Sent=FALSE"

    ' Path to Transfers.mdb
    MyConn = "J:\transfers.mdb"

    Set cnn = New ADODB.Connection
    With cnn
        .Provider = "Microsoft.Jet.OLEDB.4.0"
        .Open MyConn
    End With

    Set rst = New ADODB.Recordset
    rst.CursorLocation = adUseServer
    rst.Open Source:=sSQL, ActiveConnection:=cnn, _
        CursorType:=AdForwardOnly, LockType:=adLockOptimistic, _
            Options:=adCmdText

    ' Create the report in a new worksheet
    Set WSTemp = Worksheets.Add

    ' Add Headings
    Range("A1:F1").Value = Array("ID", "Style", "From", "To", "Qty", "Date")
```

```
    ' Copy from the recordset to row 2
    Range("A2").CopyFromRecordset rst

    ' Close the connection
    rst.Close
    cnn.Close

    ' Format the report
    FinalRow = Range("A65536").End(xlUp).Row

    ' If there were no records, then stop
    If FinalRow = 1 Then
        Application.DisplayAlerts = False
        WSTemp.Delete
        Application.DisplayAlerts = True
        WSOrig.Activate
        MsgBox "There are no transfers to confirm"
        Exit Sub
    End If

    ' Format column F as a date
    Range("F2:F" & FinalRow).NumberFormat = "m/d/y"

    ' Show the userform -- used in next section
    frmTransConf.Show

    ' Delete the temporary sheet
    Application.DisplayAlerts = False
    WSTemp.Delete
    Application.DisplayAlerts = True

End Sub
```

The `CopyFromRecordSet` method copies records that match the SQL query to a range on the worksheet. Note that you receive only the data rows. The headings do not come along automatically. You must use code to write the headings to Row 1. Figure 21.3 shows the results.

Figure 21.3
`Range("A2").` `CopyFromRecord Set` brought matching records from the Access database to the worksheet.

	ID	Style	From	To	Qty	I
1	ID	Style	From	To	Qty	I
2	1935	B11275	340000	340000	8	
3	1936	B10133	340000	340000	4	
4	1937	B15422	340000	340000	5	
5	1938	B10894	340000	340000	9	
6	1939	B10049	340000	340000	3	
7	1941	B18722	340000	340000	10	
8	1944	B12886	340000	340000	10	
9	1947	B17947	340000	340000	7	
10	1950	B16431	340000	340000	9	
11	1953	B19857	340000	340000	7	

Updating an Existing Record

To update an existing record, you need to build a recordset with exactly one record. This requires that the user select some sort of unique key when identifying the records. After you have opened the recordset, use the `Fields` property to change the field in question and then the `Update` method to commit the changes to the database.

The earlier example returned a recordset to a blank worksheet and then called a userform frmTransConf. This form uses a simple Userform_Initialize to display the range in a large list box. The list box's properties have the MultiSelect property set to True:

```
Private Sub UserForm_Initialize()

    ' Determine how many records we have
    FinalRow = Cells(Rows.Count, 1).End(xlUp).Row
    If FinalRow > 1 Then
        Me.lbXlt.RowSource = "A2:F" & FinalRow
    End If

End Sub
```

After the initialize procedure is run, the unconfirmed records are displayed in a list box. The logistics planner can mark all the records that have actually been sent, as shown in Figure 21.4.

Figure 21.4

This userform displays particular records from the Access recordset. When the buyer selects certain records and then chooses the Confirm button, you have to use ADO's Update method to update the Sent field on the selected records.

The code attached to the Confirm button follows. Including the ID field in the fields returned in the prior example is important if you want to narrow the information down to a single record.

```
Private Sub cbConfirm_Click()
    Dim cnn As ADODB.Connection
    Dim rst As ADODB.Recordset

    ' If nothing is selected, warn them
    CountSelect = 0
    For x = 0 To Me.lbXlt.ListCount - 1
        If Me.lbXlt.Selected(x) Then
            CountSelect = CountSelect + 1
        End If
    Next x

    If CountSelect = 0 Then
        MsgBox "There were no transfers selected. " & _
```

21

```
                        "To exit without confirming any transfers, use Cancel."
        Exit Sub
    End If

    ' Establish a connection to transfers.mdb
    ' Path to Transfers.mdb is on Menu
    MyConn = "J:\transfers.mdb"

    Set cnn = New ADODB.Connection

    With cnn
        .Provider = "Microsoft.Jet.OLEDB.4.0"
        .Open MyConn
    End With

    ' Mark as complete
    For x = 0 To Me.lbXlt.ListCount - 1
        If Me.lbXlt.Selected(x) Then
            ThisID = Cells(2 + x, 1).Value
            ' Mark ThisID as complete
            'Build SQL String
            sSQL = "SELECT * FROM tblTransfer Where ID=" & ThisID
            Set rst = New ADODB.Recordset
            With rst
                .Open Source:=sSQL, ActiveConnection:=cnn, _
                    CursorType:=adOpenKeyset, LockType:=adLockOptimistic
                ' Update the field
                .Fields("Sent").Value = True
                .Update
                .Close
            End With
        End If
    Next x

    ' Close the connection
    cnn.Close
    Set rst = Nothing
    Set cnn = Nothing

    ' Close the userform
    Unload Me

End Sub
```

Deleting Records via ADO

As with updating a record, the key to deleting records is being able to write a bit of SQL to uniquely identify the records to be deleted. The following code uses the Execute method to pass the Delete command through to Access:

```
Public Sub ADOWipeOutAttribute(RecID)
    ' Establish a connection to transfers.mdb
    MyConn = "J:\transfers.mdb"

    With New ADODB.Connection
        .Provider = "Microsoft.Jet.OLEDB.4.0"
```

```
        .Open MyConn
        .Execute "Delete From tblTransfer Where ID = " & RecID
        .Close
    End With
End Sub
```

Summarizing Records via ADO

One of Access's strengths is running summary queries that group by a particular field. If you build a summary query in Access and examine the SQL view, you'll see that complex queries can be written. Similar SQL can be built in Excel VBA and passed to Access via ADO.

The following code uses a fairly complex query to get a net total by store:

```
Sub NetTransfers(Style As Variant)
    ' This builds a table of net open transfers
    ' on Styles AI1
    Dim cnn As ADODB.Connection
    Dim rst As ADODB.Recordset

    ' Build the large SQL query
    ' Basic Logic:  Get all open Incoming Transfers by store,
    ' union with -1* outgoing transfers by store
    ' Sum that union by store, and give us min date as well
    ' A single call to this macro will replace 60
    ' calls to GetTransferIn, GetTransferOut, TransferAge
    sSQL = "Select Store, Sum(Quantity), Min(mDate) From " & _
        "(SELECT ToStore AS Store, Sum(Qty) AS Quantity, " & _
        "Min(TDate) AS mDate FROM tblTransfer where Style='" & Style & _
        "& "' AND Receive=FALSE GROUP BY ToStore "
    sSQL = sSQL & " Union All SELECT FromStore AS Store, " & _
        "Sum(-1*Qty) AS Quantity, Min(TDate) AS mDate " & _
        "FROM tblTransfer where Style='" & Style & "' AND " & _
        "Sent=FALSE GROUP BY FromStore)"
    sSQL = sSQL & " Group by Store"

    MyConn = "J:\transfers.mdb"

    ' open the connection.
    Set cnn = New ADODB.Connection
    With cnn
        .Provider = "Microsoft.Jet.OLEDB.4.0"
        .Open MyConn
    End With

    Set rst = New ADODB.Recordset

    rst.CursorLocation = adUseServer

    ' open the first query
    rst.Open Source:=sSQL, _
        ActiveConnection:=cnn, _
        CursorType:=AdForwardOnly, _
        LockType:=adLockOptimistic, _
        Options:=adCmdText
```

```
Range("A1:C1").Value = Array("Store", "Qty", "Date")
' Return Query Results
Range("A2").CopyFromRecordset rst
rst.Close
cnn.Close

End Sub
```

Other Utilities via ADO

Consider the application we created for our case study; the buyers now have an Access database located on their network but possibly no copy of Access. It would be ideal if you could deliver changes to the Access database on the fly as their application opens.

> **NOTE**
> If you are wondering how you would ever coax the person using the application to run these queries, consider using an Update macro hidden in the `Workbook_Open` routine of the client application. Such a routine might first check to see whether a field exists and then add the field if it is missing.

→ For details on the mechanics of hiding the update query in the `Workbook_Open` routine, **see** the "Using a Hidden Code Workbook to Hold All Macros and Forms" case study in Chapter 26, "Creating Add-Ins."

Checking for the Existence of Tables

If the application needs a new table in the database, you can use the code in the next section. However, because you have a multiuser application, only the first person who opens the application has to add the table on the fly. When the next buyer shows up, the table might have already been added by the first buyer's application. Because this code is a Function instead of a Sub, it returns either a True or False to the calling routine.

This code uses the `OpenSchema` method to actually query the database schema:

```
Function TableExists(WhichTable)
    Dim cnn As ADODB.Connection
    Dim rst As ADODB.Recordset
    Dim fld As ADODB.Field
    TableExists = False

    ' Path to Transfers.mdb is on Menu
    MyConn = "J:\transfers.mdb"

    Set cnn = New ADODB.Connection

    With cnn
        .Provider = "Microsoft.Jet.OLEDB.4.0"
        .Open MyConn
    End With

    Set rst = cnn.OpenSchema(adSchemaTables)
```

21

```
    Do Until rst.EOF
        If LCase(rst!Table_Name) = LCase(WhichTable) Then
            TableExists = True
            GoTo ExitMe
        End If
        rst.MoveNext
    Loop

ExitMe:
    rst.Close
    Set rst = Nothing
    ' Close the connection
    cnn.Close

End Function
```

Checking for the Existence of a Field

Sometimes you want to add a new field to an existing table. Again, this code uses the OpenSchema method but this time looks at the columns in the tables:

```
Function ColumnExists(WhichColumn, WhichTable)
    Dim cnn As ADODB.Connection
    Dim rst As ADODB.Recordset
    Dim WSOrig As Worksheet
    Dim WSTemp As Worksheet
    Dim fld As ADODB.Field
    ColumnExists = False

    ' Path to Transfers.mdb is on menu
    MyConn = ActiveWorkbook.Worksheets("Menu").Range("TPath").Value
    If Right(MyConn, 1) = "\" Then
        MyConn = MyConn & "transfers.mdb"
    Else
        MyConn = MyConn & "\transfers.mdb"
    End If

    Set cnn = New ADODB.Connection

    With cnn
        .Provider = "Microsoft.Jet.OLEDB.4.0"
        .Open MyConn
    End With

    Set rst = cnn.OpenSchema(adSchemaColumns)

    Do Until rst.EOF
        If LCase(rst!Column_Name) = LCase(WhichColumn) And _
            LCase(rst!Table_Name) = LCase(WhichTable) Then
            ColumnExists = True
            GoTo ExitMe
        End If
        rst.MoveNext
    Loop

ExitMe:
```

21

```
        rst.Close
        Set rst = Nothing
        ' Close the connection
        cnn.Close

    End Function
```

Adding a Table On the Fly

This code uses a pass-through query to tell Access to run a Create Table command:

```
Sub ADOCreateReplenish()
    ' This creates tblReplenish
    ' There are five fields:
    ' Style
    ' A = Auto replenishment for A
    ' B = Auto replenishment level for B stores
    ' C = Auto replenishment level for C stores
    ' RecActive = Yes/No field
    Dim cnn As ADODB.Connection
    Dim cmd As ADODB.Command

    ' Define the connection
    MyConn = "J:\transfers.mdb"

    ' open the connection
    Set cnn = New ADODB.Connection
    With cnn
        .Provider = "Microsoft.Jet.OLEDB.4.0"
        .Open MyConn
    End With

    Set cmd = New ADODB.Command
    Set cmd.ActiveConnection = cnn
    'create table
    cmd.CommandText = "CREATE TABLE tblReplenish " & _
        "(Style Char(10) Primary Key, " & _
        "A int, B  int, C Int, RecActive YesNo)"
    cmd.Execute , , adCmdText
    Set cmd = Nothing
    Set cnn = Nothing
    Exit Sub
End Sub
```

Adding a Field On the Fly

If you determine that a field does not exist, you can use a pass-through query to add a field to the table:

```
Sub ADOAddField()
    ' This adds a grp field to tblReplenish
    Dim cnn As ADODB.Connection
    Dim cmd As ADODB.Command

    ' Define the connection
    MyConn = "J:\transfers.mdb"

    ' open the connection
```

```
        Set cnn = New ADODB.Connection
        With cnn
            .Provider = "Microsoft.Jet.OLEDB.4.0"
            .Open MyConn
        End With


        Set cmd = New ADODB.Command
        Set cmd.ActiveConnection = cnn
        'create table
        cmd.CommandText = "ALTER TABLE tblReplenish Add Column Grp Char(25)"
        cmd.Execute , , adCmdText
        Set cmd = Nothing
        Set cnn = Nothing

End Sub
```

SQL Server Examples

If you have 64-bit versions of Office and if Microsoft does not provide the 64-bit Microsoft.Jet.OLEDB.4.0 drivers, you have to switch over to using SQL Server or another database technology:

```
Sub DataExtract()

Application.DisplayAlerts = False

'clear out all previous data
Sheet1.Cells.Clear

' Create a connection object.
Dim cnPubs As ADODB.Connection
Set cnPubs = New ADODB.Connection

' Provide the connection string.
Dim strConn As String

'Use the SQL Server OLE DB Provider.
strConn = "PROVIDER=SQLOLEDB;"

'Connect to the Pubs database on the local server.
strConn = strConn & "DATA SOURCE=a_sql_server;INITIAL CATALOG=a_database;"

'Use an integrated login.
strConn = strConn & " INTEGRATED SECURITY=sspi;"

'Now open the connection.
cnPubs.Open strConn

' Create a recordset object.
Dim rsPubs As ADODB.Recordset
Set rsPubs = New ADODB.Recordset

With rsPubs
    ' Assign the Connection object.
    .ActiveConnection = cnPubs
```

21

```
        ' Extract the required records.
        .Open "exec a_database..a_stored_procedure"
        ' Copy the records into cell A1 on Sheet1.
        Sheet1.Range("A2").CopyFromRecordset rsPubs


    Dim myColumn As Range
    'Dim title_string As String
    Dim K As Integer
    For K = 0 To rsPubs.Fields.Count - 1
       'Sheet1.Columns(K).Value = rsPubs.Fields(K).Name
       'title_string = title_string & rsPubs.Fields(K).Name & Chr(9)
       'Sheet1.Columns(K).Cells(1).Name = rsPubs.Fields(K).Name
       'Sheet1.Columns.Column(K) = rsPubs.Fields(K).Name
       'Set myColumn = Sheet1.Columns(K)
       'myColumn.Cells(1, K).Value = rsPubs.Fields(K).Name
       'Sheet1.Cells(1, K) = rsPubs.Fields(K).Name
       Sheet1.Cells(1, K + 1) = rsPubs.Fields(K).Name
       Sheet1.Cells(1, K + 1).Font.Bold = "TRUE"
    Next K
    'Sheet1.Range("A1").Value = title_string


        ' Tidy up
        .Close
    End With

    cnPubs.Close
    Set rsPubs = Nothing
    Set cnPubs = Nothing

    'clear out errors
    Dim cellval As Range
    Dim myRng As Range
    Set myRng = ActiveSheet.UsedRange
    For Each cellval In myRng
      cellval.Value = cellval.Value
      'cellval.NumberFormat = "@" 'this works as well as setting
      'HorizontalAlignment
      cellval.HorizontalAlignment = xlRight
    Next

    End Sub
```

Next Steps

In Chapter 22, "Advanced Userform Techniques," you discover more controls and techniques you can use in building userforms.

Advanced Userform Techniques

Chapter 10, "Userforms: An Introduction," covered the basics of adding controls to userforms. This chapter continues this topic by looking at more advanced controls and methods for making the most out of userforms.

Using the UserForm Toolbar in the Design of Controls on Userforms

In the VB Editor, under View, Toolbars, are a few toolbars that do not appear unless the user selects them. One of these is the UserForm toolbar, shown in Figure 22.1. It has functionality useful for organizing the controls you add to a userform; for example, it will make all the controls you select the same size.

Figure 22.1
The UserForm toolbar has tools to organize the controls on a userform.

Bring to front   Group   Alignments   Uniform Size

Send to back   UnGroup   Centering

More Userform Controls

Chapter 10 began a review of some of the controls available on userforms. The review is continued here. At the end of each control review is a table listing that control's events.

Check Boxes

Check boxes allow the user to select one or more options on a userform. Unlike the option buttons discussed in Chapter 10, a user can select one or more check boxes at a time.

22

The value of a checked box is True; the value of an unchecked box is False. If you clear the value of a check box (Checkbox1.value = ""), when the userform runs, the check box will have a faded check in it, as shown in Figure 22.2. This can be useful to verify that users have viewed all options and made a selection.

Figure 22.2
Use the null value of the check box to verify that users have viewed and answered all options.

The following code reviews all the check boxes in the language group. If a value is null, the user is prompted to review the selections:

```
Private Sub btnClose_Click()
Dim Msg As String
Dim Chk As Control

Set Chk = Nothing

'narrow down the search to just the 2nd page's controls
For Each Chk In frm_Multipage.MultiPage1.Pages(1).Controls
    'only need to verify checkbox controls
    If TypeName(Chk) = "CheckBox" Then
        'and just in case we add more check box controls,
        'just check the ones in the group
        If Chk.GroupName = "Languages" Then
            'if the value is null (the property value is empty)
            If IsNull(Chk.Object.Value) Then
                'add the caption to a string
                Msg = Msg & vbNewLine & Chk.Caption
            End If
        End If
    End If
Next Chk

If Msg <> "" Then
    Msg = "The following check boxes were not verified:" & vbNewLine & Msg
    MsgBox Msg, vbInformation, "Additional Information Required"
End If
Unload Me
End Sub
```

Table 22.1 lists the events for CheckBox controls.

Table 22.1   Events for CheckBox Controls

Event	Description
AfterUpdate	Occurs after a check box has been selected/cleared.
BeforeDragOver	Occurs while the user drags and drops data onto the check box.
BeforeDropOrPaste	Occurs right before the user is about to drop or paste data onto the check box.
BeforeUpdate	Occurs before the check box is selected/cleared.
Change	Occurs when the value of the check box is changed.
Click	Occurs when the user clicks the control with the mouse.
DblClick	Occurs when the user double-clicks the check box with the mouse.
Enter	Occurs right before the check box receives the focus from another control on the same userform.
Error	Occurs when the check box runs into an error and cannot return the error information.
Exit	Occurs right after the check box loses focus to another control on the same userform.
KeyDown	Occurs when the user presses a key on the keyboard.
KeyPress	Occurs when the user presses an ANSI key. An ANSI key is a typeable character such as the letter *A*.
KeyUp	Occurs when the user releases a key on the keyboard.
MouseDown	Occurs when the user presses the mouse button within the borders of the check box.
MouseMove	Occurs when the user moves the mouse within the borders of the check box.
MouseUp	Occurs when the user releases the mouse button within the borders of the check box.

 Tab Strips

The MultiPage control allows a userform to have several pages. Each page of the form can have its own set of controls, unrelated to any other control on the form. A TabStrip control also allows a userform to have many pages, but the controls on a tab strip are identical; they are drawn only once. Yet when the form is run, the information changes according to the tab strip that is active (see Figure 22.3).

→ To learn more about MultiPage controls, **see** "Using the MultiPage Control to Combine Forms" on **p. 190**.

Figure 22.3
A tab strip allows a user-form with multiple pages to share controls but not information.

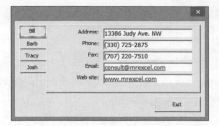

By default, a tab strip is thin with two tabs at the top. Right-clicking a tab enables you to add, remove, rename, or move that tab. The tab strip should also be sized to hold all the controls. A button for closing the form should be drawn outside the tab strip area.

The tabs can also be moved around the strip. This is done by changing the TabOrientation property. The tabs can be at the top, bottom, left, or right side of the userform.

The following lines of code were used to create the tab strip form shown in Figure 22.3. The Initialize sub calls the sub SetValuesToTabStrip, which sets the value for the first tab:

```
Private Sub UserForm_Initialize()
SetValuesToTabStrip 1 'As default
End Sub
```

These lines of code handle what happens when a new tab is selected:

```
Private Sub TabStrip1_Change()
Dim lngRow As Long

lngRow = TabStrip1.Value + 1
SetValuesToTabStrip lngRow
End Sub
```

This sub provides the data shown on each tab. A sheet was set up, with each row corresponding to a tab:

```
Private Sub SetValuesToTabStrip(ByVal lngRow As Long)
With frm_Staff
    .lbl_Address.Caption = Cells(lngRow, 2).Value
    .lbl_Phone.Caption = Cells(lngRow, 3).Value
    .lbl_Fax.Caption = Cells(lngRow, 4).Value
    .lbl_Email.Caption = Cells(lngRow, 5).Value
    .lbl_Website.Caption = Cells(lngRow, 6).Value
    .Show
End With
End Sub
```

The tab strip's values are automatically filled in. They correspond to the tab's position in the strip; moving a tab changes its value. The value of the first tab of a tab strip is 0, which is why, in the preceding code, we add 1 to the tab strip value when the form is initialized.

> **T I P**
> If you want a single tab to have an extra control, the control could be added at runtime when the tab is activated and removed when the tab is deactivated.

Table 22.2 lists the events for the TabStrip control.

Table 22.2   Events for TabStrip Controls

Event	Description
BeforeDragOver	Occurs while the user drags and drops data onto the control.
BeforeDropOrPaste	Occurs right before the user drops or pastes data into the control.
Change	Occurs when the value of the control is changed.
Click	Occurs when the user clicks the control with the mouse.
DblClick	Occurs when the user double-clicks the control with the mouse.
Enter	Occurs right before the control receives the focus from another control on the same userform.
Error	Occurs when the control runs into an error and cannot return the error information.
Exit	Occurs right after the control loses focus to another control on the same userform.
KeyDown	Occurs when the user presses a key on the keyboard.
KeyPress	Occurs when the user presses an ANSI key. An ANSI key is a typeable character, such as the letter *A*.
KeyUp	Occurs when the user releases a key on the keyboard.
MouseDown	Occurs when the user presses the mouse button within the borders of the control.
MouseMove	Occurs when the user moves the mouse within the borders of the control.
MouseUp	Occurs when the user releases the mouse button within the borders of the control.

 RefEdit

The RefEdit control allows the user to select a range on a sheet; the range is returned as the value of the control. It can be added to any form. When you click the button on the right side of the field, the userform disappears and is replaced with the range selection form that is used for selecting ranges with Excel's many wizard tools, as shown in Figure 22.4. Click the button on the right of the field to show the userform once again.

Figure 22.4
Use RefEdit to enable the user to select a range on a sheet.

22

The following code used with a RefEdit control allows the user to select a range, which is then made bold.

```
Private Sub cb1_Click()
Range(RefEdit1.Value).Font.Bold = True
Unload Me
End Sub
```

Table 22.3 lists the events for RefEdit controls.

> ┌ C A U T I O N ───
> RefEdit events are notorious for not working properly. If you run into this problem, use a different control's event to trigger code.

Table 22.3 Events for RefEdit Controls

Event	Description
AfterUpdate	Occurs after the control's data has been changed by the user.
BeforeDragOver	Occurs while the user drags and drops data onto the control.
BeforeDropOrPaste	Occurs right before the user drops or pastes data into the control.
BeforeUpdate	Occurs before the data in the control is changed.
Change	Occurs when the value of the control is changed.
Click	Occurs when the user clicks the control with the mouse.
DblClick	Occurs when the user double-clicks the control with the mouse.
DropButtonClick	Occurs when the user clicks the drop button on the right side of the field.
Enter	Occurs right before the control receives the focus from another control on the same userform.
Error	Occurs when the control runs into an error and cannot return the error information.
Exit	Occurs right after the control loses focus to another control on the same userform.
KeyDown	Occurs when the user presses a key on the keyboard.
KeyPress	Occurs when the user presses an ANSI key. An ANSI key is a typeable character, such as the letter A.
KeyUp	Occurs when the user releases a key on the keyboard.
MouseDown	Occurs when the user presses the mouse button within the borders of the control.
MouseMove	Occurs when the user moves the mouse within the borders of the control.
MouseUp	Occurs when the user releases the mouse button within the borders of the control.

Toggle Buttons

A toggle button looks like a normal command button, but when the user presses it, it stays pressed until it is selected again. This allows a True or False value to be returned based on the status of the button. Table 22.4 lists the events for the ToggleButton controls.

Table 22.4   Events for ToggleButton Controls

Event	Description
AfterUpdate	Occurs after the control's data has been changed by the user.
BeforeDragOver	Occurs while the user drags and drops data onto the control.
BeforeDropOrPaste	Occurs right before the user drops or pastes data into the control.
BeforeUpdate	Occurs before the data in the control is changed.
Change	Occurs when the value of the control is changed.
Click	Occurs when the user clicks the control with the mouse.
DblClick	Occurs when the user double-clicks the control with the mouse.
Enter	Occurs right before the control receives the focus from another control on the same userform.
Error	Occurs when the control runs into an error and cannot return the error information.
Exit	Occurs right after the control loses focus to another control on the same userform.
KeyDown	Occurs when the user presses a key on the keyboard.
KeyPress	Occurs when the user presses an ANSI key. An ANSI key is a typeable character, such as the letter *A*.
KeyUp	Occurs when the user releases a key on the keyboard.
MouseDown	Occurs when the user presses the mouse button within the borders of the control.
MouseMove	Occurs when the user moves the mouse within the borders of the control.
MouseUp	Occurs when the user releases the mouse button within the borders of the control.

 Using a Scrollbar As a Slider to Select Values

Chapter 10 discusses using a SpinButton control to enable someone to choose a date. The spin button is useful, but it allows users to adjust up or down by only one unit at a time. An alternative method is to draw a horizontal or vertical scrollbar in the middle of the userform and use it as a slider. Users can use arrows on the ends of the scrollbar like the spin button arrows, but they can also grab the scrollbar and instantly drag it to a certain value.

22

The userform shown in Figure 22.5 includes a label named Label1 and a scrollbar called ScrollBar1.

Figure 22.5
Using a scrollbar control allows the user to drag to a particular numeric or data value.

The userform's Initialize code sets up the Min and Max values for the scrollbar. It initializes the scrollbar to a value from cell A1 and updates the Label1.Caption:

```
Private Sub UserForm_Initialize()
    Me.ScrollBar1.Min = 0
    Me.ScrollBar1.Max = 100
    Me.ScrollBar1.Value = Worksheets("Scrollbar").Range("A1").Value
    Me.Label1.Caption = Me.ScrollBar1.Value
End Sub
```

Two event handlers are needed for the scrollbar. The Change event triggers when users click the arrows at the ends of the scrollbar. The Scroll event triggers when they drag the slider to a new value:

```
Private Sub ScrollBar1_Change()
    ' This event triggers when they touch
    ' the arrows on the end of the scrollbar
    Me.Label1.Caption = Me.ScrollBar1.Value
End Sub

Private Sub ScrollBar1_Scroll()
    ' This event triggers when they drag the slider
    Me.Label1.Caption = Me.ScrollBar1.Value
End Sub
```

Finally, the event attached to the button writes the scrollbar value out to the worksheet:

```
Private Sub btnClose_Click()
    Worksheets("Scrollbar").Range("A1").Value = Me.ScrollBar1.Value
    Unload Me
End Sub
```

Table 22.5 lists the events for Scrollbar controls.

Table 22.5   Events for Scrollbar Controls

Event	Description
AfterUpdate	Occurs after the control's data has been changed by the user.
BeforeDragOver	Occurs while the user drags and drops data onto the control.
BeforeDropOrPaste	Occurs right before the user drops or pastes data into the control.
BeforeUpdate	Occurs before the data in the control is changed.

Event	Description
Change	Occurs when the value of the control is changed.
Enter	Occurs right before the control receives the focus from another control on the same userform.
Error	Occurs when the control runs into an error and cannot return the error information.
Exit	Occurs right after the control loses focus to another control on the same userform.
KeyDown	Occurs when the user presses a key on the keyboard.
KeyPress	Occurs when the user presses an ANSI key. An ANSI key is a typeable character, such as the letter *A*.
KeyUp	Occurs when the user releases a key on the keyboard.
Scroll	Occurs when the slider is moved.

Controls and Collections

In Chapter 9, "Creating Classes, Records, and Collections," several labels on a sheet were grouped together into a collection. With a little more code, these labels were turned into help screens for the users. Userform controls can also be grouped into collections to take advantage of class modules. The following example selects or clears all the check boxes on the userform, depending on which label the user chooses.

Place the following code in the class module, clsFormCtl. It consists of one property, chb, and two methods, SelectAll and UnselectAll.

The SelectAll method selects a check box by setting its value to True:

```
Public WithEvents chb As MSForms.CheckBox

Public Sub SelectAll()
chb.Value = True
End Sub
```

The UnselectAll method clears the check box:

```
Public Sub UnselectAll()
chb.Value = False
End Sub
```

That sets up the class module. Next, the controls need to be placed in a collection. The following code, placed behind the form, frm_Movies, places the check boxes into a collection. The check boxes are part of a frame, frm_Selection, which makes it easier to create the collection because it narrows the number of controls that need to be checked from the entire userform to just those controls within the frame:

```
Dim col_Selection As New Collection
```

22

```
Private Sub UserForm_Initialize()
Dim ctl As MSForms.CheckBox
Dim chb_ctl As clsFormCtl

'Go through the members of the frame and add them to the collection
For Each ctl In frm_Selection.Controls
    Set chb_ctl = New clsFormCtl
    Set chb_ctl.chb = ctl
    col_Selection.Add chb_ctl
Next ctl
End Sub
```

When the form is opened, the controls are placed into the collection. All that's left now is to add the code for labels to select and clear the check boxes:

```
Private Sub lbl_SelectAll_Click()
Dim ctl As clsFormCtl

For Each ctl In col_Selection
    ctl.SelectAll
Next ctl
End Sub
```

The following code clears the check boxes in the collection:

```
Private Sub lbl_unSelectAll_Click()
Dim ctl As clsFormCtl

For Each ctl In col_Selection
    ctl.Unselectall
Next ctl
End Sub
```

All the check boxes can be selected and cleared with a single click of the mouse, as shown in Figure 22.6.

Figure 22.6
Use frames, collections, and class modules together to create quick and efficient userforms.

> **T I P**
>
> If your controls cannot be placed in a frame, you can use a tag to create an improvised grouping. A tag is a property that holds more information about a control. Its value is of type string, so it can hold any type of information. For example, it can be used to create an informal group of controls from different groupings.

Modeless Userforms

Have you ever had a userform active but needed to manipulate something on the active sheet or switch to another sheet? Forms can be *modeless*, which means they don't have to interfere with the functionality of Excel. The user can type in a cell, switch to another sheet, copy/paste data, and use the ribbon—it is as if the userform were not there.

By default, a userform is modal, which means that there is no interaction with Excel other than the form. To make the form modeless, change the ShowModal property to False. After it is modeless, the user can select a cell on the sheet while the form is active, as shown in Figure 22.7.

Figure 22.7
A modeless form enables the user to enter a cell while the form is still active.

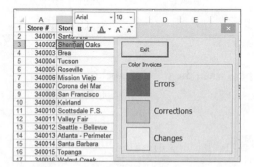

Using Hyperlinks in Userforms

In the userform example shown in Figure 22.3, there is a field for email and a field for website address. It would be nice to click these and have a blank email message or web page appear automatically. You can do this by using the following program, which creates a new message or opens a web browser when the corresponding label is clicked.

The application programming interface (API) declaration and any other constants go at the very top of the module.

> **CAUTION**
>
> The following API call is for use with the 64-bit version of Excel 2013. If you are using the 32-bit version, refer to Chapter 23, "Windows API," for information on how to modify the call.

```
Private Declare PtrSafe Function ShellExecute Lib "shell32.dll" Alias _
    "ShellExecuteA"(ByVal hWnd As Long, ByVal lpOperation As String, _
    ByVal lpFile As String, ByVal lpParameters As String, _
    ByVal lpDirectory As String, ByVal nShowCmd As Long) As LongPtr

Const SWNormal = 1
```

This sub controls what happens when the email label is clicked, as shown in Figure 22.8:

```
Private Sub lbl_Email_Click()
```

22

```
Dim lngRow As Long

lngRow = TabStrip1.Value + 1
ShellExecute 0&, "open", "mailto:" & Cells(lngRow, 5).Value, _
    vbNullString, vbNullString, SWNormal
End Sub
```

Figure 22.8
Turn email addresses and websites into clickable links by using a few lines of code.

This sub controls what happens when the website label is clicked:

```
Private Sub lbl_Website_Click()
Dim lngRow As Long

lngRow = TabStrip1.Value + 1
ShellExecute 0&, "open", Cells(lngRow, 6).Value, vbNullString, _
    vbNullString, SWNormal
End Sub
```

Adding Controls at Runtime

It is possible to add controls to a userform at runtime. This is convenient if you are not sure how many items you will be adding to the form.

Figure 22.9 shows a plain form with only one button. This plain form is used to display any number of pictures from a product catalog. The pictures and accompanying labels appear at runtime, as the form is being displayed.

Figure 22.9
Flexible forms can be created if you add most controls at runtime.

A sales rep making a sales presentation uses this form to display a product catalog. He can select any number of SKUs from an Excel worksheet and press a hotkey to display the form. If he selects 18 items on the worksheet, the form displays with a small version of each picture, as shown in Figure 22.10.

Figure 22.10
The sales rep asked to see photos of 18 SKUs. The `UserForm_Initialize` procedure adds each picture and label on the fly.

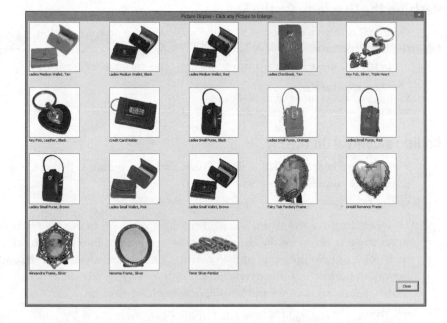

If the sales rep selects fewer items, the images are displayed larger, as shown in Figure 22.11.

Figure 22.11
The logic in `Userform_Initialize` decides how many pictures are being displayed and adds the appropriately sized image controls.

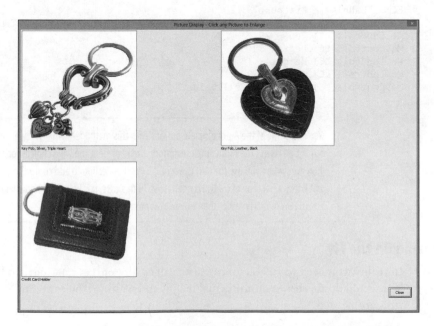

A number of techniques are used to create this userform on the fly. The initial form contains only one button, called cbClose. Everything else is added on the fly.

Resizing the Userform On the Fly

One goal is to give the best view of the images in the product catalog. This means having the form appear as large as possible. The following code uses the form's Height and Width properties to make sure the form fills almost the entire screen:

```
'resize the form
Me.Height = Int(0.98 * ActiveWindow.Height)
Me.Width = Int(0.98 * ActiveWindow.Width)
```

Adding a Control On the Fly

For a normal control added at design time, such as a button called cbClose, it is easy to refer to the control by using its name:

```
Me.cbClose.Left = 100
```

However, for a control that is added at runtime, you have to use the Controls collection to set any properties for the control. For this reason, it is important to set up a variable, such as LC, to hold the name of the control. Controls are added with the .Add method. The important parameter is the bstrProgId. This property dictates whether the added control is a label, a text box, a command button, or something else.

The following code adds a new label to the form. PicCount is a counter variable used to ensure that each label has a unique name. After the form is added, specify a position for the control by setting the Top and Left properties. You should also set a Height and Width for the control:

```
LC = "LabelA" & PicCount
Me.Controls.Add bstrProgId:="forms.label.1", Name:=LC, Visible:=True
Me.Controls(LC).Top = 25
Me.Controls(LC).Left = 50
Me.Controls(LC).Height = 18
Me.Controls(LC).Width = 60
Me.Controls(LC).Caption = Cell.Value
```

> **CAUTION**
>
> You lose some of the AutoComplete options with this method. Normally, if you would start to type Me.cbClose., the AutoComplete options would present the valid choices for a command button. However, when you use the Me.Controls(LC) collection to add controls on the fly, VBA does not know what type of control is referenced. In this case, it is helpful to know you need to set the Caption property rather than the Value property for a label.

Sizing On the Fly

In reality, you need to be able to calculate values for Top, Left, Height, and Width on the fly. You would do this based on the actual height and width of the form and on how many controls are needed.

Adding Other Controls

To add other types of controls, change the `ProgId` used with the `Add` method. Table 22.6 shows the `ProgId`s for various types of controls.

Table 22.6 Userform Controls and Corresponding `ProgId`s

Control	ProgId
CheckBox	Forms.CheckBox.1
ComboBox	Forms.ComboBox.1
CommandButton	Forms.CommandButton.1
Frame	Forms.Frame.1
Image	Forms.Image.1
Label	Forms.Label.1
ListBox	Forms.ListBox.1
MultiPage	Forms.MultiPage.1
OptionButton	Forms.OptionButton.1
ScrollBar	Forms.ScrollBar.1
SpinButton	Forms.SpinButton.1
TabStrip	Forms.TabStrip.1
TextBox	Forms.TextBox.1
ToggleButton	Forms.ToggleButton.1

Adding an Image On the Fly

There is some unpredictability in adding images. Any given image might be shaped either landscape or portrait. The image might be small or huge. The strategy you might want to use is to let the image load at full size by setting the `.AutoSize` parameter to `True` before loading it:

```
TC = "Image" & PicCount
Me.Controls.Add bstrProgId:="forms.image.1", Name:=TC, Visible:=True
Me.Controls(TC).Top = LastTop
Me.Controls(TC).Left = LastLeft
Me.Controls(TC).AutoSize = True
On Error Resume Next
Me.Controls(TC).Picture = LoadPicture(fname)
On Error GoTo 0
```

After the image has loaded, you can read the control's `Height` and `Width` properties to determine whether the image is landscape or portrait and whether the image is constrained by available width or available height:

```
'The picture resized the control to full size
'determine the size of the picture
Wid = Me.Controls(TC).Width
Ht = Me.Controls(TC).Height
'CellWid and CellHt are calculated in the full code sample below
WidRedux = CellWid / Wid
HtRedux = CellHt / Ht
If WidRedux < HtRedux Then
    Redux = WidRedux
Else
    Redux = HtRedux
End If
NewHt = Int(Ht * Redux)
NewWid = Int(Wid * Redux)
```

After you find the proper size for the image so that it draws without distortion, set the AutoSize property to False. Use the correct height and width to have the image not appear distorted:

```
'Now resize the control
Me.Controls(TC).AutoSize = False
Me.Controls(TC).Height = NewHt
Me.Controls(TC).Width = NewWid
Me.Controls(TC).PictureSizeMode = fmPictureSizeModeStretch
```

Putting It All Together

This is the complete code for the Picture Catalog userform:

```
Private Sub UserForm_Initialize()
    'Display pictures of each SKU selected on the worksheet
    'This may be anywhere from 1 to 36 pictures
    PicPath = "C:\qimage\qi"

    'resize the form
    Me.Height = Int(0.98 * ActiveWindow.Height)
    Me.Width = Int(0.98 * ActiveWindow.Width)

    'determine how many cells are selected
    'We need one picture and label for each cell
    CellCount = Selection.Cells.Count
    ReDim Preserve Pics(1 To CellCount)

    'Figure out the size of the resized form
    TempHt = Me.Height
    TempWid = Me.Width

    'The number of columns is a roundup of SQRT(CellCount)
    'This will ensure 4 rows of 5 pictures for 20, etc.
    NumCol = Int(0.99 + Sqr(CellCount))
    NumRow = Int(0.99 + CellCount / NumCol)

    'Figure out the height and width of each square
    'Each column will have 2 points to left & right of pics
    CellWid = Application.WorksheetFunction.Max(Int(TempWid / NumCol) - 4, 1)
    'each row needs to have 33 points below it for the label
    CellHt = Application.WorksheetFunction.Max(Int(TempHt / NumRow) - 33, 1)
```

22

```
PicCount = 0 'Counter variable
LastTop = 2
MaxBottom = 1
'Build each row on the form
For x = 1 To NumRow
    LastLeft = 3
    'Build each column in this row
    For Y = 1 To NumCol
        PicCount = PicCount + 1
        If PicCount > CellCount Then
            'There is not an even number of pictures to fill
            'out the last row
            Me.Height = MaxBottom + 100
            Me.cbClose.Top = MaxBottom + 25
            Me.cbClose.Left = Me.Width - 70
            Repaint 'redraws the form
            Exit Sub
        End If
        ThisStyle = Selection.Cells(PicCount).Value
        ThisDesc = Selection.Cells(PicCount).Offset(0, 1).Value
        fname = PicPath & ThisStyle & ".jpg"
        TC = "Image" & PicCount
        Me.Controls.Add bstrProgId:="forms.image.1", Name:=TC, _
          Visible:=True
        Me.Controls(TC).Top = LastTop
        Me.Controls(TC).Left = LastLeft
        Me.Controls(TC).AutoSize = True
        On Error Resume Next
        Me.Controls(TC).Picture = LoadPicture(fname)
        On Error GoTo 0

        'The picture resized the control to full size
        'determine the size of the picture
        Wid = Me.Controls(TC).Width
        Ht = Me.Controls(TC).Height
        WidRedux = CellWid / Wid
        HtRedux = CellHt / Ht
        If WidRedux < HtRedux Then
            Redux = WidRedux
        Else
            Redux = HtRedux
        End If
        NewHt = Int(Ht * Redux)
        NewWid = Int(Wid * Redux)

        'Now resize the control
        Me.Controls(TC).AutoSize = False
        Me.Controls(TC).Height = NewHt
        Me.Controls(TC).Width = NewWid
        Me.Controls(TC).PictureSizeMode = fmPictureSizeModeStretch
        Me.Controls(TC).ControlTipText = "Style " & _
                ThisStyle & " " & ThisDesc

        'Keep track of the bottommost & rightmost picture
        ThisRight = Me.Controls(TC).Left + Me.Controls(TC).Width
        ThisBottom = Me.Controls(TC).Top + Me.Controls(TC).Height
        If ThisBottom > MaxBottom Then MaxBottom = ThisBottom
```

22

```
            'Add a label below the picture
            LC = "LabelA" & PicCount
            Me.Controls.Add bstrProgId:="forms.label.1", Name:=LC, _
              Visible:=True
            Me.Controls(LC).Top = ThisBottom + 1
            Me.Controls(LC).Left = LastLeft
            Me.Controls(LC).Height = 18
            Me.Controls(LC).Width = CellWid
            Me.Controls(LC).Caption = ThisDesc

            'Keep track of where the next picture should display
            LastLeft = LastLeft + CellWid + 4
        Next Y ' end of this row
        LastTop = MaxBottom + 21 + 16
    Next x

    Me.Height = MaxBottom + 100
    Me.cbClose.Top = MaxBottom + 25
    Me.cbClose.Left = Me.Width - 70
    Repaint
End Sub
```

Adding Help to the Userform

Even though you designed a great userform, there is one thing missing: guidance for the users. The following sections show four ways you can help users fill out the form properly.

Showing Accelerator Keys

Built-in forms often have keyboard shortcuts that allow actions to be triggered or fields selected with a few keystrokes. These shortcuts are identified by an underlined letter on a button or label.

You can add this same capability to custom userforms by entering a value in the Accelerator property of the control. Alt + the accelerator key selects the control. For example, in Figure 22.12, Alt+H selects the VHS check box. Repeating the combination clears the box.

Figure 22.12
Use accelerator key combinations, like ALT+H to select VHS, in order to give userforms the power of keyboard shortcuts.

Adding Control Tip Text

When a cursor is waved over a toolbar, tip text appears, hinting at what the control does. You can also add tip text to userforms by entering a value in the `ControlTipText` property of a control. In Figure 22.13, tip text has been added to the frame surrounding the various categories.

Figure 22.13
Add tips to controls to provide help to users.

Creating the Tab Order

Users can tab from one field to another. This is an automatic feature in a form. To control which field the next tab brings a user to, you can set the `TapStop` property value for each control.

The first tab stop is zero, and the last tab stop is equal to the number of controls in a group. Remember, a group can be created with a frame. Excel does not allow multiple controls within a group to have the same tab stop. After tab stops are set, the user can use the Tab key and spacebar to select/deselect various options.

> **TIP**
> If you right-click the userform (not one of its controls) and select Tab Order, a form appears listing all the controls. You can reorder the controls from this form to set the tab order.

Coloring the Active Control

Another method for helping a user fill out a form is to color the active field. The following example changes the color of a text box or combo box when it is active. `RaiseEvent` is used to call the events declared at the top of the class module. The code for the events is part of the userform.

Place the following code in a class module called `clsCtlColor`:

```
Public Event GetFocus()
Public Event LostFocus(ByVal strCtrl As String)
Private strPreCtr As String

Public Sub CheckActiveCtrl(objForm As MSForms.UserForm)
With objForm
```

```
    If TypeName(.ActiveControl) = "ComboBox" Or _
        TypeName(.ActiveControl) = "TextBox" Then
        strPreCtr = .ActiveControl.Name
        On Error GoTo Terminate
        Do
            DoEvents
            If .ActiveControl.Name <> strPreCtr Then
                If TypeName(.ActiveControl) = "ComboBox" Or _
                    TypeName(.ActiveControl) = "TextBox" Then
                    RaiseEvent LostFocus(strPreCtr)
                    strPreCtr = .ActiveControl.Name
                    RaiseEvent GetFocus
                End If
            End If
        Loop
    End If
End With

Terminate:
    Exit Sub

End Sub
```

Place the following code behind the userform:

```
Private WithEvents objForm As clsCtlColor

Private Sub UserForm_Initialize()
Set objForm = New clsCtlColor
End Sub
```

This sub changes the BackColor of the active control when the form is activated:

```
Private Sub UserForm_Activate()
If TypeName(ActiveControl) = "ComboBox" Or _
    TypeName(ActiveControl) = "TextBox" Then
    ActiveControl.BackColor = &HC0E0FF
End If
objForm.CheckActiveCtrl Me
End Sub
```

This sub changes the BackColor of the active control when it gets the focus:

```
Private Sub objForm_GetFocus()
ActiveControl.BackColor = &HC0E0FF
End Sub
```

This sub changes the BackColor back to white when the control loses the focus:

```
Private Sub objForm_LostFocus(ByVal strCtrl As String)
Me.Controls(strCtrl).BackColor = &HFFFFFF
End Sub
```

This sub clears the objForm when the form is closed:

```
Private Sub UserForm_QueryClose(Cancel As Integer, CloseMode As Integer)
Set objForm = Nothing
End Sub
```

CASE STUDY: MULTICOLUMN LIST BOXES

You have created several spreadsheets containing store data. The primary key of each set is the store number. The workbook is used by several people, but not everyone memorizes stores by store numbers. You need some way of letting a user select a store by its name. At the same time, you need to return the store number to be used in the code. You could use VLOOKUP or MATCH, but there is another way.

A list box can have more than one column, but not all the columns need to be visible to the user. In addition, the user can select an item from the visible list, but the list box returns the corresponding value from another column.

Draw a list box and set the ColumnCount property to 2. Set the RowSource to a two-column range called Stores. The first column of the range is the store number; the second column is the store name. At this point, the list box is displaying both columns of data. To change this, set the ColumnWidths to 0, 20—the text automatically updates to 0 pt;20 pt. The first column is now hidden. Figure 22.14 shows the list box properties as they need to be.

Figure 22.14
Setting the list box properties creates a two-column list box that appears to be a single column of data.

The appearance of the list box has now been set. When the user activates the list box, she sees only the store names. To return the value of the first column, set the BoundColumn property to 1. This can be done through the Properties window or through code. This example uses code to maintain the flexibility of returning the store number (see Figure 22.15):

```
Private Sub UserForm_Initialize()
    lb_StoreName.BoundColumn = 1
End Sub

Private Sub lb_StoreName_Click()
lbl_StoreNum.Caption = lb_StoreName.Value
End Sub
```

Figure 22.15
Use a two-column list box to allow the user to select a store name but return the store number.

22

Creating Transparent Forms

Have you ever had a form that you had to keep moving out of the way so you could see the data behind it? The following code sets the userform at a 50 percent transparency (see Figure 22.16) so that you can see the data behind it without moving the form somewhere else on the screen (and blocking more data).

Figure 22.16
Create a 50 percent transparent form to view the data on the sheet behind it.

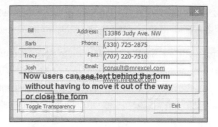

C A U T I O N

The following API call is for use with the 64-bit version of Excel 2013. If you are using the 32-bit version, refer to Chapter 23 for information on how to modify the call.

Place the following code in the declarations section at the top of the userform:

```
Private Declare PtrSafe Function GetActiveWindow Lib "USER32" () As Long
Private Declare PtrSafe Function SetWindowLongPtr Lib "USER32" Alias _
    "SetWindowLongA" (ByVal hWnd As Long, ByVal nIndex As Long, _
    ByVal dwNewLong As Long) As LongPtr
Private Declare PtrSafe Function GetWindowLongPtr Lib "USER32" Alias _
    "GetWindowLongA" (ByVal hWnd As Long, ByVal nIndex As Long) As Long
Private Declare PtrSafe Function SetLayeredWindowAttributes Lib "USER32" _
    (ByVal hWnd As Long, ByVal crKey As Integer, _
    ByVal bAlpha As Integer, ByVal dwFlags As Long) As LongPtr
Private Const WS_EX_LAYERED = &H80000
Private Const LWA_COLORKEY = &H1
Private Const LWA_ALPHA = &H2
Private Const GWL_EXSTYLE = &HFFEC
Dim hWnd As Long
```

Place the following code behind a toggle button. When the button is pressed in, the transparency will be reduced 50%. When the user toggles the button back up, the transparency is set to 0.

```
Private Sub ToggleButton1_Click()
If ToggleButton1.Value = True Then
    '127 sets the 50% semitransparent
    SetTransparency 127
Else
    'a value of 255 is opaque and 0 is transparent
    SetTransparency 255
End If
End Sub
```

```
Private Sub SetTransparency(TRate As Integer)
Dim nIndex As Long
hWnd = GetActiveWindow
nIndex = GetWindowLong(hWnd, GWL_EXSTYLE)
SetWindowLong hWnd, GWL_EXSTYLE, nIndex Or WS_EX_LAYERED
SetLayeredWindowAttributes hWnd, 0, TRate, LWA_ALPHA
End Sub
```

22

Next Steps

This chapter showed you how to take advantage of API calls to perform functions Excel can't normally do. In Chapter 23 you'll discover more on how to access these functions and procedures hidden in files on your computer.

Windows API

What Is the Windows API?

With all the wonderful things you can do in Excel VBA, there are some things that are out of VBA's reach or are just too difficult to do, such as finding out what the user's screen resolution setting is. This is where the Windows application programming interface (API) can help.

If you look in the Windows System directory \Windows\System32 (Windows NT systems), you will see many files with the extension .dll. These files, which are dynamic link libraries (dll), contain various functions and procedures that other programs can access, including VBA. They give the user access to functionality used by the Windows operating system and many other programs.

> **CAUTION**
>
> Keep in mind that Windows API declarations are accessible only on computers running the Microsoft Windows operating system.

This chapter does not teach you how to write API declarations, but it does teach you the basics of interpreting and using them. Several useful examples have also been included. You can find more online by searching for terms like "Windows API List."

Understanding an API Declaration

The following line is an example of an API function:

```
Private Declare PtrSafe Function GetUserName _
    Lib "advapi32.dll" Alias "GetUserNameA" _
    (ByVal lpBuffer As String, nSize As Long) _
    As LongPtr
```

There are two types of API declarations:

- **Functions**—Return information
- **Procedures**—Do something to the system

The declarations are structured similarly.

Basically, what this declaration is saying is this:

- It is Private; therefore, it can be used only in the module in which it is declared. Declare it Public in a standard module if you want to share it among several modules.

> **CAUTION**
>
> API declarations in standard modules can be public or private. API declarations in class modules must be private.

- It will be referred to as GetUserName in your program. This is the variable name assigned by you.
- The function being used is found in advapi32.dll.
- The alias, GetUserNameA, is what the function is referred to in the DLL. This name is case sensitive and cannot be changed; it is specific to the DLL. There are often two versions of each API function. One version uses the ANSI character set and has aliases that end with the letter *A*. The other version uses the Unicode character set and has aliases that end with the letter *W*. When specifying the alias, you are telling VBA which version of the function to use.
- There are two parameters: lpBuffer and nSize. These are two arguments that the DLL function accepts.

> **CAUTION**
>
> The downside of using APIs is that there may be no errors when your code compiles or runs. This means that an incorrectly configured API call can cause your computer to crash or lock up. For this reason, it is a good idea to save often.

Using an API Declaration

Using an API is no different from calling a function or procedure you created in VBA. The following example uses the GetUserName declaration in a function to return the UserName in Excel:

```
Public Function UserName() As String
Dim sName As String * 256
Dim cChars As Long
cChars = 256
If GetUserName(sName, cChars) Then
    UserName = Left$(sName, cChars - 1)
End If
End Function

Sub ProgramRights()
```

```
Dim NameofUser As String
NameofUser = UserName
Select Case NameofUser
    Case Is = "Administrator"
        MsgBox "You have full rights to this computer"
    Case Else
        MsgBox "You have limited rights to this computer"
End Select
End Sub
```

Run the `ProgramRights` macro, and you will learn whether you are currently signed on as Administrator. The result shown in Figure 23.1 indicates that Administrator is the current username.

Figure 23.1
The `GetUserName` API function can be used to get a user's Windows login name—which is more difficult to edit than the Excel username. You can then control what rights a user has with your program.

Making 32-Bit and 64-Bit Compatible API Declarations

The examples in this book are 64-bit API declarations and might not work in 32-bit Excel. For example, if in a 64-bit version you have the declaration

```
Private Declare PtrSafe Function GetWindowLongptr Lib _
"USER32" Alias _
"GetWindowLongA" (ByVal hWnd As LongPtr, ByVal nIndex As _
Long) As LongPtr
```

it will need to be changed to the following to work in the 32-bit version:

```
Private Declare Function GetWindowLongptr Lib "USER32" Alias _
"GetWindowLongA" (ByVal hWnd As Long, ByVal nIndex As _
Long) As LongPtr
```

The difference is that `PtrSafe` needs to be removed from the declaration. You might also notice that there is a new variable type in use: `LongPtr`. Actually, `LongPtr` isn't a true data type; it becomes `LongLong` for 64-bit environments and `Long` in 32-bit environments. This does *not* mean that you should use it throughout your code; it has a specific use, such as in API calls. But you might find yourself using it in your code for API variables. For example, if you return an API variable of `LongPtr` to another variable in your code, that variable must also be `LongPtr`.

If you need to distribute your workbook to 32-bit and 64-bit users, you don't need to create two workbooks. You can create an If, Then, Else statement in the declarations area, setting up the API calls for both versions. So, for the preceding two examples, you could declare them like so:

```
#If VBA7 And Win64 Then
Private Declare PtrSafe Function GetUserName Lib "advapi32.dll" _
    Alias "GetUserNameA" (ByVal lpBuffer As String, nSize As Long) As LongPtr
#Else
Private Declare Function GetUserName Lib "advapi32.dll" _
    Alias "GetUserNameA" (ByVal lpBuffer As String, nSize As Long) As LongPtr
#End If
```

The pound sign (#) is used to mark conditional compilation. The code only compiles the line(s) of code that satisfy the logic check. #If VBA7 And Win64 checks to see whether the current environment is using the new code base (in use only since Office 2010) and whether the environment (Excel, not Windows) is 64-bit. If both are true, the first API declaration is processed. Else, the second one is used. For example, if Excel 2013 64-bit is running, the first API declaration is processed, but if the environment is Excel 2013 32-bit or Excel 2007, the second one is used. Note that in the 64-bit environment, the second API declaration will be colored as an error, but will compile just fine.

The change to 64-bit API calls is still new and there is some confusion as Microsoft continues to make changes. To help make sense of it all, Jan Karel Pieterse of JKP Application Development Services (www.jkp-ads.com) is working on an ever-growing web page listing the proper syntax for the 64-bit declarations. You can find it at www.jkp-ads.com/articles/apideclarations.asp.

API Examples

The following sections provide more examples of useful API declarations you can use in your Excel programs. Each example starts with a short description of what the example can do, followed by the actual declarations, and an example of its use.

Retrieving the Computer Name

This API function returns the computer name. This is the name of the computer found under Computer, Computer name:

```
Private Declare PtrSafe Function GetComputerName Lib "kernel32" Alias _
    "GetComputerNameA" (ByVal lpBuffer As String, ByRef nSize As Long) _
    As LongPtr

Private Function ComputerName() As String
Dim stBuff As String * 255, lAPIResult As LongPtr
Dim lBuffLen As Long

lBuffLen = 255
lAPIResult = GetComputerName(stBuff, lBuffLen)
If lBuffLen > 0 Then ComputerName = Left(stBuff, lBuffLen)
End Function

Sub ComputerCheck()
Dim CompName As String
```

```
    CompName = ComputerName

If CompName <> "BillJelenPC" Then
    MsgBox _
    "This application does not have the right to run on this computer."
        ActiveWorkbook.Close SaveChanges:=False
End If
End Sub
```

The `ComputerCheck` macro uses an API call to get the name of the computer. In the preceding example, the workbook refuses to open on any computer except the hard-coded computer name of the owner.

Checking Whether an Excel File Is Open on a Network

You can check whether you have a file open in Excel by trying to set the workbook to an object. If the object is `Nothing` (empty), you know that the file is not open. However, what if you want to see whether someone else on a network has the file open? The following API function returns that information:

```
Private Declare PtrSafe Function lOpen Lib "kernel32" Alias "_lopen" _
    (ByVal lpPathName As String, ByVal iReadWrite As Long) As LongPtr
Private Declare PtrSafe Function lClose Lib "kernel32" _
    Alias "_lclose" (ByVal hFile As LongPtr) As LongPtr
Private Const OF_SHARE_EXCLUSIVE = &H10

Private Function FileIsOpen(strFullPath_FileName As String) As Boolean
Dim hdlFile As LongPtr
Dim lastErr As Long

hdlFile = -1
hdlFile = lOpen(strFullPath_FileName, OF_SHARE_EXCLUSIVE)

If hdlFile = -1 Then
    lastErr = Err.LastDllError
Else
    lClose (hdlFile)
End If
FileIsOpen = (hdlFile = -1) And (lastErr = 32)
End Function

Sub CheckFileOpen()
If FileIsOpen("C:\XYZ Corp.xlsx") Then
    MsgBox "File is open"
Else
    MsgBox "File is not open"
End If
End Sub
```

Calling the `FileIsOpen` function with a particular path and filename as the parameter will tell you whether someone has the file open.

Retrieving Display-Resolution Information

The following API function retrieves the computer's display size:

```
Declare PtrSafe Function DisplaySize Lib "user32" Alias _
    "GetSystemMetrics" (ByVal nIndex As Long) As LongPtr

Public Const SM_CXSCREEN = 0
Public Const SM_CYSCREEN = 1

Function VideoRes() As String
Dim vidWidth
Dim vidHeight

vidWidth = DisplaySize(SM_CXSCREEN)
vidHeight = DisplaySize(SM_CYSCREEN)

Select Case (vidWidth * vidHeight)
    Case 307200
        VideoRes = "640 x 480"
    Case 480000
        VideoRes = "800 x 600"
    Case 786432
        VideoRes = "1024 x 768"
    Case Else
        VideoRes = "Something else"
End Select
End Function

Sub CheckDisplayRes()
Dim VideoInfo As String
Dim Msg1 As String, Msg2 As String, Msg3 As String

VideoInfo = VideoRes

Msg1 = "Current resolution is set at " & VideoInfo & Chr(10)
Msg2 = "Optimal resolution for this application is 1024 x 768" & Chr(10)
Msg3 = "Please adjust resolution"

Select Case VideoInfo
    Case Is = "640 x 480"
        MsgBox Msg1 & Msg2 & Msg3
    Case Is = "800 x 600"
        MsgBox Msg1 & Msg2
    Case Is = "1024 x 768"
        MsgBox Msg1
    Case Else
        MsgBox Msg2 & Msg3
End Select
End Sub
```

The CheckDisplayRes macro warns the client that the display setting is not optimal for the application.

Customizing the About Dialog

If you go to Help, About Windows in File Explorer, you get a nice little About dialog with information about the File Explorer and a few system details. With the following code, you can get that window to pop up in your own program and customize a few items, as shown in Figure 23.2.

Figure 23.2
You can customize the About dialog used by Windows for your own program.

```
Declare PtrSafe Function ShellAbout Lib "shell32.dll" Alias "ShellAboutA" _
    (ByVal hwnd As LongPtr, ByVal szApp As String, ByVal szOtherStuff As _
    String, ByVal hIcon As Long) As LongPtr
Declare PtrSafe Function GetActiveWindow Lib "user32" () As LongPtr

Sub AboutMrExcel()
Dim hwnd As LongPtr
On Error Resume Next
hwnd = GetActiveWindow()
ShellAbout hwnd, Nm, vbCrLf + Chr(169) + "" & " MrExcel.com Consulting" _
    + vbCrLf, 0
On Error GoTo 0
End Sub
```

Disabling the X for Closing a Userform

The X button located in the upper-right corner of a userform can be used to shut down the form. You can capture the event with QueryClose, but to prevent the button from being active and working at all, you need an API call. The following API declarations work together to disable that X, forcing the user to use the Close button. When the form is initialized, the X button is disabled. After the form is closed, the X button is reset to normal:

```
Private Declare PtrSafe Function FindWindow Lib "user32" Alias "FindWindowA" _
    (ByVal lpClassName As String, ByVal lpWindowName As String) As LongPtr
Private Declare PtrSafe Function GetSystemMenu Lib "user32" _
    (ByVal hWnd As LongPtr, ByVal bRevert As Long) As LongPtr
Private Declare PtrSafe Function DeleteMenu Lib "user32" _
    (ByVal hMenu As LongPtr, ByVal nPosition As Long, _
    ByVal wFlags As Long) As LongPtr
Private Const SC_CLOSE As Long = &HF060

Private Sub UserForm_Initialize()
Dim hWndForm As LongPtr
Dim hMenu As LongPtr
'ThunderDFrame is the class name of all userforms
hWndForm = FindWindow("ThunderDFrame", Me.Caption)
hMenu = GetSystemMenu(hWndForm, 0)
DeleteMenu hMenu, SC_CLOSE, 0&
End Sub
```

The DeleteMenu macro in the UserForm_Initialize procedure causes the X in the corner of the userform to be grayed out, as shown in Figure 23.3. This forces the client to use your programmed Close button.

Figure 23.3

Disable the X button on a userform, forcing users to use the Close button to shut down the form properly and rendering them unable to bypass any code attached to the Close button.

23

Running Timer

You can use the NOW function to get the time, but what if you need a running timer displaying the exact time as the seconds tick by? The following API declarations work together to provide this functionality. The timer is placed in cell A1 of Sheet1.

```
Public Declare PtrSafe Function SetTimer Lib "user32" _
    (ByVal hWnd As Long, ByVal nIDEvent As Long, _
    ByVal uElapse As Long, ByVal lpTimerFunc As LongPtr) As LongPtr
Public Declare PtrSafe Function KillTimer Lib "user32" _
    (ByVal hWnd As Long, ByVal nIDEvent As Long) As LongPtr
Public Declare PtrSafe Function FindWindow Lib "user32" _
    Alias "FindWindowA" (ByVal lpClassName As String, _
    ByVal lpWindowName As String) As LongPtr
Private lngTimerID As Long
Private datStartingTime As Date

Public Sub StartTimer()
StopTimer 'stop previous timer
lngTimerID = SetTimer(0, 1, 10, AddressOf RunTimer)
End Sub

Public Sub StopTimer()
Dim lRet As LongPtr, lngTID As Long

If IsEmpty(lngTimerID) Then Exit Sub

lngTID = lngTimerID
lRet = KillTimer(0, lngTID)
lngTimerID = Empty
End Sub

Private Sub RunTimer(ByVal hWnd As Long, _
    ByVal uint1 As Long, ByVal nEventId As Long, _
    ByVal dwParam As Long)
On Error Resume Next
Sheet1.Range("A1").Value = Format(Now - datStartingTime, "hh:mm:ss")
End Sub
```

Run the StartTimer macro to have the current date and time constantly updated in cell A1.

Playing Sounds

Have you ever wanted to play a sound to warn users or congratulate them? You could add a sound object to a sheet and call that sound. However, it would be easier to use the following API declaration and specify the proper path to a sound file:

```
Public Declare PtrSafe Function PlayWavSound Lib "winmm.dll" _
    Alias "sndPlaySoundA" (ByVal LpszSoundName As String, _
    ByVal uFlags As Long) As LongPtr

Public Sub PlaySound()
Dim SoundName As String

SoundName = "C:\Windows\Media\Chimes.wav"
PlayWavSound SoundName, 0

End Sub
```

Next Steps

In Chapter 24, "Handling Errors," you'll find out about error handling. In a perfect world, you want to be able to hand your applications off to a co-worker, leave for vacation, and not have to worry about an unhandled error appearing while you are on the beach. Chapter 24 discusses how to handle obvious and not-so-obvious errors.

Handling Errors

Errors are bound to happen. Even when you test
and retest your code, after a report is put into daily
production and used for hundreds of days, something unexpected will eventually happen. Your goal
should be to try to head off obscure errors as you
code. For this reason, you should always be thinking
of what unexpected things could happen someday
that could make your code not work.

24

What Happens When an Error Occurs?

When VBA encounters an error and you have no
error-checking code in place, the program stops and
presents you or your client with the "Continue, End,
Debug, Help" error message, as shown in Figure
24.1. If Debug is grayed out, then someone has protected the VBA code and you will have to call the
developer.

Figure 24.1
An unhandled error in an
unprotected module pres-
ents you with a choice to
end or debug.

Microsoft Visual Basic

Run-time error '1004':

Sorry, we couldn't find C:\NotHere.xls. Is it possible it was moved,
renamed or deleted?

Continue | End | Debug | Help

When presented with the choice to end or debug,
you should click Debug. The VB Editor highlights
in yellow the line that caused the error. When you
hover the cursor over any variable, you see the current value of the variable, which provides a lot of
information about what could have caused the error
(see Figure 24.2).

Figure 24.2
After clicking Debug, the macro is in break mode. Hover the cursor over a variable; after a few seconds, the current value of the variable is shown.

Hover over the x for a tooltip

Excel is notorious for returning errors that are not very meaningful. For example, dozens of situations can cause a 1004 error. Seeing the offending line highlighted in yellow and examining the current value of any variables helps you discover the real cause of an error. You might note that many error messages in Excel 2013 are more meaningful than the equivalent message in Excel 2010. This extends to the VBA error messages.

After examining the line in error, click the Reset button to stop execution of the macro. The Reset button is the square button under the Run item in the main menu, as shown in Figure 24.3.

Figure 24.3
The Reset button looks like the Stop button in the set of three buttons that resembles a DVD control panel.

If you fail to click Reset to end the macro and then attempt to run another macro, you are presented with the annoying error message shown in Figure 24.4. The message is annoying because you start in Excel, but when this message window is displayed, the screen automatically switches to display the VB Editor. You can see the Reset button in the background, but you cannot click it due to the message box that is displayed. However, immediately after you click OK to close the message box, you are returned to the Excel user interface instead of being left in the VB Editor. Because this error message occurs quite often, it would be more convenient if you could be returned to the VB Editor after clicking OK.

Figure 24.4
This message appears if you forget to click Reset to end a debug session and then attempt to run another macro.

Debug Error Inside Userform Code Is Misleading

After you click Debug, the line highlighted as the error can be misleading in one situation. For example, suppose you call a macro that displays a userform. Somewhere in the userform code, an error occurs. When you click Debug, instead of showing the problem inside the userform code, Excel highlights the line in the original macro that displayed the userform. Follow these steps to find the real error:

1. After the error message box shown in Figure 24.5 is displayed, click the Debug button.

Figure 24.5
Select Debug in response to this error 13.

```
Microsoft Visual Basic

Run-time error '13':

Type mismatch



   Continue        End         Debug         Help
```

You see that the error allegedly occurred on a line that shows a userform, as shown in Figure 24.6. Because you have read this chapter, you know that this is not the line in error.

24

Figure 24.6
The line in error is indicated as the frm-Choose.Show line.

```
Sub PrepareAndDisplay()
    ' sometimes an error happens in a userform
    ' yet the editor reports it as the next line
    Dim WS As Worksheet
    Set WS = Worksheets("Sheet1")

    FinalRow = WS.Cells(Rows.Count, 1).End(xlUp).Row
    WS.Cells(1, 1).Sort _
        Key1:=WS.Cells(1, 1), Order1:=xlAscending, Header:=xlYes

    frmChoose.Show

    MsgBox "Macro complete"

End Sub
```

2. Press F8 to execute the Show method. Instead of getting an error, you are taken into the Userform_Initialize procedure.

3. Keep pressing F8 until you get the error message again. Stay alert because as soon as you encounter the error, the error message box is displayed. Click Debug and you are returned to the userform.Show line. It is particularly difficult to follow the code when the error occurs on the other side of a long loop, as shown in Figure 24.7.

Figure 24.7
With 25 items to add to the list box, you must press F8 53 times to get through this three-line loop.

Loop

```
Private Sub UserForm_Initialize()
    Dim WS As Worksheet
    Set WS = Worksheets("Sheet1")

    FinalRow = WS.Cells(Rows.Count, 1).End(xlUp).Row
    For i = 2 To FinalRow
        Me.ListBox1.AddItem WS.Cells(i, 1)
    Next i

    ' The next line is actually the line that causes an error
    Me.ListBox1(0).Selected = True



End Sub
```

Imagine trying to step through the code in Figure 24.7. You carefully press F8 five times with no problems through the first pass of the loop. Because the problem could be in future iterations through the loop, you continue to press F8. If there are 25 items to add to the list box, 48 more presses of F8 are required to get through the loop safely. Each time before pressing F8, you should mentally note that you are about to run some specific line.

At the point shown in Figure 24.7, the next press of the F8 key displays the error and returns you to the frmChoose.Show line back in Module1. This is an annoying situation.

When you click Debug and see that the line in error is a line that displays a userform, you need to start pressing the F8 key to step into the userform code until you get the error. Invariably, you will get incredibly bored pressing F8 a million times and forget to pay attention to which line caused the error. However, as soon as the error happens, you are thrown back to the Debug message, which returns you to the frmChoose.Show line of code.

At that point, you need to start pressing F8 again. If you can recall the general area where the debug error occurred, click the mouse cursor in a line right before that section and use Ctrl+F8 to run the macro up to the cursor. Alternatively, right-click that line and choose Run to Cursor.

Sometimes an error will occur within a loop. Add Debug.Print i inside the loop and use the Immediate Pane (Ctrl+G) to locate which time through the loop caused the problem.

Basic Error Handling with the On Error GoTo Syntax

The basic error-handling option is to tell VBA that in the case of an error you want to have code branch to a specific area of the macro. In this area, you might have special code that alerts users of the problem and enables them to react.

A typical scenario is to add the error-handling routine at the end of the macro. To set up an error handler, follow these steps:

1. After the last code line of the macro, insert the code line Exit Sub. This makes sure that the execution of the macro does not continue into the error handler.

2. After the Exit Sub line, add a label. A label is a name followed by a colon. For example, you might create a label called MyErrorHandler:.

3. Write the code to handle the error. If you want to return control of the macro to the line after the one that caused the error, use the statement Resume Next.

In your macro, just before the line that might likely cause the error, add a line reading On Error GoTo MyErrorHandler. Note that in this line, you do not include the colon after the label name.

Immediately after the line of code that you suspect will cause the error, add code to turn off the special error handler. Because this is not intuitive, it tends to confuse people. The code to cancel any special error handling is On Error GoTo 0. There is no label named 0. Instead, this line is a fictitious line that instructs Excel to go back to the normal state of displaying the End/Debug error message when an error is encountered. This is why it is important to cancel the error handling.

Note that you can have multiple error handler labels at the bottom of your macro. Be sure that each section ends in Exit Sub or Resume Next so that the code from the first error handler does not continue into the second error handler.

> **NOTE** The following code includes a special error handler to handle the necessary action if the file has been moved or is missing. You definitely do not want this error handler invoked for another error later in the macro such as division by zero.

```
Sub HandleAnError()
    Dim MyFile as Variant
    ' Set up a special error handler
    On Error GoTo FileNotThere
    Workbooks.Open Filename:="C:\NotHere.xls"
    ' If we get here, cancel the special error handler
    On Error GoTo 0
    MsgBox "The program is complete"

    ' The macro is done. Use Exit sub, otherwise the macro
    ' execution WILL continue into the error handler
    Exit Sub

    ' Set up a name for the Error handler
FileNotThere:
    MyPrompt = "There was an error opening the file. It is possible the"
    MyPrompt = MyPrompt & " file has been moved. Click OK to browse for the "
    MyPrompt = MyPrompt & "file, or click Cancel to end the program"
    Ans = MsgBox(Prompt:=MyPrompt, Buttons:=vbOKCancel)
    If Ans = vbCancel Then Exit Sub

    ' The client clicked OK. Let him browse for the file
    MyFile = Application.GetOpenFilename
    If MyFile = False Then Exit Sub

    ' What if the 2nd file is corrupt? We do not want to recursively throw
    ' the client back into this error handler. Just stop the program
    On Error GoTo 0
    Workbooks.Open MyFile
    ' If we get here, then return the macro execution back to the original
    ' section of the macro, to the line after the one that caused the error.
    Resume Next

End Sub
```

> **NOTE** It is possible to have more than one error handler at the end of a macro. Make sure that each error handler ends with either Resume Next or Exit Sub so that macro execution does not accidentally move into the next error handler.

24

Generic Error Handlers

Some developers like to direct any error to a generic error handler to make use of the Err object. This object has properties for error number and description. You can offer this information to the client and prevent her from getting a Debug message:

```
On Error GoTo HandleAny
Sheets(9).Select

Exit Sub

HandleAny:
    Msg = "We encountered " & Err.Number & " - " & Err.Description
    MsgBox Msg
    Exit Sub
```

Handling Errors by Choosing to Ignore Them

Some errors can simply be ignored. For example, suppose you are going to use the HTML Creator macro from Chapter 18, "Reading from and Writing to the Web." Your code erases any existing index.html file from a folder before writing out the next file.

The Kill (FileName) statement returns an error if FileName does not exist. This probably is not something about which you need to worry. After all, you are trying to delete the file, so you probably do not care whether someone already deleted it before running the macro. In this case, tell Excel to just skip over the offending line and resume macro execution with the next line. The code to do this is On Error Resume Next:

```
Sub WriteHTML()
    MyFile = "C:\Index.html"
    On Error Resume Next
    Kill MyFile
    On Error Goto 0
    Open MyFile for Output as #1
    ' etc...
End Sub
```

> **NOTE**
>
> Be careful with On Error Resume Next. You can use it selectively in situations in which you know that the error can be ignored. You should immediately return error checking to normal after the line that might cause an error with On Error GoTo 0.
>
> If you attempt to have On Error Resume Next skip an error that cannot be skipped, the macro immediately steps out of the current macro. If you have a situation in which MacroA calls MacroB and MacroB encounters a nonskippable error, the program jumps out of MacroB and continues with the next line in MacroA. This is rarely a good thing.

CASE STUDY: PAGE SETUP PROBLEMS CAN BE OVERLOOKED

When you record a macro and perform a page setup, even if you change just one item in the Page Setup dialog, the macro recorder records two dozen settings for you. These settings notoriously differ from printer to printer. For example, If you record the PageSetup on a system with a color printer, it might record a setting for .BlackAndWhite = True. This setting will fail on another system on which the printer does not offer the choice. Your printer might offer a .PrintQuality = 600 setting. If the client's printer offers only a 300 resolution setting, this code fails. For this reason, you should surround the entire PageSetup with On Error Resume Next to ensure that most settings happen but the trivial ones that fail do not cause a runtime error. Here is how to do this:

```
On Error Resume Next
Application.PrintCommunication = False
With ActiveSheet.PageSetup
    .PrintTitleRows = ""
    .PrintTitleColumns = ""
End With
 ActiveSheet.PageSetup.PrintArea = "$A$1:$L$27"
 With ActiveSheet.PageSetup
    .LeftHeader = ""
    .CenterHeader = ""
    .RightHeader = ""
    .LeftFooter = ""
    .CenterFooter = ""
    .RightFooter = ""
    .LeftMargin = Application.InchesToPoints(0.25)
    .RightMargin = Application.InchesToPoints(0.25)
    .TopMargin = Application.InchesToPoints(0.75)
    .BottomMargin = Application.InchesToPoints(0.5)
    .HeaderMargin = Application.InchesToPoints(0.5)
    .FooterMargin = Application.InchesToPoints(0.5)
    .PrintHeadings = False
    .PrintGridlines = False
    .PrintComments = xlPrintNoComments
    .PrintQuality = 300
    .CenterHorizontally = False
    .CenterVertically = False
    .Orientation = xlLandscape
    .Draft = False
    .PaperSize = xlPaperLetter
    .FirstPageNumber = xlAutomatic
    .Order = xlDownThenOver
    .BlackAndWhite = False
    .Zoom = False
    .FitToPagesWide = 1
    .FitToPagesTall = False
    .PrintErrors = xlPrintErrorsDisplayed
End With
Application.PrintCommunication = True
On Error GoTo 0
```

VBA code to handle printer settings will run much faster by turning off PrintCommunication at the beginning of the preceding code and turning it back on at the end of the code. This trick was new in Excel 2010. Before this, Excel would pause for almost a half-second during each line of print setting code. Now, the whole block of code runs in less than a second.

24

Suppressing Excel Warnings

Some messages appear even if you have set Excel to ignore errors. For example, try to delete a worksheet using code and you still get the message "You can't undo deleting sheets, and you might be removing some data. If you don't need it, click Delete." This is annoying. You do not want your clients to have to answer this warning; it gives them a chance to choose not to delete the sheet your macro wants to delete. In fact, this is not an error but an alert. To suppress all alerts and force Excel to take the default action, use `Application. DisplayAlerts = False`:

```
Sub DeleteSheet()
    Application.DisplayAlerts = False
    Worksheets("Sheet2").Delete
    Application.DisplayAlerts = True
End Sub
```

Encountering Errors on Purpose

Because programmers hate errors, this concept might seem counterintuitive, but errors are not always bad. Sometimes it is faster to simply encounter an error.

Suppose, for example, that you want to find out whether the active workbook contains a worksheet named Data. To find this out without causing an error, you could code this:

```
DataFound = False
For Each ws in ActiveWorkbook.Worksheets
    If ws.Name = "Data" then
        DataFound = True
        Exit For
    End if
Next ws
If not DataFound then Sheets.Add.Name = "Data"
```

This takes eight lines of code. If your workbook has 128 worksheets, the program loops through 128 times before deciding that the data worksheet is missing.

The alternative is to try to reference the data worksheet. If you have error checking set to resume next, the code runs, and the `Err` object is assigned a number other than zero:

```
On Error Resume Next
X = Worksheets("Data").Name
If Err.Number <> 0 then Sheets.Add.Name = "Data"
On Error GoTo 0
```

This code runs much faster. Errors usually make programmers cringe. However, in this case and in many other cases, the errors are perfectly acceptable.

Train Your Clients

Suppose you are developing code for a client across the globe or for the administrative assistant so that he can run the code while you are on vacation. In both cases, you might find yourself trying to debug code remotely while you are on the telephone with the client.

For this reason, it is important to train clients about the difference between an error and a simple MsgBox. Even though a MsgBox is a planned message, it still appears out of the blue with a beep. Teach your users that even though error messages are bad, not everything that pops up is an error message. For example, I had a client who kept reporting to her boss that she was getting an error from my program. In reality, she was getting an informational MsgBox. Both Debug errors and Msgbox messages beep at the user.

When clients get Debug errors, train them to call you while the Debug message is still on the screen. This enables you to get the error number and description. You also can ask the client to click Debug and tell you the module name, the procedure name, and which line is in yellow. Armed with this information, you can usually figure out what is going on. Without this information, it is unlikely that you will be able to resolve the problem. Getting a call from a client saying that there was a 1004 error is of little help—1004 is a catchall error that can mean any number of things.

Errors While Developing Versus Errors Months Later

When you have just written code that you are running for the first time, you expect errors. In fact, you might decide to step through code line by line to watch the progress of the code the first time through.

It is another thing to have a program that has been running daily in production suddenly stop working because of an error. This can be perplexing. The code has been working for months. Why did it suddenly stop working today?

It is easy to blame the client. However, when you get right down to it, it is really the fault of developers for not considering the possibilities.

The following sections describe a couple of common problems that can strike an application months later.

Runtime Error 9: Subscript Out of Range

You set up an application for a client and you provided a Menu worksheet where some settings are stored. Then one day this client reports the error message shown in Figure 24.8.

Figure 24.8
The Runtime Error 9 is often caused when you expect a worksheet to be there and it has been deleted or renamed by the client.

Your code expected there to be a worksheet named Menu. For some reason, the client either accidentally deleted the worksheet or renamed it. When you tried to select the sheet, you received an error:

```
Sub GetSettings()
    ThisWorkbook.Worksheets("Menu").Select
    x = Range("A1").Value
End Sub
```

This is a classic situation where you cannot believe that the client would do something so crazy. After you have been burned by this one a few times, you might go to these lengths to prevent an unhandled Debug error:

```
Sub GetSettings()
    On Error Resume Next
    x = ThisWorkbook.Worksheets("Menu").Name
    If Not Err.Number = 0 Then
        MsgBox "Expected to find a Menu worksheet, but it is missing"
        Exit Sub
    End If
    On Error GoTo 0

    ThisWorkbook.Worksheets("Menu").Select
    x = Range("A1").Value
End Sub
```

Runtime Error 1004: Method Range of Object Global Failed

You have code that imports a text file each day. You expect the text file to end with a Total row. After importing the text, you want to convert all the detail rows to italic.

The following code works fine for months:

```
Sub SetReportInItalics()
    TotalRow = Cells(Rows.Count,1).End(xlUp).Row
    FinalRow = TotalRow - 1
    Range("A1:A" & FinalRow).Font.Italic = True
End Sub
```

Then one day, the client calls with the error message shown in Figure 24.9.

Figure 24.9
The Runtime Error 1004 can be caused by a number of things.

Upon examination of the code, you discover that something bizarre went wrong when the text file was transferred via FTP to the client that day. The text file ended up as an empty file. Because the worksheet was empty, TotalRow was determined to be Row 1. If you assume that the last detail row was TotalRow - 1, the code is set up to attempt to format Row 0, which clearly does not exist.

After an episode like this, you find yourself writing code that preemptively looks for this situation:

```
Sub SetReportInItalics()
    TotalRow = Cells(Rows.Count,1).End(xlUp).Row
    FinalRow = TotalRow - 1
    If FinalRow > 0 Then
        Range("A1:A" & FinalRow).Font.Italic = True
    Else
        MsgBox "It appears the file is empty today. Check the FTP process"
    End If
End Sub
```

The Ills of Protecting Code

It is possible to lock a VBA project so that it cannot be viewed. However, this is not recommended. When code is protected and an error is encountered, your user is presented with an error message but no opportunity to debug. The Debug button is there, but it is grayed out. This is useless in helping you discover the problem.

Further, the Excel VBA protection scheme is horribly easy to break. Programmers in Estonia offer $40 software that lets you unlock any project. For this reason, you need to understand that office VBA code is not secure and get over it. If you absolutely need to truly protect your code, invest in Visual Studio and learn how to develop COM add-ins.

24

CASE STUDY: PASSWORD CRACKING

The password-hacking schemes were very easy in Excel 97 and Excel 2000. The password-cracking software could immediately locate the actual password in the VBA project and report it to the software user.

Then, in Excel 2002, Microsoft offered a brilliant protection scheme that temporarily appeared to foil the password-cracking utilities. The password was tightly encrypted. For several months after the release of Excel 2002, password-cracking programs had to try brute-force combinations. The software could crack a password such as blue in 10 minutes. However, given a 24-character password such as *A6%kJJ542(9$GgU44#2drt8, the program would take 20 hours to find the password. This was a fun annoyance to foist upon other VBA programmers who would potentially break into your code.

However, the next version of the password-cracking software was able to break a 24-character password in Excel 2002 in about 2 seconds. When I tested my 24-character password-protected project, the password utility quickly told me that my password was XVII. I thought this was certainly wrong, but after testing, I found the project had a new password of XVII. Yes, this latest version of the software resorted to another approach. Instead of using brute force to crack the password, it simply wrote a new random four-character password to the project and saved the file.

Now, this causes an embarrassing problem for whoever cracked the password. The developer has a sign on his wall reminding him the password is *A6%kJJ542(9$GgU44#2drt8. However, in the cracked version of the file, the password is now XVII. If there is a problem with the cracked file and it is sent back to the developer, the developer can no longer open the file. The only person getting anything from this is the programmer in Estonia who wrote the cracking software.

There are not enough Excel VBA developers in the world, and there are more projects than there are programmers. In my circle of developer friends, we acknowledge that business prospects slip through the cracks because we are too busy with other customers.

Therefore, the situation of a newbie developer is common. In this scenario, this new developer does an adequate job of writing code for a customer and then locks the VBA project.

The customer needs some changes. The original developer does the work. A few weeks later, the developer delivers some requested changes. A month later, the customer needs more work. Either the developer is busy with other projects or he has underpriced these maintenance jobs and has more lucrative work. The client tries to contact the programmer a few times before realizing he needs to get the project fixed, so he calls another developer—you!

You get the code. It is protected. You break the password and see who wrote the code. This is a tough call. You have no interest in stealing the new developer's customer. In fact, you prefer to do this one job and then have the customer return to the original developer. However, because of the password hacking, you have created a situation in which the two developers have different passwords. Your only choice is to remove the password entirely. This will tip off the other developer that someone else has been in his or her code. Maybe you could try to placate the other developer with a few lines of comment that the password was removed after the customer could not contact the original developer.

More Problems with Passwords

The password scheme for any version of Excel from 2002 forward is incompatible with Excel 97. If you protected code in Excel 2002, you cannot unlock the project in Excel 97. As your application is given to more employees in a company, you will invariably find an employee using Excel 97. Of course, that user will come up with a runtime error. However, if you locked the project in Excel 2002 or newer, you are not able to unlock the project in Excel 97, which means that you cannot debug the program in Excel 97.

Bottom line: Locking code causes more trouble than it is worth.

> **NOTE** If you are using a combination of Excel 2003 through Excel 2013, the passwords transfer easily back and forth. This holds true even if the file is saved as an XLSM file and opened in Excel 2003 using the file converter. You can change code in Excel 2003, save the file, and successfully round-trip back to Excel 2013.

Errors Caused by Different Versions

Microsoft improves VBA in every version of Excel. Pivot table creation was improved dramatically between Excel 97 and Excel 2000. Sparklines and slicers were new in Excel 2010. The Data Model is introduced in Excel 2013.

The `TrailingMinusNumbers` parameter was new in Excel 2002. This means that if you write code in Excel 2013 and then send the code to a client with Excel 2000, that user gets a compile error as soon as she tries to run any code in the same module as the offending code. For this reason, you need to consider this application in two modules.

Module1 has macros ProcA, ProcB, and ProcC. Module2 has macros ProcD and ProcE. It happens that ProcE has an `ImportText` method with the `TrailingMinusNumbers` parameter.

The client can run ProcA and ProcB on the Excel 2000 machine without problem. As soon as she tries to run ProcD, she gets a compile error reported in ProcD because Excel tries to compile all of Module2 when she tries to run code in that module. This can be incredibly misleading: An error being reported when the client runs ProcD is actually caused by an error in ProcE.

One solution is to have access to every supported version of Excel, plus Excel 97, and test the code in all versions. Note that Excel 97 SR-2 was far more stable than the initial releases of Excel 97. Even though many clients are hanging on to Excel 97, it is frustrating when you find someone who does not have the stable service release.

Macintosh users will believe that their version of Excel is the same as the Excel for Windows. Microsoft promised compatibility of files, but that promise ends in the Excel user interface. VBA code is not compatible between Windows and the Mac. Excel VBA on the Mac in Excel 2011 is close to Excel 2010 VBA but annoyingly different. Excel 2008 for the Mac uses AppleScript instead of supporting VBA. Further, anything you do with the Windows API is not going to work on a Mac.

Next Steps

This chapter discussed how to make your code more bulletproof for your clients. In Chapter 25, "Customizing the Ribbon to Run Macros," you'll learn how to customize the ribbon to allow your clients to enjoy a professional user interface.

Customizing the Ribbon to Run Macros

25

Out with the Old, In with the New

If you have been working with a legacy version of Excel, one of the first changes you notice when you open Excel 2013 is the ribbon toolbar that was introduced in Excel 2007. Gone are the menus and toolbars of old. And this change isn't just visual—the method of modifying custom menu controls was changed just as radically. One of the biggest bonuses of the ribbon is that you no longer have to worry about your custom toolbar sticking around after the workbook is closed because the custom toolbar is now part of the inner workings of the workbook. One thing to keep in mind is that with the change to a single document interface (SDI), the custom ribbon tab attached to a workbook is visible only when that workbook is active. When you activate another workbook, the tab will not appear on the ribbon. The exception is with an add-in; its custom ribbon is visible on any workbook open after the add-in is opened.

→ **See** Chapter 28, "What's New in Excel 2013 and What's Changed," for more information on SDI.

→ **See** Chapter 26, "Creating Add-Ins," for more information on creating an add-in.

The original `CommandBars` object still works, but the customized menus and toolbars are all placed on the Add-ins tab. If you had custom menu commands, they will appear on the Menu Commands group, as shown in Figure 25.1. In Figure 25.2, the custom toolbars from two different workbooks appear together on the Custom Toolbars group.

Figure 25.1
Legacy version custom menus will be grouped together under the Menu Commands group.

Figure 25.2
Custom toolbars from legacy versions of Excel appear in the Custom Toolbars group.

If you want to modify the ribbon and add your own tab, you need to modify the Excel file itself, which isn't as impossible as it sounds. The new Excel file is actually a zipped file, containing various files and folders. All you need to do is unzip it, make your changes, and you're done. Okay, it's not *that* simple—a few more steps are involved—but it's not impossible.

Before beginning, go to the File tab and select Options, Advanced, General, and select Show Add-In User Interface Errors. This allows error messages to appear so that you can troubleshoot errors in your custom toolbar.

➔ **See** the "Troubleshooting Error Messages" section, **p. 548**, for more details.

> **CAUTION**
>
> Unlike programming in the VB Editor, you won't have any assistance with automatic correction of letter case; and the XML code, which is what the ribbon code is, is very particular. Note the case of the XML-specific words, such as `id`—using `ID` will generate an error.

Where to Add Your Code: `customui` Folder and File

Create a folder called `customui`. This folder will contain the elements of your custom ribbon tab. Within the folder, create a text file and call it `customUI14.xml`, as shown in Figure 25.3. Open the XML file in a text editor; either Notepad or WordPad will work.

Figure 25.3
Create a custom-uUI14.xml file within a customui folder.

Insert the basic structure for the XML code, shown here, into your XML file. For every opening tag grouping, such as <ribbon>, there must be a closing tag, </ribbon>:

```
<customUI xmlns="http://schemas.microsoft.com/office/2009/07/customui">
  <ribbon startFromScratch="false">
    <tabs>

      <!-- your ribbon controls here -->

    </tabs>
  </ribbon>
</customUI>
```

startFromScratch is optional with a default value of false. It's how you tell the code the other tabs in Excel will not be shown, only yours. True means to show only your tab; false means to show your tab and all the other tabs.

> **CAUTION**
>
> Note the case of the letters in startFromScratch—the small *s* at the beginning followed by the capital *F* in From and capital *S* in Scratch. It is crucial you do not deviate from this.

The <!-- your ribbon controls here --> you see in the previous code is commented text. Just enter your comments between <!-- and -->, and the program ignores the line when it runs.

> **NOTE**
>
> At the time this was written, an updated schema (http://schemas.microsoft.com/office/2009/07/customui) for Office 2013 was not available. Although the ribbons in 2010 and 2013 are very similar, there are some differences. For the purpose of creating your own ribbon tab, this is not an issue. But if you want to modify a part of the 2013 ribbon, such as File, Save As, you might need to find the new Office 2013 schema.

25

Creating the Tab and Group

Before you can add a control to a tab, you need to identify the tab and group. A tab can hold many different controls on it, which you can group together, like the Font group on the Home tab.

We'll name our tab MrExcel Add-ins and add a group called Reports to it, as shown in Figure 25.4:

```
<customUI xmlns="http://schemas.microsoft.com/office/2009/07/customui">
  <ribbon startFromScratch="false">
    <tabs>
      <tab id="CustomTab" label="MrExcel Add-ins">
        <group id="CustomGroup" label="Reports">

          <!-- your ribbon controls here -->
```

```
            </group>
          </tab>
        </tabs>
      </ribbon>
    </customUI>
```

Figure 25.4
Add Tab and Group tags to your code to create a custom tab, MrExcel Add-Ins, and group, Reports.

The id is a unique identifier for the control (in this case, the tab and group). The label is the text you want to appear on your ribbon for the specified control.

Adding a Control to Your Ribbon

After you've set up the ribbon and group, you can add controls. Depending on the type of control, there are different attributes you can include in your XML code. (Refer to Table 25.1 for more information on various controls and their attributes.)

The following code adds a normal-sized button with the text Click to run to the Reports group, set to run the sub called HelloWorld when the button is clicked (see Figure 25.5):

```
<customUI xmlns="http://schemas.microsoft.com/office/2009/07/customui">
  <ribbon startFromScratch="false">
    <tabs>
      <tab id="CustomTab" label="MrExcel Add-ins">
        <group id="CustomGroup" label="Reports">

          <button id="button1" label="Click to run"
              onAction="Module1.HelloWorld" size="normal"/>

        </group>
      </tab>
    </tabs>
  </ribbon>
</customUI>
```

Figure 25.5
Run a program with a click of a button on your custom ribbon.

The id is a unique identifier for the control button. The label is the text you want to appear on your button. Size is the size of the button. normal is the default value, and the other option is large. onAction is the sub, HelloWorld, to call when the button is clicked. The sub, shown here, goes in a standard module, Module1, in the workbook:

```
Sub HelloWorld(control As IRibbonControl)
MsgBox "Hello World"
End Sub
```

Notice the argument control As IRibbonControl. This is the standard argument for a sub called by a button control using the onAction attribute. Refer to Table 25.2 for the required arguments for other attributes and controls.

Table 25.1   Ribbon Control Attributes

Attribute	Type or Value	Description
description	String	Specifies description text displayed in menus when the itemSize attribute is set to Large
enabled	true, false	Specifies whether the control is enabled
getContent	Callback	Retrieves XML content that describes a dynamic menu
getDescription	Callback	Gets the description of a control
getEnabled	Callback	Gets the enabled state of a control
getImage	Callback	Gets the image for a control
getImageMso	Callback	Gets a built-in control's icon by using the control ID
getItemCount	Callback	Gets the number of items to be displayed in a combo box, drop-down list, or gallery
getItemID	Callback	Gets the ID for a specific item in a combo box, drop-down list, or gallery
getItemImage	Callback	Gets the image of a combo box, drop-down list, or gallery
getItemLabel	Callback	Gets the label of a combo box, drop-down list, or gallery
getItemScreentip	Callback	Gets the ScreenTip for a combo box, drop-down list, or gallery
getItemSupertip	Callback	Gets the Enhanced ScreenTip for a combo box, drop-down list, or gallery
getKeytip	Callback	Gets the KeyTip for a control
getLabel	Callback	Gets the label for a control
getPressed	Callback	Gets a value that indicates whether a toggle button is pressed or not pressed
		Gets a value that indicates whether a check box is selected or cleared
getScreentip	Callback	Gets the ScreenTip for a control
getSelectedItemID	Callback	Gets the ID of the selected item in a drop-down list or gallery

25

Attribute	Type or Value	Description
getSelectedItemIndex	Callback	Gets the index of the selected item in a drop-down list or gallery
getShowImage	Callback	Gets a value specifying whether to display the control image
getShowLabel	Callback	Gets a value specifying whether to display the control label
getSize	Callback	Gets a value specifying the size of a control (normal or large)
getSupertip	Callback	Gets a value specifying the Enhanced ScreenTip for a control
getText	Callback	Gets the text to be displayed in the edit portion of a text box or edit box
getTitle	Callback	Gets the text to be displayed (rather than a horizontal line) for a menu separator
getVisible	Callback	Gets a value that specifies whether the control is visible
id	String	A user-defined unique identifier for the control (mutually exclusive with idMso and idQ—specify only one of these values)
idMso	Control id	Built-in control ID (mutually exclusive with id and idQ—specify only one of these values)
idQ	Qualified id	Qualified control ID, prefixed with a namespace identifier (mutually exclusive with id and idMso—specify only one of these values)
image	String	Specifies an image for the control
imageMso	Control id	Specifies an identifier for a built-in image
insertAfterMso	Control id	Specifies the identifier for the built-in control after which to position this control
insertAfterQ	Qualified id	Specifies the identifier of a control whose idQ property was specified after which to position this control
insertBeforeMso	Control id	Specifies the identifier for the built-in control before which to position this control
insertBeforeQ	Qualified id	Specifies the identifier of a control whose idQ property was specified before which to position this control
itemSize	large, normal	Specifies the size for the items in a menu
keytip	String	Specifies the KeyTip for the control
label	String	Specifies the label for the control

25

Attribute	Type or Value	Description
onAction	Callback	Called when the user clicks the control
onChange	Callback	Called when the user enters or selects text in an edit box or combo box
screenTip	String	Specifies the control's ScreenTip
showImage	true, false	Specifies whether the control's image is shown
showItemImage	true, false	Specifies whether to show the image in a combo box, drop-down list, or gallery
showItemLabel	true, false	Specifies whether to show the label in a combo box, drop-down list, or gallery
showLabel	true, false	Specifies whether the control's label is shown
size	large, normal	Specifies the size for the control
sizeString	String	Indicates the width for the control by specifying a string, such as "xxxxxx"
supertip	String	Specifies the Enhanced ScreenTip for the control
tag	String	Specifies user-defined text
title	String	Specifies the text to be displayed, rather than a horizontal line, for a menu separator
visible	true, false	Specifies whether the control is visible

25

Table 25.2 Control Arguments

Control	Callback Name	Signature
Various controls	getDescription	Sub GetDescription(control as IRibbonControl, ByRef description)
	getEnabled	Sub GetEnabled(control As IRibbonControl, ByRef enabled)
	getImage	Sub GetImage(control As IRibbonControl, ByRef image)
	getImageMso	Sub GetImageMso(control As IRibbonControl, ByRef imageMso)
	getLabel	Sub GetLabel(control As IRibbonControl, ByRef label)
	getKeytip	Sub GetKeytip (control As IRibbonControl, ByRef label)
	getSize	Sub GetSize(control As IRibbonControl, ByRef size)
	getScreentip	Sub GetScreentip(control As IRibbonControl, ByRef screentip)
	getSupertip	Sub GetSupertip(control As IRibbonControl, ByRef screentip)
	getVisible	Sub GetVisible(control As IRibbonControl, ByRef visible)

Control	Callback Name	Signature
button	getShowImage	Sub GetShowImage (control As IRibbonControl, ByRef showImage)
	getShowLabel	Sub GetShowLabel (control As IRibbonControl, ByRef showLabel)
	onAction	Sub OnAction(control As IRibbonControl)
checkBox	getPressed	Sub GetPressed(control As IRibbonControl, ByRef returnValue)
	onAction	Sub OnAction(control As IRibbonControl, pressed As Boolean)
comboBox	getItemCount	Sub GetItemCount(control As IRibbonControl, ByRef count)
	getItemID	Sub GetItemID(control As IRibbonControl, index As Integer, ByRef id)
	getItemImage	Sub GetItemImage(control As IRibbonControl, index As Integer, ByRef image)
	getItemLabel	Sub GetItemLabel(control As IRibbonControl, index As Integer, ByRef label)
	getItemScreenTip	Sub GetItemScreenTip(control As IRibbonControl, index As Integer, ByRef screentip)
	getItemSuperTip	Sub GetItemSuperTip (control As IRibbonControl, index As Integer, ByRef supertip)
	getText	Sub GetText(control As IRibbonControl, ByRef text)
	onChange	Sub OnChange(control As IRibbonControl, text As String)
customUI	loadImage	Sub LoadImage(imageId As string, ByRef image)
	onLoad	Sub OnLoad(ribbon As IRibbonUI)
dropDown	getItemCount	Sub GetItemCount(control As IRibbonControl, ByRef count)
	getItemID	Sub GetItemID(control As IRibbonControl, index As Integer, ByRef id)
	getItemImage	Sub GetItemImage(control As IRibbonControl, index As Integer, ByRef image)

Control	Callback Name	Signature
dropDown	getItemLabel	Sub GetItemLabel(control As IRibbonControl, index As Integer, ByRef label)
	getItemScreenTip	Sub GetItemScreenTip(control As IRibbonControl, index As Integer, ByRef screenTip)
	getItemSuperTip	Sub GetItemSuperTip (control As IRibbonControl, index As Integer, ByRef superTip)
	getSelectedItemID	Sub GetSelectedItemID(control As IRibbonControl, ByRef index)
	getSelectedItemIndex	Sub GetSelectedItemIndex(control As IRibbonControl, ByRef index)
	onAction	Sub OnAction(control As IRibbonControl, selectedId As String, selectedIndex As Integer)
dynamicMen	getContent	Sub GetContent(control As IRibbonControl, ByRef content)
editBox	getText	Sub GetText(control As IRibbonControl, ByRef text)
	onChange	Sub OnChange(control As IRibbonControl, text As String)
gallery	getItemCount	Sub GetItemCount(control As IRibbonControl, ByRef count)
	getItemHeight	Sub getItemHeight(control As IRibbonControl, ByRef height)
	getItemID	Sub GetItemID(control As IRibbonControl, index As Integer, ByRef id)
	getItemImage	Sub GetItemImage(control As IRibbonControl, index As Integer, ByRef image)
	getItemLabel	Sub GetItemLabel(control As IRibbonControl, index As Integer, ByRef label)
	getItemScreenTip	Sub GetItemScreenTip(control As IRibbonControl, index as Integer, ByRef screen)
	getItemSuperTip	Sub GetItemSuperTip (control As IRibbonControl, index as Integer, ByRef screen)
	getItemWidth	Sub getItemWidth(control As IRibbonControl, ByRef width)
	getSelectedItemID	Sub GetSelectedItemID(control As IRibbonControl, ByRef index)
	getSelectedItemIndex	Sub GetSelectedItemIndex(control As IRibbonControl, ByRef index)
	onAction	Sub OnAction(control As IRibbonControl, selectedId As String, selectedIndex As Integer)

25

Control	Callback Name	Signature
menuSeparator	getTitle	Sub GetTitle (control As IRibbonControl, ByRef title)
toggleButton	getPressed	Sub GetPressed(control As IRibbonControl, ByRef returnValue)
	onAction	Sub OnAction(control As IRibbonControl, pressed As Boolean)

Accessing the File Structure

The new Excel file types are actually zipped files containing various files and folders to create the workbook and worksheets you see when you open the workbook. To view this structure, rename the file, adding a .zip extension to the end of the filename. For example, if your filename is Chapter 25 - Simple Ribbon.xlsm, rename it to Chapter 25 - Simple Ribbon.xlsm.zip. You can then use your zip utility to access the folders and files within.

Copy into the zip file your customui folder and file, as shown in Figure 25.6. After placing them in the XLSM file, you need to let the rest of the Excel file know that they are there and what their purpose is. To do that, modify the RELS file.

Figure 25.6
Using a zip utility, open the XLSM file and copy over the customui folder and file.

Understanding the RELS File

The RELS file, found in the _rels folder, contains the various relationships of the Excel file. Extract this file from the zip file and open it using a text editor.

The file already contains existing relationships that you do not want to change. Instead, you need to add one for the customui folder. Scroll all the way to the right of the <Relationships line and place your cursor before the </Relationships> tag, as shown in Figure 25.7. Insert the following code:

```
<Relationship Id="rAB67989"
Type="http://schemas.microsoft.com/office/2007/relationships/ui/_
extensibility"
Target="customui/customUI14.xml"/>
```

Figure 25.7
Place your cursor in the correct spot for entering your custom ribbon relationship.

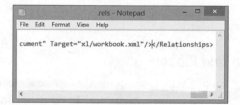

Id is any unique string to identify the relationship. If Excel has a problem with the string you enter, it might change it when you open the file. `Target` is the `customui` folder and file. Save your changes and add the RELS file back into the zip file.

→ **See** the troubleshooting section "Excel Found a Problem with Some Content," **p. 549**, for more information.

> **CAUTION**
>
> Even though the previous code appears as three lines in this book (not including the underscore character being used as a continuation character), it should appear as a single line in the RELS file. If you want to enter it as three separate lines, do not separate the lines within the quoted strings and do not use a continuation character as you would in VBA. The preceding examples are correct breaks. An incorrect break of the third line, for example, would be this:
>
> ```
> Target = "customui/
>     customUI14.xml"
> ```

25

Renaming the Excel File and Opening the Workbook

Rename the Excel file back to its original name by removing the `.zip` extension. Open your workbook.

→ If any error messages appear when you rename an Excel file, **see** "Troubleshooting Error Messages," **p. 548**.

It can be a little time-consuming to perform all the steps involved in adding a custom ribbon, especially if you make little mistakes and have to keep renaming your workbook, opening the zip file, extracting your file, modifying, adding it back to the zip, renaming, and testing. To aid in this, OpenXMLDeveloper.org offers the Custom UI Editor Tool, which you can learn more about at `http://openxmldeveloper.org/blog/b/openxmldeveloper/archive/2009/08/07/7293.aspx`. The tool also updates the RELS file, helps with using custom images, and has other useful aids to customizing the ribbon.

Using Images on Buttons

The image that appears on a button can be either an image from the Microsoft Office icon library or a custom image you create and include within the workbook's `customui` folder.

With a good icon image, you can hide the button label but still have a friendly ribbon with images that are self-explanatory.

Using Microsoft Office Icons on Your Ribbon

Remember how, in legacy versions of Excel, if you wanted to reuse an icon from an Excel button, you had to identify the faceid? It was a nightmare to do manually, though thankfully there were many tools out there to help you retrieve the information. Well, Microsoft must have heard the screams of agony because they've made it so much easier to reuse their icons. Not only that, but instead of using some meaningless number, they've provided easy-to-understand text!

Select File, Options, Customize Ribbon. Place your cursor over any menu command in the list, and a ScreenTip will appear, providing more information about the command. Included at the very end in parentheses is the image name, as shown in Figure 25.8.

Figure 25.8
Placing your cursor over a command, such as Insert Hyperlink, brings up the icon name, HyperlinkInsert.

To place an image on your button, you need to go back into the customUI14.xml file and advise Excel of what you want. The following code uses the HyperlinkInsert icon for the HelloWorld button and also hides the label, as shown in Figure 25.9. Note that the icon name is case sensitive.

```xml
<customUI xmlns="http://schemas.microsoft.com/office/2009/07/customui">
  <ribbon startFromScratch="false">
    <tabs>
      <tab id="CustomTab" label="MrExcel Add-ins">
        <group id="CustomGroup" label="Reports">

          <button id="button1" label="Click to run"
            onAction="Module1.HelloWorld" imageMso="HyperlinkInsert"
            showLabel = "false" />

        </group>
      </tab>
    </tabs>
  </ribbon>
</customUI>
```

Figure 25.9
You can apply the image from any Microsoft Office icon to your custom button.

Reports

You aren't limited to just the icons available in Excel. You can use the icon for any installed Microsoft Office application. You can download a workbook from Microsoft with several galleries showing the icons available (and their names) from `http://www.microsoft.com/en-us/download/details.aspx?id=11675`.

Adding Custom Icon Images to Your Ribbon

What if the icon library just doesn't have the icon you're looking for? You can create your own image file and modify the ribbon to use it:

1. Create a folder called `images` in the `customui` folder. Place your image in this folder.

2. Create a folder called `_rels` in the `customui` folder. Create a text file called `customUI14.xml.rels` in this new folder, as shown in Figure 25.10. Place the following code in the file. Note that the `Id` for the image relationship is the name of the image file, `mrexcellogo`:

```
<?xml version="1.0" encoding="UTF-8" standalone="yes"?>
<Relationships xmlns="http://schemas.openxmlformats.org/package/2006/_
relationships"><Relationship Id="mrexcellogo"_
Type="http://schemas.openxmlformats.org/officeDocument/2006/relationships/_
image"
Target="images/mrexcellogo.jpg"/></Relationships>
```

Figure 25.10
Create a `_rels` folder and an `images` folder within the `customui` folder to hold files relevant to your custom image.

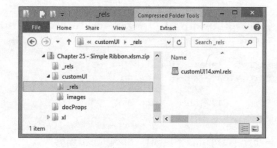

25

3. Open the `customUI14.xml` file and add the `image` attribute to the control, as shown here. Save and close the file.

```
<customUI xmlns="http://schemas.microsoft.com/office/2009/07/customui">
  <ribbon startFromScratch="false">
    <tabs>
      <tab id="CustomTab" label="MrExcel Add-ins">
        <group id="CustomGroup" label="Reports">

          <button id="button1" label="Click to run"
            onAction="Module1.HelloWorld" image="mrexcellogo"
            size="large" />
```

```
            </group>
          </tab>
        </tabs>
      </ribbon>
    </customUI>
```

4. Open the [Content_Types].xml file and add the following at the very end of the file but before the </Types>:

```
<Default Extension="jpg" ContentType="application/octet-stream"/>
```

5. Save your changes, rename your folder, and open your workbook. The custom image appears on the button, as shown in Figure 25.11.

Figure 25.11
With a few more changes to your customui, you can add a custom image to a button.

CASE STUDY: CONVERTING AN EXCEL 2003 CUSTOM TOOLBAR TO EXCEL 2013

25

You have a workbook and custom toolbar designed in Excel 2003 with several buttons. You're now ready to transfer over to Excel 2013. When you open the workbook in 2013, the toolbar appears on the Add-ins tab, but you don't want it there. You could create a custom Quick Access Toolbar and attach it to the workbook, but you would prefer a custom ribbon tab.

After saving the workbook as an XLSM file, create the customUI14.xml file as shown here. The tab is called My Quick Macros, and it has two groups: Viewing Options and Shortcuts. Place the file in the customui folder and add it to the workbook.

```
<customUI xmlns="http://schemas.microsoft.com/office/2009/07/customui">
  <ribbon startFromScratch="false">
    <tabs>
      <tab id="customMacros" label="My Quick Macros">
        <group id="customview" label="Viewing Options">

          <button id="btn_r1c1" label="Toggle R1C1"
             onAction="mod_2013.myButtons" />

           <button id="btn_Headings" label="Show Headings"
              onAction="mod_2013.myButtons" imageMso="TableStyleClear"/>

           <button id="btn_gridlines" label="Show Gridlines"
              onAction="mod_2013.myButtons" imageMso="BordersAll"/>

           <button id="btn_tabs" label="Show Tabs"
              onAction="mod_2013.myButtons" imageMso="Connections"/>
        </group>

        <group id="customshortcuts" label="Shortcuts">

          <button id="btn_formulas" label="Highlight Formulas"
```

```
            onAction="mod_2013.myButtons" imageMso="FunctionWizard"/>
        </group>
      </tab>
    </tabs>
  </ribbon>
</customUI>
```

While looking at the workbook structure, go to the xl folder. If you see the file `attachedToolbars.bin`, delete it. That file was where the previous custom toolbar was stored. If you don't see the file, your original toolbar was created in another way. Next, update the RELS file and then open the workbook to see the new tab, as shown in Figure 25.12.

Figure 25.12
Re-create your Excel 2003 toolbar in Excel 2013 as its own ribbon.

→ **See** the "Understanding the RELS File" section, **p. 542**, to review how to update the RELS file.

Now it's time to update the code in the workbook. Notice that the `onAction` in the `customui` code all pointed to the same sub, `mod_2013.myButtons`, instead of each having a custom call. Because all the controls are of the same type, buttons, and have the same argument type, `iRibbonControl`, you can take advantage of these facts. Create a single sub, `myButtons`, in a module called `mod_2013` to handle all the button calls using `Select Case` to manage the IDs of each button:

```
Sub myButtons(control As IRibbonControl)
Select Case control.ID
    Case Is = "btn_r1c1"
        SwitchR1C1
    Case Is = "btn_Headings"
        ShowHeaders
    Case Is = "btn_gridlines"
        ShowGridlines
    Case Is = "btn_tabs"
        ShowTabs
    Case Is = "btn_formulas"
        GoToFormulas
    End Select
End Sub
```

The `control.ID`s are the `ids` assigned each button in the `customUI14.xml` file. The action within each `Case` statement is a call to the desired sub. Here is a sample of one of the subs, `ShowHeaders`, being called. It is the same sub that was in the original 2003 workbook.

```
Sub ShowHeaders()
If ActiveWindow.DisplayHeadings = False Then
    ActiveWindow.DisplayHeadings = True
Else
    ActiveWindow.DisplayHeadings = False
End If
End Sub
```

Troubleshooting Error Messages

To be able to see the error messages generated by a custom ribbon, go to File, Options, Advanced, General, and select the Show Add-in User Interface Errors option.

The Attribute "*Attribute Name*" on the Element "*customui Ribbon*" Is Not Defined in the DTD/Schema

As noted in the "Where to Add Your Code: `customui` Folder and File" section of this chapter, the case of the attributes is very particular. If an attribute is "mis-cased," the error shown in Figure 25.13 might occur.

Figure 25.13
Mis-cased attributes can generate errors. Read the error message carefully; it might help you trace the problem.

The code in the `customUI14.xml` that generated the error had the following line:

```
<ribbon startfromscratch="false">
```

Instead of `startFromScratch`, the code contained `startfromscratch` (all lowercase letters). The error message even helps you narrow down the problem by naming the attribute with which it has a problem.

Illegal Qualified Name Character

For every opening <, you need a closing >. If you forget a closing >, the error shown in Figure 25.14 might appear. The error message is not specific at all, but it does provide a line and column number to indicate where it's having a problem. Still, it's not the actual spot where the missing > would go. Instead, it's the beginning of the next line. You have to review your code to find the error, but you have an idea of where to start.

Figure 25.14
For every opening <, you need a closing >.

The following code in the `customUI14.xml` generated the error:

```
<tab id="CustomTab" label="MrExcel Add-ins">
  <group id="CustomGroup" label="Reports"
```

```
<button id="button1" label="Click to run"
    onAction="Module1.HelloWorld" image="mrexcellogo"
    size="large" />
```

Note the missing > for the group line (second line of code). The line should have been this:

```
<group id="CustomGroup" label="Reports">
```

Element *"customui Tag Name"* Is Unexpected According to Content Model of Parent Element *"customui Tag Name"*

If your structure is in the wrong order, such as the group tag placed before the tab tag as shown here, a chain of errors will appear, beginning with the one shown in Figure 25.15:

Figure 25.15
An error in one line can lead to string of error messages because the other lines are now considered out of order.

```
<group id="CustomGroup" label="Reports">
  <tab id="CustomTab" label="MrExcel Add-ins">
```

Excel Found a Problem with Some Content

Figure 25.16 shows a generic catchall message for different types of problems Excel can find. If you click Yes, you then receive the message shown in Figure 25.17. If you click No, the workbook doesn't open. While creating ribbons, though, I found it appearing most often when Excel didn't like the relationship id I had assigned the customui relationship in the RELS file. What's nice is that if you click Yes, Excel will assign a new ID file, and the next time you open the file, the error should not appear.

Figure 25.16
This rather generic message could appear for many reasons. Click Yes to try to repair the file.

Figure 25.17
Excel lets you know whether it has succeeded in repairing the file.

25

Original relationship:

```
<Relationship Id="rId3"
Type="http://schemas.microsoft.com/office/2007/relationships/ui/extensibility"
Target="customui/customUI14.xml"/>
```

Excel modified relationship:

```
<Relationship Id="rE1FA1CF0-6CA9-499E-9217-90BF2D86492F"
Type="http://schemas.microsoft.com/office/2007/relationships/ui/extensibility"
 Target="customui/customuUI14.xml"/>
```

In the RELS file, the error also appears if you split the relationship line within a quoted string. You might recall that you were cautioned against this in the "Understanding the RELS File" section, earlier in this chapter. In this case, Excel could not fix the file, and you must make the correction yourself.

Wrong Number of Arguments or Invalid Property Assignment

If there is a problem with the sub being called by your control, you might see the error in Figure 25.18 when you try to run code from your ribbon. For example, the `onAction` of a button requires a single `IRibbonControl` argument such as the following:

```
Sub HelloWorld(control As IRibbonControl)
```

It would be incorrect to leave off the argument as shown here:

```
Sub HelloWorld()
```

Figure 25.18
It's important for the subs being called by your controls to have the proper arguments. Refer to Table 25.2 for the various control arguments.

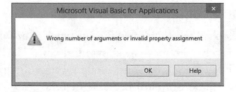

Invalid File Format or File Extension

This error message in Figure 25.19 looks rather drastic, but it could be deceiving. You could get it if you're missing quotation marks around an attribute's value in the RELS file. For example, look carefully at the following line to see that the `Type` value is missing its quotations marks:

```
Type=http://schemas.microsoft.com/office/2007/relationships/ui/extensibility
```

The line should have been this:

```
Type="http://schemas.microsoft.com/office/2007/relationships/ui/extensibility"
```

Figure 25.19
A missing quotation mark can generate a drastic message, but it's easily fixed.

Nothing Happens

If you open your modified workbook and your ribbon doesn't appear, but you don't get any error messages, double-check your RELS file. It's possible you forgot to update it with the required relationship to your `custumUI14.xml`.

Other Ways to Run a Macro

Custom ribbons are the best ways to run a macro; however, if you have only a couple of macros to run, it can be a bit of work to modify the file. You could have the client invoke a macro by going to the View tab, selecting Macros, View Macros, and then selecting the macro from the Macros dialog and clicking the Run button, but this is a bit unprofessional—and tedious. Other options are discussed in the following sections.

Using a Keyboard Shortcut to Run a Macro

The easiest way to run a macro is to assign a keyboard shortcut to a macro. From the Macro dialog box (Developer or View tab, click Macros, or press Alt+F8), select the macro and click Options. Assign a shortcut key to the macro. Figure 25.20 shows the shortcut Ctrl+Shift+C being assigned to the `Clean1stCol` macro. You can now conspicuously post a note on the worksheet reminding the client to press Ctrl+Shift+C to clean the first column.

Figure 25.20
The simplest way to enable a client to run a macro is to assign a shortcut key to the macro. Ctrl+Shift+C now runs the `Clean1stCol` macro.

CAUTION

Be careful when assigning keyboard shortcuts. Many of the keys are already mapped to important Windows shortcuts. If you would happen to assign a macro to Ctrl+C, anyone who uses this shortcut to copy the selection to the Clipboard will be frustrated when your application does something else in response to this common shortcut. Letters J, M, and Q are usually good choices because as of Excel 2013, they have not yet been assigned to Excel's menu of "Ctrl+" shortcut combinations. Ctrl+L and Ctrl+T used to be available, but these are used to create a table in Excel 2013.

Attaching a Macro to a Command Button

Two types of buttons can be embedded in your sheet: the traditional button shape that can be found on the Forms control and an ActiveX command button. (Both can be accessed on the Developer tab under the Controls, Insert option.)

To add a Forms control button with a macro to your sheet, follow these steps:

1. On the Developer tab, click the Insert button and select the button control from the Forms section of the drop-down, as shown in Figure 25.21.

Figure 25.21
The Forms controls are found under the Insert icon on the Developer tab.

2. Place your cursor in the worksheet where you want to insert the button and then click and drag to create the shape of your new button.

3. When you release the mouse button, the Assign Macro dialog displays. Select a macro to assign to the button and click OK.

4. Highlight the text on the button and type new meaningful text.

5. To change the font, text alignment, and other aspects of the button's appearance, right-click the button and select Format Control from the pop-up menu.

6. To reassign a new macro to the button, right-click the button and select Assign Macro from the pop-up menu.

Attaching a Macro to a Shape

The previous method assigned a macro to an object that looks like a button. You can also assign a macro to any drawing object on the worksheet, as shown in Figure 25.22. To assign a macro to an Autoshape (Insert, Illustrations, Shapes), right-click the shape and select Assign Macro.

This method is useful because you can easily add a drawing object with code and use the OnAction property to assign another macro to the object. There is one big drawback to this method: If you assign a macro that exists in another workbook, and the other workbook is saved and closed, Excel changes the OnAction for the object to be hard-coded to a specific folder.

Figure 25.22
Macros can be assigned to any drawing object on the worksheet.

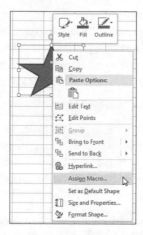

Attaching a Macro to an ActiveX Control

ActiveX controls are newer than Form controls and slightly more complicated to set up. Instead of simply assigning a macro to the button, you will have a `button_click` event where you can either call another macro or have the macro code actually embedded in the event. Follow these steps:

1. On the Developer tab, click the Insert button and select the Command Button icon from the ActiveX Controls section.

2. Place your cursor in the worksheet where you want to insert the button, and then click and drag to create the shape of your new button.

3. To format the button, right-click the button and select Properties or select Controls, Properties from the Developer tab. You can now adjust the button's caption and color in the Properties window, as shown in Figure 25.23. If nothing happens when you right-click the button, enter Design mode by clicking the Design Mode button on the Developer tab.

Figure 25.23
Clicking the Properties icon brings up the Properties window, where you can adjust many aspects of the ActiveX button.

4. To assign a macro to the button, right-click it and select View Code. This creates the header and footer for the `button_click` event in the code pane for the current worksheet. Type the code that you want to have run or the name of the macro you want to call.

> **NOTE**
>
> There is one annoying aspect of this Properties window: It is huge and covers a large portion of your worksheet. Eventually, if you want to use the worksheet, you are going to have to resize or close this Properties window. When you close the Properties window, it also hides the Properties window in the VB Editor. I would prefer that I could close this Properties window without affecting my VB Editor environment.

Running a Macro from a Hyperlink

Using a trick, it is possible to run a macro from a hyperlink. Because many people are used to clicking a hyperlink to perform an action, this method might be more intuitive for your clients.

The trick is to set up placeholder hyperlinks that simply link back to themselves. Select the cell with the text you want to link to, and from the Insert tab, select Links, Hyperlink (or press Ctrl+K). In the Insert Hyperlink dialog, click Place in This Document. Figure 25.24 shows a worksheet with four hyperlinks. Each hyperlink points back to its own cell.

Figure 25.24

To run a macro from a hyperlink, you must create placeholder hyperlinks that link back to their cells. Then, using an event handler macro on the worksheet's code pane, you can intercept the hyperlink and run any macro.

When a client clicks a hyperlink, you can intercept this action and run any macro by using the `FollowHyperlink` event. Enter the following code on the code module for the worksheet:

```
Private Sub Worksheet_FollowHyperlink(ByVal Target As Hyperlink)
Select Case Target.TextToDisplay
    Case "Widgets"
        RunWidgetReport
    Case "Gadgets"
        RunGadgetReport
    Case "Gizmos"
        RunGizmoReport
    Case "Doodads"
        RunDooDadReport
End Select
End Sub
```

Next Steps

From custom ribbons to simple buttons or hyperlinks, there are plenty of ways to ensure that your clients never need to see the Macro dialog box. In Chapter 26, "Creating Add-Ins," you'll find out how to package your macros into add-ins that you can easily distribute to others.

Creating Add-Ins

Using VBA, you can create standard add-in files for your clients to use. After the client installs the add-in on his PC, the program will be available to Excel and will load automatically every time he opens Excel.

This chapter discusses standard add-ins.

Be aware that there are two other kinds of add-ins: COM add-ins and DLL add-ins. Neither of these can be created with VBA. To create these types of add-ins, you need either Visual Basic.NET or Visual C++.

Characteristics of Standard Add-Ins

If you are going to distribute your applications, you might want to package the application as an add-in. Typically saved with an .xlam extension for Excel 2007–13 or an .xla extension for Excel 97–2003, the add-in offers several advantages:

- Usually, clients can bypass your Workbook_Open code by holding down the Shift key while opening the workbook. With an add-in, they cannot bypass the Workbook_Open code in this manner.

- After the Add-Ins dialog is used to install an add-in (select File, Options, Add-Ins, Manage Excel Add-Ins, Go), the add-in will always be loaded and available.

- Even if the macro security level is set to disallow macros, programs in an installed add-in can still run.

- Generally, custom functions work only in the workbook in which they are defined. A custom function added to an add-in is available to all open workbooks.

- The add-in does not show up in the list of open files in the Window menu item. The client cannot unhide the workbook by choosing View, Window, Unhide.

C A U T I O N

There is one strange rule for which you need to plan. The add-in is a hidden workbook. Because the add-in can never be displayed, your code cannot select or activate any cells in the add-in workbook. You are allowed to save data in your add-in file, but you cannot select the file. Also, if you do write data to your add-in file that you want to be available in the future, your add-in code needs to handle saving the file. Because your clients will not realize that the add-in is there, they will never be reminded or asked to save an unsaved add-in. You might add `ThisWorkbook.Save` to the add-in's `Workbook_BeforeClose` event.

Converting an Excel Workbook to an Add-In

Add-ins are typically managed by the Add-Ins dialog. This dialog presents an add-in name and description, which you control by entering two specific properties for the file before you convert it to an add-in.

NOTE

If you're modifying an existing add-in, you must make it visible before you can edit the properties. See the later section "Using the VB Editor to Convert a File to an Add-In."

To change the title and description shown in the Add-Ins dialog, follow these steps:

1. Select File, Info. Excel displays the Document Properties pane on the right side of the window.
2. From the Properties side of the window, select Show All Properties.
3. Enter the name for the add-in in the Title field.
4. Enter a short description of the add-in in the Comments field (see Figure 26.1).

Figure 26.1
Fill in the Title and Comments fields before converting a workbook to an add-in.

5. Click the arrow at the top left to return to your workbook.

There are two ways to convert the file to an add-in. The first method, using Save As, is easier, but has an annoying byproduct. The second method uses the VB Editor and requires two steps, but gives you some extra control. The sections that follow describe the steps for using these methods.

Using Save As to Convert a File to an Add-In

Select File, Save As. In the Save as Type field, scroll through the list and select Excel Add-In (*.xlam).

> **NOTE**
> If your add-in might be used in Excel 97 through Excel 2013, choose Excel 97-2003 Add-In (*.xla).

As shown in Figure 26.2, the filename changes from `filename.xlsm` to `filename.xlam`. Also note that the save location automatically changes to an `AddIns` folder. This folder location varies by operating system, but it will be something along the lines of C:\Users*username*\ AppData\Roaming\Microsoft\AddIns. It is also confusing that, after the XLSM file is saved as an XLAM type, the unsaved XLSM file remains open. It is not necessary to keep an XLSM version of the file because it is easy to change an XLAM back to an XLSM for editing.

Figure 26.2
The Save As method changes the `IsAddin` property, changes the name, and automatically saves the file in your `AddIns` folder.

> **TIP**
> If, before selecting the Add-in file type, you were already in the folder to which you want to save, then just click the back arrow in the Save As window to return to that folder.

> **CAUTION**
> When the Save As method is being used to create an add-in, a worksheet must be the active sheet. The Add-In file type is not available if a Chart sheet is the active sheet.

Using the VB Editor to Convert a File to an Add-In

The Save As method is great if you are creating an add-in for your own use. However, if you are creating an add-in for a client, you probably want to keep the add-in stored in a folder with all the client's application files. It is fairly easy to bypass the Save As method and create an add-in using the VB Editor:

1. Open the workbook that you want to convert to an add-in.

2. Switch to the VB Editor.

3. In the Project Explorer, click ThisWorkbook.

4. In the Properties window, find the property called IsAddin and change its value to True, as shown in Figure 26.3.

Figure 26.3
Creating an add-in is as simple as changing the IsAddin property of ThisWorkbook.

5. Press Ctrl+G to display the Immediate window. In the Immediate window, save the file, using an .xlam extension:

```
ThisWorkbook.SaveAs FileName:="C:\ClientFiles\Chap26.xlam", _
FileFormat:= xlOpenXMLAddIn
```

> **NOTE**
> If your add-in might be used in Excel 97 through Excel 2003, change the final parameter from xlOpenXMLAddIn to xlAddIn.

You've now successfully created an add-in in the client folder that you can easily find and email to your client.

> **TIP**
> If you ever need to make the add-in visible, for example, to change the properties or view data you have on sheets, repeat the previous steps, except select False from the IsAddin property. The add-in becomes visible in Excel. When you are done with your changes, change the property back to True.

Having Your Client Install the Add-In

After you email the add-in to your client, have her save it on her desktop or in another easy-to-find folder. She should then follow these steps:

1. Open Excel 2013. From the File menu, select Options.

2. Along the left navigation, select Add-Ins.

3. At the bottom of the window, select Excel Add-Ins from the Manage drop-down (see Figure 26.4).

Figure 26.4

The Excel 2013 Add-Ins tab in Options is significantly more complex than in Excel 2003. Select Excel Add-Ins from the bottom and click Go.

4. Click Go. Excel displays the familiar Add-Ins dialog.

5. In the Add-Ins dialog, click the Browse button.

6. Browse to where you saved the file. Highlight your add-in and click OK.

The add-in is now installed. If you allow it, Excel copies the file from where you saved it to the proper location of the AddIns folder. In the Add-Ins dialog, the title of the add-in and comments as specified in the File Properties dialog are displayed (see Figure 26.5).

Figure 26.5

The add-in is now available for use.

26

Standard Add-Ins Are Not Secure

Remember that anyone can go to the VB Editor, select your add-in, and change the IsAddin property to False to unhide the workbook. You can discourage this process by locking the XLAM project for viewing and protecting it in the VB Editor, but be aware that plenty of vendors sell a password-hacking utility for less than $40. To add a password to your add-in, follow these steps:

1. Go to the VB Editor.

2. From the Tools menu, select VBAProject Properties.

3. Select the Protection tab.

4. Select the Lock Project for Viewing check box.

5. Enter the password twice for verification.

Closing Add-Ins

Add-ins can be closed in three ways:

- Clear the add-in from the Add-Ins dialog. This closes the add-in for this session and ensures that it does not open during future sessions.

- Use VB Editor to close the add-in. In the VB Editor's Immediate pane, type this code to close the add-in:

```
Workbooks("YourAddinName.xlam").Close
```

- Close Excel. All add-ins are closed when Excel is closed.

Removing Add-Ins

You might want to remove an add-in from the list of available add-ins in the Add-In dialog box. There is no effective way to do this within Excel. Follow these steps:

1. Close all running instances of Excel.

2. Use Windows Explorer to locate the file. The file might be located in %AppData%\ Microsoft\AddIns\.

3. In Windows Explorer, rename the file or move it to a different folder.

4. Open Excel. You get a note warning you that the add-in could not be found. Click OK to dismiss this box.

5. Go to File, Options, Add-Ins, Manage Excel Add-Ins, Go. In the Add-Ins dialog box, clear the name of the add-in you want to remove. Excel notifies you that the file cannot be found and asks whether you want to remove it from the list. Click Yes.

Using a Hidden Workbook as an Alternative to an Add-In

One cool feature of an add-in is that the workbook is hidden. This keeps most novice users from poking around and changing formulas. However, it is possible to hide a workbook without creating an add-in.

It is easy enough to hide a workbook by selecting Hide from the View, Window menu in Excel. The trick is to then save the workbook as Hidden. Because the file is hidden, the normal File, Save choice does not work. This can be done from the VB Editor window. In the VB Editor, make sure that the workbook is selected in the Project Explorer. Then, in the Immediate window, type the following:

```
ThisWorkbook.Save
```

There is a downside to using a hidden workbook—a custom ribbon tab will not be visible if the workbook it is attached to is hidden. This isn't an issue if you use VBA code to create custom menus or toolbars that will appear on the Add-Ins tab.

CASE STUDY: USING A HIDDEN CODE WORKBOOK TO HOLD ALL MACROS AND FORMS

Access developers routinely use a second database to hold macros and forms. They place all forms and programs in one database and all data in a separate database. These database files are linked through the Link Tables function in Access.

For large projects in Excel, I recommend the same method. You use a little bit of VBA code in the Data workbook to open the Code workbook.

The advantage to this method is that when it is time to enhance the application, you can mail a new code file without affecting the client's data file.

I once encountered a single-file application rolled out by another developer that the client had sent out to 50 sales reps. The reps replicated the application for each of their 10 largest customers. Within a week, there were 500 copies of this file floating around the country. When they discovered a critical flaw in the program, patching 500 files was a nightmare.

We designed a replacement application that used two workbooks. The data workbook ended up with about 20 lines of code. This code was responsible for opening the code workbook and passing control to the code workbook. As the files were being closed, the data workbook would close the code workbook.

There were many advantages to this method. First, the customer data files were kept to a very small size. Each sales rep now has one workbook with program code and 10 or more data files for each customer. As enhancements are completed, we distribute new program code workbooks. The sales rep opens his or her existing customer data workbook, which automatically grabs the new code workbook.

Because the previous developer had been stuck with the job of trying to patch 500 workbooks, we were extremely careful to have as few lines of code in the customer workbook as possible. There are maybe 10 lines of code, and they were tested extremely thoroughly before being sent out. By contrast, the code workbook contains 3,000-plus lines of code. So if something goes wrong, I have a 99 percent chance that the bad code will be in the easy-to-replace code workbook.

26

In the customer data workbook, the `Workbook_Open` procedure has this code:

```
Private Sub Workbook_Open()
 On Error Resume Next
    X = Workbooks("Code.xlsm").Name
    If Not Err = 0 then
        On Error Goto 0
        Workbooks.Open Filename:= _
            ThisWorkbook.Path & Application.PathSeparator & "Code.xlsm"
    End If
    On Error Goto 0
    Application.Run "Code.xlsm!CustFileOpen"
End Sub
```

The `CustFileOpen` procedure in the code workbook could also handle adding a custom menu for the application. Because custom tabs for hidden workbooks are not visible, you have to use the legacy `commandbars` method to create a menu that appears on the Add-ins tab.

This dual-workbook solution works well and allows updates to be seamlessly delivered to the client without touching any of the 500 customer files.

Next Steps

Microsoft has introduced a new way of sharing applications with users, Apps for Office. These are programs that, simply put, use JavaScript, HTML, and XML to put a web page on a sheet. Chapter 27, "An Introduction to Creating Apps with Office," introduces you to what is involved in creating these apps and deploying them over a network.

26

An Introduction to Creating Apps for Office

With Office 2013, Microsoft has introduced Apps for Office, applications that provide expanded functionality to a sheet, such as a selectable calendar, or an interface with the Web, such as retrieving information from Wikipedia or Bing. Like add-ins, once installed, the app is always available. But unlike add-ins, the app has limited interaction with sheets and does not use VBA.

An app consists of an HTML file that provides the user interface on a task or content pane, a CSS file to provide styles for the HTML file, a JavaScript file to provide interactivity to the HTML file, and an XML file to register the app with Excel. Sounds like a lot of new programming skills, but it's not. I've only designed the most basic web pages, years ago, but was able to apply my VBA programming skills to JavaScript, which is where the brunt of the programming goes. The language is a little different, but not so different that you can't create a simple, useful app.

This chapter introduces you to creating an app to distribute locally and to the basics for the various programming languages. It is not meant to be an in-depth instruction, especially to JavaScript.

Creating Your First App—Hello World

Hello World is probably the most popular first program for programmers to try out. It's a simple program, just outputting the words "Hello World," but that simplicity introduces the programmer to the basics required by the application. So, with that said, it's time to create a Hello World app. Follow these steps to create the files for the app:

27

> **CAUTION**
>
> A network is used to distribute the app locally. You cannot use a local drive or a network drive mapped to a drive letter. If you do not have access to a network, you will not be able to test your app. See the section "Napa Office 365 Development Tools" for an alternative location for creating apps.

> **NOTE**
>
> In the following steps, you enter text into a text editor. Unlike with the VB Editor, there isn't a compiler to point out mistakes before you run the program. It is very important that you enter the text exactly as written, such as the case of text within quotation marks.
>
> To open a file for editing, such as with Notepad, right-click the file and select Open With, Choose Default Program. From the dialog that opens, find Notepad. Make sure that Use This App for All *filetype* Files is *not* selected (if you're in Windows 8, do this before selecting Notepad). The next time you need to edit the file, Notepad appears in the quick list of available programs in the Open With option. Then use the following steps to create your app:

1. Create a folder and name it `HelloWorld`. This folder can be on your local drive while you are creating the program. All the program files will be placed in this folder. When finished, you will move it to the network.

2. Create the HTML program.

   a. Insert a text file in the folder and name the file `HelloWorld.html`.

   b. Open the HTML file for editing and enter the following code in it. When done, save and close the file.

   ```
   <!DOCTYPEhtml>
   <html>
       <head>
           <meta charset="UTF-8"/>
           <meta http-equiv="X-UA-Compatible" content="IE=Edge"/>
           <link rel="stylesheet" type="text/css" href="program.css"/>
       </head>
       <body>
           <p>Hello World!</p>
       </body>
   </html>
   ```

3. Create the CSS file. This is a file that holds the styles used by the HTML file.

   a. Insert a text file in the folder and name the file `program.css`. Note that this is the same filename used in the HTML file in the `<link rel>` tag.

   b. Open the CSS file for editing and enter the following code in it. When done, save and close the file.

   ```
   body
   {
       position:relative;
   }
   li :hover
   {
       text-decoration: underline;
   ```

```
    cursor:pointer;
}
h1,h3,h4,p,a,li
{
    font-family: "Segoe UI Light","Segoe UI",Tahoma,sans-serif;
    text-decoration-color:#4ec724;
}
```

4. Create the XML file.

   a. Insert a text file in the folder and name the file `HelloWorld.xml`.

   b. Open the XML file for editing and enter the following code in it. Do not close it just yet.

> **CAUTION**
>
> The following code sample and others that follow extended beyond the width of the page and so a carryover (_) was added, much like VBA. But unlike VBA, you should not type in the underscore. Instead, remove the underscore and bring in the next line to be with the previous line.

```
<?xml version="1.0" encoding="utf-8"?>
<OfficeApp xmlns="http://schemas.microsoft.com/office/appforoffice/1.0"
    xmlns:xsi="http://www.w3.org/2001/XMLSchema-instance"
    xsi:type="TaskPaneApp">
    <Id>08afd7fe-1631-42f4-84f1-5ba51e242f98</Id>
    <Version>1.0</Version>
    <ProviderName>MrExcel.com</ProviderName>
    <DefaultLocale>EN-US</DefaultLocale>
    <DisplayName DefaultValue="Hello World app"/>
    <Description DefaultValue="My first app."/>
    <IconUrl DefaultValue=
        "http://officeimg.vo.msecnd.net/_layouts/images/general/ _
officelogo.jpg"/>
    <Capabilities>
        <Capability Name="Document"/>
        <Capability Name="Workbook"/>
    </Capabilities>

    <DefaultSettings>
        <SourceLocation DefaultValue="\\workpc\MyApps\HelloWorld\ _
HelloWorld.html"/>
    </DefaultSettings>
    <Permissions>ReadWriteDocument</Permissions>
</OfficeApp>
```

5. While the XML file is still open, note the Id 08afd7fe-1631-42f4-84f1-5ba51e242f98. This is a globally unique identifier (GUID). If you are testing on a private network and not distributing this file, you can likely use this GUID. But if you're on a business network with other programmers or if you're distributing the file, you must generate your own GUID. See the section "XML Use with Your App," later in this chapter, for more information on GUIDs.

> **NOTE**
>
> GUID stands for *globally unique identifier*. It is a unique reference number used to identify software. It's usually displayed as 32 alpha-numeric digits separated into five groups (8-4-4-4-12) by hyphens. So many digits are included that it's rare for identical ids to be generated.

27

6. Move the `HelloWorld` folder to a network share folder if it's not already there. Note the path to the folder and to the HTML file because you will be making use of this information. The path to the folder should be *myserver**myfolder*. For example, my `HelloWorld` folder is located at \\workpc\MyApps\HelloWorld.

7. Open the XML file for editing and change the `<SourceLocation>` (located near the bottom of the code) to the location of the HTML file on your network. Save and close the file.

8. Configure your network share as a Trusted Catalog Address:

> **CAUTION**
>
> Only one network share at a time can be configured to show in the catalog. If you want users to have access to multiple apps at once, the XMLs for the apps must be stored in the same network share. Otherwise, users will have to go into their settings and select which catalog to show.

   a. Start Excel and go to File, Options, Trust Center and select Trust Center Settings.

   b. Select Trusted App Catalogs.

   c. Enter your folder path in the Catalog URL field and click Add Catalog. The path is added to the list box.

   d. Select the Show in Menu box.

   e. Click OK. You should see a prompt indicating that the app will be available the next time Excel starts (see Figure 27.1). Click OK twice.

   f. Restart Excel.

Figure 27.1
Configure the location of your apps under Trusted App Catalogs.

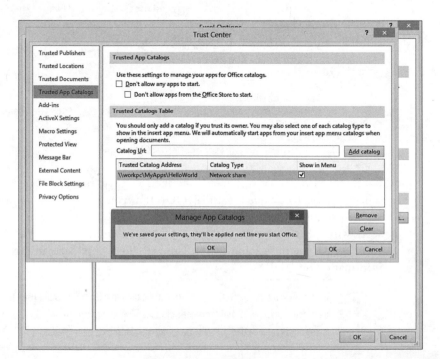

9. Insert the app you just created into Excel.

    a. Go to Insert, Apps, Apps for Office. Select See All from the drop-down menu.

    b. From the Apps for Office dialog, select Shared Folder. If you don't see anything when you've selected the link, click Refresh. The Hello World app should be listed, as shown in Figure 27.2.

Figure 27.2
The Shared Folder in the Store lists any apps it finds in the active catalog.

> **NOTE** If you still do not see anything after refreshing, there is something incorrect in the files or setup. Carefully review all the code and steps. If you do not see anything incorrect, try changing the GUID.

    c. Select the app and click Insert.

    d. A task pane on the right side of the Excel window should open, as shown in Figure 27.3, displaying the words "Hello World!"

Figure 27.3
Hello World is the first step to creating interactive apps.

27

Adding Interactivity to Your App

The Hello World app created in the preceding section is a static one—it doesn't do anything except show the words in the code. But as you browse the Web, you run into dynamic web pages. Some of those web pages use JavaScript, a programming language that adds automation to elements on otherwise static websites. Follow these steps to modify the Hello World app by adding a button to write data to a sheet and another button that reads data from a sheet, performs a calculation, and writes the results to the task pane.

> **TIP** You don't have to restart Excel if you are editing the code of an installed app. Instead, right-click in the app's task pane and select Reload.

1. Create the JS file that will provide the interactivity for the two buttons, Write Data to Sheet and Read & Calculate Data from Sheet, created by the HTML file in the next step.

   a. Insert a text file in the folder and name the file program.js.

   b. Open the JS file for editing and enter the following code in it, and then save and close the file. Note that in JavaScript, lines prefixed by // and /* are comments.

```
Office.initialize = function (reason) {
//Add any needed initialization
}
//declare and set the values of an array
var MyArray = [[234],[56],[1798], [52358]];

//write MyArray contents to the active sheet
function writeData() {
    Office.context.document.setSelectedDataAsync(MyArray, _
{coercionType: 'matrix'});
}

/*reads the selected data from the active sheet
so that we have some content to read*/
function ReadData() {
    Office.context.document.getSelectedDataAsync("matrix", _
function (result) {
//if the cells are successfully read, print results in task pane
        if (result.status === "succeeded"){
            sumData(result.value);
        }
//if there was an error, print error in task pane
        else{
            document.getElementById("results").innerText = _
result.error.name;
        }
    });
}
```

```
/*the function that calculates and shows the result
in the task pane*/
function sumData(data) {
    var printOut = 0;

//sum together all the values in the selected range
    for (var x = 0 ; x < data.length; x++) {
        for (var y = 0; y < data[x].length; y++) {
            printOut += data[x][y];
        }
    }
//print results in task pane
    document.getElementById("results").innerText = printOut;
}
```

2. Edit the HelloWorld.html file to point to the JavaScript file, program.js and add the two buttons used by the JavaScript code.

   a. Replace the existing code with the following. The actual changes are the addition of <script> tags and the replacement of the code between the <body> tags. Comment tags, <!--comments-->, are included to show where the changes are. Save and close the file.

```
<!DOCTYPEhtml>
<html>
    <head>
        <meta charset="UTF-8"/>
        <meta http-equiv="X-UA-Compatible" content="IE=Edge"/>
        <link rel="stylesheet" type="text/css" href="program.css"/>
<!--begin pointer to JavaScript file-->
        <script src = "https://appsforoffice.microsoft.com/lib/1.0/ _
hosted/office.js"></script>
        <script src= "program.js"></script>
<!--end pointer to JavaScript file-->
    </head>
    <body>
<!--begin replacement of body-->
        <button onclick="writeData()">Write Data To Sheet</button></br>
        <button onclick="ReadData()">Read & Calculate Data From _
Sheet</button></br>
        <h4>Calculation Results: <div id="results"></div> </h4>
<!--end replacement of body-->
    </body>
</html>
```

After creating the JS file and updating the HTML file, reload the app and test it by clicking the Write Data to Sheet button. It should write the numbers from MyArray onto the sheet. With those cells selected, click Read & Calculate Data from Sheet, and the results of adding the selected numbers together will appear in the Calculation Results line of the task pane, as shown in Figure 27.4.

27

Figure 27.4
Use JavaScript to create an app that can perform a calculation with data from a sheet.

A Basic Introduction to HTML

The HTML code in an app controls how the task or content pane will look, such as the text and buttons. If you open the HTML file from either Hello World sample, it opens in your default browser, looking as it did in Excel's task pane (though without any functionality). You can design the app as you would a web page, including images and links. This section reviews a few basics to get you started in designing your own app interface.

Tags

HTML consists of elements, such as images, links, and controls, that are defined by the use of tags enclosed in angle brackets. For example, the starting tag `<button>` tells the code that what follows, inside and outside the tag's brackets, relates to the button element. For each start tag, you have an end tag, which is usually use the same tag with a slash—like `</button>`—but some tags can be empty—like `/>`. A browser does not display tags or anything within the tag's brackets. Text that you want displayed needs to be outside the tags.

Comments have a tag of their own and don't require your typical end tag. As in VBA, commented text does not appear on the screen. Add comments to your HTML code like this: `<!--This is a comment-->`. A multiline comment would appear like this:

```
<!--This is a multiline comment.
Notice that nothing special is needed -->
```

Buttons

The code for a button is a combination of labeling the button and linking it to a function in the JavaScript file that will run when the button is clicked. For example:

```
<button onclick="writeData()">Write Data To Sheet</button>
```

The first part, `<button onclick="writeData()">`, identifies the control as a button and assigns the function, `writeData`, to the click event for the button. Notice that the function name is in quotes and includes argument parentheses, though they are empty. The second part, `Write Data To Sheet`, provides a label on the button. The label name is not in quotation marks. The line ends with the closing tag for the button.

By specifying other attributes of the button, you can change them. For example, to change the button text to red, add the `style` attribute for color, like this:

```
<button onclick="writeData()" style="color:Red">Write Data To Sheet</button>
```

To add a ToolTip that appears when the mouse is placed over the button, as shown in Figure 27.5, use the `title` attribute, like this:

```
<button onclick="writeData()" style="color:Red"
    title = "Use to quickly add numbers to your sheet">
    Write Data To Sheet</button> </br>
```

Use a space to separate multiple attributes. After the attribute name, such as `style`, put an equal sign and then the value in quotation marks. Also notice that HTML is rather forgiving about where you put your line breaks. Just don't put them within a string or you might also get a line break on the screen in that position.

Figure 27.5

Add other attributes to your button to change colors or add tip text for the users.

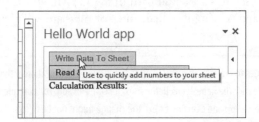

CSS

CSS stands for Cascading Style Sheets. You create styles in Excel and Word to make it easy to modify how text looks in an entire file without changing every single occurrence. You can do the same thing with an app by creating a separate style file (CSS) that your HTML code references. In the file, you set up rules for various elements of the HTML file, such as layout, colors, and fonts.

The CSS file provided in the Hello World example can be used for a variety of projects. It has a style for `h1`, `h3`, `h4` headings, hyperlinks (`a`), paragraph tags (`p`), and bullets (`li`) configured.

Using XML to Define Your App

The XML defines the elements needed to display and run the app in Excel. This includes the GUID, app logo, and location of the HTML file. It also configures how the app will appear in the app store and can provide a version number for the program.

> **CAUTION**
>
> XML tags are case sensitive. When you make changes to the provided Hello World sample, be sure you don't change any of the tags, only their values.

Two types of user interfaces are available for an app: a task pane or a content pane. A task pane starts off docked on the right side of the Excel window, but a user can undock it and

27

move it around the window. A content pane appears as a frame in the middle of the Excel window. Which type you use is up to you. To tell your app which type of pane to use, set the xsi:type value to either TaskPaneApp or ContentApp.

You should always use a unique identifier when creating an app. Websites are available, such as http://www.guidgen.com, that will generate a GUID for you.

In our Hello World sample, the store icon used is an online icon Microsoft has made available. But you can also use your own jpg file. The image should be small, about 32×32 pixels. Update IconURL with the full path to the image, like this:

```
<IconUrl DefaultValue="\\workpc\MyApps\HelloWorld\mrexcellogo.jpg"/>
```

The SourceLocation tag is used to set the full path to the HTML file. If the HTML file cannot be found when the app is being installed, an error message will appear stating that the file couldn't be found.

> **NOTE** If you make changes to the XML after you've already configured the location of the catalog or installed the app, be sure to click the Refresh link in the Apps for Office dialog. For example, if you switch between TaskPaneApp and ContentApp, the change might not be reflected even if you select to install the app again. To be safe, refresh the store.

Using JavaScript to Add Interactivity to Your App

JavaScript (JS) provides the wow factor behind an app. You can create a very useful reference with just HTML, but to make an interactive app, such as a function calculator, you need JavaScript. One limitation, though, is that you cannot specify cell addresses. The program interacts with what is selected on the sheet.

The following is a basic introduction to JS. If you are already familiar with JS, you can go ahead to "JavaScript Changes for Working in the Office App."

> **NOTE** The document.getElementById("results").innerText command used in the examples in this section is the command for the code to put the returned value in the place reserved by the "results" variable in the HTML file.

The Structure of a Function

Your JS code will consist of functions called by the HTML code and by other JS functions. Just like VBA, each function starts with function followed by the name of the function and any arguments in parentheses. But unlike VBA, there is no End Function at the end; instead, curly braces are used to group the function. See the following subsection, "Curly Braces and Spaces," for more information.

JS is case sensitive, including variable and function names. For example, if you create a function called writeData, but then try to call WriteData from another function, the code does not work. In one case, *write* is in lowercase and in the other it has a capital *W*. JS recognizes the difference. Create case rules for yourself, such as initial caps for each word in a variable, and stick to them. This helps reduce troubleshooting of JS code issues.

Curly Braces and Spaces

Curly braces ({}) are characters used by JS but not in VBA. They're used to group blocks of code that should be executed together. You can have several sets of braces within a function. For example, you would use them to group all the code in a function; then, within the function, you would use them to group lines of code such as within an if statement.

After you have finished typing a line in VBA and gone to another line, you might notice that the line adjusts itself, adding or removing spaces. In JS, spaces don't usually matter; the exceptions are spaces in strings and spaces between keywords and variables in the code. In the code samples in this section, notice that sometimes I have included spaces (a = 1) and sometimes I have not (a=1).

Semicolons and Line Breaks

You've probably noticed the semicolons (;) used in JS code. They might have appeared at the end of every line, or maybe only on some. Perhaps you noticed a line without a semicolon or you noticed a semicolon in the middle of a line. The reason the use of semicolons appears inconsistent is that, under normal circumstances, they are not required. A semicolon is a line break. If you use hard returns in your code, you are already placing line breaks and so the semicolon is not needed. If you combine multiple lines of code onto one line, though, then you need the semicolon to let the code know that the next piece of code is not part of the previous code.

Comments

There are two ways to comment out lines in JS. To comment out a single line, place two slashes (//) at the beginning of the line, like this:

```
//comment out a single line in the code like this
```

If you want to comment out multiple lines in VBA, you have to preface each line with an apostrophe. JS has a cleaner method. At the beginning of the first line to comment out, place a slash and asterisk (/*). At the end of the last line to comment out, place an asterisk slash (*/), like this:

```
/* Comment out
multiple lines of code
like this */
```

Variables

In VBA, you have the option of declaring variables. If you do declare them, you don't have to declare the variable type, but after a value is assigned to the variable, it's not always easy to change the type. In JS, you don't declare variables, except for arrays (see the later subsection "Arrays" for more information). When a value is assigned to a variable, it becomes that type, but if you reference the variable in another way, its type might change.

27

In the following example, the string "123" is assigned to myVar. But in the next line, a number is subtracted. JS just goes with it, allowing you to change the variable from a string to a number. After the code has run, myVar would be 121. Note that myVar + 2 would not deliver the same result. See the next subsection, "Strings," for more information.

```
myVar = "123"
myVar = myVar-2
```

If you need to ensure that a variable is of a specific type, use one of these functions to do so: Boolean, Number, String. For example, you have a function that is reading in numbers imported onto a sheet. As is common in imports, the numbers could be stored as text. Instead of having to ensure that the user converts the data, use the Number keyword when processing the values like this to force the number to be a number:

```
Number(importedValue)
```

Strings

As in VBA, in JS you reference strings using double quotations marks ("string"), but, unlike in VBA, you can also use single quotation marks ('string'). The choice is up to you—just don't start a string with one type and end with another. The capability to use either set can be useful. For example, if you want to show quoted text, you would use the single quotes around the entire string, like this:

```
document.getElementById("results").innerText = 'She heard him shout, "Stay away!"'
```

The result in the pane would be this: She heard him shout, "Stay away!"

To concatenate two strings, use the plus (+) sign. This is also used to add two numbers. So what happens if you have a variable hold a number as text and add it to a number. For example,

```
myVar = "123"
myVar = myVar+2
```

You might think that the result is 125. After all, in the previous example in which we had -2, the result was 121. In this case, concatenation has priority over addition and the actual answer would be 1232. To ensure that the variable is treated like a number, use the Number function. If the variable it is holding cannot be converted to a number, the function returns NaN, Not a Number.

Arrays

> **NOTE** If you are unfamiliar with using arrays in VBA, see Chapter 8, "Arrays."

Arrays are required for processing multiple cells in JS. Arrays in JS are not very different from arrays in VBA. To declare an unlimited size array, do this:

```
var MyArray = new Array ()
```

To create an array of limited size, for example, 3, do this:

```
var MyArray = new Array(3)
```

You can also fill an array at the same time that you declare it. The following creates an array of three elements, two of which are strings and the third of which is a number.

```
var MyArray = ['first value', 'second value', 3]
```

The array index always starts at 0. To print the second element, second value, of the preceding array, do this:

```
document.getElementById("results").innerText = MyArray[1]
```

If you've declared an array with a specific size but need to add another element, you can add the element by specifying the index number or by using the push() function. For example, to add a fourth element, 4, to the previously declared array, MyArray, do this (because the count starts at 0, the fourth element has an index of 3):

```
MyArray [3] = 4
```

If you don't know the current size of the array, use the push() function to add a new value to the end of the array. For example, if I don't know the index value for the last value in the preceding array, I can add a new element, fifth value, like this:

```
MyArray.push('fifth value')
```

Refer to the section "How to Do a For each..next Statement in JS" if you need to process the entire array at once. JS has other functions for processing arrays, such as concat(), which can join two arrays together, or reverse(), which reverses the order of the array's elements. Because this is just a basic introduction to JS, these functions are not covered here. For a tip on applying a math function to an entire array with a single line of code, see the section "Math Functions in JS."

JS for **Loops**

In the interactivity of the Hello World app, the following code summed the selected range. The two for loops processed the array, data, that was passed into the function, x being the row and y the column.

```
for (var x = 0 ; x < data.length; x++) {
    for (var y = 0; y < data[x].length; y++) {
        printOut += data[x][y];
    }
}
```

A for loop consists of three separate sections separated by semicolons. When the loop is started, the first section, var x=0, initializes any variables used in the loop. Multiple variables would be separated by commas. The second section, x < data.length, tests whether the loop should be entered. The third section, x++, changes any variables to continue the loop, in this case, incrementing x by 1 (x++ is shorthand for x=x+1). This section can also have more than one variable, with a comma separating each one.

27

TIP

To break out of a loop early, use the break keyword.

How to Do an if Statement in JS

The basic if statement in JS is

```
if (expression){
//do this
}
```

Here, *expression* would be a logical function that would return true or false, just as in VBA. If the expression is true, the code would continue and do the lines of code in the //do this section. To execute code if the expression is false, you need to add an else statement, like this:

```
if (expression){
//do this if true
}
else{
//do this if false
}
```

How to Do a Select..Case Statement in JS

Select..Case statements are very useful in VBA as an alternative to multiple If..Else statements. In JS, similar functionality is found within the switch() statement. Typically, the syntax of a switch statement is:

```
switch(expression){
    case firstcomparison : {
        //do this
        break;
        }
    case secondcomparison : {
        //do this
        break;
        }
    default : {
        //no matches, so do this
         break;
        }
}
```

Here, *expression* would be the value you want to compare to the case statements. The break keyword is used to stop the program from comparing to the next statement, after it has run one comparison. That is one difference from a Select statement—whereas in VBA, after a comparison is successful, the program leaves the Select statement, in JS, without the break keyword, the program continues in the switch statement until it reaches the end. Use default as you would a Case Else in VBA—to cover any comparisons not specified.

The preceding syntax works for one-on-one comparisons. If you want to see how the expression fits within a range, the standard syntax won't work. You need to replace the expression with true, forcing the code into running the switch statement. The case statements are where you use the expression compared to the range. The following code is the BMI calculator UDF from Chapter 14, "Sample User-Defined Functions," converted to JS.

27

It compares the calculated BMI to the various ranges and returns a text description to post to the task pane.

```javascript
Office.initialize = function (reason) {
//Add any needed initialization.
}

function calculateBMI() {
    Office.context.document.getSelectedDataAsync("matrix", function (result) {
//call the calculator with the array, result.value, as the argument
        myCalculator(result.value);
    });
}

function myCalculator(data){
    var calcBMI = 0;
    var BMI="";
    //Do the initial BMI calculation to get the numerical value
    calcBMI = (data[1][0] / (data[0][0] *data [0][0]))* 703

/*evaluate the calculated BMI to get a string value because we want to
evaluate range, instead of switch(calcBMI), we do switch (true) and then
use our variable as part of the ranges */
    switch(true){
        //if the calcBMI is less than 18.5
        case (calcBMI <= 18.5) : {
            BMI = "Underweight"
            break;
            }
        //if the calcBMI is a value between 18.5 and (&&) 24.9
        case ((calcBMI > 18.5)&&(calcBMI <= 24.9)):  {
            BMI = "Normal"
            break;
            }
        case ((calcBMI > 24.9)&&(calcBMI <= 29.9)) : {
            BMI = "Overweight"
            break;
            }
        //if the calcBMI is greater than 30
        case (calcBMI > 29.9) : BMI = "Obese"
        default : {
            BMI = 'Try again'
            break;
            }
    }
    document.getElementById("results").innerText = BMI;
}
```

How to Do a `For each..next` Statement in JS

If you have a collection of items to process in VBA, you might use a `For each..next` statement. One option in JS is for `(... in ...)`. For example, if you have an array of items, you can use the following code to output the list. You can do whatever you need to each element of the array. In this example, you're building a string to hold the element value and a line break so that when it prints to the screen, each element appears on its own line, as shown in Figure 27.6.

```
//set up a variable to hold the output text
arrayOutput = ""
/*process the array
i is a variable to hold the index value.
Its count starts as 0*/
for (i in MyArray) {
/*create the output by adding the element
to the previous element value.
\n is used to put in a line break */
    arrayOutput += MyArray[i] + '\n'
    }
//write the output to the screen
document.getElementById("results").innerText = arrayOutput
```

Figure 27.6
JavaScript has its own
equivalent to many VBA
looping statements, such
as the for..in loop.

```
Calculation Results:
first value
second value
3
```

Mathematical, Logical, and Assignment Operators

JS offers same basic operators as VBA plus a few more to shorten your code. Table 27.1 lists the various operators. Assume x = 5.

Table 27.1   JavaScript Operators

Operator	Description	Example	Result
+	Addition	x+5	10
–	Subtraction	x–5	0
/	Division	x/5	1
*	Multiplication	x*5	25
%	Remainder after division	11%x	1
()	Override the usual order of operations	(x+2)*5	35, whereas x+2*5=15
–	Unary minus (for negative numbers)	-x	-5
==	Values are equal	x=='5'	True
===	Values and types are equal	x==='5'	False since the types don't match. x is a number being compared to a string
>	Greater than	x>10	False
<	Less than	x<10	True

Operator	Description	Example	Result
>=	Greater than or equal to	x>=5	True
<=	Less than or equal to	x<=4	False
!=	Values are not equal	x!='5'	False
!==	Values and types are not equal	x!=='5'	True
&&	And	x==5 && 1==1	True
||	Or	x=='5' || 1==2	False
!	Not	!(x==5)	False
++	Increment	++x or x++	6
--	Decrement	--x or x--	4
+=	Equal to with addition	x += 11	16
-=	Equal to with subtraction	x-=22	-17
*=	Equal to with multiplication	x*=2	10
/=	Equal to with division	x/=30	6
%=	Equal to with the remainder	x%=11	1

The increment and decrement operators are two of my favorite ones; I wish we had them in VBA. Not only do they reduce your code, but they offer a flexibility VBA lacks (post- and pre-increments). You might remember the use of x++ in the Hello World interactivity. This was used in place of x=x+1 to increment the for loop. But it doesn't just increment the value. It uses the value and then increments it. This is called a post-increment. JS also offers a pre-increment. That is, the value is incremented and then used. So if you have x=5, both of the following lines of code return 6:

```
//would increment x then post the value
document.getElementById("results").innerText = ++x //would return 6
//would post the value of x (now 6 after the previous increment) then increment
document.getElementById("results2").innerText = x++ //would return 6
```

Math Functions in JS

JS has several math functions available, as shown in Table 27.2. Using one of the functions is straightforward. For example, to return the absolute value of the variable myNumber, do this:

```
result = Math.abs(myNumber)
```

27

Table 27.2   JavaScript Math Functions

Function	Description
Math.abs(a)	Returns the absolute value of a
Math.acos(a)	Returns the arc cosine of a
Math.asin(a)	Returns the arc sine of a
Math.atan(a)	Returns the arc tangent of a
Math.atan2(a,b)	Returns the arc tangent of a/b
Math.ceil(a)	Returns the integer closest to a and not less than a
Math.cos(a)	Returns the cosine of a
Math.exp(a)	Returns the exponent of a (Euler's number to the power a)
Math.floor(a)	Rounds down, returns the integer closest to a
Math.log(a)	Returns the log of a base e
Math.max(a,b)	Returns the maximum of a and b
Math.min(a,b)	Returns the minimum of a and b
Math.pow(a,b)	Returns a to the power b
Math.random()	Returns a random number between 0 and 1 (but not including 0 or 1)
Math.round(a)	Rounds up or down, returns the integer closest to a
Math.sin(a)	Returns the sine of a
Math.sqrt(a	Returns the square root of a
Math.tan(a)	Returns the tangent of a

TIP

If you need to apply a math function to all elements of an array, you can do this using the map() function and the desired Math function. For example, to ensure that every value in an array is positive, use the Math.abs function. The following example changes each element in an array to its absolute value and then prints the results to the screen as shown in Figure 27.7:

```
result = 0
arrayOutput = ""
arrNums = [9, -16, 25, -34, 28.9]
result = arrNums.map(Math.abs)
for (i in result){
    arrayOutput += result[i] +'\n'
}

document.getElementById("results").innerText = arrayOutput
```

Figure 27.7
Arrays are a common way of storing data in JavaScript, which offers many functions for simplifying working with those arrays.

```
Calculation Results:
9
16
25
34
28.9
```

Writing to the Content or Task Pane

After you've processed the user's data, you need to display the results. This can be done on the sheet or in the app's pane. To write to the pane, do this:

```
document.getElementById("results").innerText
```

It writes data to the app's pane, specifically to the `results` variable reserved in the HTML code. To write to the sheet, see the later subsection "Reading From and Writing To a Sheet."

JavaScript Changes for Working in the Office App

The incorporation of JavaScript into Office Apps isn't 100 percent. For example, you cannot use the `alert` or `document.write` statements. There are also some new statements for interacting with Excel provided in a JavaScript API you linked to in the HTML file with this line:

```
<script src = "https://appsforoffice.microsoft.com/lib/1.0/hosted/office.js">
</script>
```

As with APIs used in VBA, it gives you access to objects, methods, properties, and events JS can use to interact with Excel. This section introduces some of the more commonly used objects. For more information on these and other available objects, go to `http://msdn.microsoft.com/en-us/library/office/apps/fp142185.aspx`.

Initializing the App

The following event statement must be placed at the top of the JS script. It initializes the app to interact with Excel. The reason parameter returns how the app was initialized. If the app is inserted into the document, then the reason is `inserted`. If the app is already part of a workbook that's being opened, the reason is `documentOpened`.

```
Office.initialize = function (reason) { /*any initialization*/}
```

Reading from and Writing to a Sheet

`Office.context.document` represents the object the app is interacting with—the sheet. It has several methods available, most important the two that enable you to read selected data and write to a range.

The following line uses the `setSelectedDataAsync` method to write the values in `MyArray` to the selected range on a sheet. The first argument, `MyArray`, is required. It contains the values to write to the selected range. The second argument, `coercionType` is optional. Its value, `matrix`, tells the code that you want the values treated as a one-dimensional array.

```
Office.context.document.setSelectedDataAsync(MyArray, {coercionType: 'matrix'});
```

The method to read from a sheet, `getSelectedDataAsync`, is similar to the write method. The first argument, `matrix`, is the `coercionType` and is required. It tells the method how the selected data should be returned—in this case, in an array. The second argument shown is an optional callback function, with `result` being a variable that holds the returned values (`result.value`) if the call was successful, and an error if not.

27

```
Office.context.document.getSelectedDataAsync("matrix", function (result) {
    //code to manipulate the read data, result
});
```

To access the success of the call, use the status property, result.status. To retrieve the error message, do this: result.error.name.

Napa Office 365 Development Tools

You don't need a fancy program to write the code for any of the files used in an app. The Notepad program that comes with Windows will do the job. But when you consider the case sensitivity of some programming languages, like JavaScript, using a program that will provide some help is a good idea. I spent a couple of hours in frustration over some of the samples in this chapter, wondering why they didn't work when the code was perfect. Except the code wasn't perfect. Again and again I missed the case sensitivity in JS.

To help you create distributable apps, Microsoft has released Napa Office 365 Development Tools. After you sign up for a developer site, Microsoft provides you with space on a SharePoint server and the tools for developing your app. Go to dev.office.com to get started. The tool also helps you release your apps through the app store.

Next Steps

Read Chapter 28, "What's New in Excel 2013 and What Has Changed," to learn about more features that have changed significantly in Excel 2013.

27

What Is New in Excel 2013 and What Has Changed

28

If It Has Changed in the Front End, It Has Changed in VBA

If you were using Excel 2003 (or older) before Excel 2013, almost everything you knew about programming Excel objects has changed. Basic logic still works (for loops, for example), but most objects have changed. This chapter reviews changes since Excel 2007–2010. In conjunction with reviewing those sections, you should also review information in this book on tables, sorting, and conditional formatting.

If you have been using Excel 2007 or 2010, there are still a few changes to consider, and they are noted in this chapter. For most items, it's obvious, because if the Excel user interface has changed, the VBA has changed.

The Ribbon

If you have been working with a legacy version of Excel, the ribbon is one of the first changes you'll notice when you open Excel 2013. Although the `CommandBars` object does still work to a point, if you want to flawlessly integrate your custom controls into the ribbon, you need to make some major changes.

→ **See** Chapter 25, "Customizing the Ribbon to Run Macros," for more information.

Single Document Interface (SDI)

For years, if you had multiple documents open in Word, you could drag each document to a different monitor. This capability was not available in Excel, until now. With Excel 2013, Excel changes from a *multiple document interface* to a *single document interface*. What this means is that the individual workbook window no longer resides within a single application window. Instead, each workbook is in its own standalone window, separate from any other open workbook.

Changes to the layout of one window won't affect any previously opened windows. For example, open two workbooks. In the second workbook, enter and run the following code, which adds a new item, Example Option, to the bottom of the right-click menu:

```
Sub AddRightClickMenuItem()
Dim cb As CommandBarButton
Set cb = CommandBars("Cell").Controls.Add _
    (Type:=msoControlButton, temporary:=True)
cb.Caption = "Example Option"
End Sub
```

Right-click a cell in the second workbook and the option appears. Right-click a cell in the first workbook and the option does not appear. Return to the second workbook and press Ctrl+N to add a new workbook. Right-click a cell in this third workbook and the menu item appears. Go to the first workbook, create a new workbook, and check the right-click menu. The option does not appear.

Now, delete the custom menu. Go to the third workbook, and paste and run the following code:

```
Sub DeleteRightClickMenuItem()
CommandBars("Cell").Controls("Example Option").Delete
End Sub
```

The menu item is removed from the third workbook, but when you check the right-click menu of the second workbook, the item is still there. Although Excel copied the menu from the active workbook when creating new workbooks, the logic to remove the menu item does not propagate.

> **NOTE** Don't worry about having to delete all instances of the sample menu item. It was created to be temporary and will be gone when you restart Excel.

Another change to keep in mind is that making a change to the window of one workbook, such as minimizing it, doesn't affect the other workbooks. If you want to minimize all windows, you need to loop through the application's windows, like this:

```
Sub MinimizeAll()
Dim myWin As Window
For Each myWin In Application.Windows
myWin.WindowState = xlMinimized
Next myWin
End Sub
```

Quick Analysis Tool

New to Excel 2013, the Quick Analysis tool appears in the lower-right corner when a range of data is selected. This tool suggests what the user could do with the data, such as apply conditional formatting or create a chart. You can activate a specific tab, such as Totals, when the user selects a range, like this:

```
Private Sub Worksheet_SelectionChange(ByVal Target As Range)
Application.QuickAnalysis.Show (xlTotals)
End Sub
```

Charts

Charts have gone through a few incarnations since Excel 2003, and with those changes to the interface have been changes to the object model. The greatest change is in Excel 2013, with a completely new interface and a new method, AddChart2, which is not backward compatible, not even to Excel 2010. With this compatibility issue in mind, the chapter on charts provides examples for Excel 2003, 2007–2010, and 2013.

There's also a new type of minichart, called Sparklines, that can be inserted within a cell. Sparklines are available only in Excel 2010 and 2013.

→ **See** Chapter 15, "Creating Charts," for more information.

PivotTables

Each of the previous three versions of Excel offered many new features in PivotTables. If you use code for a new feature, the code works in the current version but crashes in previous versions of Excel.

- Excel 2013 introduced the PowerPivot Data Model. You can add tables to the Data Model, create a relationship, and produce a pivot table. This code does not run in Excel 2010 or earlier. The function xlDistinctCount is new. Timelines are new.

- Excel 2010 introduced slicers, Repeat All Item Labels, Named Sets, and several new calculation options: xlPercentOfParentColumn, xlPercentOfParentRow, xlPercentRunningTotal, xlRankAscending, and xlRankDescending. These do not work in Excel 2007.

- Excel 2007 introduced ConvertToFormulas, xlCompactRow layout, xlAtTop for the subtotal location, TableStyles, and SortUsingCustomLists. Macros that include this code fail in previous versions.

→ **See** Chapter 12, "Using VBA to Create Pivot Tables," for more information.

28

Slicers

Slicers were a new feature in Excel 2010 for use on pivot tables. They aren't backward compatible, not even to Excel 2007. They're useful in pivot tables, allowing for easy-to-see and -use filtering options. If you open a workbook with a slicer in an older version of Excel, the slicer is replaced with a shape, including text explaining what the shape is there for and that the feature is not available.

In Excel 2013, slicers were added to Tables. The functionality is the same as that of the slicers for pivot tables, but these new slicers are not backward compatible, not even to Excel 2010.

→ **See** Chapter 12 for more information on pivot table slicers.

SmartArt

SmartArt was introduced in Excel 2007 to replace the Diagram feature of legacy versions of Excel. Recording is very limited, but it will help you find the correct schema. After that, the recorder doesn't capture text entry or format changes.

The following example created the art shown in Figure 28.1. The name of the schema used is hChevron3. I changed the schemecolor for the middle chevron, leaving the other two with the default colors.

```
Sub AddDiagram()
With ActiveSheet
    Call .Shapes.AddSmartArt(Application.SmartArtLayouts( _
        "urn:microsoft.com/office/officeart/2005/8/layout/hChevron3")).Select
    .Shapes.Range(Array("Diagram 1")).GroupItems(1).TextEffect.Text = "Bill"
    .Shapes.Range(Array("Diagram 1")).GroupItems(3).TextEffect.Text = "Tracy"
    With .Shapes.Range(Array("Diagram 1")).GroupItems(2)
        .Fill.BackColor.SchemeColor = 7
        .Fill.Visible = True
        .TextEffect.Text = "Barb"
    End With
End With
End Sub
```

Figure 28.1

The macro recorder is limited when recording the creation of SmartArt. You need to trace through the object's properties to find what you need.

Learning the New Objects and Methods

When you click the help button in Excel, you're brought to Microsoft's online help resource. On the left side of the browser window, select What's New for Excel 2013 Developers to open an article reviewing some of the changes. Select Welcome to the Excel 2013 Developer Reference then Object Model Reference to view a list of all objects, properties, methods, and events in the Excel 2013 object model.

Compatibility Mode

With all the changes in Excel 2013, now more than ever it's important to verify the application's version. Two ways you can do this are `Version` and `Excel8CompatibilityMode`.

Dealing with Compatibility Issues

Creating a compatibility mode workbook can be problematic. Most code will still run in legacy versions of Excel, as long as the program doesn't run into an item from the Excel 2013 object model. If you use any items from the Excel 2013 object model, however, the code will not compile in legacy versions. To work around this, comment out the 2013-specific lines of code, compile, and then comment the lines back in.

If your only Excel 2013 issue is the use of constant values, partially treat your code as if you were doing late binding to an external application. If you have only constant values that are incompatible, treat them like late binding arguments, assigning a variable the numeric value of the constant. The following section shows an example of this approach.

→ **See** "Using Constant Values," **p. 456**, for more information on using constant values.

Version

The `Version` property returns a string containing the active Excel application version. For 2013, this is 15.0. This can prove useful if you've developed an add-in to use across versions, but some parts of it, such as saving the active workbook, are version specific:

```
Sub wkbkSave()
Dim xlVersion As String
Dim myxlOpenXMLWorkbook As String

myxlOpenXMLWorkbook = "51" 'non-macro enabled workbook

xlVersion = Application.Version

Select Case xlVersion
    Case Is = "9.0", "10.0", "11.0"
        ActiveWorkbook.SaveAs Filename:="LegacyVersionExcel.xls"
    Case Is = "12.0", "14.0", "15.0" '12.0 is 2007, 14.0 is 2010
        ActiveWorkbook.SaveAs Filename:="Excel2013Version", _
            FileFormat:=myxlOpenXMLWorkbook
End Select
End Sub
```

28

> ┌─ C A U T I O N ──
> Note that for the `FileFormat` property of the Excel 2013 case, I had to create my own variable,
> `myxlOpenXMLWorkbook`, to hold the constant value of `xlOpenXMLWorkbook`. If I were to try
> to run this in a legacy version of Excel just using the Excel 2013 constant, `xlOpenXMLWorkbook`,
> the code would not even compile.

Excel8CompatibilityMode

This property returns a Boolean to let you know whether a workbook is in Compatibility mode—that is, saved as an Excel 97–2003 file. You use this, for example, if you have an add-in using the new conditional formatting, but you wouldn't want the user to try to use it on the workbook. The following function, `CompatibilityCheck`, returns `True` if the active workbook is in Compatibility mode and `False` if it is not. The procedure, `CheckCompatibility`, uses the result to inform the user of an incompatible feature.

```
Function CompatibilityCheck() As Boolean
Dim blMode As Boolean

Dim arrVersions()

arrVersions = Array("12.0", "14,0", "15.0")

If Application.IsNumber(Application.Match(Application.Version, _
    arrVersions, 0)) Then
    blMode = ActiveWorkbook.Excel8CompatibilityMode
    If blMode = True Then
        CompatibilityCheck = True
    ElseIf blMode = False Then
        CompatibilityCheck = False
    End If
End If
End Function
Sub CheckCompatibility()
Dim xlCompatible As Boolean

xlCompatible = CompatibilityCheck

If xlCompatible = True Then
    MsgBox "You are attempting to use an Excel 2013 function " & Chr(10) & _
    "in a 97-2003 Compatibility Mode workbook"
End If
End Sub
```

Next Steps

28

If we as authors have done our job correctly, you now have the tools you need to design your own VBA applications in Excel. You understand the shortcomings of the macro recorder yet know how to use it as an aid in learning how to do something. You know how to use Excel's power tools in VBA to produce workhorse routines that can save you hours of time per week. You've also learned how to have your application interact with others so that you can create applications to be used by others in your organization or other organizations.

If you have found any sections of the book that you thought were confusing or could have been spelled out better, we welcome your comments, and they will be given consideration as we prepare the next edition of this book. Write to us:

Bill@MrExcel.com and

Tracy@MrExcel.com

Whether your goal was to automate some of your own tasks or to become a paid Excel consultant, we hope that we've helped you on your way. Both are rewarding goals. With 500 million potential customers, we find that being Excel consultants is a friendly business. If you are interested in joining our ranks, this book is your training manual. Master the topics and you will be qualified to join the team of Excel consultants.

Index

B

N